NASHVILLE
AN AMERICAN SELF-PORTRAIT

NASHVILLE

AN AMERICAN SELF-PORTRAIT

EDITED BY **JOHN EGERTON**

AND **E. THOMAS WOOD**

ILLUSTRATED BY PHOTOGRAPHERS OF *THE TENNESSEAN* AND OTHERS
NANCY RHODA, PHOTO EDITOR

PRINCIPAL CONTRIBUTING WRITERS

LEON ALLIGOOD • PHILIP ASHFORD • LARRY DAUGHTREY

JEAN BETHKE ELSHTAIN • BRUCE FEILER • CHRISTINE KREYLING

AMY LYNCH • DANA PRIDE • JIM RIDLEY

RICHARD SCHWEID • REGINALD STUART • RAY WADDLE

SUSAN CHAPPELL, CHIEF COPY EDITOR

BEATEN BISCUIT PRESS, NASHVILLE, TENNESSEE

NASHVILLE: AN AMERICAN SELF-PORTRAIT

This book is an all-Nashville production created between July 2000 and August 2001. Virtually all of its editors, writers, photographers, artists, designers, researchers, proofreaders, indexers, printers, binders, marketers, and investors are individuals or enterprises living in or based in Nashville, presently or previously.

The editors extend special thanks to four Nashville institutions:

• Solidus Company, and its chief executive, Townes Duncan, for investing in this project, providing fiscal oversight and accounting, providing extensive logistical support (including dinner for 15 and a proofreading "bucket brigade," both on very short notice), and generally offering wise counsel and encouragement throughout.

• Davis-Kidd Booksellers, for early support of the idea of this book, commitment to assist in the pre-publication marketing of the Patrons Edition, and timely advice both at the corporate level (through Audrey Seitz) and at every level of the Nashville store.

• Ingram Book Company, for lending timely guidance, advice, and encouragement from the start, particularly through the counsel of Ron Watson and Craig Pollock.

• The Nashville Public Library—specifically and especially the Reference Department, the Nashville Room, the Metro Archives, and the administrative offices of the director, Donna Nicely.

Library of Congress Catalog Number: 2001088241

International Standard Book Number (ISBN): 0-9706702-1-4

CONTENTS

CONTENTS

PHOTOGRAPHS

More than 300 images, most from staff photographers of *The Tennessean* or from the newspaper's archives; edited by **Nancy Rhoda**, with an assist from **P. Casey Daley**. Both are veteran staff photographers of the newspaper.

Cover and title page photograph: The Tennessee State Capitol at 5 a.m., January 1, 2001, by professional photographer **Aubrey Haynes** of Nashville.

Frontispiece: Nashville sculptor Alan LeQuire's statue of Athena in the Parthenon, photograph by Lisa Nipp.

CONTENTS

ORIGINAL ART

Original art by Nashville artists:

Newton Holiday, *page 182*
Nancy Blackwelder, *page 304*
W. J. Cunningham, *page 336*

OF RECORD: THE DAILY NEWS OF 2000

Beginning in the margin on the second page of each chapter is a continuous ribbon of the month's news, selectively and succinctly edited by **Jim Ridley**, and assisted by **D. Michelle Adkerson**. Ridley is a film and music critic and senior writer of the *Nashville Scene*.

CROSSINGS

by JOHN EGERTON

Saturday, December 25, 1999: In the predawn half-light of the last Christmas morning of the 1900s, there is not a single person in sight here on the west bank of the Cumberland River, where Nashville was born on this day in 1779. At the foot of Broadway, in Riverfront Park, the Tennessee Fox Trot Carousel is shuttered against the forbidding arctic air. Just up First Avenue to the north, the gates of old Fort Nashborough are closed, too, locking out the founding fathers, James Robertson and John Donelson, who stand frozen in a bronze handclasp on a limestone pedestal nearby. Farther up the hill, near the spot where the original pioneer station stood, sculptor Alan LeQuire's 1996 statue of Timothy Demonbreun, a fur-trading forerunner of the Anglo-Saxon settlers, keeps a lonely vigil on the craggy bluff above the river. There are no graven images or less-grand memorials to the indigenous people—Shawnees, Chickasaws, Cherokees, Creeks, Choctaws—whose Edenic hunting ground this bowl-shaped river valley was for centuries before the traders and land claimants arrived.

When the first golden glint of sunlight escapes the horizon at 6:55 a.m., the temperature is a bracing 15 degrees Fahrenheit. Up and down both sides of the river, there is a perfect stillness, a frigid silence. Then, just past the seven o'clock hour, a solitary denizen of the streets, looking more like a lumberjack than a vagabond, emerges from beneath the Woodland Street Bridge and strides across the avenue toward Church Street, where, if luck is with him, a hot mug of coffee waits in some cozy waystation over the hill.

The crest of First Avenue—or Front Street, as it was called for well over a century—is an ideal place from which to view both the modern city and the Nashville of old. If you have passed this way on any recent Fourth of July evening (you and tens of thousands of others), you've seen this street filled to overflowing with people, churning like a river of humanity at floodtide. And if you could have stood here on the bluff with James Robertson on that Christmas morning 220 years ago, you would have been counted among the 400 or so people who had walked with him across the frozen Cumberland that day to begin building a new community—a frontier outpost that would become by turns a river village, a railroad town, a highway and airport city, and a consolidated urban government jurisdiction officially known by the cumbersome name of Metropolitan Nashville-Davidson County, Tennessee, but more commonly and popularly called Nashville, or Metro. In the upcoming Census of 2000, it is expected to retain its ranking among the 25 largest cities in the United States, with a modest population increase over the 1990 total of 511,000.

On a big, round-numbered birthday like this, you'd think longevity would be reason enough for celebration—but no party is planned, and there's no mention of the milestone in the morning *Tennessean*. All the more reason, perhaps, to take note of it here, at the beginning of what is intended to be a full-dress display, in words and pictures, of contemporary life in Nashville. Think of it as a time capsule in print, an intentional artifact, a conscious attempt to capture the heart and soul of a place and a time—not just for those who live here now, but for future generations curious to know from whence they came.

When Nashville celebrated its bicentennial twenty years ago, a mayoral task force called the Century III Commission sponsored publication of a narrative history highlighting the city's transformation from a frontier outpost in the era of the Revolutionary War to a budding metropolis on the eve of the 1980s. *NASHVILLE: The Faces of Two Centuries* was published in November 1979. Its bicentennial theme suggested a standard history, with the primary focus on the farthest corners of the past. In contrast, this new volume—*NASHVILLE: An American Self-Portrait*—uses history to set the stage for a wide-ranging collection of contemporary essays about life in the city at the turn of the 21st century, and for some speculations about the future. This is not a sequel to the prior volume, not a direct descendant or even a close relative—but it is a companion, and a kindred spirit, and it does reach back, here at the beginning and sporadically after that, to pick up a few threads from the past and draw them forward to the present.

The town that started spreading outward from the riverside fort at the beginning of the 1780s would grow in ever-widening circles over the ensuing two centuries. Arching outward from the walls of Fort Nashborough like the irregular age rings of a hardwood tree, the town moved by fits and starts through war and peace, boom and bust, wind and fire and flood. It is still shaped more by such unpredictable and uncontrollable events than by any political or economic deliberation. Some of its growth rings were intentional, of course—surveyor Thomas Malloy's rectangular 2-square-mile town boundary, drawn in 1783, was the first example—but the consequences of major change sometimes exceed the most thorough calculations, for better or worse. Where a railroad line is laid or a highway routed or a landfill sited or a prison or a stadium built tells much about the concentration and strength of any city's power bases over time, and Nashville's configurations certainly reflect that reality.

Still, compensating forces do give the wheel an eccentric spin from time to time. The incidental and accidental ways in which a particular combination of people or a sequence of events comes together to shape the character and personality of a place is a process beyond our comprehension, much less our control. Only on the Red Grooms carousel, with its whimsical images of rich and famous Tennesseans whirling in carefree rings, is the merry-go-round of Nashville life a perfect and unchanging circle.

At a groundbreaking ceremony for the new Nissan plant in 1981, local United Auto Workers Union members demonstrated against the nonunion policies and foreign ownership of the company. Mitsuya Goto (fifth from left), a Nissan public relations executive, got caught up in the demonstration. Four years later, when word of Saturn's landing reached Tennessee, Spring Hill farmer J.C. King reflected the positive response of most area residents.

Looking back on the last two decades of the 20th century, it is easy to see that Nashville has enjoyed one of the most sustained periods of productivity in its history. Not since the 1920s have good times seemed so good (and even the best of times are usually sweeter in remembrance than in reality). The 1980s began inauspiciously, with former Governor Ray Blanton, a Democrat, being pursued by federal prosecutors and his successor, Governor Lamar Alexander, a Republican, striving to keep the ship of state afloat in a political hurricane.

Blanton was subsequently convicted of mail fraud, conspiracy, and extortion and went to prison for 22 months. (Several other leading Tennessee Democrats also served time during this period). Alexander was out of town a lot, too, but he was traveling free—and his trips yielded much more impressive results. He went early and often to Japan, where he sold dozens of Japanese corporations—Nissan most conspicuously—on the viewpoint that his state and their nation had a lot in common (a similar climate, a strong sense of family and history, personal qualities of politeness and good humor, dogwoods and maples and cherry trees). He also took note of the fact that three of the most popular American cultural icons among the Japanese were Elvis Presley, Jack Daniel's whiskey, and "The Tennessee Waltz," and every time he received visitors here from the East, Alexander made sure they got a taste of those "three from Tennessee."

And so it was that, on a cold February day in 1981, Nissan broke ground for a huge manufacturing facility in Smyrna, less than 25 miles from the heart of Nashville. At the time, the company projected an outlay of $450 million to create a modern, high-tech workplace where 2,200 employees would be turning out 10,000 Nissan pickup trucks a month. Now, after twenty years on the site, Nissan employs about 6,000 workers, produces an average of 30,000 vehicles a month, and counts its total capital investment over the period at about $1.5 billion.

Before he left office, Alexander scored another coup when he coaxed General Motors to locate its new Saturn automobile works in Spring Hill, south of Nashville. That plant opened in 1990, and since its inception has put up numbers similar to Nissan's: a workforce of over 7,000, production averaging about 20,000 vehicles a month, and capital outlays (spent or projected) of close to $1.5 billion. These two manufacturing facilities have had an enormous long-term impact on the greater Nashville economy—holding up the area's wage and employment averages, adding a strong manufacturing element to the already diversified economy, giving both union (Saturn) and nonunion (Nissan) forces reasons for hope,

Even in the best of times—perhaps especially in the best of times—stark contrast between the splendor and the spoils of an affluent society is never far from view. Scores of men and women like Tom Colletta and Don Brandt (below) regularly scavenge for throwaway treasures in junkpiles near Adelphia Coliseum.

and generally enriching the mix of local culture with infusions of new accents, tastes, and talents.

Governor Alexander's two terms in office dominated the early 1980s. A graduate of Vanderbilt, he glided smoothly through Nashville's eccentric configuration of elites centered in Belle Meade and Brentwood, the chamber of commerce, the professional and academic communities, the state legislature and Metro government, the music industry, the churches, and the political parties—his and the jail-spooked Democrats'. At times, the governor seemed to fit every party label, and none; he was an expansionist in a boom era, and everything he touched seemed to grow. When American Airlines announced in 1985 that it was opening a major hub at the Nashville airport, Alexander was front and center, a step ahead of the city's elected and anointed leaders. "Nashville is hot as a firecracker," he told a *Wall Street Journal* reporter near the end of his second term—and, indeed, the city did seem on the verge of becoming one of the nation's most vibrant urban areas.

All the while, a background chorus of admonition was rising softly offstage, and it would hang there like a low-frequency alert. John Tune, a Nashville attorney and civic leader, gave it voice in 1980, early in Alexander's first term. "Nashville is the new America, a city whose time has come," said Tune, a former president of the chamber of commerce. "The next few years will set the pattern for the next century. But if we're not careful, we could wind up like New York, Cleveland, Detroit. We've got to learn how to say 'No' to the temptation of the almighty dollar, and be more concerned about the quality of life than the quantity." Tune counseled strongly against offering tax incentives and other inducements to lure new businesses to Nashville.

It was differences such as these—Alexander's style and philosophy versus those more closely represented by Tune's remarks—that defined the economic profile of Nashville in the 1980s. Party politics had come to mean little or nothing in this equation. Ned Ray McWherter would put the Democrats back into the governor's office in the 1986 election, and life on Capitol Hill would continue without skipping a beat; as far as big business was concerned, McWherter and Alexander were practically interchangable. The real conflict was between those who sought to protect their wealth by keeping it close to the vest, and those (like the two governors) who preferred the more free-wheeling, entrepreneurial style that was in the air all around Nashville, spinning off new companies and new concepts with the casual daring of competitive opponents in a game of Monopoly.

By the time McWherter arrived on the scene (he had been there right along, actually, as the powerful Speaker of the House in the state General Assembly), the game was already over, and the entrepreneurs had won. Jack Massey, a Georgia country boy who had come to Nashville in the 1920s with little but the clothes on his back and worked his way up to a secure power position in banking and Belle Meade, was masterminding an amazing array of ventures—not because he knew anything about medical practice or the first thing about cooking chicken, but because he had a natural instinct for the many uses of money. It is more than merely coincidental that Kentucky Fried Chicken (with a little help from McDonald's) revolutionized the concept of "fast food cheap for the masses," or that Hospital Corporation of America changed forever the notion that health care is a "nonprofit" enterprise.

Nashville came out of the 1980s riding high on a wave of prosperity, and there was more waiting where that came from. But beneath all the euphoria lurked unsettling signs of approaching trouble. The number of personal and corporate bankruptcies in the city was rising at an alarming rate. Mergers were erasing some of the oldest names in the Nashville pantheon of corporate gods—Life & Casualty and National Life in insurance, Commerce Union and Third National in banking. Not long after National Life sold out to American General in Houston, that insurance company decided to dump the most hallowed symbols of Music City U.S.A.—the Grand Ole Opry, Opryland (the park and the hotel), WSM radio, and The Nashville Network. They were spun off to another absentee owner, Gaylord Entertainment in Oklahoma. All the while, Music Row was on a roll, but its boom-and-bust cycles were legendary—and, like hurricanes, both certain and unpredictable.

Probably the most unnerving development in the music sector of the local economy, from the Old Guard's perspective, was the conspicuously soaring affluence of country superstars who were now outsiders by choice, having developed their own mansions and country clubs in the rolling meadows and pleated hills of suburbia. This was the first old money-new money dichotomy to emerge in Nashville, but it would not be the last. It surfaced soon after World War II, when Hank Williams started a parade of stars that quickly became too big to be ignored. With some ambivalence, a few of Belle Meade's more progressive citizens began to acknowledge that peaceful coexistence would eventually be forced upon all of Nashville's wealthy, old and new alike, lest they fall into a self-destructive power struggle that no faction could win.

They reached out gingerly to draw in a few of the music world's more urbane and sophisticated stars, and some of them responded positively with an unaffected dignity. In 1973, when the descendants of Cornelius Vanderbilt were having a reunion in Nashville at the namesake university of their ancestor, the renowned guitarist Chet Atkins was invited to perform after dinner at the Swan Ball, Belle Meade's *de rigueur* social event. Atkins opened with some classical riffs reminiscent of Andrés Segovia, much to the delight of the Vanderbilts and a standing-room-only crowd. He paused then to tune his guitar, bending to catch a sound beyond the hearing of mere mortals, and as he listened, he chatted with his audience. "I think I'd been playing about twenty years before I found out I couldn't tune too well," he said softly, in his East Tennessee drawl. The crowd chuckled politely. Then, without looking up from his task, Atkins finished his thought: "By then, I was too rich to quit."

Parallel with the rise of Nashville as a "hot" city going into the 1990s were two public spectacles that disturbed the local mood of peace and tranquility. One defied explanation. The mayor, Bill Boner, was not simply caught in a sexual entanglement with a woman other than his wife; in a national television talk-show appearance with her, he flaunted the affair. The giddy couple got married and then divorced in a matter of months, and the mayor decided not to seek a second term.

The other drag on Nashville's continuing good fortune was the state General Assembly's chronic and worsening misfeasance. As Tennessee slipped ever further down the rank of states in education, health care, and other vital services, the lawmakers were stymied by an antiquated rules manual of their own making. It gave lobbyists virtually free rein, allowed deliberation and decision-making in secret, encouraged unrecorded voting, and defied all efforts to change the system except those initiated by the top leaders of each house. Not even Governor McWherter, a master of the process himself when he ran the House, could break the grip of the ensconced bosses, Senator John Wilder and Representative Jimmy Naifeh.

In 1991, the first year of his second term, McWherter saw his plans for education and health-care reform going up in the smoke that hung in the stale air of both houses. Despite healthy growth in the private sector, the state's economy was suffering from overreliance on a sales tax that was already too high and too inequitable (collected, for example, on food bought at the grocery but not food for livestock). The governor's majority leader in the House, Democrat Bill Purcell of Nashville, expressed a frustration that would echo beyond the moment when he said, "I think all this [gridlock] has resulted in a basic distrust and loss of confidence by the public in the ability of state government to solve problems."

A few blocks down the street, in the Metro Courthouse (where Purcell would find himself in a few years), Phil Bredesen began his first watch as mayor in 1991, after winning the election to replace Bill Boner. A New Yorker and a Harvard graduate, Bredesen had come to Nashville in the 1970s looking for opportunities to make money and make an impact—and like Jack Massey, he did both. He got rich from a company in the burgeoning for-profit health-care industry that Massey's money had helped to spawn, and then he decided to get into public service. After one false start (a losing race against Boner in 1987), he was elected mayor—and he took his free-wheeling business skills with him.

Bredesen couldn't stop American Airlines from reneging on its Nashville hub plans, but that was just about the only prize he went all out for and failed to get. With generous tax-waiver incentives, he coaxed HCA back to Nashville after it had merged with Columbia Healthcare and moved to Louisville. He persuaded the Metro Council to come up with funds for a $100-million arena to stimulate the revival of the downtown area, and then got a National Hockey League team to take up residence. The arena came in far over budget and operated at an expanding loss in each of its first few years, but neither Bredesen nor the general public seemed too concerned. He swung a complex deal to bring the Houston Oilers franchise of the National Football League to Nashville, and after two years in borrowed stadiums the team was reborn in 1999 as the Tennessee Titans, playing its home games in all-new Adelphia Coliseum, right across the Cumberland from Fort Nashborough and the awakening downtown district.

As an outsider himself, and a "new money" millionaire, Bredesen further weakened the Old Guard's once-solitary grip on power. His tenure as mayor filled most of the '90s—a decade of unprecedented prosperity for the greater Nashville area—and most of the new wealth locally was generated in enterprises that were new to the city, from Dell Computer and other high-tech firms to the professional sports teams.

Motorists waiting in traffic on Broadway stood outside their vehicles to study the ominous storm clouds all around. Within an hour on that day, April 16, 1998, a massive tornado bounced through the city, destroying or heavily damaging more than 1,000 homes and businesses and injuring more than 100 people.

On June 1, 1996—its 200th birthday—Tennessee celebrated in grand style with the dedication of the Bicentennial Capitol Mall, a "living history" park on the northern approach to Capitol Hill. Former Gov. Ned Ray McWherter, who steered the project to completion, and his successor, Gov. Don Sundquist, joined Vice President Al Gore, other guests and a crowd of thousands in a stirring tribute to the old state and its new park.

The "Dell deal" struck by Bredesen in the waning months of his last term was by any measure a colossal giveaway of public funds—free land, a pass on most taxes, and even a sort of reverse head tax under which Metro agreed to pay Dell an annual sum for each person it employed locally. But, the mayor's strongest supporters argued, in a single bold stroke he had brought one of the biggest names in a non-polluting growth industry to town, and the concessions he had yielded in order to land Dell would pale to insignificance as the company added more and more jobs in years to come.

Taken as a whole, Nashville's big-ticket ventures during Bredesen's eight years in office moved the city farther in less than a decade than it had ever moved before in twice the time. It could be persuasively asserted that some of the projects were ill-advised, or too costly, or someone else's doing; it might even be argued that if they moved us farther, it was in the wrong direction, as John Tune and others had warned years earlier. But for breadth and magnitude, the list was unprecedented, and whether or not they approved of Bredesen's priorities or his style, even his detractors had to acknowledge that he had made things happen.

In some respects, his business deals were less impressive than three not-for-profit endeavors that were high on his priority list: public school revitalization, public library development, and the merger of Metro General and Meharry-Hubbard hospitals into a single public hospital (later to be strengthened through an alliance between historically black Meharry and predominantly white Vanderbilt medical schools). All three of these projects made significant advances in the 1990s.

When shown against the longest period of sustained economic expansion in U.S. history, the contrast between Metro Nashville's government and the state of Tennessee's in this period was striking. While Nashville was booming right along with the nation, Tennessee saw its Medicaid expenditures for the poor more than triple during McWherter's administration, leading in 1993 to the creation of an in-state managed-care program called TennCare. It was destined for hard times. The state desperately needed an overhaul of its tax structure to better handle such massive problems, but neither McWherter nor Lamar Alexander had been able to get the legislature to move in that direction.

Don Sundquist, a former congressman from Memphis, won the election for governor in 1994, running on an anti-income tax promise, but to the dismay and outrage of many Republicans (and not a few Democrats), he too saw the light that had frightened his predecessors and came out in 1999 (soon after his re-election) in favor of a state income tax, paired with a general reduction of the sales tax and its exclusion from food. Sundquist and a handful of legislators in both parties took the heat for this proposal, but all that came of the effort was sound and fury signifying nothing. Tennessee dropped further—in comparative rankings with other states, in credit ratings, in morale. There were rallies, protest marches, and drive-by honkings at the Capitol, but most were against tax reform, not for it. Things would have to get worse before they got better.

Bill Purcell had given up his state House seat before these shenanigans began, but he had been there long enough to recognize the familiar pattern. From the mayor's office, to which he was elected in

For virtually all of his 77 years, Charlie Primm has lived and worked on the same 200-acre farm on Moores Lane in Brentwood, sleeping in the same bed, rising to look out the same window. In 2000, the farm's days were numbered; a subdivision of half-million-dollar "McMansions" was being plotted across the road from Primm's house, on half the family acreage. The rest will go after his death.

1999, he indicated to some of his friends the sense of relief he felt to be working for a viable, functioning government, one that could get something done.

Purcell was another outsider who had found his stroke in Nashville. It was starting to look like a pattern: music company executives and even country stars from somewhere else, followed by entrepreneurs, by football and hockey owners and players, and now by successful politicians. All the big local banks and insurance companies, meanwhile, had flown to headquarters in other cities. Blacks and women had ended white male exclusion in virtually every place that mattered. Even some recent immigrants were getting into the flow. Lots of old money was quietly retiring to the back benches to watch instead of play. New faces and new money were here to stay.

The age rings around this 220-year-old living organism called Nashville have spread far beyond the tiny thumbprint of Fort Nashborough. State Road 840—Interstate 840 in every particular except its name—is a huge circle on the map, a hoop with an irregular radius about 35 miles from the old fort beside the Cumberland. A fourth of the highway is either open to traffic or under construction; another quadrant, most of it in Williamson County, is tied up in court. The northern half is still in the preliminary drawing stage. As the 2000s begin, no consensus is in sight that could reconcile the opposing points of view on where the highway should be routed, or even if it should be finished at all. Like dozens of burning issues in American life, this one begs for compromise from two or more sides that have a sense of certitude about the rightness of their cause. No doubt there were some in this little frontier village who objected when Thomas Malloy surveyed a boundary around it in the 1780s. Forty years later, the arrival of steamboats ended Nashville's isolation, and unpaved turnpikes helped, too, and the railroads competed for dominance for almost a century; all of these ventures were championed by some, challenged by others.

There are people still living here who were part of the railroad era. I'm one of them; with a few other romantics, I was aboard the last passenger train through Nashville in October 1979, just for the memories. Many of us also watched, with deeply mixed feelings, the so-called "urban renewal" of downtown that cleaned up a cesspool of slums around Capitol Hill—and razed hundreds of splendidly crafted Victorian homes and businesses in the process. People who knew how difficult and time-consuming it was to drive through the city before the 1950s (U.S. Highways 31 and 41 north and south and 70 east and west all funneled through the intersection of Eighth Avenue and Broadway) were delighted to see Interstates 40 and 65 come on line—unless Jefferson Street was the center of their universe.

And all the other big changes since then—the inner loop of the interstates, Briley Parkway, Ellington Parkway, I-440, the suburban malls, Gaylord Arena, Adelphia Stadium—have had impassioned and dedicated proponents and opponents. That's the way things tend to happen in this country. There being no king or dictator to make the calls for us, and no political or religious or corporate factions powerful enough to work their will on all the rest of us, we are free to take sides, to speak and write for or against whomever or whatever we choose.

Upon this national heritage we overlay some others—a little South, some Tennessee, whatever we bring with us from elsewhere, and finally this hometown, this Nashville. Over a half-million of us claim it now, and we're all over the park: men and women and children, old-timers and newcomers, white and black and all shades in between, the rich and the rest of us, NASCAR and NASDAQ, scores of different nationalities and primary languages, just about every known religious faith (including the faith of unbelief), Democrats and Republicans and a-curse-on-both-your-houses.

For reasons beyond our understanding, this place has always been a welcome sight to travelers. The first visitors came often to hunt, and traders in canoes followed, and longhunters, and Robertson crossing on the ice, and Donelson by flatboat, they with their charges. Many crossings later, when the paths had become paved roads and the character of the place was etched deep in the hills and trees, people came anticipating, expecting, to find something good here—a chance, a start, a stake. There was conflict, yes, but also compromise, even reconciliation. "Go to Nashville," we've been told, for over two centuries now. "You'll find something there." And now, after all the tree rings have grown out, there is still life at the center, at the heart.

Everyone is coming these days, or so it seems, and houses are filling the pastures, and highways are blazing the forests, and people who are kind and polite to you in person will run you down in a rage on the road, out there between, say, the I-65 bridge and the I-40/I-24 split, where more than 160,000 vehicles a day do battle. And the question on the table is this: Can we squeeze enough community out of all this to sustain a democracy? The answer is a definite maybe.

VALLEY OF THE TITANS

by RICHARD SCHWEID

The year 2000 is either the beginning or the end of a century, the first year of a new millennium or the last of an old one. You can argue it either way, so take a number and wait your turn—we may need a few years to sort this all out.

While you're waiting, you might reflect upon the many marvels and perils of our brave new electronic world. Technology is the two-sided coin of the realm. We are enthralled by it, obsessed with it, fearful of it. Just think of our run-up to this year of ending and beginning. The non-news story of the eon has got to be Y2K, a.k.a. Year 2000—the technological bug that didn't bite. After endless months of dire warnings that cataclysmic malfunctions would follow the phenomenon of numerical conversion as it circled the planet, nothing more eventful than the usual merrymaking and overindulgence marked the turn of the clock and calendar.

By the time the big moment finally arrived in Nashville, Tennessee, and the rest of the Central time zone of the United States, its anticlimax had long since been heralded on television, radio, and the internet. That left little for this city's one million-plus residents to do but watch the fireworks, sip something festive, make a few noble but meaningless resolutions, and shuffle off to bed.

For a place that has come to be known around the nation and even abroad as Music City U.S.A., a tourist attraction and center of entertainment, Nashville seemed surprisingly subdued on this night of nights. There was a big bash at the Opryland Hotel, of course, and at scores of other venues across the city. And the honky-tonk bars of Lower Broadway, from the legendary Tootsie's Orchid Lounge to the stylized and imitative Wildhorse Saloon, pulsed with the energy and cacophony of legions of wanna-bes, has-beens, and never-wases, plus a bona fide country star or two, dropping in for a quick beer and a photo op. But nights like this are hardly millennial on Lower Broad.

So what's the big deal? There isn't one, apparently—just the usual throb and rumble of a downtown Saturday night in the capital of American music. (Quieter than normal, in fact: In the 48 hours bridging the old and new years—all of Friday, December 31, and Saturday, January 1—the Metro police blotter recorded no homicides and only 54 felony arrests. The "war room" of the city's emergency management agency was overrun with thoroughly bored disaster specialists, and even in the city's hospitals, birth and death were on slowdown, though not entirely on holiday.)

Nashvillians took it all in stride. Only one truly novel development would accentuate their millennial celebration: the meteoric rise of their new National Football League team, which was in serious contention for the U.S.—and thus the world—championship of "our kind of football." At the end of its premiere season as the Tennessee Titans, Nashville's first-ever big-league team was in the playoffs, vying for a trip to the Super Bowl on January 30. Its players had scratched, clawed, and muscled their way through a perilously thrilling season, punctuated by several heart-stopping last-minute victories—virtual miracles—that swept this city of newborn true believers into a near-religious delusion of destiny, if not divine guidance. As the playoffs began, football fever was building into a tidal wave of sports excitement, the single biggest athletic spectacle ever to unfold in the city.

1—**And it is written:** Baby Jesus is born. Jesus Yeager, the first new child of the millennium in Nashville, makes his debut at Centennial Medical Center just one minute and 40 seconds into the year 2000. The mother, Andrea Renee Yeager, and the father, Mauricio Martinez Garcia, smile happily for a photographer, while little Jesus sleeps. Even as the healthy infant draws his first breath, another century is dawning all around him. At the city's new downtown sports arena, Faith Hill and Tim McGraw, married country singers, are toasting a crowd of 17,000 with champagne and song. Trish and Glenn Nash, drag-racing enthusiasts, are becoming Nashville's first newly-weds of 2000 in a witching-hour ceremony at the Music Row Wedding Chapel. Jason Ringenberg, lead singer of Jason and the Scorchers, Nashville cowpunk heroes for almost 20 years, sings "Auld Lang Syne" to 350 revelers at the Exit/In, a venerable West End-area night spot. "Male Order Brides"—men in dresses and combat boots—puff cigars at the Opryland Hotel's Mardi Gras-style millennial celebration. Jerry Barlar, a cameraman for WKRN-Channel 2, reports live from a Salt Lake City-bound plane, where he is testing fears that the dreaded Y2K bug will cause airliners to drop from the sky at the stroke of midnight. When the intrepid reporter and millions more don't die, survivalists across Middle Tennessee and around the country gaze ruefully at their 50-pound sacks of flour, cases of condensed milk and potted meat. At St. Thomas Hospital, 90-year-old Mary Louise Holt, who until quite recently was still adding to her 60-year record of once-weekly volunteer service at the Veterans Administration Hospital, dies peacefully after a brief illness. In the Woodbine section of southeast Nashville, fireworks echo amid excited shouts in Spanish and the power chords of the Ramones' "Do You

At its best and most electric, sport is an experience to be shared, not only by the athletes who practice it but by the community they represent. A winning team can unite citizens from one end of town to the other. I'm a Nashvillian who lives in Barcelona, Spain, so there's no need to explain major-league fever to me. Barcelona's soccer team, *el Barça*, is a perennial world-class contender with a stadium that seats 130,000, and it is frequently chockablock with rabid partisans in full throat. In years when the team wins the Spanish league championship, the city vibrates with excitement, and victory parades on its mile-long pedestrian boulevard, Las Ramblas, are legendary. Now Nashville was getting its first taste of that thrill, starting the new century as a contender for what is arguably the most prestigious sports title in America.

The franchise that would become the Titans had moved from Houston to Nashville in 1997. It spent a couple of anchorless years drifting through borrowed stadiums, first in Memphis and then here, while waiting for its new home field to be finished—East Bank Stadium, as it was unofficially called, a $300-million showplace looming directly across the Cumberland River from the heart of downtown. Getting it built had taken a huge gamble by then-Mayor Phil Bredesen: a bitterly-contested referendum, the displacement of more than 40 businesses, bond issues and other public funds sufficient to launch a battleship—or save a school system, as critics pointed out. And then, when the stadium was finished, a cable television provider based in the Northeast agreed to pay $30 million for the privilege of putting its name—Adelphia—on the facility, and the team's owner, Houston businessman Bud Adams (not the stadium's owner, the city), gets to keep all the money. Some deal, huh?

And yet, tenuous though their link to Nashville was, the Titans quickly became a household word around Middle Tennessee, and Adelphia Coliseum is now almost a second home to the 67,000 ticketholders, give or take a few, who show up every time the gates open. In just one season, memories of the Houston Oilers evaporated into thin air as the Titans won their way into the hearts of tens of thousands of Mid-South football lovers. Money could indeed buy a new team, a new stadium, new uniforms, and paraphernalia, but only the fans could give the enterprise a new and lasting identity, and they have done that with great gusto. After generations of yearning for big-league status, the "Athens of the South" finally has a coliseum of classical Greco-Roman size (if not style), and its own gladiators to enliven the crowds. You may need a program to

Professional football has found a wildly enthusiastic following in Nashville and throughout the Mid-South—and the surprising success of the Titans has added to the excitement.

In the shadow of the Nashville skyline, 67,000 cheering fans regularly fill Adelphia Coliseum whenever the home-standing Tennessee Titans play. The stadium also serves as the home field of the Tennessee State University Tigers.

tell the lions from the Christians, but the cheering throngs of grateful and worshipful spectators need no prodding to make their joyful feelings known.

They might have been almost as faithful had the Titans kept up their mediocre Oiler ways. But the team responded to its new look and its new lease on life with a style of play that aroused admiration from Memphis to Bristol. Moving into the race for the national championship, the "Miracle Titans" were on everyone's lips, if not in their prayers. "Miracle" is a word that Nashville's avid churchgoing folk take seriously, and they took their football team that way, too.

If ever a city deserved a miracle team, local boosters must have felt it would have to be ours, for this is a city of the Word, with more churches per capita than almost any other, and so many religious publishing houses and church headquarters that it is widely perceived as the Holy City of American Protestantism. Somehow it seemed only right that the Titans should be making believers out of doubters, Sunday after Sunday; after all, the preachers have been trying to do that for generations. With pro football, Nashville now offered a potent and heady mixture of Sunday fervors, a two-for-one package of public passion: the steeple and the stadium.

It was a great story for the nation's sports media, too—a rewritten fairy tale spun out of the timeless Cinderella theme. As the January 8 playoff game against the Buffalo Bills approached, the city basked in the warm glow of television lights and celebrity anchors. Their attentions would be richly rewarded when the on-field drama was finally played out.

The seasoned and playoff-wise Bills, cool under pressure, came from behind to take a 16-15 lead with just sixteen seconds remaining in the game. It appeared that all

Remember Rock 'n' Roll Radio?" Local and federal law enforcement officers are investigating the theft of 270 pounds of explosives from a construction firm in suburban Millersville, northeast of the city. Across town in the Bellevue area, a mysterious blast in a creekbed shortly before 1 a.m. shatters windows in some houses and sets off the fire alarm in a nearby school. Discarded Christmas trees lie in tinsel-festooned heaps in parks around the darkened city, awaiting the chipper trucks. Whether asleep or awake in these last hours before dawn, we the living hang by a slender thread between our history and the unknowable future. Welcome to Nashville, baby Jesus. . . .
Today's weather forecast: partly

sunny, near-record warmth, high in the upper 60s. . . . *The Tennessean,* Nashville's morning newspaper, kicks off the millennium by printing a list of the state's "most interesting, talented or influential people of all time . . . people with strong Tennessee ties who had or are having an impact on their times." Included in the top 25 (rank in parentheses): Elvis Presley (1), Andrew Jackson (2), Alex Haley (3), Sequoyah (7), Cordell Hull (8), Andrew Johnson (13), Sam Houston (14), W.E.B. Du Bois (23), and Nathan Bedford Forrest (25), all deceased; among the living: Dolly Parton (10), Al Gore Jr. (15), Oprah Winfrey (16).

2—At 9:04 a.m., windows rattle and the earth shudders as a mild earthquake skitters across Giles County, about 90 miles south of Nashville. The tremor is brief and harmless, but residents have reason to be jittery. Much of West Tennessee lies within a danger zone known as the New Madrid fault, where a series of massive quakes in 1811-12 permanently changed the landscape and sent shock waves as far as Canada and the Mississippi Gulf Coast. That apocalyptic "act of God" spared Nashville, but it added evangelical fuel to an ongoing religious revival among Middle Tennessee and central Kentucky Baptists, Methodists and Presbyterians. As they vied for conversions among the unwashed masses from Nashville to Louisville, these three denominations and the various splinter groups that broke off from them collectively became the movement of evangelical Protestantism that still dominates religious life in Nashville and throughout the South today, almost two centuries later. The Great Awakening, historians named it. . . . **At the Gaylord Entertainment Center,** Nashville's new sports arena, some 7,500 evangelical Christians from scores of Middle Tennessee churches stage a contemporary "awakening" of their own: a late-Sunday service of prayer and thanksgiving on the second day of the new millennium. With a

was lost for the young and relatively inexperienced Titans. In desperation, Coach Jeff Fisher sent in a trick maneuver involving a cross-field lateral on the kickoff. The team had dutifully practiced this sandlot scenario once a week, for just such do-or-die situations as this. The chance of success seemed one in a million. But then, magically, the unbelievable happened, and there was wide receiver Kevin Dyson sailing down the sideline on a 75-yard flight to glory. The Music City Miracle had fallen from the sky. Had there not been close to 70,000 witnesses—and many millions more on television—it might have been declared a fantasy, or even a hoax. But there it was, and it was only the beginning. On consecutive weekends to follow, against Indianapolis and Jack-

In the waning seconds of their January 2000 playoff game against Buffalo at Adelphia, the Titans' Kevin Dyson took a kickoff lateral 75 yards to the winning touchdown.

In the end zone, Dyson was mobbed by his teammates while unbelieving fans and sportswriters searched for words to describe "the Music City Miracle." The scoreboard shows just three seconds remaining in the game.

sonville, the inspired Titans kept on winning—until only they and the St. Louis Rams remained to face off in Super Bowl XXXIV in Atlanta.

The story just got better and better. Near the end, it was as if the entire nation had focused its undivided attention on Our Team and Our Town. Nashvillians from across the spectrum of society seemed to float in a dazed and giddy euphoria, their lives lifted above the ordinary and held there in ecstatic suspension for the duration of this improbable dream. The Tennessee Titans were putting Nashville on the map.

The reality, of course, is that Nashville has been on the map all along, right in the same spot it has occupied for the past two centuries, and where it is likely to be in another hundred years, if the world endures. It is, in 2000, essentially what it was in 1900—a second-tier center of population rising on the banks of an Ohio River tributary and spreading out across the rolling green hills of Middle Tennessee. Fertile soil, a bearable climate, a tradition of gracious and relaxed living: What more could anyone ask?

But for many of the city's residents, all this has never been enough. Unfortunately, Nashvillians—being all too human—have been cursed with a perennial desire to

100-piece orchestra and a 750-voice choir performing while spotlights sweep the crowd, this "Gathering 2000: Embracing Jesus, Uniting Nashville" is suffused with a charismatic tingle of excitement. More than one witness likens the spectacle to a championship football game. "The Lord has blessed this gathering," a minister declares, and another adds, "It's a great prelude to heaven." It's certainly a prelude to good fortune for 10 local charities, each of which in time will receive $25,000 to further their work among the needy—all of it raised on this day of new beginnings.

Nashville's attractiveness as a place to live is enriched by the combination of Middle Tennessee's bucolic charm and the bustle of a growing urban cityscape. Less than an hour's drive separates 19th-century farmhouses (above) from noisy urban construction sites (below).

3—**A mini-retrospective** at Fisk University's Carl Van Vechten Gallery exhibits 34 paintings, prints, collages, drawings and woodcuts by David Driskell, the celebrated artist whose work addresses themes of nature, spirituality and his African-American heritage. Displayed are works from all facets of his career, including the 10 years he headed Fisk's art department, from 1956 to 1966. The Georgia-born artist now serves as a commissioner at the Smithsonian's National Museum of African Art.

4—**The Tennessee Supreme Court** sets an Apr. 6 execution date for Philip Workman, a death-row inmate at the state penitentiary in Nashville. Workman was convicted of killing a Memphis police officer in 1981. Both he and Robert Glen Coe, a convicted child-killer, now face spring execution dates (Coe's is Mar. 23). They are two of the 97 men and two women awaiting capital punishment in the state. The last official execution in Tennessee was almost 40 years ago, in 1960.

see their city move up in the world, to join the richest and most powerful on their own terms, to be a big-league city in every sense of the phrase. Nashville's long infatuation with celebrity probably goes back to the beginning of the Grand Ole Opry in 1925, when the new technology of radio first wafted across the airwaves in what was to become our signature musical form. By 1950, what would come to be known as the "Nashville Sound" already had cachet as a widely recognized and envied style of play.

Then in 1975, filmmaker Robert Altman looked at all of this through his cameras and produced a controversial movie that bore the city's name and pushed it closer to the national stage. Now, after another 25-year interval, there are some indications that Nashville is beginning to believe its press clippings and its fantasies.

That's the scary part. The good part may be that this unquenchable and overweening ambition has never been fully realized, never managed to shape what is essentially a country town to fit the Hollywood or New York mold. All efforts to let unbridled growth drive us into the front rank of major American urban centers have been graced, one could say thankfully, with repeated failure. In spite of all the changes that came along in the last quarter of the 20th century—and there were many, some of them desperately needed and long overdue—Nashville has somehow retained its best qualities and its reputation as an excellent place to live. It is still a manageably small and friendly city displaying such amenities as deep woods and quiet waters, houses with neatly kept yards, some front porches presided over by people who know how to use them, neighbors who visit back and forth, families and friends who love to socialize, strangers who chat about the Titans and the weather—in short, a relatively relaxed hometown with a measured pace of life.

Notwithstanding some strenuous and at times impressive efforts to break out of the pack, Nashville is entering the new century pretty much as it spent the last one—as a city with an encrustation of old manners and money, highlighted by the academic and social correctness of Vanderbilt and Fisk universities, historically pre-eminent educational institutions; a city with an African-American community rich in its own traditions, and a European-American community where the rich live very well indeed, deeply ensconced in the luxury and comfort of conspicuous wealth, some of it inherited and some freshly minted. Nashville's diversified commerce has kept it well-poised for the shift to the electronically driven "new world economy" that is the wave of the present and future, even in second-tier Southern cities. The country music industry, obviously, is Music City's own particular distinction. It brings revenue and national visibility, and even a measure of international notoriety—but Nashville's movers and shakers generally are not the millionaires of Music Row, nor have they ever been.

Even though Metro Nashville's population grew from about 450,000 in 1975 to almost 570,000 in 2000, it continues to look like a tree-covered town from the air, a smallish community nestled among man-made lakes and rolling green hills. There are more woods than people, and passengers on arriving flights can hardly see the houses for the trees. (There's a skyline, but you have to be on the right side of the plane to see it.) Even so, some profound changes have come about in the past quarter-century, and the growing population has been accompanied by a corresponding surge in the city's ambitions and an expansion of its horizons.

In 1956, for white Nashvillians, the biggest local football game after any of Vanderbilt's was the high-school league championship named the Clinic Bowl (proceeds went to the Children's Clinic at Vanderbilt Medical Center). It brought the two top teams of white schoolboys in the city to a showdown at Dudley Field, the university's venerable stadium. The game was held annually on Thanksgiving afternoon, and it was a big deal. More often than not, the holiday turned out to be a cold, crystal-clear day washed in brilliant colors as fall eased toward winter. At halftime, the men gathered beneath the Dudley Field grandstands in their long, wool overcoats and hats, to sip from pocket flasks and smoke cigarettes. I was 10, and I knew in my bones that this was the real male sports thing: to pass halftime standing around talking and sipping discreetly, each spoken word a puff of breath expired into the cold air. Masters of the world these men were, somehow, and this ritual confirmed and celebrated the fact. "Go on back to your seat," my father urged me, his long, beautiful fingers fanned out across the small of my back, giving me a gentle shove to get me started. A holiday football game, male bonding—that was the life.

Thirty-five years later, almost 70,000 people were jammed into Adelphia Coliseum on a January afternoon to watch one of the most amazing and unforgettable comebacks in NFL history—that phenomenal lateral and 75-yard run as the clock expired—and then to wait an interminable two minutes more for the official review of the videotape to make the miraculous win legal. All day, the Bills' quarterback had trouble barking signals over the roar of Titans fans. This was a boisterous crowd, a yeasty

. . . **Kaia Jergenson,** a freshman member of the David Lipscomb University women's basketball team, is rushed to the emergency room at St. Thomas Hospital after a period of extreme suffering from flulike symptoms. She is diagnosed with spinal meningitis. The appearance and severity of the communicable disease triggers fears of an outbreak. After weeks fighting the ravages of the disease, Jergenson ultimately will lose both her legs above the knee. Her courage and resilience in the face of the tragedy make her the subject of weeks of attention in the city's press.

5—The unthinkable happens: After years of arguing the demerits of chain journalism, as practiced by the Gannett-owned morning daily, the alternative newsweekly *Nashville Scene* joins . . . a chain! Editor Bruce Dobie and publisher Albie Del Favero, who have co-owned the paper since 1996, announce that they are among the investors in a new company, Village Voice Media, that will own the *Scene* and six papers purchased from pet-supply potentate Leonard Stern. Among the latter is New York's *Village Voice*, the combative weekly co-founded by Norman Mailer in 1956. The deal earns Dobie and Del Favero a feature in the *New York Times*—and raises suspicions that the home team has become the "bizpigs" they once ridiculed.

6—TennCare, the state's federally approved alternative to Medicaid since 1994, may be forced to drop 500,000 otherwise uninsured and uninsurable Tennesseans from its rolls because of rising costs and falling state revenue, say the top health and finance officials in Gov. Don Sundquist's administration. The largest managed-care organization, BlueCross/BlueShield of Tennessee, announced earlier that it will pull out of TennCare July 1 because of doubts about the viability of the program.

7—A state income tax is not in the cards for the 2000 General Assembly when it convenes in mix of white and black, wealthy and working-class men and women—computer specialists, doctors, bricklayers, clerks, factory workers, lawyers, all welded together in deafening celebration of the same thing, something the city had long lacked: a reason to come together, to scream, to get rowdy as a civic duty.

Nashville has never been a party town like, say, Memphis, where the big-spending residents from that western slice of Mississippi and Tennessee called the Delta have done their uninhibited carousing for generations. Communal celebration has always been something that Memphians took to as easily as ducks to the fountain water in the Peabody Hotel lobby, but Nashvillians never seemed to develop much of a flair or talent for public flaunting of the baser instincts. Beginning around the turn of the last century, when saloons and brothels and gambling clubs dotted the slopes of Capitol Hill (conveniently located to serve our public servants), the properly pious city fathers of Nashville made a show of keeping a lid on the sin dens, confining them to Printer's Alley and a few private clubs that paid protection money for the privilege of doing business. Over the years, not many people came to Nashville just to party, unless they lived within 50 miles in some little place too small to have much more than a convenience store and a post office. In 1965, judicious halftime sips from a hip flask among small groups of middle-class white guys huddled under the grandstand was about as close as they got to partying.

Not anymore. Those are Middle Tennesseans filling Adelphia Coliseum, painting their faces, waving those flags, pasting Titans logos over the paint jobs on those expensive cars they are so deep in debt for, flying Titans banners in little flag-holders mounted on their vehicles, coming to the east bank of the Cumberland for pregame tailgate parties, roaring their support for the gladiators. Major league fan-dom.

Tickets for the first playoff game against Buffalo were sold out in eighteen minutes. People camped all night in front of the stadium for a chance at them, and scalpers were getting respectably big-league prices in the $200 to $300 range. By midweek following the victory, at least a dozen buses were chartered and fully reserved for the trip to Indianapolis to play the Colts for the right to advance to the American Football Conference championship and a shot at the Super Bowl. Those who were unable to make the trip, for one reason or another, spent the week talking about the game ahead. And a week later, they had even more to talk about after the Titans dispatched the Colts, 19-16, with a true-to-form second-half comeback.

As the century turns, pro football and hockey (the Nashville Predators, a new franchise in the National Hockey League) aren't the only emblems of metropolitan life in Nashville; other big-city trappings are visible, and they're a predictable mix of the good, the bad, and the ugly. Traffic is not yet in the Atlanta class of gridlock, but it's plenty bad if you have to be on the interstate highways or other main arteries around the morning and evening rush hours. Road construction work has become an everyday reality, taxing the patience of commuters and causing some to commit aggressive, violent, even deadly acts of road rage. Still, there are lots of "back ways" to get most places, and longtime Nashvillians who know their way around can easily cross the city in a half-hour or less.

The choice of restaurants continues to improve, with some fine new dining establishments that would hold their own in Miami or Dallas or Cincinnati. There's variety, too—Old Southern and nouvelle American, Italian, French, Mexican, Indian, Jamaican, Japanese, Chinese, Korean, Thai, Middle Eastern—and new places seem to open every week. And, if it happens to be a lunchtime hunger that needs satisfying, Nashville is still home to some of the best meat-and-three cafes in the South (which is to say in the world, because no other region or nation features quite this Southern country/soul combination that typically includes a main dish, three vegetables, hot bread, sweet tea, and pie). Until recently, a five-dollar bill would buy that feast; now it takes most of a ten.

Certainly there is no lack of places to eat out. But make no mistake: This is not New Orleans, never was, never will be. People come from afar to hear Nashville music,

Besides pro football, Nashville also has the Predators, a major-league hockey team. As one of many promotions to help introduce the sport locally, team officials offered game tickets to every junior high school student in the city. Thousands of kids came, riding buses to the Gaylord Entertainment Center at Broadway and Fifth Avenue to watch the ice warriors in action.

and now to watch football, but not many come here just for the food. Chain restaurants dominate, and informal dinner with company at home is preferred by many over a more expensive dinner out. Given a warm weekend afternoon, what many folks still mean when they talk about eating out is eating in the back yard, with the grill fired up and some friends and neighbors invited over for a cookout. For a still large but diminishing number of Nashvillians, this is the apogee of social life; steaks and barbecue, beer and iced tea, coleslaw and potato salad and Tennessee home-grown tomatoes, ice cream and cake often hold greater attraction than an air-conditioned, well-appointed restaurant. The simpler pleasures retain their appeal, and the city continues to work for those who pursue them. It still runs by their rhythms.

With each new interstate that carves up yet another neighborhood or stretch of farmland, each new tax break offered to entice large multinational corporations here, each new bid to corner some segment of the entertainment market, a certain element of the local populace forecasts Nashville's imminent degradation into "the next Atlanta." Another faction, seeing great financial opportunity riding on the wings of rapid growth, views the prospect with undisguised pleasure.

There is no need for either camp to get too worked up, because neither extreme is apt to happen. Unlike Nashville, Atlanta has been an international city for a good many years. It has a developed history of resident black political power, thanks to the presence of an African-American community large and influential enough to be full players in the city's present and its future. It is a metropolis with a developed public transportation system and a large enough infrastructure to host the Olympic Games. The busiest airport in America is there. It has fielded major-league sports teams for almost 40 years (one being the Braves, a perennial powerhouse in baseball). Atlanta is the home of Ted Turner's multichannel broadcasting empire, the birthplace and headquarters of Coca-Cola, and the most populous city in the Southeast.

event helps police in the nearby city raise money for the Special Olympics. Mayor Don Fox and 13-year-old Jackie White are among the swimmers who describe the numbing experience as a shock to the system, but Vantrease takes it in stride. "It was fun," he says, shrugging while the others shiver. "I'm in pretty good health."

9—**Nashville's downtown arena,** built with taxpayer funds and opened in 1996, was touted by then-Mayor Phil Bredesen as a spotlight facility that would turn a profit of about a million dollars in its first year and keep right on raking it in. Bredesen landed a major-league hockey team for the arena (now named the Gaylord Entertainment Center, for the Oklahoma-based conglomerate that now owns, among other things, the Grand Ole Opry and

Opryland Hotel in Nashville). But in spite of steady bookings, "big city" ticket prices and high attendance, the arena has posted an ever-larger annual deficit in each of its first three years. In the current fiscal year, operating losses and debt service will bleed an estimated $3.5 million from the Metro treasury, which is already staggering under a $12.5-million shortfall left by Bredesen to new Mayor Bill Purcell and the Metro Council. Meanwhile, the hockey team—named, with no intended irony, the Predators—is raking in hefty profits for its private owners, largely because the lion's share of revenue from luxury-suite rentals, ticket sales and concessions goes directly to them. So does all of the $80 million Gaylord will pony up over the next 20 years for "naming rights" to the arena.

10—**Dell Computer Corp.**, having established a presence in Middle Tennessee, now wants to back off a promise to keep at least 1,000 jobs at one of its new factories, in suburban Wilson County. But county officials are retaliating, saying they will block a $100-million bond issue and rescind a waiver of Dell's property taxes if the company fails to keep its word. The Texas-based computer giant's main operations in Tennessee will be inside the city of Nashville, where Mayor Bredesen has given them free land, big tax breaks, and other inducements. . . . **The merger of America Online** and Time Warner Inc., creating the world's largest media and entertainment corporation, is being seen as a mixed blessing in Nashville. Some local music industry executives say it will open the way to huge sales in international markets by big-name country music stars. Others fear it's another step toward the consolidation and homogenization of all music, making country a minnow in an ocean of sound. . . . **Nashville's first homicide** of the year is a grisly public assault in the 1000 block of Second Avenue South. Wanda Inez Jones, 36, runs screaming into the street, with her estranged

Nashville, by comparison, is definitely minor-league. It has never risen higher in the television network hierarchy than the now-defunct TNN (The Nashville Network) and Trinity Broadcasting, each with a small niche in a vast industry (the one featuring *Dukes of Hazzard* reruns, the other marketing Christian faith healers)—and those produce small creeks compared to the real rivers of television money that run through Atlanta. What's more, this city has never elected a black mayor or sheriff, and the ratio of African Americans in the population (about 1 in 4) has not translated into proportionate room for nonwhites in the upper circles of privilege. True, Nashville does have an elected black membership of eleven in the 40-seat Metro Council, and as the year 2000 began, a black police chief was in office—but at that very moment, his department was under critical scrutiny for alleged systematic abuse of another minority (Hispanics) by some of its officers. The city has never been renowned for forward-looking police chiefs; judging by some of his current problems, Chief Emmett Turner seemed caught in the same web as his predecessors.

The fact is that every time Nashville has hailed the imminent arrival of big-city status, it just hasn't quite happened. American Airlines opened a major hub here to great fanfare in 1985, and later added daily nonstop flights to London, but now almost all of that is gone, and the "International" in the airport's name should, in all fairness, be changed to "Domestic." The Opryland theme park, once viewed as a great tourist attraction and distinguishing mark of the city, was closed in 1997 by Gaylord Entertainment, and the city was sent reeling by the subsequent plunge in tax revenue as waves of entertainment-seekers took their money elsewhere. Now Gaylord has sold The Nashville Network, and its new owner, another media conglomerate, has renamed it The National Network and moved it to New York. One after another, the various projects that were inaugurated with fine words about how they would lift the city to another level have disappeared—and each time, the city has drawn on its tried and true qualities to find a new comfort level not far from where it has always been. For a great many of the old city's longtime residents, life still works at a Triple-A, minor-league level, where the pace is comfortable and manageable. There, on a slower clock than New York and Los Angeles, Nashville quietly assimilates the kinds of changes that are coming inexorably to 21st-century urban centers across the South and nation.

But to say this city isn't locked on track to become an Atlanta clone does not mean that it's content to rest on its laurels and remain essentially the same place it has been for two centuries. Its motion is definitely forward, and at times swift. In just one generation, Nashville has experienced a sea change in urban philosophy. The city came almost all the way through the 1960s as an oligarchy, its destiny in the hands of a small group of wealthy local families and their political operatives. The first and foremost rule of this prosperous elite was to keep things as they were whenever possible, and to avoid crisis and big changes and loss of control at all cost.

Their way of doing things was represented by shadowy institutions such as the Watauga Club, whose all-male, all-white membership was drawn from Old Nashville, and among whose members were the men who would pick the politicians to implement whatever future the Wataugans envisioned for the city. Politicians were chosen for their team spirit and their ability to cooperate, not for their innovative thinking.

"For many years, I sort of looked at the power structure of Nashville as being focused in three interlocking directorates," said John Seigenthaler, former editor in chief and publisher of *The Tennessean*. "The Vanderbilt University Board of Trust, the Belle Meade Country Club Board of Directors, and the Nashville Area Chamber of Commerce Board of Directors. Those three basically represented the Watauga Society. To get into it, you had to be a CEO with decision-making powers over your institution.

"The truth of the matter is, it was a way that the competing banks, insurance companies, and pillar institutions in the city could get together and decide on a general plan. My guess is that small groups of these people met and approved political candidates and made other important decisions—but as far as I ever knew, they never did those things formally, in the larger group. I refused to join, because I didn't think it was appropriate for me as an editor or publisher to do so."

Seigenthaler said that "for a long period of time, the three banks [First American, Third National, Commerce Union] and two insurance companies [National Life, Life & Casualty] basically alternated the presidency of the chamber of commerce. That's where the power structure of Nashville resided, and for the most part, it was a reasonably progressive power structure. They basically wanted no trouble for the town. Of course, it closed out anyone from the country music industry or from the minority community. Then, all that began to change when the banks were bought up by outside interests, and American General bought both insurance companies. The power has been dispersed—some. And it has been diminished—some."

Most longtime Nashvillians have their own set of important dates in the city's 20th-century history—watershed moments that made it clear the times had changed irrevocably. The opening of Union Station and rising dominance of the Louisville & Nashville Railroad was easily the most significant change at the turn of the last century. The two world wars, sandwiched around the Great Depression, marked subsequent eras. Since 1950, the one change that makes almost everybody's list is the end of legalized racial segregation. Long after the "Whites Only" signs were taken down from public places and people became accustomed to the fact that black and white Nashvillians were entitled to the same rights and privileges of citizenship, latent prejudices lingered in the hearts and minds of many. Not all the changes engendered by desegregation have been altogether harmonious, productive, and beneficial. For instance, as black Nashvillians took advantage of new federal civil rights laws, thousands of white families who had been living in the city fled to the suburbs, abandoning schools, churches, and other urban institutions. Their exodus would only make it harder to reclaim that deserted terrain when it became evident a quarter-century later that without a true renaissance of downtown Nashville, there was no possibility of shaping a successful 21st-century metropolitan community.

Another momentous development of the 20th century was the merger of Nashville and Davidson County in 1963, following approval by the voters of both jurisdictions in a referendum the previous year. This was the first such urban consolidation in the nation, and it paved the way for many of the political, economic, and social advances made by "Metro" (Metropolitan Nashville-Davidson County government) in the past four decades. Attorney Cecil Branstetter, who served on the special commission that gave shape and substance to the new entity, is more convinced with each passing year that this change has given Nashville a permanent advantage over the more duplicative and fragmented urban communities typical of modern American society. "We don't fully appreciate what a positive difference consolidation has made here," he said.

Still another change that many residents remember as a defining moment in Nashville history—for good or ill—came in 1967, when the city passed a liquor-by-the-drink referendum. That represented a departure from the ingrained habit of waiting on religious voices for legislative guidance. Before that, there was relatively little dining in public places, and social life was largely a private affair. Few good restaurants could be persuaded to operate if they could not serve liquor.

"We didn't pass liquor-by-the-drink in Tennessee until 1967, and it was another ten years before we knew that the change was here to stay," said Frank Sutherland, *The Tennessean*'s current editor, who replaced Seigenthaler in 1989. "Then the good restaurants and the big hotels that bar service made economically feasible began to come in, and conventions followed, and that was a major turning point."

A fourth big change that most longtime Nashville watchers consider important has had a more subtle impact than the others, but it may be equally as important. That was the change in the state's banking laws that allowed out-of-state banks to buy up Nashville's financial institutions. "The state legislature had a thing about banks," recalled Sutherland. "Tennessee law said there could be no regional banking—you could only operate in your home county—whereas most of the nation was going to regional banking. The law was finally repealed in 1985, and that's when old Nashville money gave way to corporate money. No longer could a few families run Nashville, and decide its fate.

"When I had the Metro beat as a *Tennessean* reporter in the 1960s and 1970s," Sutherland continued, "I could go down to the courthouse and find out everything I needed to know about the government of Nashville. All the people who knew were either there, or they were represented there. Now you go to the courthouse, and a lot of people don't have a clue what's going on. The power has shifted away from the political arena. The old families were very political, in an indirect way, but many of the corporations were apolitical, so the power became more dispersed. Metro government

husband, James Earl Jones, 40, in pursuit. He stabs her in the back with a butcher knife. A neighbor knocks the enraged assailant unconscious with a metal pipe, and a passing motorist tries to stanch the flow of blood from the victim's wound, but their help comes too late. Until two months ago, James Earl Jones was doing time in a West Tennessee jail. His crime: an earlier attempted murder of his wife.

11—**The 101st Tennessee General Assembly** may be hobbled by a projected $382-million budget shortfall, but adversity hasn't killed the spirit of charity in its heart. The assembly makes its first order of business a bill granting sales-tax exemption to a private company, Spallation Neutron Source, if it will base a $1.3-billion federally funded research project at Oak Ridge in East Tennessee. With bipartisan support and no visible opposition, the bill moves at warp speed toward passage. Tax exemptions for scores of goods and services, from haircuts to heart surgery, already cost Tennessee an estimated $2.7 billion a year in lost revenue. . . . **A day after its job-cuts** trial balloon was shot down in Wilson County, Dell Computer decides it will maintain its payroll of at least 1,000 workers there, and thus protect the bond issue and tax waiver it had been promised as a trade-off.

12—**Just days before** the Tennessee Titans' big NFL playoff game in Indianapolis, with a shot at the Super Bowl awaiting the winner, a news story breaks that Titans cornerback Denard Walker, 25, was arrested the previous July on charges of assaulting the 21-year-old mother of his child during a domestic argument, leaving bruises and strangulation marks on her. Not only was the sports star allowed to wait outside in the booking area after his arrest, unlike other offenders, but the officers who booked him actually loaned him money for bail. The previously unreported story breaks in the *Nashville Scene* just days before the team leaves for Indianapolis. It's the first negative press about personal behavior since the team moved here in 1997. The public reaction is instant fury and outrage—toward the *Scene*—for almost ruining the Titans' preparation for and concentration on the Big Game. This incident notwithstanding, the Titans as a group come out squeaky-clean in comparison with NFL personnel overall. According to a published report, 1 in every 5 NFL players has at least one incident of violent criminal behavior on his record. In this winter alone, the millionaire 20-somethings who dominate the game must count in their ranks two men charged with murder and more than a dozen others whose crimes range from vehicular homicide to assault and rape.

13—Suspensions, firings and resignations are mounting in the 1,200-officer Metro Police Department, prompting Chief Emmett Turner to make administrative changes, including the creation of an office of professional accountability, to be headed by a civilian attorney. (The department has never had a civilian review board.) A year after Turner became chief in 1996, Nashville recorded a record 112 criminal homicides, but a two-year decline in the murder rate followed, and the department seemed to be getting its footing. Now, within the past two months, at least a dozen alarming incidents have riddled the ranks and shaken public confidence. Among them: a patrol officer fired for operating a "swingers club" where customers dance naked and engage in sex; serious allegations voiced by Hispanic residents of an apartment complex who say they were routinely abused and harassed by off-duty police officers working for a private security company; the resignation of a top murder-squad detective after he failed a random drug-screening test; the resignation of a nationally recognized domestic violence expert after in-house squabbling led to his transfer from the special unit he had helped to form; a burglary detective suspended for selling beer without a license; and three off-

has had a lot to do with that, and for the better. But whether you see the shift as a plus or a minus, there's no question that the old power structure has given way to something more diverse, less organized, and more volatile."

It is the corporate model that works today, not just in Nashville, but all across a world shaped by globalization. A big-city mayor needs to be a manager, someone who runs the place as if it were a successful business, or so the thinking goes—and that is precisely what Phil Bredesen brought to city government when he was elected Metro's fourth mayor in 1991. The shift to a corporate mentality now dominates in a multitude of places, not just in city government and the banks. By the year 2000, Nashville's major bookstores, movie theaters, television channels and, indeed, the very daily paper over which Frank Sutherland presides had all been acquired by corporate owners.

The chamber of commerce has clearly made a transition into a different era from those oligarchic days of the "three interlocking directorates." The chamber's interests are not automatically those of the banking and insurance industries. These, in turn, are being run currently by people who may have been in Nashville for only a brief time, and whose ties to the town are far more tenuous than to their corporations, which may be headquartered in another state, or even another country.

How about the other two boards, those of the Belle Meade Country Club and Vanderbilt University? In Belle Meade, not a lot has changed, nothing beyond the usual life-and-death dramas and scandals. Some families have risen, of course, while others have fallen. There has been token change here and there. One difference is that the club's members don't run quite as much of "Greater Nashville" as they used to. After all, two of the Metro Council's five at-large seats are held by African Americans. The club has hardly changed its character, but not all of the most important people in the city are among its members, as once was the case.

Like the country club, Vanderbilt has often been criticized for its insular character, for a seeming lack of interest and engagement in the larger Nashville community. And, the reverse can also be noted: most Nashvillians (besides hospital patients, sports fans, and movie buffs attending Sarratt Cinema) pay little attention to what is happening on the campus. Historically, Vanderbilt answered to a wealthy elite; that is less so now, but the perception lingers that the campus feels no urgent need to link itself with the city, and the city considers itself big enough and important enough without the university's prestige.

Local government and private enterprise meet cooperatively through such organizations as the Greater Nashville Chamber of Commerce. HCA chairman Tommy Frist (left) has served as president of the chamber, and Metro Mayor Bill Purcell, an attorney, was formerly a state legislator.

Inside the campus walls, Vanderbilt has certainly changed. It came into 2000 with a new chancellor, Gordon Gee, who had been boldly hired away from Brown University, and of whom great things were expected. The university's graduate and professional schools (particularly the medical school) are highly regarded nationally, while the undergraduate programs, always strong, have kept their high standing. Vanderbilt prospers in other ways, too, and Nashville is a prime beneficiary. With more than 15,000 people on its payroll, the university is the second largest private employer in Tennessee. Its endowment has been soaring above the $2-billion mark, and its annual operating budget of more than $1.25 billion is actually larger than that of Metro Government itself. Former Mayor Bredesen may have had these figures in mind when he notoriously referred to Vanderbilt as "an 800-pound gorilla," the inference being that it loomed over the city but took little interest in its activities. The town-gown divide has always existed, and it remains, in spite of individual efforts on both sides of the wall to reach across. The opportunity for cross-fertilization now seems greater than ever, with the garrulous Gee in one command post and Vandy law school grad Bill Purcell in the other. (The mayor also ran a research institute at the university prior to his election.)

And then there is that other distinctive Nashville industry, country music. It, like the banks and insurance companies and newspapers, has been absorbed into corporate culture to an ever-increasing degree. More and more economic clout in the music industry is being consolidated into fewer and fewer hands, and those hands usually belong to a corporate body that has no ties to Nashville. A far cry from the old days, when the executives who ran the country music divisions for the various record labels

Under the watchful gaze of Cornelius Vanderbilt, whose 1873 benefaction spawned the Nashville institution that bears his name, the new chancellor of Vanderbilt University, Gordon Gee, greeted his faculty in February 2000.

In the long tradition of so many musicians who come to Music City in search of fame and fortune, guitar picker Steve Daniels tried out his repertoire on the streets near the Nashville riverfront.

duty officers suspended after they wheeled out of a bar parking lot into the path of a state patrol car.

14—**In a rare civil judgment** with criminal implications, Davidson County Circuit Judge Frank Clement Jr. rules that Janet Levine March, missing since 1996 from her Forest Hills home, is dead, and her husband, Nashville lawyer Perry March, is responsible. Police have never charged March with a crime in the case but have named him a prime suspect in her "disappearance and/or homicide." Now living in Mexico, March has refused to return to Nashville for questioning, or to allow the couple's two small children to visit their grandparents here, Lawrence and Carolyn

could pretty well expect to grow old and die in Nashville, because while they worked for national companies like Decca or RCA Victor, these labels generally left their country music operations alone, in the hands of those who knew the market and the music.

Country musicians generally lived and recorded in Nashville, but traditionally did not perform here (except at the Grand Ole Opry). It was a safe place for them to repair to, offstage and off the road. While they tended to disappear into nouveau riche communities like Hendersonville, where they could build big homes by the lake, some were also scattered throughout the city. One, I vividly recall, lived near our family.

It happened that on a Saturday morning in 1951, when I was 5, I wandered with my 3-year-old brother a few doors down the block from our house on Westwood Avenue to see where, so we had heard, the famous singer Hank Williams was renting a house with another rising country music performer, Ray Price. I knew nothing about music, of course, but even little kids are drawn to the stars.

As I recall, Roy Acuff was standing in the yard when we stopped and stared. "Wanna see Mister Williams, boys?" He invited us into the house. We followed him down a darkened hallway and into a small bedroom. There, on a narrow bed, Hank Williams lay stretched out fully clothed, except for his boots and hat. He appeared to be in great distress—looking, I know now, like a man gripped by the worst hangover of his life. I remember seeing a pair of fallen-over cowboy boots beside the bed.

"Couple of young fans wanted to meet you, Hank," said his handler and ours, in a sarcastic voice no doubt meant as a judgment on the young singer's delicate condition. When no answer was forthcoming, Acuff took mercy on the supine form and shuffled us out.

Of course, there are lots of players in Nashville who never become stars. I also remember an elderly gentleman who lived on Westwood in one of the houses between my parents' and Webb Pierce's. He would sit outside on his front porch on sunny weekends with a fiddle under his chin and play. Occasionally, he would be joined by a guitar player of a similarly advanced age. They would tolerate a kid if he crept up quietly to watch and listen and kept his mouth shut. How beautiful to see those old hands make music, to notice the fiddle tucked up under the man's grizzled chin on its folded square of white handkerchief, to watch the bow dance across the strings. All the music in Music City doesn't belong to the record companies, but sometimes that's an easy thing to forget.

For a while, it looked as if country music might be the key to open the door so Nashville could enter into the urban major leagues. *The Johnny Cash Show*, extremely popular in the late 1960s, brought Nashville onto TV screens all across America, and Nashvillians got used to seeing cameras and sound trucks and long limousines all over town. But television consumes material like a glass furnace, and the Cash show, like all others, slid off into the rerun morgue, to be replaced onstage by numerous other "country" acts (as defined in New York and Hollywood)—by *The Glen Campbell Show, Hee Haw*, and others. All the while, of course, the country music business was changing faster than a Charlie Daniels fiddle riff. Now, the laid-back local management style is gone. Most of the record labels have been bought by multinational corporations more interested in micromanagement and money than in the music. In their view, nothing sings like a strong bottom line, and those who can't deliver it on demand, be they artists or executives, need to keep their résumés up to date.

This attitude had led to a repetitious and discordant replay of musical chairs by the end of the 1990s, because country music's sales numbers had slid from robust to anemic. By 1998, growth was flat—and then 1999 was worse, with total album sales falling off 4.5 percent, even as the rest of the recording industry was experiencing a better than 6 percent rise.

Ironically, these more unstable times have had one beneficial effect in

Guitar legend Chet Atkins was one of many Nashville music stars whose presence was avidly sought in the new music-food-entertainment venues clustered in the Lower Broadway area.

Levine. . . . **Anglican Archbishop** Desmond Tutu of South Africa, a hero of the black liberation movement there, is warmly received by an overflow crowd in Fisk University's Memorial Chapel. The heralded cleric, whose daughter works at Fisk's Race Relations Institute, holds his audience spellbound throughout a 30-minute speech. . . . **Mayor Purcell's** systematic review of Metro government procedures and performance is raising anxiety among employees. Internal audits are being conducted, department by department. The queries are not only about money (as in how to balance budgets without raising taxes) but also about the work climate (as in personnel policies, productivity, efficiency and morale). Purcell has already made personal visits to almost half of Metro's 127 public schools since he took office in September. He promises to get around to every one of them during his first year.

15—**Finally, some good news** on the fiscal front: The state pension fund, benefiting from a roaring bull of a stock market, has grown so much that the state now needs to put in less money to maintain the same level of retirement benefits. A windfall of $10-$15 million thus will go into the Tennessee treasury, where it will certainly come in handy as a down payment on the looming $380-odd-million deficit.

16—**For several years,** two Nashville churches have held a joint worship service on the Sunday before Martin Luther King's birthday—but not today. The reason: The time conflicts with the nationally televised NFL playoff game between the Titans and the Colts. But the two congregations—one mostly white and Unitarian, the other black and Baptist—will still sit down together this afternoon, say the Rev. Mary Katherine Morn of First Unitarian Universalist and the Rev. Enoch Fuzz of Corinthian Baptist. The place: Miss Cloudie Mae's BBQ restaurant on Trinity Lane, where they will watch the game on TV. Fuzz says King would heartily approve: "This is another way to celebrate the dream he died for." . . . **Their prayers** presumably answered, an estimated 10,000 delirious fans meet the victorious Titans at Nashville International Airport after their 19-16 victory over Peyton Manning and the Colts. One woman is seriously injured on an escalator as the celebratory frenzy careens momentarily out of hand.

17—The Metro Fire Department is reeling from the shock of a $1-million budget deficit this fiscal year, and the pain is also being felt and heard in other city departments. The state's money woes are even more acute. The commissioner of environment and conservation, former state Sen. Milton Hamilton, says he will be forced to close 10 of Tennessee's 54 parks or begin charging user fees unless the legislature appropriates $1.3 million more for his department.

18—After 38 years on the air as WDCN-Channel 8, Nashville's public television station is adopting a new name and a new identity. Starting Feb. 22, the station will call itself NPT, which stands for Nashville Public Television. In a mailing sent to members, new WDCN president/CEO Steven M. Bass says the change signals the station's departure from a "conventional, safe approach to programming."

19—Another petitioner weighs in as the University of Tennessee's new president, Wade Gilley, pleads for a one-time, $30-million special appropriation from the state to help boost UT into the ranks of the nation's 25 top public research universities. The UT athletic program (which perennially ranks among the top 10 in football) would match the state's $30 million from its own separate stash, Gilley says, and the university would raise $60 million more from private gifts and yet another $30 million from administrative streamlining. . . . **Federal funds** would pay most of the $30 million cost of a 32-mile commuter rail line on existing

Nashville: They have brought more of the performers onto local stages, the better to be seen and heard (and bought, in the record shops). It has always been easier to bump into country music stars at the corner grocery than to find them performing anywhere nearby. In the year 2000, you may still run into them doing their shopping (depending on what neighborhood you shop in), but you may also hear them playing an occasional gig around Music City. The industry, as before, remains only marginally engaged in Nashville's civic life (apart from its role as a revenue generator), but there are unmistakable signs that this picture is changing.

For its part, the city has certainly been reaching out, as witness its substantial financial contribution to the cost of building the new Country Music Hall of Fame on Demonbreun Street downtown, and the financing of a roundabout and other traffic improvements on Music Row. In reciprocation, more and more star performers are doing benefits for worthy causes.

Rashawn Crayton was "a bouncy little 9-year-old kid" when he started piano lessons with Clarice Hargrove at the W.O. Smith Community Music School. Pupil and teacher, they personify the school's success since its start in 1982.

Consider the W.O. Smith Nashville Community Music School, where musicians from the industry volunteer their time and talent in a rigorous program of small-group and one-on-one music lessons for talented kids who couldn't otherwise afford them.

"When Del Sawyer [then the dean of Vanderbilt's Blair School of Music] first went to Music Row with the idea of such a school back in the late 1970s, he didn't get much of a reception," said Frank Sutherland. "But finally he got to Buddy Killen [president of Tree Publishing, then an industry leader], and when Buddy got interested, he made it work. Buddy said, 'This reinforces what we're about, and here's a chance for us to make a contribution to the city.' The W.O. Smith School was the first crack in the wall. If you look today, you'll see Vince Gill in every charity event coming down the pike. And Reba McEntire, Mark Collie, Mark O'Connor, Collin Ray, just to name a few—these folks have become a very visible and supportive part of the community. For them to do that, their companies have to be behind them."

Any way you cut it, Nashville still throbs to the beat of music—and the music is spilling out of its traditional borders and flowing through almost every imaginable genre, including bluegrass, jazz, rock, rap, gospel, blues, folk, pop, salsa, classical, and techno. There are more world-class studio session players and independent songwriters doing their semi-anonymous thing here now than there ever were at any time in the

Music City's signature is country, but its total showcase contains anything and everything musical, including O.J. Ekemode, leader of the Nigerian All-Stars, who play an eclectic mix of jazz and "Afro-beat."

past, not to mention well-known stars from the rock world, such as Donna Summer, Peter Frampton, and Steve Winwood, who make their homes here. On almost any given night, you can hear the strains of African, Mexican, Middle Eastern, Asian, and South American music somewhere in the Nashville night. Music City lives.

Most other facets of the arts in Nashville also have grown and matured, according to John Bridges, a longtime arts journalist and writer who is Mayor Bill Purcell's choice as the city's first-ever director of cultural affairs. One of his jobs is liaison with the country music industry—the first local government outreach to the record companies. "I've always maintained that Nashville is already a major-league city culturally, if for no other reason than because we're the home of country music," Bridges said. "Now, however, we can seize a moment that will carry us to that level in other cultural aspects, as well as in major-league sports. We can have it all."

Within 60 days in the spring of 2001, he said, three major institutions will open new venues that will significantly raise Nashville's standing in the world of culture: the Frist Center for the Visual Arts, on Broadway; the downtown public library, on Church Street; and the Country Music Hall of Fame and Museum, on Demonbreun Street. Collectively, they represent an investment of more than $160 million in public and private funds (hardly small change, but still only about half what it took to get Adelphia Coliseum up and running).

By fits and starts, Nashville is indeed changing, and mostly in the direction of a major-league model. A yearning has grown up among its citizens for more of the amenities expected of a metropolitan population center. Tranquil, staid, stable, and quiet are wonderful qualities, as far as they go—but not in themselves enough to bring productivity, prosperity, and pleasure to an urban hub of more than 1.2 million people.

track right-of-way between Nashville and Lebanon, say local officials who are touting the plan, and the trains could be running by the end of 2001. Passengers would pay $3 for the 50-minute one-way trip. Four more legs of this "innovative response to our highway congestion problems" would be added by 2010, giving commuters in the Gallatin, Murfreesboro, Franklin and Kingston Springs areas a new way to get to and from work in the city. Sixty years ago, 44 passenger trains a day chugged in and out of Nashville's Union Station; none do now.

20—**Edward J. McKeown,** a former Catholic priest in Nashville now serving a prison sentence for child molestation, draws two multimillion-dollar lawsuits against himself, the local Catholic diocese and the Metro government. The suits allege that both the church and Metro's juvenile court division negligently allowed the priest to keep working with children after they learned that he had a history of child sexual abuse. . . . **In an impassioned editorial,** the *Nashville Scene* calls for the resignation of Metro Police Chief Emmett Turner, citing his apparent lack of leadership and his scandal-rocked department. Turner stays, but calls in his top brass for what is described as a "come-to-Jesus meeting."

21—**Sam M. Fleming,** eulogized as "one of the great financial leaders of Nashville and the nation," dies at 91 years of age, after half a century in the vortex of power created by the major local banks (now all absentee-owned), Vanderbilt University, the city's chamber of commerce and Belle Meade, the bluestocking residential community. . . . **On Printer's Alley,** another death is mourned. A candlelight vigil is held to commemorate the second anniversary of the murder of colorful club owner David "Skull" Schulman in his nightclub, Skull's Rainbow Room. The club, opened in the mid-1940s, featured exotic dancers in its heyday, and Schulman made it a honky-tonk in 1989. But he was perhaps best known for his behind-the-scene role in the creation of the country music TV series *Hee Haw*. He was often seen sitting on a bench in Printer's Alley in his *Hee Haw* overalls and a cap, stroking his ubiquitous poodle Sweetie. Schulman, 78, was found stabbed during working hours, the victim of an apparent robbery. The crime remains unsolved. . . . **During a total lunar eclipse,** a blood-red moon arcs over the city.

22—**Nashvillians wake up** to a beautiful freak snowfall that dumps up to 3.5 inches of wet, slushy snow in the area. It will melt quickly, but it nonetheless rouses the hair-trigger survival instincts of the Midstate's snow-fearing folk, who stampede to the

On virtually every construction site, there are many Hispanic laborers like Jaime Del Rio (above, preparing concrete forms at the Hilton Suites Hotel in downtown Nashville).

Cities—all living things—must grow and change, or die. The question is not whether Nashville goes on growing and changing, but how.

Many Nashvillians have lived here all their lives, and can trace more than a century of family history in this place. To them, there may seem nothing special about being a second-tier Southern city with plenty of work available and lots of open green space. But now, a growing number of people from faraway places come here and see all this as something just short of paradise. They are people who have come to the United States looking for work and a chance to better their lives, and for one reason or another, they don't want to live in one of the big cities where Hispanic or Asian or Middle

Eastern immigrants traditionally have settled—New York, Boston, Chicago, Miami, Houston, Los Angeles. As the Nashville job market expanded toward the end of the 1990s, the city grew increasingly attractive to immigrants and refugees, documented and undocumented, and the numbers of people arriving in Nashville from underdeveloped nations began to rise.

This meant that Nashville finally had to deal with the diversification of its population, just as larger cities had already been doing for decades. There have been resident populations of foreigners, usually professionals, in this city for a long time (often people who came to study at one of the colleges or universities), but their numbers were small and their impact on the city was minimal. Many were Asians grateful for the chance to be studying or teaching here, and they worked hard without much desire to participate in community life outside of their own circles. But now a new wave of immigrants and refugees is sweeping in, and they are not from such well-educated backgrounds, nor do they have much intention or hope of ever returning to their homeland. They are in Nashville to stay and, by the start of 2000, they were already at work converting the city into something a little more comfortably international.

Nashville's Latino community is growing by leaps and bounds. The city has an unemployment rate of only 2.4 percent, and employers are desperate for workers. Large companies like Opryland Hotel are using labor contractors to recruit and hire people in Mexico and Latin America and bring them here for the busy seasons.

The world is in rapid forward motion—and for its own competitive health, not to say survival, Nashville is becoming increasingly intertwined with the global economy. This means filling jobs with people from other countries who are willing to work for low

nearest supermarket and fortify themselves with stashes of Swiss Miss Cocoa, candles and cough drops. . . . **The city also awakens** to news of the deaths of two Middle Tennesseans who made their lasting marks outside the city. Celebrated former *Life* magazine photojournalist Ed Clark has died in Sarasota at age 88, leaving a gallery of subjects that includes President John F. Kennedy and actress Marilyn Monroe. And in New York City, Murfreesboro native Jean Faircloth MacArthur, the widow of Gen. Douglas MacArthur, dies at the age of 101 after a lengthy illness. Her longevity is reflected in her inclusive dates: born 1899, died 2000.

23—**The Tennessee Titans'** improbable march to the Super Bowl is a dream come true after the team scores a decisive 33-14 victory over Jacksonville at the losers' home stadium. The Nashville team will meet the St. Louis Rams in Super Bowl XXXIV in Atlanta next Sunday. Upwards of 35,000 wildly exuberant fans turn out to welcome the Titans home—not at the airport this time but in the stadium, where crowd control is easier. A high-octane mix of young and old, white and black, drunk and devout, they all appear to be in full agreement with one among them who shouts to reporters, "This is the greatest thing that ever happened to Nashville!" No one dares disagree. . . . **At *The Tennessean,*** the entire front page and most of the sports section of tomorrow's editions will belong to the Titans. As the editors busily make up the front page, an executive from the marketing department comes in to inspect. Disapproving of the chosen headline and top photograph as too horizontal for the T-shirt they're planning as a promotion, the executive pulls rank on the layout editor—and prevails on appeal to the higher-ups. . . . **In an 11-hour operation,** doctors at Vanderbilt University Medical Center replace the heart, lungs and liver of Darrell Hedgecoth, an 18-year-old high-school senior from nearby Ashland City, with organs from a donor who died

The New Testament in Spanish holds the attention of Nelva Luz Ventura and her husband, José Alfredo Dominguez, at the Nashville Union Rescue Mission.

in a car accident. Hedgecoth, suffering from cystic fibrosis, had been given only a few months to live; now, says one of his surgeons, Dr. Davis C. Drinkwater Jr., he should be able to live a normal life. Only about a dozen triple-organ transplants have been reported anywhere in the world.

24—The morning paper's "all Titans" front page—a strong vertical that fits perfectly on the "limited-edition T-shirt . . . available for only $15" (plus $6 shipping and handling and 8.25% sales tax, so make that $22.73 each)—is a triumph for the marketing department and looks impressive in the full-page advertisement on page 13A. In the newsroom, though, there is deep gloom and distress. Many reporters and lower-level editors complain bitterly among themselves and to others outside the company that the paper (a link in the suburban Washington-based Gannett chain since 1979) has become so obsessively profit-driven that its credibility and effectiveness as an independent voice are seriously eroded. . . . **Police Chief Emmett Turner** names a Metro legal department attorney, Kennetha Sawyers, as the civilian head of a new "Office of Professional Accountability" to oversee investigations of all complaints against police employees. This is in lieu of an external review process. . . . **Convicted murderer Robert Glen Coe** is scheduled to be executed in less than two months. But before he can be put to death, he must be found mentally competent— the subject of today's hearing in Judge John Colton's Memphis courtroom. Coe, in shackles, is belligerent and enraged, screaming obscenities, but the judge appears to ignore the outbursts. Before the hearing ends four days hence, a parade of expert witnesses will testify to Coe's mental state, most of them concluding that he is indeed disturbed, but understands what is happening. By the third day, Coe's erratic behavior— spitting, cursing, threatening—causes Judge Colton to have him gagged, and finally removed to a nearby room where the court proceedings are showing

wages and no benefits. This is not exactly stop-the-presses news in big metropolitan areas where Hispanic immigration began generations ago—but for Nashville, it's an eye-opening revelation.

Lest anyone doubt that increased numbers of immigrants are good for, and even vital to, Nashville's continued development, note that among the groups most eager to see a U.S. Immigration and Naturalization Service office established here was the local chamber of commerce. By the year 2000, there was virtually no labor pool of native Nashvillians willing to do the heavy lifting; anyone seriously looking for work could find other jobs that paid more and didn't require such strenuous effort. Immigrants were desperately needed to fill those day-labor jobs.

An altogether different kind of worker from Central America and the Middle East was also finding a niche in Nashville: craftsmen and artisans, those who still practiced professions that were dying in this country for lack of young people willing to learn and practice them. It didn't take long for Nashville contractors and home builders to discover that Mexican immigrants were still capable of doing the kind of masonry work that a diminishing number of local artisans still knew how to do.

While there are some things, such as their darker skin and different language, that make Latinos stand out in Nashville, there are other things that make them fit right in. The Mexican and Central American cultures practice, on a daily basis, a devotion to family that many North Americans only preach. In addition, the combination of traditional Catholicism and contemporary evangelical Christianity so completely dominates all of the Americas south of Florida and Texas that new arrivals from south of the border know their Bibles every bit as well as your average Nashville Christian—which is to say, very well indeed. Many Mexicans, Hondurans, Columbians, and others would no sooner think of missing Sunday mass or Wednesday-night prayer meeting than would any devout Davidson County Catholic or Baptist.

Freeways, feeder roads, shopping malls and subdivisions (as witness the Cool Springs area from the air) follow one after another, as surely as the seasons follow the calendar.

Of course, immigrant labor is not always going to be in such demand, and the economy, being cyclical in nature, will not always be as good as it was when 2000 began. What lies ahead after the inevitable economic slowdown is sure to be bumpy for everyone, and especially turbulent for immigrants. They will be the first to be fired and the last to be rehired. Nevertheless, there are many immigrants and refugees who have settled into Middle Tennessee, who have car payments and house loans, and kids in school here, and these people will stay on. The large numbers of single men, only temporarily living outside Mexico or Central America while they send money home to families with no prospect of any kind of work, will move on to places where jobs are more plentiful or pay is higher. But many families will stay behind and put down roots and become Nashvillians in the fullest sense. These are people who know what really hard times are all about, and who

One sure sign of rapid growth in the Nashville area is congestion on the interstate highways that spoke out in six directions from the city. Traffic snarls can turn a normal 30-minute drive into a two-hour standstill.

have a developed capacity for hunkering down and weathering the worst (good qualities in any environment). Most of them will be able to wait until the city enters its next phase of economic growth.

As for the long-established population of Nashville, what the future holds is, of course, unknowable—but it does seem likely that if the city is to maintain controlled growth and continue to prosper, it must embrace the smaller towns around it and shape a destiny that includes and benefits the adjacent counties that, with Nashville-Davidson, make up the Greater Nashville metropolitan district. Davidson County's population grew by almost 12 percent during the 1990s, while the seven surrounding counties grew by an average of more than 35 percent. Without regional cooperation, the problems caused by such unbalanced growth will only intensify.

In the 21st century, Nashville will face many of the same challenges as Charlotte, Louisville, Birmingham, Jacksonville, and other Southern cities where the car is king. They all have big-league pretensions, but a city is more than an aggregation of suburbs. Nashville illustrates this point only too well, sitting as it is in the middle of the country and at the junction of several interstate highway routes. The combination of cars and trucks passing through and commuters going to and from work in the central city has all but gridlocked the highways. But Nashvillians have an attachment to their cars that sometimes seems bred in the bone, and enticing people off the highways is a tough task, to say the least. The city has grown up and spread out along the interstates, so much so that from the 1950s through the mid-1990s, it was consistently defined by moves farther and farther from downtown. Malls and residential developments required longer and longer drives to reach. Nashvillians like to drive to where they

on closed-circuit television.

25—**Remember that $382-million budget deficit** forecast by Gov. Sundquist? The good news is, it has been lowered by about $40 million because of brighter revenue estimates, says the state's commissioner of finance, John Ferguson. The bad news: The sum needed to fix the crippled TennCare medical program will be $40 million higher than expected—so the total shortfall remains the same. "Rome is burning," says Sen. Bob Rochelle (D-Lebanon), the most vocal supporter of the governor's state income tax proposal, "and there's still a lot of fiddling going on."

26—**In a bizarre promotional stunt** gone awry, country station shop, and they don't like to mix retail and residential functions, preferring to keep their stores and their houses distinctly separated. (In contrast, European cities routinely require a mix of residential and commercial development.) When Opryland decided to close its theme park, the rides and funhouses were replaced with a shopping mall, even though the location was far off the beaten path for Nashville shoppers, in a place that basically is inaccessible except by car. Nevertheless, the developers confidently predict-ed that upwards of 17 million people would visit the mall within a year of its spring 2000 opening.

The first tentative steps toward regional transportation had already begun, with buses running daily schedules between Nashville and several towns, including Clarksville and Murfreesboro. They were doing a thriving business, and other routes were planned. There is even talk that commuter rail service will return after an absence of some 50 years. Meanwhile, a lot of work remained to be done on existing public transportation within Nashville. It has one of the worst bus systems of any city its size. Routes are infrequent, and a one-way ride costs $1.40. "If you look at other cities we compete with economically," said the Metro Transit Authority's Bob Babbitt, "most of them invest two, three, or even four times as much in their bus systems as we do—and charge less per rider."

It will, no doubt, be many years before the pie of power in Nashville is more equitably divided among all its residents, and the city becomes a comfortable place to live for everyone. But swept along on the tide of Titan jubilation, it was just possible to imagine that it might one day happen, that with lots of work and dedication Nashville would grow into a city with the best to offer all its people, wherever they live and work.

One day in 1999, when I was back in town for a visit, I drove downtown to the Bicentennial Mall to do some shopping at the Farmers Market. Now this is what I call a mall! How great to have it here—the whole layout designed to be inviting and attrac-tive to stroll through, and at the same time, a useful lesson in the colorful history of this grand state, with its wealth of human and natural resources from the mountains to the delta.

Many of the state's products are in fact available for sale right in the market. You can buy almost anything to eat here, from catfish and country hams to pickled garlic by the ounce and turnip greens by the bushel, from frijoles and cilantro to taro root, curry, and a bazillion other things.

For some reason, though, it seemed quiet in the place—too quiet. Maybe things hadn't changed as much as I thought. Late on this lovely Saturday afternoon, there was almost no one strolling on the mall. The sun gleamed on empty benches, the light fell warm on the deserted pathways. A thin straggle of shoppers drifted out of the Farmers Market, where the vendors were straightening shelves and packing up their produce, getting ready to go home for the evening. Compared to any supermarket or any mall around the city at that moment, the place was virtually empty. Maybe Nashville wasn't ready for this quintessentially urban scene: a richly variegated international market, smoothly interlaced with the traditions and history of Tennessee.

Leaving the mall area, I drove along James Robertson Parkway (named for the father of Nashville, a woodsman and pioneer who walked here from upper East Ten-nessee in the winter of 1779-80). Stopping at the curb, I got out and gazed up from the foot of a steep slope of grass to the State Capitol at the crest, soaring against the sky.

On the hillside I saw two boys—they couldn't have been more than 14—sitting with their knees drawn up to their chests. Each was puffing a cigarette. They looked buzzed and rebellious, furtive, guilty. I thought back 40 years to when my young friend and I passed our Saturday afternoons coming downtown on the bus to that special drugstore we knew where the woman behind the counter sold cigarettes to one and all, no ID required. The mystique and the thrill of a pack of smokes! Yorks, Springs, King Sanos—even the names sang of forbidden pleasures.

After the buy, we'd head off to that hilltop perch behind the capitol. From there, you could see for miles all around, or so it seemed. We were far enough above the park-

At the Bicentennial Mall, just to the north of Capitol Hill, sunny-day strollers are reflected in the black stone floating globe commemorating Tennesseans who fought in World War II.

way that passersby could not quite make out our faces—that little precaution just in case someone who knew us should drive by, and then tell our parents what unspeakable crimes we were committing.

How we lived in the moment then, so full of certainty that the world was pregnant with possibilities, just waiting for us to show our stuff. A couple of teenagers being cool—laughing, talking, smoking cheap cigarettes on a grassy slope of downtown turf in a second-tier urban center in the heart of the South, a little city on a little river, right in the middle of Tennessee.

January 30, 2000: Super Bowl Sunday. The St. Louis Rams versus—Omigod! Here come the Tennessee Titans running out onto the field at the Georgia Dome in Atlanta, in front of 72,625 fans and almost a billion viewers worldwide. That's Nashville's team! The relocated, reinvented, reconstructed, rejuvenated Titans! Omigod! It must be a dream!

But it's true, and real, and almost unbelievable, right down to the last agonizing second. As the climax of a season in which nothing has been easy, this is a typical game. Trailing 16-0 in the third quarter, the Titans come roaring back to tie the game in the final minutes, only to have the Rams strike quickly on a touchdown bomb, leaving our heroes down by seven with just 1:48 remaining. Titans' fans have lived through Sunday after Sunday when it seemed that only a miracle could save the team from defeat, and that miracle has been forth-

ethics board majority contends that accepting such special treatment compromises council members' ability to make independent judgments on issues concerning the team or the stadium. Metro's legal department will investigate.

28—*Tennessean* **reporter and columnist** Jerry Thompson, 59, a likable and mischievous practical joker with countless friends in high and low places, dies peacefully in a local hospital, ending his 12-year fight against cancer. In the 1960s, he covered the notorious Commerce Street red-light district, and as an investigative reporter, he went undercover in the Ku Klux Klan. In a fond remembrance, Vice President Al Gore, his former

29—**William Edmondson,** a son of slaves, never traveled outside of Tennessee in his lifetime. Yet the haunting, vividly detailed sculptures he chiseled at his home at 1434 14th Ave. S., most crafted between 1934 and 1948, are displayed today in the Museum of Modern Art, the Smithsonian and other famed galleries. Edmondson's work is the subject of a major touring retrospective opening this week at Cheekwood. When this traveling exhibition ends, more people will have seen his work than in all the decades combined since his seminal 1937 show at the MOMA.

30—Titans' receiver Kevin **Dyson** is tackled one yard short of the end zone on the last play of the Super Bowl, and St. Louis escapes with a 23-16 victory in what sportswriters call the most exciting game in the 34-year history of the championship. For the Nashville team and its newfound legion of fans, the "miracle season" ends just one miracle short.

31—In his State of the State **address,** Gov. Sundquist once again defies his party by proposing a 3.75 percent flat-rate income tax as the key element in his efforts to reform the state's overburdened and inequitable tax system. "Many have pronounced my vision for the future dead on arrival," he acknowledges, "but I refuse to accept that pronouncement." In a rare act of bipartisanship, the assembled Republicans and Democrats greet this remark with dismissive silence.

coming, again and again. Who could blame them for believing it would happen one more time? Just this once, for the football championship of the world.

Starting on his own 13-yard line, quarterback Steve McNair coolly and quickly guides the men in blue tantalizingly close to the tying touchdown. With time expiring, McNair eludes several St. Louis defenders and tosses a short pass to receiver Kevin Dyson, who grabs it and lunges for the goal line. But he is slammed to the turf just one yard short of the Promised Land—and suddenly, heartbreakingly, it's all over.

One yard short. Sportswriters around the nation would call it "the most unforgettable of Super Bowls," and "among the all-time great finishes in the big-game annals of sports." There on the artificial turf, for want of a single yard, the Titans miracle finally died.

Or did it? Even without the championship, Middle Tennessee still adored its Titans. This had been a fan-tastic season, unlike anything else the city had ever known. Win or lose, the team had made it all the way to the Super Bowl. And the city had, too. What better way to inaugurate the new year, the new century, the new millennium?

It would be prudent not to make too much of it. Nowhere in the record books is there an example of a city so uplifted by a big sports championship that it pulled itself together, healed its sick, housed its homeless, fixed its schools, offered its poor a leg up. Those kinds of miracles are not within the province of athletes. A different sort of strength is called for.

Nashville is still searching for that strength, for the vision and the will to become a productive and interdependent 21st-century community. The Titans came through their crucible proudly, the bigger and better for having faced the challenge. As a symbol of what trying hard can get you, they are valuable beyond measure to their home city. Thanks in part to the team and its accomplishments, Nashville blew into the new millennium a year early and a yard short, but on a full head of civic steam. Now we will see how far it gets us.

It snowed confetti at the end of Super Bowl XXXIV, but for a dejected and weary Eddie George and his Tennessee Titans, it was a bitter blizzard.

"Bury Me in an Old Press Box"

by FRED RUSSELL

If you had told me back in 1990 that Nashville would send a National Football League team to the Super Bowl by the beginning of the new century, I'd have thought you were absolutely crazy, simply crazy.

Don't get me wrong—I loved that fantasy. I chased major-league teams and their stars for more than 70 years. I've been the luckiest man in the world. My first big story at the *Nashville Banner* was an interview with the great Ty Cobb in 1929. I got to cover about 50 World Series and as many Kentucky Derbies, four Olympics, and more football and basketball games than I can count.

Except for an occasional exhibition here, most of the really big sporting events I've witnessed were on the road. So you're asking me, ten years back, to imagine a team called the Tennessee Titans winning an NFL conference title? And winning a playoff game with a last-minute touchdown in a brand new stadium in Nashville? And coming within a yard of a tie in the 2000 Super Bowl? Never. Impossible.

You couldn't have made me believe it. But that's just what happened, and I'm delighted to say I was alive to see it. This ranks right up there with the all-time great stories to come along since I started writing about sports.

I must have written more than 17,000 columns for the *Banner*. My 1957 book, *Bury Me in an Old Press Box*, looked back on almost 30 years of covering the great ones. I've enjoyed close friendships with Grantland Rice (who was born in Murfreesboro), Red Smith of the *New York Times*, and other fine sportswriters, and such exceptional athletes as golf legend Bobby Jones, football's Red Grange, and boxing champ Jack Dempsey. Those people and those experiences enriched my life and left me with memories I wouldn't trade for anything.

Today the Tennessee Titans are creating lasting memories like that for their fans everywhere. In their short but sensational time here, they have become the toast of the town, the number-one sports story in our city.

Take it from a guy who was born here in 1906—having this pro team has been a wonderful thing for Nashville. There's more to life than sports, of course, but all you have to do is look around, and listen—people love this team. I am reminded that there is nothing like winning to give you a positive attitude. The Titans, led by their superstar running back Eddie George, have captured the hearts of their new fans, and I'm right there in front of the TV set whenever the team lines up for the kickoff.

The only shadow over it all, as far as I'm concerned, is the death of the *Nashville Banner*. The afternoon paper was a vital part of this city from 1876 until 1998, when it was sold to Gannett and ceased publication. We all took its demise pretty hard, almost like a death in the family—a family I'd been part of since the 1920s. I'd love to be out there today with the old *Banner* sports staffers, covering this memorable story.

Most of my old pals are gone now, and here I am, still having my say in the 21st century. It bears repeating: I'm the luckiest man in the world.

Reminds me of a little verse, probably from the pen of Granny Rice:

> *Time marches on, you say?*
> *Ah, but no,*
> *It is not time,*
> *But we, who go.*

—30—

Fred Russell was still writing for the Nashville Banner *when it folded. His byline graced the sports pages during eight decades of the 20th century. With this reflection, he extends his writing streak to nine.*

Oh, Brother! It's Nashville

by Roy Blount Jr.

"I never met a Southerner who didn't hate the movie," the critic Pauline Kael is quoted as saying in *The Nashville Chronicles: The Making of Robert Altman's Masterpiece*, "and it's hard to understand. There is a kind of reaction, as if the movie is meant to be critical of them." I would be one of the Southerners who has given her that impression. And if there's anything I hate, it's the notion of hating something that's good, or being regarded as hating something that's good, because of where I'm from.

I have, in fact, met a number of Southerners who loved *Nashville*. I would argue with them till I was blue in the face. Sometimes I got pretty worked up about it. But now, I believe, I am finally able to speak of this movie calmly. In part because I am mature and tired, and in part because I now have another movie to love, which many other Southerners hate.

Nashville marked its 25th anniversary in the year 2000. It is also the year that *Oh Brother, Where Art Thou?* has appeared. Both films are set in the South, were shot on location in the South, and have much to do with Southern music. Both were directed by non-Southerners—in the first case Robert Altman of Kansas City, in the second the Coen Brothers of Minnesota. I couldn't wait to see *Brother* so I could denounce it as a crude, heartless caricature of persons representing my ethnic background. I sat there scowling at it for fifteen minutes. And then . . .

It's a funny movie. And it's got feeling. And Charles Durning does just enough of a little dance to retain his title as the best-dancing fat man there ever has been. I would sit through a musical tribute to Newt Gingrich by Billy Ray Cyrus if I thought that at some point Charles Durning would get up and dance. And I like George Clooney in movies.

Maybe you think I have forsaken all vigilance. Well, maybe I just have bad taste. Let me confess that I have found much to enjoy over the years in *Hee-Haw*, and also in *Amos 'n' Andy*. Then too, maybe I like a little Northern smart-ass mixed in with my country pleasures. Purely Southern funnin'-of-ourselves sometimes gets too cozy. As sharp and funny as Mrs. Sarah Cannon (Minnie Pearl) was as a person, check out some of her old "Grinder's Switch"

monologues if you want to hear Southern people being portrayed as embarrassingly dumb.

But the main virtue of *Brother* is how lovingly and respectfully it involves real, weird, ecstatic, piercing, rootsy Southern music—from "You Are My Sunshine" and "I'll Fly Away" to the wonderfully spooky-erotic (and new to me) folk lullaby, "Didn't Leave Nobody But the Baby." You might well say that any movie with any sense set in the South would take advantage of the good music. But that is what *Nashville*, the music-filled movie, does not do. Of course neither does Nashville, the music industry. If only Altman had been grounded enough in the music to give that disjunction the business.

As soon as *Nashville* came out I rushed to see it. The other day I watched the DVD of it to make sure I hadn't just been in a bad mood that night in 1975. The movie still puts my nose out of joint. It has some great stuff in it, to be sure. Lily Tomlin's Nashville housewife has what the character supposedly based on Loretta Lynn lacks: character. Her scenes with Ned Beatty playing her husband and with Keith Carradine as the young musician who seduces her (it is she, however, who comes out on top), and Beatty's scenes with Gwen Welles as the aspiring, untalented singer who has to strip for a political smoker, all flow together the way only a semi-improvised, actor-friendly Altman syncopation can, when it's got some fiber to it. But you can't flambé fried chicken. As a concept, *Nashville* has too much literal and metaphorical specific gravity, good and bad, to be served up just any old whichaway à la Altman.

In his directorial commentary on the DVD, Altman says *Nashville* "is a microcosm of the Hollywood problem." This is an excuse for him to fill out his cast of characters with a melange of L.A. drifter types looking for fame. After *Nashville* came out, documentarian Ray Farkas made a brief film that captured the sort of obsession that, in fact, draws more dreamers to Nashville than to Hollywood. It seemed that every third Nashvillian he met, beginning with the rent-a-car lady in the airport, had a song that he or she had written, hoped to get recorded, and was happy to sing, badly, for Farkas' camera.

These days creative Nashville may think of itself as a microcosm of Hollywood, but what that amounts to is road-show Hollywood, a contradiction in terms. "The Hollywood problem" that Altman presents as Nashville verité is nothing more than his scattershot vision of mid-'70s American Zeitgeist. In his DVD commentary, he readily admits that he knew nothing about Nashville or country music, and that his screenwriter, Joan Tewkesbury, didn't either, except what she picked up in two atmosphere-gathering visits. He keeps insisting, however, on the movie's "realism." Altman didn't want to deal with record companies (understandably), so his actors wrote their own songs. Carradine's are catchy, but they don't smack at all of Nashville or of Jerry Jeff Walker, the hell-raising outlaw-country icon who supposedly inspired his character. Henry Gibson's songs are droll, as is his performance as a Hank Snow sort of fella, but they aren't as funny as Snow's explanation of why he wouldn't go to the movie: "I have better things to do than to go see a movie where somebody's supposed to be playing me. . . . I'm not pompous at all. I'm just a quiet, bashful country boy."

When Vassar Clements appears on the screen, Altman in his voice-over commentary identifies him as "a great jazz violinist." No, he's a great country fiddle player. As is Johnny Gimble, who pops up a couple of times gamely trying to play along with whatever the hell is going on, and who isn't even mentioned in the credits. Johnny Gimble is a man who has played and hung with—and can tell you great stories about—Bob Wills and Willie Nelson.

In *Nashville*, Altman was trying to make some kind of grand political point which, as a British reviewer of the movie put it snottily, "looks stuck in for a significance that it could never have in a place so traumatized by its self-importance that minutes after gunshots have left a bloody body onstage, the townsfolk are nodding and clapping again in time to their staple music." This is really infuriating to me, because that indifference to reality seems to be Altman's theme, when in fact it is a matter of his own indifference.

The supposed Loretta Lynn character breaks down while singing at Opryland, and her audience responds by groaning nastily. "Those are the faces of the audience," says Altman on the CD. "You can go there today and that's what you'll see." No realistic country music audience witnessing anybody as beloved as Loretta Lynn breaking down would respond like that.

Then in the final, climactic scene of the movie, the one adverted to by the British reviewer, this same character is shot by an assassin, and her audience responds by singing over and over the refrain of a song written by Carradine, "You may say that I ain't free. Well it don't worry me."

When they filmed that scene in Centennial Park back in 1974, the production company gathered a big crowd by advertising 10-cent hotdogs, and, more significantly, a chance to be in a movie. That's what I went for. I don't know that I even got a hotdog. I happened to be in Nashville at the time (covering a Protestant ministers' golf tournament), and some friends and I joined the multitude. We saw an actress get shot a couple of times, and then all we were directed to do was sing along, for more than an hour, with this mindless ditty. What were we going to do, act? I tell you what, if it had been Loretta Lynn shot we wouldn't have been nodding and clapping. We would have been weeping and looking to kill the sumbitch that shot her. But since it was a movie, we were smiling and playing along with whatever the gag was.

"We couldn't stage this," says Altman on the DVD. "So that's the . . . the faces of Nashville."

It was the faces of Nashville trying to be helpful to the Hollywood folks, is what it was. At one point the camera passed through us and the resultant crush knocked an elderly woman next to me off her feet. "Wait a minute," I said, "this lady's about to get trampled!"

"Don't stop 'em," she said from the ground, her eyes alight. Maybe that was a microcosm of Hollywood—but was it art?

No, I am not visible in the movie. If there's anything I hate, it's being accused of hating a movie because I got cut out of it.

Noted humorist and writer Roy Blount Jr. is a Georgia native, a Vanderbilt graduate, and a New York resident who frequently returns to Nashville to fill up on Southern energy.

"Nashville Was My Graduate School"

Excerpts from a conversation with DAVID HALBERSTAM

I've kept some very close friendships in Nashville ever since my days as a young reporter at *The Tennessean* back in the 1950s. That was a very significant period of my life. I had graduated from Harvard in 1955, as the civil rights clashes were just beginning to capture national attention, and I drove to Mississippi that summer in a '46 Chevy packed with all my belongings, including a hi-fi player, some records, and a copy of Gunnar Myrdal's *An American Dilemma*. I was full of idealism and eagerness to cover what I thought would be a big story that was just then beginning to unfold. My destination was Jackson, but the job I had been sent there for didn't materialize, so I ended up as the only reporter at the *Daily Times Leader* (circulation 4,000) in West Point, Mississippi.

I lasted ten months. The fact that I lasted any time at all seems amazing to me even now, considering that I was a 21-year-old Jewish kid just out of Harvard and deeply interested in a subject that Henry Harris, the editor, didn't think was a story at all and didn't want covered. One day when I came in to work he gave me a few hours to clean out my desk. He had already hired my replacement. I still remember his exact words: I was "free, white, and 21" and could go wherever I wanted.

I called Hodding Carter, the great editor over in Greenville, and he told me about an opening at *The Tennessean*, which he called "the best stepping-stone paper in the country." Carter recommended me to his counterpart there, Coleman Harwell—and so I drove into Nashville on a beautiful April day in 1956, and I stayed on to spend four wildly happy years there, years that remain as good in the recollection of them as they were in the living.

Nashville was a wonderful place to grow up as a journalist. In a way, it was as if I had picked the finest of graduate schools—in the best place, at the right time, with the greatest colleagues and mentors. *The Tennessean* was arguably the best paper in the South (or so we who worked there like to remember it). In the late 1930s and early '40s, the paper had crusaded to end the poll tax, and the eventual repeal of that tax broke the back of the "Boss" Crump political machine based in Memphis. It also allowed many more blacks and poor whites to vote, and that changed the entire political fabric of the state, making many of its politicians more sensitive to race and class issues than their Deep South peers. One of *The Tennessean*'s editors, Jennings Perry (who was also my landlord), led that fight, and wrote a book about it in 1944.

The newspaper boasted a proud tradition as an aggressive, combative, fearless voice of the people, a public trust. Compared to Mississippi, which was a de facto police state, Nashville was a nice, livable little city—the state capital, a university town, a pretty literate place, where you could say what you wanted (if you didn't mind being unpopular in some quarters). The atmosphere had not congealed in fear, as had happened farther south. And best of all, the newspaper was right in the thick of every fight, and I was like the proverbial kid in the candy store, just devouring everything I could get my hands on.

You wouldn't recognize that Nashville if you saw it today. For all its amenities compared to the deeper South, it still seemed backward and much less modern than Northern cities, which had been receiving the benefits of a booming wartime and postwar economy far longer than Nashville and the South. Segregation, poverty, air pollution, and public health were glaring problems that most people seemed to take for granted. Everything was closed on Sunday (except churches, of course), and restaurants couldn't serve alcohol so there were few good restaurants. But there was an underground nightlife of private clubs, illicit gambling and drinking and sex, smoky jazz and blues dives and country honky-tonks, cops and politicians on the take—and all that seamy behavior got translated for me by my older and wiser colleagues at the newspaper. The South was exotic and mystifying, like another world, suspended in isolation from the rest of the country—until the race issue blew the lid off.

Coleman Harwell was an emotionally conservative man running a liberal paper for Silliman Evans, who had owned it since the 1930s. Behind his crusty formality, Coley was a very likable man, a Southern gentleman. He had grown up in a society that treated white supremacy as a birthright, and when he had to confront the reality of racial discrimination, it became a religious challenge for him. He knew that both he and the paper would be judged by how they handled this story, and he was determined to play it right down the middle—not crusading about it, but not dodging it either. Harwell was not going to look away; he was determined to confront the contradictions of his social heritage—and so would other white citizens if they read the paper. That must have caused him a lot of grief at the Belle Meade Country Club.

Coley assigned Wallace Westfeldt to cover the developing race story, and I was one of numerous reporters periodically sent out to work with him. Wally was a marine veteran, about ten years older than I, and we got along well. He went on to be news director and then producer for *NBC News*, with Chet Huntley and David Brinkley.

The paper was loaded with talent. Creed Black ran the editorial page, on his way up to bigger things, and when he left, a young North Carolinian named Tom Wicker replaced him. We had great reporters—Nat Caldwell and Gene Graham (they shared a Pulitzer Prize one year), John Seigenthaler, Mac Harris, Wayne Whitt, Lee Winfrey. Fred Graham, who later went to the *New York Times* and CBS, shared an apartment with me next to a funeral home on West End Avenue. He had grown up in Nashville. We ran around together in a crowd that included some other local people—Gil Merritt, John Nixon, George Barrett, and Nancy Gore, Al's big sister. They were all students at Vanderbilt, or in law school, or already lawyers.

There was some mingling of white and black in that subterranean culture I mentioned, but not out in the open. I got to know some black guys who played jazz together—pianist Brenton Banks, bass player W.O. Smith, drummer Morris Palmer, sax man Andy Goodrich. They were talented and very elegant men who exuded dignity in spite of the constant humiliations and outrages of the segregated culture. Andy was close to my age, and we got to be pals—even covertly double-dated a few times. The quartet played a long gig at Jimmy Hyde's Carousel in Printer's Alley. I still remember the last song they played on their last night there: "Bye Bye Blackbird." A few years ago, I came back to Nashville to introduce some of those guys at a benefit concert for the W.O. Smith Music School, after Smitty died.

It was in 1959 and '60 that a group of students from the black colleges—Fisk and Meharry, American Baptist and Tennessee A&I—started meeting with the Reverend Kelly Miller Smith of First Baptist Church-Capitol Hill and Jim Lawson, who was a student at the Vanderbilt Divinity School. The sit-ins grew out of those training sessions in nonviolence. I got to cover the start of all that, the clashes at lunch counters downtown. That was the the beginning of what would be the student part of the civil rights movement. It was also my first big, running story as a reporter—the story I had been wanting to cover since I set off for the South five years earlier. I learned a lot from those young people. Their families had been in this country so much longer than mine and had been given far fewer benefits and opportunities, yet they were fearlessly prepared to take enormous risks for democracy. How could I, who had been given so much more in terms of education and the right to vote, take fewer risks? It was a lesson that served me well in Vietnam two years later.

We worked hard at the paper, long hours—and then we went out to dinner or to the Alley and kept right on talking shop. I loved every minute of it. In fact, it's hard for me to recall a single unhappy memory from my Nashville days.

The day after the election of 1960, I went to work for James Reston in the Washington bureau of the *New York Times*, and within six months I was in the Congo as a foreign correspondent. Those assignments came to me, I'm convinced, because I had been so well trained in Nashville. By 1962 I was in Vietnam for the *Times*, and I won the Pulitzer in 1963 for my reporting from there. The first person I called after I learned about the prize was Coley Harwell. I wanted to tell him that he and others at the paper had made me a reporter. That's who I owed. So many good people. I still think of Jack Corn, for instance—a great photographer and a great teacher. He could talk to anyone on an equal plane. Working with him on assignment, I learned how to read people—not just how to do my job, but why it mattered, why you needed to be open and respectful and patient. Those are the things that stay with me—how generous so many people were to me, how much trust I was granted, how much they taught me.

Nashville made an indelible impression on me back then. It's very different now, of course—a lot like Atlanta was in the '50s: bigger, richer, lots of outsiders, pro sports moving in, things changing right before your eyes. Old blood and old money mattered more then than they do now. You can look at that from both sides, the old and the new. Either way, it's a mixed bag of gains and losses.

I can't say how it would feel to live there now, though I always enjoy my return visits. But living there 40 years ago was a lucky break for me, and I'll always remember it that way.

David Halberstam's prize-winning newspaper career has been followed by a long string of best-selling books, including The Children, *his 1998 account of the Nashville sit-ins and the students who made them a major achievement of the civil rights movement.*

As regular as clockwork, freight trains pass back and forth across the century-old railroad bridge and trestle at the south end of Shelby Park. Beyond the trestle to the east lies an 800-acre expanse of undeveloped land nestled in a sweeping bend of the Cumberland River. The wooded area, known as Shelby Bottoms, is an important link in the Metro Parks Department's long-range plan to develop a greenways belt throughout Davidson County.

THE THINGS OF SHAPE TO COME

by CHRISTINE KREYLING

O n a cold morning in early February, I stand in the gold-brown floodplain of Shelby Bottoms and watch a freight train cross the Cumberland River toward the Omohundro waterworks. The train stretches the length of the trestle, which serves as a monumental entrance gate into the Bottoms, dividing the nature preserve from the chain-linked playing fields of Shelby Park. The hills stepping up from the floodplain to the north are patterned with small ranch houses whose chimneys exhale wisps of smoke, cozy signs of domestication on this snow-dusted day. Both park and bottoms are named, like the avenue, for John Shelby, a physician, state senator, and postmaster of the 19th century who owned much land within the bend of the Cumberland that inscribes East Nashville.

Across the river, the Omohundro water filtration complex lies near the water's edge, its sturdy red-brick profile recalling the textile mills of New England's Blackstone River valley, mills that brought the Industrial Revolution to America. The facade of Omohundro's 1889 pumping station resembles that of a Romanesque basilica, while the interior of the 1920s filtration plant, with its brick arcades, diamond ter-razzo floor, light-shedding clerestory, and hardwood truss ceiling, suggests the basilica's nave and side aisles. The architecture of Omohundro reminds us that the gospel of Jesus and the gospel of technologi-cal progress were once complementary theologies, sanctifying the materialistic urge of the New World.

I spend an hour of most every morning in the Bottoms, waving to the engineer to blow his whis-tle as my dogs course through the brush, sniffing for rabbits they never catch, digging for moles they fail to unearth. My mind is drawn to the tableau of river and train and fields.

In 1850, just 30 years after the first steamboat docked at the Nashville wharf, the first steam loco-motive arrived in the city (ironically enough, by boat). Soon the natural routes of waterways would yield supremacy to the man-made trails of tracks and trestles. The scene before me summons up those paint-ings of the mid-19th century that recorded the entrance of the machine called the iron horse into the gar-den of the American landscape. The trains appeared discreetly in the middle distance or in the back-ground, their man-made steam and smoke blending into the clouds. The artists tailored the machine and its effects to the pastoral dream.

It's unclear whether the ambivalence about technology we read into these paintings resided in the lens of the 19th century, or is a case of 21st-century hindsight. We have come a long way since the loco-motive first chugged across the canvas of America, and we recognize the implications carried in the box-cars. Our wilderness is no longer one of forests to be felled for fields to be plowed. Today's wilderness is a man-made one of strip malls and interstates and asphalt parking lots. And nature is seen as a diminish-ing treasure, the conservation of which requires deed restrictions and easements, public acquisition and private foundations, and green-friendly Tennessee license plates on the cars that have brought nature to its knees. But the American identity—and that of Nashvillians by implication—is still rooted in an unset-tled debate about what is more sublime: technology or nature.

Shelby Bottoms is one of those rare and ideal settings where natural habitat and human habita-tion congrue in a harmonious landscape. In 1997 we removed the machine from this small part of the

Of Record
February 2000

1—A parade through the streets of downtown Nashville and across the Woodland Street Bridge to Adelphia Coliseum gives a joyous crowd, estimated at more than 50,000, a close-up opportunity to heap praise on their homecoming Titans. Wedged elbow to elbow on the sidewalks, leaning precariously from office windows and rooftops, the revelers fill the air with nonstop noise and a confetti storm fashioned from punch-holed computer printout scraps, shredding-machine leavings and

garden, allowing nature to reclaim 800 formerly cultivated acres—acres periodically threatened by development schemes for landfills, subdivisions, and golf courses—a mere twenty blocks from downtown Nashville. And every morning that I walk there I thank God (and former Mayor Phil Bredesen, and the folks of Metro's greenways program) for painting this picture for Nashvillians.

In reclaiming the Bottoms, we have also reclaimed a small stretch of the Cumberland. The river, which loops through Nashville like a party necklace carelessly tossed onto a dresser, was once the main commercial artery into the city, turbulent with traffic. Then we turned away from it, toward the web of train tracks, the spokes of highways, the runways of the airport. We dammed the river into tranquility, cut down the trees that held its banks, and polluted it with the runoff of our lives. Except for the soundstage that is Riverfront Park, and the small sliver of park on the opposite bank near the stadium, we have looked away from the river.

With Shelby Bottoms we face the Cumberland once again, this time not to use it to make a living, but to apprehend the sense of freedom waterways convey. When I stand in the Bottoms on the river's banks, I imagine traveling on the river—stepping from solid earth onto a medium that moves like quicksilver, and rushing all the way to the sea. This sense of liberty from the cares of dry land still persists all along the Cumberland and its tributaries, an overlooked frontier waiting to be reclaimed. The greenways plan for Davidson County maps the reclamation. The central chain of the green necklace is the 57 miles of the river that flow through the county, with a nature park like the Bottoms in each bend of the river. These jewels are linked by trails along the

In the summer months especially, the Cumberland still draws fishing enthusiasts to its banks, albeit less so than in times past. For casters and cane-pole fishers alike, some of the choice spots are near the Shelby Park railroad bridge.

Undisturbed by development, the Shelby Bottoms tract is an enchanted forest for city children brought up on concrete and asphalt. The wooded floodplain looks much as it did a century ago.

torn newspapers. Celebrants playing hooky from work or school mug for passing news cameras, oblivious to the thought that their bosses and teachers might see them on the evening news. When the parade reaches the stadium, another 30,000-plus who have waited there for their heroes emit a roar that echoes back across the river. Police later describe the swarm of humanity as "jubilant but orderly." . . . **A more reserved audience** of about 350 gathers in the evening at Vanderbilt's Langford Auditorium for a speech by Kweisi Mfume, president of the National Association for the Advancement of Colored People (NAACP). In a wide-ranging oration that focuses on wage discrimination, white supremacy and a rash of arson fires at black churches, Mfume asserts that "Jim Crow Sr. is dead, but Jim Crow Jr. is alive and well." The many African-American students on hand lead the applause. . . . **Public higher education** in Tennessee suffers at the hands of a legislature preoccupied with other matters. Less than one-fifth of the state's top high-school graduates apply to their own colleges and universities. Last year, a special task force addressing such problems called for a five-year infusion of almost a half-billion in new funds to make these institutions competitive with other states. Noting that Tennessee ranks 48th in the graduation rate of both high school and college students, state Finance Commissioner John Ferguson pleaded with the legislature to pick up the slack. They took the plea under advisement. . . . **At the Exit/In** on Elliston Place, Billy Block's Western Beat Roots Revival celebrates its fourth anniversary. Hosted by Block, a drummer, showman and tireless promoter, the Roots Revival has become a sort of weekly Tuesday-night Grand Ole Opry for "alternative-country," the recombinant strain of honky-tonk music defined by one wag as "country music for rock critics." On this night, however, the lineup that includes country crooner Rodney Crowell, Lower Broadway hillbilly

riverbanks. Other greenways—along the Stones and Harpeth rivers, along Richland, Seven Mile, and White's creeks—feed into the central system as these streams flow into the Cumberland. The greenways plan is not a pipe dream, because the land for the system is still there, much of it floodplain that has so far inhibited development. Just as the Cumberland River was the first road to Nashville two centuries ago, so in this new century can the river be the path to regaining a small part of the paradise of open space, if we have the collective will to follow it.

Shelby Bottoms is a victory balanced by many defeats. As the 20th century makes its broad turn into the 21st, the shape of Nashville fluctuates restlessly—between gain and loss, reclamation and destruction. We saved Union Station but lost its train shed, renovated the Bennie Dillon building into urban apartments but destroyed the Jacksonian apartments. We have gained an ever-expanding system of roadways, but in the process we have carved up the traditional neighborhoods surrounding the central core of the city, and jerry-rigged an architectural wasteland in the far-flung suburbs. Now the old urban neighborhoods are being reclaimed by successive waves of resettlers, but the tidal wave of new subdivisions swells ever larger.

Some of us, seeing in the current flux of the Nashville landscape mostly threat and destruction, have retreated to gated communities, taking refuge in massive houses where the functional spaces for eating and sleeping and socializing have been joined by theaters and gyms, pool rooms and lap pools—privatizing once-public activities and guarding them with alarm systems worthy of a bank vault. The McMansion—with its so-called "lawyer foyer" sporting a second-story pseudo-Palladian window displaying a pseudo-Colonial chandelier—has become a Brentwood staple; the teardown of one house to replace it with a larger one a common tactic in Belle Meade. The big house is now as ubiquitous in Nashville as big hair once was on the album covers of Music Row.

Others among us have looked beyond our private fences and begun to reimagine the public realm. That realm includes sports palaces and libraries, an arts center and a country music museum, sidewalks and boulevards, a connective tissue of neighborhoods and greenways instead of the dead ends of cul-de-sacs.

Whichever way we choose to live—and whatever compromises we make between nature and culture, private and public space—the places in which we live will mold our character for the next century and beyond. To find the past and present shapes—public and private, sacred and profane—molding Nashville's future, it is best to start at the center and work our way outward, mimicking the way the city grew from a frontier outpost into a metropolitan region. The point of origin is the public square.

Whostrickland arrived at Nashville's public square in 1845, he must have thought he had come to the edge of the frontier. Most of the city's notable buildings were gathered near the square. The City Hall and Market House and the Davidson County Courthouse were all together in the square. Facing them on the periphery were the City Hotel, the Bank of the United States, the Nashville Inn, and several other substantial structures. Strickland was to live at the inn for the remaining years of his life. Beyond the square, Nashville quickly lapsed into a town of low-rise brick and wood structures punctuated by the spires of churches, and then into country. The city probably seemed primitive to Strickland, who had been designing elegant Greek Revival structures in Philadelphia and now had been hired to architect another as a statehouse for Tennessee.

But Nashville already had a plan that mapped a town from wilderness, and it was as logical and hierarchical as Strickland's design for the Capitol—and five decades older. In 1794, before Tennessee was even a state, the North Carolina legislature passed an act laying out Nashville in 200 one-acre lots, with a four-acre public square on the bluffs above the Cumberland River, near Fort Nashborough, as its center. Surveyor Thomas Molloy had mapped the town-in-embryo as simply and as surely as William Faulkner, 150 years later, would trace the town center of his mythical city of Jefferson, in his mythical Yoknapatawpha County, in the pages of *Requiem for a Nun*:

"With stakes and hanks of fishline, the architect laid out in a grove of oaks opposite the tavern and the store, the square and simple foundations, the irrevocable design not only of the courthouse but of the town too, telling them as much: 'In fifty years you will be trying to change it in the name of what you will call progress. But you will fail; but you will never be able to get away from it.' "

Molloy's square seemed irrevocable for more than a century and a half. After the Civil War, the square was surrounded by two- and three-story mercantile buildings in an eclectic mixture of Victorian styles. Besides providing a place to gossip and barter, to

William Strickland's son, Francis, designed Davidson County's second permanent courthouse in 1856 in the Greek Revival style reminiscent of his late father. The pitched roof was removed in 1906 to add a fourth story to the building, and thereafter its roof was flat. Facing the Public Square on all sides were many of the city's leading business houses.

lobby a politician and buy a tomato, the square was the setting for most civic events guaranteed to draw a crowd.

The first permanent structure to be erected in the square as a courthouse for Davidson County was opened in 1802. It was destroyed by fire in 1856 and was soon replaced by what came to be known as "the Strickland courthouse," designed by William Strickland's son, Francis. It was remodeled and enlarged 50 years later, and lasted until 1937, when the present Davidson County Courthouse was completed. Architects Emmons Woolwine of Nashville and Frederick C. Hirons of New York designed a solid block of a building, embellished by heroically scaled Doric columns and a Roman-inspired cornice, to declare that our government stood rock-solid in the midst of the Great Depression. Retail stores had long since spread west along Church Street, and hotels and restaurants had migrated in the direction of Union Station as rails of iron replaced the river as the main path for people and products. But the square still worked as a public living room.

It was not until the late 1970s that the public square—not just its walls of buildings, but its identity as a civic gathering place—was fully revoked. What appeared instead were the high-rise First American Center (now AmSouth Center), the bland behemoth Criminal Justice Center, the Gay Street Connector, and a parking lot. Each of these constructions is discretely functional in the manner of suburban planning, which is why they fail to cohere into communal living space.

Nashvillians have been looking for common ground ever since. For Thursday's "Dancin' in the District" during the warm months, and on the Fourth of July, we gather at the river. We seek out Legislative Plaza for the Southern Festival of Books and occasional concerts. Some of us mall-walk in climate-controlled comfort; others prefer the earthier air of the Farmers Market and the history lessons of the Bicentennial Mall.

But these spaces, worthy as they may be, do not embody our identity as citizens of Nashville, and the city without its square remains a mouth missing its two front teeth. In 1964, hundreds of black and white citizens of Nashville joined hands in the

Tera M. Daniels, stemming from a lease dispute between Daniels and the building's owner, Lee Harrison. Daniels' friend, Janis Loman, filed for the writ of seizure, since Daniels herself is not around. In November 1998, Daniels was indicted on federal charges of money laundering, racketeering and embezzlement. A month ago, on New Year's Eve, she disappeared from the Nashville halfway house where she was awaiting trial; in January she was arrested in a Houston hotel; now she's in an Oklahoma City jail. Says Loman, "We're just protecting her good name.". . . **Actress Reese Witherspoon**, a Nashville native and Harpeth Hall School graduate, begins a featured role as the sister of Jennifer Aniston's character on the TV sitcom *Friends*. . . . **Memphis Criminal Court Judge** John Colton issues a 28-page opinion that Robert Glen Coe is mentally competent to be executed. "While the

A thriving farmers' market operated daily on the Public Square until well after World War II. It was then relocated to the Sulphur Dell area north of Capitol Hill, now an integral part of the Bicentennial Mall. The market has evolved into an indoor-outdoor complex with a rich mixture of local and international foods and flavors.

defendant's actions [during a court hearing last month] were unpleasant, vile and disruptive," the judge writes, "they did not appear to be involuntary reactions. Throughout all the testimony given, one fact has been constant: that (Coe) realizes he is facing execution, and that he knows it is because he has been convicted of murdering a little girl." The ruling will be automatically appealed to the state Supreme Court.

public square to call for an end to racial segregation. Two decades later, our cars stood there side by side, demonstrating for the inalienable right to park. In 1996, when Mayor Phil Bredesen attended the Mayor's Institute on City Design to get some opinions on the best site for a new downtown library, he was asked by the mayor of Cincinnati, "Where is the town center of Nashville?" The mayor couldn't answer. We still can't.

Yet we need our public square, now more than ever. Increasingly isolated inside the personal armor of our private vehicles, and segregated by zoning and advertising into focus groups of class and race, we need space that can shape us into a common culture, a place where we can once again join hands across the historic fault lines of skin color and the economic divide of income. After a quarter-century of civic heartlessness, it's time to bury the parking lot and remake our square. The makeover will not be an exercise in nostalgia, but the practice of civic repair. In building on the history of our city—not necessarily its architectural style, but how it once worked—we learn from the past to embrace the present and future.

But if the historic center of the city of Nashville has failed to hold, the same cannot be said for the physical hub of the state of Tennessee, four blocks away. The State Capitol's Greek temple form instantly transformed the hill called Cedar Knob into

In 145 years of harvest moons, the Tennessee State Capitol has weathered civil war, tornadoes, depression and prosperity and numerous peaceful changes of the political guard. Its classical symmetry can be read as architect William Strickland's way of expressing the permanence and stability of the state.

Nashville's acropolis when it was completed in 1855. In 1996 the state infused visual stamina into its most important structure with the opening of the Bicentennial Mall, preserving the lone surviving optical avenue to Capitol Hill. In the process, the mall revived a definition of public works (long hijacked to the strictly functional purposes of street paving and maintenance) that Nashville had not seen since the state's Centennial Exposition in 1897.

The best way to understand the Mall is to stand on the crest of Capitol Hill and gaze north. At your back is the temple of Tennessee democracy designed by William Strickland. Halfway down the slope at your feet is the overlook known as the Belvedere, where lie remnants of the Capitol's original columns. Straight ahead stretches the Mall itself. Taken in conjunction, the Capitol, old columns, and new Mall articulate in three dimensions the past, present, and future of the classical spirit in Nashville and in Tennessee.

That classical spirit is a way of perceiving the world and using the arts to persuade others to see it likewise. The nation's founding fathers—Washington and Jefferson in particular—thought that social meaning, not everyday function, should determine the form of public buildings. The Greek and Roman styles had the right symbolism, with allusions to Greek democracy and the Roman republic, and no religious overtones. Classical architecture also had the right formal properties; its symmetry and hierarchy, clarity and predictability were the instruments that could tame a wilderness.

William Strickland was one of the nation's leading advocates of the Greek Revival form of classicism in the first half of the 19th century and the most prominent architect ever to live in Nashville. Today's communication and transportation systems allow a nationally known architect—such as Robert A.M. Stern, the New York-based designer of Nashville's new downtown library—to do a project in the architectural hinterlands while maintaining a practice in a major urban center. Strickland had to move here to build here.

The architect came to Nashville on the rebound. Design commissions in his hometown of Philadelphia had dried up due to a recession, and drawings he had submitted to Congress for the renovation and expansion of the U.S. Capitol and for the Washington Monument were not accepted. Strickland prepared a preliminary sketch for

4—A woman remembered for introducing pizza to Nashvillians is dead of a heart attack at age 87. Ruby Marchetti and her late husband, Gino, opened their popular Italian restaurant, Marchetti's, off West End Avenue in 1946 and quickly built a reputation around Ruby's pizzas, which her grandson claims were probably the first to grace a menu in Middle Tennessee. The restaurant burned down in 1982. . . . **Lynette Cole, 21,** the reigning Miss Tennessee U.S.A. and the queen of Columbia's 1994 Mule Day celebration, is crowned Miss U.S.A. at a glitzy gala in Branson, Mo. She receives a silver convertible Camaro, a diamond tiara, a pearl necklace, an apartment for one year in Manhattan's Trump Plaza, a year's supply of makeup, a $5,000 scholarship and $7,000 in phone cards. . . . **Seven police officers** are needed to break up a fracas at McGavock High School, where the annual Wacky Olympics, a day of goofy student games, turns into a melee. A coach, a student and a police officer are involved in a scuffle. . . . **The public flocks** to the Nashville Zoo to see quintuplets—five Bengal tiger cubs, to be exact. The cubs, named Amal, Kiri, Gita, Amoli and Rajah, go on display in the zoo's nursery. They were born Dec. 8 to mother Johnette and father Raj at the zoo.

5—Vice President Al Gore, *Tennessean* Editor Frank Sutherland, and columnist Dwight Lewis are among the 500 friends, family members and loyal readers who fill the Tennessee Performing Arts Center's Jackson Hall to say goodbye to the late Jerry Thompson, last of the daily newspaper's roguish, old-school characters. Sutherland recounts a whopper of a practical joke his zany colleague pulled on the editor's wedding day in 1974—a prank that involved convincing some rural deputies that Sutherland and his new bride, Natilee Duning, were actually fleeing in a stolen car. Country singer Ricky Van Shelton, once managed by Thompson,

The mounted presence of Andrew Jackson's looming figure dominates the east slope of Capitol Hill, much as the man himself dominated public life in Nashville and beyond for more than 50 years, until he died at The Hermitage in 1845.

performs a ballad called "Decisions," co-written by his late friend and former business associate. Gore, who is campaigning for the White House, gives an off-the-cuff tribute that many in the hall say is the best speech of his career. Afterward, the mourners celebrate Thompson's life and legacy in a style he would have appreciated: beer and barbecue. . . . **For the first time** in more than a month, there is no mention of the Titans above the page-one fold in *The Tennessean.* The 32-day string falls just six days short of the paper's all-time booster record, set in 1998-99 with a 38-day trumpet blast for the University of Tennessee Volunteers when they won the National

a new statehouse at the request of the Tennessee Capitol Board of Commissioners because he needed work. The commissioners hired him to carve from local limestone the symbol of a new golden age that proclaimed: The glory that was Greece is ours.

The belief in the classical style, with its rationalist ideology, had already been professed in domestic architecture by Andrew Jackson. Jackson had commissioned classical architecture for both the second and third versions of his Hermitage, as well as for Tulip Grove, the home he built for his wife's nephew in the 1830s. With his design for Tennessee's Capitol, Strickland extended the premises of the Greek style to our civic architecture as the country was extending its grasp of the new land to the southwest.

When the Capitol's cornerstone was laid on Independence Day, 1845, Nashville was one of the largest English-speaking communities west of the Appalachians. It was during this period that Philip Lindsley, president of the University of Nashville from 1825 to 1850, began using the term "Athens of the West" as a metaphor for the city. Lindsley, like other Nashville leaders, saw the opportunity to dignify capitalistic and cultural endeavors by applying a classical moniker to a frontier setting.

Athens as a metaphor for Nashville has always been more a naive exercise in provincial chutzpah than a description of fact. But then, Athens in the age of Pericles was probably not as golden as later culture-consumers cracked it up to be, either. In using a classical and Old-World metaphor for Nashville's cultural physiognomy, however, Lindsley was expressing a belief—that the man-made was preferable to the natural world—as well as an aspiration. Pioneers like Jackson, Lindsley, and Strickland saw the expansion of the white presence across the continent as logical and inevitable steps of progress. And they thought the natural world needed the discipline of axe and plow and chisel to yield its wealth of promise. They had little sense that they would, or even could, obliterate the untouched nature that distinguished the New World from the Old.

The relentless destruction of the American wilderness in the first half of the 19th century paradoxically coincided with a new significance given to nature. Some Americans regretted that, with clearing and cultivation, the sublimity of the wilderness should pass away. This attitude is a romantic way of seeing the world, and the very opposite of the classical spirit. Romantic ideology contends that a human being is at his or her best when closest to nature. Classicism celebrates the obviously man-made in a language of right angles and symmetrical facades, producing an impression, not of sublimity, but of calm and order designed to encourage people to think clear thoughts and believe in the perfectibility of mankind. The myth of America has always vibrated between these two opposing visions.

By the last decade of the 20th century, the force of nature could no longer be read in the landscape north of the Capitol. The French Lick stream that once drew the animals that drew the Native Americans and longhunters to the area lay 25 feet below the surface of the earth, flowing into the Cumberland River through a massive brick-lined culvert. The machine had obliterated this garden beyond reclamation, and the romantic spirit had to seek consolation in a reminder that human intervention is subject to the same forces of erosion as a riverbank.

That reminder lies in the memorial garden on Capitol Hill's northern flank, with its fragments of the Capitol's original columns. Pulled down in 1955 because the Tennessee limestone had weathered poorly, these time-blurred relics of our classical heritage prophesy the inevitable ruin of all things man-made. Sculpted from the earth, they are now slowly subsiding back into it. Look closely at a fluted column and you can see in the striations the history of the planet itself. As rough to the touch as a cat's tongue, they feel of time, grainy and dissolute.

These scarred and shaling pieces lay, like Shelley's Ozymandias, in random heaps in a field near the Tennessee State Penitentiary until Charles Warterfield of the Mall planning team brought them back to public view. That Tennessee at 200 created from them a memorial to the Capitol's original stone carvers adds a cautionary hyphen between the confident assertions of Capitol and Mall.

The positioning of the Capitol on downtown's tallest hill originally conveyed the message that we should look up, literally and figuratively, to our government. The fact that our Capitol no longer dominates the Nashville skyline, or can even be seen from most angles, may indicate that we no longer need, or perhaps even want, our government to be so visible. Perhaps we now assume the stability and permanence of government that the Capitol was designed to convey, and we find the skyscrapers of private capitalism more necessary to our sense of progress. Or maybe we now feel that the less we are reminded of our elected officials, the better.

The "permanent" Parthenon and the War Memorial, completed in the 1920s, were the last buildings in Nashville to reflect a confident identification with the ancient world until the end of the century. But for the state's bicentennial, an act of piety to Tennessee's classical past that preserved the sight line to the icon of that past seemed in order. Governor Ned McWherter and the Bicentennial Commission hired a team led by Tuck Hinton Architects to devise a plan for the flat, nineteen-acre plain to the north.

The Bicentennial Mall's ground plan filters the classical principles of order, symmetry, and clarity through the practices of Baroque and subsequent Beaux Arts planning. Within its rectangle, paths laid out in diagonals of diminishing perspective worthy of a Renaissance painting lead to a carillon bending in 280 degrees of a circle that relays the focus back to the Capitol.

The Mall's history walk, and its topographical representation of the state as it climbs from the floodplains of the Mississippi River to the mountains in the east, function as an open-air museum—recalling the Acropolis of Athens, the Forum of Rome, and other ancient sites that used civic monies to sanctify places of collective gathering, commemoration, and ceremony. As a massive public works project undertaken for the education and edification of the citizens of Tennessee, the Bicentennial Mall is a revival of the American City Beautiful movement, which brought classically inspired purpose to the planning of our public spaces (and also brought Thomas Jefferson's plan for an academic village to the campus of George Peabody College for Teachers) before World War I.

Collegiate Athletic Association football championship.

6—**Darrell Hedgecoth,** the Ashland City teenager who underwent triple-organ transplant surgery at Vanderbilt Medical Center less than two weeks ago, is at home after his discharge from the hospital. Hedgecoth was dying of cystic fibrosis when doctors replaced his heart, liver and lungs. Now he's sporting a Titans cap, a foot-long chest scar and a big smile. "He looks great," says one of his surgeons, Dr. E. Wesley Eli. "This kid has just walked through the coals."

7—**There is joy once again** at the Tom Joy Head Start Center. The day-care facility has been closed since Jan. 10, when a driver for the center dropped off a 4-year-old charge at his grandmother's house, unaware that the woman wasn't home. No harm resulted, but under the state Department of Human Services' new zero-tolerance policy— adopted after two unattended children in Memphis died one day in separate incidents due to sweltering heat—Tom Joy was immediately shut down. The closing of this, the largest of Nashville's eight Head Start Centers, left the parents of its 271 children scrambling for alternative day care. On Feb. 4, Chancery Court Judge Ellen Hobbs Lyle told a courtroom of cheering parents that the day-care center could reopen today. . . . **A statue of the angel** Moroni is hoisted atop the spire of the long-delayed Nashville Temple of the Church of Jesus Christ of Latter-day Saints. Their five-year effort to build the suburban temple having finally succeeded against residential-zoning opponents, many in the gathered throng weep for joy. The 11,000-square-foot Nashville temple, which is actually in Williamson County, will serve 25,000 Mormon Church members in Middle Tennessee and Kentucky. However, unlike churches that host weekly worship services, the temple will be used only for sacred rites such as

The conversion of a 19-acre eyesore at the foot of Capitol Hill into a place of memory, history and hope ranks as one of the most significant public-works improvements in the history of the city and state. Dedicated in the state's 200th year by Gov. Ned McWherter, the Bicentennial Capitol Mall is designed to embrace the state's past and to grow in stature as a focal point of public life.

Reaching beyond these obvious classical parallels, the Bicentennial Mall demonstrates how the classical tradition can be used to reclaim social meaning from a maze of metal sheds and parking lots. It defines a space in which Tennesseans and visitors can pause and reflect on the longevity of civic identity, on democracy's reliance on an educated citizenry, and on the way topography shapes history. The Mall reaches into the future as well. Its construction generated a master plan for the surrounding area that, if brought to three-dimensional reality, will reweave the urban fabric—its grid of streets and mixture of living and working places—as a fitting and necessary complement to the Mall's public realm. The Mall is a hybrid construction, looking backward to the state's past, yet reinforcing for the future the concept of civic space as central to our built environment.

Tradition requires reinterpretation and revision to remain alive. The creation, maintenance, and revision of sacred space collaborates with civic space in shaping the character of Nashville. And one of Nashville's most sacred spaces is the Ryman Auditorium.

Hugh Cathcart Thompson designed the "mother church of country music," but his portrait doesn't hang on the Ryman's wall of fame, and his name doesn't ring a bell, even among the most knowledgeable country music fans. Thompson came to Nashville from Monroe County in East Tennessee in 1849, just four years after Strickland. He rose from the carpenter ranks to draw blueprints for the carpenters before architecture became a profession that required a college degree. During the Federal occupation of Nashville in the Civil War, he complained in an ungrammatical and misspelled letter to

baptisms for the dead and marriage ceremonies. . . . **E. Gordon Gee,** a devout Mormon who looks like popcorn magnate Orville Redenbacher and owns more than 600 bow ties, stuns the faculty and trustees of Brown University in Rhode Island by announcing he is stepping down as president after only two years. The reason: Gee (pronounced like "glee" without the "l") has quietly secured the chancellorship of Vanderbilt University. He will replace the retiring Joe B. "Invisible Man" Wyatt, who leaves an 18-year record all but unblemished by public appearances. Brown cries foul, but the *New York Times* reports that the university did not make a counteroffer to Vanderbilt's lucrative pay-and-

Military Governor Andrew Johnson that his Unionist sympathies were costing him work and earning him threats in the Confederate-leaning city. But after the war, in 1892, Thompson had the good fortune to design a building that would carve itself a place in Nashville's soul.

The Ryman Auditorium's status as one of Nashville's best-loved buildings has little to do with the quality of its architecture. Thompson designed buildings that spoke the common language of the time. The Ryman is, however, a strong building, and its strength lies in its simplicity. Nothing but red brick, bone-colored limestone, and white-painted wood fashioned into a clear gable shape pierced by plain Gothic windows, its triangular profile stands in stark contrast to the slick skins and complex textures of the rest of downtown.

During its early history, the Ryman's 2,200 seats made a splendid assembly hall for Nashville, hosting everything from opera arias to fire-and-brimstone preachers shouting about sinners in the hands of an angry God. As the city grew, however, the Ryman's use as a civic auditorium waned. If the Grand Ole Opry hadn't moved in in 1941, the Ryman would probably have ceased to be. The congruence of common-touch architecture with the common-touch musical language of the Opry made for a perfect partnership.

But that marriage dissolved in 1974, when the Opry moved to a new home in suburban Pennington Bend, the next turn of the Cumberland east of Shelby Bottoms. It's ironic that the face of Opryland mullah Bud Wendell hangs in sanctified splendor on the Ryman's wall of fame, because he wanted to level the place. Wendell planned to use some of its bricks to construct the "Little Chapel of Opryland" out in the new theme park. This gesture of architectural pseudo-piety would have, for capitalistic convenience, eliminated any musical competition the Ryman might have posed to the new venture. Now that a shopping mall has replaced the theme park, we might have the "Little Chapel of Opry Mills."

A fierce and sometimes uncivil war broke out between the historic preservationists determined to save the Ryman, and the prominent Nashville families who owed

Hugh Cathcart Thompson designed Union Gospel Tabernacle in 1892 as a Gothic temple where saved souls (such as riverboat captain Tom Ryman, who put up the money) and seekers alike could congregate for services. In time it evolved from a house of worship to a civic auditorium, and in 1941, it became the home of the Grand Ole Opry.

benefits package—which totals almost $1 million, factoring in Gee's salary as chancellor and his wife, Constance's, as a tenured professor. (A couple of raises and they'll be right up there with the Titans' second-stringers; an estimated 30 of 150 employees of the NFL franchise earn more than $1 million a year.) The chancellor-to-be displays a departure from Wyatt's leadership style almost immediately by meeting publicly with students.

8—**Tying Nashville Together,** a grassroots community action group, is pushing the mayor and council and the Metro Transit Authority to improve services, and a new report card on the MTA lends credence to the TNT critique: The bus system is under-equipped, understaffed, under-funded, underutilized—and over-priced (one-way fare, $1.45). TNT is giving MTA a 26-point improvement list, and as street congestion worsens daily, officials are listening. "Everyone is treated equally badly by our transportation system," says Mayor Purcell, once a regular rider himself. While he waits for results from a performance audit of the 104-bus system, Purcell is already serving notice that improvements had better come soon, or heads will roll. Noting that almost no one rides now except those who have no other alternative, the mayor says bluntly: "I wouldn't recommend anyone use them" as long as service is so poor.

9—**A sudden break** brings swift closure to one of the city's high-profile unsolved homicides—after only two years. In Lincoln, Neb., 26-year-old Jason G. Pence is arrested and extradited to Nashville. He is charged with the 1998 slaying of Skull Schulman, the colorful proprietor of the Skull's Rainbow Room nightclub in Printer's Alley. Two days later, a second man, 19-year-old James Charles Caveye, confesses his own part in the crime while being held on another charge in San Francisco. . . . **Gov. Don Sundquist** tells the Tennessee their fortunes to the National Life and Accident Insurance Company, which owned the building. In a city—and a nation—that likes to envision itself as aggressively bulldozing problems while constantly striding forward into the future, the preservationist position was widely characterized as muddled-headed nostalgia at best, anti-progress at worst. But the turning point came when the architecture critic of the *New York Times*, Ada Louise Huxtable, attacked National Life's position as "a mixture of architectural igno-rance and acute business venality." The national stature of the *Times* accelerated mounting public pressure to keep the Ryman standing. The building survived, pad-locked shut except for token tours, until the downtown revival caused Opryland to see new revenue opportunities in the old structure; renovation began in 1993.

On a hot summer Tuesday—Bluegrass Night—in 1994, I sat in one of the pews shortly after music returned to the Ryman. I listened to the mournful sounds of Alison Krauss' violin float into the darkness from the stage. And I thought about what the music was telling me—that other people have been happy or sad for the same reasons that I've been and will be happy or sad. The music made connections between my life and other lives, so that mine assumed its relative importance, which is not that great. That didn't make me feel small, it made me feel cushioned.

Despite the hardness of its seating, the Ryman's architecture makes for a similar sort of cushion. Just like bluegrass music, the Ryman reminds us that where we sit thou-sands of others have sat, and the accumulated emotions of the accumulated generations resonate as warmly as the acoustics. That's what old buildings are good at, absorbing the present moment into a larger context. After a bad trip on the interstate, it's com-forting to trade in rampant individualism for a good dose of community.

Hugh Cathcart Thompson designed and built a number of structures for Nashville in the second half of the 19th century, most of them as long gone and for-gotten as the architect's reputation. But the generation before ours saved his best to last. In the process these preservationists saved more than architecture. Just think about where we'd be if they had lost.

Today country music seems like a carefully calculated industry churning out crossover country pabulum, and the Opry is nostalgia served up on a platter as generic as the plastic tray of a frozen dinner—except for the program's vacations at the Ryman. The entire Opry campus on Briley Parkway is a muddled mixture of anywhere subur-biana—the Opry Mills shopping mall, and the Southern kitsch combination of bas-tardized Williamsburg and bastardized New Orleans, and magnolias in hair nets that is the Opryland Hotel. The soul of country music lives elsewhere.

It lives on Fifth Avenue, half a block off Broadway, in a place whose basic geom-etry is both a reminder of its old-fashioned origin and a wellspring that continually nourishes country music's roots. In saving the Ryman, we saved a place—in the words of a song sung on that summer night in 1994 by Alison Krauss & The Cox Family—"Where No One Stands Alone."

The Ryman is five blocks from the courthouse and five blocks from the Capitol. This triangulation suggests the way in which the instincts and energies of Nashville have played in anything but harmony throughout our city's history. Nashville first asserted itself as the Athens of the West (later South) in The Hermitage, the State Capitol, and the Strickland courthouse and reinforced this self-image with the Parthenon in Cen-tennial Park, the Depression-era courthouse, the Bicentennial Mall, and every house with a classical portico. In the 1920s, Nashvillians proclaimed Union Street to be the "Wall Street of the South," where banking and insurance monies flowed into the vaults of taller and taller buildings.

In 1978 the Chamber of Commerce adopted "Music City U.S.A." as a popular cul-ture metaphor for the city, a metaphor residing in the mixture of bungalows and office buildings that is the "campus" of Music Row. But in the last ten years, Nashville has stretched its sense of self beyond any one theme, and a climate of heightened civic self-consciousness has shaped and been shaped by a new inventory of buildings rising in the center of the city. And these buildings—arena, stadium, Frist Center for the Visual Arts,

Nashville's contemporary architectural profile is an eclectic mix of styles, with Victorian structures such as the Ryman Auditorium slipping ever deeper into the shadows of taller buildings. Many have simply disappeared. At the zenith in the late 1920s, more than 1,000 substantial 19th-century homes and businesses gave the 2-square-mile area of the original Nashville its own distinctive architectural personality; today, only about two or three dozen of those structures remain.

steak house reopens. . . . **Across town**, 300 Hillsboro High School students—nearly one-fourth of the enrollment—are sidelined by a nasty stomach virus. They did not eat at the Fifth Quarter.

11—**An electrical fire** quickly rages out of control in the kitchen of Mary Frances Holbert at her home at 924 29th Ave. N. Neighbors say Mrs. Holbert, 100, known as "Granny," has lived on 29th Avenue for as many as 80 years. Her great-grandson-in-law, William Darden, and her neighbor, Reggie Phillips, manage to pull her from the blaze and perform CPR, but she is taken to St. Thomas Hospital in precarious condition from smoke inhalation. . . . **Adam AnKarlo, 18,** son of WWTN-FM talk-radio host Darrell AnKarlo, is arrested after running buck-naked through a pep rally at Franklin High School. The temperature outside, where he is caught: 40 degrees. . . . **Police arrest a Nashville developer** on charges that he raped a child under 13 years of age and used minors for sexually charged material. Larry J. Lafferty Jr., 57, is facing 13 counts involving three female minors. Lafferty built and developed Lakeshore Pointe Condominiums; he is also the author of two children's books. . . . **A surprise guest** shows up for a writers-in-the-round show at the Bluebird Cafe: country superstar Garth Brooks, who sits in with the writers of some of his biggest hits. After the show, he signs autographs and poses for pictures with the 90 or so folks on hand. . . . **At the Blair School of Music's** Turner Recital Hall, the Blair String Quartet performs an evening of music by modern classical composer John Harbison. No one sticks around for after-concert autographs.

12—**Reformers, reform thyselves.** In the ballroom of the Nashville Marriott Hotel, a meeting of the Reform Party National Committee quickly degenerates into screaming matches and chaos. At issue: the direction of the party, its leadership, the site for its nominating convention and—most significantly—the party's $12-million subsidy from the Federal Election Commission. Earlier in the week, the notoriously volatile third party, associated most closely with Texas billionaire H. Ross Perot's 1992 bid for the presidency, was rocked by the withdrawal of one of its highest-profile members, former professional wrestler Jesse Ventura, now the governor of Minnesota. Today, when the smoke clears, at least two delegates have been thrown out of the room, and national chairman Jack Gargan has been booted out of office by a vote of 109 to 31. "This was not the Reform Party I know," Gargan declares, as he is escorted away from the hostile crowd. "This is not the party of honesty and integrity. This is a sham!" With Ventura supporter Gargan out of the way, the controlling Perotistas shift their support to Pat Buchanan. Those with long memories recall that a Nashvillian, political gadfly John Jay Hooker, helped engineer Perot's 1992 run. Those with short memories may vote for Buchanan, the antigovernment roughneck who covets the feds' hard-money subsidy.

13—**Cody Patrick Timmons,** a 26-year-old state social worker, vanishes. His wife Misty calls police. A preliminary investigation yields no clues to Cody Timmons' whereabouts. . . . **An afternoon storm** turns ugly and ominous, and by 6 p.m., the city is being savaged by 60 to 70 mph winds. A tornado is said to have touched down in Bordeaux. Power-line poles are bent like drinking straws on Eighth Avenue South. An uprooted magnolia tree is pitched onto Arthur Avenue in North Nashville, where 600 Nashville Electric Service customers are left without power. Gusts rake Germantown while sirens wail on the Vanderbilt campus, sending students racing for cover. During its evening newscast, WTVF-Channel 5 is knocked temporarily off the air, just as it was during the infamous tornado of April 1998, which left a billion-dollar mess in

Country Music Hall of Fame and Museum, downtown library—were brought to life by Mayor Phil Bredesen. From 1992 to 2000, this Harvard-educated entrepreneur, who had made millions in the for-profit health-care industry, was the master builder who raised the city's vision and boosted its self-confidence.

Bredesen was not Nashville's first ambitious builder in the post-World War II period. In 1957, the Life and Casualty Insurance Company placed what was then the tallest skyscraper in the Southeast on the corner of Fourth and Church streets. The L&C Tower asserted that Nashville was once again the Wall Street of the South, and it remains the most expressive tower on the skyline. Designed by Nashville architect Edwin Keeble, L&C's smooth limestone walls and aluminum fins race corniceless into the sky, possessing all the streamlining that our later skyscrapers have lacked. Yet in spite of its height, the tower rests urbanely on its corner, its entrance and lobby retaining a comfortable sense of the human scale.

Edwin Keeble had ambitions to raise the entire profile of architecture in Nashville. During the early phase of his career, he hoped to establish a school of architecture at Vanderbilt University, writing in a 1932 letter, "if we would realize our own strength and the possibilities of it, Southern architecture would follow Southern literature up the road to an enviable position." In 1930, Keeble had founded the Nashville Atelier in response to the desire of many young men of the city to study architecture with him. For two years, the studio met in a classroom at Vanderbilt, but when Keeble tried to push the program into a formal affiliation with the university, administrators balked. This missed opportunity still inhibits the seriousness with which the design of the built environment is taken in the city.

Beverly Briley led the fight to weld city and county into Metro government in 1963, providing a more secure financial base for government but also accelerating the sprawl that had begun after World War II. In the late '60s, Briley, Metro's first mayor, gave the council a proposal for a six-lane roadway stretching from 21st Avenue, south of Hillsboro Village, to Demonbreun Street. The purpose of this boulevard—informally referred to as "Briley's Boulevard"—was to give the music business a prestigious address. Protests against all the demolition the road would have required, and excessive land speculation that drove up the cost of right-of-way acquisition, led to the modification of the plan into Magnolia Boulevard and the one-way pairs of 16th and 17th avenues. But Briley had given the country music industry a more consolidated presence and a higher profile in Nashville.

Mayor Richard Fulton was certainly devoted to downtown, but his administration suffered from poor timing. The 1970s philosophy of urban renewal by suburban means dominated Fulton's building initiatives. During his terms in office, Church Street became a wavy lane and lost a block of human-scale architecture. A shopping mall was built to stem the exodus of downtown retail; nine years later the mall came down. Fulton built a convention center that turned its back to Broadway; today there is talk of tearing it down, too. His most lasting contributions to downtown are Riverfront Park and the saving of Union Station. As master-builder, Fulton was a case of good intentions, but some misguided actions.

As our master-builder of the '90s, Phil Bredesen capitalized on public sentiment; a big question of the 1991 campaign was "Who will do the most for downtown?" Urban consciousness had risen in Nashville. More Nashvillians were singles or empty nesters who cared little for big lots and school districts; more were nonnatives with experience of urban living in other cities, just like Bredesen. A loose confederation of design professionals, preservationists, and interested bystanders formed the Nashville Urban Design Forum to discuss how to repair the central city.

Bredesen responded to this climate of heightened expectations. Within the boundaries of Thomas Molloy's old city he chose to devise a series of big places "where people can come together. There are negatives to living in a city—traffic, higher taxes. The people who live there should get something back in return." For Bredesen, the best "something" was the ability "to go out and interact with all sorts of other people. That's what the arena was all about, not about professional sports." He points out that the arena was conceived "as much more for performances; we didn't have a hockey team. And I never planned to have an NFL team."

The key strength of Bredesen-the-builder was not unique thinking but the

From the air, the L&C Tower (center-left, with sign on roof) is hard to pick out from the newer and larger buildings around it. When the Life and Casualty Insurance Company built it in 1957, it was the tallest skyscraper in the Southeast.

its wake. This time, the city considers itself lucky to escape with relatively minor damage.

14—**Valentine's Day in Nashville.** Cost of a dozen roses from Emma's, the "supoilative" florist: 40 bucks and tax. . . . **While other men** are scrambling to send their significant others flowers or candy, Stephen Anderson gives his wife, Sharon, a once-in-a-lifetime Valentine present: a kidney. For years, Sharon Anderson has undergone dialysis treatment for a rare hereditary disease, and her own kidneys have nearly failed. Doctors at Centennial Medical Center have determined, though, that her husband can donate one of his own kidneys to save her life. He chooses Valentine's Day as the target date. News of the selfless gesture travels well beyond the city limits: The couple is interviewed before surgery by the *Today Show*'s Katie Couric on NBC-TV. "We're off to see the wizard," Stephen Anderson says, just before heading to the operating table. The surgery is performed by doctors Peter Minich and Luft Rehman in four hours. It goes off without a hitch. . . . **Normally, Fox's Barber Shop** in Spring Hill would be closed on Monday. Today, though, the shop's only employee (besides owner Larry Fox) has decided she doesn't want the day off. Since Fox has recently suffered a severe stroke, Dianne Colley has started opening the shop for "Larry Fox Mondays," cutting hair for donations toward his medical expenses. Regardless of the length of their hair, patrons wait in line to be shorn.

15—**More than a year** after the discovery of his wife's body, Thomas Farr, 45, is indicted on murder charges. Farr, who has been living in North Carolina, has long been the chief suspect. Donna Farr, mother of two, disappeared March 28, 1998, when she left for church but never arrived. Seven months later, on Oct. 5, her body was found in a wooded section of Williamson County near the Davidson County line. A single bullet was found in the ground beneath her body.

capacity to select from a host of competing blueprints, and turn his picks into three dimensions. Bredesen's personal favorite of his downtown deals is the new library. "But what's done the most for the city's psyche is the Titans, without doubt. If a hundred people comment on what I did as mayor, at least 95 of them thank me for getting the Titans," he says. "We actually spent more money on the schools than on any one of the downtown projects, but nobody seemed to notice."

Everyone noticed the arena in 1996 when it landed on Broadway like a flying saucer. The result of a design competition won by Hellmuth, Obata & Kassabaum of Kansas City, a firm that does sports facilities for much of the nation, what's now called the Gaylord Entertainment Center is a '90s L&C—a symbol of our city's futuristic ambitions.

Adelphia Coliseum, on the other hand, is a concrete ashtray of a structure. It works just fine, but it looks better on *Monday Night Football* than on Sunday afternoons, when the hard light of high noon exposes its functional homeliness. The point of the stadium was not to make architecture, but to make a stage for the Titans, quickly—and it shows. From the standpoint of the built environment, the stadium's significance is to annex the East Bank into downtown.

Exploding onto the downtown scene like a string of firecrackers in the spring and early summer of 2001, the Frist Center for the Visual Arts, the Country Music Hall of Fame, and the downtown library will add cultural offerings to the civic menu. The arts center in the old downtown post office gives new purpose to a white marble elephant. The Country Music Hall of Fame, which Bredesen lured downtown from its holy barn on Music Row, places Nashville's musical heritage front and center south of Broadway. Designed by Tuck Hinton Architects as an architectural abstraction of the values inherent in country music, the hall's heavy, stable materials—stone, brick, rough aggregate concrete—symbolize the earthy soil from which country music grew. During the last decade, Seab Tuck and Kem Hinton have gone from their reputation as Nashville's "bad-boy architects"—because they pushed the edge of the city's conservative design envelope—to a status as movers and shakers in the architecture establishment.

The new downtown library, a competition-winning design by Robert A.M. Stern of New York, is a more obvious nod to tradition. Standing on Church Street directly facing the State Capitol, Stern's quiet classicism speaks to Strickland's more ornate classicism of 150 years before. But if the exterior is a revival, the interior, with quadruple the

The old Nashville Post Office, built in the early 1930s as much to generate construction jobs as to expand postal service, is finding a second life as the Frist Center for the Visual Arts, opening in April 2001. Just west of the Frist is the 100-year-old Union Station.

A model of the new Country Music Hall of Fame and Museum on Demonbreun Street gets a slight adjustment from architect Chip Jones of Tuck Hinton Architects, designers of record for the facility. Its opening is set for May 2001.

space of the current main library and double the collection, is an aggressive gesture of confidence in Nashville's willingness to support the library's shift from minor to major league.

In the architectural language of the library we hear the quiet, genteel drawl of the more conservative city that garbed itself in the robe of Athens. The arena and the Country Music Hall of Fame speak in a hipper, less formal tongue. But the collective contents of all these new constructions reflect Nashville's ambition to speak the dominant dialect of American cities. It's as if our civic leaders looked around at other cities of comparable size in the United States, made a list of what they had that we didn't, and began to check off the items, one by one.

Bredesen agrees that what he built implies his recognition that cities compete, but says his concept of the nature of that competition has changed. "I thought when I came into office that cities competed for businesses, for investment," Bredesen explains." I decided that

The new Nashville Public Library extends and enlarges the classical style that comes closest to giving Nashville an architectural identity. The building fronts on Church Street between Sixth and Seventh avenues.

restaurant on Jefferson Street is closed after less than a year of operation. The $1.1-million, minority-owned venture, touted as an anchor for Jefferson's revitalization efforts, won high praise for its cuisine. Its building, formerly the national headquarters of the Church of God Sanctified, will remain padlocked while the owners search for more financial backing. . . . **Mary Frances Holbert,** 100, succumbs to injuries sustained in her house fire Feb. 11. She is survived by four children, 23 grandchildren, 51 great-grandchildren, 22 great-great-grandchildren and two great-great-great-grandchildren. . . . **Dozens of limousines** line the side streets off Lower Broad. Men in top hats and capes and women in pearls and evening gowns hurry along the Broadway sidewalk past the barflies in Tootsie's Orchid Lounge and the Bluegrass Inn, on their way to the Gaylord Entertainment Center, where Luciano Pavarotti is performing with the Nashville Symphony Orchestra. Tickets range up to $300. Pavarotti keeps his audience of more than 16,000 waiting for close to an hour, but they honor him with a standing ovation before he has sung his first note. The renowned tenor, clearly delighted by the reception, launches into his program with gusto and good humor, displaying top form with selections from Puccini's *La Boheme* and Leoncavallo's *Pagliacci*, plus a gratifying four encores. While the adoring throng was awaiting his arrival, Pavarotti held a 45-minute dressing-room reunion with a longtime fan and close personal friend, Nashville-area librarian Clarice DeQuasie, who has been diagnosed with progressive atrophy of the cerebellum.

17—Helen Lane, also known as "the Crab Orchard Lady" or "the woolly-worm lady," dies at 79 of complications from bone cancer. For more than four decades as the Crossville *Chronicle*'s correspondent from the community of Crab Orchard, Lane sagely predicted the severity of the area's winters. No meteorologist, she relied upon such signifiers as the thickness of corn husks, the color of woolly worms and the number of fogs in August. Her reputation grew after her predictions on the harsh winter of 1959 were close enough to quiet her doubters. She had been profiled in *Life* and other national magazines, and the Public Broadcasting System even made her the subject of a documentary. . . . **The Eggplant Faerie Players,** a radical gay theater troupe with an artists' commune on Short Mountain, ventures down from the hills to the Darkhorse Theater on Charlotte Avenue to perform its latest opus, *Swishing Channels*. . . . **Motorists across the Midstate** are grousing because gasoline prices have soared to an average of $1.31 a gallon. Gas is currently at its highest prices since the 1991 Gulf War, driven upward by a combination of fuel shortages, lower output by oil producers and a severe winter in the Northeast that has boosted production of heating oil at the expense of other fuels. "Surging gas prices may soon peak," reads an optimistic front-page headline in *The Tennessean*. Little do they know.

18—**An exhibit of simulated dinosaurs** draws hundreds of kids and parents to the Cumberland Science Museum. At the Dino Rumble exhibition, tots unearth fossils in a sandbox with archaeological tools, while a mechanical Tyrannosaurus Rex and an animatronic Triceratops move and make ferocious noises nearby.

19—Abandon all hope, ye who enter Demonbreun Street hoping to reach Music Row. Between 14th and 16th avenues, the street will be closed for 18 months while the new Music Row Roundabout is under construction. When finished, the $2.78-million roundabout will entice visitors to Music Row with a statue, a fountain and a piano-key design, while purportedly solving the intersection's perennial traffic confusion. For the time being, the mix of rubble, dust and redirected streets is leaving motorists cursing—though not

somewhere in the middle, cities compete for people. In this mobile age, if the sons and daughters of Nashville return [after college], and new people relocate here, then we'll prosper. If they say, 'I'd rather live in Seattle,' then we won't."

In building people-magnets for Nashville, Bredesen didn't get to all the items on his list, including a town center for downtown, and a continuous greenway from the county line. "I also think Metro needs to do some serious sidewalk building—not scattered fragments in every council district, but a whole system," he says. "And we need to make a major investment in public transportation."

Some planners criticize Bredesen as being so focused on plopping big boxes into downtown that he blinded himself to the need to integrate the boxes into the streetscape, and to tie the boxes together with more subtly-scaled infill. On his watch we got the BellSouth headquarters designed by Earl Swensson Architects, with its pointy profile recalling the logo for the movie *Batman*. The building put more workers into downtown and simultaneously created a new, kid-friendly—and TV-blimp-friendly—architectural icon for the skyline. But the widescraper way that Batman hits the ground ignores the make-nice-to-the-street lessons of the L&C.

The absence of retail in the central city, the ubiquitousness of surface parking, and the fact that most new private projects built downtown have been subsidized by Metro monies, leave open the question of whether Nashville's central city is marching forward into the future, or is staging the dance of one step forward and one step back that characterized the Fulton years. But what remains on Bredesen's list of "things to do" would be a good starting point for present and future mayors intent on raising the level of Nashville's civic game. "Being mayor isn't a revolution but an evolution," Bredesen says. "You're putting more bricks into the structure that already exists."

Unlike our major monuments, old and new, there are places now shaping Nashville more definitively than any civic icon. You'll never see them on the postcard rack, but they're all around us. To find them, you have to go to the suburbs. The suburb is not a modern phenomenon. The Roman patricians located leisure villas—daytime getaways—outside the city walls. These places of diversion and leisure grew out of a mythic belief in the benefits and pleasures of country life cultivated by the urban aristocrat, not the farmer or the serf.

The spatial remove of the Roman suburban villa from the urban masses is consistent with the element of class definition central to the suburb from its beginnings. It was only the wealthy who could afford to seek respite from the dense mixture of classes, the democracy of filth and disease in the city center. In the 19th century, this geographical gap between urban and rural would prove to be a perfect place for a new class—the middle class—to emerge in the social gap between rich and poor.

The first American suburbs developed in the mid-19th century as a place to shelter private family life from the noise, muck, congestion, and debauchery of the city. In Nashville, thousands of people lived within easy walking distance of the Capitol and the Public Square—and in the midst of squalor. The city was filthy. Coal fires to heat the buildings and power the locomotives blackened the air and left a ubiquitous patina of soot. Hogs roamed and rooted in the muddy streets and alleys, outhouses reeked, open privys leached waste directly into streams supplying drinking water, cholera and typhoid epidemics were a constant threat. Along Cherry Street (now Fourth Avenue North) and elsewhere in the heart of the city, gambling, drinking, and prostitution flourished in hotels and saloons with such names as the Utopia, the Climax, the Southern Turf. Nashville's earliest commuters had ample reason to seek living quarters outside the city center.

The first suburb was located on Rutledge Hill, overlooking the Cumberland immediately south of the central city. Incorporated separately as South Nashville from 1850-54, this area was a fashionable residential neighborhood of elegant 19th-century homes and townhouses (Captain Ryman made his home here) and early educational institutions. Vanderbilt University, George Peabody College for Teachers, and Montgomery Bell Academy all had their origins on Rutledge Hill. The subsequent suburb

Symbolic of the booming 1990s were scores of sprawling suburban mansions surrounded by golf courses, private pools and acres of lawn—or, conversely, squeezed onto lots too small for them. They popped up like mushrooms in the six counties adjacent to Metro—but in Nashville-Davidson County alone, more than 600 homes, old and new, had seven-figure valuations at the turn of the century.

Only a few Victorian houses remain on Rutledge Hill, Nashville's first suburb, and most of them are now offices. The area, a few blocks south of Broadway, was initially incorporated as South Nashville in 1850. Two other 19th-century residential districts—Germantown on the north and Edgefield on the east, across the river—enjoyed great popularity through the streetcar era and are reviving neighborhoods now.

north of Nashville called Germantown was also a primarily residential district within walking distance of the commercial center. East of the city, Edgefield's residential development was spurred by the opening of a suspension bridge in 1853 at the present site of the Woodland Street bridge. The suburbs to the west of downtown Nashville—Hillsboro-Belmont, Hillsboro-West End, Richland—had to wait on the electric streetcar,

as loudly as merchants such as MotoPhoto, which must still conduct business there. . . . **The Vanderbilt men's** basketball team slam-dunks their archrivals, the fifth-ranked Tennessee Vols, in an 85-72 upset at Memorial Gym.

20—**A controversial front-page story** in *The Tennessean* says that black Nashvillians are ticketed by police with greater frequency than white motorists. While African Americans account for only 22 percent of licensed drivers in Davidson County, the paper explains, they account for 30 percent of the traffic tickets. What's more, the paper adds, they're also more likely to be charged with multiple offenses when they're ticketed.

21—**Expressing little confidence** in the state Democratic Party, U.S. Rep. Harold Ford Jr. (D-Memphis), tells the Memphis *Commercial Appeal* that he will not oppose incumbent Republican Sen. Bill Frist for his seat. Without a candidate of Ford's name recognition and party support, Frist is all but assured of victory in November. . . . **No need to worry** about Cody Patrick Timmons, the Nashville social worker and husband who disappeared on the eve of Valentine's Day. Timmons places a call to his mother and informs her that he went gambling in Tunica, Miss., before visiting his former home state of Texas. He tells her he may not come back to Tennessee. He needn't come back for his job, which is terminated. Police wonder whether his wife, Misty, actually knew more about his disappearance than she let on, since Timmons took with him a shaving kit and their TV set. . . . **On a national holiday** to celebrate the birthdays of former presidents George Washington and Abraham Lincoln, someone has hanged Lincoln in effigy from a flagpole in a private park facing Interstate 65 south of the city. Park owner William Dorris, a staunch devotee of the late Confederate States of America, has been displaying the Confederate battle flag and a which appeared in 1889. Mule-drawn trolleys did cross the railroad gulch to go west, but it was a hard pull. Nashville's park system had its origins in the suburban migration; land owners saw parks as an attraction that would draw home buyers to their lots.

These Nashville suburbs were all built to a similar pattern: relatively small lots flanking a connected grid of streets and sidewalks and alleys. Corner stores and commercial nodes supplied daily needs; schools and churches served each neighborhood. Because almost everyone walked—children to school, women to the neighborhood stores, commuting men to the trolley stop, families to church—land uses were intermingled, and buildings were clustered to make it easy on the shoe leather. It is important to note, however, that when cars arrived, these traditional neighborhoods could accommodate them. Residents built garages off their alleys or parked next to the curb. Traffic was dispersed through the grid network. If one route was blocked or congested, a driver could turn right or left and take an alternate path.

The architecture of these early suburbs was dominated by the detached, single-family home in a variety of sizes and in a vaguely organic style within each block (the largest usually occupied the corner lots). These houses sported the irregular profiles and elaborate textures that appear in nature because their buyers wanted to escape from the city into nature. Most houses had front porches, the transition between the private and public life of the neighborhood. Commercial buildings were plain, one- to three-story structures built to the sidewalk. Civic buildings—schools, libraries, churches—were more obviously architected; North and East Nashville, for example, had Classical Carnegie libraries. The exceptions were the fire halls, whose styles mimicked that of the surrounding residences. The Holly Street Fire Hall of 1914 was designed in a Classical revival style that would not have been inappropriate for an imposing home. Nashville continued this tradition with the later Tudor bungalow fire station on 21st Avenue South.

As early as the 1920s and '30s, international visionaries like the architect Le Corbusier concluded that cities would have to be redesigned for the automobile. A 1928 Le Corbusier diagram of the city of the future looks much like the suburbia of today—a few large arterials going directly into a pod of land use. The fine-grain network disappears. What is also absent is a storage place for all the vehicles in the diagram, and the notion that once you put all these people in cars on a single road, someone is going to sell them something. The two uses that visually dominate our landscape today, parking and big-box retail, are missing. Le Corbusier tailored the car to the 20th-century technological dream much as the 19th-century American artist tailored the railroad to the pastoral vision.

It was after 1945 that Le Corbusier's dreamscape appeared in Nashville. On the city's edge we began to lower the density of new residential development, and locate retail and commercial buildings farther away from homes, segregated in the larger nodes of shopping centers. The post-World War II subdivision typically features lots of the same size and houses with similar amounts of square footage—effective definitions of an economic class. Multifamily structures grew into blocks of apartments and were restricted by zoning to buffer areas between commerce and single-family dwellings. In Nashville's suburbs, the large lot size was in large part the result of so much impermeable limestone lying close to the surface. Water and sewer lines were too expensive to install, and it took a half-acre or more to accommodate a septic tank.

The lower density and compartmentalized land use were made possible by a car in every garage and an expanding inventory of roads. When you could drive directly from home to wherever you had to go, distance between destinations was no obstacle. Lawns grew; sidewalks disappeared. These new subdivisions did more than accommodate cars; they completely depended on them. Now you had to drive to the grocery, the hardware store, the dry cleaner, the drugstore, the post office. Children needed buses to get to school. Traffic increased, and cul-de-sacs were introduced to restrict cars in residential neighborhoods only to the residents themselves.

The architecture of these newer suburbs reflects the traditional primacy placed on the single-family home and the new primacy placed on the car. Through a columned portico here and a Palladian window there, residential design expresses a vague nostalgia for the suburban villas of the past. But garages have come out front, in the form of what designers call "snout houses," and porches have gone out back, in the form of decks. Commercial buildings express the generic, drive-by ethos of the national chain: building

Whether in straight lines or serpentine curves, clusters or cul-de-sacs, the modern suburbs of greater Nashville, and American cities everywhere, reflect a society that is totally dependent on automobiles; instead of front porches, front garages—and in the back, decks, patios, pools.

as billboard. The architecture of the few suburban civic buildings, with parking in the front, expresses the values of consumer friendliness.

The road pattern serving cul-de-sac subdivisions and shopping malls does not disperse traffic, but concentrates it onto major arterials because there are so few through-streets. It's no coincidence that eleven of the twelve most congested intersections identified in a 1999 report by Metro traffic engineers were not in downtown Nashville, with its 70,000 workers, but in the newer suburbs.

The limited-access highway is another manifestation of design-for-autos that appeared on the Nashville landscape in the early 1960s. The father of the modern American freeway was Norman Bel Geddes, a stage and industrial designer who crafted the General Motors Futurama exhibit for the 1939 World's Fair in New York. (The legislative father of the U.S.

up $2.3 million a year in lost revenue from the school board, convert to a digital format ($4.8 million) and boost annual donations from viewers substantially beyond the present level of $1.6 million.

23—**Ashes to ashes:** By a vote of 80-12, the lower house of the Tennessee General Assembly passes legislation that requires a 24-hour waiting period for all cremations. The only exceptions are for pre-purchased cremation plans. The waiting period, quietly slipped into a 1999 bill, has been sharply criticized for giving funeral directors (whose number includes Democrats John Ford of Memphis in the Senate and Tim Garrett of Goodlettsville in the House) extra time to guilt-trip

Less than four decades after the interstate highway system reached Nashville-Davidson County, almost 200 miles of limited-access freeways and parkways crisscrossed the area, and more such roads are coming. The spaghetti-like configuration of overpasses at the junction of Interstates 65 and 440 south of Nashville is far more functional than most major intersections in the system.

grief-stricken families into buying caskets. However, one group is very happy with the outcome: the well-funded funeral industry lobby. Lucky stiffs. . . . **The poor General Assembly!** So many problems to worry with: endless committee meetings, the incessant harangue of lobbyists, one budget crisis after another—and all this for just $16,500 a year in salary. What would motivate anyone to public service under such conditions? Associated Press reporter Phil West may have found some answers. His scrutiny of the legislature's $26-million annual budget reveals a cornucopia of perks for the 99 representatives and 33 senators: generous pensions and 401(k)

interstate system, two decades later, was Senator Albert Gore Sr. of Tennessee, who is credited with steering an Eisenhower administration plan through Congress.) The Bel Geddes exhibit, which projected how the United States would look in 1960, was remarkably similar to today's interstate system, with one notable exception. In his 1939 book, *Magic Motorways*, Bel Geddes said that the limited-access motorway "should not be allowed to infringe on the city" because the motorway is basically hostile to the form of cities. His idea was that the motorway should be kept 30 to 40 miles outside, to be used strictly for long-distance travel. Commercial development along these cross-country roads should be restricted to gas stations, motels, restaurants, and the like. The motorway would be connected to the city by boulevards and surface streets.

The American traffic engineer accepted the motorway idea, but brought it right into the city. The express thoroughfare was the great "urban renewer," carving up neighborhoods—often African-American and always low-income—such as Interstate 40 did in North Nashville and I-65 did in East Nashville. Zoning was changed to permit massive commercial development at interchanges.

The expressway is not inherently bad, but as a design for long-distance travel adapted to provide local circulation, it does not perform well. Neither does the major arterial lined with strip shops, curb cuts, and cul-de-sacs. Their basic dysfunctionality is apparent in Nashville in the congestion and growing length of our rush hours. What these roads did do well was allow the commuter seeking a vision of country living to travel farther and farther to find it.

At a certain point in the nation's history—around 1990 in Nashville—the larger and more far-flung suburbs ceased to be dependent on the urban core for jobs, goods, and services and began evolving into an "edge city." But there is little that is civic about such places. The best local example is Cool Springs. The name, like so many suburban developments, memorializes what it has destroyed, in this case a farm called Cool Springs. This edge city has all the components of a traditional town: a major transportation corridor in I-65, single- and multifamily housing in a variety of price ranges, restaurants and retail, education and health care. Mid-rise office towers seem to spring up like daffodils in what is perhaps the hottest market in the Nashville region.

Cool Springs may be the land of opportunity for the developer; it is also one of the biggest missed opportunities in the region's planning history. A typical day in Cool Springs is an exercise in dysfunction. If you work in one of the office blocks, you drive to the lot and park. Lunch with a friend involves another car trip and a parking space, as do shopping after lunch, a trip to the gym after work, dinner with a friend, a movie with a spouse. Requiring six trips for one car just to get one person through the day is a congestion generator and a waste of time for the car

Cool Springs, the newest and largest of Nashville's suburban "edge cities," is larger than all but a handful of Tennessee's traditional cities, yet it is a sprawling commercial and residential entity, not a municipal one; the towns of Brentwood and Franklin and Williamson County government all claim partial jurisdiction.

owner; providing these spaces is a waste of money for the developers, as well as a waste of land. The construction of the shopping mall that sparked all the development also caused the channeling of Spencer Creek, a free-flowing stream with high-quality water, into a concrete box, effectively killing it—which is a waste of a natural resource.

Taking the same assemblage of farm land on which Cool Springs grew, a town could have been platted next to the interstate in the manner that Nashville once was platted next to the river. Effective planning could have yielded a grid of streets and sidewalks, a mixture of land uses in a variety of building sizes, nodes of parking—one trip and you've parked the car for the day, or ridden mass transit to a central location. But the zoning of Cool Springs would not have allowed for a real town plan because of the mandates for a division of land uses and separate parking for each enterprise. These mandates reflect an anti-urban bias that is at the heart of the suburban mind-set.

In *Town and Countryside*, published in 1932, Thomas Sharp warned against using the suburb to resolve the conflict between culture and nature inherent in the American character. "The antithesis of town and country is already breaking down," he wrote. "Two diametrically opposed, dramatically contrasting, inevitable types of beauty are being displaced by one drab, revolting neutrality. Rural influences neutralize the town. Urban influences neutralize the country. In a few years all will be neutrality. The strength of the town; the softer beauty, the richness, the fruitfulness of the countryside, will be debased into one sterile, hermaphroditic beastliness."

Sharp might well have been describing Nashville in 2000 when he wrote, "The crying need of the moment is reestablishment of the ancient antithesis. The town is

retirement plans, comprehensive health and life insurance, $525-a-month expense allowance (no itemization necessary), $114-a-day per diem for every day they're in Nashville on official business, additional travel reimbursement, lodging discounts and more. All in all, the benefits amount to roughly double the salary—and that's not counting the cost of office space and staff. Not bad for a part-time job, some legislators say. One, Sen. Douglas Henry (D-Nashville), a wealthy attorney, returns to the state every penny he is paid for his services. But a clear majority of both houses think the compensation is inadequate. They search tirelessly for quiet ways to ratchet it up.

24—**A domestic violence complaint** leads to death, tragedy and controversy in the community of Bear Creek near Leiper's Fork. Two Williamson County deputies are dispatched to arrest Bruce Gilbert, 35, a Bear Creek resident with a police record dating back to 1989. Gilbert, who has been deaf since birth, reportedly turns belligerent and strikes one of the deputies. He is doused with pepper spray and subdued with a baton, but manages to break free. A shovel rests nearby where he has been moving gravel. He reaches for the shovel and swings at one of the officers. They shoot Gilbert five to six times in the chest and hands. Shortly thereafter, he dies. His mother, Martha Faye Raines, tells *The Tennessean* that she swore out the warrant on her son because she thought he needed help. She, like other friends and family members, considers the deputies' force excessive. The deputies, Terrence Demerest and Robert Durbin, are placed on administrative leave without pay but later cleared of any wrongdoing.

25—**In a sold-out show** at the Gaylord Entertainment Center, country singer Alan Jackson gives the crowd of 17,000 a taste of his next single, a duet with fellow country traditionalist George

Strait. To the crowd's surprise, the song is a blistering indictment of the watered-down crossover country coming off Music Row's assembly line. "Nobody saw him runnin' from Sixteenth Avenue/They never found a fingerprint or the weapon that was used," sings Jackson. "But someone killed country music, cut out its heart and soul/They got away with murder down on Music Row." The crowd cheers Jackson on as he lambastes the current state of country stations, especially when he sings that his idol, George Jones, "wouldn't stand a chance on today's radio." The song, "Murder on Music Row," co-written by Larry Shell and bluegrass artist Larry Cordle, becomes both an anthem of traditionalist dissatisfaction and the subject of much Sixteenth Avenue tut-tutting. It also becomes a hit. **. . . 25 years ago today,** 9-year-old Marsha Trimble left her Green Hills home to deliver Girl Scout cookies and never returned. The search for her grew to massive proportions and stretched over 33 days, until Mar. 30, when her body was found in a garage in the same neighborhood. No one was ever brought to justice for the abduction and death, and the case remains, in the words of one Metro police detective, "the biggest murder mystery in Nashville history.". . . **Dr. Charles W. Ingram,** the founder of Nashville's Interfaith Dental Clinic, is tending his home garden when he suffers a fatal heart attack. He was 75. The Interfaith Dental Clinic, a boon to low-income Nashville families, provides dental care for hundreds of patients at nominal cost. . . . **Belmont University** announces that Robert C. Fisher, vice president of academic affairs at Arkansas State University, will become its new president effective Apr. 13. Fisher replaces William Troutt, under whose tenure the Baptist school's enrollment swelled to more than 3,000 students. . . . **Specialties listed** in *The Tennessean*'s two-page Saturday spread of church advertising: "Healings. . . Deliverance. . . Miracles. . . Tongues. . . Prophecy."

State Road 840 is cutting a circular swath around Nashville some 35 miles out from the heart of the city. Most of the southern half of the circle was open or under construction in 2000; one section in Williamson County was tied up in court. The northern half was still in the preliminary planning stage. The entire circle, when completed, would be about 175 miles around.

town: the country is country. Only in the preservation of the town as town can the countryside be saved; and only through the limitation of rurality to the country can the town be preserved."

On a balmy afternoon in late February, I can hear the water running down the western Highland Rim. Even in a dry summer, there's lots of liquid in the Kelley Creek watershed of southwest Williamson County—seeping from limestone crevices, bubbling up from springs, flowing over the descending series of limestone shelves that form the streambeds that empty into the Harpeth River. On a day when sun induces thaw—a false promise of imminent spring often made but never kept in Middle Tennessee—the rush of water is like the whispered promise of eternal life.

But the sound of running water on the Highland Rim may soon fade to a whisper. State Road 840 beltway, if completed, will encircle the Metro Nashville region an average distance of 35 miles out from the city center. Much of the road will lie on the slope of the rim, disrupting the watershed with leached earth and concrete culverts. And if past practice is any predictor of future form, the highway will carry the sprawling patterns of development that the interstates first delivered to the basin in the 1960s.

The watershed within the Highland Rim—a rough, hilly, almost mountainous land gouged by narrow river valleys—is what made the Central Basin the garden of Middle Tennessee. The waters carved a filigree of veins and arteries in the basin's bed of solid limestone, depositing silt in the 600-foot depression running north-south through the state. Silt and streams made a hunting park for the nomadic natives, and a rich agricultural land for the settlers who followed. Today the floodplains of the basin and the rocky slopes of the rim—two topographies that have so far discouraged development—present us with complementary opportunities to preserve some balance between natural habitat and human habitation.

The shape of Middle Tennessee has never displayed the drama of the West—which is perhaps why it called out to James Robertson, John Donelson, and the other Nashville founders for domestication. But there is a big difference between domestication and devastation. What the landscape heralds now is a homogenization of city and country that retains the character of neither.

The Central Basin is where most Middle Tennessee families have made their homes, established farms, and built businesses. For 150 years, the patterns in which they settled kept a rough sense of proportion: town squares and commercial centers surrounded by homes, the towns connected by the spokes of roads that ran through a greenbelt of forest and farm. But 50 years ago, this pattern began to disintegrate.

The inner loop of the interstates formed a relatively tight collar around Nashville, defining a center city that we are now trying desperately to repair. But these limited-access highways separated the old city from its support system of neighborhoods, and became escape routes to the sprawling developments that were invading the greenbelts. Interstates 40 and 65 and 440 drove concrete canyons through the old streetcar suburbs. Briley Parkway, Old Hickory Boulevard, and now 840 each define successive stages of our growing appetite for land. Metro Planning Department statistics show that in the decade of the 1990s, new residential development in Davidson County gobbled up land at a rate five times greater than the increase of population. This phenomenon of spatial obesity threatens to resolve definitively for the Nashville metropolitan region the tension between sublime nature and the material progress of the engineered landscape that has defined the American character from inception.

Nashville has historically fudged the tension. While the big cotton planters of the Deep South seemed intent on working people and soil to exhaustion, those who migrated into this basin had other dreams. From the beginning, Nashville has been a place settled to sustain a diversity of crops and a diverse economy for the long haul. Today's possessors of basin and rim have a choice, as all who preceded them once had: to be stewards or looters of the land. The myth of America encompasses both.

It requires bipolar vision for Americans to see their land as a heaven on earth. We feel entitled to the goods and services of cities, with all their convenience and

26—**Animal-rights activists** get on their high horse over a "donkey ball" fund-raising event at Madison Academy, a private school. The sport of donkey ball is much like basketball, with the added attraction that the players sit on their asses. Activists claim the donkeys are mistreated, but their owners counter that the donkeys have been trained for just such a purpose. Not heard from are the donkeys. . . . **Much more vocal** are supporters of the wild turkey—the kind found in woodlands, not liquor stores. Having released 13 wild turkey hens the day before on a Mt. Juliet farm, the National Wild Turkey Federation stages the main event of its convention at the Opryland Hotel: the Grand National Turkey-Calling Championship. Some 1,500 people gather amongst the chandeliers and stuffed birds in an Opryland ballroom to hear 14 contestants practice their most authentic turkey calls. "Cutting yelp of excited hen," demands emcee Mark Bunting, resplendent in hunter's green. Contestants dutifully squint their eyes, stalk about the stage and emit rasping squawks and trills. When the smoke clears, Chris Parrish of Mexico, Mo., is the senior division champ. The moment is witnessed by representatives from the National Wild Turkey Federation's official publication, *Turkey Call.* . . . **Cost of a 10-pound** fresh turkey at Kroger: $13.90.

27—**Surgeons at Vanderbilt Medical Center** are performing more operations on fetuses to treat such debilitating conditions as spinal bifida, and their success is changing the way society views the fetus as a patient, a person and as part of a woman's body. Medical writer Bill Snyder of *The Tennessean* reports that debates over abortion and the meaning of "God's will" are raging among surgeons, medical ethicists, religious leaders and others because of these surgical interventions. . . . **The digital age** has arrived. *The Tennessean*'s closely-watched obituaries go online.

28—**Lest anyone accuse** the state Senate of shirking its duty, Sen. Jerry Cooper (D-McMinnville), asks that his colleagues postpone voting for a week on a bill of vital importance. At issue: what kinds of foods can actually be considered the first meal of the day. To fast-food restaurants near interstate exits, the distinction is crucial: Dining spots that serve three meals a day get first crack at the coveted slots on service signs near off-ramp exits. Representatives of McDonald's, which is pushing the bill, are McHacked that pizza parlors sometimes lay out trays of doughnuts and coffee to protect their space on the signs. People should be allowed to determine their own breakfasts, counters a Taco Bell shill in a stirring defense of eaters' rights. What rough beast slouches toward McDonaldland, waiting to be born? . . . **Saturn Corp.** is shutting down its car manufacturing plant in Spring Hill this week to reduce inventories due to falling demand for its compact autos, but the 7,200 members of the United Auto Workers union will draw full pay due to a "no-layoff" clause in their contract. Sales of the Spring Hill-built S series compact were down for the third straight year in 1999. . . . **A provision of the Tennessee** abortion statute requiring pregnant girls under 18 to have parental consent before they can have an abortion has finally cleared court challenges going all the way back to 1988. Today, the provision goes into effect.

Before construction comes deconstruction: To clear space for expansion in the Cool Springs area, hundreds of large trees were uprooted and removed.

abundance and quality. Yet we also feel entitled to go it alone in a single-family home and a single-occupant vehicle, to escape from community into the individual experience of open space, and to enter it both visually and physically. If Nashvillians fail to come together to set patterns for the region's expansion that respond to topography rather than destroying it, if we fail to cluster ourselves on the land in a way that sustains both poles of the American vision—city and open space, culture and nature—we may lose everything, and our sense of entitlement will become a sense of permanent loss.

On the horizon are faint but hopeful signs that Nashville may be beginning to face up to past mistakes and the potential for future problems. The founding of Cumberland Region Tomorrow is evidence of the growing acknowledgement that the infrastructure of roads and sewers and water lines today channel where and how we grow as surely as the rivers once did. Citizens from Davidson and ten surrounding Middle Tennessee counties founded this not-for-profit organization in 2000 to consider growth and planning issues with an emphasis on land use, transportation, and preservation of the rural landscape, as well as the character of the region's communities.

What legacy will Nashville leave to the next century? Will we have more Shelby Bottoms or more Wal-Marts? More subdivisions or more neighborhoods? Will we fill in the gaps within the existing city—the parking lots and empty lots, the brown fields abandoned by industry and the gray fields left by commerce—or will we continue to consume the green fields at the edge? Will we keep the best architecture of the past 50 years, or lose it? Will the arena and the Country Music Hall of Fame be landmarks or new construction sites? Will we still be Nashville, or will we have become Nashlanta?

The questions come easier than the answers. But this much seems clear: The next 100 years will see a struggle for the soul of Nashville more intense and self-conscious than that of the last 200 years, or even the last twenty. We now have a better sense of what we have to gain and lose, because we have gained and lost so much. The art of architecture, of civic design, is not primarily the art of the thing itself, but the effect of structure on the human spirit. The shape we give to our city, in turn, shapes us.

Animal Kingdom

by ANNE PAINE

Archaeological evidence shows that people and animals have coexisted here in the Central Basin of Middle Tennessee for at least thirteen millennia. The first 98 percent of that time can be reviewed by sifting through artifacts. Only the most recent 2 percent—the last three centuries, since about 1700—gives us any sort of recorded history. Over that relatively short period of time, the human history of the region has been captured in ever-lengthening detail. Not so well known, though, is the animal history.

The abundance of wildlife caused indigenous people—descendants of the Paleo-Indian hunters and gatherers who arrived after the last Ice Age—to return seasonally to this wilderness Eden. Near the beginning of the 18th century, small numbers of hunters, trappers, and explorers from east of the mountains found their way here—they, too, attracted by the game. Middle Tennessee teemed with woodland bison, elk, deer, and other four-footed animals, smaller descendants of prehistoric creatures.

Here in the heart of present-day Nashville, herds of beasts numbering in the thousands crowded around a great salt-tinged spring in the vicinity of our Bicentennial Mall—the French Lick, as it would be named. The bison were the grumpy master race of the animal world. Mature males could weigh over a ton (and they were puny compared to their ancestors). They wallowed in the mud to coat their shaggy hides for protection against vast clouds of buffalo gnats. Prairie grasses that provided the herds with unlimited food grew tall in places where Indian farmers of an earlier age may have cultivated corn and other crops. Because the human presence was both small and seasonal prior to the mid-1700s, with Indians and Europeans alike coming mainly to hunt, not settle, the herds multiplied faster than the hunters could thin them. But over time, more people and deadlier weapons turned the tide; the bison were decimated, many to have only their tongues cut away for food and their tallow taken for candles. Carcasses rotted where they fell. Natural selection also applied: Wolf packs followed the growing herds, waiting for the weak to fall or stray; bears and panthers lurked at the edge of the French Lick.

With permanent settlement, the fate of the beasts was sealed. "People are a major change organism on the earth," said naturalist Mack Prichard of the Tennessee Department of Environment and Conservation. "We're very successful hunters." No animals had protection; they were either commodities to be exploited or pests to be eradicated. The bison, which had created the first wilderness roads as herds moved from place to place, were by 1800 a rare sight in Middle Tennessee. Fifty years later, no elk or bear remained. If any large wild animals managed to survive after that, they were hunted down by all parties when civil war came.

At the turn of the 20th century, few wild deer survived in Davidson County. Their shoulders, loins, and hams were coveted as meat, and their hides were a source of clothing. Fewer than 2,000 roamed the entire state, and those mainly in East Tennessee. Now, a century later, the Tennessee Wildlife Resources Agency estimates the number of white-tailed deer in Davidson County alone at 8,000. Hunting regulations and the release of deer brought in from other states beginning in the 1940s caused this population explosion. Now the graceful animals have attained pest status as they nibble gardens and shrubbery and dart across roads in front of cars.

In part to ensure the continued presence of a natural habitat, Nashville leaders in the 1920s took some positive steps. Luke Lea donated the first large chunk of what would become the 2,600-acre Warner Parks. A special commission began to assemble the public park system that would eventually ring the city with green.

The coyote, a newcomer from the West, has entered this region in the last few decades, prowling subdivisions from Joelton to Old Hickory, dining on dishes of pet food left outside—and sometimes on the pets themselves. Their presence is known mainly from their excrement and the occasional yipping and falsetto howls rippling through the night air.

The largest predator in the area now—as in the settlers' day—is the bobcat, spotted rarely in the Warner Parks and other woods. They're quiet, camouflaged, nocturnal—and their numbers are dwindling. They might not be around in another 100 years. "It's going to get harder and harder," said Sandy Bivens, Warner Park Nature Center director. "This park used to be a lot bigger, in the sense that all the acres around us were like part of the park. Now they're subdivisions."

The newly arrived night-traveling armadillo is expected to become a regular sight in the years ahead, most often as road kill. Starlings, a European import not present in the settlers' day, fill trees by the tens of thousands, as do crows in the waning light of winter afternoons. The city, where hunting is prohibited, provides overnight protection for their roosts. Canada Geese that once only migrated through here now congregate in fussy, defecating masses on golf courses and on lawns near ponds. Gulls weren't to be found here at all until Old Hickory, Percy Priest, and other man-made lakes were created after World War II. This chain of waterways, our "Great Lakes of the South," caused several varieties of shore birds to take up full-time residency.

The most exotic wild animals to be found around here now are in the Nashville Zoo at Grassmere. And the greatest modern-day addition to the animal kingdom is not a product of nature but a consequence of the rise in human population. Domesticated animals, most of them house pets, are thought to number close to a quarter-million in Nashville and Davidson County, with dogs outnumbering cats by about 2 to 1. That's roughly one pet for every two people.

Anne Paine, a native Nashvillian, has been writing about environmental issues and other subjects for The Tennessean *since 1983.*

A Place Remembered

by PAUL CLEMENTS

Some ten thousand years ago, nomadic people arrived in the region where Nashville now stands. Life was a continual quest for food, and the members of those wandering communities depended on one another for survival. After hundreds of generations, their descendants became farmers, and villages appeared along what would eventually become known as the Cumberland River. Although food was more abundant, there were periods of warfare with rival groups, and the inhabitants continued to depend on each other for survival. The rich and intricate patterns of human activity unfolded day by day, season by season, and century by century, until that long-enduring culture passed away.

With the arrival of frontier families in the late 1700s, much of the interdependence that was so deeply woven into the fabric of ancient settlements returned to the region. Neighbors helped clear and plant land, and they harvested crops together. When a family needed to build a house or a barn, others from the community helped with the work. People married close to home, looked after each other's children, learned together, worshiped together. Through the long years of warfare with Indians, the settlers fought and mourned together, and some who survived grew old together.

When my great-great-grandfather came to Nashville in 1839, a few of those survivors and some of the intimacy that had existed on the frontier remained. Whether through living in the same neighborhood, working side-by-side, or buying and selling from each other, everyone in town knew almost everyone else. Nashville was a close-knit place—but my ancestor had not found Utopia. There were inequities and hardships. Slavery was firmly entrenched, epidemics brought death, and work could be a lifelong succession of grueling, indistinguishable days. Still, he had found what seemed a good place to earn a living and raise his family, and he stayed.

He was a carriage maker, and though he struggled at times, he was eventually able to provide his family with a measure of comfort. His sons and daughters were largely free to explore the place where they lived. Just beyond the lightly traveled streets of their neighborhood were the familiar stores and merchants around the public square, and there was the river, where children could swim, fish, or watch steamboats come and go.

Change came slowly until the 1850s when, through the exertions of those whose fortunes were tied to the rapid growth of Nashville, the railroads arrived and crime swelled along with the population. The sense of community eroded further during the Civil War. Nashville became a military center, and the sense of place that Nashvillians had always shared soon broke apart and was scattered into the various neighborhoods of what had become a city.

By the time the war ended, my great-great-grandfather was in his mid-50s, and his oldest daughter had a family of her own. His grandchildren, one of whom was my grandmother, were raised in an environment that was far more crowded, more dangerous, and dirtier than it had been a generation earlier. There were still familiar faces, but also more strangers, more crime, and more places where children were not allowed to go. Nashville grew less and less habitable. The business center was still downtown, but the extension of streetcar service made it easier to live farther away.

In the early 1900s, soon after their marriage, my grandparents joined the growing number of people moving out of the city. They built a modest home just south of Nashville, and my mother and four older brothers were all born there. Residents knew each other and children were free to roam, but with the automobile allowing more people to flee the city, the neighborhood gradually became crowded. In the mid 1920s, my mother's family moved out between Hillsboro and Harding roads. New houses would be built across the countryside, but for a number of years there would also be clear streams, woods, and open fields.

Woodmont School was built in 1931 to accommodate the growing number of area children. It quickly became the center of the neighborhood. My mother grew up and married, and after World War II, she and my father bought a house a few hundred yards from the place where my grandparents had moved twenty years earlier. Downtown Nashville would remain the commercial hub, but it had long since ceased to be a community.

The Woodmont neighborhood of my boyhood was similar to other communities that surrounded Nashville in those years following the war. Roads were largely free of traffic. People knew their neighbors, and there were numerous places for children to play. The school had an excellent reputation, and was the reason many families moved into the area. Almost every child in the neighborhood attended Woodmont, and most walked or rode bicycles to school. There was a grassy lot called Herbert's Field where children played baseball and football, and there were two places to fish within a five-minute bicycle ride of my house. I could leave home on Saturday morning and be gone for hours without giving my parents cause for concern. There were backyard sleepouts in summer, and on clear nights we could look up and see the multitude of stars.

The Woodmont neighborhood flourished through the 1960s, but unwanted changes were on the way. Those institutions and individuals with the most to gain from the growth of Nashville were extremely powerful—and no less energetic than their railroad-hungry counterparts of a century earlier.

Some lobbied the federal government to bring arteries of the interstate highway system through Nashville. Others pushed to consolidate the governments of Nashville and Davidson County, or to legalize the sale of liquor by the drink. And at times they chose to move silently, appearing uninvolved as they eased the way for land developers and their other allies to take control of local land-use policies. Whether visible or not, their efforts always focused on bringing more business, more people, and more capital to Nashville.

The Woodmont School neighborhood was one of many communities that became a casualty of the grand design being pursued by the financial and political leaders of Nashville. The vast majority of residents wanted their neighborhood to remain as it was, but when they appeared before the governmental agencies that made decisions about development, they were consistently ignored.

An ever-increasing density of housing was robbing the Woodmont neighborhood of its character, as was the decline of public education. Those who were so effective in promoting growth failed to exert their influence when it came to supporting the public school system. School desegregation was inevitable, but education officials, who seemed to reflect the attitudes of area leaders, were purposefully slow to enact the needed changes. In 1971, court-ordered busing was instituted to bring racial balance to the city's classrooms, and Woodmont ceased to be a neighborhood school. It closed in 1981, and was torn down a few years later.

With the school gone, neighborhood children, and then their families, lost their connection to each other. Herbert's Field and other open areas had long since been covered by houses. There were fewer places where young people could play together and learn, independent of adults, the most lasting lessons of childhood. Automobile traffic intensified, and as the area population increased, neighborhood children stayed closer to home. With one of the fishing holes drained for development and the other fouled by commercial pollution, children on bicycles were no longer seen pedaling home with a freshly caught fish or two. And with streetlights along each thoroughfare casting their dull collective glow across the neighborhood, anyone looking up into the night sky could see only a few stars.

In the 1970s I moved out to Williamson County and later built the house where my wife and I would raise our family. For a few years the rural setting remained intact, but then a familiar pattern began to unfold. There were protests against unwanted development, but those making land-use decisions ruled more and more in favor of developers, at the expense of regular citizens. A few well-planned developments were built, but the usual result was merely massed housing that lacked the rich possibilities offered by traditional neighborhoods.

Those with the most to gain from the economic development of the county dismissed protest with the same arguments used earlier by their counterparts in Nashville. They said that development would minimize property tax increases, but taxes rose and debt spiraled. They claimed that growth brought about improved roads and schools, but failed to add that regular taxpayers, not developers, funded most such improvements. The benefits of rising property values were put forward, but nothing was said about how those selling their property were rarely better off after paying an increased price for their next home.

Then it was solemnly declared that any area would die unless it grew. But no examples were provided of places as economically viable or well-located as Nashville or Williamson County where cautious growth policies had caused civic death. And those trying to create hyper-growth had no answer when they were asked how, if an area must either grow or die, Nashville and Williamson County had remained healthy through long periods of little or no growth.

But what if there had been some truth to the statement that the end of growth brought economic death? Given that growth within any finite area must ultimately reach its limit, would it not be better to have slower, carefully controlled growth? No one would give an answer. The population was rising, and there were legitimate questions about where new housing should be built and how dense it should be. Suburban sprawl was an issue. But those pushing for maximum growth had no interest in dialogues about how much growth to allow and how best to deal with it. Instead there was the familiar argument that any effort to limit growth was unfair to those wanting to move into the county, but no mention was made about local areas such as Belle Meade, Oak Hill, and Forest Hills, where growth had been managed through strict zoning. Growth proponents would shrug and say people needed new places to live—but would not discuss the wisdom of developing massive amounts of fertile farmland in the face of an exploding world population.

If pushed hard enough, the purveyors of rampaging growth indignantly fell back to the argument that to limit growth was to oppose property rights. But nothing was ever said about the rights of those who had their property condemned so roads could be constructed or widened, so schools and fire stations could be built, or so electrical substations and power lines could be installed to accommodate burgeoning development. And there was no acknowledgement that headlong growth is almost always accompanied by increased traffic, more air and water pollution, and a rising rate of crime.

So twenty years after I built my house in Williamson County, the boomtown mentality that ravaged Nashville has taken root in all the counties surrounding Nashville. Crowded plots of housing, along with massive commercial developments, continue to spring up. And with the seemingly inevitable completion of State Road 840, a project initiated by road builders and land speculators, a semicircular swath of sprawl to the south seems inevitable.

The old city of Nashville is at the center of an enormous metropolis-in-the-making, and as that metropolis continues to swallow up communities and countryside alike, there is the prospect that future residents might become urban nomads. Will they someday be isolated, not by the vastness of nature, but by the vastness of humanity? Having little access to the natural world, and with only vague connections to those living around them, what sort of people will they be? Will they occupy a place so indistinguishable, so lacking in character, that although they do not wander, they will be, like the nomads who arrived so long ago, people without a home?

Paul Clements is the author of A Past Remembered *(1987) a two-volume microhistory of 72 antebellum houses in Davidson County, of which seven no longer exist.*

SUNG AND UNSUNG

by LEON ALLIGOOD

I t was one of those parties where you don't know anyone but the host—a dull affair, because every-body's afraid to talk about anybody else in the room for fear that the person you decide to chat up is the cousin or co-worker or spouse of the person across the room about whom you make some catty remark.

One of those parties. And so, effectively constrained from talking about one another, we turned in pairs and foursomes to the evergreen and ever-safe subject of celebrities. At many a Nashville gather-ing, stargazing is standard fodder for small talk, if only because there are so many stars in our universe. People here tend to be somewhat ambivalent about fame—casually unimpressed, even jaded, from so much exposure to it, but at the same time drawn to it, like bees to blossoms.

". . . so I was just standing there in the checkout line, and I turned to look at a magazine cover and you'll never guess who was right behind me—NAOMI," said a woman in a St. Patrick's-green pantsuit. All she had to say was the first name; her listeners understood that it was Naomi Judd she had seen K-Marting. The woman accentuated each vowel of the nurse-cum-country superstar's name as if it were a wartime password for entrance to a secret bunker.

Between judicious sips of her zinfandel, Ms. Irish tossed in the rest of her spy tale: "She was buy-ing lip gloss." Her listeners nodded sagely—and with that, a lively round of celebrity one-upmanship began in earnest.

". . . and there was Charley Pride, just strolling through the mall like anybody else."

"Dolly was so nice. She barely even got to touch her salad because of all the people coming up to talk to her."

"You wouldn't believe how good-looking that Faith Hill is when you're practically standing next to her—well, no farther than a couple of rows . . ."

Soon the game had expanded from the recent-time to the all-time list, and the sightings report rambled on: Little Jimmy Dickens coming out of a Cracker Barrel restaurant . . . Oprah Winfrey greeting home folks at the airport . . . George Jones two days before he wrecked his Lexus . . . Amy Grant cheering for her daughter at a softball game umpired by Bill Boner . . . Anne Holt having dinner with her husband at a little restaurant on Franklin Road . . . Garth Brooks playing with his kids in the park . . . a rumpled Marvin Runyon leaving Kroger on a rainy Sunday evening . . . Fate Thomas and Gayle Ray, the once and future sheriffs, sitting back-to-back at separate breakfast tables at the Pie Wagon . . . Eddie George schlep-ping a bag of dog food in the checkout line at PetSmart . . . Garrison Keillor having lunch at Arnold's . . . Marty Stuart riffling through the CDs at the Great Escape . . . Martha Ingram and Kenneth Schermer-horn doing some last-minute Christmas shopping at Target . . . perennial political candidate John Jay Hooker tacking into a stiff breeze at the Bicentennial Mall, his clawhammer coattails flapping . . . Al Gore baring his funny bone and his soul at a memorial service for his old *Tennessean* pal, Jerry Thompson.

Names of the famous, the notorious, the so-Nashville tumbled forth like shrimp tails on the plas-tic cocktail plates we were dropping into the trash can in the kitchen. No one seemed to notice what had

1—**Amid frantic construction** of Opry Mills, the outlet mall-run-amok on which Gaylord Entertainment is staking the city's tourism future, some 1,200 disc jockeys, programmers and consultants begin trickling, then flooding, into the lobby of the Opryland Hotel. It's time for the annual Country Radio Seminar, which started as a disc-jockey convention in 1952 when WSM decided to throw a birthday party and schmoozefest for the Grand Ole Opry. The event has evolved into an annual pulse-taking of country radio's health. Panelists prepare for a week of hand-wringing. . . . **Another panel,** the Amtrak Reform Council, has bad news for Nashville rail proponents. The federally formed independent panel concludes that it is not feasible at this time to extend train service the 180 miles from Louisville to Music City. A passenger train hasn't stopped in Nashville since October 1979, when Amtrak's *Floridian* passed through on its Chicago to Miami run.

2—**No need to worry** anymore about flying the Tennessee state flag upside down. Sen. Bob Rochelle (D-Lebanon) introduces a bill that would label which end of the state flag is up. Naysayers fear that the instructions will deface the three-starred flag, but Rochelle has anticipated their concerns—he demonstrates that the label can be printed on the flag's nylon border. The bill passes, 25 to 3. . . . **An unspeakable word** echoes through the corridors of the Country Radio Seminar: crossover. Many country deejays loathe the prospect of having hits such as Lonestar's "Amazed" co-opted by contemporary hit radio stations. Yet such hits are good for country radio, argues researcher Rick Torcasso, because they advertise the format to noncountry listeners. Torcasso says the format suffers from a distinct lack of superstars, or "icons."

happened—that an hour had passed, during which the party's focus had shifted from internal to external, from us to them, and to the who-when-where of celebrity sightings. Nor is it likely that the assembled star-watchers were aware that their stories possessed a single common denominator: Every one of them had happened here in greater Nashville, a town that until half a century ago was an unimpressive little backwater burg on the banks of the Cumberland River, no more a lure to the rich and famous and celebrated than any other mid-sized city with middling appeal—Birmingham, say, or Charlotte, or Columbus.

Music changed that. The Grand Ole Opry probably got the ball rolling in the 1920s when it started broadcasting on WSM radio, and they ramped it up when the Opry moved to the Ryman Auditorium in 1943. Great instrumental artistry by fiddlers and guitar pickers changed it. After World War II, the smooth, citified, crossover country sounds of people like Eddy Arnold changed it, in tandem with lonesome ramblers like Hank Williams and Ernest Tubb, in their pointed-toe boots and wide-brimmed Stetsons. Women got in the act, too. Patsy Cline went from wholesome cowgirl to supperclub siren—and all the while, Minnie Pearl's cornpone "How-dee!" lingered as a lyrical challenge to the world to take us as we are. Nashville went national with a savvy blend of all these sounds.

Music has given Nashville name recognition across the country and beyond. Tourists are drawn to the city for many reasons now, but country music fans are still the most numerous. They come to hear their favorite performers, to see celebrities in the hall of fame or in person and to have their pictures taken at such legendary watering holes as Tootsie's Orchid Lounge on Lower Broad.

In time, the world did accept the town that Timothy Demonbreun had seen in his mind's eye when he deemed this a suitable spot for settlement back in 1769. By 2000, Nashville had emphatically declared its eligibility to join the major league of American cities. It had a population in excess of half a million (more than twice that within the greater urban orbit) and a national visibility that most cities its size could only envy. A vigorous and sustained revitalization was in progress downtown; two pro sports teams were drawing big crowds to new venues; the diversified economy was humming along at a pretty good clip; and, within a half-mile radius of Eighth and Broad, three important new institutions would soon be opening their doors—a fine arts center, a 21st-century library, and a thoroughly modern museum celebrating the music for which the city is famous. All this ferment was jump-started in 2000 when the Tennessee Titans emerged as the Cinderella team in pro football's Super Bowl XXXIV, and this brand-new collection of local celebrities and heroes came within a tippy-toe of wearing the golden slippers back to Nashville.

This oh-so-close reach for professional football's crown jewel would be followed some months later by another event for the masses: Billy Graham's last stand against the forces of darkness right here in Music City. He packed Adelphia Coliseum for four balmy June nights. In fact, unless the stadium is enlarged, the octogenarian preacher will hold the attendance record: 71,800 people—almost 5,000 in excess of its official capacity—squeezed inside on the third night of the crusade, before the fire marshal ordered the gates shut.

Religion, music, and football—not necessarily in that order—appeared to be the talk of the town as the 20th century drew to a close. The new millennium arrived with Nashville's prestige as a music center still intact, despite sluggish sales of country CDs and dire forecasts that country wasn't cool anymore. For all its sales and marketing troubles, the Nashville music scene remained the single most distinctive facet of our collective personality. Though other regions of the country have labored to be music cities, the Nashville Sound couldn't be replicated, it seems, not even in the larger venues of New York and Los Angeles.

Sufficient proof of Nashville's musical magnetism can be witnessed at the Greyhound Bus station on Eighth Avenue South. Would-be Garths and Trisha Yearwoods continue to arrive weekly, guitar cases and dreams in tow. Only a very few make the transition from washing dishes in restaurants to the big time, but because Randy Travis did it almost twenty years ago, a legion of true believers follows his lead.

Rags-to-rhinestones stories like this are woven into the Music City psyche. Many people will swear on their grandma's King James that they saw Travis, or one of a multitude of other stars in their dishwashing days, belting out sad songs while scrubbing pots. In many ways we are modern-day Walter Mittys, living our lives vicariously through those brave enough to state their dreams aloud. You've seen them singing on Second Avenue, with the empty guitar case at their feet unfolded like open palms to receive loose change and an occasional piece of paper money. These hardy souls go boldly where most of us fear to tread, because we have neither the courage nor the talent to bare our hearts and our hopes to strangers.

We ordinary Nashvillians may take passing notice of the true celebrities and the wannabes among us, but we tend not to be obsessive about it, like bird-watchers with their life lists. What seems worth remembering about all this is not that we have stars among us; it's that we all happen to call Nashville home, and when musicians or athletes or politicians give

The only icons that registered with the 800 people his company surveyed were Garth Brooks, George Strait, Shania Twain and the Dixie Chicks. His conclusion: More superstars are needed. . . . **Across town**, later in the evening, the present fortunes of country music are a world away. College professors, community activists and whole families clad in color-splashed African garb are among the more than 300 patrons who file into the historic Belcourt Theatre in Hillsboro Village. There, Roy "Futureman" Wooten, percussionist for the bluegrass-jazz group Bela Fleck and the Flecktones, is warming up a hand-picked ensemble for the debut of his new work, "Evolution d'Amour." Wooten performs the multimedia piece using a customized musical instrument whose tones are said to match the periodic table of elements, a concept that befuddles even some of his musicians. But the audience gives him a standing ovation after the climax, which involves dancers, a breathing fabric sculpture and a performance artist smearing red paint on the stage. The last word on anyone's mind is "crossover."

3—**Fewer men are listening** to country music, while women's numbers are up. So goes today's round of hand-wringing at the Country Radio Seminar, where industry researcher Larry Rosin tells the faithful that men are tuning out on sugary pop-accented hits such as Lonestar's "Amazed." The guys like their country pepped up with rock beats, explains Rosin, citing Dwight Yoakam's "Guitars, Cadillacs and Hillbilly Music" as an example. . . . **Heal thyself:** Hospital operator Community Health Systems agrees to pay $31 million as part of a fraud settlement with the U.S. Department of Justice. . . . **The critical break** in the David "Skull" Schulman murder investigation came from a Lower Broadway janitor, according to testimony today in Metro Juvenile Court. Metro Detective E.J. Bernard says that Jule Tabor, a former custodian at the Legends Corner watering hole, called in a tip that he had seen defendant James Caveye in bloody clothes, just after Schulman was beaten and stabbed at his Printer's Alley nightclub in February 1998. Acting on the tip, Metro detectives reopened the case, which resulted in the arrest of Caveye and his accused accomplice, Jason Pense. The case is being heard in juvenile court because at the time of the murder, Caveye was 17. . . . **Tonight in Printer's Alley,** near where Skull Schulman lay bleeding two years before, scattered costumed revelers slip in among those downing beer and jambalaya at the Bourbon Street Blues and Boogie Bar. As patrons whistle inside from the cramped upstairs balcony, the spry Koko Taylor, Chicago's reigning Queen of the Blues, ushers in the club's annual Mardi Gras celebration by belting out her trademark tune, "Wang Dang Doodle.". . . *Today Show* **weatherman** Willard Scott helps Marie Freeman blow out the candles on her birthday cake at the McKendree Village retirement home. Scott wishes her a happy birthday—her 102nd.

4—**Alison Krauss,** the vocalist, fiddler and bandleader who has triggered a surge of commercial interest in bluegrass music, performs before a Ryman Auditorium audience that includes Vince Gill, his date Amy Grant, Irish vocalist Maura O'Connell and actress Ashley Judd. Krauss is almost an hour late coming onstage, prompting restiveness in the crowd. "Even Pavarotti didn't keep us waiting this long," grouses one impatient patron. . . . **Thousands of Middle Tennesseans** dreading their tax returns next month get a sorely needed laugh from a story on the front page of *The Tennessean*'s business section, which offers tips from an august panel of experts. The group's name is misprinted as "the Tennessee Society of Certified Pubic Accountants."

5—**James Cromwell,** the Oscar-nominated character actor, warmly greets a full room at the Bluebird Cafe, a rarity on a Sunday afternoon. The occasion is a

Nashville got its own marathon in April 2000—not exactly a celebrity event in itself, but one that attracts participants and spectators from other places. The first Country Music Marathon sent more than 7,000 runners down West End Avenue into the city on the first leg of the 26.2-mile course.

Nashville cachet, some of it rubs off on the rest of us. Whether we want to admit it or not, most of us like being from a town that has widespread name recognition and appeal, not just across this country but far beyond.

Even so, vital communities are not built on celebrity, or on the sound bites of the charmed. We acknowledge the big names, past and present, whose fame has fostered the Nashville mystique—from Andrew Jackson to Al Gore, from Adelicia Acklen to Oprah and Dolly—but they don't begin to say all there is to say about Nashville, or even about who among us truly is famous, or deserves to be. All the big names can do is affirm the city's reputation as an interesting, engaging, exciting place to live or visit, an upbeat city that is presently enjoying a spin in the fast lane. Think of it this way: Johnny Cash isn't here because he's famous, or famous because he's here; he's both here

and famous because he discovered in Music City a favorable climate for his musical gifts and his creative spirit to grow and flourish.

And so in their own distinctive ways have countless others, most of whom could not be called celebrated or famous, in the common meaning of those terms. Generally they're not rich, not entertainers or athletes, not seen on television or radio or in the papers, not recognized in the aisles at Wal-Mart—and they're never plagued by Gray Line tour buses taking tourists past their homes. But their voices resonate nonetheless, providing a strong contrapuntal beat to the city's countrypolitan rhythm. When you get down to the nub of it, Nashville is as much about the unsung as about those who sing and play.

Guided tours have long been a feature of Music City life. The main attraction is "the homes of the stars," featuring a drive-by viewing of Nashville's residential equivalent of the Hollywood hills.

benefit for Hecel Oyakapi, a charity Cromwell has founded to promote and preserve the culture of the Lakota people of South Dakota. Those in attendance have paid $30 to hear sets by country artists Suzy Bogguss, Pam Tillis, Bryan White, Collin Raye and The Wilkinsons. Cromwell's most recent movie, *The Green Mile*, was partially filmed at the old Tennessee State Prison facility. The film has been nominated for the upcoming Academy Awards.

6—**Martha Ingram,** billionaire leader of the Ingram Industries fortune, tops *Business Nashville* magazine's annual list of the city's most powerful people. Current Nashville Mayor Bill Purcell comes in at No. 3—a notch below his predecessor, Phil Bredesen. Other selections at random (with rank in parentheses): Freedom Forum head John Seigenthaler (13), WTVF-Channel 5 anchor Chris Clark (36), WSMV-Channel 4 anchor Dan Miller (52), former *Banner* publisher Irby Simpkins (62), WKRN-Channel 2 anchor Anne Holt (66), *Tennessean* editor Frank Sutherland (92) and *Nashville Scene* editor Bruce Dobie (100). . . . **With their client's scheduled execution** little more than a month away, lawyers for convicted Death Row inmate Philip Workman ask the U.S. 6th Circuit Court of Appeals to reopen Workman's case. They cite an X-ray taken during the autopsy of Lt. Ronald Oliver, the Memphis police officer whom Workman was convicted of killing during a 1981 robbery. The X-ray shows that the bullet that killed Oliver passed through his body intact. Workman's attorneys argue that the 45-caliber hollowpoint silvertip bullets their client used would have fragmented upon impact. They accuse Shelby County officials of withholding the evidence. The story makes headlines across the state. . . . **Meanwhile, the Tennessee Supreme Court** finds that Robert Glen Coe, the Death Row inmate convicted of the 1979 rape and murder of Cary Ann Medlin, is mentally competent to be executed. Options are running out for his attorneys. Coe is scheduled to die in 17 days.

Dr. Ming Wang is hardly unknown. Thousands of Tennesseans refer to him as the "Laser Liberator," the man who emancipated them from the burden of eyeglasses with a penetrating beam of excited electrons.

What most people see when they look at this 39-year-old man with the quick and easy smile is an accomplished young professional (doctorate in laser physics from the University of Maryland, medical degree from Harvard). His patients seldom learn that the witty, articulate ophthalmologist is also light on his feet (he's a champion ballroom dancer), or that he arrived in this country just two decades ago with $50 in his pocket and a mere handful of English words and phrases in his head. Today he moves through the corridors of Vanderbilt Medical Center with the fluid stride of a waltz master, speaks English with the ease of a linguist—and restores lost vision with a high-tech precision instrument that is revolutionizing the field of eye surgery. To say that Ming Wang has come a very long way in a very short period of time is to grossly understate the magnitude of his journey.

When he was growing up in China, he was held out of high school by his parents, both physicians, because Mao Tse-Tung's Cultural Revolution was sending all high-school graduates into military service, or to work camps in the remote provinces. He turned to music, hoping somehow to fashion a career, but again he was stymied. Finally his parents, who taught at a medical school, arranged for their 14-year-old son to attend classes there. He finished the course work in just two years, but not being officially graduated, he was denied a chance to go further.

Angry but powerless, Wang ended up wrapping books in a printing plant, a menial task that paid little. He might have spent the rest of his life there, had it not been for an important turn of events: the death of Mao, and the subsequent dismantling of the repressive Cultural Revolution. Soon Wang was enrolled in a science and technology university, where he studied physics and laser science. On the strength of his outstanding grades, he was invited in 1982 to pursue graduate study in the United States. At the University of Maryland, he honed his English skills by going to the movies, mouthing the words silently to himself, and repeating the dialogue on the way

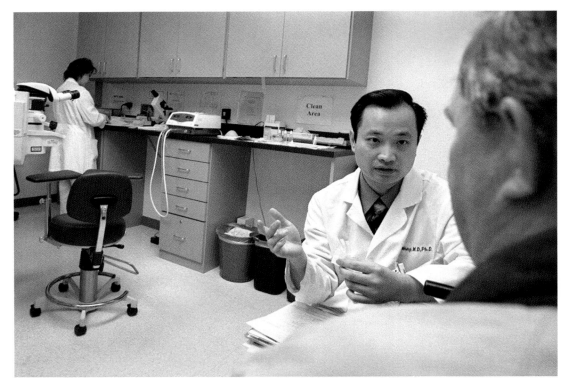

Dr. Ming Wang's combined expertise as an eye surgeon and a specialist in laser technology has brought him many patients. Few of them would guess from his easy-going, conversational style that he had no grasp of English when he arrived in this country two decades ago.

When he isn't performing eye surgery, Ming Wang likes to hone his skills as a ballroom dancer. With his dance partner and fiancée, Suyudn Liu, Dr. Wang dances competitively, sometimes winning—and always enjoying the spirited activity.

home. Wang was just 26 when he completed his doctorate. He could have stayed to teach physics there, but his dream was to become a medical doctor—and at Harvard in 1991, he reached that goal.

Combining his medical training with his expertise in laser technology, Wang found himself on the cutting edge, so to speak, of a type of advanced eye surgery that used laser beams instead of scalpels. In addition to his practice of corrective laser surgery, Wang is one of the few surgeons in the country to experiment with the use of amniotic membrane tissue in the repair of severely damaged eyes. With these advanced methods and materials, he is literally giving sight to the blind.

When he came to Nashville in 1997 to be the first director of the Vanderbilt Laser Sight Center, he took an immediate and positive liking to the city. "This was a great opportunity for me," he said. "Nashville is an up-and-coming city. I looked at it this way: If you go to Los Angeles, it's almost like a ten-story building that you are adding an extra brick to. Nashville is at three or four stories, but actively growing. I thought I would have a better opportunity here to participate in the construction.

"We are becoming another Atlanta.". . . **While 10 clergymen** representing faiths from Judaism to Buddhism to Christianity are launching a "Do Not Kill in My Name" postcard campaign to Gov. Don Sundquist, Philip Workman drops the bid for clemency that a state parole board was expected to hear today. Instead, Workman gambles that a federal appeals court will reopen his case. . . . **Second Harvest Food Bank**, which began collecting and distributing surplus food to hungry Middle Tennesseans 22 years ago, announces plans to build a

120,000-square-foot warehouse in MetroCenter. The charitable organization now gives away more than 8 million pounds of food a year. In the new facility, it will be prepared to handle more than 20 million pounds.

9—**More than 1,000** Middle Tennessee Eagle Scouts gather for an "Evening of Honor" ceremony at the Opryland Hotel. The oldest, Wilbur F. Creighton Jr., 93, tells how he joined Nashville's Boy Scout Troop 3 as a 12-year-old, just two weeks after Armistice Day ended World War I on Nov. 11, 1918. He remembers suiting up in his Scout uniform and marching alongside the doughboys returning from France. The youngest Eagle, Jon Eric Doliana II, 13, was just given the Scouts' highest honor last week. . . . **A musical benefit** for David Lipscomb University basketball player Kaia Jergenson, who was stricken in January with a severe case of meningitis, raises $5,000 to help pay her medical expenses. The show, which features Michael McDonald, legendary soul sideman Steve Cropper and other Nashville musicians, brings the total raised in Jergenson's behalf to $136,000. She remains at St. Thomas Hospital in stable but fair condition.

10—**More than 20,000 Southern Baptist teens** crowd into Vanderbilt's Memorial Gymnasium for one of the largest youth religious events in the nation, the Tennessee Baptist Convention Youth Evangelism Conference. Part pep rally, part rock concert, the event is so large that it can only be managed in two-person shifts. Amid fog machines and grid lighting, Christian vocalist Rebecca St. James, 22, exhorts teens who have dabbled in premarital sex to become "recycled virgins." Reads one T-shirt in the crowd: "Satan Is a Nerd." . . . **A sterling production** of Henrik Ibsen's *A Doll's House,* starring Nashville actors David Alford and Denice Hicks and adapted and directed by Mark Cabus, opens at the War Memorial Auditorium. The raised stage causes some

"It has been an experience beyond my wildest expectations. I often wonder what my patients would think if they knew all this had happened to me, that I was not some golden boy growing up in a well-to-do family with a silver spoon in my mouth. I do not know if they would believe it. Sometimes I find it hard to believe, too."

It seems safe to say that most Nashvillians probably would not recognize the name of John Lozier. He's not on the radar screens of the social set, the club crowd, the "beautiful people." But below First Avenue and Broadway—that is, under the bridges—they know him. At Meharry-General, they know him. At the clinics and shelters and soup kitchens, they know him.

Lozier first came to Nashville from his native Atlanta in 1975 to enroll at Vanderbilt University in a multidisciplinary graduate program that combined law and divinity. He didn't complete the program, but he did find a new home, and a calling: working with and on behalf of society's outcasts.

Today, he is executive director of the National Health Care for the Homeless Council, an umbrella agency that helps to coordinate health-care initiatives for homeless people around the country. The council, with 49 member organizations, lobbies for funding for homeless health care and offers training for health-care clinicians—the doctors, nurses, and social workers who do the hands-on work with America's homeless. "When you've got a career like mine, it just sort of unfolds before you," he said.

Lozier left Vanderbilt to work with Death Row prisoners and their families. His involvement with housing issues for these families led him inevitably to the multiple needs of the homeless. "Nobody knows how many of them there are, but almost by definition, they're uncountable." In Nashville, shelter providers report an average of about 1,000 people a night; service providers know the number is much larger, and rising.

In 1984, Lozier belonged to a group of social activists who combined their efforts to seek grant money to target health care for the homeless. Their first major success was a $1.4-million grant from the Robert Wood Johnson Foundation. Nashville was one of nineteen cities in the U.S. to receive the grant money. With part of the windfall, a medical clinic was opened downtown to serve Nashville's homeless population,

For the past 20 years, John Lozier has been focusing on health-care issues for homeless people in Nashville. Since 1990, he has headed a national coalition of local agencies engaged in such work.

which had grown steadily as the city metamorphosed from big-town wannabe to a big town in fact.

In 1990, Lozier was appointed by his colleagues to head the newly formed National Health Care for the Homeless Council. "We had to have a director, and I got the job," he said with a shrug. But he almost turned them down because his colleagues didn't feel Nashville was the proper venue from which to launch the group's concerns.

"They said maybe I ought to live in New York or Washington, and I said maybe they ought to hire somebody else. This is home," Lozier said. "I don't want to live in New York or D.C. When I go to New York, in three days I've got sensory overload. Nashville always has plenty to get involved in, and you can handle it. The theater is good, the arts scene is good, the social activism scene is good. We live in an East Nashville neighborhood where people sit on their front porches and visit with one another. Plus, I walked to work this morning," he said.

Growing up in Atlanta, Lozier saw what Georgia's capital city lost as it grew, and he didn't particularly like it: "Where our house used to be, there's now a church playground. All the woods where I played are gone. I share the fears of so many that growth will undo Nashville. One does get attached to a place, and it's nice to count on some stability, even as the world changes around you."

There is probably no way of knowing just how many Nashville residents must contend with some kind of disability. Thousands, maybe tens of thousands. Many more besides them are dedicated to their support and service. And probably no one hereabouts is a stronger advocate for this scattered community and their network of services than Jackie Page. For nearly a quarter of a century, this articulate, sensitive, good-humored woman has been an inspiration and a constant comfort to countless hundreds of disabled citizens in the city.

She works for Metro's Disability Information Office. Though her title and the specific Metro department she answers to have changed several times over the years, Page's zeal has remained constant, despite the effects of a birth condition that has left her a quadriplegic in a wheelchair. As some have said about her, Page is the ablest disabled person they know, accomplishing much in behalf of those who must overcome disadvantages in order to live independent lives. "I've had the privilege of working with a lot of good people in a number of agencies," she said. "It's been a lot of hard work to widen the envelope a little bit for people with disabilities, but I've loved the challenge, still do. For me, dreams do come true."

Page, an only child, was born in Asheville, North Carolina, during the Great Depression. Doctors had a name for the rare birth defect that fused her joints together—arthrogryposis multiplex congenita, usually abbreviated to AMC—but they couldn't cure it or explain what caused it. "They understand more about it now, but they still don't have a reason why," said Page, who long ago decided to concentrate on what she could do despite her condition, rather than lamenting what might have been.

In 1965, when her parents moved to Nashville, her mother's hometown, she was not thrilled with the idea, believing she was leaving behind her friends and her support. What, she thought, could Nashville have to offer her? Where would she find enlightened people who understood the hopes and fears—and rights—of the disabled? The answers surprised her. Through correspondence with various groups about what programs and activities might be available for her here, she was put in touch with Henry and Elsa Ellis, a Nashville couple who had taken up the cause of the disabled. They became Page's mentors in her journey to independence.

When Page's parents took her to regular meetings with the Ellises at their church, they would strap her in the front seat of the car with an army belt. "We invented seat belts," said Page, laughing. "The Ellises encouraged me to believe I could do things outside the home, that I could go to college, which was a dream I had never told anyone about," she recalled. "I had tried selling things over the phone—what a disaster that was, just terrible. It was almost beyond my imagination to think that I could work, really work, but the Ellises and my parents stuck that idea in my head, and it didn't leave me.

neck strain, but the cast makes the audience forget with a captivating performance. . . . **Frederic Minns,** a custodian for 22 years at University School of Nashville, is to be honored with a surprise "King for a Day" event at the school on his 90th birthday. Unfortunately, Minns has taken the day off. A staffer runs out and brings him back to school. . . . **Singers Vince Gill and Amy Grant** are married in a private ceremony on a farm in Williamson County. The bride is barefoot, the groom dressed in a dark suit. Their evening reception at a home Grant has been renting off of West End draws much of Music Row's A-list. . . . **The Tennessee Supreme Court** denies Robert Glen Coe a 90-day stay of execution. He now has 13 days to live.

11—Excitement over the Billy **Graham Crusade** this coming June officially cranks up with a morning kickoff rally for women at the Grand Ole Opry House. The only hitch: The featured guest, Graham's daughter Gigi Graham Tchividjian, can't attend because of her mother's hip surgery. Undeterred, singer CeCe Winans keeps the sold-out crowd entertained, and Tchividjian addresses the audience by speaker phone. . . . **Ad copy** for Highland Park Church in *The Tennessean's* two-page Worship Services Directory: "Jeans at Church!? That's fine with us. One Hour. . . Casual Dress. . . Great Music. . . Christ-Centered. . . Pressure-Free." . . . A *Nashville Scene* "BackBoard" ad promises past-life regression at individual and group rates. . . . **On CBS'** *Meet the Press*, GOP phrasemaker Mary Matalin calls Vice President Al Gore "a phony-baloney political pervert." . . . **The cost of gasoline** in Nashville is at $1.49 a gallon and rising. Even so, it's still cheaper than a half-gallon of milk or a loaf of name-brand sandwich bread.

12—The good news: Vanderbilt's Lady Commodores basketball team will advance to the NCAA's Division I "March Madness" tournament. The bad news:

Jackie Page was born with a rare and incurable form of paralysis that would have stopped most people. With the encouragement and help of family and friends, she earned two college degrees. Page has worked for Metro government since the late 1970s.

The men 'Dores will not, even though their 19-10 record includes some significant upset victories. However, the men are asked to play Wake Forest in the National Invitational Tournament two days from now in Vanderbilt's Memorial Gym. . . . **Matthew Barrett,** the only employee on duty at a Subway sandwich shop at 1414 Charlotte Ave., is making a sandwich when a robber bursts into the restaurant. The gunman shoots Barrett once in the head. Barrett manages to stagger across the street to an Exxon Tigermarket for help; he is rushed to Vanderbilt University Medical Center in critical condition. The restaurant has a security camera, but no tape is found. . . . **Alive Hospice,** which has given care to more

I don't know if that would have happened if I had been anywhere else." Page did go to college. She completed her undergraduate degree at Peabody College in 1963—the first wheelchair graduate ever at that school—and went on to earn a master's degree at Peabody. In the mid-1980s, feeling that her mind was "getting a little rusty," she decided to return to the classroom to work on a post-master's degree, Education Specialist,which she completed in 1990.

"With the encouragement I was getting, I saw education as the way I needed to go. I really felt the only way I was going to be able to stay out of a nursing home or some kind of an institution was to be employed, earn a living, and eventually have a personal-care assistant and be on my own." She has stuck to that plan. "I've been with Metro for 23 years. The mortgage company and I are paying off my condo, and I do have someone who now lives with me as a personal assistant. I count my blessings."

From her unique perspective as an advocate for those with special needs, Page has witnessed many positive changes in Nashville with regard to the disabled, but she remains unsatisfied. "Once you start to open things up, you want to push it a little more. We're not where we need to be yet, but we're moving in that direction. As long as we're making progress, I want to stay involved." Jackie Page isn't thinking about retiring. At least not until she turns 70. Next year.

Luis A. Bustillos is 5-foot-2 and weighs 140 pounds, a compact dynamo of a man who has left an indelible imprint on many aspects of Nashville life, especially for those who move here from south of the border. During the past 22 years, Bustillos has become an authoritative and familiar voice to Spanish-speaking citizens trying to forge a life in a non-Spanish speaking society. At school board meetings he has highlighted concerns about cutbacks in English as a second language (ESL) programs. Through churches and social agencies he has organized support for Hispanic families in need. To new immigrants, lured by a steady paycheck and opportunity, Bustillos has explained the American way and how Latinos can find their place in Nashville. Just as he found his.

Born and raised in Bolivia, Bustillos always dreamed, even as a child, of moving to America. He was educated in a private school where the teachers were from the United States and England. After graduating from high school with an adequate grasp of the English language, he followed his older brother to the States. After several years he met and married his wife, an American, and moved with her to Nashville when she was transferred south by her employer. "I came with her. I didn't know Nashville. I didn't know what to expect, but I liked it almost immediately," he recalled.

As a resident of Nashville for 22 years, Bolivian native Luis Bustillos says he has never seen so much growth among nonnative people as the city experienced in the last five years of the 20th century. Particularly the Hispanics, he said: "We are everywhere."

than 17,000 terminally ill patients since its founding 25 years ago in Nashville, announces plans to build a $12-million facility at 17th and Charlotte avenues.

13—A Clarksville housewife, identified only as Gretchen, is whisked away to a deserted island in the South China Sea. She has been selected as one of 16 contestants for a new CBS television series called *Survivor.* The person who remains on the island for all of the show's 13 episodes without being voted off by the other contestants will receive $1 million. Displaying surprising investigative skills, local radio stations piece together information that "Gretchen" is Gretchen Cordy, a 38-year-old mother of two and former Air Force survival instructor. . . . **Chanting** "We want what's right, not what's left," 3,000 teachers from across Tennessee march on the State Capitol. They urge the legislature not to slash $210 million of their salaries and retirement benefits from the state budget. Unfortunately, by the time the marchers arrive at 7 p.m., most of the legislators have already gone home. Average teachers' salaries in Tennessee are about $5,000 below the national average. . . . *The Tennessean* polls 10 of the 12 jurors who voted to convict Philip Workman of first-degree murder in 1982. Five say they now have doubts and believe he should get a new trial. One remains convinced that Workman is guilty; four won't comment.

14—In as dull a presidential primary finish as anyone can recall, Vice President Al Gore and Texas Gov. George W. Bush clinch their parties' respective nominations. Turnout is so low that some Nashville precincts have fewer than 100 voters. . . . **Dorothy Polly Haskins** becomes the first woman elected to a Berry Hill public office in the "satellite" city's 50-year history. Haskins, wife of the late mayor, James Haskins, is elected to the Berry Hill City Commission. . . . **A major snag** has developed in plans for the proposed

$3.7-million sculpture fountain at the Music Row Roundabout, now under construction at the intersection of 16th Avenue South and Division and Demonbreun streets. An anonymous donor has already pledged $2 million, and Metro has agreed to chip in an additional $400,000, but unless the project's supporters can raise the remaining $1.3 million, Metro will scrap plans for the fountain. Andree LeQuire, wife of sculptor Alan LeQuire, schedules a last-ditch meeting with city officials. . . . **Songwriter Tommy Collins**, 69, who helped establish the loping "Bakersfield Sound" of California country music, dies at his home in Ashland City. Among his trademark tunes was the Faron Young hit "If You Ain't Lovin' (You Ain't Livin')."

15—**Old Hickory** doffs his top hat once more on the steps of the Hermitage, thanks to a group celebrating Andrew Jackson's 233rd birthday at his historic home. Beneath balconies draped with bunting, actor Dave McArdle reenacts speeches from Jackson's 1828 run for president and subsequent victory over John Quincy Adams. Folklorist Oscar Brand regales visitors with Jackson's campaign song. . . . **The fountain goes**, the sculpture stays. That's the ruling of MDHA Director Gerald Nicely, who decides that the sculptural part of the Music Row Roundabout can proceed without its centerpiece fountain. Plans by sculptors Alan LeQuire and David Preston Allard call for a 30-foot bronze sculpture with seven dancing figures, as well as six bronze columns with reliefs depicting the history of jazz, blues and other musical genres. The roundabout is scheduled to open in one year; the sculpture will be installed in three. . . . **Calling all artists:** Officials for the new Frist Center for the Visual Arts, currently being transformed from the old downtown post office building on Broadway, are asking local artists to submit proposals for two installations at the new facility. One will be a $40,000 commission for four

Bustillos now operates a Spanish translation service, working primarily for the Davidson County courts and other governmental agencies. The Spanish-speaking population here has exploded in the two decades since he arrived. By his estimate, there were only a few hundred Hispanics in the Nashville area then. Today, the official total for Davidson County alone is about 26,000, according to Census 2000. But Bustillos, like many other Hispanic community workers, feels the count is much higher, perhaps twice or even three times that many. "I stand amazed at how many people are moving here from Mexico, from Central America, from South America," he said. "Hispanics pass the word along among themselves that there are jobs in the area, and they are coming. I never thought our population would be as big as it is." A Hispanic soccer program he helped to organize has grown from one team to three leagues with dozens of teams. "And the restaurants and bakeries and stores that have opened, almost all owned by Hispanics—seeing all this, that's when I knew that our numbers were really growing," Bustillos added.

What began as a modest enclave of Hispanics along Nolensville Road has now spread into other sections of the city: Woodbine, Murfreesboro Road, Hickory Hollow, Gallatin Road. "We are everywhere," he said, but he acknowledged that such a rapid infusion into the Music City melting pot comes with certain costs. "For the most part

Her impressive experience as a trial lawyer earned Aleta Trauger an appointment in 1998 to the U. S. District Court for the Middle District of Tennessee—the trial court level of the federal judiciary.

we are accepted, but we're still having problems with some people who refuse Hispanics the credit they deserve. There is some discrimination, but I hope with time that we'll be able to dissipate that mentality. People have to learn that in every culture there is a bad element and a good element. Because a few of them are doing things wrong, all Hispanics tend to get blamed for it."

The hopes and dreams Bustillos carries for his Hispanic brothers and sisters center on two things: education and unity. "We need to get together," he asserted. "We are getting separated into groups instead of uniting as a community of Latin-Americans. We don't need one group working against another; we should all work together. We are here to stay, and we are here to work and to make this country a better place to live.

"My other main goal is for the Hispanic community to learn English as a second language. We are here in the United States, and the official language is English, not Spanish." Bustillos, an American citizen and Nashville resident since the mid-1970s, is proud to see ESL classes filled to capacity with men, women, and children of all ages, all eager to learn English so they might become better residents of the United States. "When you see the progress people are making in their lives, it's very heartwarming. I am happy to have been a part of such a movement and to see all of this happening in Nashville, Tennessee. We should all take great pride in our city. I certainly do. This is my home," he said.

On a Friday afternoon at the end of a busy week, U.S. District Court Judge Aleta Arthur Trauger paused for a short break in her seventh-floor office at the Federal Courthouse on Broadway. Around her on the walls and shelves were framed photographs of family and friends, and of the day in 1998 when she took the judicial oath, after her appointment to the federal bench by President Bill Clinton. Her office decor is a study in blue, against which the judge, dressed in a dark ensemble, was a walking exclamation mark as she moved about the room. Her intense, black-olive eyes behind squarish reading glasses gave her a countenance that was at once professorial and motherly. Convicted felons must torment themselves trying to read her face just before she imposes sentence.

She came to Nashville after graduating from Cornell College, and earned a master's degree at Vanderbilt. She taught school briefly, but found that education was not her calling. A friend suggested she go into law, a career she had never considered. She took the law school entrance exam and scored higher than she thought she would. Trauger was accepted at Vanderbilt Law School in the fall of 1973.

While she didn't much like the rigors of law school, she did enjoy the duties of being a lawyer. After her first year, she began clerking for a small but highly regarded local firm—Barrett, Brandt, and Barrett. "It was one of the best experiences I could have had. They took me to court. They took me to depositions. They let me see the practice of law in Nashville, and I looked around and I said, 'I can do this. I may not have been number one in my law school class, but I can practice law in Nashville, Tennessee.' That gave me lots of confidence."

She might have stayed longer with the firm if Hal Hardin, the U.S. attorney here, hadn't asked her to join his staff. For five years (including one spent in Chicago), she was an assistant U.S. attorney. She loved trial work and eventually became a go-to person in the Nashville office's criminal division. That's how one of the state's most celebrated trials, the political corruption case of former Tennessee Governor Ray Blanton, came to her in 1981. "When we went into the Blanton trial we thought we would probably lose," she recalled. "In fact, one of the lawyers involved in the case predicted that we were going to be ridden out of town on a rail. Famous last words I guess."

The trial lasted six weeks. Her closing argument took four hours, an extraordinary amount of time that she doubts she would tolerate in her court today. As anyone who

works of sculpture incorporating a fountain; the other will be a $60,000 "donor recognition wall" to contain the names of 150 major patrons, which must be readable from 10 feet away. The deadline is Apr. 10. . . . **At a birthday soiree** for Vice President Al Gore, country singer Pam Tillis serenades the Democratic presidential contender with an original birthday song. She encourages the wooden veep to "party hearty."

16—**Robert Glen Coe** has one week to live. U.S. District Judge John Nixon withdraws from hearing Coe's request for a stay of execution, on grounds that Coe is raising issues he did not hear previously. Nixon incurred the wrath of voters in 1996 when he reversed Coe's conviction and death sentence; the decision was later overturned. The case goes to Judge Aleta Trauger. . . . **After he has already waited** two years in jail for his trial, Mack Taylor Jr., 28, is acquitted of charges that he killed amateur boxing champion Edward Taj Ledford in a 1998 altercation. The fight was over a fender bender that damaged Ledford's 1978 Cadillac outside the Quiet Side Lounge at 2037 Jefferson St. Taylor's father, Mack Taylor Sr., says he couldn't afford to pay 10 percent of his son's $150,000 bail to set him free. When Taylor is released, he weighs 100 pounds less than when he went in.

17—**The solemn faces** of John and Patsy Ramsey are splashed across the city's media. The Ramseys are here promoting their book, *The Death of Innocence*, about the still-unsolved 1997 murder in Denver of their 6-year-old daughter, JonBenet. For many local readers, the larger mystery is why Thomas Nelson, the Nashville-based publisher of Bibles and religious texts, published the book. . . . *Mr. Death: The Rise and Fall of Fred A. Leuchter Jr.*, a documentary by Errol Morris, opens for a week-long run at the Regal Green Hills theaters. Leuchter, a controversial "execution expert" embraced by

Holocaust revisionists, has made headlines lately for his restoration work on the Tennessee State Prison's electric chair. . . . **Green beer,** green shirts and green teeth are among the sights on display as the city celebrates St. Patrick's Day. At Nashville's official Irish bars, the cozy Sherlock Holmes Pub on Elliston Place and the cavernous Seanachie on Lower Broadway, the green is flowing, in every sense. At the cinder-block bluegrass club the Station Inn, where local string band The Rogues is playing, the sound of fiddles and Celtic reels wafts outside each time the door opens. At The Sutler, the Franklin Road watering hole whose walls carry photos of past performers and saucy saloon gals, veteran Nashville songwriter Cletus Haegert—a.k.a. Clete O'Hagerty—performs on the same stage where he proposed to his wife exactly five years earlier.

18—**While U.S. Supreme Court** Justice Sandra Day O'Connor deliberates over a mock-trial competition at Vanderbilt University, District Judge Aleta Trauger declines to issue a stay of execution for Robert Glen Coe. He now has five days to live.

19—**Former State Sen.** John T. Hicks, 74, dies of a heart attack at his home in Old Hickory. An East High School graduate and World War II Navy veteran, Hicks served in the state House of Representatives from 1965 to 1976, when he successfully ran for the state Senate in the 20th District. He resigned in 1992 when he and fellow Democrat and political ally Sen. Joe M. Haynes were reapportioned to the same district.

20—**Tennessee's credit rating** is in trouble. Moody's Investors Service has downgraded the state's long-term financial outlook from stable to negative. If Tennessee's triple-A bond rating slips, taxpayers could face millions in additional expenses from raised interest payments. . . . **Craig Baldwin,** underground San Francisco filmmaker, hosts a no-frills 16mm screening of his work at

has followed Tennessee politics knows, Blanton was forced to leave the governor's office three days before his term ended, and was later convicted of public corruption in connection with the granting of liquor licenses to friends. "It was a fascinating, challenging, engrossing endeavor," said Trauger. "It was a good experience for me, and the impact it had on my career was immeasurable—but I was glad when it was over."

For a decade after the Blanton trial, Trauger was largely out of public view. She joined one of the city's law firms, then moved to South Carolina as counsel for the College of Charleston, and returned to Nashville to work for another firm that represented numerous entertainment clients. Along the way, she married attorney Byron Trauger. Content and happy in both her public and private life, Trauger believed she was "settled" when incoming Mayor Phil Bredesen asked her to be his chief of staff in 1991. "This was totally out of the blue," she said. "I knew nothing about being a chief of staff for a mayor, but the fact that he thought I could do it gave me confidence, and I really wanted to help him succeed." Trauger stayed with the mayor for about a year, learning at close range what it's like to run a big city.

In 1993 a new bankruptcy judgeship was created, and Trauger was chosen. Five years later she was elevated to the U.S. District Court for the Middle District of Tennessee. "Everything I've done in my legal career has prepared me for the job I have now," she said. "For me, it feels like coming home. This is where I should be—in Nashville, doing what I do," she said.

Patricia Nalini Paiva came to the United States from her native Ceylon (now Sri Lanka) in 1963, when she was 11 years old. By the time she moved to Nashville in 1994, she had lived in a half-dozen cities, but never in the South. "I didn't know a soul," said the woman with eyes the color of coffee. In fact, there was much she didn't know when she arrived here. For example, she didn't know Spanish, except for the few phrases she remembered from a college course. Today, Paiva is fluent in Spanish, having taken a conversational course and informal "lessons" from her many Spanish-speaking friends; in English, which she learned as a girl in school; and Sinhalese, her native tongue.

She also could not have known in 1994 that the new century would find her happily engaged as the proprietor of La Favorita, a popular Hispanic bakery on Nolensville Road. "And with twelve employees, can you believe it?" she exclaimed. "I love Nashville. I have decided this is where I want to be. This city has been so good to me." Who would have thought this uncommon story possible—that a Sri Lankan native could move to Nashville, be "adopted" by the city's burgeoning Hispanic population, and open a successful business on her first try as an entrepreneur? It can only be explained, said Paiva, as one of life's wonderful mysteries.

Her Ceylonese family could trace its roots back for centuries. They were Tamils, a minority ethnic group. They were even more in the minority because they were also Catholic, as opposed to the majority of Tamils in Sri Lanka, who are Hindu. Meanwhile, the country's largest ethnic group, the Sinhalese, are Buddhist. When the country won its independence from Britain, the last in a long list of countries to colonize it, Tamils felt the brunt of discrimination.

Her father lost his position at a government-run school. "He was a Tamil and a Catholic," she explained, "so they would never give him a job." After their arrival in America, political unrest in her homeland continued to escalate. Tamils became the subject of much prejudice and discrimination, as did other minorities. Soon it was apparent that they would never be able to go home again. "We didn't know that when we came to this country. When I think of all the stuff we left behind, all our favorite possessions . . . To this day, anything that's important and dear to me is kept within, inside of me. We thought we would return for our things, but we never did."

Paiva's father moved to this country ahead of his family and earned an advanced degree in social work at Brandeis University in Boston. Paiva, her mother, and three siblings booked passage on a Norwegian freighter, enduring close quarters and a hurricane on the 28-day voyage.

In the United States, she earned a bachelor's degree in psychology and a mas-

Patricia Paiva, an Asian-American native of Sri Lanka, is the unlikely proprietor of a Hispanic bakery on Nolensville Road. When she moved to Nashville in the mid-1990s, Paiva knew almost no Spanish; now she's fluent and an "adopted" member of the local Latino community.

the Fugitive Art Center. The venue is located in an industrial district off Fourth Avenue South, in a block of factory buildings with broken windows, where artists have started to reclaim run-down structures in the area as studio space. Baldwin, a garrulous, wild-eyed fellow in a worn bushman's hat, introduces his found-footage science-fiction epic *Spectres of the Spectrum* before approximately 90 viewers seated on rickety folding chairs. . . . **Steve Highfill**, former manager of Feed the Children, pleads guilty to taking donated items from the relief organization's warehouse. As manager, Highfill, 48, encouraged employees to supplement their incomes by helping themselves to food, clothes, cosmetics and hardware. Last May, a WTVF-Channel 5 news crew caught staffers on camera loading their cars with loot intended for the less fortunate. In the ensuing explosion of civic outrage, Highfill quit and other staffers were canned. Highfill gets two years' probation, a $1,000 fine and 96 hours community service. . . . **Back in January,** Robert Glen Coe taunted Judge John Colton that "old Judge Nixon" would block his execution no matter what. Today, just 58 hours before Coe's scheduled execution by lethal injection, Senior U.S. District Court Judge John T. Nixon does just that. Questioning the constitutionality of the methods that determined Coe's competency, Judge Nixon grants him an indefinite stay of execution. But the 6th Circuit U.S. Court of Appeals lifts the stay, and the Tennessee Board of Probation and Parole votes unanimously not to give him a clemency hearing. Coe, who was moved to Riverbend Prison's never-used "death-watch" unit before dawn this morning, remains there with 48 hours to live.

21—**Strange but true:** Despite near-perpetual road construction and blockage, not to mention potholes the size of lunar craters, Nashville has the third best roads in the nation out of 50 major urban areas, according to a Washington-based research group.

ter's in education at the University of Missouri in Columbia. She has lived in the cities of Boston, New York, and St. Louis, as well as in smaller towns in Ohio, Missouri, and Illinois. For a while, she also lived in Quebec. In every location she played three roles: a wife (she is now divorced), mother to her three children, and a catalyst in the international community.

One of the first things she did after settling in Nashville was to look for ways she could become involved. She was referred to the Catholic Charities Refugee Reset-

Only Atlanta and Fort Lauderdale rank higher. Nashville motorists are skeptical, to put it mildly.

22—**Less than 16 hours** before Robert Glen Coe's scheduled execution, U.S. District Court Judge Aleta Trauger announces that she needs time to review the way Tennessee courts have handled his lawyers' claim that he is mentally unfit to be executed. She grants Coe a temporary stay of execution. . . . **Bill Hall,** WSMV-Channel 4's avuncular weatherman, has signed a four-year contract worth $1 million, according to *The Tennessean*. The deal makes Hall one of Nashville's highest-paid television personalities. Hall's Q rating, which measures favorable audience recognition, almost equals that of all his competitors combined.

23—**In a meeting** of the House Finance Committee, Rep. Tommy Head (D-Clarksville), all but accuses Gov. Don Sundquist of shifting the route of the controversial State Road 840 (or I-840, as it should be called) to please a major Republican contributor. Head tells reporters that the interstate's path has been rerouted from the west side of Lebanon to the east side—7 miles off course—and thus safely removed from valuable property belonging to Cracker Barrel honcho Dan Evins. Sundquist responds with outrage that anyone would accuse him of politicking. The new outer loop, under construction since 1996, has been under attack by environmentalists and communities along its route from Lebanon to Dickson. In a letter to the *Nashville Scene*, community activist Gene Cotten offers to cut Sundquist a check if that is all it takes to divert the project. . . . **Dean Fearing,** award-winning chef at The Mansion on Turtle Creek in Dallas, presides over a $750-a-plate dinner of smoked pheasant at Loews Vanderbilt Plaza Hotel. While in town, Fearing tells Thayer Wine, the *Tennessean* food critic, that Nashville palates are being dulled by a preponderance of chain restaurants with bland menus. . . . **Kaia**

tlement office, where she was promptly hired as a liaison with a diverse group of refugees and immigrants, including Haitians, Sudanese, Vietnamese, Bosnians, and Hispanics. "It was apparent that Nashville wasn't ready for the bombardment of all these different people, but I feel we were able to be a part of the process by helping the refugees to fully assimilate and the community to accept them. It's exciting to me because I was there from the beginning. I kind of feel like I'm an old Nashvillian now, because I've been a part of this tremendous growth and change," she said.

Her bakery grew out of her friendships and connections in the Hispanic community and her love of bread-baking, something she learned at her mother's knee. Several of her friends were opening a store, and she asked to have "a little part" in the project. La Favorita opened in August of 1999 and soon developed a growing trade, offering a variety of fresh sweet breads, pastries, and cakes, including a store specialty, *tres leches* cake. "It means three-milks cake. The recipe calls for regular milk, condensed milk, and evaporated milk," she said.

Paiva is now the sole proprietor of the bakery, having bought out the other partners. Because nearly all of her workers are Latinos who speak Spanish only, she finds that her role as facilitator for Nashville's international community has taken on a new dimension. "I'm still teaching, in a way, and learning," she said. "My employees are Mexicans and one Guatemalan, a Salvadoran, one white American and one black American. It's been a learning experience for them. They all have limited ideas about groups of people, stereotypes that come from the unknown. I'm trying to dismiss a lot of that. It gives me the opportunity, in the widest, most challenging way, to put into action what I'm really interested in, which is communication between various ethnic and cultural communities."

She sees signs of progress—several of her employees are taking English classes. And, while most of her customers are Mexican, some of her customers are Afghanis, Ethiopians, and Somalis, as well as born and bred Nashvillians. "The Hispanics accept me as one of their own, and I'm honored that they do. They respect me and I respect them," she said. "It doesn't matter that I'm really an Asian woman, not someone from Mexico. To them it doesn't matter. In business, it's not about numbers and finance, it's about people—and if you don't like people, you cannot succeed."

Actor Barry Scott's dark eyes float in glistening pools of ivory, and his mellifluous voice is spellbinding. In combination, these features of his persona give him a stage presence that is compellingly familiar to serious Nashville theater patrons of the past two decades—a devoted though small audience. Live theater has had a long and continuous presence in Nashville, but it has never flashed atop the local arts marquee. That's no fault of Barry Scott's. If this were New York or Chicago—or even a good theater town like Louisville—his star power no doubt would have been brighter (not that he's complaining).

The 46-year-old actor's signature role is his portrayal of the Reverend Martin Luther King Jr. As a teenager in the late 1960s, he started reciting King's "I Have a Dream" speech at churches. He had become fascinated with the speech when his father, a school teacher, brought home a movie projector and showed his family a film of the 1963 March on Washington. Scott watched it several times. He was entranced by the tenor and cadence of King's voice, the musicality of his phrasemaking. The grainy image of King in that sea of black faces was branded indelibly on the youngster's psyche, as if he had been born with the movie imprinted in his brain. He replays it at will now in the theater of his mind; the 16-millimeter projector whirs gently in the background.

Nashville is the actor's hometown, as well as his workplace. He met with a measure of success in Los Angeles when he moved there in 1978, during the height of the Norman Lear sitcom revolution, but California wasn't a good fit. All the same, his return to Nashville came as something of a surprise, considering what had happened on a summer evening some years earlier, when a Nashville cop decided to scare the bejesus out of a young black kid.

Barry Scott was in his mid-teens when he first recited Martin Luther King's "I Have a Dream" speech at his family's church in North Nashville. It was to be the beginning of his career as an actor.

The car was a Pontiac Le Mans, turquoise green, with a black landau top and a gearshift on the floor, even though it was an automatic. As cool as the car looked to a 16-year-old going out on his first date, it had a tendency to choke down and stall. On this evening, of all times, it happened again, on a lonely stretch of road.

Scott had seen his father handle the situation. Wait a while, pat the accelerator, and turn over the ignition. As he waited, a man approached, a man with a gun. "Nigger, out of the car!" he commanded.

Scott froze. The man took a Nashville police badge out of his pocket and held it to the window.

"Thank God officer, I thought you were going to rob me," Scott exhaled in a rush of words and emotion.

"Shut up, nigger, and get out of the car!"

The young black man stepped out, and the interrogation began. Rapid-fire questions spilled out on top of one another, each coated with bigotry and rage: "Where are you going? Who are you going to rob? What trouble are you getting into, boy?"

Scott said he was only going to pick up his date.

"Who's your mother?"

Scott answered. Then the cop said, "Oh, I know her. She's a whore, isn't she? Isn't that right, boy? Say, 'My mother's a whore.'" Scott repeated the phrase, trembling.

"Who's your father?" the plainclothes cop demanded.

He replied that he was a school teacher.

"No, he's a drunk, a lazy bastard, never had a job in his life. Isn't that right, nigger?" This time, Scott shook his head no.

Jergenson is transferred from St. Thomas to the Rehabilitation Institute of Chicago, where she will begin rehabilitation therapy. She was admitted to the Nashville hospital Jan. 4 with a severe case of bacterial meningitis. She has been in the hospital now for more than two months.

24—To passersby on Fifth Avenue South, the new Country Music Hall of Fame, catercorner from the Gaylord Entertainment Center, resembles a tall undulating wave of concrete and girders—the sweeping fin of Webb Pierce's Cadillac writ large against the city skyline. Today, though, a select group of civic bigwigs that includes Mayor Bill Purcell and retired Gaylord CEO E.W. "Bud"

"Yes it is! Say 'Yes Sir,' nigger!" the man shouted. He held the gun inches from the teen's head. Scott repeated the words, but it didn't seem to satisfy the cop. "One day you're going to grow up to hurt society, so I'm going to help society by killing you tonight," he told the boy.

Scott thought of running. It occurred to him that if he was going to be shot he wanted to be shot in the back—a posthumous signal to his family and friends, a clue to the unjustness of this moment. But just as Scott was about to run, the cop let him go.

The car cranked on the first try, and Scott drove home to tell his parents. The three of them then went downtown to the police department. The officer on duty lis-tened to the story. He asked Scott to repeat it for another officer. When he finished, they laughed and told the family to go home. "I remember seeing the look on my father's face, seeing him see me see him," Scott recalls. "It was all there on his face—the shift from anger to frustration to bitterness and shame." They drove home in silence.

Scott went into the living room and sat down. A few minutes later, his father brought in the film projector. Without saying a word, he threaded the film through to the take-up reel and flipped the "on" switch. "It was Martin King. We watched and we didn't talk. It played through and he rewound it and we watched it again. He rewound it again. Three times we watched without talking.

"I knew in that moment that my life was changed. Somehow I felt that a new part of me had been born, some new entity had come into me, some new understand-ing about who I was. I wanted to tell people, and that's basically what my career has been about—searching for ways to describe what I learned," he said. "I do what I do from Nashville because if I can make it here, I can make it anywhere."

Decades ago, following his first performance of King's "I Have a Dream" speech at his family's church, Barry Scott was approached by an elderly woman. Her eyes were filled with tears. "Keep saying those words," she told him. The young man had his marching orders for life. "I intend to do just that. I hope I'll never quit."

Bob Hatcher considered the question: In his 38 years as a wildlife biologist, includ-ing more than two decades as coordinator of Tennessee's endangered species program, was there one accomplishment that gave him the most satisfaction and pride? He didn't have to think long. His answer, in a gentle drawl as soft as goose down, went straight to the point: "The successful reintroduction of bald eagles in Tennessee. That's what I'm most proud of. When you go out on an eagle tour, it's gratifying to be able to see these magnificent birds flying and nesting here again. There's pure ecstasy on the faces of those on the tour."

Hatcher, like many other uncommon Nashvillians, has done his work out of the limelight. In fact, he's quick to point out that the success of the eagle project—from zero nesting sites in 1980, when the program began, to 44 nests in 2000—is the result of hard work by many people. But groups like the Tennessee Ornithological Society credit Hatcher with being the catalyst: He sustained the project through fiscal hard times, when budget makers didn't see much use in spending money for an initiative that didn't pay its own way through fees the way other wildlife management programs are funded through fishing and hunting licenses. One of the ways he earned funds for the endangered-species program was through sales of the popular bluebird license plate, an idea that originated in his office.

Born on a River Road farm in western Davidson County, Hatcher moved with his family to Williamson and later Rutherford County, where he graduated from, natu-rally, Eagleville High School. His interest in animals, however, was formed long before high school. From fifth grade on, he nourished a curiosity for the natural sciences, the flora and the fauna, and the charm has never faded.

Hatcher graduated from Middle Tennessee State University with a degree in biolo-gy and then attended Auburn University (where the gridiron battle cry is "Go War Eagle!") and received a master's degree in fisheries and zoology. After working in Alabama for a year, he returned to his home state to take a supervisory job with the Tennessee Fish and Game Commission. In 1978, he was placed in charge of nongame and endangered

The eagle has landed in Tennessee again, thanks in large measure to Bob Hatcher. When he started working on endangered-species issues for the Tennessee Wildlife Resources Agency in 1978, the bald eagle had not been seen in the state for almost a decade; in 2000, more than 40 active nests of the national bird were known to exist, most of them in West Tennessee.

species for the Tennessee Wildlife Resources Agency, the agency from which he retired.

In the mid-1970s, it had been more than ten years since a bald eagle had been seen in Tennessee. DDT, an agricultural chemical used from 1940 until it was banned in 1972, was the primary culprit blamed for almost wiping out the country's premier bird of prey. Under Hatcher's supervision, young eagles from other states were brought to Tennessee and held temporarily in "hacking" towers before being released. The idea was to imprint the surrounding area on the migratory birds, in the hope that they would return to nest in the same area in four or five years. "We felt all along that we could be successful, that the eagles would come back. It was a good feeling when they did," he said. Bald eagles have since been removed from Tennessee's endangered list.

Hatcher's expertise was not limited to bald eagles. He implemented programs to reintroduce osprey, peregrine falcons, and golden eagles, all of which had been affected by DDT in the food chain. Other endangered species, including some fish, are living in greater numbers today because of his restoration work. Nearly 500 river otters were released into the state's waterways after the species had almost been trapped to extinction in Tennessee. The new otters came from states where there were plentiful populations. In addition, thousands of warm-water fish, such as the spot fin chub and the yellow fin madtom, were bred in captivity and released into their native waters.

In the upper reaches of Center Hill Lake, TWRA scientists found a new species of yellow throat darter, a small fish. They honored Hatcher with the highest compliment a biologist can receive: a species named for him. The data books now record the discovery of *Etheostoma Hatcheri*.

charged on a single bill from one of the companies. Maybe now when something goes wrong, you'll know who to call.

26—A Jeep carrying five Brentwood High School seniors returning from spring break in Florida spins out of control on I-65 in Giles County. It rolls over several times, throwing all five passengers from the vehicle. Killed instantly are Kristen L. Smithson, 17; Shannon M. Mannix, 17; Andrea N. Dierks, 17; and Andrea N. Ward, 18. The fifth passenger, Christini Carey, remains in critical condition at Huntsville Hospital. The tragedy plunges the school into mourning. . . . **A 4-year-old boy** is shot while his parents are attempting to buy drugs. Paul Herity Jr. is in fair condition at Vanderbilt University Medical Center, as is his father, Paul Herity Sr., 44. The boy was sitting between his mother, 35-year-old Claudia Dixon, and father in the front seat of a pickup; the family went to Hadley Park looking for a local dealer. When an argument ensued over whether the drugs were real, the dealer fired several shots into the cab, hitting both father and son in the legs. Both parents are expected to be charged with child abuse and felony reckless endangerment.

27—**Five hundred Nashvillians** pledge to fast for the entire day and donate the money they would spend on food to charity, in tribute to those who go hungry without choice. The citywide "Fast for the Hungry" is sponsored by Nashville's Table, the organization that redistributes unused food from local restaurants to the needy. . . . **A Stratford High School** junior is nabbed with a loaded 9mm semiautomatic pistol on school property. This is the 10th gun-related incident in Metro schools thus far this year. . . . **Yo La Tengo,** the acclaimed New York indie-rock trio, performs tonight at the Belcourt Theatre before a sold-out crowd. The group has recorded its last three albums in Nashville; each record contains a reference to Prince's Hot Chicken Shack, the Ewing Drive eatery renowned for its fiery fried chicken.

28—**A Somalian family** is beset by a tragic blaze at their Edgehill Avenue apartment. The fire begins near the family's living-room sofa; the mother, Fatuma Salah, 32, collapses outside while trying to reach help. Neighbors rush in and fight the billowing black smoke, but the smoke has already taken the life of Khadija Jeylani Haji, just one day after her first birthday. Mohamed and Muna Jeylani Haji, ages 2 and 3, are rushed to Vanderbilt University Medical Center, where they cling to life. The family's other three children escape unharmed. . . . **Having lost four employees** to corporate consolidation two weeks ago, Asylum Records now loses six of its remaining 12 staffers. Until recently a subsidiary of Elektra Records, Asylum is now a partner under the Warner Bros.

Bernice Hicks turned 100 in July of 2000. Her Nashville home is filled with photographs of successful men and women who left rural Tennessee for the city and got their start toward adult life while living with Mrs. Hicks and her late husband, the Rev. W.L. Hicks.

Bernice Hicks has always been an educator, always looking to pass along bits of wisdom to young people. It was a trait she shared with her late husband, the Reverend W.L. Hicks. Mrs. Hicks had moved to Nashville from Perry County, 80 miles to the west, to attend Walden University, a teacher-training institute for blacks, and taught school for four years before she married in 1929. Her husband, a Davidson County native, was called to the ministry and with his wife, founded two churches in Nashville—Hicks Tabernacle and Watson Grove Baptist—both of which continue as active congregations. They also owned and operated a grocery and restaurant on South Street.

But their most amazing accomplishment, begun soon after their marriage and continued by Mrs. Hicks after her husband's death, was to provide an opportunity for dozens of black teenagers from rural counties to complete high school. Over the years, they came in ones and twos and sometimes more to live in the couple's home while attending school in Nashville. "I never thought about putting down how many," she said. "Probably well over a hundred. I just really don't know."

Hicks and her husband opened their Nashville home to a steady stream of rural youngsters who wanted more education than they could get in Perry County at the time. Until the late 1950s, the county provided no instruction for black students past the eighth grade. "It was very rural," the soft-spoken centenarian said. (It also fit a pattern common in Tennessee and across the South. Until a decade or more after 1954, the year the U.S. Supreme Court declared school segregation unconstitutional, more than one-third of Tennessee's 95 counties, including Perry, provided no place, segregated or otherwise, for black students to go to high school.)

Bernice and W.L. Hicks ran a 20th-century version of the Underground Railroad. Instead of escorting young blacks from slavery to freedom, as Harriet Tubman had done, they saw them safely from isolation and ignorance to unlimited horizons. At first it was just Perry Countians; then others came, and almost all of them were not related to the couple. They just appeared at the door, coming in the fall and leaving in the spring when the school term ended. They called her "Aunt Bernice," all of them. A similar pattern also developed for rural out-of-towners who had sick relatives in Nashville hospitals. There were no hotels for blacks, but the Hickses were always there.

But it's the students she and her husband befriended that she remembers with special fondness. Although they never had children of their own, the couple felt they had played a role in the raising of the high-school students who came their way. "We tried to give them a model for how to live your life, to love one another and to love God," she said. Many of the students worked at the grocery store and restaurant and attended church with the couple on Sundays.

On the mantle and walls inside her Villa Place living room are photographs of smiling men and women, the beneficiaries of the couple's generosity. "This one earned a doctorate, that one is a lawyer, this one's a teacher," she noted, pointing picture by picture. "They live in all directions, from California to the East Coast." When she celebrated her 100th birthday, cards arrived bearing postmarks from about half the states.

"I'm blessed," said Bernice Hicks, who turned 100 on July 17, 2000.

The silver and blue dream chaser pulled into the Greyhound station, and a blue-eyed man with shoulder-length hair the color of freshly baled hay stepped off the bus. He had his belongings on his back and a guitar case in one hand. No one was there to meet Doug Ellwanger, a 45-year-old refugee from life as most people know it. He was fresh from Lexington, Kentucky, via upstate New York. Before that—well, he'd been in a lot of places, and his old Washburn guitar and the tunes tumbling from his head had been his only reliable companions.

He had never been to Music City. "It was kind of a fluke actually," Ellwanger said, slipping into a story with ease. He had followed a girlfriend to Lexington. "There's always a woman involved," he said with a smile. "You see, she wigged out on me, just lost it, and broke it off. The wind was knocked out of my sails, so I decided to leave. A

corporate umbrella. At the last minute, the label abandons plans to move into a building next to the Warner Bros. headquarters on Music Row; instead, it moves into a smaller office space in the Warner Bros. building. The label is best known as the current home of country great George Jones. . . . **Supporters of Union Hill** Elementary School win a victory tonight with the Metro school board: The 50-year-old school will remain open, at least through the 2000-2001 school year. The small brick school had been considered too small to be cost-effective, but a public effort by parents keeps it open with a skeleton staff of six teachers, no physical education or music classes and a total of 110 students.

29—**Tennessee State University** is hosting its first open house aimed specifically at attracting white students. A 1984 federal court order mandated that the historically black institution must increase its while enrollment to 50 percent. But the number of white students has declined yearly, from 22.1 percent in 1996 to 15.4 percent last year. (To keep things in perspective: At the historically white University of Tennessee in Knoxville, blacks make up less than 5 percent of the undergraduate enrollment.) TSU President James Hefner cites an "unfair perception" that the school suffers from inferior quality. But Amanda R. Jones, a white senior at Nashville's Martin Luther King Magnet School, tells *The Tennessean* that "some people are just scared to go to a predominantly black school." She will attend TSU in the fall on a minority scholarship. . . . **The Edgehill Avenue** fire that killed a 1-year-old child claims another young victim. Mohamed Jeylani Haji, 2, dies at Vanderbilt University Medical Center of complications arising from smoke inhalation. One child, 3-year-old Muna Jeylani Haji, remains in critical condition. . . . **Metro's Health Department** releases results from a national Youth Risk Behavior survey in which 1,266 Nashville-area high-school students participated.

Among the findings: 25 percent of "our kids" said they never wear a seat belt, 30 percent claimed to have smoked marijuana within the past month, and 40 percent claimed to have had sexual intercourse within the past three months. . . . **After seven days** of deliberation, Judge Aleta Trauger finds that Robert Glen Coe meets federally mandated standards of mental competency. She lifts his stay of execution.

30—**Shannon Wood**, wife, mother and co-founder of the Darkhorse Theater, formally announces her candidacy for the U.S. Senate. She will face perennial loser John Jay Hooker and others in the Democratic primary. Wood makes her political debut from the Darkhorse's stage in a former church on Charlotte Avenue. The 31 supporters on hand cheer her unabashedly liberal platform, which supports universal health care, gay rights, abortion rights and gun control. If Wood wins in August, she will face U.S. Sen. Bill Frist in the November election. . . . **Adam AnKarlo**, the streaker who disrupted a Feb. 11 pep rally at Franklin High School, agrees to serve time clearing trees from his attorney's farm as punishment. He is also sentenced to a pair of suspended 10-day jail terms, four months of supervised probation, a 5,000-word essay and a tour of the county jail. . . . **The Tennessee Supreme Court** sets a date for Robert Glen Coe's execution by lethal injection: Apr. 5, one week from today.

31—**The "Fly Jock,"** Tom Joyner, soul station WQQK's syndicated morning man, leads a jubilant early-morning census rally on the Tennessee State University campus before an estimated crowd of 5,000. Listeners begin arriving as early as 4 a.m. Joyner, who was profiled the previous Sunday on CBS' *60 Minutes*, is urging his listeners to "represent" in the ongoing 2000 census to demonstrate the true economic strength of African Americans.

Doug Ellwanger stepped off a bus onto the streets of Nashville and tried his hand (and voice) at public entertainment, hoping to catch the attention of country music scouts. It is a route traveled by many a troubadour before him.

friend told me that Nashville was a great place for a street musician, and I got on the bus."

A week later, he had cornered a high-traffic spot at the south entrance to the Farmers Market. His face was sunburned, but he was still smiling. In the open guitar case at his feet, a few dollar bills fluttered in a mild breeze. He was living from night to night in a low-rent hotel—on those nights when he made enough to eat and pay the hotel bill. "If I don't, then I stay at the [Union] Mission," he said, reaching for a nub of a cigarette pinched between the strings on an upper fret. The jury is still out on whether this town likes me, but I'm not complaining. I'm not suffering from delusions that I'm going to make it big—but I know that I'm good enough if I do."

The itinerant musician savored the last draw on his cigarette, extinguished the the butt in an ashtray, and begun to strum a song of his own composition. Some of the Nashvillians who came to the Farmers Market to buy what was in season stopped to listen to the struggling musician. A few stayed for a song or two. Ellwanger closed his eyes and played his best. Coins and bills fell little by little into his felt-lined kitty.

"What's his name?" one woman asked another.

"Ellwanger," was the reply.

"That's a funny name for a singer," the first woman observed. "Wonder what the 'L' stands for?"

Confessions of an Expatriate New Yorker

by WILLY STERN

Two days after I decided to quit my job at *Business Week* in midtown Manhattan, I went in to tell my boss. It was not a duty I faced eagerly. You know the type: Ivy League degree, monogrammed shirt and bow tie, with a stick up his butt thicker than Jevon Kearse's thigh. Highly intelligent but humorless, a living embodiment of East Coast haughtiness, as limited by his provincialism as any Pulaski pig farmer.

I told him I was giving up my job as a roving writer for the flagship of weekly business magazines and moving to what he considers a backwater Southern town to write for a giveaway tabloid weekly that runs personal ads for ménàge a trois.

He was speechless. "You know, Willy," he finally managed, "that's the most extraordinary example of downward Jewish mobility I've ever witnessed." In his world view, who in his right mind would give up the prestigious business card, the 4 Train to Yankee Stadium, the Broadway shows, the late-night home delivery of moo shi pork—for Nashville, Tennessee?

Next I trotted down the hall to break the news to the managing editor, a mild-mannered and decent man who had, after a fashion, taken me under his wing. He could play New York power politics with the best of them, but still jogged in Central Park at lunch with lowly staff writers. When I told him of my plans to head to Nashville, he got up and shut the door. It turned out he had grown up in Texas. Nary a day went by that he didn't wonder what the heck he was doing trying to raise a family in the hellhole of New York City. He was proud of me, and envious. "I wish I'd had the balls to do it, Willy," he said, "but now I'm stuck here."

In the responses of these two high-IQ New Yorkers—both leading, at the time, very similar lives—you see the paradox of every expatriate big-city type who ever ended up in Nashville: We're all conflicted. Sure, we tell native Nashvillians how much we love it here. We all can spout the mantra of short commutes, knowing Phil and Bill by their first names, grilling slabs of meat in our huge back yards, and having our groceries walked out to our Subaru wagons at Kroger. Get stuck next to us at a Nashville dinner party and you'll eventually hear us confide that it's really flattering to be asked to sit on these local boards, and how our kids are a shoo-in for admission to Yale (what with geographical diversity quotas and all). We'll rave about being able to leave work early on a Thursday afternoon and be on the Harpeth in an hour. We'll wax eloquent about how our colleagues at Vandy and Waller are every bit as smart as the ones we left behind at Harvard and Skadden.

And, in our own way, we believe it. We ex-pats understand the virtues of what only we could consider small-town life here. To build credibility, we'll segue into how the rush-hour traffic on West End rivals anything on the Upper West

Side. We'll laugh about all those Sunday-morning preachers on TV, and the black waiters in white coats at Jimmy Kelly's who still call you "suh." We'll joke about picking up *The Tennessean* at the end of the driveway and having it read by the time we get to the trash can in the back. We'll poke fun at those 92 platters of sugar-coated fried glop that pass for Chinese food in Lion's Head.

But we get far more catty when talking among ourselves. We snicker at those cars zipping around town with Titans stickers and flags all over them. Sports loyalty to us means being a third-generation Red Sox fan. Nashville's collective infatuation with its fledgling football team strikes us as juvenile. Think of a pimply-faced college kid who finally gets lucky and then drives around honking his horn and telling all his buddies how much he loves this girl he's known for two weeks. That's how we feel about Titansmania.

It's the same with all those black and gold sweaters you see on adult men (and women) at Vandy games. Most of us outgrew our need to wear the school colors by about sophomore year. And we don't know whether to laugh or cry when we meet Nashville women who know the name of the third-string quarterback at UT—women who didn't even go to UT.

But we get real defensive when our inside-the-beltway friends inquire—as they inevitably do—if we have found any "intelligent friends down there." They don't even realize how smug and condescending they are. Our crowd here includes drummers, novelists, politicians, screenwriters—and they're a helluva lot more interesting (and low-key!) than those we left behind. When we try to explain why we adore living here, the cognoscenti roll their eyes. Eventually, we just stop trying.

Herein lies the peculiar internal ethos of Nashville's ex-pat community: *We* can make fun of our fair city—but pity the poor sumbitch up East who tries it. In our own way, we're very, very loyal. We get offers for more money to head back to Boston or Los Angeles or Chicago, and we don't even think about it (much) anymore. We know Nashville is a town with far too many strip malls, narrow-minded preppies in Duck Heads, and unnaturally blond women. Yet, the day comes for all of us when we wake and realize that we have become deeply attached to this slow-paced, eminently manageable little city on a little river. It's a damn good life here. We know it. But we're still of another culture. That's us. We love this town—but God forbid our kids grow up to have Southern accents. Hope y'all don't take offense.

Nashville Scene investigative reporter Willy Stern lived in New York, Boston, Washington, Chicago, London, Tokyo, and Johannesburg before coming to Nashville—where he has (gasp!) roots.

Dolly and Lee, Dishing the Dirt

by HAL CROWTHER

In his 1975 film *Nashville*, Robert Altman scouts the borderland between fact and fantasy in this venerable Southern city that's become less a state capital than a state of mind. The film is never praised and seldom mentioned in Nashville, Tennessee. The local consensus is that Altman exaggerated, missed the subtle charm, and zeroed in on the paranoia he could understand. What more or less would you expect from a Hollywood director?

But Altman's nose did not entirely deceive him when he settled on Nashville for his disturbing logical portrait of the American condition. This is a schizoid town where straight and twisted cohabit, where cultural opposites attract and repel. Tax attorneys write country songs on their Palm Pilots, Opry backup singers study French literature at Vanderbilt. Everyone but the governor is in a band. At one cultural pole there's the Opry and its singing cowboys. At the other stands Vanderbilt University, high and hatless, the reputed Harvard of the literary South.

Modern Nashville bridges this pair of rich traditions, side-by-side but scarcely intertwined. Between the world of books and the world of banjos, cross-fertilization isn't something you take for granted—but it happens. Songwriter Tom T. Hall and country blue blood Rosanne Cash have pursued literary interests; singer-songwriter Lucinda Williams is the daughter of a distinguished poet. Donald Davidson, the most unbending conservative in Vanderbilt's original band of Fugitives, wrote a country music novel, *The Big Ballad Jamboree*, published after his death.

Great country songs are often novels in miniature—Townes Van Zandt's "Pancho and Lefty," Robert Earl Keen's "The Road Goes on Forever," Bobby Braddock's "He Stopped Loving Her Today," Don Schlitz's "The Gambler," and Matraca Berg's "Back When We Were Beautiful" come quickly to mind. Even the best novelists have failed to capture the lyric immediacy of the best Southern music.

Between songwriters and other writers there's a tentative kind of courtship, a mix of mutual respect, curiosity, and caution. In the spring of 2000, when Vanderbilt hosted 44 Southern writers for "A Millennial Gathering of the Writers of the New South," musicians shared the bill. Marshall Chapman, the towering cult goddess of redneck rock, read from her Nashville memoir-in-progress. Among the local heavyweights with literary connections are Bob McDill and Steve Earle, gold-standard songwriters of two different Nashville generations. They consented to sit on a panel with some poets—and suffered with the audience through several literary excesses, including a white poet who testified that she was part African American, at least in the marrow of her bones, because her ancestors had black wet nurses. Political correctness, praise the Lord, has yet to rear its ugly head in country music.

The most fertile connections between music and literature don't occur on panels but one-on-one, between entertainers who love to read and writers who love to listen. At another engagement I had in Nashville that weekend—an invitation to lunch with Dolly Parton—I witnessed a bonding of that kind, and I can testify to its power on many levels. Of the several writers in my family, it turns out that one of them is Parton's favorite writer, and it's not me. After only 30 seconds in a crushing hammerlock, with my knee wedged firmly against her spine, my wife was kind enough to suggest that I join her and Dolly for lunch.

Here was a memorable meeting of opposites who turned out to be more like twins. When you say that my wife—Lee Smith—is a novelist and a professor of English, you haven't begun to paint her portrait. When you say that Dolly Parton is a legendary country singer, songwriter, entrepreneur, and Hollywood actress, you've only scratched the surface of the smartest woman who ever grew up in Sevier County, Tennessee.

What's relevant is that they're both shrewd mountain girls with old-fashioned manners, and watching them recognize each other was a privilege I'll remember. I know one well, the other just slightly and recently. But my take on this pair of sisters is that if Dolly Parton had also been sent to Hollins College, they'd be virtually the same person. It's not surprising that each claims to have been the other's fan "forever."

"I've got a confession—I tried to dress down a little today because you're a famous writer and I didn't want to look too cheap," says Dolly, who's wearing a black skirt slit almost to the thigh, and a purple sequined body sweater you could substitute for your Christmas tree.

"I've got a confession, too," says Lee. "I put on a little extra makeup to meet you so you wouldn't think I was too mousy."

By the time we reach the restaurant at Belle Meade Mansion, they're talking about their daddies. When we walk in, Dolly draws a round of applause from the lunch crowd, and I turn and wave—a lame joke I've managed to keep in mothballs since 1969, when I walked into a Times Square restaurant in the entourage of Muhammad Ali.

Two hard-breathing autograph vultures hit her before she gets to her table, and Dolly treats them like kin, like royalty. The waitress requests a laying-on of hands, and Dolly indulges her, too. "They love for me to touch them," she says, without condescension, and we contemplate the demands of serious A-list celebrity. At 54, this is a woman who seems to love her work, her fans, and the considerable responsibility of being Dolly Parton. Her fans are polite but hungry to make a connection, any connection, and the lady isn't stingy with herself. She doesn't know it, but there isn't one "famous writer" in the world who gets spontaneous ovations at lunch.

Lee Smith wanted to be a country singer even more than she wanted to be a writer—and she started writing at 9. Unfortunately she was born with crippling musical disabilities. One of her family nicknames is "Tuneslayer." She made it to Nashville through the quiet uptown end, as a Vanderbilt faculty wife and a seventh-grade teacher at Harpeth Hall School. But read her Nashville novel, *The Devil's Dream*—or compare her novel *Oral History* with Dolly Parton's ballad "Mountain Angel"—and you'll grasp that they come from the same litter, these two, and understand the same people, the same songs.

Over at Vanderbilt, the New South writers were quick to agree that the marketplace starves talent and smothers genius. Modesty restrains me from testifying for my wife. But Dolly Parton is a walking, glittering rebuttal to all this grousing (in which I often join) that the cream never rises to the top. Sometimes it rises. Parton came to Nashville as a starstruck teenager, went through the wringer like all the country girls, and found herself in the deep and troubled waters of celebrity. Instead of drowning, she learned to swim real well. Pressed into a Grand Ole Opry stereotype, a singing version of Lil' Abner's Daisy Mae, she took it to a level beyond imitation.

"The dumb blond act didn't bother me, because I know I'm not dumb," she says, "and I know I'm not blond either." As Dolly tells it, she was never shy about learning the business side of Music City, which has burned so many big talents to smoking ruins. "Many an old boy has found out too late that I look like a woman but think like a man," she recalls with a satisfied cackle.

Parton's latest CDs, returning to her roots in bluegrass, gospel, and old-time mountain string bands, have won extravagant praise from the most exacting critics. She also markets wigs and cosmetics, and her Dollywood theme park is ever-expanding. A serious reader and a philanthropist for literacy programs, Parton may be more comfortable with Nashville's splintered consciousness—pickers and poets, rural roots and rhinestones, high standards and hard cash—than anyone I've ever met.

She looks good and works at it. Dolly's always approached the word "authentic" with humor and artistic license. What you see is not exactly what time and gravity would have produced, unchecked. In her autobiography she gives her plastic surgeon's phone number and writes, "My spirit is too beautiful to live in some dilapidated old body if it doesn't have to. . . I look in the mirror, and if I see anything that doesn't look like Dolly, I tell 'em, 'Cut it off.' " She doesn't know how long it takes to do her hair, she likes to say, because she's never there when it happens. Dolly wears her image the way Minnie Pearl wore her hat, like a favorite joke among old friends.

"Authentic" is a word you hear a lot around Nashville, from critics and publicists alike. I couldn't help noticing some new criteria for authenticity at the Vanderbilt conference. Where the Fugitive generation might have claimed ancestors who carried swords and planted cotton, these Subterfugitives (credit: Tony Earley) claim recent ancestors who dipped snuff and lived without benefit of plumbing. One of my litmus tests for Southern authenticity would be the ability to appreciate the paradox of Dolly Parton: Beneath a blinding surface of deliberate, exaggerated, self-satirizing artifice lurks one of the most engagingly authentic individuals in the Nashville pantheon.

Mountain girls don't lose much sleep over what the neighbors might say, or the *New York Times* either. When she restored her parents' old homeplace in the Smoky Mountains, Dolly got a big kick, she says, out of designing her new toilets as faux outhouses. It's a private joke and a wide-gauge irony she understands on the same level that Lee Smith would understand it—or Robert Penn Warren for that matter.

Hal Crowther writes social commentary for the popular press. Two collections of his columns have been published as books: Unarmed but Dangerous *and* Cathedrals of Kudzu. *He lives in Hillsborough, North Carolina.*

After his retirement from the National Basketball Association, Charles Davis returned to Nashville. Coaching and business held his interest for a while, but closest to his heart were hundreds of inner-city children who needed a hand up—as he did 30 years ago, coming of age in the J.C. Napier Homes on Lafayette Street.

SOMEWHERE UNDER THE RAINBOW

by REGINALD STUART

As a youngster growing up in a public housing project on the south side of Nashville in the early 1970s, Charles Davis learned early what limits his home city placed upon him. "I saw Nashville as the world," he recalled. "I didn't experience much racism firsthand, but I knew it was there. As a young black boy, I knew what was expected of me."

Not much: no achievement, no competition, no trouble.

Davis was not one to follow the beaten path. Undeterred by the game of low expectations, by all the seen and unseen hurdles thrown into his path, he made it to McGavock High School, largely on the strength of his potential as an athlete. By graduation time, he was a smoking-hot basketball talent, a sought-after star.

The hurdles were still there. "I was told I couldn't go to Vanderbilt," he recalled. "When I asked why, they said, 'blacks just don't go there.' " True, Perry Wallace had broken the athletics segregation barrier at Vandy, and in the Southeastern Conference, a decade earlier. Still, it wasn't routine for a black person to go to Vandy. The challenge appealed to Davis, and he pursued it.

Not only did he attend Vanderbilt; he became one of its all-time best basketball players, graduated with his class in 1981, and went directly into a twelve-year professional career in the National Basketball Association. From an unpromising start on a crumbling asphalt court in the projects, he soared to stardom with the Washington Bullets, the San Antonio Spurs, and the Chicago Bulls. He won fame and fortune, and nourished both with prudence and sound judgment.

Professional sports also took him to Italy and Japan, literally worlds away from the streets of South Nashville. Over the years he worked with people of different races, learned different languages and cultures, gained a greater sense of himself and the rest of the world community.

When his professional career ended in 1994, Davis returned to his roots, keeping a promise he had made to himself years earlier. He served as an assistant coach at Vanderbilt for a couple of years. Then he moved on to start his own business, CDC Incorporated, a company that distributes a variety of products, from pasta and bottled water to surgical supplies and even doors. No beer, wine, liquor, drugs, or guns.

In every way imaginable, Charles Davis has made a spectacular success of his life—and at 42, he's just reaching his prime. Not bad for a lanky youngster from the J.C. Napier Homes who, but for his own belief in himself, the unyielding love of his mother, and timely advice from others along the way, might just as easily have wound up behind bars at the state prison in West Nashville.

Davis is ever mindful of that. It is one of the main reasons he decided to return to Nashville. Only someone who has lived the life could possibly know how slim the margin is between making it and missing it in the projects. It's as thin as a cigarette paper, as fragile as a whiskey bottle, as hazardous as a hypodermic needle. Maybe lots of kids could make it safely past the hazards, Davis reasoned, if they just had a little more help and encouragement—so he came home to give back to his community some of what he had taken with him and some of what he had gained along the way.

After his rookie year as a professional basketball player, Davis had established a small foundation

1—At the YMCA's 47th-annual Youth Legislature, neophyte lawmakers tackle an issue their adult counterparts would never touch: the uninhabitable atmosphere of the State Capitol. Appalled by the toxic stench and choking fog of cigarette smoke on Capitol Hill, the young lawmakers vote to ban smoking in the State Capitol and Legislative Plaza. "Since the adults aren't doing it, we're taking charge," says 18-year-old Speaker Pro Tem John Thomas of Hume-Fogg Magnet School. Not surprisingly, the cause isn't taken up by the adult legislators. Blowing smoke is something this General Assembly does only too well.

2—**For the second time,** Death Row inmate Robert Glen Coe is moved in the early morning hours to a "deathwatch" unit in Riverbend Prison. As it now stands, Coe is to be executed by lethal injection at 1 a.m. Apr. 5. His attorneys will ask Judge Aleta Trauger for a stay of execution. . . . **For reasons unknown to police,** 26-year-old Christopher Wolfe flies into a rage and shoots three people at his home. The Antioch man kills his wife, Stephanie Wolfe, 25, and injures a visiting couple, Nicole and Joseph McCullen, before fleeing the scene. At approximately 9:15 p.m., he is spotted driving down Robertson Street near Lafayette Street. Police attempt to pull him over, but Wolfe veers into a parking lot, jumps out and runs. Less than two hours later, a police dog leads officers to a shed on Claiborne Street, where Wolfe has apparently killed himself.

3—**Andrea Bocelli**, the blind Italian tenor beloved of swooning fans and PBS pledge drives, performs for more than 9,000 patrons at the Gaylord Entertainment Center. . . . **Paving the way** for a scary new wave of karate killers, the Tennessee Supreme Court rules unanimously that hands and feet are not deadly

in his name for the purpose of helping youngsters in Nashville who face the same low expectations he did growing up here. This nonprofit venture has become his consuming interest, evolving into a major Nashville philanthropy that touches the lives of about 3,500 children a year in thirteen city schools. They get mentoring, tutoring from area college students, introductory training for future careers—and most importantly, a genuine sense of possibility, of hope. "I really wanted to come back and focus, concentrate, on making a difference in people's lives," Davis said. "I want to be known not as an athlete but as a humanitarian. We're not trying to fix anybody—I just don't want to see any more kids fall through the cracks."

In the spirit of a small but significant number of black and poor Nashvillians before him, Charles Davis has overcome poverty and prejudice to establish himself as a successful citizen committed to making a difference with his time and money. He is deeply invested in helping to reshape his hometown as a better place for all its residents, regardless of their standing in life. Davis has seen Nashville grow and mature since the 1960s. Progress has been made. Still, it's easy for him to be reminded of how slowly white Nashville has matured in its perception of the black one-fourth of the population. He related this experience to make the point:

Heavily recruited as a senior coming out of McGavock High School, Davis chose to stay in Nashville and play for Vanderbilt University. When he graduated in 1981, he was the second-leading scorer in Commodore basketball history.

"Just yesterday, at the Mercedes Benz dealership, as I was dropping my car off to be serviced, a [white] lady pulled in catercorner to me. She looked over and said, 'When you're done, could you park my car?' I was polite. I said, 'Pardon me, but you should not assume that every black person you see here works here.' " Davis said the lady looked embarrassed and quickly tried to pass the encounter off as if she were joking. The damage had been done.

Lingering particles of subtle racism still float like radioactive dust in the atmosphere of contemporary Nashville. They continue to affect and infect those of us, black and white, whose ties to the city and to the South run deep. Now, we are beginning to see newcomers from other regions and other races falter from exposure to the same low-grade poison.

The atmosphere is somewhat deceiving. This is not a time of pervasive tension and hostility in Nashville. No alarm bells are ringing, no violent confrontations are imminent, no screams of rage disturb the surface harmony. Instead, a vague disquiet hovers beneath the surface of our thoughts, causing even the most well-meaning of longtime residents to question our collective ability—and our will—to move the city up a notch, to transform it into an equitable, vibrant, multiethnic, and productive 21st-century community.

At the starting gate for this journey, questions beg answers: Are we prepared—mentally, socially, politically, educationally, economically—to transform ourselves into a community of interdependent citizens, or even a reasonably progressive and productive small city attuned to its cross-cultural strengths, like Seattle or Portland? Can

Nashville overcome its racial and cultural bonds and rifts? Can it move on to embrace, or at least respectfully tolerate, an avalanche of new languages, cultures, lifestyles, folkways, and mores? Or are we so saddled with the baggage of the past that we will fail to seize the opportunities still open to us, disintegrating instead into another Sarajevo, a city doomed to decades of ethnic and religious strife and preyed upon by one faction of political and economic interests after another?

The questions are not ours alone. Every American community faces them. Nashville's real test at this point in its history is to adjust its thinking from negative to positive—to see its problems as opportunities. The future prospect for Nashville's evolution into a multiethnic city of ever-new possibilities now takes on complex dimensions that could hardly have been imagined during most of the last century, when issues of race were sharply etched in black and white. Until the 1950s, legally enforced separation of the two races governed all facets of life in this and every other Southern community. Most people, whatever their race, understood and accepted "their place." Few would acknowledge, much less confront, the economic, social, and moral costs of segregation, or its mindlessly self-destructive consequences.

By 1955, the transparent racism of segregation was being exposed across America, and particularly in the South, where it had the sanction of law. Nashville was among the first Southern communities to be compelled to respond. Black attorneys Z. Alexander Looby and Avon N. Williams Jr. sought formal relief from school segregation in 1954. The Reverend Kelly Miller Smith, a black minister, and Vanderbilt divinity student James Lawson (soon to be expelled for his involvement), coached a host of socially conscious college students in nonviolent civil disobedience, giving birth to the sit-ins of 1960. John Lewis, Diane Nash, James Bevel, Bernard Lafayette, and others in that group went on to play leading roles in the fight for civil rights nationwide. Remaining here to carry on the local struggle were such middle-class activists as Agnes Hayes, Curley McGruder, and Andrew White. They had a few white allies in their fight, among them social activists Bill Barnes and Fred Cloud, Baxton Bryant and Carleen Waller, Molly Todd and Will Campbell, and John Seigenthaler, editor of *The Tennessean*.

As a Nashville college student almost a half-century ago, John Lewis was arrested numerous times for demonstrating against segregated public accommodations. He lived in Nashville from 1957 until 1963, by which time he was, at the age of 23, a hero of the civil rights movement. Lewis was elected to the U.S. House of Representatives from Atlanta in 1986 and was still serving in that office at the turn of the century.

weapons. The ruling grants a new trial for Eric Flemming, who had appealed his conviction for especially aggravated robbery in the 1995 holdup and beating of Derrick Lamont Smith. Prosecutors had argued that Flemming's hands and feet were weapons as lethal as any firearm.

4—**Mayor Bill Purcell** delivers his first State of Metro address, and it comes off as the antithesis of the big-picture, big-spending ways of his high-rolling predecessor, former Mayor Phil Bredesen. Addressing some 800 people at Gaylord Entertainment Center, Purcell calls for reuse of existing office space to shave building costs; conversion of an 800-acre green space at Bell's Bend into a park or greenway, not a landfill; and solutions to jail overcrowding and the lack of affordable housing. . . . **A Bellevue Middle School** eighth-grader who fought off a teacher's attacker is among the more than 75 civic heroes honored by Mayor Purcell and Metro Police Chief Emmett Turner at the Metro Police Department's annual awards banquet. The previous July, Tradd Hampton-Lemacks Staecker, 14, was at a local gas station when a knife-wielding man tried to rob a kindergarten teacher of her cash and checkbook. Although the attacker was larger, older and armed, Staecker rushed to the woman's aid, shoving the man off her and preventing the robbery. Also honored: Officer Marvin Rivera, who receives the department's highest honor for a living officer, the Distinguished Service Award, for his part in thwarting the robbery of employees at a Sonic restaurant by a murder suspect. . . . **Bearing signs** that read "Find the Money" and "I Knede Edukasun," more than 300 students descend on the Metro Courthouse for a sit-in to protest Metro's projected $10.4-million budget shortfall. . . . **Knology Inc.**, a Georgia company offering bundled cable, telephone and internet services, has applied to Metro officials for a cable television franchise. In its filing, Knology announces a five-year plan to build a 2,400-mile cable network throughout Davidson County. This would make Knology the first company to provide the bundled services, as well as the first rival to challenge Nashville's entrenched cable provider, InterMedia. . . . **Condemned men** Robert Glen Coe and Philip Ray Workman win temporary stays of execution from the U.S. Court of Appeals for the 6th Circuit in Cincinnati. Coe's stay stops the clock just 15 hours before he is scheduled to be killed by lethal injection. Workman wins a rare "en banc" hearing before the entire circuit court to determine whether his lawyers can introduce newly discovered evidence. His execution was to take place just 24 hours after Coe's.

5—The *Nashville Scene's* 11th annual Best of Nashville issue hits the streets, mixing readers' polls with writers' choices. For the 11th year in a row, the Elliston Place diner Rotier's gets voted Best Cheeseburger; WSIX-FM morning man Gerry House (Best Radio Deejay) and WSMV-Channel 4's Bill Hall (Best Local TV Weatherperson) and Rudy Kalis (Best TV Sports Reporter) continue their unbroken winning streaks. This year's readers-poll winners include the Second Avenue fondue parlor The Melting Pot (Best Restaurant in Nashville); the Clifton Avenue soul-food restaurant Swett's (Best Meat-and-Three); and the Centennial Park-area watering hole Springwater (Best Dive Bar). . . . **After last week's incident** in which a 20-month-old toddler was accidentally overdosed with prescription cough medicine, a Department of Human Services official says the Merry-Go-Round Day Care Center on Currey Road will remain closed indefinitely. . . . **The Warner Park Nature Center** shows off its new $1.3-million indoor learning facility, designed to serve classes of schoolchildren rain or shine.

6—**Darn!** The Reform Party rejects presidential candidate Pat Buchanan's bid to shift the contentious third party's national convention to Nashville.

Throughout the decade of the 1960s, white Nashville yielded grudgingly to black demands for equality under the law. It was during this time that Interstate 40 was routed through the heart of North Nashville, splitting apart the principal black district of the city. Black leaders Harold Love (left) and Z. Alexander Looby joined Dr. Edwin H. Mitchell and others in a futile attempt to reroute the highway.

Being a city that liked to think of itself as intellectually and morally superior—the Athens of the South, the buckle of the Bible Belt—Nashville was anxious to distance itself from racist extremism. Prodded by the student sit-ins, it moved in the early 1960s to voluntarily dismantle racial segregation (symbolically, if not substantively) in areas of commerce. Much of the rest was done in the courts—a fiercely resisted public school desegregation case, and formal complaints to various federal agencies about racial exclusion in housing, job discrimination, affirmative action, and numerous other issues. The city's supposed moderation and sweet reasonableness aside, it has taken many years and much effort for Nashville to get where it is today.

The one major battle lost by the local black community in the past half-century—despite relentless efforts led by Edwin Mitchell, a Meharry Medical College radiologist turned passionate community preservationist—was over the routing of Interstate 40 through the heart of North Nashville. As an economic bludgeon and a destroyer of neighborhoods, it was devastating. As a wound to the dignity of black Nashville, it is as raw in the year 2000 as when the bulldozers began plowing away four decades ago.

Reasonable minds will acknowledge that it is easier today than half a century ago for people of color to buy or rent a home where they choose, dine where and with whom they please, stay at hotels, go to movies, get into the educational programs of their choice and, in all circumstances, expect to be treated with dignity and respect. One could make a marginal case that it is also easier for a person of color—*a* person, not *all* persons—to get a job as something other than a teacher, preacher, or laborer.

These were rights derived from the battles fought between blacks and whites in the last century. Both races talk of the personal sacrifices they have made to reach this point of more peaceful coexistence (though not genuine community). In those years, the entire fabric of Southern society was woven in black and white. But what does the new wave of ethnic groups converging upon Nashville in the 21st century know of that history? They have their own histories, many of which are at least as complex and troubled as ours. To these new neighbors, Nashville may simply be a place they happened into, hoping to start their lives anew. If so, it's hard to imagine they could possibly know how our city has evolved to this point.

The familiar sight of eateries that advertise their wares in languages other than English is a sure sign of Nashville's ongoing makeover from a small Southern city to an international one. Tony's Taco Stand on Thompson Lane would not seem out of place in any part of Mexico.

Signs abound that Nashville is finally becoming what our airport promoters were trying to persuade people we were years ago: a cosmopolitan, international city, not a one-note country town. Drive along Murfreesboro or Nolensville roads and you'll see scores of storefronts with names few Nashvillians can pronounce. Many of the city's recent settlers are living between these two major thoroughfares, or along Gallatin Road. The more prosperous have already moved on to affluent suburban communities.

By day and by night, these new Nashvillians are everywhere to be seen, as laborers, clerks, students, teachers, artisans, white-collar professionals, shopkeepers, and restaurant operators. Not so long ago, the Mexican and Asian eateries in greater Nashville could be counted on the fingers of one hand. They were pale imitations of authentic establishments, yet they were the closest we could get to Hispanic and Asian food and culture. Now, the national cuisines of two or three dozen countries can be found faithfully rendered in the city, along with the native tongues of perhaps a hundred nationalities.

Pass almost any major construction site, and you'll see Mexican laborers doing the work that blacks and poor whites once fought over and eventually shared. Park downtown, and you'll find Somalian men managing most of the parking lots. Visit a beauty supply store, such as Kim's on Jefferson Street, and you'll meet Korean owners. Shop at Kroger, and you'll be asked "paper or plastic?" in countless accents. Dine at the Belle Meade Buffet on Harding Road, and you'll find "new" people dispensing Southern cooking and comfort—the same familiar black men carrying trays, but mostly Asian cooks and servers, and a quietly efficient team of Asian managers in place of the whites

Buchanan's campaign manager and sister, Bay Buchanan, says they favor Nashville for its "middle-America" image, but some worry that a large religious conference booked here for the same week would interfere with the convention. In the end, the party's executive committee votes down the idea—perhaps remembering the Reform Party's disastrous Music City convention in February, in which meetings degenerated into chaos and police had to restore order. The convention will proceed as scheduled in Long Beach, Calif. . . . **In broad daylight**, with a Metro police sergeant sitting in full view, a gunfight erupts among several men at the Porter Road Save-A-Trip market. When the shooting stops, Larry who used to be in charge. (This hasn't set well with many longtime patrons, some of whom have abandoned the buffet for other restaurants.)

At least three local Spanish-language radio stations are now on the dial, airing Latino music and lively debate on current issues within the booming Hispanic community. On local newsstands, you'll see more than the morning *Tennessean*, the new daily *City Paper*, the weekly *Nashville Scene*, and black weeklies such as the *Tennessee Tribune* and *Nashville Pride*. Today's local news also comes via *Actualidad Hispana*, *Tennessee Latino*, *La Campana*, and *Tennessee Chinese Times*, among others.

Old Nashville is receiving its new neighbors (the estimated 1 in 7 born outside the U.S.) with reactions that range from hospitable to hostile. In general, the more affluent of Nashville's white citizens tend to take a neutral or even positive view of the new wave of legal immigrants, seeing net gains from any infusion of working- and merchant-class residents. Even some undocumented workers—bricklayers, say, or skilled laborers—often get a wink and a nod from contractors ready to hire able and willing hands at below-market wages. In contrast, the African-American population—the other part of Old Nashville, and the main losers when new competition enters the job market—still has unfinished business to settle with the white majority. Many blacks see the new residents as something of a threat to the thin sliver of economic pie they have battled so long to secure.

Old Nashville—white and black native Nashville—really isn't prepared to offer any sort of unified response to the sudden flood of newcomers. "We" enjoy "their" food, but few of us understand their languages—Spanish, Thai, Korean, Kurdish, Chinese, Sudanese, and many others. Even fewer of us can begin to fathom their histories, cultures, lifestyles, and mannerisms. All too predictably, human nature being what it is, we whites and blacks tend to generalize about the new residents, making sweeping assertions, just as we have painted each other with broad strokes for nearly two centuries.

For black Nashvillians, the trauma goes deeper. As the new century turns, we seem caught in a post-segregation-era depression that causes extreme dysfunction in an alarmingly high number of households. The signs are painfully apparent: the toxic spread of illegal drugs; domestic violence; violence against, and by, juveniles; unmarried teenagers producing children out of wedlock for others to raise; a lost sense of community and work ethic, two vital strengths in the struggle against segregation.

Having no unified plans of its own, black Nashville finds it all too easy to resent

The only international market in Nashville 25 years ago was the Oriental Food Store in the 1500 block of Church Street. It's still there, but no longer alone. Almost 100 ethnic food dispensaries, including the Middle Eastern market above, were operating in the Nashville area as the new century began.

Expansion of the Nashville Union Rescue Mission's facilities for the homeless at the turn of the century provided one measure of a widening separation between "old" and "new" Nashvillians. Relatively few of the latter—that is, immigrants—show up among the homeless men who check in daily for free food and shelter at the mission.

or ridicule the solidarity and the idealistic dreams of new residents. This dismissive attitude is like a mask covering a core fear: "They" are taking "our" jobs, "our" security—our stake—without so much as a nod of acknowledgement that the opportunities they enjoy were made possible by the African-American minority long before the newcomers arrived. White Nashville, meanwhile, reacts as if it has too little at stake and no desire for a '60s-style confrontation in any case. Fifty years from now, will the New Nashvillians outnumber the rest of us? Outwork us? Outvote us? So far, Old Nashville, white and black, hasn't seriously pondered the questions. We still can't roll our R's, so we just roll our eyes.

It's probably just as hard for most new Nashvillians to figure us out. Our Southern speech makes it difficult for them to understand our English. Language barriers, immigration status, cultural histories, and stereotypes make it even harder for most new residents to build coalitions outside their own communities—to pick up the vernacular and subtleties of Nashville talk, Nashville life. Meanwhile, the Hispanics, Asians, and others aren't exactly inviting us to come into theirs.

Conversation and dialogue, so important a part of daily life in Nashville and the South, are hindered by so many real or imagined barriers between New and Old Nashvillians. So we fret separately, too caught up in our own concerns to worry much about the consequences of a new style of segregation.

We have been counting colors for a very long time. When the first census of the United States was conducted in 1790, newly founded Nashville was part of the "Territory South of the Ohio River," a landholding claimed by the state of North Carolina. Six years later, this real estate would become Tennessee, the sixteenth state in the new American nation, its title a derivation of *Tanasi*, the name of a Cherokee village in the eastern mountains. Place names are just about the only thing left to remind us that tribes of native people inhabited this vast territory long before the Europeans came.

man Virgis Colbert. Throughout the ceremony, Smith is greeted with several standing ovations as he pledges to help "move Fisk to a higher mountaintop." It won't be an easy climb. The renowned, historically black institution has an endowment of $13 million—just one-sixth of what Smith says the school needs. Even so, morale at the 134-year-old university, which enrolls 850 undergraduates and 35 graduate and professional students, is high now that the school officially has a new president. . . . **The cold fails** to drive away some 900 Middle Tennessee youths participating in Nashville Youth PULSE 2000, a communitywide cleanup effort that draws schoolkids from all across Nashville. Pearl-Cohn Comprehensive High School alone posts 130 student volunteers, more than any other school in the city. Several volunteers paint wooden flowers to be planted in the Children's Memorial Garden in Centennial Park. . . . **Cumberland Gallery**, the tony Bandywood art space, commemorates its 20th anniversary with a gala opening and exhibition. When the gallery opened in 1980, in the doldrums of an economic recession, it was one of Nashville's only contemporary art venues. It grew, under the guidance of owner Carol Stein, to become a cornerstone of the city's visual arts community. Over the years, its featured artists have included John Baeder, Marilyn Murphy, Barry Buxkamper, Terry Williams and Tennessee Fox Trot Carousel creator Red Grooms. Several of these artists are on hand for the opening and exhibition, which spotlights 43 signature pieces, many created for the occasion.

9—What begins as an ordinary traffic stop in the early morning hours on Ellington Parkway, ends with a man dead after allegedly attempting to run over a Metro police officer. A 1999 Chevrolet Concorde races through a radar post manned by Metro traffic officer Scott McGonigle, who pulls the vehicle over on Ellington just before the Trinity Lane exit. Inside the car, McGonigle finds the

At Overton High School, a dozen members of the wrestling team had international roots. Left to right around the circle: Ari Ibrihim, Armen Mailyan, Joey Petrone, Matt Moss, Jonathan Drinkwine, John Kim, Irdis Dosky, Alan Muhammet, Herman Ibrihim, Kunle Adewole, Gudar Abdbullatif and Bower Tayip.

The New Nashvillians defy stereotypical description, ranging across the spectrum of occupations, cultures and socioeconomic classes. Edna Caldwell (left) of the Philippines and Aram Ferdowsi of Iran (right) are in an international women's luncheon club that meets monthly at the home of one of its members, all of whom either originated from or have lived in another country.

According to the numbers duly reported to Secretary of State Thomas Jefferson, there were 35,691 people in the "Southwest Territory." The vast majority were whites, but 361 free blacks (1 percent) and 3,417 black slaves (10 percent) were also counted among the first "official" Tennesseans. The Indians still present at that time were not included at all.

There was already a Davidson County in 1790 (an area embracing much of Middle Tennessee). Then as now, Nashville was at the center of it. The population estimate for Nashville-Davidson County in that year was about 500, of whom fewer than 10 percent were slaves or free blacks, the rest being of European extraction (Indians, again, being excluded). It seems logical to assume that virtually all of these early Nashvillians were "native born," meaning that their forebears had lived somewhere in the American colonies, not in another land.

Fast-forward more than a century to the census of 1900, when Tennessee recorded a population of just over 2 million, and Nashville-Davidson County had about 120,000 people. The rest of the profile was much the same as it had been in 1790: a white-black ratio of about 85 to 15, with no Indians and a foreign-born fragment of less than 1 percent.

Given this history, contemporary Nashville is a significantly different place now than ever before—than even ten years ago. It is more urban, more densely populated, more diverse, more international, much richer (and at the same time more at risk financially), better educated, and growing faster in the lower- and upper-age brackets than in the middle.

From the 2000 census, we learn that Metro Nashville-Davidson County's whites (67 percent) and blacks (26 percent) account for almost 95 percent of the population of 570,000. But in census lingo, race is an inexact and elusive term. Most Hispanics, for example, are counted as whites; so are most Canadians, Brazilians, western Europeans; so too are Iraqis, Iranians, Saudis, Palestinians, Israelis, Greeks, Turks, and Kurds. (Nashville reportedly has the second-largest Kurdish population in the U.S., totaling close to 10,000.) By most accounts, there are at least 15,000 Asians living in the

driver, Larry Demetriu Davis, and a large plastic bag bulging with cash. Officer Jeff Bauer arrives on the scene and spots a brick-shaped bag in Davis's car, partially obscured by a floor mat. After questioning, Davis tries to speed off while Bauer is standing by the left front tire. Bauer shoots once, McGonigle four times. Davis, 25, is hit in the head and lower neck and killed. He is unarmed. The car contains more than $30,000 and 4.4 pounds of a white powder believed to be cocaine.

10—**Huldah Warfield Cheek Sharp**, a Nashville philanthropist whose gifts have changed the city in countless ways throughout the last half of the century, dies at her home in Williamson County of causes that include congestive heart failure. She was 85. Mrs. Sharp is perhaps best known for donating her family's Belle Meade estate to create the Cheekwood Fine Arts Center and Botanical Gardens, which opened to the public in 1960. With her husband, Walter B. Sharp, whom she married at the Cheekwood estate on Valentine's Day 1942, she helped found the Nashville Symphony, which gave its first public performance in 1946. . . . **Pauline LaFon Gore,** the 88-year-old mother of Vice President Al Gore, receives her bachelor's degree from Union University at a Nashville City Club luncheon held in her honor. The degree comes 67 years after Mrs. Gore left Union in 1933 to attend Vanderbilt Law School, which then required only two previous years of college. Her son attends the function and mentions little about his ongoing campaign for the presidency. This is just as well: motorists grumble yet again about the veep's motorcade clogging downtown traffic, as motorcycle police block exits onto West End Avenue. . . . **Karen Lynne Deal,** the Nashville Symphony's popular assistant conductor, announces that she will leave when her contract expires in July 2001. Her new post: music director/conductor of the Illinois Symphony Orchestra and the Illinois Chamber Orchestra. She has been

The four charter members of Nashville's first Hispanic Boy Scout troop—from left, Rene Rodriguez, Ramon Rodriguez, Arnold Valdez and Byron Burgos—repeated the Scout's pledge along with Hispanic volunteers who organized the meeting in May 1998.

Nashville area—Chinese, Japanese, Koreans, Indians, Pakistanis, southeast Asians. And finally, the classification "black" includes not only Americans of African descent but immigrants from Africa, of whom there are said to be 10,000 here, perhaps more.

The key identifier is not color, as it was when the entire local population was native-born and racial discrimination was embedded in the law; the biggest change in Nashville is that, in a few short years, we have ceased to be an insular aggregation of natives, white and black. As the new century opens, upwards of 85,000 Nashvillians—15 percent of us—were born in another country, another culture, another mother tongue. Collectively, they are the new minority, the New Nashville. The rest of us, the majority, are Old Nashville—whites and blacks and a handful of Native Americans thrown together by history and given the awesome responsibility of fashioning a workable society that serves us all.

The questions persist: Are we ready for this? Can we make a go of it? Have we learned anything from our history—or enough, at least, to keep us from repeating it?

The early signs are not promising. Consider this brief deposition of "street sociology": Hispanics far outnumber Asians among the new population groups in Nashville (by at least 4 to 1, some say), yet Asians are much more visible in a broader range of roles at the upper end of the economic scale—they're physicians, scientists, and educators at area hospitals and universities, business executives at manufacturing facilities, prosperous merchants, computer wizards. They have a visibility out of all proportion to their numbers. At the blue-collar end of the spectrum, meanwhile, the sheer number of Hispanic laborers and craftsmen would lead you to believe that without them, no new buildings or roads or major landscaping could possibly be finished.

These two distinct variations on the visibility theme generate a single familiar refrain among Old Nashville's populace: "Those Asians and Hispanics are stealing our jobs and taking over the city!" It is a worn-out lament heard all too often today, as it was in reference to blacks during the past 50 years, when racial segregation was being dismantled brick by brick. Each time black Nashvillians achieved a breakthrough—the first policemen and firefighters, the first city bus drivers, the first car salesmen—a chorus of white Nashvillians could be heard sighing that disaster was near, that "something has got to be done to stop them." And sighing rather than shooting was often noted by the powerful elite as reassuring proof that the city had a good heart, and it would come around to change gradually, in its own sweet time.

This time around, the sighs may be loudest in black Nashville. We have come so far—and yet, it seems, we have learned so little. It is not the Asians and Hispanics who threaten our advancement; it is Old Nashville.

James Sun, a native of China, came to the United States in 1989 and to Nashville in 1992. He and Kim, his Korean wife of ten years, fit the stereotype of hard-working, success-minded Asians. Within three years they had opened a produce business at the Farmers Market, and now they have added a grocery store on Nolensville Road. Both enterprises are thriving.

"When I quit my clothing import-export business in Florida, I traveled all around the East for two months looking for a place that was quiet and safe and had business potential," Sun recalled in an interview one April afternoon. He understands English well, and speaks it well enough to get his thoughts across. "A friend who works for NationsBank suggested I try Nashville. 'It has nice weather. The people are nice.' We came. We stayed."

He decided to go into the food business, but it was a struggle finding local brokers and distributors who would import the Chinese food items he wanted to sell at his market, so he worked with a broker in Georgia. Things eventually got better. Skeptical merchants had warned him that his business, called Oriental Farmers Market, probably wouldn't last more than a few months. Too different, they said. To prove them wrong, Sun worked longer hours and pushed harder. Five years later, Oriental Farmers Market was a vibrant complement to the array of food vendors who represent a rainbow of ethnic and racial groups from around the world.

with the local symphony since 1992. . . . **Will John Smith,** the organizer of last year's troubled Street Nic event, get another chance to stage a community festival? Not unless he can convince Police Chief Emmett Turner, who makes his misgivings known publicly about the planned Easter-weekend event. Last year's Street Nic, an outdoor fest at Riverfront Park modeled somewhat on Atlanta's annual Freaknik blowout for vacationing black students, was tainted by shootings at an Antioch after-party that left seven wounded. The new event, Nashville Street Fest 2000, is to be held in a shopping plaza at Clarksville Highway and 25th Avenue North, but Chief Turner worries that it will still draw "a certain element of people.". . . **Billy Pilgrim,** the hero of Kurt Vonnegut Jr.'s *Slaughterhouse Five*, may be unstuck in time, but he'll remain put in Brentwood. The novel will not be crossed off Brentwood High School reading lists, despite efforts by concerned parent Rich Hinson. The book was assigned to Hinson's daughter in her 10th-grade English class, and Hinson is displeased by its adult language. So is Scott Goodrich, the president of Brentwood High's parent-teacher organization. At a review committee meeting today, Goodrich tells teacher John Rich, "Read *Humpty Dumpty*. Philosophize about that." Nevertheless, the committee votes 4-1 in favor of the book, with Goodrich casting the sole nay. Hinson is not happy. "What will there be in another 10 years in our schools?" he asks. "A triple-X porno film?"

11—**The Tennessee Supreme Court** sets a new date for convicted child killer Robert Glen Coe's execution. Coe will be killed by lethal injection on Wednesday, Apr. 19. His attorneys prepare a last-ditch round of appeals arguing that Coe's life should be spared by reason of his mental incompetence. . . . **At Club K,** a Hermitage facility where some 700 girls take instruction in softball, an 11-year-old girl warms up with her fielding and hitting teacher, Jennifer McFalls. McFalls

Nashville has proved to be a good place for James and Kim Sun to live and work. Sun, a native of China, and his wife, who is from Korea, operate an Asian food market at the Farmers Market and an international grocery store on Nolensville Road.

Next, Sun and his wife rented a vacant store on Nolensville Road, poured their savings into it, and opened an ethnic grocery, K&S International. The Suns' new store offers a wide variety of food items from around the world. Patrons of all colors come in a steady stream. Since the store opened, Sun said, he has not taken one day off from work.

He's not complaining. On the contrary, like many Asian merchants here, Sun is proud of his total commitment to success. He sees it as a critical part of his contribution to the community: "For myself, I try to do my best. For them (Old Nashville) to see how hard Asian people try and how we succeed, then the people believe we also support the city. When I see success, I'm happy."

Sun's approach to helping the community, in other words, is simply to make sure he succeeds in his pursuits and doesn't become a drain on any public or private resources. Their life, in that respect, mirrors one of the key teachings of Reverend Ike, the legendary radio evangelist well-known to black listeners a generation ago. He always reminded his followers: "The best way to help the poor is not to be one of them."

Despite his personal success, Sun says candidly that he encounters more than a few Americans who "don't like Oriental people," who "look at me as an Asian face." He has also had a hard time in his Franklin neighborhood, an upscale area where houses generally go for a quarter-million and up. He said one neighbor in particular seizes any occasion to criticize something about the Suns. She even made snide (if not racist) comments about his Lincoln Continental.

"I moved there because of the neighborhood, and good schools," said Sun, whose 16-year-old stepson goes to public school in Franklin. "But some people resent us. They don't think we should live in this community." Another Asian family moved

serves as shortstop on Team U.S.A., the Olympic women's softball team. Remember her name.

12—Rocker Bruce **Springsteen** performs with his reunited E Street Band before a capacity crowd at Gaylord Entertainment Center. Flanking the Boss all night is Nashvillian Garry Tallent, Springsteen's bassist since the mid-1970s. Initial grousing about the $70-plus ticket price is gone by the time Springsteen and company finish their encore of "Born to Run," near the end of a two-hour-and-45-minute show. Spotted in the audience: Wynonna Judd, members of the Oak Ridge Boys and a lone figure in a Bush 2000 T-shirt.

13—The General Assembly is reeling this morning from an unexpected death. State Sen. Kenneth N. "Pete" Springer (D-

Centerville) died yesterday of an apparent heart attack at his apartment in The Cumberland on Church Street. He was 55. His body was found by Sen. Ward Crutchfield (D-Chattanooga) in the two-bedroom apartment the two shared while the legislature was in session. The legislature commemorates Springer by suspending business for the day. Unfortunately for state Democrats, Springer's death comes during an especially volatile election year, as Republicans need just two seats to win back control of the Senate. . . . **The Freedom Forum**, Gannett's well-endowed spin-off center for the study of First Amendment issues, is known as "the Feed-'em Forum" to ink-stained ingrates who regularly sup gratis at its media luncheons and receptions. The forum garners plaudits by announcing its newest project: a minority journalism center at Vanderbilt University. The institute will train nontraditional students such as those at colleges without journalism programs; it could be open as soon as fall 2001. . . . **La Vergne-based** Bridgestone/Firestone Corp., in celebration of its 100th year in business, completes a two-year transfer of 10,000 wilderness acres to the Tennessee Wildlife Resources Agency. The land, a wilderness treasure of forests, caves and craggy bluffs, is in White County, about 100 miles east of Nashville.

14—Forget the Bible Belt. According to a Middle Tennessee State University poll, the region is statistically no more religious than the rest of the country, despite the number of churches and church-related industries here. . . . A **37-year-old** Massachusetts administrator named Mark Reynolds becomes the eighth person in six years to try to manage the state's perpetually embattled, $4.3-billion TennCare medical services program for 1.3 million low-income and uninsured Tennesseans. Reynolds will be paid $180,000 a year—the highest salary of any state employee, including Gov. Sundquist, who makes less than half as much.

In the tradition of "mom and pop" merchants that once was the backbone of American free enterprise, Korean-Americans Joong and Hyun Mi Seo operate a successful dry-cleaning establishment in Green Hills. Joong Seo envies Hispanic immigrants' language bond—an advantage Asians lack.

out, he said; a black family moved in. Things change slowly. Sun remains hopeful his hostile neighbors will change, if only because "they will appreciate how hard we work."

Ironically, Sun is less optimistic about relations among Nashville's Asian communities, and the Asian population's relations with the rest of the city. "They're all divided," he said of the various nationalities represented here (Laotian, Japanese, Vietnamese, Chinese, Korean, Filipino, Indian, Cambodian, Thai and others). "Not much contact. Each group has its own churches, its own parties. I think language is the problem." There is no common language among Asians, as there is for all Hispanics, and for most blacks and whites.

Besides language barriers, the political and social history of Asia is full of conflicts that still divide people. Even their propensity for hard work gets in the way of solidarity. "Everybody is busy," said Sun. "Not much time to get together. Sometimes I sleep just three or four hours. Even Christmas Day, I worked," he said with a mixture of embarrassment and pride.

Joong Seo, who moved to Chicago from Korea with his parents in 1982 at age 12, offered additional insight. "Most immigrants coming here are highly educated," Seo said. "So other than language barriers, they have the necessary skills to succeed. This is still the land of opportunity for most immigrants. Even the less-educated come here believing they will succeed."

Seo earned a degree in economics at DePaul University, worked at the Chicago Mercantile Exchange, and became a certified public accountant before moving to Nashville in 1995. The 30-year-old businessman, who grew up in a family of dry-cleaning merchants, owns Town and Country Cleaners on Hillsboro Road in Green Hills. His wife, Hyun Mi, is from Nashville. They met in college.

Seo drew on his Chicago experience to help his visitor sort through what may be happening in Nashville. "Hispanics have a single language," he explained, "and they can organize under a term like Hispanic or Latino. But Asians? Each country has a different language. Asians are also very nationalistic. Filipinos don't like Japanese, and so on. Other people look at us and say we're all Asians, all immigrants, but there is very little cohesion."

A Korean merchants association has tried to organize businessmen, Seo noted, but only ten or fifteen people show up for meetings. In his view, the closest Koreans can get to bonding is in Christian churches. "The community can't function without the church," Seo said. "There are about fifteen churches here and about 70 percent of all Koreans attend one."

Just as black and white Nashvillians have had their own perpetual disagreements, Seo says there are many such disputes among the Asian people. It is very hard, for example, for many Koreans to even think of bonding with the Japanese. Too much historical baggage, just like many blacks and whites who still clash over slavery and the Confederacy. It was the Japanese who occupied Korea during World War II and forced many young Korean women into camps to provide sex for Japanese soldiers. "The animosity and mistrust rest in my grandfather's generation," said Seo. "He would never trust a Japanese person. If my children had Japanese friends and they wanted to marry, I wouldn't have a problem with that. But not many would unite and say, 'Let's do something as Asian people.' "

What about Asians and Old Nashvillians?

"The white community embraces Asians a lot better than the black community," Seo said, "probably because of stereotypes. White people say, 'they [Asians] won't beat us up, rape us. They are smart and work harder.' Black people think Asians are taking their money and don't care about us.' Koreans say, 'black people just want to rob and kill us.' It's very tough to get beyond that. But the only way to make things better is through education. It is very important. The black community has to get out of poverty and empower themselves. Kids 12 and 13 years old should be in school. Immigrants come here and say 'hey, they're not our equals because all they do is drink and shoot. They are not our friends, not our equals.' It is sad that so many people come here with such fixed notions."

Is Nashville ready to become a culturally diverse community?

"Most people think it's probably more ready than it really is," said Seo. "As my business expands, I meet more city leaders. I visited the City Club once. My brother and I were the only minorities there, except the servers. At a Pavarotti concert, there were about ten minorities. Who runs this city?"

By the year 2000, Martha Salazar, a native of Colombia, had been in Nashville only four years. Already, though, she was operating a very busy storefront called Hispanic Community on Nolensville Road. From this perch, Salazar, who came to the United States in the mid-1970s, provides translation services, immigration forms, tax assistance, and publishes the magazine *Tennessee Latino*. In the process, she sees and hears what's happening among Latinos in Nashville.

By Salazar's estimate, the Hispanic population here numbers far more than the 26,000 counted by the census—perhaps three times that many, or more. Her total, she said, reflects the huge number of "economic refugees," most of whom live here illegally.

"The biggest part of the population welcomes Hispanics, but not all," said Salazar. "Some police treat them like animals because they don't speak the language. Landlords don't want to rent to them; they bring a lot of excuses, or they have these awful places to rent because the tenants won't complain. People back away in restaurants when Mexicans come in for lunch. At the driver's license bureau, a black clerk looked perturbed every time I brought Mexican men in to get their licenses."

The one area where there are relatively few problems is employment. "Hispanics are hard workers," Salazar said. "The illegals are taking jobs that nobody else wants"—as construction hands, landscapers, hospital orderlies, day labor. Most natives can't begin to make distinctions among Hispanics based on nationality, social class, or legal status, and to fall back on the lame "they all look alike" response muddies the water of community acceptance even more.

Nashville's news media don't help matters much, Salizar complained: "The coverage is very poor. They reinforce false stereotypes of Hispanics as Democrats who are big on welfare, don't have a work ethic, and don't pay taxes." Salazar takes strong offense at these assumptions, but acknowledges there is little the Hispanics can do because of the language barrier.

. . . **Spotted on a Geo Prism** in the parking lot behind the Fido coffeehouse in Hillsboro Village: a metallic fish that looks like the Christian symbols often seen on the backs of cars—only this one bears two little feet and the word DARWIN.

15—**The stretch limos** creep like caterpillars down Belle Meade Boulevard and file through the gates at Cheekwood. The occasion is Nashville's most exclusive social event of the year, the Swan Ball. Unless you were invited—and unless you could pay the $600 per person to attend—you are not here. Those who do attend represent the city's grandees: Cheeks, Frists, Armisteads, Masseys, Dudleys. Former Secretary of State Alexander Haig rolls up in a white limo. Newlyweds Amy Grant and Vince Gill appear. Under the big tent in Cheekwood's Swan Garden, vases brim with 7,000 long-stemmed white tulips imported from France. Natalie Cole, the daughter of the late Nat King Cole, favors the crowd with her father's signature song "Unforgettable." She tells the well-heeled revelers to "kick off your shoes. Slap your thighs. Slap somebody else's thighs." . . . **The bodies** of Metro Police Capt. Barry Touchstone, his wife, Sharon, and his 5-year-old grandson, Michael Sean, are found in the family's West Nashville home. The coroner determines they died from accidental carbon-monoxide poisoning, the result of a car left running in their closed garage. Fumes seeped from the garage into the house. Touchstone, 51, was a 30-year veteran of the force.

16—**A tuneful War of Northern Aggression** occupies the stage of TPAC's Jackson Hall for one last time before marching on. The touring company of *The Civil War*, the dramatic musical by hit Broadway composer Frank Wildhorn, ends its five-day run today in Nashville. The cast includes country singer Larry Gatlin and gospel superstar BeBe Winans, as well as Music City studio singer Mike Eldred, who appeared in the

Martha Salazar is the publisher of *Tennessee Latino,* a magazine for the rapidly growing Hispanic population. She believes the 2000 census count of 26,000 Hispanics in Davidson County is far too small. There could be 80,000 or more Spanish-speaking residents in the greater urban area, she says, including a huge number of "economic refugees" who have not established residency. These undocumented workers were flooding into the local labor market at the turn of the century; for every individual or group caught in the act of illegal entry (below), at least two slipped through, often with the knowledge of employers.

show on Broadway. Local Civil War historians, of whom there are a few, grouse that the show refers to Murfreesboro's Battle of Stones River as "the Battle of Stone River." Others wonder if rigorous accuracy is a bit much to ask of a show with singing Rebels and dancing Yankees.

The surge in the immigrant population has fueled an entire new economy aimed at Hispanics, most of whom are Catholic and speak little if any English. Catholic and Methodist churches are offering services in Spanish. Local banks are trying to work with immigrants. Some employers, like Gaylord Entertainment, have helped newcomers find housing and transportation to and from work. All this against a national backdrop of a new president, former Texas Governor George W. Bush, who is promoting even easier access across the border for Mexicans, in hopes of stimulating greater economic growth for the United States.

"I do have a lot of hope because people are listening and trying to do something to accommodate everyone," said Salazar. Her three sons, all of whom have spent some time at Overton High School, like living in Nashville: "They are very open-minded. They go out with anybody. They are friends with black Americans, whites, Asians. That process is what we need to see more of." Salazar had done her own share of trying to reach out. She got involved in Leadership Middle Tennessee and made friends with the publisher of one of the city's black newspapers. That has helped her grasp the feelings of whites and blacks in Nashville toward Latinos moving here in large numbers. It has helped her educate them as well, and defuse some misguided notions.

Meanwhile, the evolving Hispanic community is sorting through its own growth pains. At one point, Hispanic business leaders got on the radio to air their dispute over which Hispanic chamber of commerce was the "real" one. "This division is hurting us," Salazar said, "because people in the community are asking, 'Who are the good guys?' We don't know."

If there is anything the diverse communities of Old and New Nashville have in common, it is the police. Long a source of angst for black and poor white Nashville, the Metropolitan Police Department marked the turn of the century in familiar territory—at the center of one controversy after another.

This was not the same old bunch of hard-nosed white cops, for sure. The department had changed, ostensibly for the better. Emmett Turner, a Nashville native and a graduate of Tennessee State University, was the city's first black chief of police. More blacks were on the force, along with whites of more moderate thinking than many of those who preceded them in the days of racial segregation. Efforts were being made to recruit Hispanics and Asians as well. Crash courses in so-called "survival Spanish" were being offered.

The nature of crime in the city had changed, too. Increasingly, there were widespread and violent drug-related crimes the likes of which the city had rarely known. Black-on-black crime surged. Crime and fear of more crime prompted thousands of families to turn their happy homes into small, barred prisons of self-defense. The police force, politicians, and otherwise reasonable rank-and-file citizens seemed at times to operate from a siege mentality, a zero-tolerance law enforcement mode.

By 2000, violent crimes had fallen significantly. At the same time, the jails were bursting at the seams, filled mostly with people of color and others who couldn't afford legal counsel. Meanwhile, some community leaders who were once angered over crime found themselves increasingly angry over police tactics and the overpopulation of jails. Order may have broken down in the city—but was reasonable law enforcement quickly following suit?

The police respond effectively to thousands of calls each month. It's only the few that appear to have been grossly mishandled that fuel a public sense of irresponsibility. It doesn't take many. Blacks were protesting police tactics in general—and four incidents that proved fatal for nonwhite males—in a two-month period of 2000. Hispanics in a southside apartment complex were complaining of harassment by off-duty police and private security guards. Asians railed against the police shooting of a Korean merchant as he stood in front of his store firing at fleeing robbers.

"The police don't have to answer to anybody," said Mansfield Douglas, a charter member of the Metro Council who retired in 1999 after 36 years of service to his South Nashville neighborhood. An experienced mediator in police-community relations, Douglas is accustomed to hearing complaints from constituents about objectionable police conduct. This time, though, it was Douglas who was sour about police misconduct and disappointed with neighborhood reactions.

"Just down the road in Lebanon recently, the police crashed into the wrong house on a drug raid," Douglas said over breakfast at an off-Broadway pancake shop. "The resident, a black man, jumped up in surprise, and the cops—white—shot and killed him, right there in his own home. You would think that the greater Nashville black community would be up in arms about that, but nobody ever raised any fuss over it. One member of the council told me nobody even brought it up to him."

Douglas shook his head. "We don't have leadership like we did in the 1960s. That black chief is worse than Joe Casey ever was," the reference being to a tough but fair-minded chief in the post-segregation era. "At least Joe would come out in public and talk. Turner has almost guaranteed there will never be another black chief."

Not everyone was as pointed in their criticism of Chief Turner as Douglas, but

17—Tax day! Even with the deadline delayed two days, since the 15th fell on Saturday, Nashville's post offices are jammed with procrastinators filing last-minute tax returns. . . . **Local callers** can't dial 1-877-TRA-7030 fast enough. The toll-free number, introduced today by the Tennessee Regulatory Authority, allows state residents to make their home telephone numbers off-limits to telemarketers. . . . **An admitted prostitute,** three shift managers and a security guard are among the six defendants who plead guilty to assisting the operation of a reputed Nolensville Road brothel disguised as a health spa. All have been employed at Dawn's Whirlpool and Health Spa, owned by Tera M. Daniels, who has herself been in jail since January, awaiting trial May 1 on multiple counts of money laundering, embezzlement and racketeering. . . . **On the front page** of The Tennessean, the family of Larry Davis, the 25-year-old Nashvillian shot and killed by police Apr. 9, demands an inquiry to determine if deadly force was justified. Davis was the second person killed by Metro police in 10 days on grounds that he tried to run over officers at the scene, causing them to fear for their lives. "This is not over here," says Davis' aunt, Melanie Boleyjack. On an Ellington Parkway embankment, a memorial of flowers and a plastic Bible marks the place where Davis died.

18—At the command of technician Dwayne Brankiewicz, workers begin hoisting a 70-foot-by-90-foot screen onto its seven-story frame at Regal Cinemas' new IMAX theater. The IMAX is the showpiece of Regal's newest megaplex, the Opry Mills 22, scheduled to open next month at the hotly touted new Opry Mills shopping center. The IMAX, a large-format movie-screening system, has proved to be highly successful and popular in the relatively few places it has been introduced across the country. The screen alone weighs 1,000 pounds. . . . **One person** isn't pleased with Tennessee's new toll-free anti-telemarketer number:

Renee Lansdem. Lansdem answers phones for a Fargo, N.D., bank that has a toll-free number almost identical to the one Tennesseans call to ward off telemarketers. In one day, Lansdem receives more than 500 misdirected calls. . . . **Metro Council** passes on second reading a key initiative that will make public art a reality in Nashville. The measure will set aside 1 percent of any general obligation bond issued for a newly built or heavily renovated public building, park or parking facility. That money will then be used for a work of public art to be incorporated into the finished design. It is a major victory for the Nashville arts community, which has long considered the lack of public art a civic failing. . . . **At Centennial Park**, a memorial service is held for Cary Ann Medlin, the 8-year-old girl Robert Glen Coe confessed to raping and killing in 1979. Charlotte Stout, Cary Ann's mother, carries her daughter's bronzed baby shoes, a photo of Cary Ann as a toddler and a card the young girl wrote to her family. Soon the victim's family will go to Riverbend Prison to witness the execution. In the park, the girl's white lace dress hangs from a wire hanger. "You can look at that dress and you can see reality, that she is in the grave, that there is evil in the world," Charlotte Stout tells *The Tennessean*," and that evil has consequences." Coe has seven hours to live. . . . **All systems are go** for Nashville Street Fest 2000, the successor to last year's troubled Street Nic. Organizer John Smith wins a permit for the three-day festival tailored to African Americans, despite reservations by Metro Council member Morris Haddox, who says he has collected more than 100 signatures from his constituents protesting the event. Police agree to patrol the event the first day and increase their presence if needed. . . . **As the clock nears midnight**, protesters both for and against the death penalty converge on Riverbend Prison. Reporters swarm the area outside. Sherman Novoson, a fringe figure in the Capitol Hill press corps, uses the

In 36 years as a Metro councilman, Mansfield Douglas frequently clashed with police over issues of fair and equitable treatment of minorities. Though he retired from office in 1999, Douglas kept speaking out for an independent civilian review authority over the police department

numerous others spoke unfavorably of the department, even as the crime statistics were falling. What didn't happen, though, was a closing of the ranks among the various groups of citizens with complaints about police misconduct. When Asians protested the shooting of the merchant, they were on their own. The same was true with Hispanics. An opportunity for the city's ethnic groups to reach out, to share and bond from a position of strength, spiraled into a divisive issue when the local branch of the NAACP abruptly decided at the last minute not to join Hispanic activists in a downtown march to protest alleged police misconduct. While some black leaders defended that decision and later admonished the Hispanics for

Instead of a civilian review board, the mayor and police chief chose Kennetha Sawyers, a civilian attorney in the Metro legal department, to head a new Office of Professional Accountability to oversee internal investigations of alleged misconduct by police officers.

seeking Chief Turner's resignation, Douglas and others feared the incident only fueled more ill will and mistrust among the "new minorities" of Nashville.

"Black people still have issues with the police; the hostility is deep," said Kennetha Sawyers, head of the police department's new Office of Professional Accountability. "The perception that force is going to be out of proportion is strengthened" with every new incident, she said. "Now Hispanics have issues. Asians have issues."

Sawyers, a black woman, a native Nashvillian with a law degree from Ohio State University and seventeen years of experience practicing law, was hired by Turner to help restore credibility and accountability to the department—and to ward off calls for a

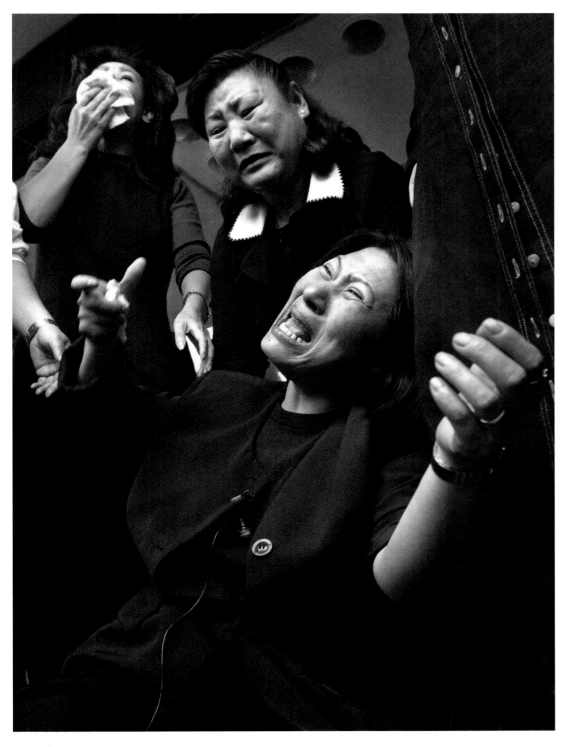

Two Metro policeman mistakenly gunned down a Korean merchant as he was attempting to stop two armed robbers in April 2000. The anguished cries of Chong Hwan An's widow, Young An, were echoed elsewhere in the city after four fatal encounters between white police and nonwhite "subjects."

occasion to sell bowls of beef stew out of his car for two bucks. On Death Row, Coe's last meal consists of a fried catfish dinner with sweet tea and pecan pie.

19—**At 1:01 a.m.,** five guards arrive at Coe's cell, cuff his hands and feet and walk him to a gurney. He tries to make small talk, but the guards are trained not to respond. He is rolled 50 feet to the execution chamber. Eight minutes later, he is in place for the execution. By arrangement with Riverbend's warden, Ricky Bell, Cary Ann Medlin's family watches the execution directly, not over closed-circuit television. At 1:32 a.m., the first of seven syringes begins pumping into Coe's body the chemicals that will kill him. "I'm gone," he says. "I'll see you in heaven. Bye-bye." Robert Glen Coe's 44 years on earth end at 1:37 a.m. on Apr. 19, 2000. In less than an hour, *The Tennessean*'s massive high-speed presses are rolling. "COE EXECUTED," the banner headline announces. . . . **The family of Larry Davis,** the Nashville man killed by Metro police during a traffic pullover, leads some 60 protesters from the Bicentennial Mall on Jefferson Street to Metro police headquarters. They demand to know why deadly force was used when Davis was unarmed, and they call for the removal of officers Jeff Bauer and Scott McGonigle, the police involved in the shooting. "Murder is murder," reads one protester's sign, "no matter who commits it—the police, the governor.". . . **In the old Nashville City Cemetery,** historian Carol Bucy walks a tour group of 60 people through the rows of crumbling monuments. Nashville's first cemetery was opened in 1822, and it houses some 20,000 of the city's dead. It is the week before Easter, and all around, in the details of upraised hands and crosses and crowns, the hope of resurrection is chiseled in stone. Bucy explains how the dead were buried with their feet toward the east, in the hope they'd be facing Jesus on Judgment Day. Today turns out not to be that day.

civilian review board. There was a time when Sawyers was seen by police as their friend. That was when she worked as a senior litigator for the city, defending police officers. Now she is seen by many in the department as the enemy. Her office replaced the department's secretive Internal Affairs Division, which for decades handled all police misconduct complaints and meted out discipline (such as it was).

Predictably, Sawyers defended Turner, saying "he has taken a beating in the press" for his handling of the department's internal and external woes. Still, she is not blind to the internal problems he faces, as well as the public relations nightmares that

20—Singer-songwriter **Steven Curtis Chapman** is the night's big winner at the Dove Awards, the contemporary-Christian music industry's version of the Grammys, held at the Grand Ole Opry House. Thanks to his *Speechless* album and its hit single "Dive," Chapman takes home six of the winged trophies. He has bagged 44 Doves, total. Chart-topper Michael W. Smith wins Songwriter of the Year honors for "This Is Your Life," a song inspired by the tragic high-school shootings at Columbine High School in Littleton, Colo. Those shootings occurred exactly one year earlier to the day. Sixpence None the Richer, the Nashville pop group whose ethereal song "Kiss Me" reached the top of *Billboard*'s pop charts in 1999, picks up two Doves. Two high-profile presenters set aside their rivalry for the Dove ceremony, but only barely: St. Louis Rams quarterback Kurt Warner and Nashville's coach Jeff Fisher, whose Tennessee Titans lost to the Rams in a squeaker of a Super Bowl in January. Warner lets Fisher announce an award, ribbing him, "I'll let you handle this trophy. I got the last one." Fisher's reply brings down the house: "At least the recipient earned this one.". . . **Supporters of the liberal Green Party** are still fired up about the previous day's visit by their presidential candidate, Ralph Nader. The veteran activist appeared yesterday at Fisk University to rally his Green troops. Even he acknowledges he doesn't have a prayer in the November election. But Nader's unexpected popularity has caused Al Gore's local Democratic machine to worry that the Greensman is a "spoiler" who will siphon away enough votes to assure a Bush victory. That hardly dissuades Nader from pledging a vigorous campaign. The rally also gives a whisper of name recognition to the Green Party's U.S. Senate candidate Tom Burrell, a Covington, Tenn., community activist who is opposing Republican incumbent Sen. Bill Frist. Frist is not exactly quaking in his Guccis.

When he joined the police force in 1996, Guillermo Guerrero was one of the first Nashville officers in a new category: "other" (neither white nor black). Four years later, only 25 of the more than 1,200 officers were in this group, along with 170 blacks (14 percent) and over 1,000 whites (84 percent).

stem from just the appearance of police misconduct. She did not take on her job to work miracles. "I'm not the knight in shining armor, but I think a change of perception was necessary," said Sawyers. "The police perceive themselves as under siege in all corners. That causes you to become insular. Sometimes you need to see things from a different perspective."

If the department were getting a report card from the community at about this time, it would probably receive a "D" from people of color and not much higher than a "C" from whites, she said. "Frequently people base their opinions on anecdotal accounts of encounters with the police, and the negative ones are usually repeated more than the positive ones." Sawyers added that in some parts of the city people are ridiculed if they have anything positive to say about the police.

"Much of the problem stems from the failure to adequately explain things," Sawyers said. "You can do everything right, by the book, but if you do it in such a way as to seem disrespectful, the reaction from the citizen becomes entrenched at the point of contact. People don't buy the explanations given later. They don't want to hear what you have to say then."

There are other realities about the police department—familiar ones— that await resolution. One is manpower. The force in 2000 was about 100 uniformed officers short of its authorized size of 1,300. Efforts to raise the standards for new recruits (requiring two years of college, for example, or the equivalent in military training) were advancing, but the starting pay of $29,998 was not competitive with other Southern cities, let alone with other kinds of work. Recruiters were searching far and wide for people with speaking and writing skills in Spanish and for prospects coming out of historically black colleges—but so was everyone else. Asians, Hispanics, and Native Americans made up a combined total of just 2 percent of the force, and black officers about 14 percent; the rest were white.

Meanwhile, the number of police recruits without local ties is on the rise. In many respects, they are like most other New Nashvillians: They have no real understanding of the city's history beyond stereotypical generalities and what they see upon arrival. Most of the present patrol force is relatively inexperienced, with five years or less on the job. Few speak Spanish; even fewer speak any Asian language. All are out trying to enforce the law in a quickly changing city that even long-term residents are finding harder and harder to understand.

If life in the post-segregation era had attained even a fraction of what was envisioned by young blacks during the sit-ins, stand-ins, boycotts, and marches of the 1960s, Nashville would indeed be a different city today. Blacks and whites who were seniors in Nashville high schools then would be law partners now, or doctors in joint practice, or in business together all over town. Hardly anything like that happened. We would all be living in more integrated neighborhoods, redefining community while retaining heritage and values. Never happened. Our kids would be walking to integrated neighborhood elementary schools, never having needed a court order to define equality or enforce the principle of equal protection of the law—but that didn't happen either.

Downtown Nashville might have been spared a couple of decades of looking like an abandoned gold-mining town, since white flight would not have been the driving social force of the 1970s and '80s, and we wouldn't have had to reinvent the vision of a vibrant central business district. Jobs and job training would have been more accessible to all. The Centennial Park swimming pool would still be a pool, not a botanical garden created to avoid integrating the pool.

Reality didn't live up to those dreams. Today, Nashville may be a better place to live than it used to be—but in many respects we are further apart than most well-meaning folks would have thought we'd be by now. Somehow the dream has faltered.

Much of white Nashville sees it a different way: "We surrendered a lot in the past century to give black Nashvillians access to all public schools and higher education, public accommodations, job opportunities, and political power. What more do they want?"

The answers are short and long, simple and complex, inspired and impossible. Such as: Rip up Interstate 40 and restore the thriving community that once grew there in the heart of North Nashville (it might have died of integration anyway, but it would have been a much slower and less painful death). Make good on still-unfulfilled promises, over the past century, to invest generously in Fisk University and Meharry Medical College, two of Nashville's best-known institutions of higher learning. Get more color into the pale complexion of professional music in the city, from the recording studios to the management offices to the symphony orchestra. Let Tennessee State University develop into the premier state university in Middle Tennessee. Make the criminal justice system fundamentally fair to all, from the squad car to the courtroom to the jail cells.

Old baggage. Old baggage that white Nashville kept out of sight as it raced to build professional football stadiums and monuments to music and art. Old baggage that black Nashvillians with long memories will never forget.

There is another painful reason why the dream has foundered. It's true that whites have failed blacks, but blacks have also failed themselves. "My generation as a whole—the '60s and '70s—has made the worst generation of parents in history," said T.B. Boyd III, leader of the fourth generation of Boyds involved in the printing and publishing industry here. "We, black folks in general, lost that level of respect for our elders that we had at one time. The children of today are not being indoctrinated with that respect. I don't think we are prepared at all for what is ahead," he said.

Boyd grew up in North Nashville, attended public schools here, and now runs the family's businesses. At 53, he is president and chief executive officer of Boyd Publishing, producer of hundreds of thousands of pieces of religious literature each year; chairman of Citizens Savings Bank and Trust Company, the oldest continuously operating black bank in America; and vice chairman of the board of Meharry Medical College, a school that at one point in the last century had educated nearly half the black physicians and dentists practicing in America. He is in a position to know whereof he speaks. Reviewing the prospects for black Nashville, Boyd expressed deep concern:

"So far, I see too much apathy and too many of our young people majoring in minors, more interested in the hip-hop scene than real-life issues that are going to make or break them in adult life. I don't see them showing enough seriousness about the competition they will face in this city. We don't take advantage of the educational opportunities. We've got schools galore and opportunities to learn, but these schools are falling behind because the parents are so apathetic."

21—**Chong Hwan An**, 49, is working at his Boutique World salon in the Madison Square Shopping Center at 7:30 p.m., when two robbers, a man and a woman, enter the store. They demand money at gunpoint from An and his wife, but when An draws a handgun they exchange shots, and the robbers flee. Two Metro police officers arrive on the scene in time to see An standing outside, firing at the escaping robbers. They shout for him to drop his weapon, but he continues to shoot. The officers open fire on the shop owner. He dies at the scene, and in the confusion, the robbers escape. (A suspect, 17-year-old Jennifer Szostecki, is captured later with some of the money on her after the robbers carjack a Jeep in a nearby parking lot.) Chong Hwan An becomes the third person shot and killed by Metro officers in less than a month. The South Korean native had been a U.S. resident for 25 years. . . . **The Overcup Oak**, the upstairs pub in Vanderbilt's Sarratt Student Center, is nobody's idea of a Delta juke joint. And yet here is Othar Turner, the legendary nonagenarian fife-and-drum musician from Mississippi, performing for a grooving crowd of hard-core blues fanatics, drunken frat boys and Turner's own boisterous entourage. Fife-and-drum is an indigenous folk music with roots dating back to slavery and beyond; Turner, now in his mid-90s, trills his hand-cut cane flute while his many drummers beat out a funky marching-band pulse. When he isn't playing, he slyly places a hand at his hip, gunslinger-style, and shimmies like a man seven decades younger. . . . **Fears that North Nashville's Street Fest 2000** (successor to Street Nic) would result in violence prove to be unfounded—as, unfortunately, do hopes of success. Bad weather and a dismal turnout leave vendors with heaps of unsold burgers and grilled chicken. Kids, meanwhile, are disappointed to learn the planned carnival rides are not running. They settle for having their bike speed clocked by Metro

T.B. Boyd III presides over a religious publishing company that was founded in Nashville by his great-grandfather more than a century ago. Boyd worries that many young blacks have lost the work ethic and the respect for elders that was the salvation of earlier generations—and is the cornerstone of life for most immigrants.

Banker William Collier Jr. grew up on Jefferson Street in North Nashville. There were 400 to 500 black-owned businesses in the city then, compared to only 100 or so now, but few recognize the significance of this reduction. Collier calls it "one of the biggest losses," not only for blacks but for Nashvillians in general.

motorcycle officers on the scene. The event's supporters look to the next day and pray.

22—**What a difference a day makes** for Nashville Street Fest 2000. A mild, dry day brings out hundreds of neighborhood residents, including children who pile onto the event's four carnival rides. There is no violence, only music, high spirits and all the grilled chicken a soul could eat.

23—**More than 125 members** of Nashville's Korean community hold a peaceful demonstration at

As a businessman, Boyd sees the new influx of market-savvy Asians taking one black business location after another and making good where blacks failed. As an employer, he sees Hispanics anxious to fill any labor job available. Young black Nashvillians may be fiddling while Rome finishes burning down, he suggested. To make the point, he recalled one of his teachers at Washington Junior High School—the band director, Don Q. Pullen. One day, Pullen was castigating his students, including trumpet player Boyd, for failing to apply themselves. He offered a comparison between them and their white counterparts: "The white boys are circling the earth and y'all are circling the alleys," Boyd quoted Pullen. The analogy may have been a stretch, Boyd said, but they all got the message.

William A. "Bill" Collier Jr., grew up in a merchant family in North Nashville and went through the city's public schools. His father owned a dry-cleaning business on Jefferson Street and a small restaurant known for its tasty hamburgers. Collier was both a beneficiary and a victim of the falling walls of employment discrimination. After college, he went into banking with the old First American National Bank. At the turn of the century, Collier was an officer at Union Planters bank downtown. The family businesses were gone, but Collier was in the mainstream. Like Boyd, he had mixed feelings about what he saw happening:

"When you look at some of the old business directories, there were 400 to 500 black businesses going from North to West to South Nashville. Now, when you look in the directories, you see 100 businesses and 400 individuals. The growing professional class of blacks is less tied to old neighborhoods and community reinvestment than earlier generations of black Nashvillians with money. There doesn't appear to be any recognition of the importance of maintaining a viable black business community in Nashville. That's one of the biggest losses to the entire community."

Collier noted that there was little if any new housing construction or remodeling of existing houses in old neighborhoods, and no new investment in business ventures. As for those dreams that drove the battle to end racial segregation and employment discrimination and gave Collier's generation hope for a whole different world, he said:

"It was the kind of freedom we were looking for, but in a lot of ways it became self-defeating. Black businesses have been shut. Entire neighborhoods in the city have been abandoned for 'better' ones in the suburbs. Schools are resegregating. Family dysfunction is as serious as neighborhood breakdown. Educators are having a hard time educating. We have frustrated teachers in a frustrating environment who can't produce the results we got 30 years ago."

Like T.B. Boyd, Bill Collier was looking for reinforcements, but not seeing many: "In the workplace, it's assumed if you are Asian you are bright and hard-working. If you're black, its assumed you are lazy, not smart, and aren't going to work hard. When I walk the streets of downtown, it's rare to run across any minorities in professional roles, wearing shirts and ties. I'm not very optimistic that things will change for the better anytime soon. If there's a change in the wind, you can't smell it, taste it, feel it, or see it. What I do see are ethnic pockets forming all around the city. They're growing by leaps and bounds, like little townships, as black communities once did."

The implication is that as the immigrants make economic gains, their voices in Nashville will become stronger than traditional black voices. Throughout black Nashville, among those who made it across the bridge from the segregated old Nashville to the desegregated new Nashville, and now face the new multicultural Nashville, the vibes of worry resound over and over.

"We have so many of our boys in the pen and on drugs, that when these Mexicans come in they get the jobs," said the Reverend James Thomas, pastor for 30 years at Jefferson Street Baptist Church. Thomas, who left his home in Texas with $4 and lunch in a sack, came to Nashville in 1964 and emerged as one of the more outspoken Nashville clergy in the final decades of the last century. He has presided over more funerals than he can count for the children of church members who became involved in trafficking and use of illegal drugs. He faults adults for encouraging too much materialism among children and not enough of a work ethic and appreciation for education.

"We've got to do something to encourage our young folks," he said emphatically. "The immigrants have the values blacks had two generations ago," Thomas concluded. "They come here willing to sacrifice for the sake of their children. They don't identify with us. They know 'bubba' and 'brother,' but they don't know us. Before they get here, they've already been taught what to think of us."

Despite the political clout black Nashvillians have gained in the past 30 years, many say the community has lost the will to flex its muscle. "There are more blacks than ever before in key political positions," said Dwight Lewis, whose 30 years as a reporter and columnist for *The Tennessean* gave him a long lens on the city's evolution. Recalling the time when Nashville had only a few black elected officials, Lewis rattled off part of the current list: two of the five council members at large, nine of the 35 districted council members, several members of the legislature and the state judiciary.

But, instead of working together, these leaders "can't get anything done except infighting over little things," said Lewis. "Maybe they're just not as hungry for change as they used to be."

the Madison Square Shopping Center, site of the fatal shooting of Madison store owner Chong Hwan An by two Metro officers. It's the second such protest in less than a week. Bearing placards demanding justice, the demonstrators line Gallatin Road for more than an hour. Byung Ho Shin, president of the Tennessee Korean Association, which represents 3,500 Koreans in Nashville alone, calls for a full investigation and an official apology to An's family.

24—**Authors Bob O'Gorman** and Mary Faulkner appear at Davis-Kidd Booksellers to sign their book, *The Complete Idiot's Guide to Understanding Catholicism.*

25—**The Saturn automobile plant,** built 10 years ago by General Motors in suburban Spring Hill, 25 miles south of Nashville, is about to get a $1.5-billion infusion of funds for expansion.

26—**WPLN-FM,** Nashville's public-radio news and classical-music station, profiles Evan Broder, the composer of an original opera being performed today by students at Eakin Elementary School. The opera, *The Ten Suns,* is based on a Chinese folktale. Broder is reserved about the performance, which is somewhat surprising, given that he is an Eakin sixth-grader himself.

27—**The good news:** Demonbreun Street, reduced to rubble by the Music Row Roundabout project, will be patched in time for Saturday's first Music City Marathon. The marathon's course, which was set before the roundabout was announced in September, passes through Demonbreun, and rerouting the expected 10,000 runners would have been a logistical nightmare. The bad news: The patch job will cost an expected $1,500—and it will be torn up as soon as the race is over. . . . **As expected,** the Nashville-based Gaylord Entertainment Company posts first-quarter losses of $15 million. . . . **More than three-and-a-half years**

after his wife Janet's mysterious disappearance, Perry March is ordered by a probate jury to pay her parents, Lawrence and Carolyn Levine, a total of $113.5 million for her wrongful death. March stays put in Mexico.

28—**During a routine truancy check,** a 15-year-old Stratford High School student shoots a Metro policeman in the face. Officer Joe Cooper, 46, a veteran with 15 years on the force, spots the student on Marina Street during school hours and stops him to see if he should be in school. The teen pulls a .32-caliber revolver and fires. Cooper is hospitalized in critical but stable condition. The suspect turns himself in hours later. . . . **In a deal** that spells the end of local ownership for Nashville brokerage giant J.C. Bradford & Co., the 73-year-old company announces it is being bought by the New York-based PaineWebber Group Inc. The price is in excess of $600 million. Bradford, founded in 1927, is the last major locally based financial-services company. . . . **KISS, t**he flame-spitting, grease-painted '70s rock 'n' roll titans who by now are older than most high-school guidance counselors, bring their "farewell" tour to AmSouth Amphitheatre. WNRQ-FM, Nashville's hard-rock radio station, hosts a citywide scavenger hunt for a voucher that guarantees two front-row tickets. The winner, Ray Balz, finally locates the voucher wedged inside a mile-marker sign near the Red Lobster on Bell Road —but not until after a search that, at one point, involved a three-hour exploration downtown with his eight-months-pregnant wife.

29—**In the 50-degree chill** of the dawn hours, a blocked-off West End becomes a carpet of bobbing heads and jostling bodies. Some 7,500 runners suit up for the first-annual Music City Marathon, running a 26.2-mile course that stretches from Music Row to Lower Broadway to East Nashville and back. Luke Kibet of Kenya wins the men's division in two hours and 12 minutes. His countrywoman, Lucia Sabato, finishes in two hours and 37 minutes to clinch the women's race. Among local runners, Clarksville's Bob

One who keeps a finger on the pulse of Old Nashville—and who counts himself as a cautious optimist as the new century begins—is businessman Nelson Andrews. A 1949 graduate of Vanderbilt University, he started a career selling building materials, and has since been a mover and shaker in Nashville through his real estate and other business interests and his involvement in public service. He chaired the state Board of Education in the 1980s, and was chosen by Mayor Bill Purcell to head a task force on education in Metro.

Andrews probably is not among the city's richest white citizens, but it's fair to say he is among the most influential. He's big on volunteerism and community building, on reaching out across racial and economic lines. He was the instigator of Leadership Nashville, a forum for dialogue that in the past two decades or so has lured and coerced more than 1,000 people—often strangers of different social, political, and economic stripes—to spend a year learning about their city and each other. "You don't get past the race issue until you create personal friendships," Andrews said emphatically. Many of his alumni agree.

Since the 1970s, Andrews said, Nashville has done a fair job of rising above its racial biases—"better than a lot of communities. We've been blessed with a steady economy, a strong religious community, an educated black middle class. That doesn't make everything rosy, but it has certainly helped. We haven't gotten what I think is a real measure of success, though."

Specifically citing the immigrant community, he said, "We've got to be very proactive at including these folks in all aspects of Nashville life, and we really haven't done very well at it. "

Hispanics are not a united group, said Andrews. Of the various Asian nationalities, he related this story: "Seven or eight years ago, a delegation of Asians came to see me. They said, 'We're all settled in Nashville, our kids do better than your kids in school, and we're going to be economically successful. But we can't seem to get any leadership positions. What can we do?'

"I said, 'You're not involved. What you're doing is your thing, and you think excellence is the key. But you've got to step out into the volunteer community. How many of you have volunteered for anything?' Not one. 'This is a community of volunteers; we share. If you don't become part of the social fabric of the community, you're not going anywhere.'

"I never heard from them again," Andrews said. "Somehow that notion of reaching across cultures is not in their background. If you want to connect cultures, somebody's got to step out. And I don't really think we've done that very much. I've said the same thing to Hispanic folks, too. It's hard to reach people who try to isolate themselves."

Isolation is where we are, however—in some ways, almost as separate as in the days of Old Nashville. Far from abandoning course, though, Andrews expressed his optimism that the city was poised to move into a new era: "We've got a very good opportunity to achieve racial harmony on a level playing field. We've got very good young people coming along in the communities who can work together, and will. I think people will step up."

Nashville is my hometown. Every time I come back to it, I'm reminded again of how it was, how it's changed, and how it hasn't. This time, I thought of it in comparison to the scores of cities and towns I have visited as a journalist over the past 30 years. In all those places, no matter their size or shape or complexion, I've witnessed essentially the same drama: people experimenting with different ways to adapt to one another and to the world around them. All have fallen short of achieving the utopian dream of total harmony. Most have been unable to share their fears, shed their fears, and deal with other people as equals. Still, many have tried and gotten impressive results.

This town is no different. Nashville is at a crucial juncture in its history. We are

What present-day Nashvillians make of their city may soon be overshadowed by what their children and grandchildren make of it. East Literature School classmates Thamesha Brewster and Lauren Andai, co-writers of a catchy tune called "The Magnet School Blues," are representative of a much more broadly defined younger generation growing up in Nashville now.

not yet a truly diverse city, but we are about to become one, and the real question is, Can we do it right? The faces of Asia, Latin America, Africa, Europe, and the Middle East will be present in all walks of Nashville life. The prayers of Hindus, Muslims, and Buddhists will echo with those of Protestants and Catholics and Jews. Spanish will be a close second to English in our classrooms and marketplaces. We can see these challenges as opportunities to grow or as threats to the status quo. The choice is ours.

Too often, I have heard Old Nashville speaking as if it had to protect the status quo in order to grow, when in fact healthy growth will be impossible if the established and privileged sections of the city are too self-satisfied or too insecure to reform themselves. Too often, I have heard the New Nashville talking as if it had already decided how to relate to Old Nashville, black and white. Our new Asian residents might want to remember that many young Americans, including some Nashvillians—one being 19-year-old George Joyce, a child of the projects like Charles Davis, and a Pearl High School classmate of mine in 1964—who died in Vietnam fighting to expand the freedoms we all enjoy here today. The world is smaller than we realize.

We—the Old and New—have within us the ability to become a city that embraces racial and cultural diversity. Doing so would make us a deeper, more interesting, more productive society. It would take sacrifice, open-mindedness, and a willingness to look at the world through new lenses, but it can be done.

Nashville could be different. It could become a city second to none in this century. For all of its faults, this big patch in the middle of Tennessee is a community. It has drawn people of varied backgrounds to this region for centuries. We might not like one another every day, all the time, but we love Nashville. For that reason alone, we need to get it right in the 21st century.

Marchinko clocks in at two hours and 26 minutes, while Nashvillian Maureen Manning leads local women with a time of two hours and 58 minutes. Along the route, runners are greeted with cheers, live music and cups of water. . . . **The Asian restaurant** The Orchid in Brentwood gives Middle Tennessee its first taste of the Chinatown lunchtime specialty, dim sum, since the old Peking Garden restaurant on Division Street closed a few years ago. Carts dispense steamed dumplings and other delicacies for $2.95 per stackable tray. At the end of the meal, the bill is calculated by counting the trays. May the sum never dim.

30—**A mentally disabled man** becomes the fourth person to die in a month's time in police-related incidents. Calvin Champion, 32, becomes agitated in a van outside a Babies R Us store on Nolensville Road, hitting his caregiver's 3-year-old daughter on the head and beating on the windows. When police arrive, he rips the caregiver's shirt and grabs an officer by the throat. Champion, whose disability has left him unable to speak, is subdued with pepper spray and pinned face-down to the ground by three officers. They call for medical help when he starts vomiting. Paramedics arrive and attempt to give him CPR, but he is pronounced dead at Southern Hills Medical Center. An autopsy will be performed. . . . **Patrons pronounce** the restoration of the East Branch Library a smashing success. Built in 1919, the Gallatin Road library was one of 1,689 public libraries across the country funded by philanthropist Andrew Carnegie. But its classic look had been "modernized" in an urban renewal frenzy back in the early 1960s. Thanks to a $778,685-renovation project, the library has recaptured its earlier glory. . . . **In Carthage, Tenn.,** Tracy Mayberry's toilet backs up. No one thinks much about it at the time.

"A New American Community"

by Carrie Ferguson

A decade ago, finding a plantain in Nashville was possible mainly through word-of-mouth. It went something like this:

"Hey, you just moved here? Miss the Cuban food? You know, they sell plantains and black beans at a little grocery on Church Street. You don't have to have food mailed to you from home."

And so there, against the market's far wall on the left, many an isolated Hispanic newcomer found an antidote for homesickness—right in front of the garlic mojo marinade sauce, Bijol seasoning, and Bustelo coffee. Food from home, sitting on shelves near seaweed for Japanese sushi, English scone mix, Australian vegemite, and Indian biryani sauce.

Today, plantains are a staple, even at Kroger. So are cactus pears, jicama, and papayas. They're as common as the sounds of Spanish, Hindi, Kurdish, and Laotian on Nashville's streets and in its schools. It took just a few short years in the 1990s for Nashville to move beyond white bread and no crust. It had to. Today, one in every seven Nashvillians is foreign-born.

As the dizzying pace of change is incorporated into the collective psyche, the city and surrounding counties are learning to bend and adapt—not without frustration—to the thousands of immigrants and refugees who have arrived, with more certain to follow. City leaders debate how—or whether—they can provide enough ESL classes (English as a Second Language), and respond to new transportation, housing, and health-care needs. Health-care workers have had to learn to recognize certain customs, like female circumcision, that to them may seem abhorrent and backward. Teachers have had to learn not to touch the heads of Asian children, for that is where the soul resides, and to remember that pork, the Southern staple, is not eaten by Muslim children. Many businesses have scrambled to keep up with the changes, too, encouraging staff to take Spanish classes and posting *Se Habla Espanol* signs in shop windows. Some employers have gone as far as Europe and Latin America looking for workers.

Organized community groups, especially in South Nashville, have embraced and welcomed these changes, offering meeting space and classes in language and finance. In return, they have experienced neighborhood revitalization, school expansion, and commercial growth.

While the citizenry adjusts, the newcomers are going about the business of settling in, finding work in everything from banking to housekeeping, enrolling in school, opening businesses. They've started community organizations like the Kurdish Watch Foundation, the Refugee Womens' Association, and chambers of commerce for Hispanics, Asians, and Africans. They've founded Buddhist and Hindu temples and Muslim mosques, and started newspapers in their own languages. In spite of the linguistic and cultural barriers, they're adapting—as this country's immigrants have always done.

"Now it feels like home," says 33-year-old Tony Perez. "There was nothing when I came here." Perez is a Mexican national who arrived in 1988 to paint houses and send money back home. He stayed to become an entrepreneur and reach for the American Dream. He's now the owner of Latino's Market on Thompson Place, in the heart of South Nashville, where nearly half of Metro's more than 25,000 Hispanics live (at least that many more live elsewhere in Middle Tennessee).

There have been immigrants in Nashville—Greeks, Germans, Italians—for well over a century. Fleeing famine, war, and political oppression, they came to America from all over the world, and in places like Nashville they blended in—finding shelter, learning English, getting an education, climbing up the economic ladder. Later they came from places like Kurdistan, Iraq, Korea, and Cuba, but the process was essentially the same.

It wasn't until the 1970s that resettlement agencies opened the doors here and began to bring in refugees fleeing turmoil and seeking personal freedom. This influx reached tidal-wave proportions in the early 1990s, when Nashville's booming economy offered an inviting contrast to unrest around the world. The resettlement of refugees locally is done mainly by three faith-based agencies—World Relief (Protestant), Catholic Charities, and Jewish Family Service—under contract with the federal government. Over the past quarter-century, these humanitarian organizations have largely molded the changing ethnic makeup of every American community, simply by directing the flow of refugee groups—Laotians here, Bosnians there, Sudanese or Salvadorans or Sikhs elsewhere.

Once in their new communities, the immigrants have filled the jobs that go begging in a full-employment economy, and also in certain skilled crafts where acute shortages exist. South and East Nashville, with the most inexpensive rentals, became target neighborhoods, and remain the areas where high concentrations of the foreign-born live. With small budgets and lots of donated goods and services, the resettlement agencies strive to get each new family on its feet and moving toward self-sufficiency.

Refugees from Iraq began arriving after the Persian Gulf War, placed here because they could easily find jobs and get a hand from those who came before them. Men and women from Somalia and Sudan came to escape mayhem and political turmoil; Russian Jews arrived seeking religious freedom; Bosnians came fleeing war and ethnic cleansing. And the young Mexicans, Salvadorans, and Guatemalans came, too—not as refugees, but as economic immigrants, most with no legal papers or right to be here. Yet they found jobs in construction, restaurants, and hotels—green card or not. Employers often turned a blind eye to the details of documentation; what they wanted was skilled and willing hands.

Nashville was building its arena in 1994, Brentwood was building fancy executive homes, and rural counties needed help picking tobacco and gutting chickens. Greater Nashville added 160,000 new jobs in just ten years, and it is widely acknowledged that without the immigrant bricklayers, drywallers, and metal workers, the projects might not have been finished on time. Many a Middle Tennessee farmer also thanked God and the government for the migrants.

"Our population would have decreased without the foreign-born. Our economy would have faltered, and building in Nashville would have been a challenge," said Carter Moody, an administrator of the Nashville Task Force on Refugees and Immigrants. Moody once worked for the Council of Community Services, and it was he who put together a directory of resources for services to immigrants and refugees. He found help—offered by church groups, city agencies, and everything in between—available in seventeen Middle Tennessee counties, showing that the reach is wide and deep. "Even little Bedford County had 8,000 new people working at the chicken plant," he said.

To be sure, it's not all about booming business and International Day celebrations here. Hispanics have complained about police harassment. They say government services aren't readily available; barriers of language and simple transportation keep them out. Africans and African Americans have clashed; often they don't relate to each other, despite the commonalities of skin color and motherland. Africans, their advocates report, have a hard time adjusting to minority status—and worse, to being a minority within a minority. Laotian teenagers are stuck with an unwanted reputation as gang members, and foreign-born women often do not know how to drive and report feeling isolated and depressed at home.

For their part, native-born Middle Tennesseans have voiced frustration about their neighbors who don't speak English. They express concern, verbally and in newspaper letters to the editor, about jobs lost to immigrants, about neighborhoods changing right before their eyes, about the assumption (incorrect) that illegal immigrants don't pay taxes. Many natives don't know the difference between refugees and immigrants, legal or not.

Lee Eby is head of the resettlement agency World Relief, which has helped thousands of refugees dig roots in Middle Tennessee soil. His office receives the occasional phone call from angry Nashvillians who claim the resettled refugees get stuff they don't get: cars from the government, a tax-free life, money to live on for years. None of it is true.

"There is a percolating and unfortunate tension between some of the original, longer-term natives and the relative newcomers, simply because newcomers are not a known factor," said Moody, a consultant who once worked for the Metro Human Relations Commission. "Blacks and whites may have tensions, but they know each other. People from other countries, cultures, and faiths certainly are benefiting the local economy and culture, but there is still some tension." Echoed 15-year-old Nereyda Barron, whose Mexican family owns a bridal and western wear shop on Nolensville Road: "I remember when we first got here, the Americans would look at us funny. They weren't used to seeing us. Now I think they're used to us." Nashville is more cosmopolitan today than it was a decade ago, and much of that credit goes to the immigrants and refugees who have painted the city in rich hues, say those who celebrate the changes. The world is reflected here at last, and not just through cuisine. Those citizens who embrace it will benefit by learning firsthand about other cultures and customs. The world is, after all, a much smaller place these days.

"My child is almost school-age, and even in prekindergarten, she plays with an international group of kids that includes children from China, Latin America, Iran, and India," said attorney Mary Griffin, who co-hosts a Spanish-language informational radio program and specializes in representing the foreign-born. "The challenge for Nashville now is to communicate and integrate. Provincialism leads to prejudice and it is based on fear," Eby said. "When you break down barriers, you break down fear."

An alliance of businesses, social service agencies, and immigrant-refugee groups calling itself the Nashville New American Coalition is seeking ways to do just that: break down barriers. With a grant from the U.S. Office of Refugee Resettlement, the coalition is engaged in a pilot venture called "Building the New American Community." Its aim: to integrate the foreign-born into the wider community and advance the voice and progress of refugees and immigrants living here.

Garrett Harper, research director for the Nashville Area Chamber of Commerce, wrote most of the grant proposal. He sees the program as a citywide opportunity "to begin new conversations and ask a deeper level of questions" about Nashville's future as a "new American community." Coalition members say they hope to involve both the foreign-born and the native-born, so that they too may be transformed into "New Americans" who welcome the opportunity to be renewed and influenced by the creativity, culture, and commerce of their new neighbors.

Carrie Ferguson, whose parents were born in Cuba, has been a feature writer at The Tennessean *since 1990.*

African-American Nashville Now

by JEFF OBAFEMI CARR

Back in the day/ when visionaries of the African-American race/graced the academic halls of Fisk University/ there existed a man/who wrote out a plan/ for his people to be free. This "Sweet Land of Liberty"/ conflicted him as he/ dared to dream of a better place/ for Africans in American history. James Weldon Johnson was his name,/ Lift E'vry Voice and Sing his claim to fame./ God's Trombones, sermons in verse, and other works of poetry, prose, and song/ placed him high up in the intellectual universe./ What brought him here to Nashville?/ A desire to teach and thereby reach/ the hearts and minds of people/—his own, and perhaps a few others./ He lived at 911 18th Avenue North./ The house stands empty now, smack dab in the midst of his brothers./ From there in 1934/ he wrote a little book/ that dared to look/ at the lives of Black folk at the time./ Titled Negro Americans, What Now?/ *it outlined specifically how/ we could overcome./ Sixty-six years later,/ the task may be greater/ for we still face a long journey home/ to that place/ where race/ is no longer the subject/ of a book/ or essay/ or poem.*

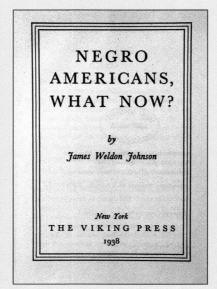

Just as James Weldon Johnson dared to take a sobering look at the state of race in America during his time, so must I embrace this opportunity to peer into the window of the house of African Americans in Nashville as the city makes a wide, sweeping turn into the next phase of its history. Let me warn you that not much has changed since Johnson's day—at least insofar as Nashville's African-American citizenry is concerned.

When Johnson's *Negro Americans* essay fell into my hands, I hungrily devoured it, hoping to get a picture of the past that would show me what *was*, so that I might better recognize and come to terms with what *is* today. I had not expected to discover that these two pictures would be as closely synchronized as they are.

Let me give you a glimpse at some of the areas Johnson explored in his book, and juxtapose them with today's state of affairs in Education, Politics, Interracial Relationships, and Stereotypes.

Education: In 1934, Johnson noted that, by and large, there was a lack of effective cultural education. Citing the field of history, he pointed out that it was taught "from a textbook that completely ignores the Negro or mentions him only in condescending or derogatory terms." He could have written that yesterday. Although a movement was launched in the late 1980s by the African-American Cultural Alliance to have Black history integrated into mainstream education, it never quite made it into all the textbooks and the classrooms. During Black History Month we hear of Dr. King, of course, and the usual cadre of "Black achievers" (Sojourner Truth, Harriett Tubman, and—since the movie—Malcolm X). But in most school systems (including Metro's), no established program is in place to assure that education and its peripheral elements (test preparation, attendance, cultural sensitivity) are fair and equitable. Although the ruse of "integration" was hatched after Johnson's day, the Metro School Board's recent "victory" in the federal courts that makes way for a return to "neighborhood schools" sets the tone for what is popularly called "re-segregation." Translation: White flight x 10.

Politics: In 1934, full voting rights were yet to be won. Thankfully, that has changed—although half or more don't exercise those rights in Nashville with any consistency, whether they be White, Black, or Other. Johnson advocated a focus on local politics as opposed to national elections, arguing that Blacks would have a more realistic chance of controlling their destiny in the areas of education, justice, and the like. The same principle applies here. Presently, the Metro Council (a body created to include all of Davidson County, in part to prevent Blacks from attaining majority status as Whites fled the city) has its highest-ever proportion of Black members—11 of 40. But how effective can this more representative city legislature be? It has been left with meager resources at the outset, following a wave of lavish spending by outgoing Mayor Phil Bredesen and the previous council on huge taxpayer-funded capital projects, such as the new arena and football stadium. The same officials also doled out a variety of subsidies to Dell Computer, HCA, the Country Music Association, and other private enterprises, also at the expense of the tax-paying public.

James Weldon Johnson in his 1934 assessment said there was a need for leaders with "unquestionable integrity, who put the best interest of the race before personal interests." Those "race leaders" were rare in his day, and they are still at a premium today. Trustworthy, issue-oriented leaders can be found here and there, but too many are more interested in being remembered for their style of dress or their verbal quips than for anything lasting they've contributed. We're still waiting for strong and effective leadership—of any race—to seize the brass ring.

Interracial Relationships: Johnson argued for the "establishment and maintenance of friendly interracial intercourse." Well, there are many more interracial couples now, and they are more openly received publicly than in Johnson's time—but somehow, I don't think that's what he was talking about. To Nashville's benefit, the Race Relations Institute at Fisk University, started in 1944 by Charles S. Johnson, Fisk's first Black president, was regenerated and began hosting summer conferences on race in 1997. With dialogues that returned the likes of Fisk alumnus and celebrated historian John Hope Franklin and Nashville native Mary Frances Berry, chair of the U.S. Commission on Civil Rights, to James Weldon Johnson's old stomping ground, the RRI sparked a renewal of discussions on the topic of race that made waves all the way up to the White House. Those discussions could hardly be characterized as "friendly," though; too few of us are able to disagree without being disagreeable. And, the Whites who attend these dialogues are not the ones who hold power in industry, banking, politics and the like. They tend instead to be old liberals or hippies from the '60s, or their descendants—who, with their tie-dyed shirts and matted dreadlocks, are as excluded from the power circles of Nashville as African-Americans in general.

Stereotypes, Art, & Money: As an artist/activist, I share a special bond with Professor Johnson. During his time, stereotyping of African-Americans in the performing arts (stage, film, radio, and later, television) was entering its Golden Age. Transparent, subservient, one-dimensional, menial Black images dominated the art of the mainstream: Mammies, Coons, Buffoons, Sex-Crazed Bucks. Nashville has kept this tradition alive and well. A quick survey of the plays produced over the past few years by the city's "premier" theatrical organizations shows that Blacks, if cast at all, were offered roles that fit snugly into one of the aforementioned categories of stereotype.

You might be led by this evidence to believe that there are few, if any, Black playwrights, directors, or technicians working in the world today. Having lived in New York and worked in other cities across the country, I know better. There is a wealth of quality art being created by African-American artists. But do we see it in Nashville, on the stages of the larger arts companies—the Tennessee Repertory Theatre, the Nashville Opera, the Nashville Ballet—or even from any of the fledgling companies whose stated purpose at first was to expose the city to new and avant-garde art? Nope.

Such perverse color blindness led Johnson, two-thirds of a century ago, to this assertion: "Instead of begging white writers and artists to treat us with more consideration, we should rear a group of Negro Americans who can smash the old stereotype." Such chronic myopia still in evidence today leads me to the same conclusion.

We see the beginning of a determined, self-actualizing African-American arts movement in Nashville. Dance companies like the Village Cultural Arts Center have begun to establish themselves as a strong, positive force in the larger community. In the theatrical world, Black Taffeta and Burlap Theatre continues in its mission to develop and showcase minority talent; the American Negro Playwright Theater promises to build a strong audience through its residency relationship with Tennessee State University; and the Amun Ra Theater, with its commitment to youth drama training and to discovering new writers and actors, as well as exposing the public to Black classics, is also becoming a major force in regional theater.

All this ferment bodes well for the future of Black art and the smashing of stereotypes. Nonetheless, these ventures don't receive a proportional share of community support, even though African-American Nashvillians pay their proportional share of taxes. Money is the acid test of fairness. The larger and more prominent organizations expect public and corporate support and private philanthropy, and for the most part they get it, while African-American organizations struggle just to keep the lights on. The more things seem to change, the more they truly do stay the same.

Sitting on the steps in front of James Weldon Johnson's slowly deteriorating home near the Fisk campus, I thought back on the past 66 years and wondered what progress has been made by and for African Americans in Nashville. It would be too negative to say that no progress has been made. But to acknowledge that the same issues Johnson confronted remain before us now is itself a damning statement about a town that is being touted by government and industry and the image-makers as a progressive community, "a city too busy to hate," á la Atlanta. We have a very long way to go before we can honestly stake that claim.

Will Nashville ever cross over into the Promised Land of equality, mutual respect, fairness, and brotherly love? We are not given to know. For myself, I can only hope and pray that when the next "century book" is written in 2100, people can read James Weldon Johnson's words, and my words, and say to their children: "This is the way it used to be. Thank God it's not that way any longer."

---

jeff obafemi carr is an actor, director, poet, and publisher in Nashville, his hometown.

Only in your dreams—and at Business Expo 2000, a two-day event at the Nashville Convention Center—is there a machine that spits out legal tender like a popcorn popper. Old money, new money, play money: It was all on the table as Nashville went careening into the 21st century.

POWER STEERING

by E. Thomas Wood

Amid plentiful signs of progress, Nashville's gainfully employed hustled through their usual workday routine on Monday, May 15, 2000. Signage crews hauling down old corporate logos and putting up new ones, office workers going through their daily motions behind the smoked glass of downtown office buildings, a crew setting up folding chairs for yet another groundbreaking ceremony on the Vanderbilt University campus—the rhythm of routine industry produced its familiar hum. If the employees carrying out these rituals invested their labor that morning with any particular emotion, an outsider probably would not have noticed.

But many hearts beat with conflicted passions that day, especially among the city's leadership caste. Some of Nashville's most powerful individuals were caught up in the activities of that Monday—an ordinary day, but also one that, in hindsight, seems momentous, a day when the balance of power in Nashville changed forever. For Nashvillians across the spectrum of class and wealth, the changes would be by turns promising, profitable, disruptive, and disturbing, all in varying measures not readily predictable by social status. By day's end, the question of who would control Nashville's future—the question of where money, power, and leadership were destined to be concentrated in the new century—would be just a little harder to answer than it had been the day before.

Ascending into the gathering heat of that morning in the buckets of cherry-pickers, workers from Cummings Sign Company were taking down the last vestiges of First American National Bank. The signage had remained temporarily on the branches and downtown headquarters of First American, Nashville's last major independent bank, after AmSouth Bancorp in Birmingham, Alabama, purchased it in 1999. By the time the work crews hauled the signs to the scrap heap, many of the hundreds of bank employees who had been laid off or who had otherwise departed in the wake of the deal had long since landed new jobs in the bustling Middle Tennessee economy. Some were plotting to compete with AmSouth by launching new, local banks.

Someday, perhaps, one of those new institutions would be as important a factor in the city's life as its major banks once were—not just holding deposits and making loans, but influencing civic affairs in manifold ways and grooming a new generation of local power brokers. Eventually, perhaps, at a homegrown bank or some other institution, there would be a forum similar to First American's executive dining room, where the city's top business people and politicians used to lunch regularly with bank officers, far from the prying eyes of the public, discussing much more than banking. Perhaps such a new forum, known only to the cognoscenti, had already been established—or perhaps leadership in Nashville would take different forms in the new century.

Downtown, at the headquarters of regional investment bankers J.C. Bradford & Company, the partners were packing up their tombstones. A tombstone is what you get after you help put together a big financial deal, such as a multimillion-dollar issue of municipal bonds, a corporate merger, or the initial public offering of a company. Just about every little etched-glass memento crowded onto the shelves of a Bradford veteran represented hundreds of seemingly endless days and nights of team effort expended, innumerable

1—**Mayday!** State legislators are rattled by the sight and sound of 250 protesters marching up Capitol Hill from the Bicentennial Mall. Their cry—"Tax reform now!"—echoes down the hallowed halls. Representing more than 25 groups, including Tennesseans for Fair Taxation and the League of Women Voters, this "May Day SOS" coalition marches to protest raising Tennessee's sales tax on food. In the throng of protesters, a man dressed as a giant empty dinner plate brandishes a knife and fork the size of hockey sticks. Three more people, including Nashvillian Marsha Hyne, place a life preserver at the Capitol's entrance. The circus on Capitol Hill is only pitching its tent. . . . **Across the street** at the War Memorial Building, a rally to protest the low wages paid to day-care workers draws about three dozen adults. The starting salary for most day-care workers in the city is $5.25 an hour—less than a first-day fry cook at McDonald's. . . . **Setting a bold new low** for sweeps-month hucksterism, WTVF-Channel 5 airs "The Spring Break Tapes," a heavy-breathing indictment of licentious behavior by Nashville-area students during spring break in Florida. The "exposé" shows bikini-clad girls baring their breasts and getting pawed and nuzzled. WTVF attracts the most viewers in the 10 p.m. time slot for the trial month, but the peep-hole footage makes the station's management an instant laughing-stock . . . . **A judge rules** that convicted killer Paul Dennis Reid is mentally competent to be tried for the murder of three people during the robbery of a McDonald's in Hermitage in March 1997. If convicted, he will likely receive his seventh death penalty. Reid was previously convicted of killings related to a string of fast-food robberies that shook the Midstate in 1997, including the murder of two employees at a Captain D's restaurant in Nashville

For over a half-century, three major banks and two insurance companies with local roots dominated the Nashville economic scene. After the last of these, First American National Bank, fell under absentee ownership, the lowering of its signs in May of 2000 was symbolic of the end of "home rule."

take-out meals consumed over conference tables, hours of delicate negotiations brought to fruition, and millions in fees earned for the investment bank. Tombstones are happy things at a place like Bradford.

Now it was time, though, to bury the tombstones in newspaper padding and cardboard boxes: a bittersweet if not funereal occasion. For Bradford was no longer the dealmaker. Its own deal had been cut at the end of April, when the large New York brokerage house PaineWebber Group bought it for $620 million in cash. Not that the tombstoners would suffer in material terms: Upon the closing of the deal later in the year, the windfalls to the company's owners would include more than $50 million for Senior Partner J.C. Bradford Jr., whose father had founded the company in 1927, at the apex of Nashville's influence as the "Wall Street of the South." At least 26 other local partners would receive amounts ranging from $2 million to $18 million each; still more would get smaller but quite substantial payouts. Perhaps inevitably, with so much money on the

In the boom-boom '90s, J.C. Bradford & Co. reached its zenith as a regional banking and investment firm. In its seven-plus decades, the firm had helped create and multiply the fortunes of local companies and investors alike. Its roster of veteran equity traders like Harold Wilson (above) was the main prize sought by New York's PaineWebber Group when it acquired Bradford in 2000.

One of the giants of the New York-based brokerage industry, PaineWebber, already had a presence in Nashville when it paid well over a half-billion dollars in cash for the J.C. Bradford firm. Just a month after it closed the Bradford deal, PaineWebber itself sold out to a Swiss conglomerate.

and the killing of two women who worked at a Baskin-Robbins ice-cream store in Clarksville.
. . . **Author and scholar** Chaim Potok, noted for his novels about the Jewish experience, speaks on the Holocaust before a packed hall at The Temple. His appearance coincides with a worldwide day of mourning and reflection on the deaths of 6 million Jews in Nazi concentration camps during World War II. "There were 103 members of our family in Europe," Potok tells the hushed audience. "No one survived."

2—R. Clayton McWhorter, former chairman of Nashville-based Columbia/HCA Healthcare Corp., the nation's largest hospital company, announces he'll step down from the health-care giant's board to focus on other ventures. McWhorter, 66, served as Columbia/HCA chairman in 1995-96 after his company, HealthTrust, merged with Columbia/HCA. He remained on the board after Dr. Thomas Frist Jr. took over as Columbia/HCA's chief executive officer in 1997, in the midst of the company's federal fraud investigation. . . . **His courtroom** clogged with 12 defendants in the same marijuana conspiracy hearing, General Sessions Judge John P. Brown sets a local record for the largest number of incarcerated defendants in court for a single case: an Apr. 19 drug bust, in which dealers with walkie-talkies negotiated the handoff of 100 pounds of pot at a Nolensville Road car wash. Seven people were arrested on the spot; the trail led to more arrests at two residences on Antioch Pike, where another 280 pounds of marijuana were found. Eleven of the 12 defendants are Hispanic and must be outfitted with headphones that translate the hearing into Spanish. Ten defense attorneys are present. . . . **West Nashville residents** heading home on Centennial Boulevard at 9 p.m. are startled to find the street blocked from 39th Avenue North to 51st and the sky flickering with the lights of emergency vehicles. An explosion at the Rhodia Company, a Nashville chemical plant,

table, some would balk at how the spoils were divided. By year's end, disgruntled ex-partners were plotting litigation, claiming the deal had shortchanged them.

A third scene that Monday morning, May 15, featured a newer variety of money and power. At the corner of Pierce Avenue and 22nd Avenue South, Vanderbilt University broke ground on the Monroe Carell Jr. Children's Hospital, funded in part by a $20-million donation from one local businessman who, unlike many in Nashville's old guard, remained firmly in control of his business.

Monroe Carell was a native Nashvillian and a member of the Belle Meade Country Club. He and his wife, Ann, moved in the social circles of the elite. Still, Carell was cut from a different cloth than many in the city's privileged class. He had earned his money the hard way. The New Nashville rightfully boasted of its entrepreneurial energy, but it still bore traces of the "son-in-law town" that was the Old Nashville, where heredity and marriage were the key determinants of power. Carell, it was true, had taken over a family business of running parking lots in the 1970s, but he had turned the sleepy little firm into something his father could not have imagined. By 2000, Central Parking Corporation operated more than 4,000 parking facilities throughout North America and Europe, and as far afield as Malaysia and Chile. No company in the world threatened its dominance in this field of business. On this day, some of Nashville's leading businesspeople must have gazed ruefully, if not enviously, at a peer who had become hunter rather than prey in the global marketplace.

Money made, money given: Do these in combination amount to power wielded? That equation, in some form, is surely part of the governing dynamic of every American city. Acknowledging as much does not mean belittling either the real accomplishment of many wealth-creators or the real altruism in the hearts of many (or most, or all) donors whose gifts help to make a city a better place. But it does invite the question: When out-of-town companies take control of industries that once accounted for a significant share (qualitatively if not quantitatively) of local wealth, do they assume a power that trumps the authority of even the wealthiest local individuals?

One by one, the headquarters buildings of Nashville financial institutions changed names around the turn of the century. Two of the oldest—the Life and Casualty and National Life insurance companies—were the first to go (though the L&C Tower retained its name), and others soon followed. First American (left) became the AmSouth Bank Building; The SunTrust Center traced back to Third National Bank; and First Union Tower (right), which had roots in the Nashville Trust Company, now is known as Firstar Tower.

has belched a cloud of phosphine gas over the area near 4600 Centennial Blvd., and the Cumberland River. The flammable gas, which packs a garliclike stench, can be lethal in high doses, and dramatic TV news reports temporarily scare the hell out of viewers. But the factory blaze is extinguished by 10:40 p.m., and residents are home by 11:15, breathing easier.

3—**Behind closed doors,** House Democrats and Republicans scramble to fix the state's fiscal woes without inciting the wrath of sundry vested interests. Both parties are happy to leave Gov. Don Sundquist crying in the wilderness about the need for a state income tax, but there is still the matter of that budget shortfall, variously estimated at between $300 million and $400 million. By the end of the day, Democrats and Republicans alike claim to be formulating remedies—but since they're meeting

One after another, the old institutional centers of moneyed power had vanished from Nashville over the past two decades, dispersing into the hands of local individuals great quantities of money and, sometimes, power—both in search of a purpose. For a great many of the beneficiaries themselves, and for many more in the community at large, these cashed-out investments were paying a dividend of anxiety.

Such were the social and economic peculiarities of the time that the millionaire tombstone collectors of J.C. Bradford & Company may have been more likely to feel disquiet over the firm's deal than others lower on the organizational chart with whom they shared a fate of impending unemployment. On May 15, rumors and gallows humor were the order of the day for employees waiting to learn how deeply PaineWebber would pare back Bradford's organization.

To former Army officer Nathan Bedford Forrest Shoaf, a partner on Bradford's corporate finance staff, military history provided an analogy for the moment. Shoaf felt a kinship with the Romans of the fifth century A.D., besieged by Alaric and his Visigoths. "We knew we were sitting there in the ruins of a once-proud empire, and that our days were almost up," he recalled. "We knew the Goths could arrive at any moment—and when they got here, there would be a vast sacking. No business going on. Most of us were just showing up every day out of a sense of meaning, a sense of community."

On Wednesday, May 17, the first wave of department closures would be announced. More would follow in June, idling several hundred employees in all ranks of the organization. Shoaf was one of them; he was picked up by the Nashville office of a Memphis-based brokerage firm, Morgan Keegan & Company—which, within a few months, would be swallowed by a bigger fish in Birmingham. "So I answer to Memphis, who answers to Birmingham," Shoaf mused. "I'm an outpost of an outpost." In July, the business formerly known as J.C. Bradford & Company would also become an outpost of an outpost when it sold out to Swiss financial conglomerate UBS AG. At the local level, the disappearance of deep-rooted companies with reliable old names was profoundly unsettling, not only for customers and employees, but for the larger community's sense of identity and well-being.

There's never a good time to lose a job, especially for workers in the midst of other important life events—like April Hayes in Bradford's bond department and Shane Steely in its mail room, who were expecting their first child within a couple of months. Yet, getting a good job had never been easier in the Metro Nashville area, where the unemployment rate stood at 2.4 percent. The more vexing question on many minds, even of those who might never need to work again, was what kind of city Nashville would be with no domestic financial structure to call its own.

Bradford was gone. The city's other major brokerage house, Equitable Securities, had sold out in 1998. First American was gone. A succession of mergers in the 1980s and '90s had devoured the other mainstay commercial banks in town, including Commerce Union, which had played a political kingmaker role rivaling First American's, and Third National, a key financial supporter of Nashville's music and health-care industries in their early days. Nashville was no longer the Wall Street of the South, just as it had ceased to be the Hartford of the South after a Texas-based insurance company, American General, bought up the National Life & Accident Insurance Company's $4.6 billion in assets in 1982.

Of all these transitions, one prominent Nashville attorney fretted late in 2000, "the banking piece of it is what causes me the most concern for the future." (Since his firm had banks as clients, he preferred not to speak for attribution.) "The next time there's a recession, what little lending is done will likely be done closer to home. We are now no longer 'home.' When things aren't going so well, you're generally more likely to apply hard formulas in the hinterlands—and we're the hinterlands now." Like many among the elite, this lawyer also worried that out-of-town owners would not support charitable causes in Nashville at the level their local predecessors had. And he saw an ill-starred precedent: "I would cite the bankruptcy of the symphony in the mid-1980s as something that would not have happened had National Life not been sold." (This insider was not the only one haunted by the Nashville Symphony's financial collapse in 1987-88; as we shall see, many in the city's white-tie-and-tails crowd were preoccupied during 2000 with one grand effort to lay that memory to rest forever.)

More broadly, in Nashville as across America, local and familiar brand names continually gave way to out-of-town control by chains and conglomerates. In 2000, grocery shoppers still saw the logo of Purity Dairies on milk cartons, but after 73 years

clandestinely in what would seem to be a clear violation of the state Sunshine Law, nobody knows what those plans entail. Meanwhile, legislators celebrate "Asthma Awareness Day" on Capitol Hill in a fog of cigar and cigarette smoke. . . . **Lebanon-based** Cracker Barrel Old Country Store lays an egg with its book-giveaway to libraries across the country. The libraries that were supposed to benefit from the restaurant's chainwide literacy drive last August are being deluged with hundreds, even thousands of copies of the same titles. One Arizona library opens a shipment of 15,000 books to find 11,796 copies of the children's book *What Would Happen If*.

4—**An e-mail message** labeled "ILOVEYOU" is a good thing, right? Not to thousands of Middle Tennesseans and millions worldwide whose computers are attacked by the "Love Bug" virus. Once opened, the innocuous-looking message replaces files with infected copies, mails itself to every address in the user's e-mail address book, and tries to relay passwords to an address in the Philippines. Along with computer systems from Tokyo to Kenya, Nashville's servers reel from the assault. Metro's nearly 5,000 government e-mail accounts are shut down while as many as 30,000 infected messages are deleted. Businesses ranging from Columbia/ HCA to Bridgestone/Firestone are hit. By day's end, love has turned to hate. . . . **Nashvillians didn't know** they had it so good. A Rochester, Minn., consulting firm says Music City ranks 50th out of 51 U.S. cities in the amount of its total per capita tax burden. Nashville families in 1999 paid an average of $11,902 in taxes on incomes of $60,000. By contrast, New Yorkers paid $16,362. . . . **Cable behemoth Viacom** completes its $50-billion takeover of CBS. This means locally based Country Music Television and The Nashville Network, a.k.a. CBS Cable Networks, will be merged under the command of MTV Networks Chairman Tom Freston.

Before being bought out by Illinois-based Dean Foods in 1998, Purity Dairies was a model of local corporate ownership. The founding Ezell family, led by chairman and CEO Bill Ezell (center), still offered such personal touches as home delivery. To its credit, Dean has continued the service.

One of the two cable networks will not survive the year in Nashville.

5—**Speak of the devil.** MTV chief Tom Freston appears in Music City at the Opryland offices of CMT and TNN to survey his new babies. Freston announces his mission to create a newer, hipper national network, which shouldn't be hard: TNN's cutting-edge programming included 20-year-old reruns of *Dallas* and *The Dukes of Hazzard*. His prescription involves adding the World Wrestling Federation, the cheesy "professional wrestling" charade that is currently the most popular program on cable. . . . **B.A. Pargh,** the Nashville-based office-supplies wholesaler, announces its sale to Texas company Daisytek International for an undisclosed sum. Founder Bernard Pargh started out selling showerheads out of a station wagon in 1973; by 1978 he had sold the business to Service Merchandise. When SM went bankrupt in 1999, Pargh bought it back for $6 million. . . . **The New Nashville** in a nutshell: Mack's Country Kitchen, the all-night 21st Avenue greasy spoon once beloved by Vanderbilt students and Metro cops on the graveyard shift, now serves sashimi. Kenji Ohno, the Osaka native and eight-year Nashvillian who won a loyal following as sushi chef at Ichiban on Second Avenue, has turned the former Mack's into Ken's Sushi. For decades, Mack's slung burgers and plate lunches at all hours. A couple of years ago, it became an upscale dining spot called Cafe Luna. Regulars of the old Mack's eyed the cappuccino machine suspiciously and prodded croissants as if they were alien spawn.

6—**One of the city's** largest and most influential congregations, the massive Christ Church in the Hickory Hollow Mall area, celebrates a trio of 50-year milestones this weekend. On its 50th anniversary, the church honors Pastor L.H. Hardwick for his five decades in the pulpit, as well as his 50th year of wedded bliss with his wife, Montelle. When Hardwick

of independence, the Ezell family had sold the dairy company in 1998 to Illinois-based Dean Foods Company—which itself was soon to be gulped down by a larger competitor. Purity milk was still for sale at the nominally independent H.G. Hill supermarkets in town, but Oklahoma-based Fleming Companies had taken over the local Hill warehouse and now controlled what the stores sold. Homey hardware stores seemed a little emptier every year as The Home Depot's superstores bustled with do-it-yourselfers. Locally owned drugstores were a thing of the past, replaced by national chains that seemed to be fighting a scorched-earth battle for prime store sites on Nashville's street corners. The most notorious example of collateral damage from that competition had been the 1999 demolition—despite fierce community protests—of the Jacksonian, an old and widely admired apartment building on West End Avenue. In its place now sat a drive-thru Walgreens.

Ah, but we still had Central Parking Corporation. Nashville was still the one place that could tell the world: "Your asphalt is mine."

Early in 2000, Central Parking had reached a settlement to end a protracted tussle with federal antitrust authorities over its intended purchase of its closest competitor, Allright Corporation of Houston. ("Joel Klein, who also beat the hell out of Microsoft, was the [federal attorney] on our case," Carell recalled. "We probably were fortunate to get out with what we did.") In a city fretting over the predations of out-of-town corporate behemoths ranging from PaineWebber to Walgreens, Central Parking represented a unique inversion of the pattern: a local company with enough global might to arouse the suspicions of anti-monopoly forces.

Carell had briefly cracked the "*Forbes* 400" list of the nation's richest individuals in 1997, before dot-com upstarts nudged him out. Investors reacted to the Allright

Monroe Carell, chairman of Central Parking Corp., was thrust into the local spotlight in the 1990s, first when he steered a home-grown enterprise into an international corporation, and then when he bestowed millions of dollars on educational, artistic and medical charities in Nashville.

After assuming control of Central Parking from his father, Nashvillian Monroe Carell took the company to the top of its field. Having bought out its closest competitor, Texas-based Allright Parking, Central was by 2000 the dominant parking management company nationwide and also had extensive holdings in Europe, Asia and Latin America. As parking-lot prices escalated in downtown Nashville, so did grumbling about "price-gouging monopolies."

became pastor in 1950, three weeks into his marriage, the church was called Woodbine United Pentecostal and housed in a single building at the corner of Rose and Church streets off Nolensville Road. By 1956, it had 56 members. In 1977, it moved to a rocky five-acre site on Old Hickory Boulevard and changed its name to Christ Church Pentecostal, ultimately dropping the "Pentecostal" to accommodate an influx of Baptist and Church of Christ members. Today, it occupies 70 acres and boasts some 7,000 active members, including local politicians (Hardwick is U.S. Rep. Bob Clement's brother-in-law) and bigwigs in the country and contemporary-Christian music industries. In Nashville, musicians often say choosing a church is a career move in itself.

7—**Excitement greets the news** that Vanderbilt University will be the first school in the country to subscribe to the "book of life"—a vast computerized database of human genetic information that will give researchers powerful new tools for conducting cancer research, studying mental disorders and locating and identifying new genes. The cost of this subscription over several years could run into millions of dollars. Celera Genomics Group, the company compiling the database, has been criticized for selling access to information that many believe should be shared freely, but for the moment, the issue is moot: Celera's rough map of the human genetic code will not be finished until summer. . . . **Circle Players**, Nashville's oldest community theater group, continues its three-week run of *One Flew Over the Cuckoo's Nest* at TPAC's Johnson Theater. Charles Howard stars as the recalcitrant asylum inmate McMurphy, the role Jack Nicholson had in the 1975 film; Cinda McCain plays the iron-willed, authoritarian Nurse Ratched.

8—**Today's guest of honor** at Fisk University is a man who wasn't allowed to set foot in this country for almost 40 years. Civil rights activist Preston King, a deal with something less than enthusiasm, and Central Parking's stock was having a rocky 2000, but the Carell family stake was still worth roughly $400 million on May 15. In the last years of the 1990s, the Carells had embarked on a highly visible series of charitable efforts involving mainstay Nashville institutions. In addition to the Children's Hospital donation, they funded a $5-million library for the private girls' school Harpeth Hall, eight full-tuition scholarships for Vanderbilt students working their way through college, the principal gift for a new Catholic high school in Hendersonville, a donation of at least $1 million to the Nashville Symphony, and a permanent outdoor sculpture installation at Cheekwood.

More than a few locals quietly remarked on the irony of the Carell Woodland Sculpture Trail's establishment at more or less the same time large swaths of the city's former urban heart, Church Street, had been flattened for use as Central Parking spaces. By 2000, Carell's company and his family owned at least a dozen downtown lots and garages, with a total tax-appraised value approaching $10 million, and managed numerous other facilities in the city's center (though the antitrust settlement would require Central to divest itself of several facilities). Nashvillians accustomed to cheap and easy downtown parking howled as prices shot up during the 1990s, many blaming Central Parking for squeezing up rates as it squeezed out competitors. Carell's personal reputation as a fearsome and demanding manager further cemented Central Parking's notoriety for something less than model corporate citizenship.

It all may have been a bum rap. Central Parking didn't cause the department stores and other merchants of Church Street to wither and die; if any villain can be blamed with certainty for the decline, it's the car-loving, suburb-dwelling public. And Carell did not write the local ordinances giving property owners tax incentives to raze any building that is not producing a good stream of income—and no incentive to preserve beautiful or historic structures until a better use can be found for them. The sniping clearly rankled Carell. He said he became most vividly aware of the undercurrent of criticism at a meeting with Mayor Bill Purcell late in 2000. "I found out from the mayor's office that some of the people who I thought were my friends were, in fact, claiming that I had, that the company had, some sort of monopoly that was adversely affecting the business community," Carell sighed. He blamed publicity from the recent antitrust case for kindling local sentiment against Central Parking. "We are being accused of things unjustly," he said.

Well, then: Were all the donations meant to put forth a kinder, gentler image of Carell in the local public eye? He was offended at the notion his detractors might take such a cynical view. "I can stand their criticism, but if they thought I did it for material purposes, that would be totally unjust. I'd fight over that one," he said. "I'm not going to buy anybody's support. I might give to the politician for that purpose, but as far as the hospital or school or churches, absolutely not." (Federal Election Commission records show that Carell family members gave at least $125,000 to candidates for federal office between 1992 and 2000, with roughly equal amounts going to Democrats and Republicans alike.) "What we do in that area is our responsibility. It's totally our choice, and we do it because we think we've been fortunate and we ought to share."

It's not as though these were hard times—not for most Nashvillians, and certainly not for most of the commercial class. There were losers among the corporate winners, to be sure, but their sad fates could generally be explained away as unrepresentative of the overall economy. Service Merchandise Company, which had its roots in the now-extinct culture of small-town Jewish merchants in the South, and which grew to become one of the nation's major catalog and showroom retailers, was now in bankruptcy after years of fruitless attempts to adjust to the fickle tastes of shoppers. Pioneering restaurant chain Shoney's Incorporated, whose unpretentious offerings were a part of the fabric of life for a generation of diners in Nashville and beyond, had lost its footing. Every few months seemed to bring more bad news for Shoney's, continuing a downward financial spiral that had lasted for most of a decade.

Some of the more ambitious publicly held companies in town, especially in

In the topsy-turvy corporate world of mergers, acquisitions and globalization, giant chain stores like Best Buy (above) dominated some fields, driving smaller retailers out of the field.

health care, were finding that the basic assumptions behind their business plans did not fully hold up to investor scrutiny. Would-be prison-management giant Corrections Corporation of America faced similar problems as investors lost faith in its mission. CCA and health-care companies Phycor, American Healthcorp (now American Healthways) and ClinTrials Research, all based at Nashville's Burton Hills office park, had each been Wall Street darlings at moments in the 1990s. Money manager Jon Shayne, also located in Burton Hills, dubbed the office complex "High-P/E Plaza" in honor of these companies' lofty market valuations. By May 2000, Phycor had swooned from a high of $41 a share to 44 cents, while ClinTrials had dropped from $50 to $3, and the others had followed similar trajectories. The collective price/earnings ratio at Burton Hills had reached a level closer to market norms.

Still, the misfortunes of these and other local businesses, including much of the music industry, which was facing crises of confidence and cash flow after years of robust growth, could not dampen the overall euphoria of the Nashville marketplace.

Middle Tennessee had never enjoyed a more sterling reputation as a place to do business. A poll of site-selection consultants, conducted in 2000 by the trade magazine *Expansion Management*, ranked Nashville as the sixth-best city in the U.S. (among 331 metro areas) for expanding or relocating corporate operations. Metro government was a good credit risk. Municipal-bond rating agencies gave Nashville excellent marks,

Service Merchandise Co. was one of several well-known Nashville companies in deep financial trouble during 2000. Overall, however, the local economy was perking along as never before.

representative of the civic mood are the handmade banners and church signs proclaiming, "Another Music City Miracle." In Middle Tennessee, there is little separation of church and sports.

10—**At long last,** a select audience of some 10,000 Nashvillians gets the chance to tour the new Opry Mills shopping center the day before its grand opening. Just getting to the Opry Mills exit on Briley Parkway from I-40 takes 70 minutes, with an additional 20 minutes spent parking. Once inside, shoppers stroll through the mall's villagelike enclaves, sampling paper cones of Thai noodles and nibbles of pizza. Among the attractions are the chocolate malts at Ghirardelli ($3.49), the huge tank stocked with fish at the Bass Outdoor Pro Shop and the mechanized hippo snorting in a makeshift lagoon outside the Rainforest Cafe. Perhaps most striking is the yahoo-chic juxtaposition of ritzy boutiques with glorified arcade attractions. . . . **Citing the "unusual circumstances"** of three killings by Metro police in a 22-day period earlier this year, District Attorney General Torry Johnson orders a grand jury investigation of the deaths. Johnson says the probe is intended more to reassure the public than to bring any kind of criminal charges against the officers. . . . **A tempest in a dog bowl** is brewing over those puppies found sweltering in the back of a broken-down transport truck. Metro Animal Control personnel say they will file suit to bar the canines' Missouri-based owner and breeder from taking possession of the 143 surviving pups.

11—**Braving traffic,** parking hassles and clowns, close to 100,000 visitors pass through the portals of Opry Mills in its first official day of business. By closing time, approximately $3 million in sales have poured into the shopping center's coffers. Yet some merchants worry that attendance is not higher. The Gaylord company's marketers are projecting 17 million shoppers a year, which works out to 46,575 a day. . . . **Nevada golfer Pat Hurst** shoots a 65 to take a two-shot lead in the Ladies Professional Golf Association's Electrolux U.S.A. Championship, currently under way at The Legends Club of Franklin. One hundred forty-four women players from Japan, Peru, Italy, Canada, Australia and points beyond converge on the Legends' links, which are sculpted replicas of famous courses around the world. The tournament was previously known as the Sara Lee Classic, until the popular pound-cake peddler ended its sponsorship last year. . . . **West Meade resident** Coleman Harwell, 57, spends two hours in jail this afternoon for his possession of grass—not marijuana, but plain old lawn grass. Harwell likes the grass in his yard tall and rangy, which has brought him citations from Metro codes inspectors. His crime: "excessive vegetation." General Sessions Judge Gloria Dumas finds Harwell in contempt of court for violating an injunction last September that ordered him to trim his yard; he receives a sentence of two days in jail. His attorney gets him released after a few hours while he appeals the ruling.

12—**A group of 35** Franklin pastors decides to set Middle Tennessee straight on what's Christian and what's not—like, for instance, the Church of Jesus Christ of Latter-day Saints, which has just opened the Midstate's first Mormon temple to public tours in Franklin. The pastors take issue with the Mormon church calling itself a Christian organization. As members of a group called the Empty Hands Fellowship, which is devoted to racial and denominational reconciliation, the pastors outline eight key differences between the Mormon faith and Christianity. Chief among these is the Mormons' erstwhile ban on African-American men becoming lay priests. (No mention of women, whose denial of priestly functions is a point of general agreement among Mormons and Empty Hands fellows alike.) . . . **The return of commuter rail service** to Nashville after a half-century absence is the goal of the new Regional Transportation Authority, which has se-cured enough federal funds to test the concept on existing tracks. In a week of trial runs

citing a broad and diverse economy, the presence of large institutional employers, and stable economic growth rates. In 2000, relocating companies continued a two-decade pilgrimage toward the Nashville area, greatly diversifying its mix of industrial activity. On April 25, General Motors announced it would invest $1.5 billion in upgrades to its Saturn Corporation plant in Spring Hill, south of town. Nissan was expanding its Smyrna operations, Dell Computer and Hewlett-Packard had each brought high-tech manufacturing operations to the region in recent years, and major telecom player Sprint PCS opened what was projected to become a large programming facility in Nashville during 2000.

When industry leader Dell Computer came looking for plant sites in 1999, Metro outbid all suitors by giving up free land next to the airport and exclusion from most taxes.

The local economy had benefited from its past misfortunes. The occasional woes of the past two decades, such as the real estate-driven recession of the late 1980s, tended to strengthen the resolve of community leaders to insulate the city from such shocks in the future. The mid-to-late 1990s were boom years for commercial property development in town, but only because growth in the overall economy was creating new demand for office and warehouse space. This was not the speculative, debt-driven boom of the 1980s, a hot streak that ended with bad loans sending First American's stock to low single digits, Metropolitan Federal Savings & Loan being taken over by federal regulators, and the Federal Deposit Insurance Corporation citing Nashville as the nation's second-worst commercial real estate market. All parties involved had been humbled by the comedown. Developers were now more conservative in their plans, and so were local bankers.

Pickets worked both sides of the issue when Mayor Bredesen brought the "Dell deal" before the Metro Council, which endorsed it after heated debate. Dell started construction immediately.

Within a year, in September 2000, Dell's assembly plant was up and running. The computer giant's 1,800 new employees assembled outside the new facility for opening ceremonies. Another 1,000 were already at work in rented warehouse space a few miles away, across the Wilson County line. In addition to tax breaks and free land, Dell would also receive from Metro a $500 annual fee—in effect, a bonus—for every person on its Davidson County payroll.

between the city and three stations to the east—Donelson, Hermitage and Mt. Juliet—free rides were taken by about 2,400 riders. This route, extending to Lebanon, is slated for regular service by 2002, with other routes to Gallatin, Murfreesboro, Franklin and Kingston Springs to follow—if funding becomes available.

13—**What was that Oscar Wilde** line on fox hunting—something about the unspeakable in pursuit of the uneatable? Banish the thought, as the 59th-running of the Iroquois Steeplechase draws more than 25,000 revelers to Percy Warner Park. So great is the turnout on this balmy spring day that Old Hickory Boulevard must be converted to one-way traffic to accommodate the flow. As always, spectators gravitate to the expensive box seats, where feathered chapeaux and goblets of chardonnay are plentiful, or to the cheaper vantage points on the hillside, where khakis and coolers prevail. The loftier patrons note with dismay the relaxed dress code (or undress code, since plunging decolletage is in). Others place bets, guzzle wine coolers and defend their sinuses against the onslaught of turf and manure.

14—**From the jazz brunch** at Bosco's in Hillsboro Village, featuring the Gypsy Hombres, to the lavish spread laid out at the Opryland Hotel's arboretum, the city's restaurants are filled for Mother's Day. Even the Cracker Barrel on Sidco Drive puts a 75-minute wait between Mom and her first white-gravy biscuit. The line outside Pancake Pantry stretches out the door and down the sidewalk, but that is nothing new for the beloved Hillsboro Village flapjack joint: It even keeps a vat of coffee stationed outside the entrance for the faithful. . . . **In solidarity** with the Million Mom March, a handgun-violence protest in Washington, D.C., that galvanizes tens of thousands of concerned parents, Nashville parents stage their own rally at Centennial Park in support of tighter gun-control laws. School shootings, handgun availability and their children's

Commercial development was booming not only in the vicinity of suburban shopping malls; there was evidence of it in downtown Nashville too: Commerce Center at Third and Commerce.

future are the key topics among the 250 people on hand, mostly women. . . . **Today's** *New York Times* has a critique of Nashville by reporter Neil Strauss. "Yesterday's Nashville, the one Tom T. Hall sang about in 'Nashville is a Groovy Little Town,' lies on a scrap heap," Strauss says. "Many of the city's oldest, quaintest attractions are either moving or closing or have already been leveled. All of this is one reason why Nashville is in a tourist slump, with 15% fewer visitors over the past two summers." Don't wait for the city boosters to make it over into an ersatz Southern Manhattan, Strauss advises. "Now may be the best time to visit, while it's in the throes of a personality crisis.". . . **Thousands** of Middle Tennessee parents make the ultimate sacrifice for their children: they sit through boy-band 'N Sync's mobbed stadium show

The rapid expansion of industry in the Nashville metropolitan area spurred high-income population growth throughout the 1990s, and that, in turn, caused a housing boom, particularly in Williamson County to the south. Scores of rambling mansions and showplaces were springing up like mushrooms in the rolling hills and farmlands, so many that a couple of generic names became attached to them: "McMansions" and "Brentwood houses."

More to the point, much of the economic risk of overbuilding in the Nashville area had been diffused far beyond its borders as real estate investment trusts (REITs) became the dominant force in commercial development. Few Nashvillians outside the realty business paid much attention as publicly held REITs—flush with cash as their stocks rose in the mid-1990s—snapped up immense chunks of Middle Tennessee property over the course of just a few years. But this transition was one case, at least, in which loss of local control in the economy appeared to be beneficial to the city. Henceforth, Nashville would be cushioned against the endemic cycles of boom, overbuild, and bust that had long plagued the area's economy. Shareholders of the REITs would feel the pain when occupancy trends turned south (as they had begun to do by 2000), but local lenders and investors would be less exposed than in the past.

For many individual Nashvillians, meanwhile, the boom times just kept on. Unemployment had been under 4 percent since 1993. Home values had shot upward, not just in the "Golden Triangle" of Belle Meade, Forest Hills, and Green Hills (where the average price of a single-family home was around $400,000), but also in parts of East Nashville that had become newly chic after decades of quiet stagnation and blight. Every home-improvement contractor worth his or her salt was booked up months in advance, as homeowners all over town cast aside old concerns about "overbuilding the neighborhood," turning cottages into mansions and mansions into palaces.

Nashville's money was not just old and gray, either. "Who could have imagined there were so many young millionaires in this town?" marveled John Hardcastle, president of H.G. Hill Realty, after most of the lots in the company's 129-acre Hill Place residential development were sold in a one-day land rush in April 1995. Buyers, most of whom were under 50 and many under 40, put down as much as $300,000 each that day—just for the lots—and nearly half paid more than the asking price for the privilege of owning raw land in what would become, by 2000, an ultra-upscale subdivision of huge and dazzling homes, right across the CSX railroad tracks from Belle Meade.

The striking thing about Monroe Carell, in both his accumulation of wealth and his community largess, was the very fact that he was far from unique in Nashville. His fortune paled next to those of at least two other clans that had made the "*Forbes* 400" list: the Ingram family (which dominated the businesses of wholesale book, video, and computer distribution) and the Frist family (which helped invent, and then dominated, the for-profit hospital industry, along the way sending a member of their clan, heart surgeon Bill Frist, to Washington as a senator). There was plenty of public-company wealth in town, and scores of Nashville families were also descended from old, private, well-invested money that had grown into nest eggs Forbes would have no way of estimating—but which, according to sometimes-reliable rumors, approached $200 million in several instances. And it occasionally seemed that people spent more energy giving money away than making it. Carell himself recounted a comment from Hugh McColl, the North Carolina banker who parlayed a regional financial institution and a lot of raw nerve into what is now the national powerhouse Bank of America (owner of what used to be Nashville's Commerce Union Bank). "He thought Nashville was the most philanthropic city, for its size, of any in the United States," Carell recalled.

To be sure, some of Nashville's nouveau riche millionaires found themselves in aberrantly generous spirits in 2000. The roaring NASDAQ stock market made many feel like pashas as the year began, and some were even wise enough to cash in their holdings before profits evaporated in the long slide of the last three quarters of the year. But the giving spirit of Nashville as a whole was nothing new. "Nashville has reached the point where there is overkill in charitable giving," moaned venture capitalist Ed Nelson, chairman of the Vanderbilt University Medical Center board and former head of Commerce Union Bank. "It's such a copycat city—whether it's the entrepreneurial starting of companies or starting a new disease ball." Examples of the extraordinary open-handedness of the city's residents were all around:

• **On campus.** Carell's $20-million gift to Vanderbilt for the children's hospital was generous, to be sure, but hardly singular. By the end of 2000, David Lipscomb

at Adelphia Coliseum. In a review on *The Tennessean*'s front page, critic Alison Embry writes, "It was loud and everybody screamed and they played all my favorite songs." She is 9. Summing up the parental consensus, a 35-year-old father of four calls it "prepubescent hell."

15—**Vanderbilt University** breaks ground on its new $150-million children's hospital, to be located at the corner of Pierce Avenue and 22nd Avenue South. The nine-story facility will more than double the current space of the children's hospital. If all goes according to plan, it will open in 2003. . . . **The final stats** on opening weekend at Opry Mills: approximately 350,000 shoppers from the U.S. and 23 other countries, and $10 million in sales. The only downside is that the mall had projected between 400,000 and 500,000 visitors.

16—**The Sundquist administration** puts a $264-million price tag on overhauling TennCare, the state's health-insurance program for the poor, uninsured and uninsurable. Sundquist's "TennCare II" program calls for reducing some benefits and sharing the risk of cost overruns with the private insurance plans that administer the program's claims. . . . **The use of deadly force** by Metro police comes in for sharp raps at a public forum on law enforcement sponsored by the Metro Human Rights Commission. The forum, part of a conference on community relations issues, draws more than 300 people to the Renaissance Nashville Hotel, and the exchanges among local business owners, religious leaders, political figures and police representatives are often heated. Many agree with commissioner Rev. James Thomas, who says, "The police are untouchable." The criticism softens a bit when the police department's critics are invited to step into an officer's shoes. A virtual-reality role-playing game used in Metro Police Academy training lets audience members act in high-risk situations, and even harsh critics take notice when they see how little time officers have to react to some challenges. When Metro Police Sgt. Bob Allen finally guns down a computer-generated suspect, the audience cheers. . . . **On trial** for racketeering, money laundering and conspiracy, accused madam Tera M. Daniels contends that she is shocked to learn her employees at Dawn's Whirlpool and Health Spa on Eighth Avenue South were offering sex for money from 1993 to 1999. Dissenting views are given by Daniels' former boyfriend, her mother and stepbrother, her former employees and a customer who claims to have made 300 visits for sex. . . . **In one stroke,** Music City loses two downtown nightclubs, including the city's premier jazz hall. To focus attention on its new Bluegrass Showcase venue at Opry Mills, guitar manufacturer Gibson Music Instruments Co. closes Gibson's Guitar Cafe and Gallery on Lower Broadway and Gibson's Caffé Milano on Third Avenue North. Of the two, the four-year-old Caffé Milano is the greater loss. Before Gibson bought the money-losing nightspot in 1998, the 250-seat dinner club hosted artists ranging from Elvis Costello and the Fairfield Four to rising jazz vocal superstar Diana Krall. For salsa great Tito Puente, patrons shoved aside tables to dance the mambo. The club's acoustics, intimacy and state-of-the-art video and audio capabilities made it one of the city's most impressive music venues.

17—**The altar rail** of downtown St. Mary's Catholic Church is lined with photographs of the 33 Metro police officers and one sheriff's deputy who have been killed in the line of duty since 1903. The occasion is a memorial service honoring Nashville's slain law enforcement officers. Sgt. Jimmy Wheeler, president of Nashville's Fraternal Order of Police, commemorates the late policemen as having the "courage, integrity, heart and guts to work in a profession that many would not." After the service, officers fire a 21-gun

University had started work on a new campus arena and a bell tower, thanks to more than $12 million in gifts from James C. Allen, a trustee and former vice president of the Church of Christ-related institution, and Baptist-affiliated Belmont University was planning to announce a $10-million donation from recording executive Mike Curb, followed in just four months by a $9-million gift from Sally Beaman, widow of longtime Nashville automobile dealer Alvin Beaman, to build a new student center. None of these gifts came close to what Martha Ingram, chair of the distribution conglomerate Ingram Industries Incorporated, had bestowed on Vanderbilt in 1998. In what may have been the largest private gift ever made to an American university, the Ingram Charitable Fund signed over shares of stock then valued at some $340 million.

• **On Broadway.** A $25-million grant from the Frist Foundation, under the aegis of Hospital Corporation of America co-founder Thomas F. Frist Jr., covered about half the cost of turning Nashville's former main post office—an imposing art-deco edifice at 901 Broadway—into the Frist Center for the Visual Arts. By May 2000, eleven months ahead of its scheduled opening, civic excitement over the "world-class" art museum was already running high. For the Frists, the city's eager anticipation was a welcome distraction from continuing legal unpleasantness surrounding the family company: During 2000, HCA agreed to pay a total of $840 million in criminal and civil penalties to the federal government, settling just part of a billing-fraud case that had been in the news since 1997.

• **In national politics.** When the *Wall Street Journal* revealed in 1999 that the Belle Meade-Green Hills-Forest Hills zip codes of 37205 and 37215 were two of the top three zips in federal campaign contributions, the rest of the country learned what political insiders have known for some time: Nashville functions as an ATM for would-be senators and presidents. (The same front-page article yielded Belle Meade resident Herb Shayne's lapidary description of his neighborhood as a "hotbed of social rest.") Middle Tennessee in 2000 was home to an improbably large collection of key money people backing Washington politicians. An outsider might have presumed that homeboy Al Gore would have a coterie of financiers in town, and the Eskinds did fit that description—longtime Democratic operative Jane Eskind personally donated $235,000 in "soft money" to the Democratic National Committee during 2000, and she and her family had contributed close to $1 million in total support for Democrats since 1992. But most of the rainmakers in Nashville were Republicans. Four past national finance chairmen of

As a record company executive in Nashville, former California Lt. Gov. Mike Curb found the community to his liking. He branched out to become an important Republican Party fund-raiser and a major benefactor of Baptist-affiliated Belmont University.

Hospital Corporation of America co-founder Thomas F. Frist Jr. (right, with senior officer Jack O. Bovender) had turned over the reins to Richard Scott when restructured Columbia/HCA got into legal hot water that eventually cost the company almost a billion dollars in fines and settlements. Frist returned to top management and changed the name back to HCA. The company has spawned many for-profit health-care companies in its image. The Frist name is prominent in local philanthropy.

the Republican National Committee lived in the city: Mike Curb (who served an embattled term as lieutenant governor of California before moving to Nashville), investor Joe M. Rodgers, real estate magnate Ted Welch, and financier David K. "Pat" Wilson. The Curb, Rodgers, Welch, and Wilson families gave roughly $800,000 to national GOP candidates during the 1990s, but they raised many times that amount by passing the plate among fellow industrialists. Welch, universally acknowledged as the most successful Republican fund-raiser in history, had arranged the financing of Lamar Alexander's failed presidential bids in 1996 and 2000 and then, each time, moved on to raise millions more for the party's nominee. People who knew Welch observed that he seemed not to seek any personal gain from his efforts, and that he showed no signs of zealotry on the great issues of the day—nor, indeed, of having any strongly articulated political beliefs at all. He just enjoyed the hunt.

• **In the pews.** Nobody had any way of reliably tracking the total sums offered up by Nashville's religious congregations every week, but in a city full of impressive houses of worship, the total can only have been immense. Local accountants, in their off hours, could occasionally be heard speaking with wonder about the number of clients who engaged in honest-to-goodness tithing.

• **At the office.** In a time when the United Way's system of workplace giving faced competition from a host of newly outstretched hands, Nashville's annual campaigns consistently ranked in the top 10 percent among United Ways nationwide in the amount donated per giver.

• **At the Y.** The YMCA of Middle Tennessee outstripped YMCAs from some of the nation's largest metropolitan areas in its fund-raising. In 1998, Nashville's Y had revenues larger than those of Dallas, Philadelphia, Boston, or Metro Washington, according to public filings with the Internal Revenue Service. From 1994 through 1998,

salute outside the church, and 27 Goodlettsville fourth-graders sing the Latin hymn "*Dona Nobis Pacem.*". . . **A U.S. District Court jury** finds Tera Daniels guilty on 35 counts of prostitution-related racketeering, money laundering and conspiracy. The jury, deadlocked over whether the convicted madam should forfeit $745,000 and her home in Mt. Juliet, eventually decides that she should. Daniels kisses her twin 9-year-old daughters goodbye and goes into custody. . . . **Those 143 puppies** whose status has been updated nightly on local newscasts are finding homes, but not with their owner in Missouri. In exchange for dropping animal-cruelty charges against the truck driver, an out-of-court settlement awards custody of the pups to the Metro Public Health Department Animal Control Facility. Eyeing the prospect of purebred pups for a song, Nashvillians eagerly await the public adoption three days hence. . . . **Legendary banjo picker** Earl Scruggs, 76, half of the famed Flatt and Scruggs bluegrass duo of the 1960s, plays the Ryman for the first time in a quarter-century. With country star Marty Stuart and others, Scruggs brings back memories of his wide-ranging career that included pairings with Joan Baez and Bob Dylan and gigs at Carnegie Hall and the Newport Folk Festival.

18—Who needs women pastors? Apparently not the Southern Baptists. For their annual convention in June, the nation's largest Protestant church body is considering a revised faith statement that says God did not intend women to ascend to the pulpit. Of the 190 congregations in the Nashville Baptist Convention, none has a female pastor. . . . **Columbia/HCA** agrees to a $745-million civil settlement of claims that it habitually inflated bills at hospitals, home-health agencies and outpatient laboratories. This speeds up but does not end the federal government's fraud case against the health-care giant, which still stands charged of overbilling Medicare and giving kickbacks to doctors who referred patients to its hospitals.

19—**King Crimson,** the British progressive-rock band whose line-up includes veteran guitarist and Nashville resident Adrian Belew, begins a three-night stand at 12th & Porter. Since this will be the group's only North American performance before its European tour, fans arrive from as far away as Japan, Canada and Australia. Every show is filled to capacity.

. . . **Donna Oquendo** pulls up outside the Metro Animal Control Facility in Bordeaux at 4:45 in the afternoon. Oquendo is the first person in line for one of the 143 purebred pups being put up for adoption tomorrow. She will wait there until . . .

20—. . .**the doors open** at 10 a.m., by which time the facility has become a madhouse. Would-be owners arrive throughout the night, and by 4 a.m., 32 people are already in line. At 5 a.m., the four police officers on the scene call for backup. A lottery system is briefly discussed but abandoned after bitter protest by those who have camped out. Adding to the frenzy is that 77 of the pups have already been adopted the previous day by volunteers and workers at the Neely Coble Co., where the pups were found. Only 28 dogs will be put up for adoption today, with an additional 30 to be released from quarantine later this week. By 8 a.m., police turn away hundreds of the approximately 1,000 people at the scene. Of those who remain, 28 get to pay the $79 adoption fee and go home with purebred terriers, shelties, Labradors and golden retrievers. Donna Oquendo's first pick is a grey-and-white Italian greyhound, to be named Troubles.

. . . **Meanwhile,** columnist Tim Chavez, *The Tennessean*'s liberal conscience, wonders why the city and its media have spent the past 10 days agonizing over the fate of some puppies, while Nashville's children face more than $10 million in possible school budget cuts. He surmises that the cuddly pups are easier to sentimentalize, and hence to save. "If only children were puppies," Chavez

the YMCA increased annual revenues 116 percent, from $19.6 million to $41.3 million (rising to $48.7 million in 1999). Bill Wilson, son of Pat Wilson, led a multiyear capital campaign that had raised almost $50 million by the end of 1999. And all this recent revenue merely added to an already impressive asset base, built up over the course of more than a century of major donations—from the grocery and real estate wealth of the H.G. Hill family, the retail wealth of Dollar General Corporation's Cal Turner family, and other leading supporters. Although many of the Y's 107,000 area members frequented the family and athletic programs of its well-appointed suburban facilities, it also operated a number of inner-city programs credited with making a positive difference in Nashville housing projects.

Given the long-standing local habit of giving, it was jolting to recall that what should have been a bedrock institution, the Nashville Symphony, had gone bankrupt a mere thirteen years earlier. The problem, in the view of symphony supporters, was that Nashville's power people didn't see it as a bedrock institution. They were tone-deaf to the part played by the arts in the life of a community. Such a lack of civic communication might have happened anywhere in the United States. Only in the South, though, would leaders like Martha Ingram blame it on the War.

Nashville had an easy War Between the States, at least compared to Atlanta. Lacking an apocalyptic legacy of physical destruction, locals tend not to notice the evidence of a profound Yankee victory hidden in plain sight all around them: the triumph of commercial boosterism. The forces that won the Civil War lost the peace, in the sense that the "reconstructed" South remained defiantly resistant to an embrace of what we now call fundamental human rights. But they succeeded resoundingly in convincing Southern elites to become acolytes of a mercantile society. The last gasp of coherent opposition to the march of boosterism expired in the impotent and largely ignored pages of *I'll Take My Stand*, the 1930 manifesto of Vanderbilt's self-styled Agrarians, whose pleas to preserve the best of antebellum Southern culture were too intertwined with shrill promotion of the very worst of it to win over civilized hearts and minds.

None of this was ancient history, even if many contemporary Nashvillians wished it so. Within living memory, the civil rights movement had offered a vivid demonstration of how commercial power could shape the city's decisions on social issues far removed from everyday business.

Whether or not Fred Harvey and John Sloan thought they were breaking new ground, there were already generations of history to guide Nashville's two leading department-store merchants when they faced a choice in 1960 between loyalty to the old racial mores and "the right thing." They finally did the right thing, opening their lunch counters to African-American diners in response to sit-ins. It does not diminish the rightness of the thing to observe that it dovetailed nicely with the immediate interest of Harveys and Cain-Sloan in letting black people spend green money in their stores, and with the longer-term interest of a broader community of commercial boosters in painting Nashville in the image of a city where moderation ruled.

The leaders in charge of Nashville industry at the turn of the millennium had faced less crucial issues on their way up, but the thoughtful among them found the burden of the deep past still weighing upon the community. Thus did Martha Ingram connect the hard times of Reconstruction with the dearth of public support that contributed to the symphony's bankruptcy. "When things were so bad in the South after the Civil War, there was little money to do anything but survive," Ingram reflected. "The arts simply got shoved aside. We've had four, five, six generations with very little exposure to the arts—other than the people whose families were wealthy enough to send them away to school. The general public has had so little exposure." And thus did Ingram resolve, in her crusade to complete the orchestra's rehabilitation, to lead a march straight into the heart of the Old Union: New York City. Her ambition, announced in 1998, was to take the Nashville Symphony to the stage of Carnegie Hall in the year 2000.

Ingram set to her task with the same steel-magnolia will and talent she had applied repeatedly in prior philanthropic efforts. Before she became the first woman chair of the Vanderbilt Board of Trust, before she played a decisive role in the development of the Bicentennial Mall in downtown Nashville, before the death of her husband, Bronson, in 1995 left her at the helm of a corporation worth as much as $4 billion—before any of that, she had long since become the go-to woman for the arts in Nashville. Back in the 1980s, when the Ingram family was merely very wealthy rather than fabulously wealthy, she had been not only a patron but also a fund-raiser and guiding presence for the city's fledgling ballet, opera, and repertory theater companies, among many other arts groups. In the late 1970s, she had led the charge to build and fund the Tennessee Performing Arts Center downtown.

Now she saw it as her task to show Nashville's sometimes out-of-touch overlords, once and for all, that the arts mattered to Nashville's future. She may or may not have been an "art for art's sake" person in her soul, but she knew that return on investment meant everything to the

More than two decades ago, Martha Ingram (with Tennessee Performing Arts Center CEO Steven Greil, above) led the campaign for development of TPAC. She has since been the driving force behind several major performing arts projects, including rescuing the symphony from bankruptcy.

writes, "then we could help those living things with the longest history of abuse and neglect in our state." Chavez's column appears on the front page of the Local section. The next day, the daily's front page features two full-color photos under the headline, "Stranded puppies touch hearts." . . . **A few blocks** from the Capitol, where tobacco lobbyists are as thick as the cigar and cigarette smoke, a new billboard on Church Street keeps a running tally of Tennessee's tobacco-related deaths and costs. Like an odometer charting the mileage to the grave, the billboard ticks off "Tobacco's Toll in Tennessee" over the past year and a half. Deaths: 13,870. Kids addicted: 35,570. Health-care costs: $2 billion. If only puppies could smoke. . . . **The city's print and PR pigs** turn out at 328 Performance Hall for the Swine Ball, the beer-and-barbecue bash founded by local media types to benefit the American Cancer Society while tweaking the chi-chi Swan Ball. The evening is dedicated to the mem-

Primarily through Ingram's efforts, the symphony made its debut at Carnegie Hall in New York on Sept. 25, 2000, with musical director Kenneth Schermerhorn conducting. The orchestra's home hall is TPAC's Jackson Theater.

ory of the late *Tennessean* columnist Jerry Thompson, who graced many a Swine Ball in years past.

21—**Forty-four years** after he arrived in Nashville with 15¢ to his name, German resident Rudolf Rischer preaches one last sermon at the East Nashville church that sheltered him, the Chapel Avenue Church of Christ. When Rischer turned 18, a missionary paid his way from war-ravaged Munich to America to study at David Lipscomb College. When he arrived in Nashville in 1956, he had little else but the phone number of Carroll Ellis, Chapel Avenue's pastor. Rischer was welcomed to Chapel Avenue, and he stayed there for two years before returning to Europe to found his own church. The church at Chapel Avenue continued to send him monthly checks for almost 15 years. But the congregation has dwindled from 300 members in 1980 to as few as 23 today, and the church building is being sold and converted into a recording studio. To ensure Chapel Avenue's legacy, the remaining members plan to put the $150,000 in proceeds into an annuity for Rischer's church in Augsburg, Germany, thus ending his years of financial struggle. Those members who remain will continue meeting at a gymnasium space owned by the church a few blocks away. . . .
The "hot" light is off at Krispy Kreme on Thompson Lane. The company is tearing down the popular doughnut den, which diverts motorists and Metro cops every day with its red neon sign—a signal that indicates piping hot doughnuts have just left the oven. Not to worry, though—the building is being leveled to make room for a larger Krispy Kreme with more seating. Cost of one last hot Krispy Kreme: 37¢

22—**Vanderbilt University** researchers may have found an important new step in the treatment and understanding of lung cancer. Studies offer evidence that solid tumors grow by usurping the functions of the body that produce new blood vessels. By squeezing off its blood supply, the

people she was addressing—and she made a plausible case about the consequences of failing to invest in the arts. "There was a real revelation that occurred when the symphony was forced to close down," she said. "The chamber of commerce was unable to attract a single company even to consider Nashville as a place where they would like to have an office or headquarters. Not even one company would look at it. That was a real wake-up call to the chamber that the arts were an economic development factor, and not just a frill. As a group, I think that's how they saw the arts before: 'If you can't support a symphony, well, who cares?' A lot of people care, because the health of a symphony is generally reflective of the health of an arts community. People don't want to move employees into an area where there is not an attractive lifestyle."

A cynic might have disparaged the whole Carnegie effort as a personal caprice of Ingram's. Her fortune had helped rebuild the symphony during the past decade, and, in recent years, she and its maestro, the debonair Kenneth Schermerhorn, had become a fixture on the social scene as a couple. But the rest of Nashville's elite clearly bought into her vision for the symphony. It wasn't just her contribution that raised the orchestra's endowment from $7 million to $20 million in a campaign leading up to September's self-financed Carnegie trip. She didn't force a thousand Nashvillians to pay more than $1,000 a head for junkets to attend the show. Martha Ingram had a plan, and the rest of blue-stocking Nashville followed her lead with a unanimity of purpose seldom if ever seen in any realm of local endeavor—and never, certainly, in support of the arts.

Despite the past decade's dramatic accomplishments, Nashville's leaders in the 21st century would inherit a catalog of unmet social needs from the current leadership cadre. All the recent progress the city's influential people had made, in working as a team to better the city, made the persistence of certain communitywide problems stand out in stark relief. The collective success of Nashville's most powerful people, in building up both civic amenities and personal wealth, often did not trickle down to the city's least powerful citizens: the working poor, the homeless, the children.

The rising tide of economic prosperity in Nashville had lifted some boats, but by no means all. The situation in three inner-city housing projects—James A. Cayce Homes, Sam Levy Homes, and Tony Sudekum Homes—offered a snapshot showing both progress and continued poverty on the bottom rungs of society. Income statistics for the years 1994, before state and federal welfare-reform initiatives came into effect, and 2000, several years into the welfare-to-work initiatives, show measurable progress. At the three sites combined, the number of employed residents nearly doubled in six years, while gross household income rose an inflation-adjusted 13 percent, outpacing the rate of the city as a whole. That performance sounds impressive, and Tennessee did earn a bonus from the U.S. Department of Health and Human Services in 2000 for its success in moving people off welfare and into the workplace. But the average gross household income in the three housing projects was still only $5,806; it had risen only from 37 percent to 41 percent of the federally defined poverty level.

Moreover, there were disturbing signs that more and more people were falling through the cracks

In Nashville during 2000, resources available for emergency food aid declined slightly, but requests for assistance went up by 25 percent. More than two-thirds of those seeking food are employed. Second Harvest Food Bank is one of several local nonprofit food-assistance programs in the city.

Well over a thousand people are homeless in Nashville, sleeping in shelters or in the open, even in the winter. Contrary to common belief, close to half of the homeless are employed but don't earn enough to afford housing.

of Nashville's social structures. Whether because of welfare reform or not (and according to advocates, only about 40 percent of the people compelled to leave the welfare rolls were employed), Nashville in 2000 was gaining the dubious distinction of being a national leader in one particular measure of poverty: the so-called "working poor." The city figured prominently in a U.S. Conference of Mayors' "Status Report on Hunger and Homelessness," covering a twelve-month period in 1999-2000. The report found that 50 percent of Nashville's homeless, and 70 percent of those seeking emergency food assistance, were employed. The latter percentage was the highest in the country, and more than twice the national average. Local resources available for food aid during the period actually decreased, while requests for emergency food assistance rose 25 percent—the highest rate of the 25 cities surveyed.

Nobody could rightfully blame Nashville's corporate leaders for this state of affairs. Still, the medieval scale of the contrasts raised questions that a future generation would have to answer: If Nashvillians were generous enough to raise a $20-million endowment for the symphony, why did the Second Harvest Food Bank go begging? What if the 1,000 people who paid $1,000 each to attend the Carnegie spectacle had applied that million dollars to the Nashville Family Shelter?

Among middle-class Nashvillians, widespread prosperity was interspersed with growing pockets of economic misery, much of it self-inflicted. As the ruling class worried about a loss of control to out-of-town financial institutions, so did many ordinary workers, but their focus was on the financial control they had ceded by succumbing to the lure of easy credit. Personal debt problems had become a nationwide epidemic, but

growth of lung cancer can be slowed. The discovery will aid in the fight against tumors of the breast, colon, prostate and lungs, which will account for more than half the nation's projected 552,000 cancer deaths this year.

23—A slender, jittery man dressed in black with graying dark hair and a narrow beard paces the downstairs lobby of Regal Cinemas' Green Hills Commons 16-screen theater. At a distance, he is easily mistaken for Nashville film and TV producer Andy van Roon. In fact, it is filmmaker Joel Coen, nervously awaiting the first local screening of his new film *O Brother, Where Art Thou?* Coen, who made such films as *Raising*

Arizona and the Oscar-winning *Fargo* with his brother and writing partner, Ethan, is showing the movie in secret for the many Nashville musicians who appear on the movie's sound track. Most of them will perform tomorrow night at a gala concert at the Ryman Auditorium. . . . **After a three-month search,** the Metro Planning Commission appoints Rick Bernhardt to direct the staff of this influential city department. Bernhardt, who worked as a planning assistant at the commission in the 1970s, is selected for his expertise in "New Urbanism," the movement that promotes a return to compact, livable, pedestrian-friendly urban neighborhoods. Bernhardt will replace longtime planning director Jeff Browning, whose resignation in January was widely viewed as a shove by Purcell. "I think the city will thank you forever," the mayor tells the search committee that recommends the new director.

24—**The Ryman Auditorium** concert commemorating the music for the Coen brothers' new movie is a star-studded showcase for some of Nashville's finest gospel and string-band music. Among the highlights: the majestic Fairfield Four; the heavenly trio of Emmylou Harris, Alison Krauss and Gillian Welch; the Peasall Sisters, three adorable Nashville moppets ages 7, 9 and 12. The room hushes when venerable bluegrass star Ralph Stanley takes the stage. In a keening, unearthly tenor, he sings an eerie a cappella version of "O Death," which in the movie is placed in the mouth of a murderous Klansman. For much of the night, the legendary documentarian D.A. Pennebaker (*Don't Look Back*) stands onstage filming with a bulky camera hoisted atop his shoulder.

25—**Yes to new libraries,** no to across-the-board raises for Metro employees. Mayor Bill Purcell sets the city's priorities in the $1.1-billion budget he presents to the Metro Council. The city has to contend with a $12-million shortfall for the coming year, and some departments must be

Tennessee led the U.S. in bankruptcy filings per capita, with one family in 43 resorting to legal protection from creditors. A typical case, one of 57 personal bankruptcies filed in the U.S. Bankruptcy Court for Middle Tennessee on May 15, 2000, involved a suburban Nashville couple who owned a $175,000 home, held $23,000 in retirement assets, and had earned a combined income of $85,000 in 1999. This family had a second mortgage on the home to almost its full value, owed more on a car note than the auto was worth, and had run up $60,000 in unsecured debt with five credit cards, six charge accounts at jewelry and department stores, a credit-company loan, and medical bills. It was no wonder that Nashville, as the epicenter of the bankruptcy boom and the Bible Belt, was also the home base of radio personality Dave Ramsey's nationally syndicated fusion of financial advice and revivalist tradition, which preached a gospel of debt-reduction that clearly had a large potential audience in Nashville.

Perhaps spiritual assistance could help debtors come to terms with their errors of judgment in spending, but better education might have prevented the mistakes in the first place. Whether or not the chronic shortcomings of public education in Nashville could be directly correlated with the pervasive evidence of personal financial mismanagement, there was abundant evidence to suggest that it was clearly in the enlightened self-interest of Nashville business to work to invest in a more effective and productive system of public schools.

Civic boosters touted Nashville's "well-educated workforce" in pitching the city to relocating employers, but cocktail-party chatter among the managerial classes told a different story, much in the vein of a letter sent to the *Wall Street Journal* in 2000 by a Nashville businessman. "Boy, did I identify with your article, 'When Just Awful Becomes Good Enough,'" wrote Warren Feld, the operator of a catalog company, in response to a story about how companies nationwide had been compelled to lower employment standards in a tight labor market. "To fill positions, I've had to play 'Let's Make a Deal.' To have Saturday coverage—a virtual impossibility—I've hired a mother and her daughter to rotate every other week. The mother is great; the daughter a dud. And of course there's an excellent chance that the employees, once hired, won't be able to do the job. I have to fire them if they can't add, count, or fill in an invoice form. Many people actively looking for jobs can't perform these tasks."

It's true that there were individuals in Nashville's corporate arena who were deeply committed to creating an educational system that would not send "duds" into the workforce. Initiatives from the business community to improve schools had undoubtedly done some good. There was certainly no shortage of rhetoric about business support for education. But Nashville's elite sent a much clearer signal by what they did than by what they said. The vast majority of prominent businesspeople with school-aged children sent them to private schools. And the parents did not just pay tuition; they often became key supporters of the schools, remaining involved even after the kids had graduated. The best-established of these schools tapped into loyal bases of alumni, parents, and ex-parents to raise huge sums of money. Private boys' school Montgomery Bell Academy received more than $7 million in contributions during the 1999-2000 fiscal year. Just by way of comparison, both MBA's annual revenues and its endowment were larger than those of 134-year-old, historically black Fisk University across town.

Without question, Nashville got a payoff from MBA's wealth, as the school had been grooming future leaders, local and national, for more than a century (since 1855, in fact, when it was conceived in the will of Montgomery Bell, a reclusive industrialist, "for the education of children . . . who are not able to support and educate themselves and whose parents are not able to do so.") But there was simply no comparable mechanism in place to promote voluntary support of public education. A nonprofit entity, the Metropolitan Nashville Public Education Foundation, existed to receive contributions on behalf of Metro schools, but it had almost no public profile and generally attracted only nominal contributions. On the other hand, some of the potential beneficiaries of any such support had wasted a chance for coalition-building by opposing the one major private fund-raising effort on behalf of a public school in recent years. Over a two-year period in the late 1990s, parents and other backers of Julia Green Elementary School in the affluent Green Hills area, raised $480,000 for improvements in the school's physical plant. Anticipating criticism that they were simply buying their way to perpetual advantage over other public schools, the planners included in their

Radio talk-show host Dave Ramsey found a national audience for his "gospel of fiscal responsibility," which he syndicates from a Nashville station. Ramsey, a Christian conservative, offers free tax advice and financial planning strategies on the air. He also has a book of money talk on the market.

fund-raising pitch an option for donors to contribute to a separate fund for public schools in general. They raised an additional $50,000 thereby, and set up the Miss Julia Green Fund through the Greater Nashville Community Foundation, urging other public school supporters to pick up the challenge. In the end, Julia Green got the improvements it wanted; the fund-raisers got criticized by some black leaders for perpetuating inequalities in resources from school to school; and the rainy-day fund for all public schools was an idea that never got rolling. Instead of action and reaction, a little more preliminary interaction might have yielded better long-term results.

Mayors Phil Bredesen and Bill Purcell had each managed to channel large amounts of new government funding to the Metro school system, much of it earmarked for long-overdue capital improvements. In 2000, though, many schools still had to use portable classrooms to supplement their overcrowded buildings, and teacher pay remained stagnant. Average teacher salaries, adjusted for inflation, were lower in 2000 than they had been in 1991.

A casual observer—or a future historian—could be forgiven for finding the city fathers and mothers of 2000 morally obtuse in their apparent neglect of hunger and need in favor of already-wealthy institutions and artistic spectacle. Yet the climate of the times suggested a different problem—not a let-them-eat-cake attitude, but rather a failure to appreciate how much power they had to do good.

The symphony's Carnegie Hall campaign was evidence that Nashville's power people could band together to bring about positive change in civic life. Where the collective will could be mustered, the elite could lead the city toward quality-of-life improvements. A few earlier episodes had showed that, besides flexing their financial muscle, they could sway the general population to their point of view. In the 1960s, businesspeople in Metro Nashville had set out to legalize liquor-by-the-drink—a necessary lubricant, as they saw it, of economic development—and won over public support against great odds. In the 1990s, business adopted the cause of NFL football in Nashville,

trimmed by as much as 10 percent, while others require additional funds. Purcell's budget sets aside $3.4 million for operating the city's new main library and branches. Popular programs such as chipper service, recycling, the Metro Human Relations Commission and a new animal-control facility remain uncut. A budget must be approved by June 30. . . . **Murray Philip,** who has earned a reputation as the mad bull of the Metro school board, announces today that he won't seek re-election this summer. The controversial Philip has been on the board for four years, during which time his tenacious stand on issues and his confrontational style have impressed some colleagues and alienated others. But after a board meeting Tuesday night, at which his was the sole dissenting vote against building a new elementary school in an industrial area off Brick Church Pike, Philip says he is tired of fighting. "I'm just burned out," he tells *The Tennessean.* "I've made a lot of enemies. So it's time to go do other things.". . . **Calvin Champion's death** was accidental, rules the Metro medical examiner's office. Champion, 32, died Apr. 30 in police custody after an altercation outside a store on Nolensville Road. The autistic man was pepper-sprayed, subdued and left facedown, but the office finds that he died of an undiagnosed heart condition.

26—Save the Belcourt! becomes the rally call of preservationists determined to save the Belcourt Theatre in Hillsboro Village, the city's last historic neighborhood cinema. The 75-year-old theater once housed both the Grand Ole Opry and the Nashville Academy Theater. The two-screen moviehouse was operated as an art-movie theater by Carmike Cinemas until 1997, when a group of investors led by developer Charles Hawkins purchased it on behalf of the Watkins Institute School of Art and Design. Faced with monthly losses, the independently owned and operated theater closed its doors in January 1999. However, a grassroots group, Belcourt YES!, has spearheaded an effort to save the theater. In January, the group signed a 10-year lease and will begin showing foreign and independent films again on June 2.

27—**Nashville clubgoers** and rock bands rally to show support for Lennon Murphy, the teenage singer-songwriter who has suffered a crushing family tragedy. The 18-year-old Hendersonville musician has become a popular attraction on the local club scene, but last month her mother, manager and indefatigable champion, Kathleen Murphy, died unexpectedly at home of an apparent allergic reaction. Murphy, who was named for John Lennon by her mother, was suddenly left to juggle her escalating career and the responsibility of raising her 8-year-old sister. To help her out, Murphy's friend, Tony Armani, a Nashville stylist and image consultant, assembles a benefit show at the Elliston Place club The End. Among the popular local acts donating their time are the Brian Kotzur Band, Chris Mitchell & The Collection, Hangman's Daughter, Kacey Jones, Phillbilly and Kim's Fable. Among Nashville's large, supportive community of club-level musicians, few of whom have health benefits or retirement plans, benefit shows take place almost daily.

28—**"When you leave** here today, hug your mother, hug your father, your grandmother, your grandfather," urges Darrell Hedgecoth, a senior at Cheatham County Central High School in Ashland City. That Hedgecoth is even here to speak at his graduation ceremony, held at Austin Peay State University in Clarksville, is remarkable. Hedgecoth, whose organs had been destroyed by cystic fibrosis, was the recipient of the first triple-organ transplant ever performed at Vanderbilt University Medical Center. The heart, lungs and liver he received on Jan. 23 are working fine. . . . **Freelance media queen** Drue Smith, the technicolor chatterbox whose news and views from Capitol Hill and local high society are the delight of

Business executive Marguerite Sallee is one of a few women who have served as CEOs of Nashville companies—and the only woman thus far to chair the Nashville Area Chamber of Commerce. The overwhelming majority of corporate leaders in the city are now, as in the past, white males.

facing vocal opposition to the sweetness of the deal being offered to Bud Adams' Houston Oilers, and helped mount a successful campaign to win a "Yes" vote in a referendum forced by the opponents.

Nashville's leadership had accomplished these things while steadily becoming more inclusive. For the moment, the city's bigwigs were still overwhelmingly white and male, but there were growing signs of diversity within the ruling class. Twenty or 30 years earlier, it had been considered progress for women and Jews to be allowed into business societies like the Exchange Club, the Cumberland Club, and the City Club. Now just about every club and social institution in town included members from varied racial and religious backgrounds. One woman, Marguerite Sallee, had served as both the CEO of a publicly held company and chair of the Greater Nashville Chamber of Commerce—and there was reason to believe that more would follow. Perhaps just as important was the increasing diversity of expertise and passions among the rising leaders of the city. To take just one category as an example, data-processing innovators Fred Goad, Rich Roberts, and Greg Daily—the latter two barely over 40—had become sought-after board members and investors as they built successful companies in the 1990s. These technology entrepreneurs were filling seats that would have belonged to old-line banking and insurance executives a generation ago.

And yet, in May 2000, behind the customary sunny optimism evident on the sidewalks of Union Street, a nagging self-doubt plagued the commercial gentry of Nashville. The subconscious origins of those feelings may have stretched back as far as the Civil War and may have been intertwined with a regional inferiority complex. But the immediate focus was the here and now, in moments of quiet reflection on the dizzy-

Business writer David Fox combined his experience as a journalist and his skills in electronic communications to create an online "magazine" of daily business news called NashvillePost.com. The website journal has attracted more than 2,000 subscribers in its first year of operation.

Mary Anne Howland (below) president of Ibis Communications, a marketing firm she founded in 1993, was honored in 2000 for five consecutive years of inclusion on the "Music City Future 50" list, a coveted designation indicating consistently strong revenue and employment growth.

fun-loving readers, gets a splashy feature from former society columnist Catherine Darnell in the Sunday *Tennessean*. The ageless (some say 80-ish) party girl, a fixture here since she moved up from Chattanooga about 30 years ago, takes the occasion to give some advice to "my fellow women." Coos Drue: "I don't want to criticize, but often they take themselves too seriously." As for herself, she says, "I've never been serious about anything."

29—**Memorial Day**. A military plane flanked by two helicopters drones high above Nashville National Cemetery in Madison, where the Al Menah Shrine and American Legion Post 5 bands play hymns to fallen defenders in wars past. Miniature American flags flutter alongside the lines of white tombstones at Stones River Battlefield in Murfreesboro. A lone bagpipe wails in the distance at Mt. Olivet . . . . **Memorial Day tourism** is looking up for the first time since 1997, when the Opryland theme park closed. The newly opened Opry Mills shopping complex gets much of the credit. At the Nashville Shores water park, which has just added a make-believe Hawaiian lagoon, attendance is up 25 percent. But not everyone is hoisting drinks with umbrellas. Says Ted Lannom, owner of the Nashville Toy Museum on Music Valley Drive in the shadow of Opry Mills, "Nobody I know is having a party tonight."

30—**Four wholesale parts salesmen** at Beaman Automotive Group on West End will never again have to settle for just taking a spin around the block. James Christian, Ronnie Mays, Andy Perry and Mike Alderdice hold the lucky ticket in the Kentucky State Lottery's Powerball drawing. Its value: $60.6 million. Christian, like thousands of other Tennesseans, trooped across the state line to buy the ticket. The four men decide to settle for the cash option, worth $31 million, or $7.75 million each. . . . **A million dollars** would help Metro's embattled English as a Second Language program. Enrollment of

Renal Care, a local company headed by Sam Brooks, has survived a wave of consolidations in its field to become the nation's fourth largest investor-owned kidney dialysis service provider.

immigrant students has risen from 737 in 1990 to 3,046 10 years later, with many more expected. Yet the position of outgoing ESL director Sue Reynolds will not be filled, and ESL teachers are overworked, spread thin across too many schools and increasingly unmanageable class sizes. . . .
Boy-wonder businessman Scott Mercy, 38, chairman and CEO of Lifepoint Hospitals, a spin-off of Nashville-based HCA, dies instantly when the four-seater Beechcraft he is piloting (with his former flight instructor, Deborah Ann Millwood, on board) plummets to earth next to a golf course in Smyrna. Millwood is also killed. Many local health-care executives say Mercy was being groomed to succeed Thomas Frist Jr., HCA's co-founder and CEO.
. . . **Fine print** in the Adelphia Coliseum lease agreement between the Titans football team and the city will require the taxpayers to fork over about $1 million a year for upkeep of the facility. City officials say their hands are tied.

31—**From his home** in Mexico, Perry March fires off a round of legal motions via Federal Express to the courtroom of Davidson County Circuit Judge Frank Clement Jr. The motions are meant to overturn Clement's $113.5-million wrongful-death judgment against March for the alleged murder of his wife, Janet Levine March, in 1996. The story soon will take yet another strange turn. . . . **The Lost Lake Gallery,** a new shop on White Bridge Road, offers a selection of Native American artifacts and remnants from prehistoric cultures. The store attracts unusual attention because of its owner: Lionel R. Barrett Jr., the legendary Nashville defense attorney who has represented clients ranging from Perry March and Byron "Low Tax" Looper to numerous Death Row convicts. At Barrett's request, the Tennessee Supreme Court put his license to practice law on "disability inactive" status May 17. As of now, he says in an interview, he has "no desire to go back into the practice of law."

ing procession of deals that had brought about a fruit-basket turnover in the ownership of Nashville institutions. There was reason to wonder whether the next generation of elite Nashvillians, regardless of wealth, would hold enough of the levers of the area's social machinery to wield control over Nashville's destiny.

"In the collection of leadership, there is a vacuum," financier Ed Nelson said. "There are a lot of people that can get together and get something done. There are many who have a lot of money, who are very generous to the community. But it's to their pet things often. The bankers that were a logical power base—that has definitely changed. Bankers are still participating, but they're not known. You can't really name the heads of the institutions. They're all smart, personable, good people. They're just not known."

Nelson, who speaks Japanese and has long-standing business interests in Japan, saw worrying parallels between the Nashville business community's response to Tennessee's state financial woes in 2000 and Japan's inability to deal with persistent economic problems. "One of Japan's major problems is political will," Nelson said. "They don't have any leaders. And we've got a hell of a mess with our tax system. I don't think there's any leadership." Nelson, who conceded that he personally would fare better under a new state income tax than under the existing Hall Tax on certain investment income, winced in patrician disgust at the rabble of protesters who descended on downtown in high and noisy dander after legislators proposed an income tax. "The hornhonkers are unelected officials—guys who want to be in the limelight and have the microphone," Nelson said. "Nobody wants to get behind the other option. But there needs to be some business leadership."

In the oligarchy of Old Nashville, things had been different. Key individuals—especially bankers like Nelson's former competitor at Third National Bank, Sam Fleming, who died in January 2000—wielded the authority necessary to begin building a consensus on public issues. "Sam Fleming could still, to the end of his life, stick his hand into something if he wanted, and things would move," Nelson recalled.

But not everybody was sorry to see that style of leadership—with its implication of backroom deal-making and elitism—on the wane. And not everyone believed the city was adrift. Many Nashvillians, including more than a few members of the privileged set, were throwing their energies into molding a new, more inclusive, more democratic model of leadership for the future. In 1993, a multiracial, multifaith group of religious congregations organized Tying Nashville Together. This grassroots effort to promote community improvement started with neighborhood audits, identifying a pothole here, a crack house there, and publicly calling for action to deal with the problems. By 2000, it had become a well-organized movement with effective programs to identify community needs and hold local politicians accountable for their promises. The year 2000 saw the creation of another broad-based organization seeking a new leadership vision, Cumberland Region Tomorrow. CRT's mandate was to encourage planned growth and the maintenance of hometown values, rather than haphazard suburban sprawl, in the multicounty Nashville area. These groups, as well as neighborhood associations and other community organizations that had come to life around the city, affirmed the possibility that Nashville might someday rely less on the wealthy residents of Belle Meade and Forest Hills to organize its community initiatives and plan its future.

Nashville in 2000 was, at various levels, a city struggling for self-control. More than a few locals spoke of the past decade—in some ways the past two decades—as "a wild ride." Roller-coasters can be fun, but there's always someone else at the wheel. Both the ups and the downs of recent years had served to reinforce a certain passivity. People had become satisfied with the status quo in some ways, and they lacked confidence in their ability to change it. The people in power had not yet reckoned with their own strength, had not yet fully grasped the responsibilities that came with the authority they did wield, and had only begun to work toward liberating the human potential of the greater community. That work remained to be done in the new millennium.

End of an Era

by BILL CAREY

Sam Fleming stayed busy. From helping out in his dad's Harpeth National Bank in Franklin in the early 1920s to helping close some major Nashville deals more than half a century later, he never was a slacker. Right to the end, he was still coming to the office regularly, keeping appointments, hurrying from one thing to the next.

He was a lucky man to have been in his heyday when Nashville was smaller and the banks were locally owned. Fleming was more than just the president of Third National Bank; he was the godfather of the Nashville business community—and when he died at 91 on January 21, 2000, no successor stepped forward to take his place. A few months before his death, I sat in Fleming's office picking his brain about various nuances of Nashville business history. He was in his element—dominating the conversation, thumping his finger on the desk, lecturing me about everything from the importance of "milling in transit" to the value of finishing schools for young ladies in Old Nashville. His hearing was poor, but his concentration was such that he could pick up on my mispronunciation of Nashville financial giant Rogers Caldwell's last name (it's CaldWELL—emphasis on the second syllable.)

After an hour, Fleming announced that time for the interview had expired; if I needed more from him, I could call his secretary and she would fit me in. "Mr. Fleming," I asked with a smile as he walked me to the door, "what could you have to do right now that's so important?" He recoiled, dumbfounded. Returning my smile, he let me know he always had something important to do—and then he closed the door.

In fact, Sam Fleming may have had more important things to do than just about anyone in Nashville business history. Because his career started so early and he never really retired, he was in business through several generations. In his time, regulators allowed bank presidents to operate venture capital companies on the side, so Fleming managed to acquire more businesses than future bank presidents could even dream of. He was personable and pragmatic—one of the few people outside Washington who was friends with both Dwight Eisenhower and Lyndon Johnson.

Just about everyone seemed to like Sam Fleming—except those who worked at competitor banks. "I think he infuriated First American," former Commerce Union president Ed Nelson once said, recalling some of his own moments of frustration when he went toe-to-toe with the agile Fleming.

Third National helped launch many companies. When a young man named Herman Lay needed a loan to expand his potato chip delivery firm, he called Fleming. When Jack Massey needed the money to buy Kentucky Fried Chicken, he called Fleming. When HCA needed capital to purchase hospitals, Tommy Frist called Fleming. After months of meeting with bankers, HCA thought it had a $35-million line of credit from a group of banks, including Third National. At the last minute, First American dropped out. "It was a near disaster," said John Neff, then HCA's chief financial officer, "but Sam Fleming saved the day."

The pinnacle of Fleming's career came in 1968, when he convinced Dan Brooks, an old Vanderbilt classmate, to merge his insurance company, the venerable National Life, with Fleming's bank, creating NLT (National Life-Third). For one brief moment, it was the largest financial institution in the South (as Caldwell and Company had been before the crash of '29). "It was one of the greatest things that ever happened here," Fleming said in 1999. "We really thought we had hit the jackpot." But it was not to be. As Nashville's Genesco had learned in the 1950s, the government balks when companies grow too big too fast. A few months after NLT was formed, the feds forced it to divest the bank. Nashville's second historic moment of leadership in the South's financial affairs would be its last.

In the final two decades of his life, Sam Fleming was no longer actively running Third National. The era of locally owned financial institutions was ending, and Nashville was a juicy plum waiting to be picked by others with more resources. American General took over NLT in 1982. Third National merged with SunTrust in 1986. First American held on until 1999, when it was merged into AmSouth. Commerce Union is now in its third reincarnation, as a Bank of America outpost.

Nashville has become a branch town. The skyline once dominated by monuments to Fleming, his friends, and his rivals (Guilford Dudley Jr.'s L&C Tower, Dan Brooks' National Life Center, Andrew Benedict's First American Center) is left without a single locally owned skyliner.

None of this seemed to bother Sam Fleming. His friends say he was an eternal optimist; he believed that a merger would lead to new opportunity, that the decline of one industry would lead to the rise of another, that Nashville would always find a way to rebound. "After the war, in 1947, we had a big downturn, and it didn't seem like we were ever going to get out of it," he said. "But things came back."

He also loved to outfox the big dogs. "During the depression, First American had nearly all of the established firms," he recalled, "so we started lending money to people who were just going into business, and we stayed with them when things got tough. We were responsible for lots of businesses getting started in Nashville." Sam Fleming loved to remember himself as a 42-year-old bank president in the 1950s: "I was very aggressive. I worked hard and built a great organization. We went after the business. And we got it."

Bill Carey's popular history of Nashville business, Fiddles, Fortunes, and Fried Chicken, *was the best-selling local book of 2000.*

The Business of Medicine in Nashville

by JOHN SERGENT

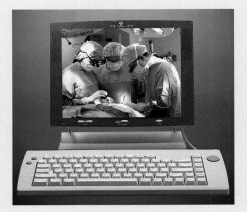

In many ways the United States health-care system is the envy of the world. Our medical schools, libraries, and information systems are probably the best anywhere. High quality primary and specialist physicians are in cities large and small, and virtually every American lives within a short drive of the latest technology, whether it's in cardiac catheterization laboratories, MRI machines, rehabilitation equipment, or ambulatory surgical facilities.

In all these particulars, Nashville and Middle Tennessee are fairly representative of the rest of the country— ahead of most places, behind a few. You can get coronary arteriography in several Nashville hospitals and in Franklin, Murfreesboro, Clarksville, and Cookeville, among other cities. MRI machines are ubiquitous. And Nashville offers full open-heart surgery programs in all four of its large central hospitals.

But all is not well. Not in Nashville, and not in the nation at large.

Despite all of our technology and education, our outcomes are not what they should be. For example, it's been proven that patients coming to an emergency room with a possible heart attack should receive aspirin immediately, yet 17 percent of the time that does not occur. And people being discharged after heart attacks should be sent home on a drug called a beta blocker—but 31 percent of Americans with heart attacks do not go home on a beta blocker. Only 65 percent of women over 65 have received a mammogram within the last two years, and less than half of diabetics have had a thorough examination by an ophthalmologist or optometrist within the past year.

Then there is the problem of random variation. The rates of all sorts of procedures, from back surgery to hysterectomy to coronary angioplasty, vary severalfold from city to city across the nation, for no apparent reason. All of this variation is expensive and sometimes dangerous. The government spends $8,414 per year on each Medicare recipient in Miami and only $3,341 in Minneapolis. The elderly in Miami undergo many more medical procedures and tests, to be sure, but this is not resulting in any apparent benefit to their their health in comparison to their counterparts in Minneapolis.

These inconsistencies exist because we have some antiquated ideas about how best to operate our enormous and complex systems of health care. It's sort of like using a mid-20th century telephone system to communicate in the new millennium. When health insurance, and then Medicare, expanded rapidly in the two decades after World War II, the overriding concern was acute illnesses and injuries requiring hospitalization. Health insurance and Medicare were designed specifically to cover the costs of expensive procedures and hospitalizations. In the 1960s that was a reasonable goal. In this new century, it is not. There are three components to health care: preventive care and health maintenance, episodic care, and chronic disease management. Our reimbursement system is geared to cover episodic care such as treatment for appendicitis, accidents, heart attacks, and cancer. It will pay some, but precious little, for preventive care and maintenance. And, by and large, it pays virtually nothing for chronic disease management.

As an example, look at congestive heart failure. It has been proven in a number of studies that disease management works in preventing unnecessary hospitalizations and in improving quality of life. But disease management is expensive. It requires nurses to call patients to check on their weight, ankle swelling, shortness of breath, and compliance with medications. It requires the development of a database on each patient in order to detect early on when things are going wrong. All of that is time-consuming and costly, yet in the vast majority of health plans, physicians or hospitals receive nothing for those services.

Now let's look at Nashville. Health care is serious business here, and a massive enterprise, with operating costs in the billions of dollars annually. We have intensely competitive systems, including the HCA hospitals, St. Thomas/Baptist and their affiliates, and Vanderbilt. All spend millions advertising this or that service. All have far-flung physician affiliates, diagnostic facilities, ambulatory surgery centers, and the like. And yet the figures on health outcomes are even worse for Tennessee than for the rest of the nation.

Unless we come to a fundamentally different mindset, it is likely that the future will simply yield more of the same, and Nashville, like the rest of the country, will continue to have a health-care system with great potential but mediocre results. If we don't want that to happen—if we truly want to make a change for the better—we have to think outside the box. So here goes:

What if the hospitals in our region, starting with the four large Nashville hospitals plus Metro General, set about collectively to improve the health of the people of our region? That's not to suggest that they stop competing with each other, but rather that they look for areas where cooperation would be clearly in the public's best interest—and theirs.

One such area of cooperation, which potentially would have a huge impact, is the creation of a unified electronic medical record. There are many advantages to electronic records. They are accessible from many areas at the same time. New data, such as laboratory reports, radiology results, and operating-room notes, can be added to the record quickly and simultaneously. And electronic records can also greatly reduce the chance for human error that now exists every time new paperwork is clipped to a patient's chart.

As valuable as these advantages are, though, they pale in comparison to the two principal advantages of a unified electronic record: It's portable, which makes it instantly accessible from anywhere; and it can be kept continually up-to-date, incorporating the latest research and guidelines for medical practice.

Portability is critical because health care in America is hopelessly fragmented and likely to remain that way. Americans have voted with their feet, and they demand two things from their health plans: the latest in high-tech specialty care, and their own choice of doctors and hospitals. In Nashville it's commonplace to find families who have their babies at Baptist, use Vanderbilt for pediatric services, get heart surgery at St. Thomas, and go to one of the HCA hospitals for emergency care. Meanwhile, their next-door neighbors choose Vanderbilt's heart program, Centennial for obstetrics, St. Thomas for cancer care, and Baptist orthopedic surgery. And so it goes.

While this ability to choose is obviously valued by the public, one of its unwanted consequences is a dangerously fragmented system in which all sorts of vital information on everything from allergies to drug interactions to major diagnoses may not be available and known by all concerned. The Institute of Medicine, the medical arm of the National Academy of Sciences, has estimated that between 50,000 and 100,000 Americans die each year because of preventable medical errors, many of which are due to the fact that doctors ordered drugs and tests that were contra-indicated, but the physician didn't have the full information.

Incorporation of the most up-to-date guidelines into the electronic record could be done fairly easily. When a patient has a mammogram, not only would the results be recorded but an automatic reminder would appear when her next one is due. That could be communicated to the patient electronically or by other means. And an endocrinologist or primary-care provider monitoring a patient with diabetes could have immediate access to the patient's file, with prompts for the next eye examination, blood tests, or visit to a kidney specialist, all based on the latest recommendations.

A unified medical record is not just cybernetic pie in the sky; it's doable now. Vanderbilt already has an electronic record, developed under the leadership of Dr. Bill Stead. It also has the nation's most sophisticated system for writing orders electronically, although to date it is used primarily for hospitalized patients. Establishing a consolidated repository for the medical records of all hospitals and medical groups in our region would cost some money, but it would not present an impossible technical hurdle. In fact, Dr. Stead has previously proposed just such a system, with appropriate checks and balances to ensure patient confidentiality.

Where would the money to do this come from? Some would no doubt come from hospitals, which would be saving the millions of dollars they now spend on paper records. The rest would have to come from insurance companies and, ultimately, employers and the insured themselves. The other major player in health and medicine, the federal government, could also be expected to cooperate in a venture of this sort.

As long as we are thinking unconventionally, let's imagine that for every enrollee in a commercial health plan in Nashville and Middle Tennessee, an insurance company must write a check for $50 each year to develop and maintain the electronic record. If there are 500,000 insured people in our region, that would generate $25 million per year. For that amount of money—$4.17 per person per month—we would be able to develop and maintain a comprehensive, current, secure record that can be utilized with the patient's permission by any authorized physician. The record would be organized in such a way that the doctor or hospital or emergency room could quickly get all the information needed to treat whatever medical problem the patient has, from a broken arm to a stroke.

And what would that mean? It would mean that our citizens would get better health care, and that once again Nashville would be showing the rest of the nation that health-care innovation starts here. It would also mean that our hospitals and medical groups, while intensely competitive in most areas, recognize that their primary mission is to improve the health of the people they serve.

And somewhere down the road, perhaps it would also mean that the seeds for a comprehensive plan to meet America's health-care delivery needs would have been planted here in Nashville. We have all the elements of a microcosm: medical schools, university research hospitals, religion-based charity hospitals, public hospitals (city, state, and federal), for-profit medical systems and patient-care facilities, private insurance companies, doctors' groups, and, of course, patients. The nation's health is too important to be left to one or a few of these. It will take all—and Nashville is an ideal place to create the model.

Dr. John Sergent is chief medical officer at Vanderbilt University Medical Center. He has practiced rheumatology in Nashville for more than 25 years.

When he opened a four-night crusade in Nashville on June 1, 2000, evangelist Billy Graham was bringing an old-fashioned message of salvation to a Video Age audience. Was contemporary Nashville in the mood to hear it?

CONFESSIONS

by RAY WADDLE

As the days and hours ticked away before 81-year-old Billy Graham was scheduled to preach at 67,000-seat Adelphia Coliseum in Nashville, his seasoned crusade staff seemed uncharacteristically anxious. This was to be the famed evangelist's first Nashville crusade in 21 years—and, in all certainty, one of the very last big revivals he would conduct anywhere in the world, after more than 50 well-chronicled years on the salvation circuit. From modest Southern roots, he had preached his way to fame among publicans and sinners, presidents and kings. No other 20th-century evangelist had so successfully met the challenges of secularism, televangelism, and overexposure. Whether as Dr. Graham, the Reverend Graham, or just plain Billy, he had won the hearts, if not the souls, of millions, overcoming all obstacles but the last: age and infirmity.

His seriously declining health had been a major issue for months. Some wondered if he would be well enough to preach to church-going Nashvillians, here in the epicenter of American Protestantism. Yet as troubling as his health was, it was not his staff's biggest worry, not today. They had eased him into town without fanfare, and gotten him snugly nestled at an undisclosed hotel (the Marriott near the airport, as it turned out). There, he was contentedly at work, going over last-minute sermon revisions. No, his handlers had a bigger problem, or so they thought. It was not whether their leader would be able to preach, but whether Nashville's faithful would show up en masse to hear him.

The big evangelical Protestant churches in town were enthusiastic supporters of the event, with pastors bonding anew as they planned the crusade over the last year and a half and raised more than $2.5 million to cover the cost of it. But from another angle, there had been signs of discontent for months. The turnout of lay volunteers had failed to meet expectations, and a surprisingly small percentage of Middle Tennessee churches (most of them Baptist, Presbyterian, Church of Christ, or nondenominational) had agreed to take on the thousand-and-one tasks that make a Billy Graham citywide crusade a success.

Not surprisingly, few black churches had volunteered to help pave the way for the crusade bandwagon; their estrangement from white, born-again Protestantism was tinged with memories of past discrimination. Catholics and liberal Protestants, having little empathy for Graham's preaching style or his political priorities, didn't show much crusade spirit, either. Despite Graham's legendary personal graciousness and goodwill, his main band of devoted followers could fairly be described as white, Protestant, and conservative.

Graham's expert detail men knew how to plan a city crusade as precisely as a military invasion or a space shot. They brought years of experience to the task, and they had an energetic local committee to connect the dots. Still, the ground seemed to be shifting beneath their feet as they tried to unravel the mysteries and complexities of Music City. As May drew to a close, it was far from certain that this Bible-Belt metropolis was ready to pack the stadium and embrace revival—not even to hear the 20th-century's master evangelist in what could be his valedictory sermons.

"Nashville was a bit of an enigma at the beginning," Rick Marshall, Graham's director of crusades, said later. "You have polarities there, theological differences. It's a town of leaders, people who are busy

1—**The Tennessee House of Representatives** okays a budget package that slashes Gov. Don Sundquist's proposed spending by $139 million. The plan includes an increase in the "sin tax" on beer, wine, liquor and cigarettes, and a higher tax on utility bills, while providing salary increases for thousands of state employees and teachers. Gov. Sundquist, who continues to push for a state income tax, warns that he will likely veto the bill if it's approved by the state Senate. The measure passes the House by a veto-proof 68-to-29 margin. Now it's up to the Senate to go along or find something better. . . . **On the first night** of the much-anticipated Billy Graham Crusade, the legendary man of God is backed up by a generational cross-section of devout musicians, from contemporary Christian pop singer Steven Curtis Chapman to Graham's 91-year-old colleague, baritone George Beverly Shea (who delivers his trademark rendition of "How Great Thou Art"). For relief from the June heat—and in the spirit of fellowship—a local Christian radio station hands out 25,000 commemorative paper fans, with a 25-cent coupon for Boomer's Barbecue printed on the back. Out in the concession stands at Adelphia Coliseum, hamburgers are going for four bucks and sodas in souvenir Titans cups for five (no beer tonight). Not exactly loaves-and-fishes rates, but sales are brisk. Later, Metro and the Titans will get into a scrape over which of them gets the money.

2—**WTVF-Channel 5** runs an evening-news segment on Tracy Mayberry, who lives with her husband and five children in a dilapidated $400-a-month rental house in Carthage. Last month, as she claims to have done for months before, she complained to the property manager that her toilets overflow, her plumbing is in constant disrepair and her walls and

or out of town a lot, and there was plenty going on at the churches already, lots of events. I see Nashville as a new Southern city, like Louisville or Jacksonville, where the demographic has shifted. The preparation was more difficult than I thought it would be."

Such uncertainty would have been completely out of place during Graham's two previous Nashville crusades, in 1954 and 1979. But that was before the life of the spirit got crowded with new distractions and pursuits—internet spirituality, come-as-you-are worship informality, immigrant religions, pluralism, cable TV evangelism, hypermaterialism '90s style. It was also before big-time professional sports landed in this relatively small-market town, making further demands on Nashvillians' passions and loyalties.

It was a clear indicator of change in Nashville, even in the past two decades, that an evangelical legend was no longer a guaranteed marquee draw. It was as though Billy Graham, the biggest name in American religion, had to be shoehorned into the busy schedule of a city so saturated with churches that it is wryly nicknamed the "Protestant Vatican." Graham's people apparently had underestimated just how over-scheduled this town could be. It was not the first time outsiders and newcomers had tried to take the measure of Nashville's spiritual scene and come up bewildered.

In this year of stocktaking and soul-searching, Nashville was a mental and physical landscape of competing faith claims, religious power centers, theological probings, and heartbreaks. It was a city stretched tight between traditionalism and postmodernism, juggling more than its share of municipal inner conflicts. Nashville had religion in its blood and money on its mind. It was an old town on the make, singing for its supper, winking at the ancient flesh trade, burnishing its country music image even as it fretted that such an image might be a glittery distortion, an empty emblem.

But it wanted to do the right thing, and so it went to weekend worship in higher than average numbers. The old faith gently beckoned. The evidence for this had an old-fashioned clarity: On Sunday mornings, the parking lots were full at hundreds of places of worship, if for a hundred reasons—love of God, ancestral duty, spiritual resuscitation, a solution to loneliness, vague mystical longings, a reliable dating service, ethical instruction for the kids, business connections, entertaining music and oratory and lightshows, the cult of personality, submission to biblical authority, a school for civic leadership, a vision of the beloved community.

Religious Nashville was a jumble of high rhetoric, innovation, spiritual passion,

Putting the Bible on videotape was the latest commercial twist in the constant search to deliver the ancient scriptural story to a new audience and a new market.

good deeds, hypocrisy, highly accomplished music, and half-mad street prophets shouting red-hot messages from an angry deity. There was no lack of big, thriving churches, some with memberships of 3,000 to 5,000 souls—but always in the background lurked worries about superficial spirituality, political injustice, teenage promiscuity, hand-gun dangers, cyber-excitements, and a growing feeling of impotence against the competing secular culture of commercialism. There was a sense that the old verities of the religious heart were cast adrift and under assault. "Nashville is experiencing what's happening across America," said Rick Marshall of the Graham crusade staff. "The culture has shifted away from the Judeo-Christian ethic in very demonstrable ways. Divorce, kids at risk, violence—the Christian community is no longer protected from these things."

Some things hadn't changed. The city's faith profile remained overwhelmingly Protestant, but there were also other communities of long standing and measurable influence. Catholic church history went back to Nashville's early days, and remained strongly rooted. In the city's four well-established synagogues, rabbis intoned the ancient scriptures in Hebrew to congregations whose liturgical response bore traces of a Southern accent. There were two growing, confident Unitarian Universalist churches in the city. Downtown, and around Vanderbilt, the serene, boxy postwar buildings that housed big-budget Protestant denominational offices still stood, casting a long shadow over the city's religious identity. The old-time religion flashed its vital signs in neighborhood pockets all over town. The steeples were everywhere—nearly 1,000 religious congregations in Davidson County alone. In many parts of town, Sunday-morning streets were ghostly empty until the noon hour of sweet benediction. Big-shouldered sanctuaries got bigger in the midst of the grandest local church building boom in a generation.

People could still drive the same route that their parents took to church and work and the grocery store, and feel reassured that the old truths held fast. Church homecomings and pastor anniversaries, crowded attendance at Easter baptisms and Christmas High Mass and weekday funerals, all were sturdy benchmarks of the passage of Nashville family life cycles in sacred time. Any night of the week, you could still see families bowing their heads in corner cafes and chain restaurants, publicly saying grace as they always had. The big congregations got the press, but the little places of worship were the ballast of stability.

"The little churches still characterize Middle Tennessee," said the Reverend Rosemary Brown, pastor of two United Methodist congregations in Nashville, Monroe

Local believers found ways to convey ancient passions of faith to a hurried city of prosperity and dreams.

floors are peeling and riddled with holes. Instead of getting repairs, she said, she got an eviction notice that cited her continuous plumbing complaints and the time needed to fix them as reasons why her family should seek housing elsewhere. The reason Mayberry is on the evening news: Her "slumlord," the house's owner, is none other than Vice President Al Gore. The story goes national overnight. Conservative pundits seize upon the Mayberrys as proof that Gore cannot be trusted to help working people. . . . **Little more than a month** after acquiring famed Nashville brokerage house J.C. Bradford & Co., PaineWebber Group announces it will eventually lay off some 550 of the company's more than 1,000 local employees. Two hundred of them will be gone by June 9; the other 350 will remain on staff until a transitional period is complete in the fall.

3—More than 1,100 patrons take advantage of the all-day 25-cent admission to the newly reopened Belcourt Theatre in Hillsboro Village. The beer served by the theater's concession stand goes over well, as do the century-old church pews loaned to the theater lobby by the Downtown Presbyterian Church. The opening film, *Croupier*, a taut British thriller, will stay by popular demand for 10 weeks. . . . **Dell Computer Corp.** is moving into its new facilities on 800 acres near the Metro airport this week, just 13 months after it cut a sweet deal for the land (how does free sound?) with former Mayor Phil Bredesen and the Metro Council. Dell will open with more than 2,000 employees and 660,000 square feet of floor space. . . . **Sixty watercolors,** engravings, etchings and oils by 19th-century American artist Winslow Homer are on display for three months at the Parthenon, starting today. . . . **Seen on a Chevy Blazer** in the Adelphia parking lot on the third night of the Graham crusade: a metallic fish labeled, JESUS devouring a two-footed metallic fish labeled, DARWIN.

With their echoes of New Testament times, baptisms in rivers or lakes (such as this one in Percy Priest Lake) were traditional expressions of holiness still honored by a substantial number of churches.

4—**A ridiculous snafu** involving country stars Tim McGraw and Kenny Chesney manages to dislodge Billy Graham from the top of the city's news agenda. After performing last night at the George Strait Country Music Festival near Buffalo, N.Y., McGraw and Chesney were in the parking area designated for performers when the daughter of a mounted-division police captain said that Chesney, the singer of "She Thinks My Tractor's Sexy," could sit on her father's horse. The country heartthrob took the saddle and reportedly started to ride away. According to Police Chief Thomas Staebell, Chesney then refused requests by police officers

and Jordonia, each with about 75 members. "They keep things quietly going, doing good deeds that don't get reported. They're the churches that sustain a sense of family continuity. This is where they baptized their babies and buried their parents. It's home to people, the place where life makes sense to them."

But there were also signs of something else around town—division, contradiction, anxiety, apathy. Nashville was home to more religious publishers than any other city, and a dozen Protestant church headquarters as well—but also to the "world's largest" adult book store and high rates of sexually transmitted disease and violent crime. Some big-name religious authors, orators, and musicians who command large crowds elsewhere had trouble scaring up an audience here. Long-held hopes that a spontaneous Holy Ghost revival would bust out in Pentecostal churches in the late 1990s, transforming the city into godliness and drawing worshipers from across the country, had failed to materialize despite tearful prayer. Living here gave many believers a peculiar daily infusion of hopefulness and melancholy, leavened by country music and Southern history—the wafting memories of Civil War battles, lonesome Hank Williams songs, the noble cadences of the King James Bible, and a breathtaking hunch that Nashville had an awesome stake in the economy of salvation.

Laid on top of that was another paradox: This was a town of centralized Protestant religious bureaucracies and authorities in the heart of a Protestant culture that was never very comfortable with either bureaucracy or centralized authority. "People told me before I came here six years ago that Nashville would be an unusual church town," said the Reverend William Buchanan of Fifteenth Avenue Baptist Church, "and I can't say my experience has contradicted that statement. There's tremendous apathy around the churches. Some things don't fly. In Memphis or Atlanta churches, you'll have city-wide revivals that attract thousands. Not here. We're highly divided religiously." Buchanan was speaking mostly about the local African-American Christian scene, notably the National Baptists, who carried long memories of splinterings within their denominations going back a century. "You have factionalism that goes back many years, and it'll take years to overcome those pathologies," he said.

White religious leaders shared in the muttering. For years, people had lamented the lack of interfaith cooperation from one side of town to another. Yes, there was the popular Room In The Inn, an interdenominational project providing church shelters for homeless people on cold winter nights, and there was the positive example of faith-based cooperative efforts to build affordable housing through Habitat for Humanity. But the list of volunteer mediators and reconcilers willing to persevere at the thankless task of diplomacy across the lines of church politics and turf-marking was short indeed; most had their hands full just trying to manage doctrinal conflicts within their own denominations. Few institutions were devoted to the values of religious unity beyond their own back yards.

Farther afield, in the gray zone where social concerns and political ideology ran together, there was more evidence of conflict. The conservative Christian Coalition had long complained about a lack of organizational momentum in Middle Tennessee. Both major political parties openly courted congregational support, with mixed success. Some denominations were burning time and energy to find compromise and resolution—and avoid nasty church splits—over such difficult social issues as homosexuality, abortion, capital punishment, and prayer in schools. And where were all the mega-churches, those 10,000-member suburban space stations that sprang up elsewhere as baby-boomer havens of heavenly assembly? They were on the maps of other thriving regional capitals, leading the way to a new spiritual style, but not here.

Nashville's spiritual enigmas were a predictable topic of conversation whenever ministerial gatekeepers got together. Whether it came from left or right of the political center, much of the complaining was merely professional license; ministers were forever denouncing the laxity of the present age and declaring the urgent need for revival. They also knew that Nashville and all of the Protestant South had long been shaped by intervals of religious revival and relapse. Local spiritual awakenings in the early 1800s, after the Civil War, around the start of the 1900s, and finally after World War II stirred up the energy necessary to launch new churches and publishing houses with renewed purpose, usually followed by consolidation and repose.

Lately the perplexity had run deeper. "In some ways Nashville is still a small place," Buchanan mused. "The contradictions are more obvious here because you can't hide them. We just don't have the numbers to absorb the ambiguities. Atlanta is big enough so you don't notice the ambiguities. They can be relatively hidden." Here, he suggested, the tug of war between old and new, tradition and innovation, was more pronounced, raw like an open wound, and it affected people's everyday thinking.

Something else was happening around town to unsettle the old sense of celestial certainties. Every weekend, new prayers could be heard in strange-sounding languages—Coptic Egyptian, Muslim Arabic, Orthodox Romanian, Catholic Spanish, and more. Here in the Protestant Vatican were new religious residents, new words for God, new orders of worship, new faiths staking a claim to freedom from economic and political chaos back home in Central America or West Africa or Eastern Europe. Kurds, Somalis, Sudanese, Vietnamese, Bosnians, Russians, Ethiopians—some here for as little as a few weeks, others for a generation or more. They followed the time-honored pattern of immigration in America, living mostly in shy isolation at first, trying to get the hang of life in a town awash in Protestant expression, putting up with their own shortages of priests and icons and native liturgical order, but keeping their identity intact as best they could, especially for the sake of the children, who were finding American culture so seductive and were soaking up the language and values instantly and indiscriminantly.

to dismount. When a sergeant tried to remove Chesney from the horse, a melee ensued among Chesney, the sergeant, an enraged McGraw and a sheriff's deputy. McGraw is free on $2,500 bail, but he could face jail time if police press forward on charges of second-degree assault and resisting arrest. Chesney is free on $100 bail. . . . **Remember those four** Beaman Automotive employees who won $31 million in the Kentucky Powerball lottery? A Springfield auto-body-shop owner steps forward to say he is entitled to a fifth of the loot. The body-shop owner, Ken Brown, says he loaned Beaman delivery man James Christian $5 for lunch on May 26, along with an additional sawbuck to plunk down on the May 27 lotto. When Christian and three buddies were announced the winners, Brown began trying to contact them, first in person, then through lawyers. Christian maintains that Brown never gave him the money or discussed the lottery with him. He is filing suit in Davidson County Chancery Court tomorrow to reject Brown's claim to any of the winnings.

5—In a special section titled "The Best and the Brightest," *The Tennessean* surveys 247 valedictorians and salutatorians at Middle Tennessee high schools on topics ranging from home life to current affairs. Of the 149 girls and 98 boys polled, 9 out of 10 have two-parent homes, while 8 out of 10 rank marriage as a high priority. In contrast to the stereotypical party animal, the vast majority of the students say that they do not drink alcohol; that school prayer is acceptable; that religion is important. The results also show that 88 percent of the students plan to vote in November, and of that group 51 per-cent plan to vote for Texas Gov. George W. Bush over 41 percent for Vice President Al Gore. . . . **The section runs** a photo gallery of the students and their chosen colleges. A few at random: Antioch valedictorian Maranda Nave will go to Harding University, Glencliff valedictorian Xuan Thi Truong is Vanderbilt-bound, Donelson

Christian co-valedictorian Christo-
pher Cropsey will attend Belmont,
Pearl-Cohn valedictorian Shameka
Hamilton is headed for Berea College, Saint Cecilia salutatorian
Greta Maureen Clinton-Selin will
attend Rhodes College, Tennessee
School for the Blind valedictorian
Rojon Garrett will go to Cumberland University, Harpeth Hall valedictorian Molly Katherine Arvin
has chosen Washington University, Hillsboro valedictorian Rachel
Bloomekatz will attend Harvard,
McGavock valedictorian Stephen
Vaughn will go to UT-Knoxville,
Montgomery Bell Academy vale-
dictorian Brent Christopher Burish
is going to Notre Dame, University School valedictorian Tiffany
Shih will attend Stanford.

6—**One of Nashville's most
famous music clubs** comes of
legal age today. Perennial local
club headliners Jonell Mosser, Lee
Roy Parnell, Pat McLaughlin and
Jimmy Hall join together to celebrate the 18th birthday of the
Bluebird Cafe, the den-sized
Green Hills listening room that
introduced local audiences to
Garth Brooks and Mary Chapin
Carpenter, among other country
superstars. Under the guidance of
owner Amy Kurland, the Bluebird
has become synonymous around
the world with Music Row
songcraft, thanks to a revolving
cast of hit tunesmiths who test
their material on the club's well-
connected patrons. Present
tonight is the Jay Patten Band, the
first act to play the Bluebird
almost two decades ago. . . .
Vanderbilt University appoints
David Williams II, who currently is
vice president of student and
urban/community affairs at Ohio
State University, to be its new
general counsel, vice chancellor
and secretary of the university.
Williams becomes the first African-
American general officer in Vanderbilt's 125-year history.

7—**The 31st annual Nashville
Independent Film Festival**
begins its five-day run on four
screens at Regal's Green Hills
Commons 16. Formerly the Sink-
ing Creek Film/Video Celebration,
the festival is screening some 275

Prayers to God in Middle Tennessee took on a new accent with the arrival of Latinos in dramatic numbers.
Overwhelmingly Catholic, they practically doubled the size of the local diocese.

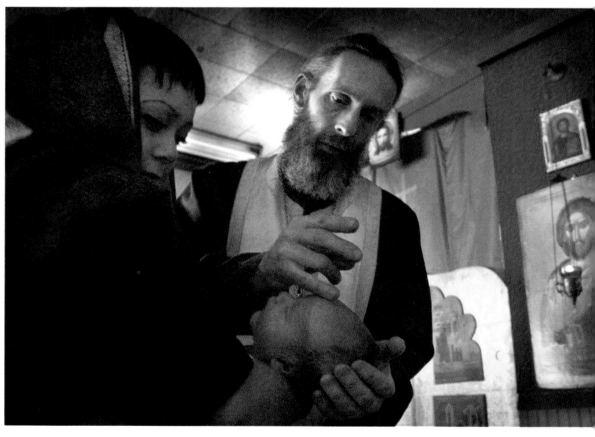

An Eastern Orthodox priest and his family brought religion to Elliston Place, setting up a cafe and chapel
on a street best known for student-oriented shops and nightlife.

Most conspicuous by their numbers were some 45,000 Spanish-speaking Catholics in Middle Tennessee, an influx that was shaking the Diocese of Nashville into new patterns of worship and identity. The number of Latino Catholics here had quintupled in just one decade, and now made up more than one-third of the Nashville diocese. Most of them were immigrants from Mexico and Central America, drawn here to work, if only for a few months at a time. Their presence prompted the local diocese to start a Hispanic mission center and find priests who could say the Mass in Spanish. A dozen Anglo parishes hosted weekly Masses for these recent arrivals. In 2000, Nashville's English-speaking Catholics and the Latino newcomers were largely parallel universes, rarely intersecting across the language gulf. But it all had theological consequences for the future. "The Hispanics here are the first group large enough to get the attention of the white middle class," said the Reverend Steve Klasek, pastor of Holy Rosary Catholic Church. "I wouldn't say whites in Nashville feel threatened. They're intrigued, maybe a little perplexed—but this is getting us to realize how universal our church really is. These are Catholics who don't look like us, who speak another language. It's been good for us."

Conversely, Nashville appeared to have been good for many of the immigrants. Valentin Serban, a member of the Saint John Chrysostom Romanian Orthodox Mission Church in Nashville, breathed a sigh of relief when the congregation finally got a priest in the summer of 2000. "Now we feel closer to God, we feel like we're home, in our own language in worship," he said. The little congregation started holding Sunday services at Calvary United Methodist Church, which allowed them use of the chapel, where they carried in icons and other symbols of Orthodox veneration. Two other small Romanian congregations—one Baptist, the other Pentecostal—were meeting elsewhere in town. "We feel like a small island in the big Nashville ocean," Serban said. "But many people have helped us. We all believe in one God. It's not an Orthodox God, or a Methodist God. It's Almighty God."

Win Myint, a native of Burma, knew that isolated-island feeling all too well. He moved here in 1965 to teach mathematics at Tennessee State University, and discovered that he was just about the only Buddhist around. "It was like a hick town—not even a Chinese restaurant," he said. "The only Oriental food we could find was at a restaurant in Smyrna." Myint and his wife, Patti, opened the International Market restaurant in 1975 to remedy that.

A few years later, he turned his attention to the lack of a Buddhist place of worship. Despite some local opposition, he bought an old Baptist church building on Treutlan Street in 1981 and converted it into a Buddhist temple, importing a couple of monks from Southeast Asia. "We wanted an ecumenical Buddhist temple so that all the Asian refugees would not forget their culture and religion," Myint said.

Steadily for 35 years, he has been a one-man Buddhist ambassador to Christian Nashville, speaking to college classes on comparative religions and taking part in fledgling interfaith study meetings. In a city where evangelism is second nature to thousands, Myint was a curiosity because, he said, "I always had to make them understand that Buddhists aren't trying to convert other people, and don't want to be converted themselves." Nashville, he said, has softened over time: "There's more interfaith dialogue now than before. I don't find opposition to Buddhism as such. But yes, there are still many Christians, and Muslims, too, who are very concerned about me. They're sure I'm going to hell. They want to preach me the truth. I ask them what the truth is. They are not able to tell me to my satisfaction. So we leave it at that."

Myint's vision of a unified Buddhist presence in Nashville fell short as later Asian immigrants brought their own ethnic and cultural interpretations of Buddhism. By 2000, Myint estimated, there were about 3,000 Buddhists in town, and three separate temples—Laotian, Cambodian, Vietnamese—as well as a small community devoted to Tibetan Buddhism.

The local Hindu experience has been different, as Myint noted with admiration. Instead of replicating the religious and political hostility that wracked the Indian subcontinent they had left behind, Hindu arrivals over the last 30 years pooled prosperous energies into one house of worship. The remarkable Hindu Temple, a decade old now, has become a proud fixture on a Bellevue hill off Old Hickory Boulevard, and a continuous fascination to other Nashvillians. The structure, resembling a monument out of

features, documentaries and short subjects. Last year's festival drew more than 7,000 people, and that was with only two screens. This one will pull in more than 10,000. . . . **Smoke 'em if you got 'em:** The state Senate approves a budget that puffs away $202 million in tobacco-lawsuit settlement funds, instead of adopting the energy tax proposed by the House. The House responds by unanimously rejecting the Senate's work, forcing a committee from both houses to seek a compromise. . . . **Ken Brown's luck** holds out. In spite of a state law from the 1800s that says a gambling contract is unenforceable, Brown reaches an out-of-court settlement with James Christian, one of four Beaman Automotive employees who split a $31-million Powerball jackpot—using what Brown claimed was the $5 he had given Christian to buy lotto tickets. Terms of the settlement are not disclosed. . . . **Mayor Bill Purcell,** focusing on long-neglected infrastructure issues in his first term, creates a pilot program to help lower-paid Metro employees buy their own homes in the city. The first year, 100 city workers with household incomes below $47,000 will get $5,000 loans to buy houses costing $120,000 or less—and the loans will be forgiven if they stay in the homes and on the Metro payroll for five years. This is part of Purcell's 10-year goal to generate 35,000 new units of affordable housing as a long-term alternative to public housing.

8—*On Music Row,* a television pilot created, cast, written and filmed in Nashville, plays to several hundred viewers as a feature of the Nashville Independent Film Festival. Directed by cinematographer and longtime Nashville film supporter Armanda Costanza, the pilot concerns a group of struggling songwriters and performers trying to get ahead on Music Row. One goes so far as to sleep with a label executive, which, in the music industry's unstable current climate, is arguably less effective than seducing a valet parker.

In ever-increasing numbers over the past three decades of the 20th century, Muslims from nearly every continent came to live in Nashville. By 2000, an estimated 15,000 practitioners of the faith were in the city's orbit, most worshiping faithfully at mosques.

The cast features country singer Lari White as well as actress Jennifer O'Neill and actors David Alford and Robert Lynn, who co-wrote the script.

9—Brentwood-based Mast Advertising is giving Nashville something it hasn't had since 1910—an area-wide business directory to compete with the BellSouth Yellow Pages. Differences in the new directory include restaurant menus, some detailed street maps, internet and fax listings for businesses—and cheaper advertising. Chuck Cinelli, owner of Cafe Coco, an all-night coffeehouse off Elliston Place, tells *The Tennessean* he pays BellSouth $750 per month for a one-column-by-one-inch ad in the Yellow Pages, while he buys a full page in the WonderBook for a monthly fee of $79. . . . **Stop the presses:** A banner headline

8th-century India, called forth craftsmen from the mother country to see it through.

The first Islamic mosque in Nashville was founded in the 1970s, and by the turn of the century, there were a half-dozen such Muslim houses of worship in the area. At Tennessee State University's Gentry Center, some 5,000 Muslims gathered one day in December 2000 for a religious observance, the biggest local assembly for Islam ever.

After an extend-

A Sikh reads from the faith's holy scriptures at home. The tiny local community of Sikhs was one religious group from the Indian subcontinent that had no temple here.

ed search, the Mormons finally found a place to build a temple for their sacred rites, settling in Franklin with a marble edifice they proudly lit at night. Practitioners of the Baha'i faith, with a passion for world peace and racial reconciliation, had outgrown their worship center in North Nashville and were building a new one in Antioch. Also scattered across the city were neopagans, psychics, freethinkers, atheists. "When I moved here 12 years ago, the first thing people would ask is, 'What church do you go

Local Hindus built a temple in Bellevue to honor ancient religious festivals that harked back to their native India and provided social unity far from home.

above the fold in *The Tennessean* blares the breaking story of the day: "You, too, can be a Survivor, if you master the art of eating bugs." It's all about the nutritional value of eating bugs if one is stranded on a desert island—just like the contestants on the top-rated "reality" TV show *Survivor*, now the Midstate's most-watched program on Wednesday nights. "You can get all the nutrients in insects that you can get in chicken," says Vanderbilt biologist Olle Pellmyr. Other nuggets of knowledge to be gleaned from the piece: Grubs taste like bacon, while water bugs are "lemony." In the story, Frank Sutherland, *The Tennessean*'s executive editor and wine columnist, recommends "a white Zinfandel" to accompany the insect repast, saying, "an ugly meal deserves an ugly wine." It's all in fun, but the maggot-munching whimsy hands plenty of ammo to media critic Henry Walker, who nags incessantly in the alternative newsweekly *In Review* that the morning paper has lost its news judgment. . . . **Facing a variety of unpleasant options,** Tennessee lawmakers resurrect a political demon: a state income tax. The General Assembly is considering a tax on those 42,000 Tennessee households making more than $100,000 a year in adjusted gross income. "It hurts so few, it helps so many and it takes Tennessee forward," says Sen. Jerry Cooper (D-Morrison). The assembly will find out quickly whom it really serves. . . . **An intertribal group of Native Americans** on a 3,800-mile walk across America stops at the intersection of Old Hickory Boulevard and Hillsboro Road to pray over five ancient graves that have been in the news. The graves were discovered when workers began widening the intersection, and local Indian organizations won a court injunction against further digging until the matter is settled. "The children buried here should be left in peace," said one of the walkers, Fred Short of Sacramento, Calif.

10— **Bearing placards** reading "Stop Genocide of Kurds," about

to?'" said Don Peterson, a native Midwesterner. "I'd tell them I'm an atheist. And they'd say, 'Why would you be something like that?' But just because people don't believe in God doesn't mean they're bad people. I don't think hell is packed with atheists."

Optimistic sociology might predict that all these attitudes and accents were somehow destined to mingle and make peace with the local religious culture of Bible adoration and Southern Sabbath graces. That sort of fusion had been going on here for 200 years already, albeit on a thoroughly Christian canvas. Previous waves of immigrants blended all sorts of notions they had brought with them—Southern cussedness and Scottish rationalism, New England severities and African spiritualism, Calvinist certitudes and Native American earth-memories, mountain poetry and delta soul, Civil War pride and prejudice—to create a Middle Tennessee way of doing religion in America. Fresh ingredients for the stew had never been lacking. The new immigrants now would spice it up further, showing what blended insights into God were conceivable to those who were prepared for the feast. But it would likely take years, decades. This prospect of local diversity was eagerly awaited by some, dreaded by others. The specter of pluralism closed in a little harder each day on a town that seemed dubious and hesitant to welcome the news.

Traditional ministers accustomed to their own denominational loyalty sometimes publicly admitted their discomfort with these new players in a spiritual marketplace gone global. In Franklin, a coalition of evangelical churches protested that the Mormons with their new temple were falsely advertising themselves as Christian. Letters to the Editor in the newspaper debated the truth-claims of various new religious arrivals in town, testing the limits of their Southern/Protestant hospitality to these new neighbors. No one is sure exactly when, but one morning Nashvillians awoke to find that religious pluralism had arrived, like a long-predicted weather front, and few churches felt prepared for the new gusts of change.

All this was happening in a broader American culture that was losing whatever unity of spiritual values it might have had—and instead of setting trends, Nashville was being swept along with the current. The paradigm of a "quest culture" was gaining currency. "Oh, I'm not religious, I'm spiritual" became an accepted shorthand self-description at cocktail parties by the mid-1990s.

"The world's getting smaller, and we're seeing a merging of ideas, scientific and religious, East and West," said Philip Self, a local yoga practitioner who grew up Methodist. He's the author of a nationally noted book, *Yogi Bare: Naked Truth from America's Leading Yoga Teachers*. "We're finding that science is supporting the mystics' intuitive knowledge. It's like a fusion of pop and country in music. This is a new merger of ideas."

One sociologist, speaking to a group of religion news writers, described "questers" as spiritual seekers who had little religious upbringing and feel "homeless" in the available faith traditions, but were now embarked on a spiritual journey. A massive new commercial sector—book publishing, massage spas, retreat centers, internet sites—catered to and reinforced that permanent restlessness. "Something about our time is deeply troubling to people," sociologist Wade Clark Roof said. "There's a sense of metaphysical homelessness. The question is whether we can dwell in a single tradition anymore."

Some of this was born of education, an exposure to the increasing diversity on the American public square. One local businessman-turned-author had done his own research. "All the people my age who grew up in the conservative churches started having children of their own and seeing that what we were told as kids wasn't real," said Ron Cook, a Nashvillian who grew up in the Church of Christ in the 1960s and is co-author of *Ground Zero: Starting All Over Again with God*. "We were told that this Southern Christianity is the only way God blesses people. But we're meeting all these people from the North who move here, and they're saying to the Bible-belters that there are other ways to think about things. I'm meeting Catholics and Jews and atheists who have bigger hearts than the angry Christians I knew."

Cook's diagnosis, after interviewing hundreds of people, is simple: "God just isn't real to people. The more denominations they check out, the emptier the places look spiritually. Church fails them. People aren't hearing the news that they are special to God. Each individual is different on purpose: That's God's plan. The only way we're ever going to find community is to see that—and truly respect each other at a personal level."

This new sensibility was settling wherever it could in Nashville, posing a perceived threat to a local religious ecology unlike any other in America. In 2000, Nashville still had reason to claim bragging-rights possession of the shiny buckle of the Bible

two dozen demonstrators march along Charlotte Avenue to protest the U.S. government's aid to Turkey, which refuses to recognize the ethnic group's right to a Kurdish state or self-governance. Several thousand Kurds, most of them Iranian refugees from the aftermath of the Gulf War, make their home in Davidson County, forming one of the largest Kurdish communities in the U.S. . . . **A sizable chunk** of East Nashville history revolves around East High School, which produced five decades of graduating classes until it became a middle school in 1986. "For me, it was my Camelot," recalls 1945 East High graduate Mary Granstaff, now a retired Metro elementary school principal. Today, the school hosts a reunion to honor 11 distinguished East High alumni, including former Nashville Mayor Richard Fulton (class of '45), former Metro Council member Tandy Wilson III ('42), former *Nashville Banner* editor Eddie Jones ('42), veteran broadcast personality Ralph Emery ('51) and Tennessee State Museum Executive Director Lois Riggins Ezell ('57). . . . **Adapting to high-tech times,** the Grand Ole Opry unveils its first new set design in 22 years. The wooden red barn that served as the Opry's backdrop has been updated and augmented with video screens and new lighting capabilities. Opry stars ranging from new country vocalist Chely Wright to 88-year-old Brother Oswald give the set a thumbs-up, but some miss the old set's rustic charm. . . . **A mysterious slice of local legend** is on display this afternoon at the Nashville Independent Film Festival. *Friends Seen and Unseen*, a documentary by WSMV-Channel 4 news anchor Demetria Kalodimos and her producing partner, Kathy Conkwright, tells the story of the Prophet Omega, the Nashville radio evangelist who taped a series of unforgettably bizarre sermons at his apartment, Q-238, at 488 Lamont Dr. throughout the late 1970s and early '80s. The sermons were taped off the radio in the mid-1980s and passed around by

As president of LifeWay Christian Resoures, Jimmy Draper headed the publishing division of the Southern Baptist Convention. LifeWay was the new name for the old Baptist Sunday School Board, a name change made to appeal to a broader range of Christian consumers.

Belt—and even claim to be the most important religious center in a nation where Protestantism remained the biggest single religious identity by far.

For this was the place where Southern Baptist, United Methodist, National Baptist, Free Will Baptist, and African Methodist Episcopal churches, among others, produced Sunday school literature, Bibles, and hymnals for some 30 million church members. Thomas Nelson Publishers, a publicly traded company, could claim to be one of the biggest producers of Bibles in the English language. And the Southern Baptists' LifeWay Christian Resources remained the world's biggest publisher of Christian materials, with the United Methodist Publishing House, a couple of blocks away, not far behind in sales volume. The National Baptist Publishing Board, run by the R.H. Boyd family for more than a century, was considered one of the most prestigious black-owned businesses in the nation. All told, religious publishing in Nashville had receipts of three-quarters of a billion dollars annually. Editorial decisions made here set the tone and subject matter for Protestant Sunday school discussions all over the nation each week. Even the Gideons, whose give-away Bibles were famously enshrined in Beatle song and hotel rooms the world over, made their headquarters here.

Such a collection of bureaucracies dictated church politics, too: This was where denominational policies got hammered out or doctrinal revisions were proposed, ministerial credentials fine-tuned, holy writ enforced. Almost every summer, the Southern Baptist Convention, with executive offices downtown, could get America talking about its latest hot-button issue, which always managed to penetrate the nation's deepest anxieties about sex, gender, or the nature of religious truth. In June 2000, the SBC revised its official faith statement to underscore its belief in an infallible Bible and, among other things, its conviction that women should not be ministerial leaders of local churches. Whether outsiders agreed or not, the SBC managed to stay in the news in ways other denominations could only envy.

This was also the place where most of contemporary Christian music, and much gospel music, was conceived and recorded—a humming and strumming and harmonizing for God, usually born-again Protestant style, that adopted every pop music current without apology. The Christian music business here exploded during the 1990s into an $800-million-plus operation employing more than 700 people in town. "Nashville is now a place with a huge creative community that's the epicenter of contemporary

musicians, ranging from country singer T. Graham Brown to the Rolling Stones and David Bowie. . . . **After 43 years** dispensing sundaes, fried chicken and wisecracks, waitress Jean Stevenson is retiring today from the Elliston Place Soda Shop, the famed luncheonette that has been serving patrons since 1939. When she started working, on July 20, 1956—her 24th birthday—a plate with meat and three vegetables and a drink cost 88¢, tax included. Today the same meal costs more than $5. When a customer asks the great-grandmother why she is leaving, she replies simply, "Because I can."

11—**Forget ratings.** This afternoon at Greer Stadium, the battle between country FM stations WSIX and WSM is all about runs. Today is the 10th-annual Celebrity Softball Challenge, which has evolved into the unofficial first event of Fan Fair. There is apprehension this year about Fan Fair's future. Next summer, the week-long country music festival is being shortened and moved from its traditional home at the Tennessee State Fairgrounds. The new location will not be announced until July, but it will likely be either Adelphia Coliseum or the new Nashville Superspeedway under construction in Wilson County.

12—"**Taxation without representation!**" The colonial rallying cry is taken up by protesters on Legislative Plaza, as Saturday's "Lexus parade" gives way to a cacophonous crawl of Cadillacs, pickup trucks and 18-wheelers. The hundred sign-waving demonstrators on hand, including former TennCare director Rusty Siebert and car dealership owner Lee Beaman, stop short of dumping tea in the Cumberland, but they vigorously boo the tax supporters across Charlotte. On the NashvillePost.com website, Bill Carey mentions a sign posted on a door at Legislative Plaza: "We're rich as hell and we're not going to take it anymore!" . . . **Coach Jeff Fisher** settles the nerves of Tennessee Titans' fans by signing a three-year contract extension. He will remain with the Titans through 2003. . . . **After six years** as Metro fire chief, a position he held without having been a fireman, Buck Dozier tenders his resignation as of Aug. 1. Dozier says he will pursue opportunities in the private sector. Less than a month ago, a personnel audit raised concerns that 16 staffing and management issues had the potential to cost the city $2 million annually. Dozier says the department still needs to fill 64 firefighter jobs.

13—The state income tax is dead. As antitax zealots maintain their vigil on Capitol Hill, legislative support crumbles in the House. Even Rep. Ben West (D-Nashville), a tax foe, has received more than 700 e-mails in two days. Reads one: "You are disgusting, disgraceful fat pigs." A man dressed as Hitler equates the income tax with Nazism. Kathryn Bowers (D-Memphis) was carried from the House on a stretcher two days ago; yesterday she learned that her father had died. She earns a standing ovation when she walks into the chamber, armed with a yes vote for the tax. Such shows of bravery are few and far between. By the end of the long day, the state is no closer to a budget than before. . . . **Run for your life!** The fire ant, the mound-building menace with the fiery bite, is said to be within 75 miles of the Nashville area. The large, dangerous, hard-to-kill pests have been advancing north and east for 80 years. Hope may reside, though, with the South American decapitating fly, whose larvae hatch in the ant's head and chew, chew, chew. Somehow these almost sound worse than the ants.

14—Renovations are under way on the west pediment of the Parthenon, the 69-year-old full-scale Athenian replica that resides in Centennial Park. Acid rain, pigeon droppings and other factors have eroded the statues on the pediments, the triangular bases of the roof at each end of the structure. The Parthenon's

Christian music," said John Styll, publisher of *CCM* magazine, the industry's leading periodical. The genre's star performers included clean-talking rock music heroes who made emotional contact with their young audiences by giving personal faith testimonies at concerts. Their calling was to keep morale high among the children of light. And sell records.

In Franklin, a short-wave radio station, World Christian Broadcasting, had a global reach, regularly producing programs in English, Russian, and Mandarin Chinese, all transmitted from a tower in Alaska. The organization, mostly Church of Christ-supported, also had offices in Saint Petersburg (Russia, not Florida) and Hong Kong, and an international audience conservatively estimated at upwards of 250,000 and rising rapidly.

Add it all up, and you get a city with religious leverage, and more influence than its small-town feel would suggest. Nashville was accustomed to this low-wattage, high-voltage role. Here, after all, was a comparatively small market for two major-league pro sports teams; a "Third-Coast" recording mecca that outdid Hollywood and New York (at least in restaurant celebrity-spottings per square foot); and, in the biblical cosmos, a kind of Southern Rome or Geneva, if not Athens, with its creativity, paradoxes, and power radiating to the four corners of God's green Protestant patch of earth.

CeCe Winans was among the more famous luminaries of the Christian music scene, which had become a merchandising colossus in Nashville.

Given Nashville's symbolic importance, it annoyed some strident Bible-believers that the city didn't get much excited about millennial calculations for the end of time as Year 2000 neared. The city seemed too vain and materialistic, too busy. It was ignoring the Book of Revelation's florid scenarios of violent divine judgment. And when January dawned and it looked like the coast was clear and Jesus had not yet appeared, that frankly suited a lot of religious professionals just fine, and for good and prudent business reasons: With so many local enterprises in the faith industry routinely turning double-digit profits, a cosmic crack-up would make for an inconvenient, not to say apocalyptic, business downturn.

Instead, many of the city's congregations were preoccupied with figuring out the changing dynamics of the world to which Jesus had not yet returned. The Holy Grail had become the psyche and soul of newcomers to town, or the teeming ranks of young people who felt spiritually adrift. More to the point, the target of the congregations was the "unchurched" folks who played hard to get, who were indifferent to the furious theological debates that defined the

Even in the Digital Age, a vivid expectation of divine judgment and the return of Christ was never far from the surface in Middle Tennessee and across the South.

past or gave denominations their identities. Many were Nashvillians numbed by divorce or downsizing or digitization, three "D's" that did not include dogma or devil. So in the name of old-fashioned evangelism, some churches tried newfangled approaches. They quietly took the "Baptist" or "Church of Christ" name off the sign out front in hopes of appealing to visitors who might be turned off by such old-line denominational tags. Or they preached the language of addiction recovery and marriage reconciliation from the pulpit. Or they placed a live band with plugged-in guitars and drum machines on stage where the altar used to be.

A couple of churches departed from an ancient Sabbath rhythm by adding a Friday-night service, since so many people now either had to work on Sundays, or perhaps as likely, were just unwilling to break up their weekend to get to church. "The day is gone when we expect the culture to shut down on Sunday and everybody's in church," said the Reverend Mike Glenn of Brentwood Baptist Church, which started a Friday-night service in August 2000. "This leaves us with an interesting choice. We can talk about how bad things are in our society, or we can try to offer an alternative."

This spirit of experimentation and adjustment marked the new freedom that many religious professionals felt inside Nashville's special milieu. It was, to be sure, a precinct crowded with thoroughly religious landmarks, but none of them could claim overpowering dominance. On the contrary, a pattern of decentralized and fragmented power was beginning to emerge, reflecting a trend that had been intensifying for a generation.

No single congregation dominated, and no one minister stood out above the others. Famed orator Kelly Miller Smith of First Baptist Church, Capitol Hill, and beloved patriarch Ira North of Madison Church of Christ both died in 1984. Pastor Bill Sherman of Woodmont Baptist Church retired from the pulpit and from his popular Sunday-morning TV worship slot in 1997. There were clergy friendships and coalitions down the West End corridor or in East Nashville or North Nashville or Brentwood, but the effect was a scattering into separate, sometimes rival, power centers. Factionalism of

east end has only recently re-opened to visitors after a $3-million restoration process; the entire structure has been surrounded by scaffolding and fences since 1994. The west pediment should be completed by May 2001. . . . **An eight-story building** at 179 8th Ave. N., vacant since 1992, is purchased by businessmen George Nason and Dee Fox for $725,000. They plan to renovate it into 10 luxury condominiums, which will run from $350,000 to more than $1 million for the top two floors. Downtown dwellings are being touted as an antidote to the suburban sprawl that decimated Church Street, which for most of the century was the hub of Nashville retailing.

15—**Two days ago,** near closing time, a masked man walked into Shintomi restaurant in Green Hills and began firing a semiautomatic weapon into the ceiling. Thus began the fourth in a string of ethnic-restaurant robberies dating back to the Apr. 24 stickups of Grand China restaurant in Bellevue and Benkay in Lion's Head. Police are on the lookout for a dark green Chevy Blazer, perhaps with temporary tags. . . . **A Davidson County grand jury** finds that Metro police officers were justified in using deadly force in three separate shooting incidents in March and April. No criminal charges will proceed against the officers who shot and killed Timothy David Hayworth, Larry Davis and Chong Hwan An. . . . **Citing a bout with diverticulitis,** Tony Coelho steps down as the chairman of Al Gore's presidential campaign. Coelho is credited with getting the Gore campaign focused on the unexpectedly strong showing of New Jersey Sen. Bill Bradley. But a recent *Newsweek* article blamed Coelho's brusque manner for the Gore headquarters' low morale, and the chairman still faces lingering questions about his personal financial dealings. Replacing him will be Commerce Secretary Bill Daley.

16—**Country singer Charley Pride** arrives at the Country Music Hall of Fame expecting to take part in a press conference about the Grand Ole Opry's 75th-anniversary celebration. Instead, when presenter Brenda Lee begins reading his biography, a tearful Pride realizes he is going to be inducted into the Hall of Fame. Pride, 62, will become the Hall of Fame's first African-American member. Also honored will be the late honky-tonk hero Faron Young, who died in 1996 of a self-inflicted gunshot wound—reportedly brought on by depression over lack of recognition for his contributions to country music. . . . **Fan Fair's approximately 21,000 visitors** are leaving the city just as about 50,000 more are expected for the three-day X Trials, which start today in the parking lot of Adelphia Coliseum. The trials are a qualifying event for the ESPN X Games, a punishing test of ability in skateboarding, inline skating, bicycle stunt riding and other extreme sports. . . . **Tennessee Dance Theatre,** the acclaimed Nashville dance company founded by Donna Rizzo and Andrew Krichels, begins a two-day run of *Ghosts of the Civil War,* an ambitious original work that features dancers clad in half-blue/half-gray costumes that represent the divided loyalties of the War Between the States. The performance is met with raves, but the company will soon face strife of its own. . . . **A proposal to turn** Nashville State Technical College from a two-year community college into a four-year school meets with sharp criticism from Tennessee State University staff and alumni. While the Nashville Area Chamber of Commerce believes Nashville Tech could offer new and expanded college options, TSU supporters argue it would undermine TSU's standing and its federally mandated efforts to attract more white students. . . . **The latest of four** budget proposals this week crashes and burns in the state Senate. When work resumes after the weekend, lawmakers will have only 12 days left to pass a budget.

17—**Vernon Winfrey,** the East Nashville barber and former councilman best known as the

Members of the Epiphany Dancers practice for a performance at Christ Church, the venerable Episcopal cathedral in downtown Nashville.

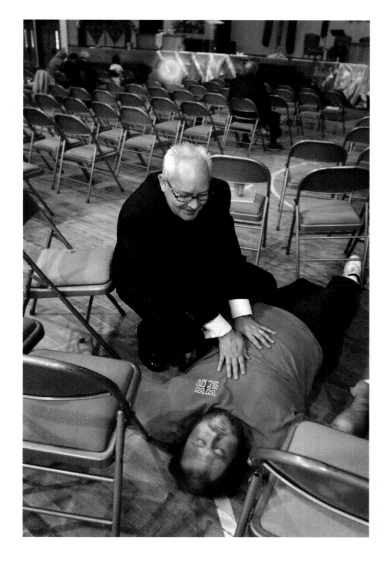

A traveling evangelist lays hands on a worshiper overcome with emotion during a Pentecostal revival. Such experiences held out the hope for a firsthand encounter with the divine.

father of multimedia superstar Oprah Winfrey, marries Brentwood High School assistant principal Barbara Williams at the downtown Hermitage Hotel before 340 guests. Oprah Winfrey and her boyfriend, Stedman Graham, attend, as do Chicago baseball hero Ernie Banks and *Essence* magazine President Susan Taylor. . . . **Meet the new Nashville:** The Grand Ole Opry begins broadcasting on the internet as part of WSM's round-the-clock streaming audio. . . . **Tracy Mayberry** and her family have announced their plans to vacate the notorious rental house owned by Vice President Al Gore. It can't be soon enough for Gore, who has endured weeks of witless wisecracks on the topic. "It's astounding to me that a man so smart he could invent the internet could be so dumb he couldn't fix a toilet," quips New York Gov. George Pataki, stumping for Texas Gov. George W. Bush before 1,200 GOP bigwigs at the Opryland Hotel. . . . **Metro police conclude** the second weekend of a crackdown on cruising teens and curfew breakers on congested Second Avenue. Ninety-one minors have been picked up, most of them from outside Davidson County. Under Metro's curfew, teens are not allowed on the street between midnight and 5 a.m. without a parent or guardian. But Second Avenue merchants regularly complain that cruising teenage drivers logjam the street, harass tourists and pick fights. On Fridays and Saturdays, it can take 40 minutes to drive one block.

18—**If all goes well,** Bellevue could be only two years away from getting its own YMCA. According to Councilman Vic Lineweaver, constituents have requested a YMCA for 10 years, but it did not seem feasible until last fall, when a donor volunteered to buy 20 acres of land near Harpeth Heights Baptist Church for the facility. The deal should be completed by the end of the month. . . . **With area blood supplies** running perilously low, the Nashville chapter of the

this sort seemed to come with the territory: With so much official religious sponsorship and incorporation, unity wasn't possible—or even desired.

In a Protestant culture that fiercely protected local congregational independence, splintering was often seen as an important engine of church growth. Congregational splits and breakaways were always part of the local drama, with new churches or temples springing out of the old, either as missionary efforts or the result of angry tumult over doctrine or clergy personality (in cases where there was no bishop in place to mediate disputes). To some people, this passion for schism exposed a deeply embarrassing side to church life, an insult to the Body of Christ; to others, it was an active indication of the stirrings of the Holy Spirit, a rejection of staid patterns of worship or leadership.

Meanwhile, some of the biggest churches had taken a generation to find their way, and were now among the leaders in contemporary Nashville. Most of these were nondenominational suburban congregations, such as Christ Church on Old Hickory Boulevard near Brentwood, signaling the new respectability of Pentecostal-oriented worship along the city's well-groomed avenues. Other sizable churches in town had not existed a generation ago—like Bellevue Community Church, a "seeker-sensitive" congregation, conservative theologically but savvy about the psychology and life situation of unchurched people, and beholden to no denominational overlords.

The venerable downtown churches—Episcopal, Presbyterian, Baptist, Methodist, Catholic—still carried a certain authority, in part because they were spiritual homes for veteran staffers from the denominational agencies and weekday denizens of the professional classes. The Covenant Association, an interfaith collection of moderate and liberal clergy, got started in the 1990s to try to reverse a perception of their declining influence in the city's public life. The Metro Pastors group, meeting regularly, had become a prime mover of most big evangelical Christian initiatives in town. The Nashville Peace and Justice Center was a haven for the city's stubbornly dedicated remnant of progressives. Scarritt-Bennett Center, an interfaith retreat campus owned by the United Methodists, had a following of its own for an alternative Christian-oriented spirituality. Tying Nashville Together, a grass-roots movement of churchmen and women advocating local public policy reforms, patiently built its base in dozens of congregations, across the lines of race and class. Quietly, a growing number of people also rallied to new forms of spiritual discipline and divine access, becoming pupils of traveling gurus or teachers of silent meditation.

Altars increasingly found new keepers of the sacred flame: women. Female ministers were joining the leadership in Presbyterian, Methodist, Episcopal, and Jewish life, even if they still were being passed over for the most prestigious congregational assignments. "I'm not afraid of talking about issues of feminine sensitivity from the pulpit," said the Reverend Becca Stevens, chaplain at Saint Augustine's Chapel at Vanderbilt. "Last year, I was pregnant during the Advent season, and I could preach about that Christmas anticipation and waiting and longing in a special way. Women have the ability to bring another side of the story of God."

Vanderbilt Divinity School remained a liberal power center of its own in a conservative Protestant culture, teaching the higher criticism of the Bible and social justice themes. Every spring, there were lots of new seminary graduates around town, further spreading, or decentralizing, the religious voice: graduates from Vanderbilt Divinity, American Baptist College, and Free Will Baptist Bible College, among others—close to 100 a year in all.

A random sampling of religious happenings in the busy summer and fall of 2000 hinted at the spiritual ferment Nashville was experiencing:

• A pope came to town for the first time—not Pope John Paul II of Rome but Pope Shenouda III of Alexandria, Egypt, spiritual leader of the Coptic Orthodox Church. He paid a visit to Saint Mina Coptic Orthodox Church in Nashville, spiritual home to 1,100 Egyptian-born local residents.

• Congregation Micah, the first new Reform congregation in Nashville in more than 100 years, saw its membership soar beyond 500 families. Signs of ferment were also evident at the three long-established Jewish congregations in the city, as well as at the Center for Jewish Awareness, the Jewish Community Center, and Akiva, the only Jewish school in the city.

• American Baptist College, under new president Forrest Harris, announced it was finding financial stability after years of uncertainty. The tiny school, the worldwide training college for ministers of the National Baptist Convention U.S.A., has a rich civil rights history but is perhaps better known in Africa than Nashville.

• Free Will Baptist Bible College put its valuable West End campus up for sale and made plans to build a new home in the countryside near Joelton.

• Rome conferred sainthood on a woman with Nashville ties: Katherine Drexel, a turn-of-the-1900s Philadelphia heiress who became a nun and started schools for African Americans. She died at 96 in 1955. Saint Vincent De Paul, a school that she and her order of nuns, the Sisters of the Blessed Sacrament, founded here in 1932, was still operating.

• Construction proceeded on the city's first new Gothic-style church in more than half a century: Covenant Presbyterian Church on Hillsboro Pike. The majestic $25-million project defied current thinking that said auditorium informality is what worshipers want. "I hope our building makes a statement about the sovereignty of God," said pastor Jim Bachmann.

• North East Church was launched—or wired—with help from its website, Godwhy.com. In temporary quarters at Volunteer State Community College in Gallatin, the nondenominational group built weekly services around subjects raised by people logging on the internet.

One final development seemed especially emblematic of the local seismic shift. A Nashville Muslim, Randall Venson, 39, ran for president of the United States. He got 535 votes in Tennessee (the only state in which he was on the ballot). So far as he knew,

Gains in the number of female ministers and rabbis broke the male monopoly on congregational leadership. In the Tennessee Episcopal diocese, for example, there were 14 ordained female priests, including the Rev. Donna Scott, associate priest at St. Paul Episcopal in Franklin.

he was the first Muslim in American history to seek the presidency. Venson did not keep his Muslim beliefs a secret on his mostly local campaign trail. His embrace of the religion of Islam was something he was proud of, something to talk about with voters in Nashville. "When I first became a Muslim in 1989, I was somewhat hesitant to tell people," said Venson, a lifelong Nashvillian who was raised Baptist. "I thought there would be a lot of negativity. I didn't feel like hearing from people that I was going to hell and all that." But things have changed in ten years. The city has certainly changed. Today I feel very comfortable being a Muslim in this city."

The influence of religion on the city's moral climate was very much on the minds of a force of born-again Christians in 2000, including a passionate core of ministers and professional musicians who wanted to shake the city back to its Judeo-Christian senses. They organized clergy meet-and-greets, prayer sessions, free concerts. Many of them were involved in launching a huge prayer gathering at the downtown arena on January 2, the day after Y2K. When representatives of this group spoke publicly, their tone was often shot through with apocalyptic grief and hope. They meant to nudge Nashville to the center of a cosmic narrative of divine redemption and release.

"I want to see this city healed and set free," said Christian musician Jeff Deyo, organizer of WorshipCityPraise, a series of free monthly music-oriented gatherings. "I think God wants that to happen." Deyo and others worried that the message of Christian music and the gospel message promoted by Christian churches were constantly threatened by the secular pressures of running a profitable business and tricking up the gospel in marquee lights and slick production values. So many people find their way to

protect the rights of students of other faiths, who often feel excluded from public prayer ceremonies.

21—**Armed with a visitation order** from a Mexican judge, Lawrence and Carolyn Levine now have temporary possession of their two grandchildren in Mexico. The Levines have not seen their grandchildren since their father, Perry March, moved to the Mexican town of Ajijic and took his children with him. While March is being questioned by Mexican officials about his immigration status, the Levines use the opportunity to take their grandchildren into custody. Whether they will remain in Mexico is not known. . . . **After days of secret**

Singers like gospel diva Aretha "Rita" Carter (singing here at Limestone Missionary Baptist Church in Franklin), put their hearts into glorifying God in worship, hoping for spiritual revival across the city.

meetings in clear defiance of the Sunshine Law—including one case in which a *Tennessean* reporter was turned away from a meeting led by House Speaker Jimmy Naifeh—terrified lawmakers may be close to hammering out a budget compromise. The budget being floated does nothing to remedy the state's fiscal woes, but strives to cover the butts of timorous incumbents, who are relieved not to hear the blare of horns honking in protest. . . . **American General Life and Accident Insurance Co**. (the National Life of yesteryear) will pay $206 million in restitution to settle a massive discrimination lawsuit. In the course of a three-and-a-half-year probe, several insurance companies belonging to American General were found to have charged African-American

Nashville to consummate their musical ambitions, he said, trying to discern the will of God along the way but often meeting with years of frustration.

"This is a city of broken-hearted people," said Deyo, "people who have sacrificed their life savings to come here and have their dreams fulfilled. Yet for many, the dreams are never fulfilled." When such heartbreak sought religious expression, he suggested, people were anguished to see the city's churches divided by in-fighting, or religious leaders failing to lead. There was the discomfiting feeling that Nashville was not living up to its presumed destiny as a chosen city of God. It might take a miracle, but it was their prayerful hope that Nashville would see fit someday, by the power of the Lord, to change its nickname from Music City U.S.A. to Worship City U.S.A.

In recent years, a sense of urgency about the morals of America in general and Music City in particular unified evangelical churches in town as never before. Hardly noticed by outsiders, it amounted to a revolutionary change in thinking when a dozen or a hundred Baptist, Pentecostal, nondenominational, and Church of Christ ministers could gather in the same room to jointly plan a meeting or parade or concert, laying aside deeply unyielding differences in doctrine and fervently praying together on their knees.

This was yet another sign of the times, a loosening of the old grip that doctrinal identities had on people. The glue of common purpose was now found in a new vocabulary spoken at evangelical rallies, services, and concerts—the language of "spiritual warfare," a form of intercessory prayer asserting that earth and human culture are under the influence of satanic forces and in need of spiritual liberation. The spiraling problems of America, for which no solutions were at hand, made the old turf wars and narrow denominational conflicts seem like small potatoes. With kids killing kids at school, parents succumbing to their own secret addictions, and pornography loosed in the bloodstream of the communications media, many of the faithful found comfort in using prayer as a new weapon of reformation. Spiritual warfare envisioned a cosmic battle for earth and society, and the possibility of cultural restoration around ancient biblical ideals. It energized some people to action, whether in a voter registration campaign, a downtown "March for Jesus," a youth rally for chastity, or a huddle of prayer warriors petitioning the Almighty to bring righteousness to Middle Tennessee.

The claim of absolute truth was indeed the coin of the realm in a community of deep professional religious loyalties and convictions. More than 3,000 people were employed here in Christian publishing, and thousands more derived their daily bread from one variation or another of the Protestant ethic. To them, it made no moral or business sense to abdicate on that claim to absolute truth. In a way, Nashville was a company town, the industry being a diversified conglomorate—call it Religion, Inc. Each denominational claim to truth had prospered on its own terms, for its own well-established audiences. For decades on end, the ingrained habits of relative isolation, class distinctions, and good Southern manners had been enough to keep friction and contradiction to a minimum, while keeping divisions intact.

Nashville, in other words, had no obvious vested interest in pushing itself to accommodate the new pluralism, even though these were emerging as millennial America's toughest religious questions, and the world's: How can the faiths get along without killing one another? How can they even get along with other religions when they are still so divided over the basic doctrines of their own faith? Can a person affirm the truth of her religion without demeaning someone else's? Can a person honor his own spiritual integrity, his urge to share the news of his faith, without declaring his neighbor's faith deficient? "The approach of the Christian community to other religions needs to be one of love," said John Styll of *CCM* magazine. "Loving people does not

and low-income families more than middle- and upper-class whites for burial and other insurance. . . . **178 students** at Martin Luther King Magnet High School are breathing easier tonight. Earlier this month, the students got word that their Advanced Placement tests had not been received by administrators; they were given the option of a refund or retaking the test. Understandably upset, the students began a campaign of calls and e-mails to get information. The missing tests were reportedly located at a Federal Express lost-and-found center.

22—Both houses of the Tennessee General Assembly sign off on a no-new-taxes budget that Gov. Sundquist derisively calls a "fudge-it budget" and vows he will veto. Only eight House members and six senators voted against it. "They're cooking the books," Sundquist declares. . . . **Lawrence and Carolyn Levine** return to Nashville bearing their grandchildren, 9-year-old Samson and 6-year-old Tzipora. Their father, former Nashville attorney Perry March, accuses the Levines of kidnapping his children. He asks judges in Nashville and Chicago to vacate contempt-of-court orders that would prevent him from returning to America to try to get his kids. . . . **Bishop T.D. Jakes,** a Dallas author and pastor, fires up a gathering of fellow ministers at the 12th-annual Higher Ground Always Abounding Assemblies Annual Convocation. The convocation, underway this weekend at the Baptist World Center, is the center of a transdenominational movement that stresses the need for black churches to effect spiritual renewal and economic improvement. . . . **A much different religious gathering** convenes today at the Nashville Convention Center: a meeting of 4,100 Unitarian Universalists, a group that encompasses Buddhists, pagans, humanists, even Christians. The liberal group offers a solid base for members such as lesbian minister Kim Crawford Harvie, who serves as a religious role model for

Some local believers renewed their faith in the power of prayer, joining hands publicly to ask God's blessings and forgiveness on the city many call the "Protestant Vatican."

mean accepting their point of view. But I hope Christians can mature to the point that they love people as children of God, even if they don't know God personally."

Historically, reaching inside to find that generosity was at odds with the temptation of religious leaders to declare or exaggerate the impending evil outside the doors of the sanctuary. Denouncing an alien faith was a reliable way of building group solidarity and maintaining clerical power and prestige. To detached observers, this was always the human tragedy of religious conflict—the itch to demonize the stranger in order to trumpet one's own claim to righteousness. But now that the mosque or ashram was just down the street and co-workers were Baptists and Buddhists and Baha'is, an enforced suspicion of the other was getting harder to maintain.

Secular pressures were eroding some of those barriers. Internet access to information gave millions of people a broader perspective on the world religion scene. Denominational loyalties weren't what they used to be. Many American believers, colored by baby-boomer sensibilities, had become pragmatic church-shoppers and -hoppers, willing to abandon the ancestral Episcopal parish or Assembly of God and join a house of worship for its friendliness and its day care. A practical impulse led some to splice East and West into their own religious outlook or practice. In Nashville it was now possible to meet yoga-practicing Baptists and meditating Episcopalians who were distinctly mellow on the subject of who owned the absolute rights to absolute truth.

The Southern Baptist Convention took on a different burden in these days of reassessment. With theologically conservative leadership firmly in control, the SBC refreshed its commitment to traditional Bible absolutism and was willing to take the abuse of critics for doing it. The 16-million-member SBC had become the premier evangelical religious voice in America to speak for Christianity's exclusive claim to truth. It was a mission, a crusade, a matter of standing up to a secular culture in moral decline, and their stern declarations were honed in downtown Nashville at the SBC executive committee's offices every working day.

"In an age increasingly hostile to Christian truth, our challenge is to express the truth as revealed in Scripture and bear witness to Jesus Christ who is 'the Way, the Truth and the Life,'" said Memphis pastor Adrian Rogers, who chaired a committee that revised the SBC's Baptist Faith and Message statement in 2000. That manifesto underscored the divinely inspired perfection of Scripture and the omniscience of God. "We are not embarrassed to state before the world that these are doctrines we hold precious," Rogers wrote. "Our generation faces the reality of a postmodern culture, complete with rampant relativism and the denial of absolute truth."

The eighteen-part statement, which exalts Jesus Christ, affirms racial diversity, and declares that women should not be church pastors, was put to a vote by the 12,000 Southern Baptist participants at their annual meeting in June 2000. It passed overwhelmingly. This formal action underscored an unbudging interpretation of the whole nature of Christian belief and evangelism, as understood by Baptists and many other believers: Having the faith means sharing it with others, because sharing the faith is the greatest act of love they know.

Several weeks later, a different vision of Bible and faith unfolded at a symposium at the Vanderbilt Divinity School. The keynote speaker, Bible scholar Marcus Borg of Oregon State University, argued that fundamentalism was destined to fade from the scene. He declared that the metaphorical meaning of biblical miracles was a more suitable option for millions of people who can no longer stomach the certitudes and simplicities of traditional Bible literalism. "It takes a lot of psychological energy to be a biblical literalist," Borg said. "The children of such church members will find it harder to sustain that energy and ward off science and pluralism." Belief in the old, closely guarded truths of Christian doctrine—the Virgin Birth, Jesus's physical resurrection, the Christmas star guiding the Wise Men to Bethlehem—was no longer so important to modern Christians, Borg argued. More crucial is a vivid faith fueled by a present-moment relationship with God, just as Jesus knew him. "Belief is not the same as faith," he said. "I can believe all the right things and still be in bondage and still be miserable and untransformed. It's relationship that transforms."

Borg's appearance was part of an Albert Schweitzer festival, a two-week affirmation of human potential honoring the legacy of the legendary medical missionary to Africa and his "reverence for life" philosophy. Beyond the Borg lecture, the Schweitzer

young gay teens. When two teenage conventioneers spot an injured homeless man lying still on the sidewalk, they are moved at 1 a.m. to take up $318 from other teens and buy groceries for the Nashville Union Mission. Adults chip in $2,700, which youth leaders end up splitting between several local charities. . . . **The three-member city commission** of Oak Hill, the affluent community that includes the governor's mansion, calls a halt to major building projects for at least six months. Among those left in the lurch is the 150-member Nashville Korean Presbyterian Church, which is in the midst of building a new home. . . . **An item in the** Nashville Scene's unsigned "City Crier" gossip column provokes an outcry from some of Belle Meade's most noted families. At issue: the lavish Belle Meade Country Club wedding reception of Ashley Weigel, daughter of Patsy and Robert Weigel, and Douglas Henry Jr., son of state Sen. Douglas Henry and his wife, Lolly. The column holds up to ridicule most every aspect of the nuptials, from the wedding cake ("a towering monument of pastel goo") to Sen. Henry's nickname "Duck" and his accompanying "waddle." Reaction is immediate and furious, typified by a letter from Anne T. Clayton that tells the Scene it has no right "to publish trash and gossip about private events." . . . **In the same** Scene **issue,** "Helter Shelter" columnist Walter Jowers, a certified home inspector, describes his recent visit to the now-infamous rental home of Carthage resident Tracy Mayberry, whose gripes with landlord Vice President Al Gore have become nightly news material. Jowers indeed finds evidence that the house is "a domestic disaster," from its "spaghetti bed of simmering wires" to its "hazard" of a water heater. But workers tell Jowers that the faulty plumbing is the result of flushed toys and debris, not to mention a lot of people using the facilities. A carload of eight people is seen leaving shortly before Jowers arrives. Mayberry, who has invited him to

At the First Unitarian Universalist Church on Woodmont Boulevard, Bernice Davidson and other members of the congregation lit a 1,000-candle mandala. Finding solidarity with Tibetan Buddhism was another way Nashvillians lit up their spirituality.

examine the house, stays inside and refuses to talk when he calls the next day.

23—**After an absence** of more than three years, a blue-eyed Siberian husky named Onyx staggers up to the home of the Hollie family in Mt. Juliet. Steve and Donna Hollie and their daughter, Heather, 15, stare in amazement at the dirty, malnourished, insect-infested dog. The Hollies have no idea where he's been since 1996, but they're certain of his identity. Onyx seems pretty clear about who they are, too. He reacts calmly to their tears and shouts, and settles back in as if he had just been out for a stroll.

24—**Actor and Oscar-winning** screenwriter Billy Bob Thornton, in town to work on a recording project, is getting input from the likes of bluegrass great Earl Scruggs, members of the rock bands ZZ Top and The Police, guitarist Peter Frampton and fellow actor Matt Damon, who stars in Thornton's new screen version of the Cormac McCarthy novel, *All the Pretty Horses.* Thornton and his bride-to-be, actress Angelina Jolie, cause heads to turn with their public display of affection at Sunset Grill in Hillsboro Village. . . . **Although it has neither a home** field nor a coach, the Nashville Dream, the city's proposed Women's National Football League franchise, attracts 80 women athletes to its tryouts at Goodpasture High School. If the team—and the league—succeed, it will face such foes as the Minnesota Vixens and the Lake Michigan Minx.

25—**More than 1,000 delegates** and observers crowd into the pews and balcony of Belmont United Methodist Church, as Mayor Bill Purcell addresses the members of Tying Nashville Together, the outreach coalition of neighborhood organizations, religious groups, political figures and community activists. Founded in 1993 with just 21 members, the group has swelled to include 60 religious and community organizations. TNT is credited with developing the Neighborhood Justice Center, creating seven after-school

Scenes of packed pews (this one at West End United Methodist Church during a 1999 rally for the faith-based organization Tying Nashville Together) were part of the local spiritual and civic identity.

day-care programs and bringing to Metro's attention a number of community concerns, from drug dealers to abandoned buildings such as the Turner School in Woodbine. Its input is now being sought on matters ranging from public transportation to affordable public housing. "Citizens are hungry for a mechanism that organizes and will move the city forward," says the Rev. Bill Barnes, a TNT founder and the retired minister of the Edgehill United Methodist Church.

26—With gas prices as high as $1.79 a gallon at some pump islands, country station WSIX-FM gives listeners an offer they can't refuse: 98-cent gasoline at the Stewart's Ferry Mapco near Uncle Bud's Catfish. (In Nashville, restaurants are always used as

Sherith Israel Rabbi Zalman Posner represented the old ways of Orthodox Judaism in Nashville throughout the last half of the 20th century.

event's emphasis on art, drama, music, and world peace was a break from the weary impasse over finding conclusive answers to debates about doctrinal truth among the professional controversialists.

In its own way, churchgoing served that purpose, too, for thousands of local residents: a weekly respite from the assaults of harsh ideology, endless culture debates, and workplace politics. It was a soulful time-out from too much talk. Weekly worship was a Nashville way of restoring the soul in a quiet place, volunteering one's time to a worthy mission, and, in some secret negotiation of the spirit, renewing a traditional pledge that promised God's blessings in the here and hereafter—eternal rewards for hard work and Bible reading and faithful church support.

On any given weekend, a thousand sermons poured forth from the city's pulpits, serving as a kind of literary jamboree in which the beloved text was not a syllabus of novels but one collection of books, the Holy Bible, the repository of truth and holy tales either in all its details or in broad outline. Their sermonic messages fell like gentle snow, an unmeasurable mystery blanketing public and private life in the city, always threatening to melt or disappear overnight but a wonder nonetheless. And when worship was over, all the heaven-pointing steeples and denominational office buildings stood as daily goads and reminders of an unspoken pact with salvation. Nashville was a city of religion-preoccupied people, some of them outright careerists for the Word, but all grasping in their own way for a spiritual center somewhere between ancient sanctities and the overheated demands of daily routine and uncertainty.

"It's still a community where religion matters, and religion still has meaning in people's lives," said Rabbi Mark Schiftan of The Temple, who arrived here from San Francisco in 1999. As a newcomer, he said he noticed "a degree of civility and human kindness that's rare for a city this size," and his hunch was religious practice had something to do with it. "It's heartening as a rabbi to see parking lots full at the churches as I drive down West End on Wednesday night—heartening as long as a religion is teaching humane values that add to people's lives without denigrating other people. When religion's values are humane, there's no greater positive impact on the community and its welfare."

Then at last came Billy Graham.

Despite anxiety about the Nashville crusade, despite every question of the shifting spiritual demographics of modern America or the state of Christian self-confidence in modern Nashville, Middle Tennesseans came in waves to hear Graham preach at Adelphia Coliseum on four balmy evenings in early June 2000. Teams of people had prayed for mild weather; rain stayed away. They prayed that worshipers would come; 227,000 showed up. Afterward, organizers saw it as a spiritual turning point for the city. "From the first day, when I saw the business and religious leaders who were going to organize this crusade, I knew it was going to work," said the Reverend Enoch Fuzz of Corinthian Baptist Church, one of the crusade planners. And it did, judging by the attendance figures, at least.

Hoping to keep the momentum, local Graham enthusiasts opened an office after the crusade—an organization called Operation Andrew, named for the disciple in Jesus's circle who was especially known for his evangelizing. The office was conceived to promote unity among the churches, do good community deeds, and reconcile the races. Fuzz, an African-American preacher, was particularly concerned about the latter issue, the racial separations of religious people. "The crusade was good medicine, but we will need follow-up care," he said. "Religiously, we're still sick. Racism is one of the greatest miseries of the human experience. Nashville has got to seize every opportunity to heal those wounds."

The Graham crusade itself turned out to be no special apotheosis of racial healing, not on any wide measurable scale, despite all the platform prayers. Predictably, the spectacle at Adelphia was something different, a ceremonial meeting ground for a revival service in the traditional Protestant mode, a sweet-spirited early summer prayer gathering under the stars—not a seminar for hammering out social policy solutions but

sweeten the deal, country stars Tracy Lawrence, Jessica Andrews, SHe-DAISY, Trace Adkins, Rascal Flatts, The Kinleys and Terri Clark man the pumps. As of 5 p.m., when the gas goes on sale, the interstate exit is blocked and a mile-long line of cars awaits.

27—To the by-now-familiar background music of shouts and car horns, Gov. Don Sundquist becomes the first governor in Tennessee history to veto the state budget. "I am vetoing a bill that robs our children of their future," Sundquist says, flushing a budget that scrupulously avoids any taint of reform by revising the state's revenue estimates upward. His state income tax will not pass; the burden of sales taxes on groceries will not be lifted from the poor. Adding insult to injury, the House strikes back two hours later, voting 78-19 to override his veto. Tomorrow's Senate vote will end the ugly fight, but not the controversy over how to fund the state's programs and services.

28—With only two days left before the state government shuts down without a legal penny to its name, the Senate votes 20-9 to override Gov. Sundquist's budget veto, clearing the way for another year of waiting for an overhaul of the outdated and inadequate tax structure. Only three of the 14 members of Nashville-Davidson County's legislative delegation—Sen. Douglas Henry and House members Edith Taylor Langster and Mary Pruitt, all Democrats—refuse to join in the gang-mugging of the Republican governor. Thus ends one of the longest, nastiest, most fruitless legislative sessions in the state's history.

29—Panhandlers for the Deeper Life Christian Church, a controversial Tampa-based denomination that ministers to homeless people and former addicts, position themselves strategically at Nashville intersections, gathering cash in orange buckets for a local church. The members do not have permits, although they wear official-looking laminated badges that are in fact homemade. The church raised concerns in Tampa because of its "cultlike" compound, its call for the worldly possessions of members and its conviction on fraud charges related to the exchanging of food stamps for cash. . . . **In the** *Nashville Scene*, editor/publisher Bruce Dobie writes an all-but-unprecedented apology to newlyweds Douglas and Ashley Henry and their families, whose wedding festivities were lampooned the week before in the *Scene*'s anonymous "City Crier" gossip column. Not only was the story "off base factually" in a number of ways, Dobie writes, "I'm not sure the paper was accomplishing anything other than throwing a pie in the faces of the people who were mentioned.". . . **Another disgruntled** *Scene* **reader** weighs in: Carthage resident Tracy Mayberry, who compiles a list of 11 objections to Walter Jowers' story the week before about his trip to her dilapidated rental house. "As for Carthage residents saying we weren't model tenants, how would they know?" Mayberry writes. "They have never been in my house or even tried to be friendly. So the fact is I don't give a damn what they think. People should sweep out their own back porches before they start on mine."

30—**It's as if the city** has gone back in time a couple of decades: The White Animals, a hugely popular local band that provided the soundtrack to many a young Nashvillian's adolescence in the early 1980s, do a reunion gig at the Exit/In. In the audience are some 40-year-old lawyers, doctors and stockbrokers who still remember the words to "Gloria."

a platform for announcing hope for the changed individual heart. Some people were there to hear the high-profile Nashville musicians on stage, or the 5,000-voice local choir; others just came to witness the spectacle of it all. Most were there, certainly, in homage to Graham himself, who in delicate health had to be helped to the podium each night but who preached with determination and humor, an evangelist who had sacrificed all else for five decades to deliver his unwavering gospel message. "God does hear your despairing cry. He's reaching out his hand tonight," Graham declared.

Each of the four evening services had a different feel, with at least 42,000 coming out nightly. The third evening, Saturday, June 3, will be remembered by local Christians as the night Graham broke attendance records at the still-new coliseum. This was youth night, a revival service the adults had designed to bring in the kids to hear Christian rock music for free, followed by an urgent sermon of salvation from Billy Graham. Officially, attendance was placed that night at about 5,000 above the stadium capacity of 67,000. But Graham organizers to this day are sure that more than 80,000 crowded in and around the stadium, a figure they believe will never be topped at the Titans' home field.

"Two things I want to leave with you tonight, just two," Graham stressed in his exhortation. "The first is, God loves you, no matter who you are or what color you are. The other is, Time is short. . . . Right now, God is ready to change you, forgive you and save you. . . . Come to Christ now while there's still time."

No matter how grim or sobering his words, no matter how amplified his image on the vast video screens near the stage, the visage of the gentle and fragile preacher at the podium was always the most poignant scene of the evening. Here he was, now in the twilight of a long ministerial calling, telling the ancient New Testament story of faith once more, and reminding his Nashville audience of their city's pivotal role as a proclaimer of the gospel news around the world. As prayers floated up into the night sky and the music commenced again, Billy Graham intoned his final benediction with quiet emotion. People sat in rapt silence, slightly swaying, or bowed with eyes closed, or leaning forward in expectation—a shepherd's flock of longing and humility, here in this commercial arena-turned-church. The moment would be long remembered as a touchstone of tradition in contemporary Nashville, with echoes of sawdust revival meetings past, ghosts of country legends, a tempestuous history of racial shames and military defeats and brilliant new football victories, all somehow stirring a renewed passion to labor in the vineyards of the Lord.

As one more stanza of "Amazing Grace" echoed up into the darkness, people seemed to hold the moment aloft a few seconds longer, hoping perhaps to glimpse a vision of some heavenly future, or a path to the "cloud of witnesses" long promised by Scripture. And then, in ones and twos, in carloads and busloads, they headed back to resume their daily lives in the sprawling metropolis that radiates beyond the skyline of downtown Nashville.

A chorus of 5,000 local choir members gave the Billy Graham Crusade some sonic heft during his Music City revival in June 2000.

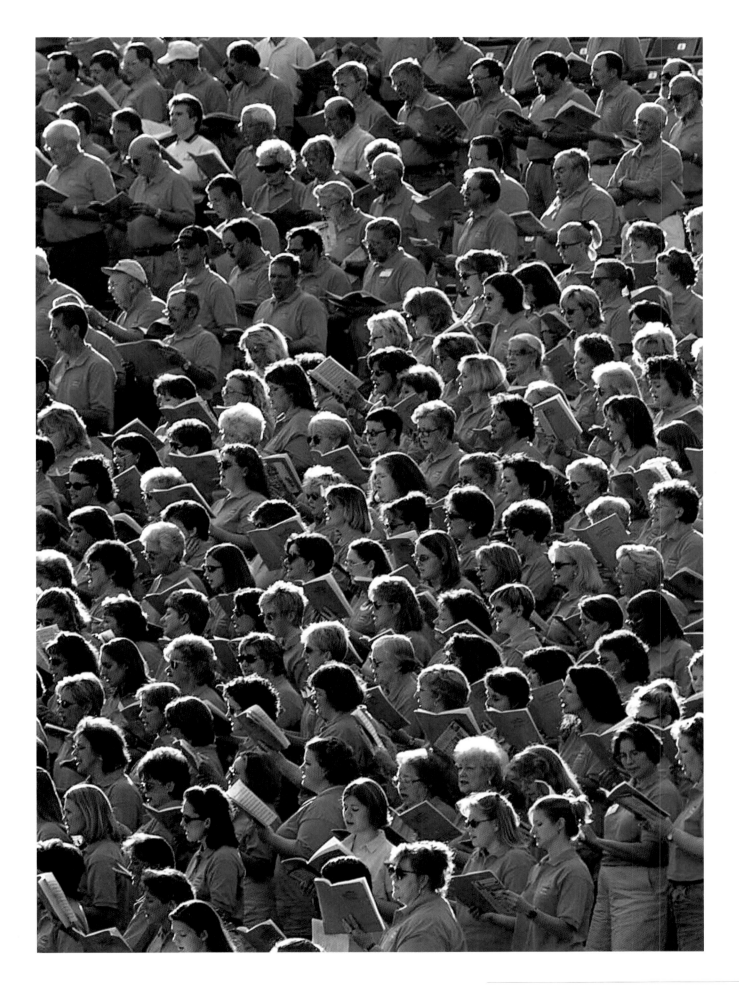

Religion in Nashville, A.D. 2050

by WILL D. CAMPBELL

> And Paul stood in the middle of the Areopagus and said, "Men of Athens, I perceive that in all things you are very religious." *Acts, 17:22*

Those were words of the Apostle Paul, speaking in the stronghold of aristocracy on his first missionary journey to the Athens of ancient Greece in about 50 A.D. They could as easily have been the words of the Reverend Billy Graham, speaking in the Nashville coliseum on his third missionary journey to the Athens of the South in 2000 A.D.

Now, as then, religion is big. In Nashville, religion is very big: more than a thousand edifices. And very rich: incalculable assets and tax-exempt real estate holdings (which if taxed would bring the city millions of dollars in revenue annually). Religion is a major economic enterprise in Middle Tennessee. In all things, we are very religious.

Through the lens of history, the Athens of the South image is a flattering self-portrait. Frontier Nashville wanted to show the nation that the glories of ancient civilization could leap over the wilderness and take root in an outpost of refinement and sophistication. By the mid-1840s, Nashville had already sent two men, Jackson and Polk, up to Washington to run the country. "This is no muddy-boots backwater," the city fathers seemed to be saying. "We're building a new Athens out here in the woods, and it's got everything the old Athens had—higher education, law, medicine, the arts, architecture, sports, religion."

Paul told the holy fathers of old Athens that their religiosity had a hollow ring to it. They made a big deal of what pious men they were, but they had idols everywhere, including one to "an unknown god"—just in case such a figure should appear among them unexpectedly. Centuries later, around 1800 A.D., the new Athens would have its own pantheon of holy fathers. They preached and prayed as apostles anointed by the various denominated fragments of Protestant Christianity—

Baptist, Presbyterian, Methodist, and continually regenerating others. These and the Catholic and Episcopalian and Jewish congregations that followed eventually erected sanctuaries of architectural splendor that would rival those seen by Paul on his missionary journey to Greece.

This new Athens had its idols, too. It worshiped land and wealth, erudition and religiosity, politics and ethnic cleansing. It dehumanized the native people hereabouts as "savages," and forcibly imported millions of others as "beasts of burden." The consequences of such imposed values, if not the fact of them, carry over to the present.

Those who believe our modern-day Athens no longer worships idols have only to sit in the coliseum bearing the Greek name Adelphia on a Sunday afternoon and witness the fervor of the throng. Sixty-some-odd-thousand zealous, spirit-filled and spirits-filled worshippers of the fierce gladiators known as the Titans. (Curiously, Adelphia is a form of the Greek verb, "to reconcile." A nice touch for owner Bud Adams and the lords of our Athens—but reconciliation is the last thing on their minds when the Baltimore Ravens come flying into town, or when the money-changers are counting the proceeds.)

Nashville has emerged in the last half-century as the central address of Protestantism in America. WASPs and AAPs—White Anglo-Saxon Protestants and African-American Protestants. This is the home base and headquarters of many religious institutions. Religion is by definition a belief system and an institutional structure. It is not the same as faith. Religion can be organized, systematized, creedalized, institutionalized; faith cannot. A belief system is passive, a recitation of words and creeds; faith is active, a laying down of life for the sake of others.

Here in Nashville in 2000 A.D., religion is big and wealthy and powerful. It also tends to be self-centered, pietistic, legalistic, absolutist. It quantifies success by the count of its membership, the size of the offering, the worth of its corpus. We are up to our steeples in politics, in recreation and enterprise, in material trappings better suited to country clubs or corporate headquarters than houses of worship. The pillars of the Areopagus and the Grecian temples of the gods could not have been more ostentatious than the physical plants of organized religion in Nashville and in all of wealthy America today. It is in the nature of self-perpetuating institutions, churches among them, to know the cost of everything, the value of nothing.

My own denominational mother church is a case in point. I was born, baptized, and ordained to preach in the largest Protestant church in America, the Southern Baptist Convention. Many of my brethren don't like to be reminded that we partially sprang from the notorious Anabaptists, the left wing of the Protestant Reformation in 16th-century Europe. Governments and other religions reviled the Anabaptists, who steadfastly refused to go to war or take an oath or participate in the political process at all. For those offenses, and for preaching and teaching counter to the state church, they were hunted down by armed horsemen and put in prison or tortured and executed. Half or more of these martyrs were women—yet to this day, Baptist women are denied the pulpit, supposedly because "man was first in creation and woman was first in the Edenic fall." By such logic, females have been doomed to outcast status since Eve ate apples. So much for the history of my people.

In the name of religion, we have taken the religionless Christianity offered by Jesus and turned it on its head, so that the institution prevails, the powers and principalities come out on top, and those whom we were called to serve—the weak, the needy, the vulnerable young and the old, the homeless, the imprisoned—are cast aside.

Is it possible that before the new century is half over, some ecclesiastical Joan of Arc will arise to lead us out of the marshland of denial? Could it be that earnest and honest Baptists (and there are many) will repent of their apostasy and reclaim their history as true protestants, men and women protesting man's inhumanity to man and woman? Who's to say? Stranger things have happened.

Jesus was a skeptic at best when it came to institutionalized religion. He contended against the chief religionists of his day. "Woe unto you, scribes and Pharisees, hypocrites!" he thundered. And those were the "good" people, not the evil ones. Jesus was not much of an organization man. He identified with the outcasts. He steered clear of a lot of rules and prohibitions. Today it is fashionable to ask WWJD—What would Jesus do? No one knows—which is where faith comes in. For myself, I find it easier to imagine what he would not do, were he here in the flesh. He wouldn't be mincing words over the value of every human life, or splitting hairs over who are the "saved" and who the "lost," and he wouldn't be any more impressed by the lords of our contemporary city than by its lay people, its multitudes.

Where is our religion heading, and our faith? I don't know. But of this much we can be certain: Whatever remains of the bricks and mortar, the institutional structure, there will always be the remnant—a Father Charlie Strobel, a Reverend Ed Sanders, a Rabbi Randy Falk, a Pastor Bill Barnes. Servants. Prophets. A remnant is all we were ever promised.

Will Campbell, preacher, writer, farmer, and father confessor to the unchurched, moved to the Nashville area from his native Mississippi in 1956 and has lived most of the time since then on a 40-acre farm in Wilson County.

"I Have Nothing . . . So Where Do I Start?"

EXCERPTS FROM A CONVERSATION WITH SISTER SANDRA SMITHSON, OSF

For as the body without the soul is dead,
so is faith without action.   *James, 2:26*

Sister Sandra (right) with her sister, Mary Craighead

I was born in Nashville 75 years ago, in the same house that I live in now, on Twelfth Avenue North. My father had come to the city from Franklin. He was brought up Baptist, but here a missionary priest befriended him, and because of that he decided to become a Catholic. My mother, who had been a Methodist, converted after they were married, and they raised ten children. I was the sixth child. We only knew two other black Catholic families living in the area.

It was only a few blocks from our house to Assumption Catholic Church, at Seventh and Monroe streets, but we couldn't go there because of segregation, so we walked about four miles to a mission church, Holy Family, near Eighth Avenue South and Lafayette Street, on Drexel. My mother and father helped the Josephites build that church. Drexel Street is named for Mother Katherine Drexel, who built missions to serve black families all over the nation. I went to Mother Katherine's schools for sixteen years, from first grade through college, graduating from Xavier University in New Orleans in 1949.

It wouldn't be accurate to say I wanted to be a nun. I really wanted to be a writer—but even as a child, I felt God calling me to a different way of life. When I was 7 and in second grade, one of the nuns asked me what I wanted to be when I grew up, and I said, "I want to become a nun." I was shocked when she replied, matter-of-factly, "Oh, you can't do that. Colored girls aren't permitted to join the order." That disturbed me a lot. The sisters were so kind, so admirable—I thought they were next to God—and yet, here was this revelation, and I couldn't make sense of it.

So for several years, I kept this big secret from my parents and my older sisters and brothers, afraid that if they knew, they might judge the nuns too harshly, lose respect for them. I wanted everyone to love them as I did. But looking back on it later, I could see the incident as a valuable lesson. It taught me to separate personalities from purposes, and that God transcends the churches that claim to speak in His name. Every time I have to deal with the church, it gets smaller and God gets bigger.

In the early 1950s, after I finished college, I wrote to all the religious communities I could find, asking if I might join. One after another, they rejected me because of my race. It was so discouraging that I began to doubt my call. But then one day, as I was talking with one of my siblings, I had what some might call a vision of a long line of nuns, one behind the other, walking through the room. One of them broke ranks and put her arm around me. It lasted only a brief moment, and then she got back in line and they all disappeared. Her face and habit were indelibly imprinted in my mind.

Soon, a letter came from the School Sisters of Saint Francis in Milwaukee, an order that had been founded to educate immigrants. The letter said, "We accept whom God sends." Later that year, in the summer of 1953, I packed up and went, half expecting to find the nun in my vision waiting there for me. But she was nowhere in sight, and what's more, the habit of the order was not the same either.

After I had been there a month or so, I was sent to the office of the Mother General for a routine introductory interview. There on the wall was a picture of "my nun," wearing the habit I had seen. "Who is that?" I asked, pointing. "That's Sister Stanislaus," said the Mother General. "She was the third General Superior of the order. They wore a different habit back then. She was the first to insist on admitting nonwhites to the order. She had to defy her bishop to do it." I was surprised. This was confirmation that I was where I belonged. It was a defining moment for me.

For almost 30 years I served with the Franciscan sisters—teaching high school English in Chicago, then spending ten years as a missionary in Costa Rica and Honduras before returning to Milwaukee to teach. In 1982, after my father died and my mother was in poor health, I got permission to relocate to Nashville so I could be her primary caregiver. I was assigned as a pastoral associate at Saint Vincent De Paul—the only surviving church and school established here 50 years earlier by Mother Katherine Drexel.

Nashville had changed tremendously since the '50s. Legal segregation was gone. Interstate 40 had cut a deep gash that divided and isolated North Nashville, and our street, once a pleasant neighborhood avenue, now dead-ended at the freeway. The area was much poorer, a depressed and dysfunctional ghetto, and it was actually more segregated than ever, because the scattered few white families (Germans, mostly) had all left. So had the middle-class blacks. And on the streets, I saw more and more little kids in trouble, skipping school, growing up illiterate. It was not the Nashville I remembered.

I struggled to understand why, and what could be done about it—what I could do to help turn things around. I thought to myself, "I have nothing—no money, no power, no friends in high places—so where do I start?"

I went to see my eldest sister, Mary, a retired school principal. This was in 1992, so she would have been 77 then. I found her out in her garden. "Why are you out here digging in your rose bed when there's so much that needs to be done?" She looked up at me kind of funny, and then went back to her roses. Mary knows me better than I know myself. "What do you want to do?" she asked. I said, "I don't know yet—but we'll do something, if you'll just get up and help me." So we got busy.

I could talk all day about Project Reflect, and the school we started—but let me just give this brief description of it. I designed the organization, incorporated it, gathered up the kids, and Mary wrote the reading curriculum for the program. It's very focused: We work with public-housing children who are not learning to read in public school; we train teachers to work with at-risk children, ten to a class, in after-school and summer sessions. That's it in a nutshell.

I wrote to every Catholic order in the country, describing our project and asking for help, and that appeal eventually brought in $110,000. The Metro Public Schools have loaned us the old Cockrill School in West Nashville, a wonderful old WPA-era building that was slated for demolition. The late Father Bill Fleming of the Cathedral on West End Avenue helped us raise $80,000 and recruit more than 600 volunteers to clean up and repair the building. We've been generously supported by grants from the United Way, the Metro Development and Housing Authority, several local foundations, various Catholic and Protestant churches, the Titans, the Predators, and on and on—all so that our "little peanut" children can learn to read and succeed in school.

When Mary and I were just getting started in the early '90s, I went to my bishop and asked for support. He seemed interested, told me to write up a plan and bring it back for review, and I did—but the leadership decided not to sponsor us. They wished us luck and have helped us with publicity—but that's about it. As I look back, I know that was a blessing. By transcending denominational lines, we've been able to give witness to the truly universal nature of God's call. There is not a clear vision in our diocese now concerning exactly what the church should be doing about the problems of minorities and the poor.

Denominational churches tend to see themselves as the keepers of eternal truth. But history shows us that institutions, even divinely inspired ones, are imperfect—they tend to degenerate, and sometimes they lose the vision and the mission for which they were created, and work instead for their own perpetuation. As I have lived my life, I've come to feel that it's a mistake to insist upon a narrow and dogmatic interpretation of truth that lets a chosen few into the kingdom and shuts out everyone else.

Religious faith, no matter how expressive or compelling dogmatically, finds its completion in the work of sincere hearts. Our most essential function in life is not to proselytize and convert others to a specific and exclusive set of beliefs, but simply to be true to the light that is within us. Somewhere it is written, "Those who have been given the law will be judged by the law they have been given, and those who have not been given the law will be judged by the law that is in their own hearts." I believe that, and I try to live by it.

Faith is vital. I know my faith is certainly very important to me. I go to Mass frequently and participate in the devotional life of my church. But our crying need here in Nashville is to live our faith—not so much in our "denominational pews" but rather, as Jesus did, in service to others, especially those less fortunate than we are.

Sister Sandra Smithson is a Franciscan nun who serves the needy children in the city of her birth.

The throb and rumble of a city in motion suffuses Fisk University artist Newton Holiday's "Nashville Rising." As a student at Fisk and an art teacher at Pearl High School, Holiday was for 15 years a mentee and adjunct under Aaron Douglas, famed artist-illustrator of the Harlem Renaissance, who had come to Fisk in 1939 and remained until his death in 1979. Inspired by "Building More Stately Mansions," a celebrated Douglas work from 1944, Holiday painted "Nashville Rising" in 2001.

ALONG THE BANKS

Edited by AMY LYNCH

from reports by Gloria Ballard, Jim Molpus,
Madeena Spray Nolan, Jeff Wilkinson, and others

I t's sweltering at Riverfront Park—92 degrees according to the radio, but definitely hotter at the core of the churning crowd that's been building along the west bank of the Cumberland River since midafternoon. There must be 20,000 people here already. All the streets leading to the park are jammed with pedestrians, and along the tiered riverbank, folks are standing, sitting, milling about, sweating. It's an amiable, congenial crowd, a party crowd. Many in the over-50 and under-10 sets are dressed in patriotic red-white-and-blue garb. Lots of miniature American flags, handed out as favors by a local bank, are attached to baby strollers, ponytail clasps, handbags and hip pockets. The dense, humid air is laced with a medley of summer picnic aromas: barbecue, hot dogs, funnel cakes, cotton candy. Music wafts up from the river stage, where one band after another with a country, pop, R&B, or soft-rock flavor is going all-out for a huge crowd of home folks. The response is good: People clap and cheer, whistle, sing along. A few dance barefoot in the grass.

The sun is still high at 5 o'clock, but the shadows cast by the looming city skyline are creeping toward the river. Along First Avenue from the park to Fort Nashborough, and on up to the crest of the bluff, where Timothy Demonbreun's pioneer visage peers westward, families and party groups have staked out choice vantage points for the fireworks to come. They're unfolding lawn chairs and off-loading coolers and baskets, preparing to spread out their picnics on the ground. A ton of fried chicken will disappear before dark.

Threading through the assemblage are all manner of men, women, and children dressed in everything from combat fatigues to sundresses and sandals. Texas-style white hats and silver-embossed belts are favored by a cluster of Latino guys who nod gravely in time to the music. A dozen Amish women, their long hair bunned under small white hats that look like upturned teacups, clap for the boldest among them, who gathers her long skirt and tries a dance step. Together, they look as if they might have just strolled out the gate of the 18th-century fort and gotten swept up in the current of humanity.

The Tennessee Fox Trot Carousel that native son Red Grooms created out of his fanciful imagination and a keen sense of history spins perpetually to the calliope sounds of "Rocky Top" and "The Tennessee Waltz." Small schools of Asian, African, and Middle Eastern immigrants, looking dazed but entranced, follow the flow of the throng. When it's oratory time, military veterans and politicians are prominent around the stage, and the music takes a more patriotic turn as a U.S. Marine honor guard presents the colors. Across the Cumberland, against the backdrop of Adelphia Coliseum, a team of detonation experts has prepared 12,000 "shots" of explosives—for a complex sequential launch to light up the night. The $60,000 cost of the pyrotechnics will be borne, as in recent years, by radio station WRVW-FM.

As dusk falls and the crowd continues to grow (ultimately to be estimated at "more than 80,000," though of course no one knows the real number), the Nashville Symphony warms up for its seventeenth-annual performance at the Fourth of July gathering. A stirring performance of classical pops suitable for the occasion is in store, and an air of positive anticipation hovers over the multitude.

On an evening like this, in an assembly so diverse and upbeat, it's hard to believe that just a few

1—**Thought the furor** over the General Assembly's budget battle had subsided? Think again. Although the state budget went into effect at the stroke of midnight, Mark Mayhew, a law clerk at the firm of Barrett Johnson & Parsley, has filed suit to nullify it. Backed by the firms of two of Nashville's most powerful attorneys, George Barrett and Cecil Branstetter, the suit charges that the secret meetings held by lawmakers violated Tennessee's Open Meetings Act. The *Nashville Scene* and NashvillePost.com soon join the suit as well. "We are putting the state on notice," says Barrett, "that they will be spending taxpayers' money that they are not authorized to spend, and they will be liable for it." No hearing date is set. . . . **College students** can thank the budget's belt-tightening measures, meanwhile, for a likely 8 percent tuition hike at state colleges and universities for the coming academic year. The raise in tuition, if approved by the Tennessee Board of Regents, could saddle undergraduates with an extra $208 in costs this year. Since misery loves company, the announcement arrives after word that Tennessee's bond rating has been downgraded by Standard & Poor's from a perfect triple A to double A plus, thus dipping the value of the state's bonds while raising interest payments. The reason: "weak budget practices." . . . **Contemporary Christian singer** and former TNN talk-show host Gary Chapman marries his fiancée, Jennifer Pittman, in a ceremony at Chapman's Williamson County home. Chapman's father, Texas minister Terry Chapman, officiates; the ring bearer is Chapman's dog Simon, who has to be lured to the altar with a raw hot dog. Guest Tom Arnold, the former husband of TV comic Roseanne Barr, tells the crowd he used the same trick on his ex-wife.

2—**With gas prices** running as high as $1.55 a gallon, local gas

The traditional Independence Day celebration at Riverfront Park draws a huge throng to hear patriotic music and oratory, pay honor to war heroes and join in a festive picnic and party that climaxes after dark with a loud and colorful fireworks display.

Hours before dark, parties begin to take shape all along the terraced embankment that stretches between First Avenue and the river. In 2000, an estimated 80,000 people watched the fireworks.

years ago, downtown Nashville was in a state of precipitous decline. It was a place people hesitated to frequent after dark. If this Fourth of July marks a turning point in time, a rounding of the river bend into a new era, it may also represent a reversal of misfortune here in the heart of the city.

Nashville seems more vigorous and hospitable in this summer of 2000 than it has in decades, and that's certainly worth celebrating. Scores of restaurants, bars, nightclubs, and shops that cater to the tourist trade are thriving in historic storefronts that had been slouching toward oblivion since the 1950s and '60s. The new interstate highways that became evacuation routes to suburban developments and shopping malls no longer feel like escape routes to Utopia; in fact, some road-weary commuters are returning to the city, not just to work and play but also to live. The ghost-town emptiness that echoed just a decade ago down Church Street and Broadway now reverberates as crowd noise. Hotels, museums and galleries, sports palaces, and even upscale living quarters are back; people are alert to the changes, waiting to see if major commercial ventures follow suit.

It is no coincidence that the public remarks of Mayor Bill Purcell and other dignitaries on this traditional holiday afternoon are focused more on the present and future than on the past. It's the present that holds the mayor's attention, anyway: the school system, urban neighborhoods, infrastructure, planning and development within the old city. The sight of thousands of people intent on business or pleasure in the downtown area pleases Purcell no end, as it did Phil Bredesen, his predecessor and

stations are losing hundreds of dollars daily to patrons who fill their tanks and speed off without paying. In response, many filling stations and convenience stores now post attendants outside, and pumps are plastered with stickers warning motorists that not paying is a punishable offense. . . . **Two Middle Tennesseans** are now in contention for the presidency. At its national convention in Anaheim, Calif., the Libertarian Party again taps Franklin investment banker Harry Browne, 67, as its candidate against Vice President Al Gore and Texas Gov. George W. Bush in November.

3—**The battle between** Lawrence and Carolyn Levine and their estranged son-in-law, Perry March, takes another sharp turn, this time in Davidson County Juvenile Court. Having taken their two grandchildren out of Mexico, March's current home, during a controversial and headline-making effort June 21, the Levines now file for permanent custody of their missing daughter's children. Juvenile Court Judge Betty Adams Green issues a restraining order giving the Levines temporary custody. March, meanwhile, has asked the Cook County Circuit Court in Illinois to declare jurisdiction over the custody proceedings, stemming from his move to Chicago after his wife, Janet Levine March's, disappearance in 1996. Hearings will be held Thursday in Nashville and Chicago, four days from now. . . . **A poll** conducted by the Knoxville *News-Sentinel* shows Vice President Al Gore leading Texas Gov. George W. Bush in Tennessee— but only by 44.5 percent to 39.5 percent, just one percentage point above the margin of error. Gore campaigners put on a brave face, but the veep's weak support in his home state raises warning flags.

4—**Independence Day.** Temperatures in the low 90s give way to mildly cloudy skies and cool breezes by evening. As always in an election year, the Whitland Avenue Fourth of July Parade and Picnic draws a crowd of Nashville pols pressing the flesh, and the annual cooking competition heats up in the food tent. Al Thomas, owner of the Belle Meade restaurant Sperry's, takes first place for picnic food with his dish, Al's Iron Skillet Baked Beans (their secret: liquid smoke.) Only those who love heat, noise, chaos and that panicky penned-up feeling plan to be among the predicted 80,000 revelers who will converge on downtown this evening for the city's annual fireworks display at Riverfront Park. At 9 p.m., all parties gaze skyward from their favorite vantage point: from sidewalks and parking lots along Woodland Street in East Nashville; from rooftops and restaurant windows along Second Avenue; from the crest of Love Circle off West End; from the Kelly Miller Smith Bridge north of downtown; from the Cumberland Science Museum and Fort Negley Hill on the south. ... **The Nashville Union Rescue Mission** hosts its annual July Fourth Community Picnic in honor of Nashville's homeless veterans, who are said to number more than 500 and comprise a quarter or more of the total estimated street population. On this day, the mission serves more than 850 meals.

5—**Two children**, left orphaned in April after a tragic crime, now have four parents. *The Tennessean* reports that Brianna Wolfe, 7, and her brother Jakub, 5, are being raised jointly by their two sets of grandparents, Charles and Barbara Graves and Jerry and Patty Austin. Apart from its apparent harmoniousness, the arrangement is unusual in another way: Christopher Wolfe, 26, Patty's son, shot and killed his wife, Stephanie Graves Wolfe, 25, the Graves' daughter, on Apr. 2 before taking his own life several hours later. What caused the shooting remains a mystery: Both sets of parents tell the morning daily they looked on the Wolfes as a devoted couple. They blame the cocaine in Chris Wolfe's system and the drug habit he could not kick for the sudden change in a man described as orderly and artistic. The two children now live

pattern-setter. Not many American cities are this alive at the core these days. Nashville is trying, and having some success.

At half past seven we're in full shadow, and the temperature has fallen a notch or two. The crowd keeps growing. They're partying up on the Second Avenue rooftops overlooking the riverfront, and hundreds of speedboats and yachts putt-putt up and down the Cumberland. The Broadway Dinner Train arrives from Donelson with 500 people aboard. Overhead, single-engine planes have been making lazy flybys for hours, some ferrying well-heeled passengers, others trailing message banners. Excitement is building for the Big Bang. There will be fireworks elsewhere in the city on this night, but nothing like this. In Nashville, July the 4th belongs to the riverfront.

And properly so. It was here on the banks of the Cumberland that Nashville's earliest communities gathered. Well over two centuries ago, the river was the main avenue most people followed to get here. The first natives, the Woodland and Mississippian people, traveled on this river; their villages were clustered on its banks. Later came French and English trappers and traders, then settlers on flatboats, and finally steam-powered riverboats. For almost a century, until the railroads came, Nashville was a river town. Any way you come at it now, the city's history always circles back to the banks of the river.

This crowd may not feel close to that history, but we are always closer than we know. The people we have been, the community we used to be, shapes who we are now and who we will be in the centuries to come. This bright and peaceful day is remarkably similar to previous Independence Days here in Nashville, each of which was both a cause for celebration and an invitation to reflection. In truth, we never reach the high ideals we espouse on this holiday. Justice and equality are always works in progress. For all our celebratory impulses, we must candidly acknowledge that this day has an underside, a counterforce. When the Robertson party walked across the frozen Cumberland on Christmas Day 1779, there were at least two dozen African slaves with them (and a few free blacks as well). The little bluffside fort the overland travelers built here, and other "stations" nearby, were a rude and unwelcome intrusion in the eyes of the Cherokee, Chickasaw, and Creek people who claimed the area as a hunting ground.

From that first day, Nashville was a house divided—an odd mixture of claimants, each pursuing what the new American nation's founders, meeting in Philadelphia just three years earlier, had defined as the "unalienable rights [of] life, liberty, and the pursuit of happiness." But whose life and liberty, whose happiness? The founders were vague on those points; they didn't mention slaves, women, or indigenous people.

The complicated and unending quest for a national (and thus local) state of "happiness," however we define that term, can never be boiled down to patriotic platitudes, neatly packaged in oaths of allegiance or renditions of "The Star Spangled Banner" and "American the Beautiful." Played on this day, those songs remind us of how high we aim, and how far short we fall. Independence Day is not about liberty and justice for all; at best, it is only an aspiration to reach such a state of grace. The Fourth of July is not now and never has been what it used to be, back in "the good old days" of our imagination.

That makes it a perfect day to take the pulse of Nashville, Tennessee, in the 221st year of its recorded history. If we could read this crowd the way we read a book, we would know the story of Nashville in 2000—the whole sprawling tale, heroic and flawed and tragic but endlessly engaging, even wondrous. The historian Will Durant must have had a place and a crowd like this in mind when he wrote:

> *Civilization is a stream with banks. The stream is sometimes*
> *filled with blood from people killing, stealing, shouting, and*
> *doing things historians usually record, while on the banks,*
> *unnoticed, people build their homes, make love, raise children,*
> *sing songs, write poetry. The story of civilization is the*
> *story of what happens on the banks.*

The normally placid Cheatham County village of Pegram, just beyond the Davidson County line, is abuzz with activities every Fourth of July. The barbecue pits fire up early, and there's food all day, as well as sports, music, crafts and a parade—this one featuring Queen Jennifer Cecil, the Tennessee Twirlers Junior Miss.

This is the one national holiday above all others when people make a point of coming together in civic celebrations. You notice that especially in a little village like Pegram, nestled in a shady valley of the Harpeth River about ten minutes west of Bellevue. They observe the Fourth with a flourish in Pegram; in fact, the number of people who show up in this quiet outpost of small-town life between 6 a.m., when the first globs of pancake batter hit the griddles at the United Methodist Church, and about 11 p.m., when the last firecracker invades the town's tranquility, far exceeds the 2,000 or so who live within the incorporated boundary of the town.

Just about everyone gets into the act. The official theme of this year's celebration is emblazoned on posters, signs, and T-shirts all around the Cheatham County community: PEGRAM—EXPLODING INTO THE NEW MILLENNIUM. Bursts of civic energy worthy of that expansive theme are everywhere. Coals were glowing in the barbecue pits well before dawn, in preparation for the midday crowds that will be waiting eagerly for their pulled pork sandwiches and chicken halves. Before lunch, though, there's breakfast, and the pancake feast gets hundreds of hearty eaters stoked for the typically hot, humid July day in store. Those who last through it all will be treated to a parade, baton twirlers, beauty pageants for girls of all ages, fire engine rides, concerts, all manner of exhibitions, contests, ball games, tournaments, booth sales—and, of course, fireworks. For many present and former residents, this is the community celebration of the year, a day of hometown pride mixed with patriotism.

Down the road in Franklin, a polished gem of a historic town, patriotic fervor always runs high. For a time during the Civil War it was a stronghold of the Confederacy, and it retained that orientation during much of the 20th century. In recent years, Franklin's rivalry with its booming cross-county neighbor, Brentwood, has set up something of an old money-new money grudge match in Williamson, the state's most prosperous county, and that preoccupation, plus the influx of thousands of new residents from outside the South, has diminished local passion for Rebel breast-beating. Into this

with their maternal grandparents in Antioch, where they attend school, and they spend weekends with their father's parents. "It never occurred to me not to forgive Chris," Barbara Graves tells a reporter. "I loved Chris just about as much as I loved Stephanie.". . . **The big top rises** in Centennial Park for the UniverSoul Circus, the country's only traveling circus owned and operated by African Americans. The show features attractions such as OnionHead the Clown, Tanzanian acrobats and trained animals. . . . **Investors take a bath** in sausage gravy when the New York Stock Exchange boots Shoney's Inc. off the big board. The NYSE says the Nashville-based stock no longer meets its requirements, including average share price, net worth and market capitalization. Although the torpid stock had made it back up to $1.63 after a positive quarterly report, the news sends its worth crashing 46 percent, to a miserable 88¢ a share. Shoney's lovers now have the option of spending $3.99 on the restaurant's famous breakfast bar, or buying 4.53 shares of its stock.

6—**A mighty voice** is stilled. James Hill, 83, the baritone anchor of Nashville's renowned Fairfield Four, succumbs to a long illness at Baptist Hospital. Born in Bessemer, Ala., Hill joined the a cappella gospel group in 1946. When the group disbanded in 1950, Hill and fellow Four member Isaac Freeman founded the gospel quartet The Skylarks; he served in the late 1940s with his band mates as co-owner of the Fairfield Four Funeral Home, and he worked as a sheriff's deputy, a Metro police sergeant and the proprietor, with his wife, Ethel, of a Third Avenue restaurant called Tombstone. But the Four reunited in 1980 to great acclaim, and under Hill's guidance the group reached new heights of international popularity, recording with artists such as Johnny Cash, Elvis Costello and Steve Earle and winning a Grammy for their 1998 album *I Couldn't Hear Nobody Pray*. At a 1998 performance with

Costello and Earle at Caffé Milano, the Four made music for the Lord that rocked harder than the devil's music ever could, leaving a sweat-soaked audience to marvel at their spirit. "They turned a nightclub into a church," Costello recalls. . . . **The day's headlines** are dominated by another death. Just hours after leaving his family home in Nashville—and three days after his indictment on misdemeanor marijuana-possession charges in Jackson, Tenn.— National Football League running back Fred Lane, 24, is found shot to death in his Charlotte, N.C., home. A former gridiron hero at Franklin High School, the 5' 10", 205-pound Lane signed in 1997 with the Carolina Panthers; he became the Panthers' leading career rusher, and he had just been traded to the Indianapolis Colts. Police say the prime suspect is Lane's wife, Deidra, who had filed a complaint against her husband back in March after he allegedly caused her to fall during an argument. A pink stork in the yard still marks the recent birth of their daughter, Pilarr. . . . **To handle all this bad news,** Nashville

The Public Square is the focal point of July Fourth festivities in Franklin. One of many popular performing groups at the 2000 event was the Rocky Top Revue, a nimble and energetic dance troupe.

relatively placid time of stasis, the all-American Fourth has quietly returned to respectability in Franklin.

The Public Square, with its monument to the Confederate dead, is the setting for what has come to be known as "Franklin on the 4th," a celebration sponsored by the city, the local chamber of commerce, and the Lions Club. Instead of a parade moving through the town, a stage in the square is the stationary focal point, and during the day it is occupied by a succession of bands, majorettes, dance troupes, church choirs, orators, and sundry local dignitaries. True to form, Brentwood has taken a

With the Stars and Stripes beside them, Nashville centenarian Norma York Hammond (left) and Sudanese teenager Nassrin Mahmoud take in the pageantry of an old-fashioned Fourth of July. Mrs. Hammond had plenty to sing about, including her health and a sunny disposition at age 100. Mahmoud, an exchange student, was a quietly fascinated spectator at the Fourth of July celebration in Franklin.

Since 1974, the Brentwood Exchange Club has hung flags along Franklin Road through the center of town to commemorate the Fourth of July.

nontraditional tack on this day, sponsoring the Cadillac Firecracker 5K Run that attracts a large number of participants and spectators. The twain may never meet in bonded bliss, but they do at least tend to share the same political philosophy (conservative Republican), patronize the same financial institutions, worship, and play golf and party together.

Other communities across Middle Tennessee have taken a variety of approaches to observing the Fourth, more or less along the lines of the two Williamson County cities, mixing patriotic respectfulness and pleasurable diversions in roughly equal measure. Numerous impromptu gatherings also get thrown together on this day. They include family homecomings, church circles, neighborhood cookouts, and what may be a new tradition for some in Nashville: a pilgrimage to the Love Circle hilltop off West End Avenue. This crowd includes a high percentage of Vanderbilt students who arrive with picnics, beer, and blankets to stake out a place to sit under the stars and watch the downtown fireworks from 3 or 4 miles away. Residents of Love Circle either join the strangers in good humor or ignore the intrusion.

One of the Nashville's most noteworthy celebrations of Independence Day takes place on Whitland Avenue. This annual party in a tony historic neighborhood started small back in 1977, when a few neighbors got together for a picnic on the Fourth. Everyone had a good time and decided to do the same the next year, and the next. Each July the party got bigger. During the 1980s, the annual gathering passed some kind of turning point and became an "event." The newspapers and television stations began to cover it, knowing they could get colorful footage and pictures on an otherwise slow news day. Now more than a thousand converge on the broad, shady avenue each year, some wearing colorful costumes, many bringing covered dishes, and all imbued with the sunny spirit of celebration.

It begins at first light with Whitland residents hustling up and down the avenue, setting up tents and tables and grills, draping red-white-blue bunting, and rounding up coolers and canoes to fill with ice and soft drinks. The orchestra, made up primarily of symphony musicians, arrives at about 10:00 a.m. to set up a temporary bandstand at its customary location in the front yard of Dan and Pat Burton's 1920s home. By 10:30, guests are trickling onto the street, bringing bowls of salad and coleslaw, platters of fruit, watermelons, pies, cakes. Around 11, the orchestra is tuning up, adding to the noise of chattering neighbors and friends and the excited squeals of children whizzing through on streamer-draped bicycles. Soon the orchestra begins a full-tilt program of heart-pounding patriotic songs. There are orations and recitations, the annual highlight being former Lipscomb University theater professor Henry

now has a fourth independent TV-news operation. At a reported cost of $3 million, the Fox TV affiliate WZTV-Channel 17 unveils its new hourlong 9 p.m. newscast anchored by Ashley Stewart and Laura Faber. Since 1997, WZTV has paid its network-affiliate rival WKRN-Channel 2 to produce its half-hour weekday newscast, sometimes going overboard in its attempt to appear edgier and more irreverent than the competition. Now, though, with a news staff increase from six to 43 and a fleet of rented satellite trucks, the station takes its place in the Nashville market seriously. . . . **Two courts** 500 miles apart issue contradictory rulings on the same matter: custody of the children of Janet Levine March. In Nashville, Juvenile Court Judge Betty Adams Green reaffirms her previous restraining order granting temporary custody to the children's grandparents, Lawrence and Carolyn Levine. In Chicago, though, Cook County Circuit Court Judge Anthony L. Young enjoins the Levines from pursuing custody in any other court but his. A federal court judge may have to settle the matter.

7—**Enough about custody;** here's to custodians. The Metro Beautification and Environment Commission names eight finalists for Custodians of the Year 1999-2000, in recognition of outstanding service in improving the learning environment of public and private schools in Davidson County. Honored are: Margaret Franklin of Lipscomb High, Antioch High's Harry Porter, McMurry Middle School's Raymond Springer, Antioch Middle School employee Howard Clark, Frank Shawn at Charlotte Park, James Lynch at Caldwell Early Childhood, Donnie Patton at Harris-Hillman and John Willie Jones in the libraries division of Metro schools. . . . **Metro Officers** Scott McGonigle and Jeff Bauer are back on active duty, almost four months to the day after their controversial shooting of an unarmed suspect, Larry Davis, who allegedly tried to run them over with his car during a traffic pullover Apr. 9. Davis had gambling receipts in his car as well as two bricks of cocaine worth $60,000, but his shooting was the first of four police-related civilian fatalities in a month's time. . . . **Two other Metro officers** draw punishment from Police Chief Emmett Turner for violating rules forbidding the brokering of outside jobs. Assistant Police Chief Robert Russell and Capt. Joe Ogg are each docked five days of vacation for their part in lining up secondary employment for officers in the same department. . . . **Able-bodied Republicans** in orange shirts show up at the rental home of Tracy Mayberry, offering their assistance in moving Vice President Al Gore's notorious tenant and her family to a new rental property in Lima, Ohio. Mayberry tells reporters she is sick of waiting for the campaigning veep to follow through on needed repairs; for help in moving, she went straight to the Republicans. During the move, Rick Martin and Donald Farmer, independent filmmakers from Cookeville, show up with a movie contract for the Mayberrys. The movie will be a spoof, Martin explains, and the accommodating Mayberrys take time out from moving to pose for a movie poster with two of their rifles.

8—**Pottermania!** Just as contemporary readers have trouble imagining the crowds that reportedly greeted Charles Dickens' serialized installments, future generations may not believe that tens of thousands of parents and children stood in line at midnight at bookstores across the country for a single title. Yet that accurately describes the fervor that greets the publication of *Harry Potter and the Goblet of Fire*, the breathlessly awaited fourth book in author J.K. Rowling's fantasy series for kids of all ages. At 12:01 a.m., bookstores from Hermitage to Hickory Hollow begin passing out reserved copies of the 734-page book, which retails for $25.95. Many a piggy bank has been raided for the occasion, and bookstores respond with midnight parties featuring magicians, entertainers, stuffed owls and

The Whitland Avenue celebration of the fourth began as a small neighborhood activity in the mid-1970s Twenty-five years later, it still featured stirring speeches and dramatic readings, and a concert band—conducted spontaneously in 2000 by 5-year-old Marcus Wanner.

Arnold's reading of the Declaration of Independence in his booming baritone, while the orchestra trumpets Aaron Copland's "Fanfare for the Common Man." The musical finale is, as always, the rousing "1812 Overture," complete with the thunderous booming of cannon fire.

Then the parade begins. The color guard, a phalanx of the party's hosts, takes up Old Glory and an assortment of other flags and banners and, with fife and drum accompaniment, marches to the end of the block. There, dozens of children with their decorated bikes, trikes, scooters, and wagons wait to follow the flag-bearers and anyone else who cares to join in a stroll back through the cheering crowd.

Gloria Ballard admits to having a mixed feelings about the annual picnic and parade. She and her husband, Henry Martin, have lived on Whitland Avenue for 20 years "among wonderful, warmhearted neighbors, many of whom we call friends." For a few years she and Martin served on the host committee for the party. "At the time," she wrote, in a turn-of-the-century reflection on the event, "it was a neighborhood gathering with a good many outsiders invited to join in. When it began to get bigger and the cost kept rising, we reluctantly decided it had outgrown us and stepped aside."

Something else was happening, too. Over time, Ballard and Martin had come to feel a level of discomfort with the incongruity of the celebration. "We are an interracial couple living in a white neighborhood," she explained. "I am African-American, my husband is white; our children are biracial. To stand in the middle of that Fourth of July crowd and see the jubilant celebration of our America—but not a cross section of Americans—began to make us feel a bit uneasy."

On this Year 2000 Fourth of July, Ballard decided to explore those feelings more deeply. She wondered if neighbors in other parts of Nashville, especially minority communities, recognized Independence Day as a patriotic occasion. She spent the afternoon of the Fourth driving around the city, searching for other signs of events like Whitland's. In the small, middle-class black neighborhood of North Nashville where she had grown up, Ballard found no indication that anyone acknowledged the most patriotic of American holidays. On she went to some of the city's favorite gathering places, such as Centennial and Hadley and Shelby parks, where many family groups had gathered for picnics—but again, there was no evidence that they were celebrating anything more than the pleasure of a midweek day off from work. Later, Ballard thought back over the day's events, and recalled her own response to the Whitland Avenue celebration earlier in the day:

"Standing in the middle of the street, surrounded by hundreds of adults and children dressed in breezy summer outfits accented by the colors of the flag, I felt I was a wary visitor in familiar surroundings. In front of me, the orchestra finished the national anthem and rollicked headlong into a medley of patriotic songs—'Yankee Doodle,' 'It's a Grand Old Flag,' 'America the Beautiful.' Spectators up front tapped their feet and bobbed their heads or sang along, while on the fringes of the crowd, people carried on conversations. I stood somewhere in the middle, listening to the talk with one ear and the music with the other. Those are songs that can make your heart pound and bring a lump to your throat. Listening to Ray Charles sing 'America the Beautiful' makes me believe those words; it's an emotional experience.

"Yet as the band pushed on through its familiar selection of tunes, I found myself growing apprehensive, ready to stop tapping my foot at the first hint of an unwelcome note. Even as I was enjoying the carefree moment, I was also thinking, Please, God, don't let them play 'Dixie.' "

In some earlier years, the orchestra had included the Confederate anthem in its patriotic medley, and that, perhaps more than anything else, had brought home to Ballard a painful reality that the overwhelmingly white assemblage seemed totally oblivious to. "Dropped into the middle of a run of catchy melodies," she wrote, " 'Dixie' may sound as right to most people as any verse that glorifies the land and the history of these United States. But to the handful of us present whose ancestors toiled under the threat of the lash in the slave South, that song will forever be an anthem of stand-up-proud white Southerners who cannot look away from Dixie. So whose independence are we celebrating here? Certainly not everyone's—or at any rate, not in the same way."

Ballard noted that at the Whitland gathering in 2000, she counted on the fingers of one hand the people besides herself whose ancestors had come to America in shackles, in the hold of a slave trader's ship. What's more, the leafy avenue to which she and her husband moved two decades ago is still, for all intents and purposes, a white neighborhood. She concluded: "As small a number as we were in the party crowd, and as we are in this neighborhood, we still feel welcome among our friends and neighbors—some of

staffers garbed in capes and top hats. *Nashville Scene* columnist Margaret Renkl captures the moment as an estimated 350 children show up for Davis-Kidd Booksellers' midnight party. Parents Wendy and Buz Martin leave a formal dinner to get their youngest child, Alex, to the bookstore in time. The Martins are present in black tie and formal wear; Alex is in gray bunny slippers. Pediatrician Betsy Triggs brings her mother, her sister, her son, her niece and two of her nephews. "For us it was much more about making a memory than buying a book," Triggs tells Renkl. "In 20 years we can say, 'Remember that night we stayed up till midnight, waiting for the Harry Potter book to come out?' "
. . . **Mixed feelings** greet today's reunion of the descendants of slaves at The Hermitage, President Andrew Jackson's plantation. "It's feelings that I can't explain," says Robert Bradley, a Nashville resident whose ancestor, Alfred Jackson-Bradley, worked as a slave at The Hermitage until his death. For Dorothy Haskins, president of The Hermitage Slave Descendants' Organization, the grounds have special significance. Haskins, 69, says that seven years of researching historic records and family tradition have convinced her that her great-grandmother, Charlotte Jackson, was the daughter of Jackson and a slave known as House Hannah, born in 1791. "It's another [Thomas] Jefferson/[Sally] Hemings," Haskins says. Unfortunately, DNA testing is impossible, since Jackson produced no known heirs. . . . **The spiritual exercise movement** Falun Gong has been suppressed in its native China as a cult that threatens public order, but at today's fifth-annual Celebration of Cultures at Scarritt-Bennett Center, Falun Gong adherent and Nashville resident Guiru Zhang says the Chinese government is merely afraid of a movement that has spread beyond its control. The festive event at Scarritt-Bennett has grown in five years from a relative handful to more than 5,000 celebrants who delight in sampling and sharing the

The Whitland festivities every Fourth of July appeal to adults and children alike, albeit for somewhat different reasons. Relatively few adults, for example, go in for face and body painting such as Anna Chappell, 10 (left), and her sister Lily, 7, found so fascinating.

U.S. District Court Judge Thomas A. Higgins, himself an Irish immigrant's son, came down from the bench to congratulate each of the 66 immigrants to whom he had just administered the oath of U.S. citizenship at the federal courthouse in Nashville on June 23, 2000.

treasures of dozens of the world's cultures . . . . **The McCabe Park** Softball All-Stars defeat the Madison Lady Titans to win Tennessee's District 7 Little League tournament. It is the first tournament win in an estimated 30 years of McCabe Park Little League ball. To get this far, the McCabe team faced some serious foes: the West Park All-Stars, the Brentwood All-Stars and a tough team from Madison. But the McCabe Park girls are unstoppable. They go on to represent District 7 in the Little League state tournament in Bluff City, Tenn., where they will ultimately be eliminated after two losses. But

whom had insisted from the start that the band not play 'Dixie.' Still, it seems important and necessary for us to remind ourselves that, for all its hospitality and pageantry and patriotism, an all-American celebration such as the one on Whitland Avenue—this portrait of America on the Fourth of July—is still missing a few of its colors."

July the Fourth carries with it the burden of American history, even as it presents the glory through star-spangled lenses. In a country as diverse as ours, the meaning of Founders Day—which is what this is—depends on who you ask and what route they and their forebears have taken to reach this place. For some, "this place" is a strange and wonderful terrain, and they view it much as the first longhunters must have looked upon the valley of the Cumberland two-and-a-half centuries ago. For new immigrants who become Americans and Nashvillians, this day is not so much about history and mythology as it is a celebration of new beginnings, of risks taken and corners turned, of setting forth to leave the old behind. Their rite of passage is played out monthly in federal courtrooms as immigrants formally declare an oath of allegiance to their new country, the United States.

A week or so before July 4, 2000, in a packed courtroom of the Federal Building in downtown Nashville, 66 people from 34 nations stood with relatives and friends when U.S. District Court Judge Thomas A. Higgins entered the room. After the clerk had intoned the quaint litany of prelude ("Hear ye, hear ye, hear ye . . . draw nigh and you will be heard"), Judge Higgins, a native Nashvillian and son of an Irish immigrant, told the soon-to-be new citizens that henceforth they would have two special birthdays to celebrate—"July 4, the birthday of your new country, and today, your own personal Independence Day."

After he had administered the oath to them en masse, the white-haired jurist stood in a receiving line and welcomed each new citizen in turn. Thus ended a formal process of preparation that takes as much as two years to complete; thus began what for most "naturalized" citizens is a permanent and mostly positive change in their lives.

Over most of the past decade, these ceremonies have been held with increasing frequency in Nashville, and the number of newly naturalized citizens in the court's jurisdiction has risen steadily, from an average of about 400 a year in the mid-1990s to almost 1,200 in 2000. Three vignettes highlight some of the challenges and opportunities facing both the newcomers from abroad and their new "hometown"—Nashville.

★ ★ ★

For Moises and Vicente Ramirez, brothers who moved to the United States from Mexico eleven years ago as legally recruited "green card" workers, July the Fourth is mostly a day to reflect on the opportunities to be found here by those who are willing to submit to endless days of hard labor. Thirty-six-year-old Vicente recalled the poverty of his years as a sharecropper south of the border. "We raise beautiful tomatoes," he said. "Rich people come and take them real cheap and send them to America. We work for nothing." Eventually, unwilling to bear the hardship any longer, the brothers followed their beautiful tomatoes north.

From agricultural work they moved up to better-paying construction jobs, and acquired skills in stucco and concrete work—skills that eventually brought them into the booming Nashville market. They are permanent residents here now, but Mexico still beckons; they try to visit their parents there once or twice a year, and they send money, too, when they can. "But it's hard," admitted Vicente, "I have a wife and a kid."

Vicente and Olga Ramirez and their daughter, Julibeth, share an apartment in Antioch with Moises and a cousin, Rosario. Theirs is one unit in a sea of apartment complexes that began to sprout up in the orbit of Hickory Hollow Mall two decades ago. Once the city's landing pads for aspiring musicians and poor whites from the South and Midwest, these complexes are increasingly the first homes of immigrants from Mexico, Asia, Africa, and Eastern Europe. On this Fourth of July, Vicente and Moises were enjoying a rare Tuesday off, grilling steaks and chicken on a small cast-iron grill under the tall oak trees outside their apartment.

"I like the Fourth," said Moises. "They give you a day off from work, and we like to go downtown and see the fireworks. Businesses and the government here create work for everybody. That's a thing to celebrate." He made a circular gesture with the barbecue fork in his hand. "Look at you. Every family has new cars. And houses, money. Maybe if the American and Mexican governments work together, they can get rid of the walls. Then it wouldn't be so necessary for people to come here for work."

It's not clear yet if the Ramirez brothers are here to stay. It takes a lot of money to buy a home, admitted Moises. And language remains a problem. "Maybe if I learn to speak better English," said Vicente, "I'll go to school."

★ ★ ★

Speaking the language and working hard are fundamental themes in the success story of Sam Hanshaly, a native of Yemen. He owns the Linbar Super Mercado at the corner of Linbar Avenue and Harding Place in Antioch. Today Hanshaly is besieged with customers grabbing last-minute supplies for holiday cookouts—charcoal, ice, beer, tortillas. The store shelves are packed with a colorful Spanish-English mishmash of items—yucca root and Coke, Gamesa Imperador and Honey Maid, Barrilitos and mi choco, pork chorizo and Armour bacon, Marlboros and El Charritos.

Most of Hanshaly's customers are Mexican workers drawn to Nashville by construction and hospitality jobs. Sometimes the Super Mercado is more bank than grocery, turning a high volume in phone cards and Western Union, wiring customers' dollars back home to Mexico. But many middle-class blacks and whites also live in the affordable

tonight, there are only giggly girls and proud parents. Fans heap praise on team members Diana Andrew, Tiffany Beckham, Kayla Clark, Gray Davis, Sara Dixon, Melissa Goad, Claire Hicks, Kristin Hines, Jess Jowers, Janelle King, Kate Mason and Ashley Stephenson, as well as coaches Jerry Dixon, Joe Beckham and Jim Davis.

9—**Friends and family** of Fred Lane tell *The Tennessean* that the slain NFL running back had been showing signs of emotional and physical abuse at the hands of his wife, Deidra Lane, the only suspect in his shooting death. Fred Lane Sr. says his son told him his wife had pulled a gun before and put it to his chest, and his allegations that Deidra had mismanaged her husband's earnings are seconded by some of Lane's former Carolina Panthers teammates. A former girlfriend also tells the morning daily that Deidra changed the couple's phone number in Charlotte a half-dozen times in recent years to discourage calls from Lane's friends. Meanwhile, at a news conference in Charlotte, Deidra Lane issues a prepared statement that suggests fame brought out a darker side in her husband. "At his best, Fred could be very good," she states. "At his worst, Fred was very different. Celebrity and the environment that comes with fame surrounded our lives and was sometimes a destructive force. I have seen it at work."

10—**"Hot as hell"** officially describes the city, as the temperature hits 98 degrees. A thick brown net of algae coats pools of water at Radnor Lake, which buzzes with clouds of mosquitoes and gnats; the triangular heads of snapping turtles poke through the brackish scum. . . . **Erinn Cosby,** daughter of actor Bill Cosby, opens the weeklong Fisk Race Relations Institute conference with an account of her 1998 journey to Senegal and to Goree Island, where African families were detained for shipment in the slave trade. This is Fisk University's 33rd-annual conference on confronting and overcoming barriers of race; the theme for this year is "Impact of Racism on the Lifecycle." . . . **Mary Phillips Gray,** a member of the Vanderbilt University School of Medicine faculty for 59 years and a pioneer for other women at the school, dies of complications from cancer. She was 86. An anatomy and pathology professor, Gray specialized in lung research; with her friend and colleague Mildred Stahlman, she studied the lung development of newborn and premature babies. She worked four days a week until shortly before her death. Her son, Bill Gray, recalls that "she used to say, 'I can go into the lab and work instead of stay home and read a mystery novel.' "

11—**If anyone** has coupons for liquid hand soap, send them posthaste to Metro Public Works. An audit investigating Mike McAllister, an assistant director there since 1996, turns up a variety of questionable spending practices. One example: Liquid soap, normally priced at $11.30 a gallon, gave taxpayers a soaking of $89.95. The audit finds that McAllister ordered thousands of dollars worth of supplies from companies that offered promotional goodies: a VCR, a CD player, gift certificates, a small TV, a coffeemaker. At the same time, he allegedly skirted Metro buying procedures by splitting many orders into amounts less than $1,000, increasing the likelihood they would be overlooked. McAllister, who has been in hot water since *The Tennessean* published an investigation almost three weeks ago, says he sent the promotional items back either the week of June 26 or the week before—and he paid the postage himself. Concludes Metro internal audit manager Joe Holzmer, "I recommend that Mr. McAllister not be allowed to resume his job responsibilities at this time."

12—**William Troy Snell,** a La Vergne High School senior, fails to come home after his closing shift at the Captain D's on North Lowry Street in Smyrna. His car is found after a caller reports a

apartments and rental houses in the area, and there are immigrants from all over. That evolving mix makes the Super Mercado a sort of mini-international crossroads, Nashville-style.

At the hub of this multiethnic operation is Hanshaly—affable but busy, constantly on the cordless phone doing business in Arabic, explaining a money order in Spanish or chatting with a customer in English. Everyone who walks through his door gets a tailored greeting. "Que pasa, amigo?" he calls out to Hispanics. "Whassup, man?" is his welcome to African Americans, and for whites there's, "Hey boss. How you doing?" Some of Hanshaly's regular customers routinely refer to the store as "Hey Boss."

Now 31, Sam Hanshaly moved to Nashville in 1992. "The Fourth of July and Thanksgiving—those are my two favorite holidays," he said. "I like to light fireworks and play with the kids, have barbecue. I go for the food." Today's grilling will begin about 4:30 p.m. if Hanshaly can get home by then, but it's after 2 and customers continue to stream into the store, so the prospects don't look good. "It's hard to close that door," he said "I would love to have a day off. But if you work hard, it pays off. Very simple. You bring the customer what they need, offer them good service. Don't try to make the money all at once. Take it one day at a time. Step by step you'll get there."

★ ★ ★

The Salimans have made steps recently—big ones. The walk to their brand-new house is lined with small American flags. In federal court just a few days ago, Mervat

Nabil Saliman, his wife, Mervat, and their two sons, Malak, 14 (left), and John, 8, had plenty to celebrate in their new subdivision home in Nashville on July 4, 2000. A few days earlier, the elder Salimans were formally declared citizens of the United States.

and Nabil Saliman pledged allegiance to their new country and were sworn in as American citizens. In their living room, American and Egyptian influences merge—an entertainment center and a computer against one wall, icons in several niches, and a floor-to-ceiling tapestry of the Virgin Mary. Nabil is a deacon in Nashville's only Coptic Christian (Egyptian Orthodox) church, and so are his sons—Malak, 14, and John, who is 8. The comfort and continuity the Salimans find in their church is a major factor in their assimilation into Nashville. "The church here is no different from our church in Egypt," said Nabil. "Every Sunday we go to church, and then we have Sunday School for the kids and teach them how to read the Bible, how to pray, and how to be good individuals. Our church from generation to generation—the same. Same songs, same prayers, same mass."

Religion wasn't the only reason the family left Egypt six years ago—"I came for opportunity," Nabil interjected—but it played a role. "In Egypt, the boys were taught the Koran in school. And they must, they *must* learn that," said Mervat. Her husband took up the story: "But here is a free country, free religions, and nobody can force him to learn something he doesn't want. Here school is good for kids."

The Salimans came to Nashville after friends told them about the religious community they'd find here. Employment, too, was a factor. Both Mervat and Nabil have college degrees, earned in Egypt. Here Nabil works in room service at a downtown hotel. Mervat has qualified for a Tennessee teaching certificate, and serves as a substitute teacher during the school year. In the summer, she works the counter at Captain D's. It's not a job she likes very much; still, she will tell you, the good things in this new place outweigh the bad. "It is hard to feel at home here," she said. "I was a little bit scared to come here. I left my home, my family, my job."

After a pause, Mervat Saliman spoke the words that mothers around the world surely have said for generations when they contemplated a move to America: "I gave up everything because I believe it will be good for my children."

Even in America, freedom is a relative thing and never a certainty. It can depend on matters beyond your control—your place of birth, your skin color, your chromosome pattern, your family's resources. No amount of wealth or advantage or pure luck can stack the deck in your favor and control the hand you're dealt. No matter what your circumstances, there are times when everything depends on how you play the cards.

Christine Wideman can attest to that. She used to be a crack addict, a prostitute married to her pimp. "I got closest to freedom," she recalled with a rueful smile, "each time I got arrested. "On the street I did things to strangers because the man who said he loved me would beat me up if I didn't. That was my life—working so I could buy the stuff to make me high, so I could forget what I'd just done, so I could wake up sick the next morning and go out and do the same things over again. It was humiliating. Who could want that?

"That was my life—that and the bruises my husband left on me. In fact, the last time I got arrested, my husband and I were just walking down the street. The

Christine Wideman (with her daughter Angel) "found a new family" at Magdalene House.

suspicious vehicle parked behind a Smyrna nail salon in the early morning hours. When police arrive, they find Snell, 18, murdered. The gruesome discoveries are just beginning. At the Captain D's where Snell worked, police find the bodies of manager Scott Myers, 42, and Bryan Speight, 29, in a walk-in cooler. The triple slaying is the worst multiple homicide in the city's 131-year history. The apparent robbery leaves police scrambling to determine how many people were involved, how they gained entry and how Snell's car and body ended up at a different location. . . . **Nebraska drifter Jason Pence** testifies in Davidson County Juvenile Court that it was his accomplice, James Caveye, who drew a knife and cut Skull Schulman's throat and then hit the bleeding man with a whiskey bottle to silence his cries. Prosecutors want Caveye bound over to Criminal Court to be tried as an adult. Caveye, now 20, was only 17 at the time of the killing in January 1998. Pence testifies that he only intended to rob the Printer's Alley nightclub owner of the bankroll he kept wadded in his trademark bib overalls. "We was tired of being on the streets, not having no money," Pence explains, "and he was rich." But his partner, Caveye, went haywire, Pence says. In his seat, Caveye shakes his head angrily. . . . **A photographic exhibit** that records the mob-led murders of African Americans draws reactions ranging from rage to stunned silence at the Race Relations Institute, now under way at Fisk University. The stark photographs of broken, burned bodies are part of "Without Sanctuary," a pictorial essay on lynchings in the United States. . . . **After narrowing its search** from more than 100 inquiries to six finalists in two categories, the Frist Center for the Visual Arts bestows a total of $100,000 on two local artists for commissioned works. Nashville metalworker P.J. Maxwell III, owner of American Ironware Inc., receives $60,000 to create the museum's donor recognition wall, while Tom Fuhrman of

Woodbury's Fuhrman Glass Studios gets the go-ahead to sculpt glass installations for the museum's four outdoor fountains at a total of $40,000. The museum will open next April.

13—**The end is near** for Union Hill Elementary School, despite the best efforts of concerned parents. Metro Schools Director Bill Wise announces this morning that the tiny, close-knit school in northern Davidson County will close for lack of students. Union Hill has operated for more than 50 years, but the Metro school board says the brick school is simply too small to justify the expense of operating it. An enrollment of 110 students was needed to keep it open, but for the 2000-2001 school year only 72 have been confirmed. Among Metro's overcrowded schools, Union Hill is a rarity: a school so intimate that the principal knows every student's name, where the great-great-great-grandsons of the school's first principal were enrolled last year. Metro Council member Bettye Balthrop, who lobbied on the school's behalf, says its closing will affect Union Hill's corner of Davidson County more than parents and residents expect. "When it finally hits them that this is going to happen," Balthrop says, "I think they're going to regret it."

14—**At noon,** the melody of "The Tennessee Waltz" peals throughout Capitol Hill, Germantown and neighborhoods along Jefferson Street, echoing off office buildings and warehouses. The sound emanates from the 95-bell Tennessee Carillon at the Bicentennial Mall, which rings out today after a lengthy silence. Funding woes kept the $4-million carillon muted for four years. Starting tomorrow, though, it will play songs representing the state's three Grand Divisions every hour on the hour from 7 a.m. to 11 p.m. . . . **For sale:** Riverstone Farm, the five-bedroom, 190-acre Williamson County home Gary Chapman once shared with his ex-wife, Amy Grant. Amenities include an airstrip and an outdoor

Vivica Peatman (foreground) and a platoon of volunteers from St. Augustine's Chapel on the Vanderbilt campus repaired a house in a near-in suburb and turned it into Magdalene House, a shelter and treatment facility where ex-prostitutes like Christine Wideman can find support.

police came up with warrants for him, but I was the one they picked up. Because they knew me, and they knew I was pregnant again. Some of the cops out there are really decent. That was the only time I didn't cry on the way to jail because I knew this could save me."

Now Wideman is out of jail and off drugs, a graduate of two innovative community programs, Chances and Magdalene House, designed to help women trapped in the subculture of drug addiction and prostitution get a new start. Still, she knows the odds against her are long. "A bunch of girls were with me in Chances," she explained. "During the six months I've been out, eight of them have relapsed, and one of them is dead." But Wideman has support now—a network of friends she made at Magdalene House, the "safe house" for troubled women started in 1997 by the Reverend Becca Stevens, the Episcopal chaplain at Vanderbilt's St. Augustine's Chapel. "There, you end up with a new family," Wideman said. "They welcomed me with open arms."

This time, Christine Wideman may be closer to freedom than she has ever been. "To me, freedom would mean standing up in court and telling them to stop looking at my past, telling them to look at how I'm doing now instead. And to be free to visit my boys and my baby girl, Angel. I'd love to watch her learn to smile and walk and talk. Then I could celebrate."

★ ★ ★

Like Wideman, the men in residence at the Campus for Human Development on Eighth Avenue South are working on basic freedoms, too. In this homeless shelter and addiction-treatment center, (which is the inspiration and ongoing mission of Father Charles Strobel), there is not much of a holiday spirit just now. The Fourth of July feels remote, irrelevant. In the windowless dining room, men mill around, talking a little and watching the big-screened television that dominates the space.

At first, Charles Moore doesn't want to talk about this holiday. He regards the world warily from under the bill of a baseball cap. His left arm and his right leg were encased in heavy bandages, and a deep gash at his temple pointed up like an arrow and disappeared under the hat. Moore, homeless and addicted, dismissed a question about the Fourth of July. "I don't do holidays," he said. "My people were farmers. It was just another day." A man seated nearby chimed in: "That's right. No real meaning to it. I don't celebrate it much. My daddy would take us on a picnic, but then he'd get drunk and fight. I'm glad we live in a great country. That's about it. And today I'm glad to be in here, in treatment, because people out there are drinking and drugging. Holidays are the worst for that."

"I remember fireworks," Moore volunteered. "I saw them one time. My parents took us to see them. The Fourth reminds me of my childhood." He beckoned to a powerfully built man walking by. "Hey Charles, what you think about the Fourth of July?" Charles Shepherd wore a red tank top and a Marine Corps baseball cap. His eyes held the same watchfulness as Moore's. "I'll take a day off," he said, "but I won't celebrate. My people were still in bondage in 1776. The first man shot in the Revolutionary War was named Crispus Attucks. He was a mulatto. And there was Pompeii, a black slave killed at the Battle of Bunker Hill. I was a history major in high college, but you don't find that stuff out in school."

Bobby Beard is a compact, thoughtful-looking guy wearing green surgical scrubs, agreed with Charles Shepherd that there was little for African Americans like him to celebrate about the Fourth. "Jefferson had a clause in the Constitution to outlaw slavery," Beard said, "but they made him take it out so the Southern states wouldn't walk out. That was the cost of getting things going. It was a big cost."

The Reverend Bruce Maxwell would know about that. He pastors Lake Providence Baptist Church, founded in the southern part of Davidson County in 1868 by former slaves. On the Fourth, the church is all but deserted, and the 49-year-old minister, usually a man in motion, wasn't very busy. He was going home to his family soon. "I'll throw a steak or two on the grill and go back in the house to keep cool," he said.

Maxwell knows firsthand why some African Americans find little to celebrate on this day. His two older brothers, Benjamin and Henry, were the first students to desegregate the county's public schools, and Bruce was one of only three African-American students who attended the otherwise all-white Antioch High School from 1967 to 1970. His father, Henry Maxwell Sr., sued the county board of education. "At that time, anyone of African-American descent here in the Providence area of town had to ride a bus all the way to Haynes High School over on Trinity Lane to get an education. My father thought it was very impractical putting kids on the bus at 5 o'clock in the morning to get them to Haynes by 8."

Maxwell remembers those years as difficult, but he and his brothers didn't learn

stereo system that plays underwater in the swimming pool. The asking price: $10.5 million.

15—**A sad day** for longtime residents of the Belmont and Hillsboro Village neighborhoods: the Compton's Foodland grocery store at the corner of Blair Boulevard and 21st Avenue South is closing its doors today after 30 years. Tearful customers wish the clerks farewell, using a pack of cigarettes or box of confectioner's sugar as an excuse to visit the nearly bare store one last time. Several take photos from the parking lot. The Compton's building will soon be razed—sooner, as it turns out, than anyone planned—to make room for a new 25,000-square-foot Harris Teeter superstore. So will the empty stores next door and two small rental houses, including one occupied for 12 years by 92-year-old Wallace Davis. Davis plans to shop at the Compton's on West End Avenue. . . . **Even with temperatures** in the 90s, tickets for the Tennessee Titans' 10 regular-season home games sell out in a matter of hours. First in line at Adelphia Coliseum are sisters Diane Reed, Charlene Moon, Doris Bonner and Ann Chabino, who staked out their lawn chairs at 6 a.m. yesterday. The first game is the preseason opener against the Kansas City Chiefs, Aug. 5. . . . **The fund-raiser** at the Wildhorse Saloon is for Vice President Al Gore, but the name on everyone's lips by the end of the evening is Bob Graham. Stumping for the veep, the Florida senator cagily downplays media speculation about a possible Gore-Graham ticket, teasing the audience with hints that he is considering a new career—"as a country-western singer." But the zingers he slings at Gore's rival, Texas Gov. George W. Bush, leave Democratic stalwarts buzzing that he has what it takes. Of course, his support in a key electoral state would not hurt either. Then again, what difference could a few Florida electoral votes make?

16—**Belmont University** graduate Ryan Leigh Chambers, 24, makes history tonight at the downtown First Baptist Church. At a time when the Southern Baptist Convention is under fire for its hard-line stance against women in the pulpit, Chambers becomes the first woman ordained into the gospel ministry in the church's 180-year history. "This is not something I chose for myself," Chambers says before the service. "God chose it for me."

17—*CBS News* reports that top brass at Fort Campbell are not being held accountable for anti-gay hostility at the post, according to a report by the Army inspector general that has not yet been made public. The report was ordered in the wake of the killing last July of Pfc. Barry Winchell, who was beaten to death after a barracks mate learned he was dating a Nashville female impersonator. In the 11 months after Winchell's murder, the post discharged 120 people for homosexuality, as opposed to six during the same period a year earlier. Yet in remarks made before he left Fort Campbell for a Pentagon post last month, the commanding officer, Maj. Gen. Robert T. Clark, stressed that "there is not, nor has there ever been during my time here, a climate of homophobia on post. The climate here is one that promotes just the opposite, respect for all.". . . **Eleven male suspects,** ranging in age from 15 to 41, are indicted in what officials call the most egregious case of sexual abuse the Metro police department has seen in years. The victim is a 13-year-old girl, whom authorities believe has been molested for more than a year. The accused victimizers include the girl's 36-year-old uncle, a South Nashville truck driver. The uncle has been in Metro Jail since May, unable to raise $200,000 bail.

18—Singer **Shelby Lynne** begins a two-night stand at the Exit/In that counts as a personal triumph—not just for the elbow-to-elbow crowds, but also for the ecstatic response she draws in a city that never quite knew what

The Rev. Bruce Maxwell (right), whose late father sued the Davidson County School Board to compel compliance with desegregation decisions of the federal courts in the 1950s, waited more than 40 years to see the issue finally resolved.

until later that their father received death threats as a result of his action. "Mostly I was aware of my own situation at school," he recalled. "You could feel the racism and hear the snide remarks. We were not called African Americans or blacks. We were called nigras or niggers to our faces, even by teachers and the principal at Antioch. It was a very tense situation."

In 2000, Maxwell sees racial tension rising again in the city—not between whites and blacks this time, but between longtime residents and newly arrived immigrants, particularly Hispanics. "It's sad," he said. "We have a real challenge to integrate this new wave of immigrants." Still, Maxwell professed hope for a diverse and harmonious city. His congregation already ministers to Hispanic women whose husbands are abusive. "They don't have any other place to turn to," he explained. And Maxwell hopes to open other areas of ministry as well. "One of the things I'm praying for is that there's going to be an Hispanic pastor. God is going to introduce us, and we can have a ministry together. There's so much we have to offer each other," he said. "Everybody brings something to the table. Maybe that's the thing we can really celebrate on a holiday like this—that this country is truly diverse. It's beautiful. It's a beautiful thing."

★ ★ ★

If a multiethnic vision of what his community could be is what inspires Bruce Maxwell, then a xenophobic vision of what it used to be seems to drive 85-year-old attorney and artist Jack Kershaw. He is the man who created the statue of Nathan Bedford Forrest on horseback that stands in a Confederate-flag-lined private park next to Interstate 65 near Brentwood. Since it was erected in 1997, the somewhat grotesque rendering of the controversial Civil War general has been the butt of many jokes, a lightning rod for scorn and, to some, a gleefully defiant symbol that the guerrilla remnant

Artist-attorney Jack Kershaw's statue of Confederate General Nathan Bedford Forrest was fashioned in his South Nashville back yard and then mounted on a rearing fiberglass steed in 1998. The creation caused a stir when it was installed at a private park next to Interstate 65 near Brentwood.

to make of her talents. In interviews, she says her frustrating Nashville career, during which she was pitched without success as a state-of-the-Row country chanteuse, almost made her pack her bags for the hotel lounges of her native Alabama. Instead, she wrote and recorded a stunning album of sultry pop songs and emerged with unprecedented acclaim and attention. She basks in the album's glow at the Exit/In.
. . . **Police arrive** at the Inglewood home of William G. Satterfield and find the door standing open and the house ransacked. Downstairs, they discover Satterfield, 82, bound and gagged in the basement. He has apparently suffocated. The police were called when a neighbor noticed Satterfield's car missing. The search begins for a 1998 white Oldsmobile.

19—**A major victory** for Lawrence and Carolyn Levine: a Chicago judge cedes jurisdiction over the Levines' suit for custody of their two grandchildren to Davidson County Juvenile Court Judge Betty Adams Green.
. . . **Outside a Super 8 Motel** in Goodlettsville, police locate the white Oldsmobile belonging to William Satterfield, the Inglewood man found murdered yesterday in his home. Behind the wheel is Jarret Guy, 27. In a motel room, police find Guy's wife and child, along with money, crack, guns and his accomplice, 24-year-old Jacob Campbell, whose grandfather is an old friend of Satterfield's. Campbell and Guy went to Satterfield's house intending to rob him. . . . **The man** charged with molesting his 13-year-old niece and offering her sexually to 11 other men is on suicide watch in Metro Jail. Two days ago, he attempted to hang himself in his cell with a bedsheet. His niece is now living with other relatives and receiving counseling.
. . . **Seen on Kirkwood Avenue,** near the Melrose Kroger: a man taking a sledgehammer to a cast-iron bathtub, pausing only to haul the pieces to the street.

of Southern partisans is still capable of major mischief, 135 years after Robert E. Lee laid down his sword at Appomattox. Most critics say Kershaw's Forrest is simply bad art. But ask Kershaw, still crusty and combative in his ninth decade, and he will tell you that the statue is a "proper memorial to Southern culture and our ancestors," by which he means specifically the white upper class that led eleven states into rebellion and war against the national government in 1861.

Kershaw can muster an occasional humorous riposte on this subject ("I've mellowed in my old age," he has been heard to say), but he's not really over the Lost Cause

20—**Tennessee** has just received its first installment of tobacco lawsuit settlement money: $202,905,080 and change. Over 25 years, the state's share of the settlement will add up to approximately $4.8 billion. At the same time, checks totaling $28.5 million from a trust fund set aside by tobacco companies are mailed to nearly 58,000 Tennessee tobacco farmers. Anyone got a light? . . . **Nashville lawyer** John Herbison, the new attorney hired to represent Perry March, says his client "is not going to stand idly by and let his parental rights be terminated." Herbison, who made headlines by working to block a Metro ordinance aimed at the city's adult-entertainment industry, says he was hired by March the same day a Chicago judge ceded jurisdiction of Lawrence and Carolyn Levine's custody suit to Nashville Juvenile Court. His first action, he says, will be to ask the judge in Chicago to reconsider.

21—**Will Fan Fair** leave Nashville? The rumors have been flying for months, but today the board of directors of the Country Music Association puts it to a vote. The result: The annual country music celebration, now in its 29th year, will stay put in Music City—just not in its longtime home at the Tennessee State Fairgrounds. Next year, Fan Fair will move to Adelphia Coliseum, with autograph and exhibit booths to be shifted to the Nashville Convention Center downtown near the new Country Music Hall of Fame. Not only does the CMA hope the new location will re-energize the aging event, it hopes to more than double this year's attendance of 21,627 die-hard country music fans. Especially since next year's Fan Fair will take place over a vacation-friendly long weekend of Thursday to Sunday, as opposed to its usual weekday schedule. . . . **The actions** of a single boxing trainer may rob Metro's at-risk children of the Police Athletic League's boxing program. Ricky Lamont Brigman, 36, was arrested last

of the Confederacy, and he insists that Southern honor, not slavery, was the primary issue that led to the war. He is a product of his time and place: the mid-20th-century South of white supremacy steered by men of means or property or family stature. A graduate of Vanderbilt and the old YMCA Law School, Kershaw joined forces with Vanderbilt Agrarian poet and right-wing extremist Donald Davidson in the 1950s to organize white opposition to desegregation, first under the banner of the Tennessee Federation for Constitutional Government and then in the forefront of the white Citizens Councils of Tennessee, the state wing of a Mississippi-based national organization characterized by its critics as "a white-collar Ku Klux Klan."

Kershaw was a defense lawyer for some school bombers in Tennessee in 1957, and a leader of the charge against integration of the state's public schools. In the 1970s he represented James Earl Ray, the convicted assassin of Martin Luther King Jr. But art was always Kershaw's first love, and in the twilight of his tumultuous life it is his one remaining solace, a grave avocation filled with visions of lost love, martyrdom, and the conflagration he calls "the War for Southern Independence."

His house in Oak Hill is a haunted castle of the Confederacy, a cavernous structure hidden by overgrown shrubbery, guarded by dogs, and filled with his work—massive sculptures of burning Southern plantations, 6-foot-tall tree trunks carved and polished into twisting forms. Nudes. Soldiers. Barren landscapes. The War. One of his most recent works is a soaring sculpture of Joan of Arc being burned at the stake, a 15-foot inferno of foam and fiberglass painted gray and gold. Many of Kershaw's works involve flame. "Anything that's fire, I do well," he declared.

The same can be said of his incendiary opinions: "Our biggest single problem is the power of the central government, which is destroying this republic every day, and has been since Lincoln. . . . Integration forced the schools to dumb down the requirements to fit the lower averages because black students simply had not performed as well as white students. . . . America should be careful about welcoming hordes of foreigners who cannot be assimilated easily. . . . Worship of diversity is a self-defeating notion that it's good for people to mingle and reciprocate, to intermarry and interbreed—but that will lead to homogenization, loss of local community, and ultimately, one-world government."

An unreconstructed rebel to the last, Jack Kershaw nevertheless admits his views have changed a little over time. He now says, for example, that freedom of association ought to be the governing principle of race relations: "If compulsory segregation is unconstitutional, so be it. Let nature take its course. Let those who want to mingle, mingle—just don't make the rest of us do it." And having said all that, Kershaw offered one more opinion. Whether it's his freedom of speech and association, the visibility of his art, the broad and lingering familiarity of his surroundings, or the people he knows and likes, Kershaw still likes Nashville: "It's been a sea change since the 1920s and '30s, a monumental change. It's gone from a small town to a metropolis. You used to say howdy to everybody. Can't do that now. But do I still like it? Yeah. I enjoy it here."

★ ★ ★

Kershaw's sentiments would ring true to Greg Cook, the 46-year-old owner of the L.A. Social Club in Antioch. The bar's real name is the L.A. Lounge, but it's commonly called the Social Club after a previous bar Cook once owned just down the road. He named it after a 1970 movie, *The Cheyenne Social Club*, in which Jimmy Stewart inherits an Old West brothel. And "L.A." stands for Lower Antioch, though no one—least of all Cook—can tell you exactly where that is. "Not a clue," he admitted, taking a break from cooking 70 pounds of ribs and 60 pounds pork shoulder to give away to his customers this Independence Day.

Antioch seems to be as much an anthropological idea as it is a place. Anyone who lives south of I-440, east of I-65, and west of an axis that runs from Hickory Hollow Mall to the airport is thrown into the Antioch hopper. Antioch claims part of Brentwood (Brentioch), as well as neighborhoods like Paragon Mills, Woodbine, Lake Providence, Tusculum Hills, and the more anonymous and sprawling residential fingers interlacing the Harding Mall area all the way to the Rutherford County line. And while Antioch has become a melting pot of Hispanics, Asians, Eastern Europeans, and Africans, it still clings to its former incarnation as a base camp of sorts for a conglomeration of whites, homegrown and transient—truck drivers and bikers, airport and mall

Bartender Jim Venus shares a laugh with customers David Whitehead and Becky Weaks (right) at the L.A. Lounge and (Social Club) in Antioch. In local parlance, L.A. stands for Lower Antioch.

workers, sales reps, music-industry infrastructure people. It is from among these, the locals and the white newcomers, that the L.A. Social Club draws its clientele.

"Antioch? It's not what it used to be," said Cook. "Now it's a mixture. It used to be country people out here. Regular people. But now you've got ever' single solitary person in the world lives in Antioch. I think it's terrible. Hell, who wouldn't? I don't like that Hispanic element, for one. I don't like it at all. Fifteen people living in one apartment? It's ridiculous. When you go to the store, you have to figure out three or four different languages to try to pull it together. Go in a restaurant and speak to someone, and they don't know what you're saying. I think it's ridiculous. 'Course, I'm kind of old-fashioned."

★ ★ ★

Within a 5-square-mile patch of South Nashville real estate, the work stations and viewpoints of Bruce Maxwell, Jack Kershaw, and Greg Cook enjoy a peaceful, unconnected coexistence. And they're just a tiny sample, so small as to grossly under-represent and perhaps distort the area's profile. Two white guys with retrograde racial views don't do justice to the large number who organized across racial lines in the mid-1980s to save Antioch High School, historically all-white, as an expanded and thoroughly integrated campus. Glencliff, the other public high school in this southeast quadrant, is similarly integrated. Nowhere else in the city is there such a United Nations in microcosm. And what about Saletta Holloway, black and female and a relative newcomer to Nashville, winning an Antioch-area seat on the Metro Council in 1995 over a white male incumbent—and getting re-elected four years later? "We've got a black council lady," Greg Cook reported, sounding amazed and almost proud. "She came in at a good time."

night and charged with two counts of rape by fraud. Police say Brigman blindfolded two teenage boys and pretended to be a woman performing oral sex on them. According to arrest warrants, Brigman had multiple sexual encounters with the boys, aged 13 and 14, at the PAL training facility and his East Nashville home. The PAL boxing league has shown guidance to several thousand kids and launched the careers of some of Nashville's top professional pugilists; among them is Jonathan Reid, the 25-0 middleweight who calls the day he started boxing at the PAL one of the most important in his life. Today, though, the PAL boxing facility at Eastland Park is padlocked, and Police Chief Emmett Turner says the boxing program is "in serious doubt." . . . **The city-owned** Gaylord Entertainment Center may have been cleaned,

Albert Bender and other Native Americans tried in vain to prevent Wal-Mart from building a new store in an area of West Nashville where many Indian burial grounds are known to exist.

but Metro taxpayers got hosed. That is the finding of an audit of Pritchard Sports and Entertainment Group, the Houston-based cleaning company that swabs down the arena. According to the audit, Pritchard overbilled the Metro Sports Authority at least $27,000 for cleaning at events over a two-year period. The company apologizes and agrees to repay the money. . . . **A 50¢** hourly raise may be Bridgestone/Firestone's "last and best offer," but the truck-and-bus tire plant's unionized employees disagree. They vote 589-14 to reject the offer, forcing negotiators to return to the bargaining table.

Elsewhere in the United Nations of Greater Antioch (a.k.a. South Nashville extended) lives Albert Bender, a middle-aged Nashvillian who doesn't like to parse phrases when it comes to identity. He describes himself as "a Cherokee Indian. Period." He would not be mistaken for one of Jack Kershaw's tribe, but like Kershaw, Bender would prefer to see his racial group—the Native American Indian population—keep its separate identity, albeit for an entirely different reason. "There are so few of us," he said. "We need to stay together, or else we'll disappear."

There were multiple thousands of indigenous people living in Middle Tennessee 300 years ago, and a few thousand in what is now Davidson County. A hundred years later, when Nashville was an established town and whites were flooding in from the East to claim Revolutionary War land grants, the Indian population hereabouts had been decimated by warfare and disease to the point of near-extinction, and that same tenuous fingerhold was all the Indians had at the end of the next century, in 1900. Policies promulgated under Nashville's own President Andrew Jackson in the 1830s and followed through the remainder of that century had driven most of the remaining Indians east of the Mississippi River to reservations in the West. Now, after yet another century has passed, the population of Native Americans is rising again; in the 2000 census, 1,679 people in Davidson County identified themselves, at least in part, as "Native American."

Bender went west to school in Oklahoma, became a lawyer, and worked for a number of years as an Indian Legal Services attorney. He moved back to Nashville in 1995, and soon became an outspoken advocate in behalf of the oldest minority group (and one of the smallest) in the area. He was a leading organizer of a multiracial effort to block construction of a Wal-Mart store on Charlotte Pike in the West Meade area after excavation turned up Indian burial sites (the protesters lost). A more recent dispute arose when graves were found at a road-widening project in southwestern Davidson County. An intertribal coalition of Indians got a court injunction to halt the work pending further review.

"We've won a few," said Bender. Mild-mannered and soft-spoken, he is also blunt in his assessment of the United States on its birthday: "Of all the people in this country, Native Americans would be the last to stand up and wave the flag on the Fourth of July. Far from being a day of independence, this date marks the occasion when white leaders got a green light to seize the rest of our land and eradicate the remaining Indians, because we stood in the way of U.S. expansion. So celebrate the Fourth? No thanks."

★ ★ ★

Ellen Wemyss also took on Wal-Mart in the 1990s—and like Albert Bender, she lost. The gargantuan superstore chain was eyeing a choice spot on the main drag into Gallatin from Nashville. Mrs. Wemyss, at age 99 a seasoned champion of historic preservation in Middle Tennessee, joined others in a lawsuit charging that the commercial giant would destroy the historic character of the highway. Wal-Mart prevailed. At Fairvue, her 1832 mansion down a shady lane not far from the highway store site, Ellen Wemyss had to content herself with preserving what was hers: the Federal-style brick home and 400 acres remaining from a 2,000-acre antebellum plantation that once backed up to the Cumberland River and shipped cotton and tobacco to the ports of Memphis and New Orleans.

Losing was not an everyday experience for Ellen Wemyss. She was born to privilege in 1895, the daughter of a prominent Nashville lawyer, Walter Stokes Sr., and she grew up with an appreciation for the finer things of life, but also with a sense that duty went along with the privilege. She was an activist for women's suffrage in her 20s, and when the 19th Amendment was ratified in 1920, she was in the first wave of new voters. She married in 1925 and moved with her husband to Alabama, but he died just nine years later, and Ellen Stokes More returned to Nashville with her young son. In 1939, she married William Wemyss, a widower with two children. He was a co-founder of Jarman Shoe Company, the forerunner of Genesco. The following year, when Wemyss was 60 and his wife 45, they turned their attention to the century-old Fairvue mansion, which William Wemyss had purchased a few years earlier, and together they set about to restore it. That launched Ellen Wemyss on a lifelong mission: the restoration of some of the great old homes of Middle Tennessee. First came Cragfont, the stately home built by Revolutionary War hero James Winchester in 1802; then Rock Castle, another Sumner County pioneer home; and both The Hermitage and Tulip Grove, on Andrew Jackson's estate in Wilson County. Others followed. Mrs. Wemyss received national recognition for these accomplishments.

Her longevity ultimately resulted in one more defeat for the spry little lady who answered to the nickname "Granny Happy." Soon after her 105th birthday in February 2000, her heirs-to-be sold Fairvue and its 400 acres to a developer with plans to turn it into a luxury lakefront community. She was left with lifetime retention of the house and surrounding acres. After her death, Fairvue will become the clubhouse of the new development.

Failing health and someone's better judgment spared the "first lady" of Tennessee historic preservation from watching new houses rise on the meadow outside her window. "She didn't see it," a close friend and fellow preservationist said, "but she realized, she knew it was happening."

The Morrison, Tenn., plant employs more than 700 workers, and when running at peak capacity it can produce 7,500 tires a day. The company's tires will soon push its labor disputes out of the headlines. . . . **Shasta Russell** and Glenn Dennis are pronounced man and wife in front of the Aisle 10 checkout lane of the Springfield Kroger, where Russell works. The officiating minister, Ed Heath, an assistant pastor at Antioch Missionary Baptist Church, is also assistant manager of the store. The processional winds through the floral department, and afterward the store serves wedding cake from the Kroger bakery. Employee Joey Siano hails the nuptials as "the best Kroger wedding I have seen in my life."

22—**If all other weight-loss programs** have failed, Weigh Down Workshop recommends a different nutritionist: Jesus. Founded by Gwen Shamblin, a Franklin dietician, Weigh Down Workshop suggests that overweight people eat to fill a God-shaped hole in their bellies. The religion-based diet program stresses spiritual sustenance as an antidote to hunger—a regimen eagerly seconded last week by the 3,000 people who attended the program's national convention at the Nashville Convention Center. Shamblin, best-selling author of *The Weigh Down Diet*, tells an interviewer that guilt can be useful for holding fast. "God is the one that gives you guilt," she explains. "He wants you to feel the pain when you aren't in his lordship. . . . **At 5:30 a.m.,** the back door smashes open at 527 Ben Allen Rd., where 23-year-old Liva Grady is spending her first night at home in two months. Her estranged husband, Jerry Grady, 28, enters with a gun. He orders everyone in the house into a back bedroom. Once there, he shoots his wife and her aunt dead and wounds one other person, a 15-year-old. Grady is subdued by his wife's uncle, and the wounded teenage girl is taken to Vanderbilt University Medical Center and released. Grady is taken into police custody and charged with two counts of homicide and three counts of attempted homicide.

23—**Ninety thousand gallons** of raw sewage spill from the city of Franklin's pumping station into the Harpeth River, killing more than 2,000 fish and producing a reek that permeates homes in the Fieldstone Farms and Cotton- woods Estates subdivisions. The casualties include carp, croppie, blue gills, darters and a small- mouth bass, a fish at least 5 years old that almost weighs his age. According to a biologist for the Tennessee Wildlife Resources Agency, the area's aquatic life will not recover fully for five years. Days will be needed to assess the damage. . . . *Tennessean* colum- nist Catherine Darnell, still famous as the paper's erstwhile "Cat in the Hat" society chronicler, pens a lengthy profile of a subject far from her usual beat: "photogra- pher extraordinaire" Queenie McEwen, who uses a small Min- olta camera to create remarkable portraits of Nashville street dwellers, addicts and drifters. McEwen, 52, grew up in extreme poverty in North Nashville; she endured years of sexual abuse, alcoholism and depression before rebounding from the brink. Now her nighttime job scrubbing toi- lets and medical labs subsidizes her consuming project: "Faces," an ongoing study shot on the streets and at Nashville's Union Rescue Mission. One photo depicts a man of indeterminate age with leathery skin and a pierc- ing stare, his wisps of long hair mashed under an unsteady base- ball cap reading, "Bredesen: It's Time." "I think the beautiful peo- ple have been taken enough," she tells Darnell. "I want people with interesting, character-type faces. It's such a hard, tough world they live in that I think it's worth talk- ing about. And worth telling. I'd like to be the one to tell their stories."

24—**For the first time** since July 12, when three employees were murdered in a triple homicide that shocked the area, the Captain D's on North Lowry Street in Smyrna is open for business. And business

Tricentenarian Ellen Stokes Wemyss, born in Nashville in 1895, spent the last six decades of the 20th century at Fairvue, a country mansion near Gallatin that she and her husband restored.

Ellen Stokes Wemyss would live for another year after the sale of the property. She died at Fairvue on June 4, 2001, at the age of 106, having saved every old home she reached out to—except her own.

★ ★ ★

They held an old-fashioned Irish wake for Lafayette Christopher "Fate" Thomas Sr. at Christ the King Church in South Nashville a few days after he died, and you would have thought Saint Patrick himself was on the marquee. The parish hall was packed with Fate's faithful—the courthouse-statehouse-workhouse crowd, present and perennial candidates for public office (Bob Clement and John Jay Hooker, to name one of each), and seemingly more Catholics than the Nashville diocese could count, suggesting that some had come from afar. After Father Charles Strobel presided at a brief and infor- mal vigil service, the evening was given over to barbecue, beer and wine, and a loud band, and the attendees at this unusual event sought catharsis by telling one another the legends of the High Sheriff, working their way back- ward, as Father Strobel put it, "from the tomb to the womb," laughing until they cried.

In an adjacent room, Fate himself, the Last Democrat, lay in state like a stranger napping. He was all but unrecognizable, silent and unsmiling in a dark suit and tie, as if his collar was too tight. It was hot in the room, but the man who had brought this crowd together, lambs and lions, donkeys and elephants, was covered chest-high under a blanket of stars and stripes, and there was not a single bead of sweat on his pale brow. "Maybe it's not him," one of his loyal retainers whispered, looking down in wonder.

Fate Thomas rose from a working-class Catholic family in South Nashville to a power base in the local Democratic Party, and then fell to the bottom, only to return to respectability before his death. He was 3 years old when the Great Depression battered the South and the nation, and from then on, he scrapped for everything he got. After high school he followed his father into railroading, becoming an engineer. In the 1950s he opened a restaurant, kept his hand in at the railroad, and got into politics, a field that had always fascinated him. Twenty years of dues-paying won him election as sheriff of Davidson County in 1972, and from that station he built the most efficient political operation in Davidson County since the heyday of ward politics a half-century ago. Until his downfall in 1990, candidates for every office from county clerk to congressman came to seek Fate's blessing—and practically everyone who received it got elected.

Thomas eventually came to grief over a long list of charges having to do, in essence, with an excess of political favors reciprocated in some manner. It was at once petty and serious, a case of overzealous generosity to others by the sheriff and several of his deputies. In July 1990, Fate pleaded guilty to three felony charges and was sentenced to two concurrent five-year terms in a federal prison. In December 1994 he finished his time and came back home.

Friends by the hundreds from every nook and cranny of the Greater Nashville landscape reached out to him, raising thousands of dollars to help pay his sundry debts to society; they bought up all the tickets to the first resumption of his rambunctious and communal Sure Shot Rabbit Hunters Association Dinner, an annual affair that had always been a popular event; and with his son, Fate Jr., he looked to the day when he could show off his pitmaster prowess in a commercial barbecue venture.

They got there in 2000 with Fate's Pig and Pie, a smoky and inviting rib joint on Charlotte Pike, in the western reaches of the county. On the Fourth of July, Fate Sr. dropped by to check the pits and chat with his son before a full day of doing for others.

Former Davidson County sheriff Fate Thomas (opposite page) was a master of local politics who turned food service into a powerful tool for building constituencies. Late in his career, after running afoul of the law himself, Thomas and his son, Fate Jr. (above), opened a barbecue restaurant and bar, but the "High Sheriff" didn't live long enough to enjoy it. Scores of politicians of all stripes were among the thousand or more people who attended his wake and funeral in July 2000.

is booming—largely because today's sales will be split among the families of the three slain employees, Troy Snell, Bryan Speight and Scott Myers. Police still have no suspects in the crime. . . . **Mayor Bill Purcell** casts a vote of confidence for embattled Police Chief Emmett Turner. "The good news is that when problems arise," Purcell says, "Chief Turner has been willing and able to address these problems and to undertake major reform." Abstaining from comment is Fraternal Order of Police President Jimmy Wheeler, who suggests the department "needs some morale boosters.". . . **Reports of outrageous spending** to the contrary, Metro Public Works assistant director Mike McAllister did not skirt buying regulations to obtain promotional trinkets, his attorney tells a closed disciplinary hearing. As McAllister's lawyer, Julian W. Blackshear, tells it, McCallister merely relied on the knowledge of his superiors about what was or wasn't kosher, and any blame rests with those who signed off on his purchases. "A man would not put his life on the line simply for baseball caps and a VCR," Blackshear argues before acting Public Works Director Randall Dunn. Well, there was a coffeemaker.

25—An era of Davidson County politics dies today with former Sheriff Fate Thomas, who succumbs to a longtime heart condition at Centennial Medical Center. He was 73. . . . **Peterbilt Motors** is downshifting. The Myatt Drive truck plant is laying off nearly 370 of its 1,150 assembly-line employees, and the company is cutting production by 30 percent. Observers blame a decline in big-rig sales after a bonanza last year.

26—Unrelenting 90-degree heat coupled with intense humidity keeps many adults indoors. But it does nothing to deter 75 teens and preteens from pounding the pavement of East Nashville, conducting a survey of the area for Mayor Bill Purcell's Youth Council. The information they gather from local business owners, on subjects ranging from handicap accessibility to property condition, will be compiled on an internet site providing data about Nashville neighborhoods. Typically, the young surveyors from the YMCA Teen Extreme camp would be visiting an amusement park or swimming in an area lake. In fact, some of the participants have never even seen Nashville's inner city, and others, such as Brentwood teens Brandon Doyle and Josh Jackson, have spent little time east of the Cumberland. Walking down Main Street between Eighth and Ninth streets, Doyle remarks that the "trashy" area would look nicer " if they cleaned it up a little."

. . . Little did Doyle know that is exactly what two East Nashville neighborhood associations are working to do. East End and Edgefield residents show up in force at a Metro Beer Permit Board meeting, urging board members to suspend the licenses of two markets that are alleged breeding grounds for criminal activity. After a stakeout of several weeks, the East End Neighborhood Association presents the board with a 46-page report detailing conditions at the East End Market on Fatherland Street and Little Rick's Market on South 10th Street. The report paints a portrait of public drunks, pissing hoboes, hookers trolling for tricks and pushers cooking up deals on store property. Attorneys and board members open a manila folder passed around by East End President Jean Harrison. Inside, they find photos of prostitutes openly conducting sex acts too graphic for the report. Worse, the playground of the nearby Head Start school is littered with glass from busted beer bottles, and vagrants approach the school asking for money and water. Attorneys for the markets' owners say the problem rests not with their clients but with the neighborhood itself. The matter is postponed until the next meeting, Aug. 23. . . . **Outside the South Street restaurant** near Vanderbilt, hundreds of listeners stand in a gravel parking lot for a free concert by punk priestess Patti Smith,

But soon an old heart ailment flared up on him again, and within days he was seriously ill. He made a couple of brief rallies, but on July 25, the affable, gregarious, cigar-chomping High Sheriff died of heart failure at the age of 73.

Attorney George Barrett, one of three longtime friends of Fate who spoke at his funeral, called him "the last of those great public servants who got elected and helped get others elected by the sweat of their brow and not by the size of their pocketbook . . . he was a unique combination of ego, swagger, and humility. Fate helped more people than most of us have known in our lives. He was a one-person, full-time social service agency."

He was also the last Democrat who might have saved Al Gore's presidential campaign, and saved the Tennessee Democratic Party from self-destruction. Nashville Democrats who had grown up taking Fate's magic touch for granted were about to learn just how desperately they needed him. No Fate, no freedom.

★ ★ ★

But life goes on, even when tall timber falls in an empty forest—or when tornados turn homes and lives upside down. Almost always (so far, at least), the sun does come up tomorrow.

In East Nashville, the notion of neighborhood is strong. The various communities on this side of the river—East End, Lockeland Springs, Edgefield, Inglewood—are communities on the rise, neighborhoods on the mend. On the east side of the river, this Fourth of July is a good time to celebrate survival and rebuilding.

Dennis O'Brien is watering the dwarf nandinas that are part of the new landscaping at his Eastland Avenue home. The shrubs have not had a chance to fill in just yet. But given time, O'Brien says, they'll grow in just fine. A columned, covered porch stretches along the front of his house. The wood clapboard siding is painted in beige hues complementary with the surroundings. Windows are large and open. Dennis O'Brien's house looks right at home with the century-old homes on the street, but his house was built just last year. "The house was about three-quarters done when we first saw it. We liked the design. We like the quality. We liked the way it fit in right here," he recalled.

What makes O'Brien's new house remarkable is not so much that it was built, but when and why. Eastland Avenue between Gallatin Road and Riverside Drive is one of East Nashville's signature streets. Lined with large almost-mansions, it is a street in transition, and has been for some time. During the 1980s, urban pioneers came to East Nashville in search of cheap historic homes in an urban setting. The found what they were seeking on Eastland. After years of effort, the old bungalows and Victorians have come back. They're now renovated and well-kept.

There were, of course, a few setbacks in the street's recovery. A tunnel of overarching tree branches was broken by an ice storm, and a handful of houses remained reluctant to give up their status as eyesores. Change was slow, but seemingly inexorable.

But Eastland's biggest challenge in a century arrived on April 16, 1998. Most of the residents were at work somewhere else on that afternoon when an ill-formed but furious F-3 tornado came through downtown, touched the east bank of the Cumberland near the site of the under-construction Adelphia Coliseum, then churned a raw trench through Historic Edgefield and Lockeland Springs before landing on Eastland. The tornado rode down the street like it was following a map. Then, as quickly as it had come, it was gone.

In the aftermath, the street looked like a war zone. Century-old trees lay in the street. Most of the homes were battered, having lost gutters, shingles, roofs, chimneys, and windows. A few unlucky parcels took the brunt. At Eastland and 17th Street, an upstairs bedroom had become an open-air porch, and the roof of Joe's Diner collapsed inside its walls. O'Brien, who lived in another part of East Nashville at the time, came to survey the damage. "This was really, really bad at that point," he remembered. "The street was really torn up."

Two years later, however, Eastland has new momentum. While damaged houses were repaired, bigger, more elaborate, architecturally appropriate houses sprang up on the graves of old homes and on previously vacant lots. Here and there, a few pieces of plywood are visible, but the ubiquitous blue tarps—temporary roofing and sign of damage after the tornado—are gone. Just as hopeful are the 15-foot maples and poplars,

Sparklers and other small fireworks occupied (from left) Blake Giles, Brandi Steady, Brittany Steady and Louie Brandon on Electric Avenue in East Nashville while they waited for the big bang on the riverfront after dark.

planted as part of ReLeaf Nashville, an initiative by the Nashville Tree Foundation and Metro Parks to plant 6,500 trees over five years. Eastland is settling back in. O'Brien's pride in the renewal is obvious. "It's amazing what's happening on this street," he said.

A few blocks away on Russell Street, Ken Anderson is sawing plywood he will use on some ceiling panels in his Victorian home. He has been working on this project during spare hours and on weekends for years. "It's a complete restoration," Anderson explained. "Before I bought it, this house had been divided up into sixteen apartments. It had been abused for many years. I'm taking it back as close as I can to what it was when it was built 125 years ago."

Russell Street took a heavy part of the wind that came from the tornado, with neighborhood churches hit particularly hard. Anderson says he was lucky. He lost thirteen trees, but they didn't fall on the home he'd worked so hard to restore. "Some of those trees we needed to lose," he joked. In an odd way, Anderson and other residents have the tornado to thank for improvements on East Nashville streets. After the storm, a Regional/Urban Design Assistance Team (RUDAT for short) brought together architects, city planners, business owners, city officials, and neighborhood residents to form a cohesive plan for rebuilding the area. But it wasn't just to repair tornado damage. The RUDAT also offered East Nashville a chance to address problems that had existed before, ranging from a lack of diverse retail to codes violations and street design. For the first time there's a broad plan in place in an area where much of the rebuilding has been done individually. The goal is to promote the unique area of the city as a distinctly urban neighborhood with a diverse residential base living in a cohesive community.

who galvanizes an audience broad enough to include documentary filmmakers, bikers, dozens of local musicians and androgynous teenage girls wearing ripped-kneed jeans slung low across their slim hips. Smith sings a protest song she wrote two years ago after seeing the slave-trade drama *Amistad*.

27—A federal judge in San Francisco rules that Napster, the controversial website that allows more than 20 million users to download music files free of charge, will have to shut down at midnight tomorrow. The injunction stems from a suit filed by the Recording Industry Association of America, which accuses Napster of costing the music industry a cool $300 million. Yet Napster users say they frequent the site to sample music they want to buy.

That suits Ken Anderson just fine. "I'm here to stay," he said. "I'll be here painting and sawing until this house is done." Then he smiled. "And a restoration is never done." Later, when the sun goes down, he'll stroll down the street to see the fireworks.

He won't be alone. On this day every year, East Nashville has a big advantage over the rest of the city. Here the neighbors can view the Riverfront Park festivities without having to cross the river, find a place to park, and brave the crowd. People lucky enough to have homes with an unobstructed view of the display put picnic tables on the lawn and invite friends over. Others fill East Park with blankets and boom boxes, waiting for the show to begin. Churches flanking the park let their parishioners park and watch. First Church of the Nazarene holds a festival with music and games for the kids. At Holy Name, a church bulletin is the price of admission to the parking lot, though a kind word or familiar face works just as well.

Barring a last-minute appeal, Napster is essentially dead—and to no one's surprise, Music Row is not decked in funeral wreaths. Nashville songwriters, publishers and label executives say Napster has gotten a free ride off their products for too long, and the decision backs the right of copyright holders to be paid for their work. The net just isn't tight enough for some folks.

28—Don't start the wake for Napster just yet. Two federal appeals court judges grant the website an eleventh-hour reprieve, just hours before it is to shut down at midnight. Until the lawsuit against Napster goes to trial, the site can continue dispensing free music files to its millions of users. No trial date is set.

29—Joe Seaton, the only Democratic candidate running for the state House in the 45th District, is likely also the only candidate in the country telling constituents not to vote for him. "I'm not interested in being a state representative," Seaton says, delivering a stump speech for an alternate universe. "I need time to recuperate and heal from my nervous breakdown. I can't do that and run." Instead of gearing up for battle against Republican incumbent Diane Black in November, Seaton, a former freelance journalist, is focusing his energies on an Aug. 18 court date. He faces charges that he assaulted his mother, father and a Gallatin police officer in an altercation May 10 that he says resulted from his nervous breakdown. Local Democrats, he says, were less than supportive. "I'm just uniquely unqualified to represent people who turned their backs on me the minute I needed them," Seaton says, but he stops short of endorsing the enemy. "Don't vote Republican," he cautions. "Don't ever do that.". . . **A crowd of 14,500 fans** cheers on the Nashville Kats as the arena-football team clobbers the Grand Rapids Rampage in playoffs. . . . **Vanderbilt football coach** Woody Widenhofer marries marketing executive Debbie Caplenor

Two poles for seven kids were not enough to go around, but the fish weren't biting anyway on this lazy Fourth of July afternoon in Shelby Park.

Gregory Carter (left) and his friend, Jamaal Cebrum, put on the gloves for a friendly sparring session in an East Nashville back yard over the 4th of July.

At 7:30, the Nashville Symphony launches into its traditional concert of patriotic songs, and the crowd gets into the spirit of the occasion. An hour passes in a blink, and full darkness descends. Finally, as 9 o'clock approaches, the signal is given for the light show to begin. For eighteen solid minutes, the barrage is incessant and deafening. Bangs and booms rattle the ground like cannon fire; cascading flares of light and simultaneous bursts of color and sound follow one after another after another; showers of sparks in brilliant hues descend like snow from a rainbow. Atop hills and tall buildings in all directions within a radius of 4 or 5 miles from the coliseum, people stop what they're doing to watch—and most of the 80,000, or however many, are impressed. They oooh and ahhhh appreciatively, leaning against one another and sticking their forefingers into their ears. Parents point skyward, directing their children's attention to the latest high-tech upgrade of this ancient art form unfolding in the night sky above them.

In these brief minutes the heat is forgotten, and with it the hassles and discomfort of too many bodies crowded together into too small a space. Momentarily lost, too, is the mundane memory of unfinished business—political conflict on Capitol Hill and in the Metro Courthouse, corporate mergers and downsizing, problems having to do with kids and schools, adults and the economy, the elderly and health care. Our worries and conflicts fade into temporary insignificance, which is probably where most of them need to stay. Lost in the spectacular display of color and sound and light, we are free to think of each other and of ourselves as we would like to be, and see our history as we wish it had been—or to see and think of nothing at all except what's happening up in the sky.

And then, after the last flicker of technicolor light has faded from the sky and the national birthday party is over for another year, Nashville seems to breathe a collective, wistful, almost audible sigh. Tomorrow is a workday, and the dog days of August are approaching, and school will begin again soon, after what seems like no more than a week or two of summer vacation. Before you know it, fall will be here.

Slowly, reluctantly, we gather up our baskets and blankets and head for home, back to our daily lives along the banks.

in a private ceremony. The couple has just enough time for a short honeymoon before football season starts next month.

30—**A state biologist** calculates the damage done by the July 23 sewage spill in Franklin, and the news is bad. According to David Sims of the Tennessee Wildlife Resources Agency, some 146,000 fish were destroyed by the spill as it seeped along a 6.5-mile stretch of the Harpeth River. The spill leaves 1-inch minnows and 14-pound catfish alike belly-up in the tainted water.

31—**The first African-American woman** to become a clerk in the Davidson County court system retires today after 36 years. When Margaret Blair started working as an elevator operator in the downtown Stahlman Building in 1963, at age 19, she could not use the restroom marked for whites or eat in the ground-floor restaurant. Blair returned to the Stahlman Building two years ago as a court clerk, when the civil division of the Davidson County General Sessions Court moved its offices there. Her boss, Circuit Court Clerk Richard Rooker, and her co-workers honor her today with a reception. "I have been a team player," Blair says. "It's a team that has had a lot of players and will have many more.". . . **Terry London, 51**, takes business observers by surprise when he announces his resignation as president and CEO of Gaylord Entertainment Co. A 22-year veteran of the company, London says he is stepping down to spend more time with his family. But observers wonder if the poor performance of Gaylord stock under London's tenure as CEO hastened his departure. . . . **Tennessee's GOP delegates** are in the City of Brotherly Love tonight for the start of the Republican National Convention. Two-time presidential hopeful Lamar Alexander has issued a pronouncement that he will not attend this year, ending a string he started in 1968. But two vice-presidential short-listers, Tennessee senators Fred Thompson and Bill Frist, will be there. So will Hank Williams Jr.!

From the time it opened on Second Avenue, just south of the Courthouse Square in 1955, the Gerst House was a popular watering hole for politicians, journalists, lawyers and sundry other street traders.

CHAPTER EIGHT

CAPITOL OFFENSES

by LARRY DAUGHTREY

I n the summer of 1999—in the run-up to the Metro mayoral election, and almost a year before the lackluster state primaries of 2000—Nashville's political community was adrift. The Gerst House, an amiably rough-hewn saloon on the eastern approach to the Cumberland River, was closing. It was a Nashville institution, dating back more than a century to the heyday of the Gerst Brewing Company, one of the city's leading German beermakers. The Gerst served up bratwurst and hot potato salad, fishbowl-sized schooners of beer, and a simmering stew of politics.

For many years the Gerst was located on Second Avenue, just south of the Davidson County Courthouse. One of the regulars was a one-eyed man of considerable political dexterity, Clifford Allen. Allen served as a state senator, ran for governor and mayor, helped establish the metropolitan form of government in Nashville, became tax assessor and, later, Nashville's congressman. All the while, his primary home, office, and campaign headquarters was a stool at the back end of the scarred and battered oak bar at the Gerst. The Second Avenue location had closed in 1970, making way for a courthouse parking lot and a skyscraper full of lawyers and money men. Later, in 1978, Clifford Allen died. The headline in *The Tennessean* marking his demise would long be remembered: "Clifford Allen Takes Turn for Worse, Dies."

The Gerst had moved a few blocks east, across the river into a windowless block building nestled between a gas station and a locksmith, a rock-throw from the growling new interstate highway that shuttled north-south traffic through the city. Making the move, along with the bar, Clifford Allen's stool, and the oversized beer schooners, was a legendary breed of cockroaches. The regular patrons noticed their comings and goings (it was difficult to do otherwise) and speculated on their ancestry. The old Gerst had been located near the site of Andrew Jackson's stables, and conventional wisdom held that these insects were direct descendants from that era. Jacksonian cockroaches, they were called.

Indeed, the Gerst seemed a lineal descendent of the uncouth taverns where Jackson and his contemporaries plotted the management of the city, the state, and eventually the nation. The old general would have felt right at home there, although the *code duello* had long since disintegrated into occasional sodden fistfights in the parking lot.

Both the old Gerst and its reincarnation had the dark, heavy interior look and feel of a protective redoubt, encrusted with the mingled stains of pork fat, baked beans, and tobacco. Faded sporting prints hung on the walls, including a picture of the racehorse Donau, which had won the Kentucky Derby for the Gerst family in 1910 (when both brewing and horse racing were illegal in Nashville). Also displayed were mounted horns from exotic beasts, a stuffed fish or two, and an electric train chugging through a Bavarian village. And then there was the smell. Many Nashville housewives could identify the distinctive odor of the Gerst—a medley of sausages, sauerkraut, cigarettes, and stale beer—that clung like a skunk's scent to their husbands' clothing. (Some of the newer breed of professional women had begun, tentatively, to stop in at the Gerst, but it remained primarily a male bastion.)

From time to time, the visitors included the likes of Bobby Knight, the legendary basketball coach from Indiana, and George Jones, the equally legendary country singer. Those were the remarkable guests.

1—**At dusk in neighborhoods** all across Nashville, residents are on the streets for the city's annual Night Out Against Crime, a show of community strength and awareness in response to the dangers of contemporary urban life. From Nebraska Avenue on the west side of the city to Woodland Street on the east, and from Edgehill Avenue south of downtown to Lischey Avenue on the north side, residents and neighbors, adults and children come out to meet, greet, eat, bond a bit. The block parties, street

It was not remarkable to find the governor of Tennessee at a center table spinning yarns for friends, or the mayor of Nashville trying to hash out some intricate zoning matter. Infrequent sightings of would-be presidential candidates like Al Gore and Lamar Alexander caused hardly a stir among the regular clientele, which included legislators winding down from their Capitol Hill exertions, councilmen and judges, the tax assessor and the Supreme Court clerk, the district attorney, and lots of cops, uniformed and plain-clothes. There were reporters and plumbers, union organizers and electricians, and a retired colonel whose long, unexplained absences were attributed to assignments from the Central Intelligence Agency.

The Gerst was the only place in Nashville where white-collar and blue-collar men (white men early on, for those were the days of segregation) mingled seamlessly, and always the talk was of politics. There was no problem or candidacy or issue that couldn't be dissected at the bar in the waning light of a workday afternoon.

But things had begun to change in the '90s. Reporters at the afternoon *Nashville Banner* had long recognized the richness of source material in the atmosphere at the Gerst and, free of deadlines by 1 p.m., had made the bar a second city room. Then the *Banner* folded, and its reporters dispersed to other cities or to public relations jobs with stricter standards, and death took its more or less predictable toll on the regulars.

The Gerst House, meanwhile, had passed from the hands of its original German-American proprietors and, like many other Nashville institutions, was now owned by newcomers to the city. Then, like its predecessor on Second Avenue, the Gerst fell victim to a new wave of progress. The cinder-block building was like a stone in the sandal

Until it vacated its Second Avenue location in 1970, the Gerst was practically an annex of the courthouse. Shortly before the move across the river, bartender Eddie Henderson and two other longtime employees, Allen Walker (left) and Carolyn Sadler (right), paused from their labors to accommodate a newspaper photographer.

Before Clifford Allen (right) won a special election in 1975 to succeed Richard Fulton (left) in Congress, he reminded his friends at the Gerst House and the Courthouse of an old political proverb: "In the land of the blind, the one-eyed man is king."

of the gleaming new gladiatorial venue for the city's recently acquired professional football team. All the combined political muscle of the regulars could not save it from the bulldozers. There was promise of a new Gerst a couple-hundred yards away, but it would be an antiseptic, professionally designed restaurant with designated non-smoking areas and actual ferns hanging inside. The restrooms would be clean, and there was no certainty that the Jacksonian cockroaches would endure.

So in that summer of prelude—before Adelphia, before the mayoral election, before the income tax war—there began a diaspora of Nashville's political community. The Gerst regulars scattered to other bars, no one of which took hold. There was no consensus on any of the candidates for mayor. And on Capitol Hill, the second-term governor and his Republican colleagues were about to come to grief over the t-word.

If there was consensus about anything among the Gerst crowd and the rest of Nashville, it may well have been about one smooth facet of the city's governmental establishment: the basic structure called Metro. Separate balloting in the old city and in surrounding Davidson County in 1962 had led, a year later, to the adoption of a single metropolitan government. The merger had been attempted before, and failed. The second time, half a dozen small municipalities within the county were allowed to retain some autonomy, and that was enough to tip the outcome toward consolidation. By the turn of the century, 37 years later, there would be no sentiment at all for going back, or even changing the structure very much. What Nashville had in this regard, other fragmented cities envied.

At first, Metro was viewed as a drastic, even radical, change. Now, it had assumed the stature of an inspired handiwork wisely crafted by founding fathers. Metro combined the old city and county governments into one, putting law enforcement, schools, courts, public works, social services, and other functions under a single public charter that gave operational authority to a mayor and a 40-member council chosen in nonpartisan elections.

The creation of this new style of government had required an epic struggle

dances, ice-cream socials and such are effective in fighting crime, police say, because neighbors who know one another watch out for each other. . . . **Statistics released** by the Metro Police Department show how badly such united resistance is needed. Crimes in seven major categories are up sharply in the first five months of 2000. Burglaries (3,663) increased by 18 percent over the same period last year; larceny (13,427), auto thefts (2,605), rapes (238), robberies (1,077), and aggravated assaults (3,146) all posted lesser but still troubling increases. Worst of all, criminal homicides are up by 31 percent; there have been 38 in five months, compared to 29 in the same period a year ago. The total number of crimes committed in these categories from Jan. 1 to May 30, 2000, is 24,194. . . . **Calls and e-mails** spread the word that American Media, the Florida corporation that publishes both *Country Weekly* magazine and the notorious *National Enquirer* tabloid, is purchasing Nashville-based *Country Music* magazine. The move is the latest in a series of shake-ups in the world of country publications, including the closing last January of the weekly *Music City News* after 37 years in business.

2—At 3 a.m., Rhonda Campbell gets up for a drink of water and glances outside at the Compton's Foodland building on Blair Boulevard, across the street from her home. She sees what she later describes as "a spectacular sight": the 72-year-old building engulfed in flames. The Belmont/Hillsboro neighborhood grocery, which closed its doors July 15 after 30 years in business, was eventually to be torn down to make room for an upscale Harris Teeter supermarket. The fire hastens the demolition process.

3—**The GOP convention** ends tonight in the City of Brotherly Love with an acceptance speech by Texas Gov. George W. Bush. But delegates from the Volunteer State are just as jazzed by the prominent placement given to

U.S. Sen. Bill Frist on the evening's agenda. The physician-senator from Nashville was considered a contender for the vice presidency until former defense secretary Dick Cheney accepted the bid. To clinch his status as a rising star, Frist has been given a key closing-night slot to advance the Republicans' health-care concerns. . . . **At home in Nashville,** only the most faithful voters turn out to cast ballots in a lackluster mix of state primaries and local races. The Democratic contenders seeking to unseat Sen. Frist in November are reduced to two: old warhorse John Jay Hooker of Nashville and Murfreesboro college professor Jeff Clark. At midnight, the race remains too close to call.

4—In Sumner County last October, an injured Hispanic migrant worker drowned in the muck of a pigpen runoff pond. Today, a Gallatin farmer, Galen Dean Eidson, 27, pleads guilty to reckless homicide in the death. Eidson was driving a pickup with three migrant workers in the back when the truck overturned. Pinned beneath was Emiliano Almaraz Monjaraz, 28. Eidson and the other two workers, not seriously injured, left the scene to seek help, apparently believing Monjaraz was dead. Eidson later returned alone and dragged the crushed man 150 yards to the pig pond. He initially denied any involvement in Monjaraz's death, but a witness told police Eidson pushed the man's body under the water with a stick until it sank. The water found in Monjaraz's lungs proved that he had survived the wreck. Eidson will be sentenced Sept. 8, exactly 11 months after the crime. . . . **Through a chain of errors,** Metro police never followed up on a statement made 10 years ago by accused child molester Ricky Brigman, in which he told a Metro detective he had "inappropriate sexual contact" with an 11-year-old boy. In a press conference today, Police Chief Emmett Turner says Brigman was questioned in 1990 on allegations that he had improper sexual contact

stretching back over a decade or more. The timing was perfect: after World War II, but before the big exodus to the suburbs. Metro probably wouldn't have worked at an earlier or a later time. It came as the city was beginning to awaken from sleepy, if charming, Southern daydreaming and gaze toward the second half of the 20th century. Looking back on it from the year 2000, it was difficult to put a finger on the most significant impact of this urban form of government. But at a time when other American cities were exploding outward into segregated suburbs, leaving their souls behind in isolated and imploding inner cores plagued by racism and poverty and crime, Nashville was different.

It had over 500 square miles under one roof, and yet there lingered a sense of a bonded whole, an organism whose extremities were bound to its innards. Nashville's population growth slowed to single digits, while the growth in the counties surrounding it was swift, if not explosive. Metro remained, for the most part, a good place to live, to work, to send children to school, and to seek culture and entertainment. It brought a measure of political stability to the city. In almost four decades, it had elected only five mayors (counting the latest, Bill Purcell, in 1999).

Nashville could look to its larger neighbor to the west, Memphis, and see one of the nation's most racially polarized cities. Its government had been dominated by African Americans long enough for competing factions to sprout, in the manner of white clans before them. Its outer ring—the rest of Shelby County—was a virtually all-white enclave of prosperity and aloofness. The two shared little in common except mutual animosity.

Or Nashville could look east, to Knoxville, where competing city and county governments had rarely been able to achieve common goals (regularly voting down metropolitan charter proposals, for example). Knoxville was a city that could not quite get its feet off the ground; as it prepared in 1982 to host a World's Fair more grand in vision than reality, a national newspaper called it a "scruffy little river city." The image was hard to shake, even when the Vols were winning most of their football games in front of 104,000 fans at Neyland Stadium.

In Nashville, two distinct political factions carried over from the old days. On the city side, the most visible representative was Mayor Ben West, a bow-tied figure with considerable talent for running both a city and a political machine. West's singular contribution was not recognized until much later. In 1961, as civil rights demonstrations were beginning in Nashville and across the South, West met a group of marchers on the courthouse steps. In a dialogue with their leaders, he grudgingly admitted that segregated lunch counters were wrong. The business community took his cue and began the desegregation process that helped Nashville avoid the deep bitterness and violence soon to plague so many other cities.

Nashville's last mayor, Ben West, earned a solid reputation as a progressive leader during his tenure prior to 1963.

Shortly before former Davidson County Judge Beverly Briley (center) won the first Metro mayoral election in the summer of 1963, he shared a banquet-table laugh with two members of Tennessee's congressional delegation, Rep. Richard Fulton (left) and Sen. Albert Gore Sr.

The other faction was headed by Davidson County Judge Beverly Briley, a mustachioed, impulsive firebrand who was one of the early proponents of a local government merger. He and West both were recognized national players in urban political circles, and both had supported consolidation on its first trip to the ballot box. But by 1962, West had soured on the idea. In the first election of Metro officials that fall, he watched from the sidelines as Briley won the mayor's race over Clifford Allen (favorite son of the Gerst gang), and went on to serve three full terms. So it was Briley who would make the nuts and bolts of unified city-county government work.

The Briley-West factions persisted, though their importance diminished with time. By 1999, one West son, Ben Jr., was a member of the state House of Representatives; another son, Jay, was the city's vice mayor. Rob Briley was a state representative, and David Briley was a rising novice in the Metro Council—both of them grandsons of the man named Beverly.

Shortly before Metro was born, another important local figure emerged. He was Richard H. Fulton, son of a railroader in the blue-collar neighborhoods of East Nashville. Fulton was handsome, not very articulate, but charming in a low-key manner. He was a formidable political campaigner. When his older brother, Lyle, died of cancer, leaving open a seat in the state Senate, Dick Fulton won the election to fill the vacancy, but he was denied the seat because he had not reached the constitutional age of 30. He had also made an unsuccessful run for Congress.

In 1962, Fulton again took on the incumbent congressman, Carlton Loser, a dour, rigid former prosecutor. This time Fulton was better prepared, with better allies, including a wiry union organizer and political wizard named Matt Lynch, who headed the statewide labor organization. Fulton also had the backing of *The Tennessean*, under the new management of Publisher Amon Carter Evans and Editor John Seigenthaler.

John F. Kennedy had been elected to the White House and was seeking help in passing his domestic programs, including Medicare and civil rights. Kennedy's friends

with two boys, ages 9 and 11. On tape, Brigman admitted contact with the older boy. But the clerk who transcribed the interview came to a long pause and thought the tape was over—thus missing the incriminating statement. Because the evidence never reached prosecutors, the case never went to trial. Turner says the department was unaware of all this when it hired Brigman as a Police Athletic League boxing trainer in 1995. Brigman is now accused of sexually abusing two boys who participated in the PAL boxing program. . . . **Jeff Clark edges past** John Jay Hooker by a whisker to win the dubious honor of facing incumbent Bill Frist in the U.S. Senate race this November. Observers say Clark's alignment with state Democrats helped him overcome Hooker's name recognition. Yet even with Hooker running largely the same lackadaisical campaign he waged against Gov. Sundquist two years ago, Clark wins by only 902 votes statewide. . . . **Modern-day Franklin** is being converted into 1915 Knoxville, complete with horse-drawn carriages and extras milling around in period attire, for the filming of a *Masterpiece Theater* adaptation of James Agee's novel *A Death in the Family*. In the lead role is Oscar-nominated actor James Cromwell. Filming moves to Nashville's Belmont and Richland neighborhoods and Sunset Studios in coming days. . . . **A long battle** with lung cancer claims the life of Khoune Chanthalavong, 70, the head monk at the Wat Lao Buddharam Temple in Murfreesboro. He had tended the Buddhist temple since 1995. Metro police credit him with opening doors between them and many of the area's estimated 6,000 Laotians after gang violence disrupted the immigrant community. . . . **Thunderstorms** down power lines, leaving 400 Nashville homes without power.

5—**Despite weather worries,** the only thunder at Adelphia Coliseum is on the field—and even that is spotty. The Tennessee Titans eke out a 14-10 victory in their preseason opener against the Kansas City Chiefs. . . . **When Melissa Shane,** a 24-year-old Vanderbilt researcher, fails to join her friends for a night of dancing, they go looking for her and discover that she and her car are missing. A message left on her mother's answering machine is the last word to be heard from her. . . . **Four people who eat** at the San Antonio Taco Co. across from Vanderbilt get something they didn't order: an apparent case of salmonella food poisoning. The Metro Health Department begins an investigation after several diners complain of illness.

6—**Who will be** the Democratic candidate for vice president of the United States? The answer will be decided today behind closed doors at the Loews Vanderbilt Plaza Hotel, where reporters covering the campaign of Vice President Al Gore have staked out the

in Nashville included Evans, Seigenthaler, Lynch, and now Fulton, who ran as an unabashed New Frontiersman. He promised to support Medicare. He openly solicited the votes of black Nashvillians—more so than any other local politician before him. He was the new face of Nashville.

Loser, an Old South Democrat, enjoyed the support of the city's conservative establishment, including James G. Stahlman and his *Nashville Banner*, most of the city's medical community, and a large chunk of the business elite. There was, at the time, virtually no local Republican organization. The city had never elected a Republican to Congress (it still hasn't). The August Democratic primary was really the general election; this time it became an all-out war for the political soul of Nashville.

When it was over, Loser appeared to have a paper-thin majority. In the wee morning hours, Lynch, Seigenthaler, Evans, and the newspaper's political reporters huddled in the back of the city room, sifting through the results. Fulton, exhausted from the campaign, dozed on a couch. "We can't let them steal the election," Seigenthaler thundered. Loser's winning margin appeared to have come from a stack of absentee ballots, most of which were known to have passed through the hands of a city councilman named Gene Jacobs, who presided over an impoverished ward in South Nashville.

Jacobs' predecessor, Charles Riley, had thrown his support to Jacobs when he retired. Asked why he did that, Riley replied: "Because he's the lesser of two evils." Thus did Jacobs have bestowed upon him an immortal nickname: Little Evil. A beer-bellied, near-illiterate man who favored a huge white Stetson, Gene "Little Evil" Jacobs seemed born to the life of a ward-heeling politician. He played his constituency like Bill Monroe played the mandolin. In the process of trying to get his daughter elected to a minor party office, Jacobs had spent days before the election canvassing his ward with about 300 absentee ballots in a satchel, signing up the unsuspecting elderly and others more illiterate than he. Since he was aligned with the faction backing Loser, Jacobs charitably marked not only his daughter's name but that of the congressman.

Tennessean reporters began a relentless, round-the-clock search for all those absentee voters in the Second Ward, Jacobs' bailiwick. Many voters said they were just doing Little Evil a favor. Most didn't know whom they had voted for. Some had simply made their mark and left the rest to Jacobs. Some half-pints had changed hands, and a few voters, of course, were found resting peacefully in the graveyard, their tombstones becoming front-page pictures in the paper. Jacobs, while trying to help his daughter, had run athwart the White House and a lot of other powerful figures.

In the roaring scandal that erupted, the state Democratic Party refused to certify Loser as the nominee. Both he and Fulton qualified to run as independents in November. Fulton won in a landslide and never lost another Nashville election for 38 years. Little Evil went to jail.

By the time Beverly Briley completed his three terms as mayor in 1975, there was no talk in Nashville of turning the Metro clock back. If there were occasional controversies and shortcomings in its execution, they appeared infinitely less serious than all that would have plagued the continuation of a dual system of government. With Briley retiring, Dick Fulton made a critical decision. He gave up what had become a safe congressional seat and rising seniority in Washington to return to Nashville and run for mayor. It was a pattern other politicians would follow over the next twenty years; the challenges and pleasures of local office, particularly in the courthouse, were more appealing than a life term in the nation's capital.

As a member of Congress, Fulton had stood by the promises of his 1962 campaign, becoming a reliable vote for civil rights, the programs of Lyndon Johnson's Great Society, and the causes of organized labor. But he had also expanded his base. Nashville's business community had grown to respect Fulton, and to appreciate his support for such issues as increased tourism and industrial growth. Nashville's African-American community, union voters, and the blue-collar workers of East Nashville and beyond had only grown more loyal in their support of him.

Metro government came in a box, unassembled, and Briley's lasting gift to the city was that he knew how to put the nuts and bolts where they belonged. Fulton saw the bigger picture—he built a new convention center downtown and spruced up Church Street in an effort (ultimately futile) to stem the exodus of retail business to the shopping malls—but he also had an eye for detail. An early riser, he would often cruise

As the city councilman from South Nashville, Gene "Little Evil" Jacobs (center) kept a tight rein on power until he was caught up in a vote-tampering scandal in the 1962 election.

the streets of Nashville at dawn, making notes about what needed to be done, then passing along instructions to the bureaucracy when he arrived at the courthouse.

When Fulton left Congress, Clifford Allen took his place, but the wise old man was on his last crusade. The will was there, but the body was almost gone; even his good eye was failing. He cut a strange and out-of-place image in the bustling hallways of Washington, like a man arrived too late for the party—and all too soon, Allen died.

The new congressman was Bill Boner, the son of a policeman (from East

lobby and surrounding environs. Gore arrives in Nashville this afternoon flanked by former Secretary of State Warren Christopher, the man heading up his veep hunt. Although Gore is not set to formally announce his choice until Aug. 8, two days from now, in a ceremony at high noon on Legislative Plaza, reporters scramble to beat the deadline—and each other—with the scoop. . . . **Speaking of scoops,** the coolest place to be is on the lawn at First Presbyterian Church on Franklin Road, standing next to a drum of homemade ice cream. Today is the 16th-annual edition of Miss Martha's Old-Fashioned Ice Cream Crankin', which dishes out frozen delights to more than 1,600 kids, parents and onlookers. At day's end, more than $25,000 is counted for the Martha O'Bryan Center, a Christian outreach ministry at the James A. Cayce public housing project in East Nashville. Along with ice cream, the center dispenses some cold facts: 83 percent of the people living in the Cayce units are African American; women ages 21 to 35 outnumber men there 11 to 1; the average family consists of a single mother and two children; the average annual net income among residents there, in the shadow of the city's multimillion-dollar NFL stadium, is only $4,757. . . . **A park ranger** spots the Volvo belonging to missing Vanderbilt researcher and psychiatric nurse-practitioner Melissa Shane in a gravel parking lot at Percy Warner Park. When the car is still parked a day later, the ranger calls in a report. There is no sign of Shane or foul play, but police treat the site as a crime scene.

7—"Gore's lips still sealed," reads a front-page headline in the morning daily. The story cites insiders' speculation that the search has narrowed to two likely nominees: Massachusetts Sen. John Kerry and North Carolina Sen. John Edwards. At the same time *The Tennessean* is landing on doorsteps, electronic media across the country are reporting that

Gore has already chosen Sen. Joseph Lieberman of Connecticut to run with him. If elected, Lieberman would become the first Jewish vice president in American history. With the official announcement still a day away, candidate Gore drops in at the Elliston Place Soda Shop with *NBC Nightly News* anchor Tom Brokaw, after a bomb-sniffing dog declares the diner clear.

8—**The Hippodrome Olds** thermometer on Broadway reads 95 degrees at 11 a.m. as a perspiring press corps sullenly convenes on the marble baking surface of Legislative Plaza to hear what they already know: that Joe Lieberman is Al Gore's running mate. As they wait, their mobile-phone chatter is a delirious multi-ethnic babble: "We'll start out with a beauty shot of the crowd. . .If you can take a little sidebar, 6 inches, on the protesters. . .Ja, ja, ja, und auch in Carthage, ja, OK, vielen Dank, tschüss!" Richard Sisk of the *New York Daily News* fairly shouts into his phone: "So I found out about Lieberman's grandson. His son—yeah, from the first marriage—married this girl from down here, some really outback shit-kicker town, and they named the kid Tennessee!"

9—**In the wake of news reports** about a possible connection between faulty treads and fatal crashes, Nashville-based Bridgestone/Firestone Inc. issues a voluntary recall of some 6.5 million tires used on more than a dozen trucks, as well as sport utility vehicles like the popular Ford Explorer. Federal investigators have received 270 complaints that the tread on the Firestone tires can peel off its casings at high speeds—a condition that may have been a factor in wrecks that caused 46 deaths and 80 injuries. The recall will cost the company hundreds of millions of dollars, but the public-relations disaster will cause incalculable damage over the coming months, especially when combined with the company's ongoing labor disputes. . . . **After a two-day effort**, searchers find a woman's

Bill Boner served in both houses of the Tennessee General Assembly, as Nashville's congressman, as Metro's mayor and again as a local delegate in the state House of Representatives—in that order—during the last three decades of the century.

Nashville, of course) and a wunderkind with the smooth manner of a door-to-door salesman. He had been elected to the state House and then to the state Senate before he won the congressional seat. He was, in name, a Democrat, and a handsome bundle of energy, the most charismatic politician Nashville had seen in many years. He had no overriding ideology except helping people, usually by cutting through the bureaucratic maze at various levels of government. On campaigns he went bouncing through neighborhoods, knocking on doors, taking notes, following up on conversations. He returned all phone calls. He seldom forgot names, or the family history connected to them. It was hard to attend a public gathering in Nashville where the garrulous man hadn't already worked the crowd.

Boner left no legislative record in Washington. Indeed, the congressional ethics watchdogs were on his trail because he accepted favors, often lavish ones, from people with business before Congress. One hopeful defense contractor gave Boner's wife a lucrative, if vague, job. Boner seemed oblivious to his ethical blind spot. He saw nothing wrong with people helping one another; after all, that was what he did for his constituents all the time. With Fulton's third term expiring in 1987, Boner made the decision to abandon Congress and run for mayor. His principal opponent was a little-known Nashville newcomer named Phil Bredesen. Boner won handily. His troubles in Washington seemed to make little impression on the local electorate.

Phil Bredesen was a New York native and a Harvard graduate who had helped pay his way through that lofty institution by delivering newspapers to dormitory rooms. (One of his customers was Al Gore.) Bredesen and his wife, Andrea Conte (who, shockingly, retained her own name), came to Nashville in 1975 in a battered Volkswagen bus.

Andrea had a job in Nashville's growing health-care industry; Phil was looking for work.

He soon started his own business, a health-care management company. Then he started another. In a very short time, he had become a millionaire. No one knew just how many millions he had; it could vary from day to day, because Bredesen traded stocks in the offhand manner that some Nashvillians played the numbers or the lottery.

In person he was not very impressive, a man of average height and appearance. He could seem aloof, even haughty. Small talk was not among his assets, and he was constitutionally unable to slap a single back. The political crowd at the Gerst House pondered over his motives and methods with some suspicion. He was not known, and he had never asked anyone if he should run for office. How, they wondered, could such a person, a first-generation Nashvillian with a Yankee background, expect to become mayor of the city? There had never been a mayor, at least not in the 20th century, without a long family history in Nashville. But Bredesen had another asset—money—his own newly minted variety. It poured like a mountain spring from his campaign headquarters on West End.

Still, Boner won, in spite of nagging concerns about his ethical compass. Bredesen did attract some interest from reform-minded politicians, though, and the new, prosperous class of entrepreneurs in town liked him a lot; he was one of them. He was also seemingly undeterred by failure. As soon as the dust settled from the mayor's election, Bredesen jumped into the race for Nashville's empty congressional seat against some of the city's oldest political names. He lost that one, too, to Bob Clement, son of a former governor. The second self-financed campaign hardly made a dent in his fortune, and he went back to doing what he did best—making more money.

Boner, who had never run anything larger than a political campaign, probably could have become an acceptable mayor, whatever his lapses. His constituents, after all, didn't seem to mind his personal financial dealings as long as he kept his hand out of the public purse. But Boner had, as they said around the Gerst House bar, a zipper problem. He loved women, and a lot of women loved him, at least for a time. He got involved with the female police officer assigned as his bodyguard, appearing with her more frequently than with his third wife. The possibilities for humor were irresistible, and all of Nashville laughed—for a time. Then the mayor fell in with an aspiring country music singer who went by the stage name Traci Peel. She was not of the upper social tiers in Nashville. The Jerry Jeff Walker tune, "I Like My Women on the Trashy Side," enjoyed a quick revival among Nashville's cheeky disc jockeys.

The singer soon confided to a *Banner* reporter, with the tape recorder running, that the mayor was fantastic in bed, good for up to seven hours of continuous passion. The laughter got a little more hollow. Then Boner announced his engagement to the singer, who would be wife number four, even though he was still married to wife number three, and the lovers agreed to make a live appearance on the nationally televised *Phil Donahue Show*, an afternoon talkfest aimed at housewives and usually featuring a guest lineup that ran the gamut of American characters. When their moment came, Hizzoner's thrush sang "Rocky Top," and the mayor of Nashville, he of the seven-hour bedroom romps, played along cheerfully on his harmonica. Nashvillians cringed and squirmed. It was the sort of psychological blow that staggered an image-conscious community. Boner had made his city a national laughingstock. It was not a damned bit funny here on the Cumberland—and the economy wasn't all that terrific, either.

In spite of his notoriety, Boner succeeded in raising a third of a million dollars for his re-election campaign in 1991, much of it from those with business connections to the city government. Still, he was a politician, and the polls soon returned a verdict of 70 percent disapproval for the one-time golden boy—not just mild dissatisfaction, but strong disapproval. It was enough to make him bow out of the race—and, in a final moment of ethical blindness, Boner pocketed most of the campaign money. The practice was technically legal under the state's casual campaign finance law, but it didn't sit well with the voters. Nashville was shaken and dispirited, believing itself branded on the national stage as "Hicksville on the Cumberland," its assets overshadowed by a harmonica and a short skirt.

Suddenly, the twice-beaten Bredesen looked pretty good to a lot of people. He didn't care about building a patronage machine at the courthouse. He was so rich that he had no need to cut corners on ethical parameters. The city could use his business

body 25 yards off a main road in Percy Warner Park. The body is identified as Melissa Shane, the 24-year-old psychiatric nurse-practitioner who has been missing for five days. An autopsy rules out homicide and suggests she died from heat stroke or a medical condition exacerbated by the heat, probably while jogging. . . . **Carmike Cinemas,** the nation's third-largest network of theaters, is reeling. Yesterday, the Georgia-based movie-house chain filed for so-called Chapter 11 protection from creditors after failing to make a $9-million interest payment to bondholders. Carmike dominated Nashville moviegoing all through the 1980s and '90s, even as the condition of its theaters declined. But when Knoxville-based Regal Cinemas opened its state-of-the-art 27-screen Hollywood megaplex at 100 Oaks in 1998, Carmike was forced to overhaul its decrepit mall cinemas hurriedly in order to compete. . . . **Metro's men in blue** get another black eye, this time over a 1998 incident documented on routine tapes of police radio transmissions. WTVF-Channel 5 investigative reporter Phil Williams says Police Maj. Carl Dollarhide, head of Metro's Patrol Division, used his influence to keep his then-brother-in-law, Brad Lewis, from getting arrested at a police roadblock. According to the Channel 5 report, Lewis, when stopped, had no driver's license but was carrying a sawed-off shotgun and paper bags full of cash. The report says Dollarhide told a police dispatcher, "Hell, I don't want the kid to get arrested," then drove to the roadblock on Ashland City Highway. No charges were filed against Lewis, the son of real-estate investor and convicted gambler Jimmy Lewis, whose ties to the police department are well documented. Dollarhide is placed on administrative leave with pay while the department investigates.

10—**War is brewing** in Cherokee Park off West End Avenue, where neighbors are bitterly divided over the issue of historic zoning. One group wants the neighborhood declared a historic area, to protect the community from commercial development. Another group opposes historic zoning on grounds that it would place too many restrictions on what residents can do with their property. Metro Council member John Summers, whose district includes the neighborhood, calls some of his no-zoning constituents "anti-government extremists." The Council will vote on the issue Aug. 15. . . . **Discriminatory hiring practices** will cost American Airlines nearly $1.7 million in the largest settlement ever obtained by the U.S. Department of Labor. The airline settled a suit filed by 96 Nashvillians and three Detroit residents, who accused American of denying them work for medical conditions that affected blood pressure, asthma, hearing and vision.

11—Tom C. Armstrong, 67, who signed himself "your humble poet," dies of a heart attack at his Antioch home. A master of the whimsical phrase, the adopted Nashvillian was a very public poet whose generosity to others won him many friends. Armstrong wrote and read aloud countless nuggets of rhyme and reason that tickled schoolchildren and adults alike. A sample from his latest collection, *Getting a Word in Edgewise*, is a one-liner titled "Nashville's Nightmare"; it reads simply, "Muzak City, U.S.A." His poem "Theist" could well serve as a creed: "I believe in God—but I don't make a religion out of it."

12—The Tennessee State Fair, an agricultural anachronism in an urban society, is struggling for relevance and a following. It may need to clone farmers like Herschel Ligon, whose 400-acre livestock farm in Old Hickory sports the second-oldest Poland China swine herd in America, producing prize-winning stock since Ligon came home a decorated soldier after World War II. The Cloyd side of his family has farmed the same land near Andrew Jackson's Hermitage since the first chapter of

skills. His wife was respectable and intelligent, now the proprietor of her own business. His birthplace was not important to the newcomers flocking to Nashville. In a flash, he was the man to beat, and no one could. Bredesen was elected Metro's fourth mayor, defeating a well-regarded Old Nashville figure, former councilwoman Betty Nixon.

The city, and the Metro Council, didn't know quite what to expect from Bredesen. What they got was little short of amazing. He showed no interest in who made sergeant on the police force and didn't care very much about the potholes in the streets. He could disappear from the courthouse for days on end, flying himself in his private jet to his Rocky Mountain retreat. He didn't apologize for putting his son in a private school. He still slapped no backs, although he sometimes made a token appearance at the Gerst House.

An unprecedented building boom marked Phil Bredesen's two terms as mayor of Metro Nashville in the 1990s. In contrast to his predecessors, Bredesen approached the job more like a businessman or a professor than a politician.

Working on a larger canvas than the political artists who preceded him, Bredesen soon tackled a problem that had persisted in Nashville for years. The city-owned hospital,

A huge crowd poured into the modernistic Nashville Arena on the day of its grand opening in December 1995. The facility later became the Gaylord Entertainment Center when the company that owned the Grand Ole Opry purchased naming rights to the arena.

The arena's jazzy, contemporary exterior joined an eclectic melange of architectural styles up and down the length of Broadway. Inside, it could be quickly converted from a concert hall to a hockey rink to a home for the Nashville Kats of the Arena Football League.

the Nashville story was played out more than 200 years ago. Today, some of Ligon's admirers are gathered at the Nashville Fairgrounds to honor their 82-year-old compatriot with the first Distinguished Service Award of the Tennessee State Fair. Pulling off his Ligon's Polands cap and brushing back sandy-gray locks with a steady hand, the honoree notes with becoming immodesty that he's been exhibiting livestock and winning prizes at the fair for 70 years. . . . **Buddy and Charlie Babb** outsmoke the competition at the Wilson County Fair's Second Annual World Barbecue Championship in Lebanon. The Babbs, a father-and-son team from Nashville, take home $11,000 in prizes, winning over such competitors as a posse of Texas 'cue-slingers, last year's winners from Switzerland and an all-female singing group from Germany. . . . **The Nashville Kats** upset the top-seeded San Jose SaberCats 51-42 in the arena-football playoff semifinals. Next: a showdown against the Orlando Predators for the league title on Aug. 20. . . . **Will Garth Brooks** convert his Goodlettsville home into Graceland on the Cumberland? *The Tennessean* reports that the country superstar has plans to turn his 20-acre Blue Rose Estate on Genelle Drive into a museum and tourist attraction. Representatives will address the matter with Brooks' neighbors on Aug. 16. . . . **Since last Saturday's** report of four salmonella food poisoning cases at the San Antonio Taco Co. on 21st Avenue, more than 300 people who ate at the Tex-Mex taco mill between Aug. 5 and 8 have called the Metro Health Department. Now 11 cases of salmonella have been confirmed. Today, the popular student hangout closes to the public, dumps hundreds of dollars worth of food, undergoes a massive scrub-down and inspection and reopens without incident.

13—**Tragedy strikes** on the first day of football practice for the Tennessee Tech Golden Eagles in Cookeville. Preston Birdsong, a 1999 Maplewood High School

On a tract of industrial acreage (foreground) across the river and directly east of downtown, Mayor Bredesen and the Metro Council chose a site for a football stadium in 1995.

graduate with no previous history of medical problems, collapses in the summer heat without warning on the field. He is pronounced dead in the emergency room at Cookeville Regional Medical Center. The cause: heatstroke. . . . **The long-ago days** of sweat-soaked Music City soul at the legendary Del Morocco and other Nashville rhythm-and-blues clubs are gone, destroyed by federally mandated urban renewal efforts and the Interstate 40 project that cut through the city in the mid-1960s. But R&B history lives on here in powerhouse vocalists Earl Gaines and Roscoe Shelton, who sing tonight at everybody's favorite roadhouse, the Belle Meade Plantation.

14—Tennessee is in the spotlight as the Democratic National Convention gets underway tonight in Los Angeles. On hand

Metro General, staffed by Vanderbilt interns and residents, was hemorrhaging financially. Meharry Medical College and its adjacent Hubbard Hospital had trained the nation's leading African-American physicians for a century, but the spread of integration in more prestigious medical schools was luring students and even some faculty away from Meharry-Hubbard. Bredesen engineered a merger of the two hospitals, complete with a new facility in North Nashville to house them.

The mayor also took a hard look at a long-neglected area of the city: the blocks south of Broadway, spreading half a mile from the Cumberland to Eighth Avenue. Once derisively called Black Bottom, the area had become a sprawl of warehouses, adult entertainment venues, and dilapidated buildings. He started leveling them, using federal urban development funds.

At the corner of Fifth and Broadway, Bredesen envisioned a new city arena to replace an aging and outdated downtown auditorium from the 1950s. It was to be a center for concerts, conventions, and even professional sports teams, although none was in sight. The arena was financed through an arrangement so complex that its actual cost would prove to be roughly twice its estimated cost. By the time the numbers were added up, no one seemed to care; the arena had set off an explosion of entertainment and tourist-oriented retail activity along Lower Broad and, most significantly, on Second Avenue between Broadway and Union. It was not Bourbon Street, but a country-flavored hybrid of it. Many Nashvillians didn't much approve, but tourists loved it. In the evening hours, downtown Nashville throbbed with energy.

Soon the arena had an anchor tenant. The National Hockey League had granted an expansion franchise for a major-league team, the Predators, in a sport little-known to

Four years later, the rechristened Tennessee Titans were drawing 67,000 fans to Adelphia Coliseum on the same site for their home games.

Nashvillians. Suprisingly, this puck craze was an instant success. Transplanted Northerners and old Nashvillians alike flocked to the raucous atmosphere, rubbing shoulders with the country music stars who adopted the team. New restaurants, a hotel, and a spacious new home for the Country Music Hall of Fame and Museum began to sprout in the vacant lots behind the arena.

Only three years into his term, Bredesen aimed higher. Al Gore, the state's brightest political star, had ascended to the vice presidency two years previously, in 1992, and Democrat Ned McWherter, the most popular governor in decades, had finished the two terms allowed him by the state constitution. The governor's office and both Tennessee Senate seats were up for grabs. The Democratic field for governor was crowded with second-tier politicians, who splintered support and made fund-raising difficult. Bredesen jumped into it, and his personal millions made him the instant favorite. He won the nomination in August. The Republican nominee was Don Sundquist, a mild-mannered moderate who had spent a dozen years in Congress. His district was anchored in Memphis but sprawled all the way to the Nashville suburbs. It was a race that featured few sharp differences. Sundquist ran on a platform promising tough action against crime and a low-tax approach to state government. In particular, he was against a state income tax. Bredesen left the door open for consideration of an income tax, if the voters assented.

It was a disastrous year for the Democrats, both nationally and in Tennessee. The state's voters elected two Republican senators: Fred Thompson, a charismatic Nashville trial lawyer and lobbyist, who had built a somewhat surprising career as a Hollywood character actor; and Bill Frist, a heart transplant surgeon and member of a prominent

to witness Al Gore's nomination for president are former Gov. Ned McWherter, Nashville Mayor Bill Purcell, U.S. Reps. Bart Gordon and Bob Clement and an unlikely guest: Irby Simpkins, former publisher of the *Nashville Banner*, the city's now-defunct, legendarily conservative afternoon daily. (He is a friend of the Gore family.)
. . . **Many Nashvillians** are gripped by a single fear as the convention opens: Will it preempt ABC's *Monday Night Football*? For one hour, but not entirely—not in Nashville, anyway. With the evening sky streaked with planes trailing banners, the Tennessee Titans are set to play a no-holds-barred grudge match (albeit just a preseason exhibition) against their Super Bowl foes, the St. Louis Rams. This is *Monday Night Football*'s first live broadcast from Nashville, and for many, it's a stamp of legitimacy that can only be conferred by

network television and beer commercials. When it's over a few
hours later, the Titans have
crushed the mighty Rams, 30-3.
. . . **At 6:19 p.m. Pacific time**, as
news of the Titans' victory reaches the West Coast, a cheer goes
up from the Tennessee delegation
at the Democratic Convention.

15—After devoting her life—
and the better part of the 20th
century—to philanthropic causes,
civic leader Mary Jane Werthan
passes away quietly at her home
at the age of 92. A Nashville
native and Hume-Fogg High
School alumna, she graduated Phi
Beta Kappa from Vanderbilt and
later became the first woman
elected to the university's board
of trust. She embarked on a lifetime of civic, cultural and religious philanthropy after marrying
Albert Werthan, chairman of
Werthan Industries, in 1932.
Among countless other distinctions, she served pro bono as a
staffer, officer, board member or
volunteer of Planned Parenthood,
Family & Children's Service, the
National Council of Jewish
Women, the Public Television
Council, the Nashville Symphony
Guild and the Friends of Cheekwood. . . . **Facing $35 million** in
civil lawsuits from two boys
molested by former priest Edward
J. McKeown, the Roman Catholic
Diocese of Nashville says it is willing to share the blame. But if the
diocese is held accountable, *The
Tennessean* reports, its lawyers
want McKeown's previous victims
to share the liability because they
did not report his crimes. In addition to the two boys he confessed
to molesting, McKeown said he
molested another 21 schoolboys
before 1995. Applying the legal
concept of "comparative fault" to
a situation like this is unprecedented, and it outrages many
local Catholics. . . . **The Metro
Council** votes to grant historic
zoning to embattled Cherokee
Park, drawing applause and
groans from its warring neighborhood groups. The decision does
nothing to ease hard feelings. A
new point of dispute is a survey
that says 66 percent of Cherokee
Park residents favor the zoning.

Nashville family who hadn't even bothered to vote until he was almost 40. Sundquist
won the governor's race over Bredesen, although the mayor did better than the Democrats' two Senate candidates, incumbent Jim Sasser and Congressman Jim Cooper.

Bredesen's fling with statewide politics hadn't hurt him in Nashville; he carried
the city handily in winning a second term as mayor in 1995. Almost as an afterthought,
he promised to devote more attention to the grubby details of running the city: potholes, leaky roofs, troubled schools, crumbling infrastructure. However, by election day,
the mayor had a challenge big enough to take his mind off potholes.

A man named Bud Adams, a quirky, self-made oil millionaire, had slipped into
town. For years, Adams had hectored the city fathers of Houston to build a new playground for his professional football team, the Oilers. In that city, he had become a
ridiculed and despised figure for what was seen as greedy grasping—on top of a
mediocre football team. He was looking for a booming city to build him the sort of
modern stadium that would maximize the profits of a football franchise.

Bredesen never blinked. In a matter of weeks, he had put together an enormously complicated financial scheme to build a stadium costing almost $300 million—
in a city whose annual budget had not yet reached $1 billion. Along the way, he cajoled
his opponent from the year before, Don Sundquist, as well as the state legislature and
a stunned Metro Council, into going along with the plans. Visions of major-league
sugar plums danced in their heads, and dollar signs swam before their eyes. Business
leaders and blue-collar fans alike plumped down $67 million (straight into Adams'
pocket) for "seat licenses"—the mere privilege to buy tickets into the stadium. Enough
disgruntled taxpayers signed petitions opposing the venture to force a referendum on
the issue, but with Adams' money and Bredesen's seductive salesmanship, voters
approved the deal by a 3-to-2 margin.

The site Bredesen chose for the stadium was the east bank of the Cumberland,
across from downtown. Like Black Bottom, it had grown up in warehouses, rusty manufacturing sites, and salvage yards. The stadium gave Bredesen an excuse to bulldoze yet
another quadrant of the downtown area, completing an urban renewal vision that had
begun in the 1950s with the clearing of the Capitol Hill area of brothels and slums.

The mayor kept wheeling and dealing on other fronts. In a city whose bonding
authority was stretched thin, he somehow found money for a $330-million upgrade of
deteriorating schools and a $75-million library, anchored on Church Street in the heart
of the city. He volunteered generous tax breaks to lure a half-dozen major corporate
headquarters to Nashville, and near the end of his second term, he threw money at Dell
Computer Corporation, one of the storied companies of the new electronic age, to get
its manufacturing presence inside the city limits.

By 1999, Bredesen had run out of time to cut more deals. There were questions
about whether a new term-limits provision in the Metro charter allowed him to seek a
third term. Bredesen instead announced that he would turn over the keys to a city that
had changed vastly in eight years.

Nashville was breathless from the speed and magnitude of the change. From the
depths of the Boner debacle, the city had soared among the stars on the national urban
horizon. There was a lot to assimilate. Someone described it as a city "with an aura of
uneasy well-being." People fretted that there had been too much growth, too fast. If
there was no sentiment for turning back the clock, there was at least a leaning toward
slowing it down. Nashville was not looking backward, but it did look inward. The city
had grown larger, but in a sense it had also grown smaller; more than 300 neighborhood groups were active, worried about things like garbage collection and sidewalks,
smaller pieces of the whole.

On paper, the 1999 mayor's race looked like déjà vu. Dick Fulton, although edg-
ing into his 70s, had decided to make a return to public life. He looked distinguished and
still seemed vigorous, and probably knew more Nashvillians than any other individual. He
had spent the thirteen years since leaving office in private business, helping to found a
bank and other enterprises. The business world knew him and felt comfortable with him.

Former state legislator Bill Purcell was the center of attention in August 1999 when he defeated former Mayor Dick Fulton and Vice Mayor Jay West in the race to choose Mayor Phil Bredesen's successor.

Fulton had no trouble raising money, and there was little doubt he would be the front-runner. He was the heir to one of the two factions that had spawned Metro, that of Beverly Briley. One of his opponents was the heir to the other side: Jay West, the son of Ben West. As a longtime councilman and a capable vice mayor, West was solid, comfortable, and clean, if a bit colorless. Between them, the names Fulton and West had held center stage in Nashville politics for half a century. But the wear and tear showed in subtle ways. Fulton looked old, and West was unimaginative and drab.

The third major candidate was a lawyer named Bill Purcell, who was 47 that year. Purcell shared some superficial things in common with Bredesen, although the two seemed to have an instinctive dislike of one another. Like Bredesen, Purcell was a Northerner, a native of Philadelphia. His wife, too, was a professional who had kept her own name. Purcell had come to Nashville to attend Vanderbilt's law school and stayed.

He had won Boner's old seat in the state legislature in 1986, the same year Ned McWherter was elected governor. After only four years, Purcell was the Democratic majority leader in the state House. In that position, he was McWherter's chief legislative

16—**Garth Brooks** appears to have lost some neighborhood friends. At a town-hall meeting tonight at the Trinity Free Will Baptist Church, closed to the media, more than 100 people belt out a chorus of disapproval over the country singer's plans to convert his Goodlettsville home into a museum and tourist attraction. "We gave this man his privacy," says neighbor Jim

Fulbright. "Now that he's leaving, he doesn't care about ours." By the end of the meeting, it is clear that the zoning change needed to create Garthland will never happen. Neither Brooks nor his wife, Sandy, attends, which is just as well. . . . **In a show of corporate loyalty** all but unseen these days, the community of Old Hickory will not rename DuPont-Hadley Middle School for the late Metro school board member Charles Gann, as current board member George Thompson has proposed. No disrespect to Gann, who died Aug. 1 of diabetes after representing the community's school district for 18 years, but the community in eastern Davidson County treasures its association with the DuPont chemical company. In 1918, E.I. DuPont de Nemours Inc. located a plant in Old Hickory to manufacture gunpowder for World War I; the company built blocks of houses and eventually sold them to workers. "Without DuPont," observes community historian Marie Tootle, "there would be no Old Hickory." Thompson respectfully withdraws his proposal.

17—**On the first day of school,** parents crowd into Julia Green Elementary in Green Hills for the opening of a spiffy new wing paid for, in part, by donations from well-heeled parents and supporters. At less privileged public schools, many kids are returning to portable units like the ones Julia Green got rid of. The policy implications of such privately funded inequity within the public school system have been raised, debated and tabled for further consideration later. . . . **To make the opening** of school less a trauma than a celebration, Mayor Bill Purcell throws a "First Day Festival" party for Metro parents and schoolchildren at the Gaylord Entertainment Center. Free bags of goodies are handed to kids, who also delight in a variety of interactive games, exhibits, booths, displays and entertainment. The festival is a bigger success than anyone expects, drawing an estimated 10,000 people. Even more successful is parents'

lieutenant. They were an odd couple: McWherter a hulking bear of a man full of country sayings and folksy mannerisms, Purcell a whip-thin intellectual with a rapid-fire mouth who didn't seem like one of the boys in McWherter's rural milieu.

Purcell tried to fit in; he displayed a tiny tattoo hidden by his watch, and sometimes stuffed a pinch of snuff in his cheek. He also steered McWherter's education and health-care reforms through the legislative meat-grinder. The two shared a disdain for Republicans. One year, three of the brighter Republican lawmakers challenged the governor's budget proposals; Purcell shredded their arguments in a packed committee room in a public, verbal flogging that became painful to watch. When the legislature drew new districts for the decennial reapportionment, Purcell stuffed twelve Republican incumbents into six districts.

Purcell studied McWherter's political skills, his ability to fit into any crowd, his willingness to sit through hours of minutiae to master the details of complex policy issues, his ways of crafting compromise. Then, toward the end of the 1996 legislative session, Purcell sent a shock through the political community by announcing his retirement from the General Assembly. He would instead run a Vanderbilt think tank on issues affecting children. He did take time that year to manage the Tennessee re-election campaign of President Bill Clinton and Vice President Al Gore. They carried the state, but it was not an easy task.

With Don Sundquist up for re-election in 1998 after a largely inert four years as governor, many Tennessee Democrats begged Purcell to run. He declined. His gut instinct, he said later, was that the cutting issues of American society had moved from statehouses to city halls. In the end, Sundquist faced only a caricature of an opponent in the faded image of John J. Hooker, a Nashville lawyer and perennial candidate. On his way to an easy victory with 70 percent of the vote, Sundquist made sure the voters remembered that he was opposed to a state income tax.

The race for mayor in 1999 seemed like the wrong time and place for Purcell. Fulton had the money and experience; West had a famous name and an office just underneath the mayor's. There wasn't a constituency for Purcell to build on—but he sensed the edgy mood of Nashville, along with its pride and contentment in a vibrant economy.

"It was a city that had realized for the first time that we could do anything we wanted to do," Purcell mused a year later at a table in the new Gerst House. "It was a situation that made us a little uneasy. There was a sense of uncertainty about our priorities, and we simply hadn't talked about that very much." He adopted in his campaign the oldest tactic in the political repertoire: For almost two years, he met with any group that wanted to hear him, sitting in kitchens, law-firm libraries, fire halls, school cafeterias. His stripes as a fiercely partisan Democrat sometimes showed, but he still attracted growing support from Republicans.

Intangibles often turn elections. Without notice, Purcell was eroding Fulton's lifetime base in East Nashville and in the African-American community. Fulton, in his growing prosperity, had sold his home in East Nashville to singer Garth Brooks and moved to a gated community off West End Avenue. Purcell still lived in East Nashville; when the 1998 tornado ravaged the area, he was on the scene with gloves and work boots, helping people clean up their neighborhoods.

Purcell also found a defining symbol, the sort of lucky talisman some politicians acquire, like Estes Kefauver's coonskin hat. A television commercial showed him working at a battered wooden desk under a shade tree on the lawn, with children and a dog coming in and out of the picture. The image embraced Purcell's themes: neighborhoods, children, safe communities, a bit of nostalgia for the past—not football stadiums and grand public works. The picture lingered long after the campaign was over.

There were few stark differences among the three major candidates, but one incident unintentionally exposed something about Nashville's soul in that year. Fulton, eyeing Purcell's upward movement in the polls, put up a negative television commercial, the sort of attack ad that had become all too common in late 20th-century American politics. It showed Purcell with a computer-drawn bandanna around his forehead, mimicking a movie tough-guy named Rambo. The message was that Purcell sounded like an action hero, but was really soft on crime.

Nashville recoiled in a visceral backlash. This city, it seemed to say, can elect a mayor without slinging mud. We are above that. Polls leading up to the election showed the candidates tightly bunched, with no one close to the 50 percent level that would bring victory without a runoff. But in the last few days, too late for the pollsters to pick up the trend, the voters made up their minds, silently but decisively. When the votes were counted, Purcell had about 48 percent, more than double the total of either opponent. His supporters roamed about in their hotel ballroom talking in hushed whispers, too stunned to celebrate. Fulton barely qualified for a runoff, but he was clearly beaten, and before the night was over he had conceded gracefully, sparing the city what might have been a brutal and ugly three weeks of fight-to-the-death campaigning. West also fell in behind Purcell, and Metro had its fifth mayor.

The charter forbade Purcell to fire Phil Bredesen's department heads, but they began to feel so uncomfortable that, one by one, they chose retirement. Rather than promoting from inside, Purcell sought new blood. David Manning, McWherter's state finance commissioner, became Metro's new money watchdog, imposing tough fiscal discipline. By the time his first budget came due in June, Purcell had taken $12 million from other departments and given it to education. The city's budget increased by just 1.5 percent, and there was no tax increase.

Within months, a $170-million supplemental budget, gleaned from savings, not only covered payments on Bredesen's big projects but also bolstered infrastructure—repairing schools, sidewalks, and, yes, potholes. The council gave unanimous consent. The city was stable; the biggest controversy on the mayor's desk was moonlighting by police officers.

Three blocks west of the courthouse, at the Tennessee State Capitol, a starkly different scene was unfolding. The state government was in deep chaos, struggling for direction in a venomous atmosphere of distrust.

Most Tennesseans paid only passing notice to the give-and-take between the legislature and the governor on Capitol Hill. State government had been a fixture in Nashville for over 150 years and was one of the city's major employers, but in a more diversified economy where people had better things to do than watch politicians at work, it seemed like a lesser player than its size suggested.

Until the 1960s, the legislature was little more than an extension of the governor's office, meeting every other year to rubber-stamp budgets and whatever else the governor might want. But change was in the wind, first on the wings of a 1962 U.S. Supreme Court ruling in *Baker* v. *Carr*, a Tennessee case that made reapportionment on the principle of equal representation the new law of the land. Then, the legislature engineered a change in the Tennessee Constitution to allow it to meet every year, and built itself an underground sanctuary—Legislative Plaza, a sunless cavern that some said resembled a bunker. For the first time, legislators had offices and a smattering of staff. The two houses began to meet longer each year, sometimes from January into June. Slowly, they freed themselves from the governor's grip.

Their outlook changed, too. Once an arena to solve political questions, the legislature had become more and more an arbitrator of business practices. Millions of dollars in private-sector profits hinged on what the legislature would or would not permit. Over a 30-year period, the number of lobbyists grew from a couple-dozen to more than 500. Men and women skilled in the arcane intricacies of lawmaking now could work full-time at the business of lobbying. Most of the major corporate interests in the state, and many nationwide, now retained their own representatives to monitor the work of the legislature. Public-interest groups involved in such issues as health care, education, and the environment vied with corporate spokesmen for the lawmakers' favor. Lobbying was a growth industry in Nashville, producing, by one calculation, more than $25 million a year in salaries.

It was sometimes an incestuous business. Under public pressure, the legislature banned gifts from lobbyists, such as free meals, hotel rooms, and bar bills. But the biggest gifts were campaign contributions, and those were untouched. It was difficult to trace under the state's campaign finance laws, but lobbying interests were providing

response to Purcell's suggestion that they go with their kids to school on the first day to meet their teachers and tour the facilities. Thousands of parents accept the invitation. . . . **The last official day** of school for retired Metro teacher Gladys Williams Waters was back in 1983, after 31 years of teaching. Waters was one of hundreds who graduated from Hampton High, an all-black Dickson County school that opened in 1936 and closed in the desegregation era in 1965. When Hampton alumni hold their 22nd-annual reunion at Montgomery Bell State Park today, Waters will be there. A member of the Class of '37, she grew up in her parents' three-room shack in the community of Hortense. One of 12 children, she went to work at 14 in a Dickson hotel, cleaning rooms and baking in the kitchen—but managing somehow to stay in school. Those hard times made her an understanding teacher who kept a bowl of fresh fruit and a bench for napping in her classroom because there were only two kinds of children she couldn't teach: a hungry child and a sleepy child. Waters tells a feature writer: "There's no greater earthly reward than an education."

18—Reel changes at the Nashville Independent Film Festival: Michael Catalano, the executive director credited with helping to re-energize the 31-year-old film fest, announces that he is stepping down after three and a half years. Under Catalano's leadership, the festival's attendance has grown from 1,500 to 10,000. The festival has also given a huge boost to local filmmakers such as Coke Sams and Bruce Arnston, whose satirical sci-fi musical *Existo* broke attendance records last year, and John Lloyd Miller, whose black-and-white short *I Still Miss Someone* toured the festival circuit. . . . **The curtain falls** on one of the city's most acclaimed arts organizations. Following the resignations of artistic directors Donna Rizzo and Andrew Krichels, the Tennessee Dance Theatre announces it will suspend operations for at least a year. Rizzo and Krichels scored a triumph in June

More than 500 lobbyists are registered to represent various interests before the legislature. Their collective influence is personified by Tom "The Golden Goose" Hensley (right), their best-known spin artist, whose hallway advice often finds its way into the chambers.

with their ambitious production *Ghosts of the Civil War*, but perpetually low audience turnout and financial woes convinced them to end their 15 years with the modern-dance company.

. . . A pregnancy-prevention agency with more than a century of ties to the Nashville area is being disbanded. Crittenton Services, which works to stem the epidemic of teen pregnancies through education and outreach programs, announces that it will farm its services out to other non-profit agencies and place most of its 15 employees with those agencies. The reason: difficulty in raising donations. The agency was an outgrowth of the Florence Crittenton Home for unwed mothers, founded in 1874; when Crittenton's homes closed some 20 years ago, the organization turned its

more than half the money used in legislative campaigns. Most of it went to incumbents; as a result, there were few involuntary turnovers in legislative membership. Most lawmakers, particularly those in leadership positions, had been on Capitol Hill for twenty years or more. Retaining seats had become both a political and personal imperative; underfunded and lesser-known challengers rarely prevailed.

The growing time demands and a low base pay had limited the diversity of the legislature. Increasingly, members were young and without heavy financial responsibilities, or older with significant wealth or professional income that permitted them to spend six months a year in Nashville. Middle-aged, middle-income lawmakers—the mirror of the state's population—were rarely in the mix.

With two brief exceptions, Democrats had controlled the legislature for more than a century. As the 1990s ended, however, party lines were often blurred, and there were deep divisions within each party. There were two varieties of Republicans. One group came largely from the counties of East Tennessee, reliable territory for the GOP since the region split off from the rest of the state and remained loyal to the Union during the Civil War. They tended to be fiscal conservatives but social moderates. When it served their interests, they were willing to deal with the Democratic majority. The other Republican faction had grown up in the formerly Democratic strongholds of Middle and West Tennessee.

The state's Democrats were an odd amalgam of those who cherished the conservative ideals of an earlier time and those who welcomed the inclusion of African Americans and had made their peace with the more liberal tone of the party's national agenda. It was these very notions that caused more and more white Democrats to shift their allegiance to the GOP.

The suburban Republicans tended to be suspicious of, if not hostile to, government at all levels. Many of their children attended private schools, avoiding the stresses of integration in the public systems. They voiced an instinctive aversion to almost all taxes. A significant number identified with the fundamentalism of the Christian right, a potent if little-recognized force in state politics. In all matters except war, they believed passionately in the supremacy of private-sector solutions over government action.

Democrats had their own divisions. One faction remained rooted in traditionally Democratic rural counties, nominally loyal to the party but far removed from its national platforms. It was difficult to tell the philosophical difference between a Democrat from Carroll County, in the west, and a Republican from Greene County, in the east. Still, there was a streak of populism running through rural Democrats—and in some districts, a black minority was all that stood between them and the Republican tide.

Both white and black Democrats from the cities tended to be more liberal than their colleagues, more willing to impose new taxes for social programs. But they retained ties to the business community, both because of proximity and to protect the source of campaign funds from the lobbying interests. At the end of the century, Democrats held an 18-15 margin in the Senate and a 59-40 advantage in the House.

For the past three decades, the most deft practitioners of legislative politics had been rural Democrats from West Tennessee, controlling the speaker's podiums in both the House and Senate, and thus the naming of committees and the control of bills flowing through the enactment process.

The speaker of the Senate for almost 30 years, far longer than any other figure in the state's history, was a Fayette County lawyer-farmer-banker-businessman named John Wilder. The position also carried the title of lieutenant governor, making him the person who would take the state's top office if there were a vacancy. Wilder was an enigma, even to those who had known him for decades. He often talked in mystical tones about the arrangement of a place he called the cosmos. Though he was approaching 80, he still flew his twin-engine airplane, nicknamed Jaybird, between Nashville and a grass strip laid out in the midst of his cotton fields. He had a profound and deep relationship with African Americans in his poor rural district. In the 1960s, many Fayette County planters had kicked blacks off their land when they tried to register to vote; Wilder provided a place for them to erect tents.

He was a Democrat, but his own party had tried to oust him from the speaker's chair fifteen years back. To retain his power, he had formed a coalition of conservative and liberal Democrats and Senate Republicans. In return, he gave Republicans control

attention to reducing teen pregnancies. Its $800,000 endowment and other assets will be folded into the Community Foundation of Middle Tennessee. . . . **6:45 p.m.,** North Nashville: A gunfight erupts at a car wash at the corner of D.B. Todd Boulevard and St. Louis Street. Accounts are sketchy and confusing, but gunmen in a speeding car apparently shot Willie Williams, then ran over him in the getaway attempt when occupants of other cars opened fire. Williams, 21, was killed. Police search for the alleged shooters, 19-year-old Marcus Graham and his 17-year-old brother, Allen, and a motive. . . . **For the fourth straight year,** Nashville leads the state in traffic fatalities, according to Tennessee Department of Safety Commissioner Mike Greene. 1998 figures show that Nashville had 239 road deaths, compared to 212 in Memphis. . . .**11:30 p.m.,** 3905 Clarksville Hwy.: Shanon Holt is sitting in his Chevrolet pickup at a self-service car wash when a round of gunfire goes off. It's either a stray shot or an intentional hit; either way, Holt, 27, dies at the hand of an unseen killer. . . . **State Democrats** are still buzzing about last night's

Speaker of the House Jimmy Naifeh (left) has ruled the lower chamber of the General Assembly for 15 years. His counterpart in the Senate, Lt. Gov. John Wilder (right), has maintained his position of authority for twice that long.

nomination of Vice President Al Gore in Los Angeles—and already, here comes his challenger. Texas Gov. George W. Bush lands on the veep's home turf for a rally in the Memphis suburb of Bartlett. Bush vows he'll carry Gore's home state in November. Unimaginable.

19—**Another car wash,** another shooting victim—the third in less than 24 hours. Jason Lamont Coleman, 20, and Terry Dowlen, 39, don't like each other. When Dowlen sees Coleman at a car wash on 10th Avenue North near Jefferson Street, the two men throw down and begin firing. Coleman, shot in the chest, staggers to nearby Fifteenth Avenue Baptist Church, where a security guard calls for help. Police pick up Dowlen at home and charge him with attempted homicide. Coleman is in critical condition at Vanderbilt University Medical Center.

20—A championship football game decided on the last play, a Nashville team handed a crushing loss—sound familiar? With no time left on the clock, the Orlando Predators get a field goal to end the Nashville Kats' championship hopes, 41-38, in Arena Bowl XIV. . . . **Backed by the Rejoice Choir** and a full band, gospel singer Fred Francis raises the rafters at the Greater Bethel AME Church on South Street. The concert is captured on tape for a live album. Francis frequently plays piano and sings at the 23rd Psalm Coffee House, but Greater Bethel, as he tells *The Tennessean*'s Peter Cooper, "is where I go to church.". . . **Suspects Marcus and Allen Graham** surrender to police in the shooting death of Willie "Pooh" Williams two nights ago at a North Nashville car wash. Their mother says both brothers had alibis; police witnesses claim they saw the Grahams shoot Williams, described as "their best friend," as he sat in his car. Marcus Graham, a former high-school tackle for the McGavock Raiders, had known Pooh Williams since seventh grade.

of some of the Senate's committees; in the House, by long practice, no Republican held a committee office.

Wilder presided over the warring factions of the Senate with a gentle touch. He rarely tried to lead on issues; he was content to wait as consensus emerged from the legislative cauldron. Despite their party differences, he enjoyed a warm friendship with Don Sundquist, the governor who had spent twelve years as Wilder's representative in Congress. In the clubby atmosphere of the Senate, incumbents had an informal agreement not to oppose each other at election time.

The speaker of the House lived only 30 miles from Wilder, in Covington. He was Jimmy Naifeh, the son of a Lebanese immigrant who became a protégé of Ned McWherter, the West Tennessee beer distributor who had served sixteen years as House speaker and eight more as governor. The Naifeh family had done well in the wholesale grocery business; despite his ethnic background, Jimmy Naifeh had become what was known in the rural precincts as a good old boy. His ruling coalition was an odd mix of rural Democrats and Memphis black lawmakers, headed by a fiery orator named Lois DeBerry. Naifeh could be a forceful and progressive legislator; he and Purcell had forged an ethics bill that put limits on the entertainment of representatives by lobbyists. But he didn't like to expose his members to unnecessary risk; controversial issues that might come back to haunt them at election time never came to the floor unless Naifeh knew he had the votes for passage.

In addition to the regulation of business, the legislature's most important chore was the passage of an annual budget. In the time Wilder had been lieutenant governor and speaker of the Senate, Tennessee had gone from its first billion-dollar budget to one that now approached $18 billion. Members of both parties took pride in their record of fiscal conservatism. The state constitution required a balanced budget, and influential legislators had long insisted that the state follow other sound business practices. In the late 1980s, for example, the legislature had doubled the gasoline tax to pay for ambitious highway projects in cash. As a result, the state had virtually no bonded debt for roads.

The budget was complex and deceptive. Unlike most other states, Tennessee tracked every dollar, ranging from fishing licenses to tuition paid by college students. State departments charged each other for rent, computer services, automobiles, and other items in order to maximize federal matching funds. With federal funds included (making up more than one-third of the total), Tennessee's budget appeared much larger than those in states of comparable size. Most of the dollars in the budget were earmarked for program continuations and federal-dollar matches. Out of the $18 billion, according to Sundquist's calculation, there was only about $600 million in discretionary funds, used for such things as state parks and industrial recruitment. Many unseen factors drove the state budget. During the past 25 years, a crackdown on criminals had been an annual legislative rite, a voter-pleasing bit of grandstanding that mostly increased sentence times. The state, which had gotten along with two prisons for almost a century, suddenly had fourteen, and was building a new one every two years to house the swelling population of inmates. And, with incarceration having become a growth industry, it seemed almost inevitable that privatization of imprisonment would follow. It did. Both present and former members of the General Assembly have been closely associated with Nashville-based Corrections Corporation of America, the first and largest of these enterprises.

A half-century ago, as the baby boomers of the post-World War II generation reached school-age, education spending also boomed. Up to 41 percent of the state's income was spent on schools, but the percentage dropped steadily from that point, even though the annual dollar expenditure kept rising. Meantime, the most dramatic growth in spending was in health care, particularly in the federal Medicaid program, a mid-1960s spinoff of Medicare designed to serve those near the poverty line. The federal government paid two-thirds of the cost, and the state paid the rest.

Medicaid compensated health-care providers for each service they rendered. In practice, many of those who were "covered" did not receive regular medical care; when there was trouble, they simply showed up in emergency rooms, the most expensive point in the health-care system. A baby's earache, treated in an emergency room, could cost ten times as much as a routine visit to a physician. The state had no control over these costs.

In some years, the growth of Medicaid expenses soared by 20 percent, and it had

With Tennessee ranking near the bottom in state spending per capita for education, teachers often rally at the Capitol to press the legislature for more funding. Members of the Tennessee Education Association staged this night demonstration in 1999.

begun to soak up state tax dollars produced by economic growth. In his last year in office, 1994, Ned McWherter and his financial experts had seen a way to control costs. They would turn Medicaid into a managed-care program. A dozen private companies would compete to provide coverage for the Medicaid population, creating service networks among hospitals, doctors, pharmacists, and other specialists. The managed-care companies would get a fixed monthly fee for each of their clients. Preventive care, a weak link in Medicaid, would become a financial incentive for the private companies.

For the same dollars, McWherter's experts calculated, the new program could cover 500,000 additional Tennesseans who had no access to health care through their employers, or who had been deemed uninsurable. Almost immediately, the new program covered 1.3 million Tennesseans out of a population of 5 million. Tennessee—small, rural, and economically modest—had come about as close as any state in America to providing universal health care.

The new program was called TennCare. Five years into it, the experts estimated that it had saved Tennessee $2.5 billion compared to the expense of continuing Medicaid. Still, the cost had soared—to $5 billion annually, more than a quarter of the state's total budget. By whatever name, health care for the poor was like a hot wire, and the state could not turn loose of it. Any cuts would lose two federal dollars for every state dollar saved. As medical costs climbed nationally, Tennessee's hospitals teetered on the brink of insolvency; taking away TennCare might send them over the edge, and drive hundreds of thousands of uninsured citizens—voters—back to the emergency rooms.

Despite its fiscal conservatism in the midst of the most robust national economic expansion on record, Tennessee found it had a cancer growing in its financial structure.

21—In a deadly instant, a collapsing trench buries two Hispanic construction workers under a mound of asphalt chunks and earth. Samuel Ramirez and Jorge Munoz, employees of the Bolden Pipe Construction Co., are within a few feet of completing a sewer trench on Ewingdale Drive when the unsupported walls give way. Members of the nine-person construction crew use shovels and picks to free the two men, but the falling rubble has already crushed them. The two men likely would have lived if safety features had been in place. One such protection, a device called a trench box that provides a fortified workspace, is found sitting unused by the roadside.

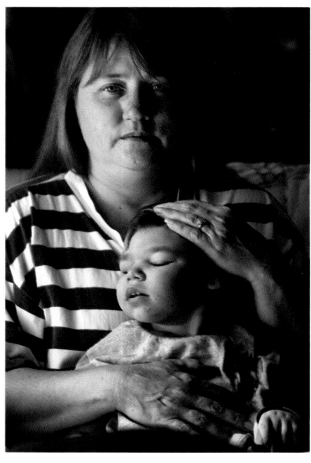

Along with education, health care for hard-to-insure residents presents state government with a powerful challenge. As 2000 began, the TennCare medical program was not only failing to serve many children and others who desperately need care; it was also facing financial collapse due to inadequate state funding.

Almost everyone on Capitol Hill knew it, and knew the prognosis if it went unchecked. In 1947, the state had abandoned the property tax to local governments and replaced it with a sales tax, a percentage of the sale of most—but not all—retail goods. The sales tax served well for a time, but as economists have warned, it is not elastic. That is, it doesn't grow as fast as the economy—only about 80 percent as fast. The demands for services, classrooms, health care, highways, and prison cells are under no such constraints. Ironically, the abandoned property tax went right on serving quite well for cities like Nashville, growing with economic development.

So a pattern developed in state government that, every six to eight years, the sales tax would be increased to continue the status quo and provide some improvements. Five of the six governors before Sundquist had been forced to raise the sales tax. It now stood at 6 percent, with local governments authorized to add another 2.75 percent. Tennessee had one of the highest sales taxes in the nation; it provided 57 percent of state dollars. McWherter had raised the tax by a half-penny in 1992, but he shrewdly earmarked it all for his secondary education improvements. By the turn of the century, Tennessee had gone fifteen years without a general sales tax increase.

Over time, the industrious lobbyists at the Capitol had riddled the tax code with exemptions for their employers. There was a tax on corn for people, but not on corn for livestock; there was a tax on automobiles, but not on tractors; there was a tax on books, but not on industrial machinery. Almost no services were taxed—and services had replaced goods as the dominant sector of the economy. The sales tax was also regressive, hitting low-wage families harder than higher-income professionals. As a percentage of personal income, low-wage earners paid five times more in sales taxes than did the wealthy.

And Tennesseans had become adept at dodging the high sales tax rate. They could cross the state line and avoid the tax on groceries; while there, they could buy a tank of cheaper gasoline and a lottery ticket (prohibited in Tennessee by the state constitution). They could also escape the sales tax by ordering catalog goods over the phone or on the internet. Economists called this tax leakage, and by 1999 it was more than a dribble.

Many citizens detested the sales tax. Liberals in particular viewed it as a tax on the poor, unfair by any definition. The exemptions were illogical and patently unfair. Applying the tax to food was especially galling. But for many others, there was a tax more intensely hated than one on sales: a tax on income, which they equated with the onerous federal income tax—the confiscatory plunder of a bullying bureaucracy, despised for its scaled-up rates and its cavernous loopholes favoring the special interests. Over the years, Tennessee politicians had routinely used the threat of an income tax as a straw tiger to frighten the electorate.

The three governors before Sundquist had realized the shortcomings of the state's revenue system and at least toyed with the idea of an income tax. Almost 30 studies, by the legislature and outside experts, had reached the same conclusion: The best way to fund government services was with an income tax; 42 other states used it. It could grow with the economy and spare the need for regular sales tax increases, always politically difficult. But the legislature would have none of it.

Sundquist's campaign for re-election in 1998, against token opposition, had been lackluster. The Republicans had effectively co-opted the Democratic Party, and their basic philosophy now reigned as completely as that of the Democrats, when the Solid South belonged to them. It was assumed by almost everyone that, in his final four years, Sundquist would be a caretaker, catering to the causes of big business, pushing economic development, running state government conservatively, and spending increasing amounts of time on his favorite golf courses. In his State of the State address in January 1999, he made no mention of a looming financial crisis.

Six weeks later, in a speech to the legislature, it was a different story. Sundquist would say later that the state's financial peril had blindsided him. Even in a prosperous economy, tax revenues were dipping far below the amount necessary to maintain services; the shortfall was close to $1 billion. He was still saying that Tennessee did not need a state income tax, but he did propose a broad revision of business taxes, reaching for the first time into the pockets of service providers. He also proposed taking the sales tax off food; some black legislators rose and applauded in the chamber when he delivered that line. Then, Sundquist pushed further: Salaries above $72,000 within businesses should be treated as profits and taxed. That was perilously close to the reviled income tax, even though it would apply to fewer than 43,000 taxpayers.

It took the business lobbyists only a few days to kill those proposals in their tracks, but legislators were beginning to squirm under the pressure of a looming shortfall and the specter of new taxes. Naifeh's inner circle whispered into the governor's ear that they could pass an income tax if he would support it. Sundquist finally agreed. He called the legislature into special session in late March, limiting its agenda to tax reform. House leaders thought they had the votes for an income tax, but the count appeared to be just short in the Senate. The special session adjourned in late April without acting.

The open discussions of an income tax had finally caught the public's attention. The idea was particularly alarming to the new breed of suburban Republican legislators and their constituents. Sundquist's own Republican Party, led by his protégés and pretenders, rose up and denounced their own governor. They even began to boo him at some public events.

After patching together a makeshift budget using reserves and one-time funds to cover recurring expenses, the legislature adjourned its regular session in June. There was an agreement that Sundquist would call yet another special session in November. Business lobbyists, realizing that an income tax not only made sense for the state but also avoided higher business taxes, agreed to raise more than $1 million for a public education campaign. But the bombardment of television commercials, intended to soften the opposition, only hardened it.

In November, the legislature wallowed again in the tax reform tar pit, and in desperation considered the old alternatives: a return to the state property tax, a tax on automobiles, higher sales taxes, eliminating some sales tax exemptions, making massive and draconian cuts in the budget. By then, Sundquist was openly backing an income tax and threatening to veto changes that fell short of what such a tax would yield.

In all the discussions about an income tax, leaders of both houses had avoided roll-call votes on the issue. But finally, six of the eleven Senate Finance Committee members voted to send an income tax bill to the floor. It was widely assumed, in the growing uproar from the public, that they had committed political suicide.

When it appeared the legislature was nearing a vote, angry taxpayers crashed the e-mail and telephone systems. Goaded by a new type of political activists—radio talk-show hosts—motorists circled the Capitol, horns blaring in protest. Hundreds of citizens packed the hallways and the rotunda of the Capitol. Thoroughly cowed, and with elections less than a year away, the legislature adjourned without any more votes on tax reform. Leaders could not find the votes in the Senate, and what had appeared to be a majority in the House was melting quicker than an early snow.

a site. An INS law enforcement team was all prepared to set up shop in Goodlettsville until today, when the town planning board nixed the chosen location. Tennessee's only INS office is in Memphis, 200 miles away.

25—One of Nashville's most famous R&B clubs is getting a new lease on life. The Modern Era at 1114 Charlotte Ave., reopens its doors tonight with a concert by soul balladeer Alexander O'Neal. The club's new owner, John Perkins, hopes to rekindle the magic of its heyday, when it was a major stop on the so-called "chitlin circuit." Originally called the New Era, the club was opened by William Sousa "Soo" Bridgeforth at Fourth and Charlotte in 1939. James Brown, B.B. King and Ray Charles all performed on its stage, but its pinnacle of fame came in 1963, when R&B legend Etta James recorded her live LP *Etta James Rocks the House* there. . . . **Financially strapped** Carmike Cinemas keeps on closing its Nashville-area theaters. From its high of 199 screens operating here a few years ago, the chain's holdings have dwindled to 74. Competitor Regal Cinemas has overtaken it with 105.

26—Actor, singer and social activist Harry Belafonte is in town to accept the 2000 Freedom in Film award given by the Freedom Forum and the Nashville Independent Film Festival. The award recognizes his long career portraying African Americans in non-stereotypical roles. Before a packed crowd at the First Amendment Center, Belafonte says Hollywood has created "a new breed of social familiarity" among races, but at the expense of meaningful debate and discussion. And until that understanding comes, he says, the country will be "put upon and plagued by the issue of race."

27—**For the fourth time** since January, residents of the Crown Chalet Apartments in Madison are unnerved by a fire, this time in a vacant apartment. The third fire, in May, was also minor, but the first two destroyed a total of eight apartments and injured 11 people. Arson is suspected.

28—**A stalled elevator** in a Vanderbilt dormitory leads to a near-tragedy and a certain miracle. Thirteen people are aboard an elevator in Vanderbilt's Carmichael Towers West when its safety sensors detect an overload. The elevator shuts down between the ninth and 10th floors, but passengers manage to pry open the interior doors. Luke Hammond, a freshman linebacker on the Vanderbilt team, attempts to wriggle through the opening to safety on the ninth floor when he loses his balance. The passengers look on in horror as Hammond slips and plummets nine stories to the bottom of the shaft. Miraculously, he lands with no broken bones, although his spleen has to be removed. He is in critical but stable condition at Vanderbilt Medical Center. . . . **After a month** of dwindling leads, the search for the I-65 Rapist is now more intense than ever. This morning, a 75-year-old woman was stopped on the Natchez Trace Parkway by a man who said her rear tire was smoking. He offered her a ride for help in his two-door, older-model white vehicle. Once she was inside, he drove her to a secluded area in Hickman County and raped her, leaving her to walk a mile and a half for help without clothes. Police now begin a desperate manhunt for a thin man with reddish hair, a shaggy goatee and a baseball cap.

29—**Maj. Carl Dollarhide**, the Metro Patrol Division commander who was the subject of a WTVF-Channel 5 exposé three weeks ago, announces that he will retire, effective Jan. 1, 2001. Dollarhide currently faces two probes on allegations that he used his influence in December 1998 to keep his then-brother-in-law from being arrested at a roadblock.

30—**Another blistering lunch hour** on Legislative Plaza, but a crowd of about 3,000 materializes

Tennessee's prolonged and emotional public conflict over state taxes in 1999 and 2000 didn't end there. Republican Gov. Don Sundquist was shunned by his own party for pushing a tax-reform strategy based on earned income, but a group called Tennesseans for Fair Taxation came to the Capitol to give him a list of organizations that supported his efforts.

By now the opponents had found their mantra: The rapid growth in the state budget was proof that the state had a spending problem, not a revenue problem. And a big culprit was the monster TennCare program, viewed by some as a welfare handout and socialized medicine. Sundquist, the supposed low tax, pro-business Republican, had become a big-spending liberal.

The 2000 legislative session was a replay of the year before. Sundquist again proposed an income tax and removal of the sales tax on food. If the legislature wanted to cut the budget instead, it would have to make the hard choices alone. To make matters worse, TennCare was threatening to come apart at the seams. Some providers were in financial trouble; increasing numbers of doctors were leaving because of slow or low or nonexistent reimbursements for their TennCare patients.

Throughout the spring, legislators huddled in private, trying to find a way out of the state's financial dilemma. Sundquist refused to budge. As the session crept into June, the House and Senate were far apart on stop-gap plans to fund the next budget, which had to be in place by July 1. Then, without any public discussion or votes or advance warning of any sort, an income tax bill was suddenly back on the table. The legislature met in a rare Saturday session on June 10. Most members spent their day waiting. And waiting. Behind the scenes, leaders tried to hammer out a compromise that could pass both houses. But word was out; hundreds of horn-honkers again circled the Capitol, and radio talk-show hosts set up shop atop the Legislative Plaza bunker. The atmosphere was a curious mix of carnival and whispered rebellion.

Finally, the legislators surrendered. As before, no public votes had been taken. Leaders began to patch together a makeshift budget by transferring funds, spending reserves, and again using one-time money for recurring expenses. That still left a gap, so the members blithely raised the estimates of tax collections. The budget they created was a financial shop of horrors. Sundquist vetoed it, calling it "a riverboat gamble." It was

Horn-honking anti-tax protesters and others on foot staged noisy demonstrations at the Capitol while the governor and the legislature were grappling with a wide range of proposed changes in the state's tax structure.

In the heat of battle over a proposed state income tax, Sen. Thelma Harper (D-Nashville) peered from beneath one of her trademark hats to make a forceful point to Rick Kuhlman, a Nashvillian who was in the Capitol to lobby against passage of a tax on six-figure incomes.

for rock star John Mellencamp, who is passing through Nashville on what is dubbed his Good Samaritan Tour—a series of impromptu, unadvertised outdoor shows from Detroit to Atlanta. For 45 minutes, Mellencamp plays acoustic guitar with a three-piece backup (accordion, violin, guitar) and belts out several of his classic hits, including "Small Town" and "Pink Houses," a Reagan-era anthem of heartland disillusionment mixed with bittersweet resignation. As Mellencamp gets to the third verse, he falls silent and lets the crowd sing; by the time he reaches the chorus, "Ain't that America for you and me?" the thousands of people on the plaza stand wedged together, swaying, singing in the noonday sun.

31—**The I-65 Rapist's** reign of terror is over. A Hickman County truckdriver confesses to raping five women along the I-65 corridor over the past year. Mark Anthony Clark, the 34-year-old married father of two young daughters, admits that he offered rides to elderly women, either pedestrians or women driving alone who thought something was wrong with their cars, as a pretext for assaulting them. Clark was arrested after a woman he pursued on the Natchez Trace several weeks ago recognized him. . . . **Nashville-based Shop At Home Inc.** announces it has laid off 20 percent of its workforce after posting a much-higher-than-anticipated $13-million loss for its fiscal year. More than 150 full-and part-time jobs have been cut in the last three months. The company attributes its problems to the poor performance of its home-shopping television network, which accounts for more than 90 percent of its revenue. . . . **In his first major address** to Vanderbilt University faculty, Chancellor E. Gordon Gee calls for a change from the school's aloof image. Noting "a lack of diversity on this campus, one that is either ignored or resented

the first budget veto in Tennessee history. The legislature just as promptly overrode the veto and headed home for one of the most uncertain election seasons since the Civil War. In a state of near-panic at the public hostility symbolized by the honking horns, incumbents and challengers alike began to sign anti-income tax pledges circulated by conservative groups. But the apocalypse feared by the members never materialized. Only one House member lost her seat over the income tax issue; no senator, not even those who had voted to send the tax bill out of committee, was defeated.

Even before the election, the jerry-built budget assembled only a few months earlier had begun to unravel. Within days of its passage, Wall Street downgraded the state's

Appealing to higher authority, some Republican senators held hands and prayed before the General Assembly's unsuccessful search for a solution to the state's budget crisis.

In the state House of Representatives, Democrats tried more informal debate rather than prayer—with the same result. When the legislative session ended, both parties and both houses had overridden Gov. Sundquist's veto of their patchwork plan for state spending.

credit and bond ratings. Tax collections sagged, foretelling a softness in the national economy. Chronic underfunding of the state's higher education system caused Tennessee to slide further behind its neighbors. State secondary-school scores continued to trail the regional and national averages, and the gap was widening. TennCare showed new signs of stress despite another infusion of funds. The state would face a shortfall of hundreds of millions of dollars in the current budget before it even began to deal with a new one in the year 2001.

Only eighteen months earlier, reform-minded lawmakers had winked knowingly at one another and sported paper lapel tags reading "Do the Right Thing"—code words for tax reform. On a half-dozen occasions, they had seemed close enough, finally, to fix the structural tax problems that doomed the state to mediocrity. Now they were returning to Capitol Hill, dispirited and frustrated. In a decade-long sonic boom of prosperity, Tennessee had failed to summon the political will to drag itself into the front rank of states entering the new century. An ominous hint of recession and retrenchment was in the wind—at just the wrong time for a state with no clue what to do about its rising expenses and its eroding tax base. Sundquist's term was waning, as was his newfound appetite for tackling tough issues. Tennessee was reduced to waiting for a new governor, but without great expectations.

Polls showed that overwhelming majorities of the voters wanted first-class schools and colleges, a viable health-care system, sustained economic growth. The same majorities opposed the kinds of taxes required to provide those things through their state government.

Around the bar at the new Gerst House, there was only one consensus: the price of beer had gone up.

or lamented," the new chancellor promises to work toward making Vanderbilt more "multiracial, multicultural and multireligious.". . . **The Tennessee Court of Appeals** agrees to hear the state's appeal of a lawsuit challenging the validity of the state budget. The lawsuit filed by former television reporter Mark Mayhew and several local news organizations, including the NashvillePost.com, the *Nashville Scene*, and now *The Tennessean*, claimed the state budget was invalid because it was formulated in secret meetings, violating the state Open Meetings Law. The state's appeal argues that under the principle of separation of powers, the courts cannot intervene in the authority of the legislature to set its own rules and procedures.

The Power of Protest

by STEVE GILL

As the conservative host of a morning radio talk-show, Steve Gill was present in June 2000 when horn-honking protesters, stirred to action by Gill and other radio personalities, circled the State Capitol to pressure the Tennessee General Assembly not to pass an income tax, This is his perspective on the tax controversy.

The seeds of the anti-tax rebellio were planted earlier, in March 1999, when Governor Don Sundquist abandoned the "no income tax" platform upon which he had just been re-elected. The governor had last voiced his firm opposition to a state income tax just six weeks earlier, when he declared that such a levy would "raise the tax burden on Tennesseans and create a way to finance the easy and endless expansion of government. Tennessee does not need a state income tax." Suddenly and inexplicably, he embraced what he had opposed.

Despite the attempt of many legislators and income-tax advocates to hide behind the euphemism "tax reform," the initial push for an income tax was essentially a frontal assault. Even when confronted with a decisively negative response from taxpayers, proponents continued to twist arms and spin the facts to convince lawmakers that the state faced a serious revenue crisis, and only two outcomes were possible: an income tax, or economic ruin. But the public wasn't buying it.

When Governor Sundquist first declared his support for "tax reform," and soon thereafter for the income tax itself, I and other hosts of call-in programs fired back with a populist anti-tax message. We had more than enough ammunition to fight a sustained battle—and the public responded. Throughout 1999, in the regular session of the General Assembly and two special sessions called by

the governor, our listeners bombarded the Capitol with a heavy blitz of phone calls, e-mails, and faxes. The immediacy of coverage afforded by talk radio, and its impact, had never before been felt in the Tennessee political process. The beleaguered lawmakers retreated behind the fortresslike walls of Legislative Plaza. Some who were used to hiding in the pack were so unnerved by this new attention and exposure that they responded by publicly denouncing the income tax and promising to vote against it. The Republican governor and the majority-Democrat legislative leadership could only watch helplessly as their potential "yes" votes peeled off one by one.

People who had never paid much attention to the political process began to tune in as a vote on the income tax issue appeared near at hand in November. On the air, we were identifying by name the apparent swing votes in both houses and encouraging our listeners to apply pressure accordingly. Then, with support from several other stations, we started a "Honk if you're against an income tax" campaign in downtown Nashville. By the morning of the scheduled vote, the protest had grown so large and noisy that the leadership declared the income tax "dead"—killed, you might say, in a "drive-by honking."

And for about six months, the tax scheme *was* dead, at least publicly. But if that first push was a direct frontal assault, the effort in June of 2000 was a calculated sneak attack on the taxpayers of Tennessee. We got a hint of the surprise on Friday, June 9, when a talk-show caller said the legislature was going to vote on a tax bill the next day. An official announcement later confirmed the rumor. A state income tax was about to be brought up for a vote, without any prior notice or involvement by the public. Most Nashvillians would know nothing of it until they read their morning paper on Saturday.

After an early-morning flurry of telephone calls,

Nashville stations WLAC and WWTN got permission to broadcast from Legislative Plaza at noon. We saw it as an emergency opportunity to call out the anti-tax troops. Shortly after we went on the air, the honkers and protesters began arriving in force. People who happened to catch the show were calling their neighbors and spreading the word. Like latter-day Paul Reveres, we were shouting, "The taxers are coming!" As word spread throughout the afternoon and the numbers steadily grew, legislative leaders found that, once again, they couldn't hold on to all the votes they needed. Late in the day, they decided to postpone the vote until Monday.

Both stations were there as the work week opened, and we remained, broadcasting from remote trucks parked outside the plaza while the ranks of demonstrators swelled in anticipation of the scheduled evening session of the House of Representatives. A close vote was expected, with the governor's forces still thinking they held a razor-thin advantage. The lawmakers, worn out by months of contentious debate, seemed ready to accept almost any proposal, if it would just get them safely out of town.

But then, dramatically, as the members began to assemble, two among them suffered stress attacks and heart problems, and were literally carried from the chamber on stretchers. The tension was unbearable. Another postponement followed, this time until noon the next day.

Sensing victory, the protesters were back in greater numbers than ever on Tuesday morning, June 13. A steady stream of vehicles circled and honked, jamming traffic in the Capitol area. Signs popped up reading "Send them ALL to the ER!" and "It's Our Money, Not Theirs." At high noon, about 500 people gathered on the Capitol steps, chanting "It's our House!" Then, streaming into the building, they formed a human gauntlet in the central hallway, forcing members of the legislature to push through, nose to nose with angry, shouting taxpayers. One protester, carrying a replica of the first American flag, with its circle of stars, was told by a state trooper that he would have to give it up because signs and displays were not permitted inside the Capitol. "You're not taking this flag!" the man replied, clutching it to his chest. The crowd grew tense. Then, spontaneously, someone started singing "America, the Beautiful," and others picked it up, and soon it was the assembled taxpayers and not the patrolman who had the upper hand. He stepped back, and then turned and walked away. The crowd cheered. The flag was safe.

The pro-tax votes that had been there just hours earlier were no longer firm. One after another, lawmakers who had been counted on as supporters of the tax publicly declared their opposition to it. At the end of the day, Senator Bob Rochelle, the Lebanon Democrat who was the primary sponsor of the income tax, threw in the towel. It would take a couple more weeks for the legislature to pass a budget based on no new or increased taxes of any kind. Governor Sundquist's promised veto was promptly and decisively overridden, and the General Assembly immediately adjourned and retreated. Thanks to the activist intervention of thousands of Tennesseans, the proposed state income tax had been stopped cold.

But winning battles isn't the same as winning a war, and the income tax war is far from over. As Republican Senator Marsha Blackburn of Brentwood, one of the leaders in the anti-tax fight, remarked right after the legislature overturned the governor's veto, "We have to win every time; they only have to win once." The struggle continues.

Nashville attorney Steve Gill, a two-time Republican candidate for Congress, carried the tax fight into 2001.

The Administration of Justice

by GORDON BONNYMAN

Over the past century, the administration of justice in our community has risen to a higher plateau. Many Nashvillians are old enough to remember when the law was largely concerned with codifying privilege and enforcing oppression. Not until 1920 did women finally win the right to vote. Less than 40 years ago, black citizens were still systematically denied the equal protection of the laws. Within living memory, scandalous miscarriages of justice allowed state protective institutions to literally steal and sell the children of the poor, and state mental health facilities to cruelly mistreat disabled persons entrusted to their care. Within the past half-century, both state and local detention agencies jailed prisoners under conditions of medieval degradation and terror. So entrenched were these injustices that lawyers who challenged them in court faced ostracism and even disbarment.

Things have changed. Nashville, the state of Tennessee, the South, and the entire nation have benefited (often in spite of themselves) from social and cultural movements and federal reforms that forced the legal system to meet a more just and humane standard. Citizens successfully petitioned their government for redress of grievances; the U.S. Supreme Court struck down Jim Crow laws and upheld individual liberties; Congress enacted civil rights laws and funded legal services for the poor; and a national sensitivity to bias and injustice finally took root. All these developments have moved us closer to our professed commitment to equality under law.

Nashville had more than a walk-on role in the dramas that have raised the standard of justice. It was here, in the Tennessee General Assembly, that the last decisive battle for women's suffrage was won 80 years ago. Our city's African-American institutions nurtured the civil rights movement in the 1960s by training a whole generation of courageous young leaders in nonviolence who went forth to change the world. It was in Nashville courtrooms that the foundation was laid for the Supreme Court's historic "one person, one vote" reapportionment ruling in 1962, thus completing a democratic evolution that can be traced to 1829, when the first Nashvillian moved into the White House.

The Nashville legal community of today would hardly be recognizable to departed members of the all-white, all-male club that once jealously guarded the perquisites of power for itself and its privileged clientele. The Nashville bar now has a record of financial and volunteer support for legal aid that is one of the most generous in the nation. Bar groups actively recruit and support women and minority lawyers and push for ongoing improvements in the justice system. High-quality legal representation is available to the poor through the efforts of dedicated, skilled advocates in the Legal Aid Society, the state and federal public defender offices, and the Nashville Bar Pro Bono program. Nashville's judiciary is better qualified and more conscientious than at any time in the city's history.

And yet, for all these advances, the civic oath of "liberty and justice for all" remains more of an aspiration than an affirmation. Every day our courts conduct business, that sober reality is exposed. We tend to believe that our adversarial system is finely honed to arrive at the truth by weighing the contending claims of equally well-prepared and zealous adversaries. But in reality, gross inequalities of power and resources frustrate the search for truth and undermine the quest for justice.

The law mirrors the society of which it is a part. Perhaps it is assuming too much to expect that, in a nation that tolerates the impoverishment of 1 in every 5 of its children and the control of more than 80 percent of its wealth by less than 20 percent of the populace, the legal system would somehow dispense equal justice without regard to distinctions of wealth and power. The very manner in which our laws are made is strongly influenced by social and economic inequities. Through campaign contributions and the ability to field skilled lobbyists, those who enjoy economic and social power wield enormous influence over the legislative process, thereby shaping to their own primary advantage the laws by which all citizens must live.

Unequal resources also closely correlate with the outcome of court cases. Litigation is generally not affordable to the poor, or even to most of the middle class, except in uncontested divorces, simple bankruptcies, personal injury cases, and a few other situations. Legal aid and charity work done by private attorneys fill only a small part of the resulting unmet need. The court system itself is highly stratified. In the most respected trial courts—the federal District Court and the state Chancery Court—judges and lawyers focus mainly on economic disputes among corporations or wealthy individuals. Sometimes these courts preside over cases of paramount public concern in which fundamental constitutional principles are at issue, but more often their energies are devoted to resolving matters in which the financial stakes are high but the impact on human lives is minimal.

It is the lower courts—General Sessions, Juvenile, and Domestic Relations—that directly touch the lives of the most people. Here, the litigants typically are from the bottom half of the economic scale. General Sessions Court is the point of entry into the criminal justice system. It also processes tens of thousands of civil cases a year, most of which involve evictions or the collection of debt. In these cases, the plaintiffs are mostly companies or individuals with money and lawyers; the defendants are usually poor and unrepresented. The plaintiffs almost invariably win. The assembly-line pace is such that it is often impossible to tell what is happening in the courtroom. Juvenile Court deals with the most dispossessed Nashvillians: the city's abused, neglected, abandoned, delinquent, or unruly children. Close to Juvenile Court in the judicial pecking order are the state circuit courts that hear divorces and domestic relations matters.

Far from the comparatively bloodless commercial disputes that occupy much of the time of their more respected counterparts, these lower courts face the most fundamental of human conflicts, relationships, and aspirations. Harried judges and lawyers must decide, literally in minutes, cases of the utmost importance to individual Nashvillians. Children are the most profoundly affected; decisions reached in these courts may affect the entire future course of their lives.

The criminal process, in which liberty and even life may be at stake, is marred by inequities that should be an acute embarrassment, but instead are accepted as the norm.

The outdated bail system explicitly conditions pretrial freedom upon a defendant's ability to buy a bail bond, with the result that poverty has more to do with whether an accused individual will be jailed than does the fact of his guilt or innocence, or the seriousness of the offense with which he has been charged. The legal system is periodically rocked by exposés involving the bail bond industry. Yet the system endures, ignored by all but its victims—and those who profit from it.

The greatest scandal of the legal system is the death penalty. Dozens of people are tried for murder in the Nashville area each year, but those who are given death sentences are nearly all poor, and a disproportionate number are black. They are assigned their punishment according to a process that owes more to caprice than to the even-handed application of any objective standard. There appears to be no way for fallible human institutions to administer the death penalty fairly; it is frighteningly prone to error. Yet Tennessee resumed capital punishment in 2000 after a 40-year hiatus, and the penitentiary in Nashville is expected to be the site of increasing numbers of executions in the coming years.

"Equal justice under law," the idealistic phrase chiseled in stone above the portals of the Supreme Court Building in Washington, remains an elusive goal, not only in the nation's capital but also here in the capital of Tennessee, and in our local seat of government. Perhaps we do assume too much when we expect equal justice to prevail in an unequal society—but that is the promise of our democratic system of government, and it is our right, our privilege, and our duty to keep on making those assumptions and holding those expectations.

To Nashvillians of future generations who may read these words, I pray you will receive them with the same sense of disquiet that we feel when we look back on prior conditions, such as child labor or chattel slavery. As you strain for a glimpse of the familiar in the Nashville of 2000—which to you will no doubt seem quaint and strange—may you find here seeds of justice that, in your own lifetime, have borne full flower.

Attorney Gordon Bonnyman directs the Nashville Justice Center, a public-interest law firm serving low-income parties before the courts. A native of Knoxville and a graduate of the University of Tennessee School of Law, he has lived in Nashville since 1970.

CHAPTER NINE

THE GREAT DIVIDE

by DANA PRIDE

September is the traditional back-to-school month in the United States, but since mid-August, about 450 yellow buses have been covering their assigned routes on the streets and roads of Nashville. The fleet transports more than two-thirds of the 70,000 students enrolled in the Metro public school system for the fall term of 2000. In this post-agrarian society, the school calendar still resembles its 19th-century model: shaped to the imperatives of planting and harvesting, not to the we-never-close character of today's work stations. In an age of television, computers, cell phones, and the internet, the modern school seems an anachronism, a throwback to an earlier and simpler time when bells clanged and children came by bus or on foot to receive the knowledge of teachers.

But appearances can be deceiving. It might be more accurate to say that the modern public school—in Nashville, in the South, in the United States—is a contradiction, an amalgam of eclectic and often conflicting resources, methods, objectives, aspirations, and legal requirements, all intended to produce, by some miraculous alchemy, succeeding generations of responsible and productive citizens. For a century and a half, America has been trying to perfect the model of the public school system as the foundation of a democratic, egalitarian society. Time and time again, the model has been tested, revised, deconstructed, retooled, and returned to service. In this opportune moment of millennial beginning, the stakes are higher than ever—and our schools are still in the design shop.

Nashville has been my home for 32 years—more than half my life. This is where I raised my children, chose a profession, made lifelong friends. It's also the place where I found myself on one side of a great chasm separating neighbors and friends, co-workers and churchgoers, rich and poor, black and white. A wedge was driven between us, and it remains. We are divided by one thing above all else: how best to educate the children of our city.

No issue in the last half-century has been more divisive than this. In the earliest days of school desegregation 45 years ago, protest marches and picket lines—and even a school bombing—exposed a deep cleavage in the city's soul. Years passed without much change, and then, at the end of the 1960s, the federal courts were compelled to take up the race-and-education issue once again. My family's arrival in Nashville coincided with this drama. Emotions were raw and volatile; no one wanted to name the problem, much less address it and resolve it.

In time, the wounds scarred over and became less visible, but still festered just beneath the surface. I can remember seeing children taunted at a private swim club because they attended public schools. I knew families who changed churches because their children had endured such ridicule in Sunday school. I knew a public school educator who felt hurt and personally rejected after parents who had praised her when she taught in a suburban elementary school would no longer trust her with their children after she and the students were assigned to an inner-city middle school. I've known friendships that stayed intact only because one topic—not religion or politics, but education—was avoided at all costs.

The schism reflects differing views about education, and about the meaning of democracy. Its roots go far back in time, but over the past 40 years or so, as the "separate but equal" myth was exposed

1—**At the 11th hour,** the United Steelworkers Union averts a nationwide strike of more than 8,000 hourly workers against embattled Bridgestone/Firestone Corp. The contract dispute has been another blowout for the Nashville-based, Japanese-owned company, which is already axle-deep in the largest tire recall in U.S. history. . . . **Vanderbilt University alumni** Jay Chawan and Ashoke Bappa Mukherji, owners of Brentwood-based ProQuest Management Services, say they regret extending two Vanderbilt football players free financial advice and guaranteed lines of credit—an offer that earned the players a smackdown from the NCAA. Linebacker Jamie Winborn and cornerback Jimmy Williams will miss the first two games of the season for violating the NCAA's extra-benefits regulation. A routine investigation revealed they had leased late-model cars and paid living expenses with lines of credit extended by Chawan and Mukherji. Chawan claims he and his business partner were unaware they were violating NCAA rules. Winborn and Williams have returned the leased vehicles, paid back the money and paid for the financial advice. . . . **U.S. News and World Report** magazine ranks Vanderbilt 22nd among 228 leading national universities. The University of the South at Sewanee ties for 25th place among 162 liberal arts colleges in the survey. . . . **A federal judge** refuses to order Lawrence and Carolyn Levine to return their grandchildren to the kids' father, Perry March. The former Nashville attorney wants the FBI to arrest the Levines on child-kidnapping charges, but that effort also fails. The Levines made a dramatic rescue of the two children from their father's current home in Mexico last June. March's lawyers argue in court documents that the Levines, longtime Nashville residents, plan to flee to Israel with the kids in tow. . . . **Mark**

and segregation laws were repealed, the impasse has been frustratingly persistent in this city and most others across the nation. On one side are those of us who see it as every citizen's duty to help provide excellent and essentially equal educational opportunities for all children, including minorities and immigrants, the poor, the mentally and physically handicapped. It is also our belief that giving children the opportunity to meet people of other races, cultures, and social classes is a positive and useful experience in a society where all will rub shoulders as adults.

On the other side are those who believe in their hearts that their sole responsibility is for the education of their own children, and that such social considerations as race and economic class are completely irrelevant to that objective. As tax-paying citizens, they automatically support the public schools. Beyond that, they may agree in principle that all children deserve a fair chance to learn, and they may even voluntarily invest money and effort to that end—but they make a clear separation between their civic and their parental roles. It tends to follow that most people on this side of the equation want their children educated in homogeneous settings, where they will be among people like themselves, separated from the lesser-privileged and protected from ideas, attitudes, and values different from their own. When the Nashville schools were desegregated, people of means who held to these views either found private schools that gave them such assurances or moved to places where they might find them.

Two points of view, two sets of values—both present in Nashville and throughout the nation.

In one sense, the issue is as old as America itself. Historically, it was about who should be given a quality education—all children, or only those born to the more advantaged families. Throughout our colonial history and for most of the nation's first century, schooling was available only to the children of the elite. Others had to get their preparation for life in whatever way they could. Such practices were challenged, however. Thomas Jefferson argued in 1800 that a free and effective public education for all children was a necessity in a democracy, it being impossible for an ignorant citizenry to make rational and responsible decisions about public affairs. Jefferson also believed that public schools would develop the leadership of those, regardless of economic status, whose innately superior capacities naturally suited them to public office.

It wasn't until almost 50 years later, in the mid-19th century, that Jefferson's notion of common schools took hold. The movement advanced slowly, and from the beginning it pitted those who would educate to preserve an aristocracy against those who would educate to strengthen a democracy. Our nation's history is filled with examples of this clash of values—excellence for a few versus opportunity for all.

It is a division I never knew in the South Dakota gold-mining town where I grew up. Admittedly, there was no dominating aristocracy present, and not even a single black family. But my hometown in the Black Hills was populated by many ethnic groups whose distinct neighborhoods persisted well into the middle of this century. Multiple nationalities were represented there, and I grew up learning about and respecting these diverse traditions. But the town's citizens were always united on one significant point: They valued education above all else and supported the local schools in every way possible. They had come to this country in pursuit of the American Dream, and in incomplete ways they had found it. The schools were a first-class ticket to the rest of it for their future generations.

Town leaders had set the tone decades earlier. In my parents' time, a free, two-year kindergarten was begun so the children of immigrants could learn to speak English before they started first grade. The same practice continued when I came of age. Our school facilities were the pride of the community; our academic and extracurricular programs were rich and varied.

And it paid off. In my graduating class of 99 students were five National Merit Scholar semifinalists, including a Native American girl and a son of the school custodian. I was not among that distinguished group, but it was a tribute to our community, as well as my parents, that my brother and I—grandchildren of four people who spoke almost no English—became graduates of Harvard and Stanford universities.

That is what I had hoped to find in the place where I came to raise my own family: a community united in behalf of all its children, one whose leadership would make certain that the fullest opportunities were available to the sons of school custodians, the daughters of immigrants, the children of every racial and ethnic group. But something happened along the way that has kept the hope from becoming a reality here in Nashville.

Soon after we arrived, I sensed an ever-widening division within the community, as one family after another opted to leave the Metro schools. The separate sides became more and more entrenched as the years passed, and I wondered how this could happen and where it would lead. I wonder still.

Nashville newspaper headlines reflect the heavy drama of desegregation: the U.S. Supreme Court's historic *Brown* v. *Board of Education* ruling on May 17, 1954 (left), and the bombing of Hattie Cotton Elementary School in East Nashville on Sept. 9, 1957.

There were several turning points in Nashville's school history when actions taken or not taken suggested that this city, like so many others, would drag its feet rather than face up to the challenge of desegregation. When the U.S. Supreme Court declared unanimously in 1954 that laws requiring racial segregation in the public schools violated the Constitution, there were two school districts in the Nashville metropolitan area, one in the city and the other serving the rest of Davidson County. Each maintained separate operations for whites and blacks, so that, in effect, there were four school systems inside the borders of the county. The long-distance bus rides that whites later would find so repugnant were all too familiar to black children, most of whom rode for an hour or more, passing many schools, to reach their designated learning place. The 25 city and county schools for blacks were typical of segregated schools everywhere: separate and grossly unequal to the schools serving whites. The buildings and equipment were in poorer condition, the hand-me-down textbooks older, materials and supplies more limited.

Within hours of the Supreme Court ruling, Z. Alexander Looby and Avon N. Williams Jr., two Nashville attorneys representing the local chapter of the National Association for the Advancement of Colored People (NAACP), formally asked the city to end segregation forthwith. Most of Nashville's Catholic schools began admitting black students that same fall. The Peabody College demonstration school (now called University School of Nashville) also desegregated promptly. While no black families sought to enroll their children in white public schools, two white professors at Fisk University tried to place their children in black schools near the campus. They were turned away.

Anthony Clark, the confessed I-65 Rapist, faces charges in two counties next week for the rape of five women and the attempted rape of three others over the past year. Arraigned yesterday in a Hickman County courtroom, the 6-foot-9 trucker weeps as he faces General Sessions Judge Samuel Smith. The judge adds a $1.5-million bond to the $1.4 million already imposed by a Maury County judge. . . . *Space Cowboys,* an outer-space action-adventure film directed by and starring Clint Eastwood, opens at theaters in Nashville and across the country. The film represents a triumph for former Nashvillian Howard Klausner, who cowrote the script. Klausner, who flunked out of Montgomery Bell Academy in seventh grade, had written 12 unproduced scripts before *Space Cowboys,* and he was about to give up when his 13th project sold. Klausner tells a *Nashville Scene* writer that he wrote much of the film's conclusion while sitting at Bongo Java on Belmont Boulevard, in the fall of 1997. . . . **Friends meet at Sunset Grill** for a last public gathering with Denver Smith, 45, a Nashville songwriter whose struggle with Lou Gehrig's disease was profiled recently in *The Tennessean.* Smith thanks his family, neighbors, workers at Alive Hospice, and Music Row acquaintances for their support—three days before his death. . . . **Picketers are marching** on Franklin Road outside the local unit of Earthgrains Co., the second-largest bakery in the country. Sixty-five Nashville employees of the St. Louis-based breadmaker are on strike for better work conditions, particularly the elimination of mandatory overtime. The strike, which involves more than 3,000 workers nationwide, is the largest in the 116-year history of the Bakery, Confectionery, Tobacco Workers and Grain Millers International Union. One motorist who passes the picket line is seen pulling into a nearby Krystal and returning with bags of square burgers for the striking workers.

This was the first lost opportunity that signaled what was to come. Rather than heeding the court ruling and preparing to fulfill its intent, many influential Nashvillians worked hard to circumvent it. A year passed. In May 1955, the Supreme Court gave school districts some latitude to work out desegregation plans locally and implement them "with all deliberate speed." The local NAACP attorneys again asked school officials to bring down the walls of segregation, and again, nothing happened. On the first day of school that fall, several white schools denied admission to black students living in their attendance zones, prompting the two attorneys to file suit against the Nashville city schools on behalf of 21 black children.

Yet another year passed without a first step being taken to end segregation. Finally, under the guidance of retiring Superintendent W.A. Bass and his chosen successor, Assistant Superintendent W.H. Oliver, the city school board approved a grade-a-year desegregation plan that would begin with the first grade in 1957 and reach all twelve grades by 1968. The plan was approved by the federal district court, despite the plaintiffs' objections to the lengthy time it would take to complete the process. This so-called "Nashville Plan" was upheld on appeal by the U.S. Supreme Court, and was quickly adopted by many Southern school systems as a model for gradual desegregation.

After three years of delay, Nashville was finally set to admit a few black first-graders to all-white schools nearest their homes. As the first day approached in that fall of 1957, Superintendent Oliver called on all teachers, employees, and parents to "carry out the mandate of the federal court with the highest respect for law and order . . . and the welfare of every little child, white and black." But an outside agitator and radical white segregationist, John Kasper of New Jersey, made provocative public statements vowing that "blood will run in the streets of Nashville before Negro children go to school with whites." Mayor Ben West, ignoring both Kasper's harsh words and those of angry parents threatening a boycott of the schools, not only supported his school officials but enrolled his 6-year-old son, Jay, in the first grade at their neighborhood public school.

At Fehr School in North Nashville, one of six white elementary schools to admit a total of 15 black first-graders on the first day of desegregation, the new students and their parents were jeered and taunted by white children and adults.

Three black children enrolled at Buena Vista Elementary on that September morning in 1957 (including this 6-year-old boy escorted by three of his elders). Some white parents showed their disapproval, but there were no disruptions, and the day passed without serious incident.

Only thirteen of the 126 rezoned black first-graders braved the taunts of hostile crowds and went with their parents to enroll in five previously all-white schools. Most of the black families, fearing physical harm, loss of jobs, and other dangers, had asked for transfers to keep their children in all-black schools. The first day ended without Kasper's predicted violence. But shortly after midnight, a dynamite blast destroyed an entire wing of Hattie Cotton School in East Nashville, where one black child had enrolled with 139 whites the day before. Although Kasper and other suspects were arrested for inciting disorder, neither he nor anyone else was ever formally charged with the bombing.

Opening day under the new plan did not prove to be much of a turning point for Nashville. Four years into the process, only 44 African-American children in grades one through four were enrolled in biracial schools; the rest—more than 15,000—remained segregated. Attorneys Looby (who also sat on the city council) and Williams, the point men for a wide range of antisegregation efforts locally, kept pressing the school board to comply with the Supreme Court mandate; the board responded by trying to hold the creeping advance of desegregation in a narrow range somewhere between the least the court would allow and the most the local white community would accept.

But the slow pace of change was hardly a sign of tranquility in the city. In the spring of 1960, dynamite thrown from a passing car blasted open the front of Looby's North Nashville home. Because their bedroom was in the rear, he and his wife were not injured in the predawn assault—nor was the quietly fearless attorney intimidated. Later

plate numbers. Now drivers across the state are objecting to their new license tags on grounds that some prefixes are humiliating. Among the offending prefixes are DUH, DUD and DUM. Giles County ends up returning half of its 600 FAT tags to the state after too many drivers refuse them. . . . **Today is the climax** of the 46th-annual Italian Street Fair, the four-day Nashville Symphony fund-raiser held each year in Centennial Park. Though scarcely tainted by anything more Italian than pizza, the fair offers carnival rides and musical entertainment galore, including '70s funksters The Spinners.

5—**In a 7-7 split decision,** the 6th Circuit Court of Appeals rejects Death Row inmate Philip Workman's request for a hearing on recently discovered evidence that his lawyers claim proves he didn't fire the shot that killed a Memphis policeman nine years ago. This puts Workman back in line for execution this year. . . . **Tom Cihlar,** an auto repair shop foreman, wins the legal right to be father to his 8-year-old biological child, even though the boy's mother is now married to another man. Cihlar's six-year battle for that right included two appearances before the state Court of Appeals and three amendments to state laws concerning paternity. The mother plans to take the case to the state Supreme Court, but for now Cihlar has visitation with his son every other weekend. . . . **Reynols, an underground** Argentine band, performs at the the dive bar Springwater near Centennial Park. The group's leader is Miguel Tomasin, a visionary drummer/vocalist who has Down's syndrome, but tonight he is represented only by a snapshot taped to a chair. Instead, his bandmates, Anla Courtis and Roberto Conlazo, create amazingly dense sonic textures with a couple of effects-laden guitars. The event will live on in the memory of the few who witnessed. . . . **A comprehensive $285,000 study** may determine the fate of Metro's 30-year-old thermal transfer plant, which heats and cools 39 downtown buildings, including the Gaylord Entertainment Center. The controversial garbage-burning facility, a longtime target of local environmental activists, faces complaints about its rising maintenance costs and the quality of its service. The study will examine whether to keep the thermal facility open or convert it to oil or natural gas. . . . **Seventeen-month-old** Isaiah J. Rhodes dies in his crib from smoke inhalation when an unlicensed Nashville day-care center catches fire. At the time of the fire, the home housed four more children than the law allows. Responding firefighters say the home also had no smoke alarms.

6—**A Lebanon man** who smothered his infant daughter last year with a teddy bear believed he was bringing about the second coming of Jesus, his attorney claims today in court. Defense lawyer Gary Vandever argues that Brian Kelley, 29, was deranged by religious fervor when he suffocated his 13-month-old daughter last August. According to Vandever, Kelley was responding to what he thought were signs calling for a human offering to God. The signs included an image of Jesus he claimed to have seen earlier that night at the Wilson County Fair. . . . **Mayor Bill Purcell** meets with Metro Police Chief Emmett Turner to make sure the short-staffed department will maintain a police presence at local schools. Purcell is responding to a report that eight Metro middle schools this semester would have no more school resource officers, and that eight more schools are expected to follow suit next semester. The police department, down by more than 70 officers, says it can no longer afford to provide resource officers at middle schools. Meanwhile, four new middle schools have been added this year. . . . **The Tennessee Performing Arts Center** celebrates its 20th birthday in downtown Nashville. The city's largest arts presenter, TPAC has at one time housed the Nashville Symphony, the Nashville Opera, the Nashville Ballet, the Tennessee Repertory

At four other Nashville elementary schools—Jones (above), Clemons, Glenn and Hattie Cotton—white and African-American first-graders were enrolled together for the first time on Sept. 9, 1957. That night, a bomb exploded at Hattie Cotton, destroying one wing of the school.

that same day, some 2,000 citizens, most of them students at four local black colleges, answered the bombing by launching the sit-in movement that would lead to the desegregation of public accommodations in the downtown business district—four years before the federal Civil Rights Act of 1964 mandated such changes nationwide.

Two more years went by without a significant increase in school desegregation. In 1962, seven years after the court ruling, Looby and Williams sued the county board of education, and that fall, after voters had approved the city-county governmental merger that created Metro, the two school desegregation cases were combined by the courts. The new school system had more than 85,000 students, 20 percent of whom were black—and all but a token few were still segregated.

In 1969, after the vaunted Nashville Plan had run its twelve-year course, the plaintiffs' attorneys took the school system back to court, pointing out that after fourteen years of litigation, almost half the system's schools had only token desegregation (if any at all), and fewer than a dozen came close to reflecting the racial makeup of the system as a whole.

Following lengthy hearings in 1969-70, Federal Court Judge William E. Miller ordered school officials to redraw zone lines and feeder-school patterns to create a "unitary, nonracial school system" for fall 1970. Enrollment the previous fall had reached an all-time high of almost 95,000 students. Miller subsequently delayed implementation of his ruling to the fall of 1971—by which time the white exodus to private schools or neighboring counties resembled a panicked flight from the plague.

And so it was that long-distance busing to achieve maximum school desegregation came to Nashville, with the intent of creating an equitable educational system for all children. It didn't have to happen in that way; busing was the last resort after almost two decades of delay, resistance, and missed opportunity. It was an imperfect solution, but the only one left to Judge Miller or his successors—L. Clure Morton, Frank Gray, and Thomas Wiseman—who would be saddled with the case, incredible as it may seem, for another quarter-century after the busing plan was initiated in 1971. In all that time, until the very end, there was never a clear indication that the white majority was ready or willing to unite with the black minority to serve the best interests of all children, let alone to obey the law of the land.

Between 1969 and 1989, while black enrollment in Metro remained stable at around 20,000, the white total fell precipitously, from 72,000-plus to half that number. Existing private and parochial schools absorbed some of the departed students, and others enrolled in the public schools of neighboring counties as their parents joined the suburban land rush. Another large group was accommodated in eighteen new schools founded by local Protestant churches in Davidson County in a 25-year span starting in the mid-1960s. Because they were self-consciously Christian, conservative, and all-white, these so-called "seg academies" appealed to many families who wanted those characteristics to be a part of their children's education. The segregation feature has softened a bit over the years, but the eighteen schools are still thriving, with enrollments totaling about 10,000.

When desegregation began in earnest in the 1970s, discussions edged with tension sometimes boiled over as parents explored both sides of the great divide. I remember one public school parent cautioning me to avoid such arguments. "We may end up being acknowledged as better citizens" she said, "but they will see themselves as better parents." Indeed, most parents who chose to flee the public school system said they were pulling out for the sake of their children, citing academic quality and safety as two of their greatest concerns. They often compared average test scores at their chosen school with those at the local public school and used the scores to prove to themselves and others that private or out-of-county schools were doing a better job of educating. The test scores, of course, didn't take into account the narrow socioeconomic range of private-school students, or the fact that a higher proportion enter their grade level with superior preparation for academic work. Nor were handicapped students commonly found in the private-school mix, nor those for whom English was a secondary language, nor those tagged as "problem kids" for one reason or another. As for the safety issue, it is true that inner-city school environments sometimes reflect the dangers that shadow much of urban life in general. But facile stereotypes about violence are no more relevant in poor neighborhoods than in suburbia, where a rash of school shootings across the U.S.—all by white males—caused virtually no one to suggest publicly that all white boys are suspect.

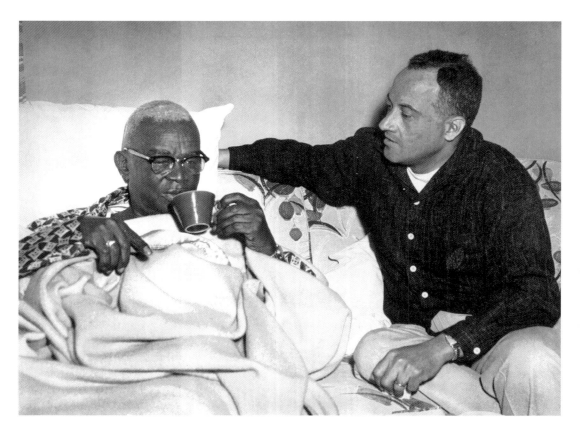

Hours after a bomb ripped off the front of his home on Apr. 19, 1960, Z. Alexander Looby, uninjured but shaken, sipped coffee and planned strategy with his law partner, Avon N. Williams Jr.

Theatre and Circle Players, as well as offering touring productions of Broadway shows. . . . **An electrical problem** likely caused the fire that killed 17-month-old Isaiah Rhodes in an unlicensed day-care center yesterday, investigators say. But the fact that 10 children were being cared for in the home means that it should have been licensed. Had it been licensed, regular fire inspections would have been routine. . . . **A Nashville flight engineer** will posthumously win the French Medal of Courage from the French government, after he dies today battling a forest fire overseas. Joe Donald Williams, 70, was one of a crew of five firefighters dumping water on an out-of-control blaze in southeastern France when their plane crashed.

7—**WTVF-Channel 5's** sweeps-month series "The Spring Break Tapes" showed plenty of flesh last May, but today it is the station's own backside that is exposed. Two teenagers shown in the report on spring-break shenanigans are suing the station, claiming that the segment portrayed them in a false light. Emily J. Barnhart and Destiny R. McCarrick, who appear briefly in the report sitting in a car in their bikinis, say that the segment damaged their reputations by showing them in the context of an exposé on salacious behavior. The teenagers say they have been harassed at school ever since the segment aired.

8—**Telia Sorrell** wears the homecoming queen's crown tonight at Macon County High School. The 17-year-old senior, diagnosed last year with cancer, is being honored by her fellow students for her courage and spirit while fighting the disease. When she graduates in 2001, Sorrell plans to enter the medical field. . . . **Clear Channels Communications Inc.,** which owns and operates more than 900 stations across the United States, is taking over one of its biggest competitors, AMFM, in a $23.8-billion merger. The significance for Nashville: further consolidation of an industry that holds the fate of Nashville music in its clutches. AMFM owns some of Nashville's top-rated stations, including country-music juggernaut WSIX-FM, pop station WRVW-FM, and classic rocker WNRQ-FM. . . . **U.S. District Court Judge** John Nixon approves American General Life and Accident Insurance Co.'s $214-million settlement of a class-action lawsuit. The Nashville-based company is accused of overcharging black and low-income policyholders for burial insurance. . . . **Mobile telephone company** Sprint PCS will open an applications development solution center near downtown Nashville that may feature as many as 400 high-end software jobs for local workers. Recruiting begins next month for the January opening of the center. . . . **Brian Kelley remains dry-eyed** when a Wilson County Criminal Court jury finds him guilty of murdering his 13-month-old daughter. He receives a life sentence. Kelley maintains God instructed him to smother her to bring back Jesus. . . . **Four of the six** surviving crew members of the *Memphis Belle*, a celebrated World War II bomber, reunite at Nashville's John Tune Airport. The first heavy bomber on the European front to fly 25 missions, the *Belle* was battered but unbowed. Today, pilot Robert Morgan, co-pilot Jim Verinis, radio operator Bob Hanson and turret gunner Harold Loch are given honorary colonel status in the state of Tennessee by Gov. Sundquist. All four men are now in their 80s.

9—**Nashvillians downtown** get a taste of 19th-century entertainment as a Wild West parade moseys from Riverfront Park to the Tennessee Performing Arts Center on Deaderick Street. Kit Cody, the grandson of Wild West legend William "Buffalo Bill" Cody, rides on horseback at the head of the parade, leading a colorful assemblage of rope tricksters, costumed Native American dancers, sharpshooters and actor Nick Riggins as a rugged Buffalo Bill. The parade celebrates tomorrow's opening of "Buffalo Bill's

When court-ordered busing began on Sept. 8, 1971, an organization of white protesters called the Concerned Parents Association set up picket lines and protest marches at about half of Metro's schools, and at the school administration offices on Bransford Avenue.

A syndrome of self-fulfilling prophecy emerged. White parents who sincerely believed they were looking out for the best interests of their children decided to enroll them elsewhere; as higher-performing students left the public schools, average test scores declined, leading to more middle-class flight justified by the lower test scores, and resulting in even lower scores—and the spiral continued downward, feeding on itself. Entire suburban communities, such as Brentwood and Hendersonville, blossomed in those years, as families moved there to escape their fears or to follow without much thought what "everybody" was doing. (The population of Brentwood, for example, quadrupled—from 4,000 to 16,000—between 1970 and 1990.)

A month after his narrow loss to incumbent Mayor Beverly Briley—and 17 years after the Supreme Court declared school segregation unconstitutional—former Metro Councilman Casey Jenkins (left) was leading the picket and boycott movement aimed at shutting down the school system in protest against busing and desegregation.

Wild West," an exhibit at the Tennessee State Museum. . . . **The Metro Council** has chosen 40 recruits for a fire academy class under new selection procedures initiated by Mayor Purcell. In a tradition that predated the establishment of the council in 1963, these jobs formerly were doled out as "spoils system" rewards for political support. Of the approximately 460 applicants who tested for the spots, nearly 400 rated outstanding. Though kinks remain, most council members agree that this is a more objective process. This year's roster includes four women and 10 African Americans.

10—**An altercation** between brothers inside a South Nashville dance club turns deadly. Albert Posada, 23, is charged in the shooting death of his brother, Ramiro, and the wounding of two other men outside the Flamingo

Police cleared pickets in front of Glencliff School to make way for parents to bring their children to school. After enduring verbal abuse from protesters, one white mother was defiant. "I told them I was going to run over them if they didn't move," she said to a reporter. "My child has a right to an education. It's not the busing they [the picketers] hate. It's the blacks."

During those emotionally charged years of the 1970s and 1980s, the issue of school desegregation consumed the lives of Nashville parents with school-age children. The preoccupation with race and education took a heavy toll—on the children and their parents, on teachers and administrators, on three directors of the school system and four federal judges, on politicians in one camp or another, and on the city's image of moderation in the face of social change. The people and institutions of Nashville are still recovering from those traumas, and the public school system is still paying dearly for its years of missed opportunity.

White flight and other migrations have dramatically altered the profile of the Metro school population. Whites are now a minority in the system, comprising 47 percent of the student population (down from 75 percent in 1969); African Americans, who make up 25 percent of the city population, account for 45 percent of the students in Metro schools; and the other 8 percent are newcomers, mostly immigrants of various racial and ethnic backgrounds. Another change is in the poverty profile. Thirty years ago, 1 of every 5 students came from low-income families (those qualifying for free or reduced-price lunches); now, the proportion is 1 of every 2. Even so, Nashville is more fortunate than many other urban school districts, where poverty now shadows close to 90 percent of all enrollees.

Here is a remarkable paradox: Whites who could afford the gamble have fled by the thousands, leaving behind other whites, blacks, and immigrants committed or compelled to make the urban experiment work for them (the timeless story of America, repeated once more)—and now, almost a half-century after it all started, we awaken to discover that our school system is still alive and functioning better than most. For many reasons (our diversified and steady economy and our metropolitan form of government being two), the Nashville public school system is, in the year 2000, more successfully desegregated, less impoverished, more stable, and more educationally productive than all but a few U.S. systems its size or larger. That may be damning with faint praise—but it does offer more cause for optimism than can be found in the troubled public schools of Los Angeles, Dallas, Atlanta, Miami, Chicago, and dozens of other cities.

Still, it's impossible not to reflect on how far we might have come by now if the epidemic of white flight had not struck the Nashville schools 30 years ago and continued ever since. No city can build a strong school system without the dedicated commitment of local leaders—and for too many years, there simply was not enough such support to be found here. Of course, there were (and are) some unsung heroes: school board members, teachers and administrators, parents and pupils, academic and religious figures, even politicians. But from the historic court decisions of the mid-1950s to the final settlement of the Nashville desegregation lawsuit in 1998, the prevailing image of public education here has been closer to that of an unwanted stepchild than to the apple of our eye or the star in our crown. It was as if the best we could muster as a city was resigned toleration of public schools as burdensome but necessary institutions.

Dance Club on Nolensville Road early this morning. The motive remains a mystery. . . . **A neighbor finds** Sherry Fay Perdue, 53, dead from multiple stab wounds at her Granada Avenue duplex. She was apparently seeking help from her brother next door when she collapsed on her front porch in a pool of blood. By day's end, police find Perdue's boyfriend, Johnny Ray Huspon, with blood still on his clothes. He is charged with the crime. . . . **Serial killer** Paul Dennis Reid, convicted in the murders of seven fast-food workers in Middle Tennessee, has been named in court documents as the likely killer of four others during the holdup of a Houston bowling alley in 1980. Reid, who was living in Houston at the time of the murders, moved to Tennessee in 1995. . . . **Viva Las Vegas!** Eleven Elvis impersonators swivel hips and curl lips at the Tennessee State Fair, vying for the $1,000 first prize and a shot at the Las Vegas finals. Among those competing to be the once and future King is John Loos, who is swathed from head to foot in black leather under a pitiless late-summer sun. Loos and his father drove 25 hours straight from Cheyenne, Wyo., for the competition.

11—Tom Baldassarre, 59, known throughout his North Nashville neighborhood as "Big Daddy," is on the phone with his wife when gunmen enter his Dickerson Road Pawn Shop on Jefferson Street. He tells her, "We're being robbed," and then she hears gunshots. One robber, 15-year-old Antonio D. Shannon, dies, and Baldassarre is critically wounded during the noon shootout. An accomplice remains at large. . . . **It takes a 90-minute struggle**, but construction workers finally dislodge a 69-year-old solid-copper time capsule from the corner of the former U.S. Postal Service building on Broadway. The contents are expected to be displayed in April when the Frist Center for the Visual Arts opens, following extensive renovation of the building, which was dedicated in 1931. A *Nashville Banner* article from that year lists

Those who remained in public schools found both advantages and disadvantages in the experience. One of the former was growth in cultural exposure and understanding. "Different but the Same," a prejudice-reduction program, gave Napier Elementary second-graders Kayla Wilson (left) and Matthew Bronson a chance to study each other's facial features.

By the end of the 1990s, so many white students had left the Metro public schools—and so many immigrants had come in—that the ratio of whites and blacks had shifted in three decades from 80 to 20 to about 45 to 45, with newcomers from abroad making up other 10 percent.

Instead of challenging the community to provide a fair start for all its children, most local leaders seemed to lose interest in the public schools after the 1971 desegregation order. Many openly supported expansion of the network of private schools; some served on boards and helped to raise funds for those efforts. At one time, the education committee of the Nashville Area Chamber of Commerce included not a single representative of the public school system—and it took a major effort by a public school advocate to change that. Realtors routinely steered middle-class newcomers with children away from Metro and into private schools or neighboring counties. As such talk spread, more and more families followed the pack. It took a very independent mind to resist assumptions and look beyond the long list of private schools that came in the mail to new residents of the city.

There have been times over the years when it appeared that general support for the Nashville schools might return. The system enjoyed a period of relative stability in the 1980s after Charles Frazier, a veteran Metro educator, was appointed director of schools. Enrollment of both white and black students inched upward, and achievement-test scores for both racial groups improved slightly. It was a tribute to Frazier's leadership that the College Board in 1990 selected Nashville as one of six cities in the nation to pilot its Equity 2000 project, an initiative designed to increase successful college performance by minority and low-income students. Specifically, the program focused on students enrolled in ninth-grade algebra and tenth-grade geometry. In 1990, less than half of those students were succeeding in these higher math classes. Eight years later, however, 80 percent were passing algebra II.

the contents, which include a Bible, a newspaper, a dedication pamphlet and a bank note signed by President Andrew Jackson.
. . . **In a move** that should bring changes to the 3600 block of Nashville's historic West End Avenue, the Free Will Baptist Bible College has secured a buyer for its land and buildings. Spiva-Hill Investments has contracted to buy the 10-acre campus, which has been a fixture in the residential neighborhood since 1942.

12—**The legislature's** Corrections Oversight Committee demands answers from Department of Corrections officials in a hearing today, after the state comptroller reports convicted felons are returning to Tennessee prisons in record numbers. The report says little is being done to rehabilitate prisoners in Tennessee. More than 43 percent of felons admitted to Tennessee prisons in 1997-98 were probation or parole violators, up from 32.6 percent in 1990-91. . . . **Stockholders approve** the proposed merger of Prison Realty Trust and Corrections Corporation of America, now the largest private owner of prisons in America. At the same time, U.S. District Court Judge Todd A. Campbell refuses to stop huge payouts to Nashville insiders Jack H. Dalton and Peaches Simpkins as a result of the PRT-CCA merger, despite the plunge in PRT's stock over the past year. Most of the money has already changed hands, rendering the legal filing in part improper, according to Campbell. Outside the stockholder meeting, more than 100 protesters, including Tennessee State Employees Association members, demonstrate against the state's reliance on private prisons.

13—**A baby girl** is abandoned outside Trevecca Community Church. Left in a car seat in front of the Murfreesboro Road church, the infant is surrounded by bags of belongings, including a photo of the child with two women in a frame inscribed, "I love my Mommy." Police seek clues to the child's identity, starting with papers found in the bags. . . . **In a 2-1 reversal,** the 6th Circuit Court of Appeals reinstates the death sentence of Abu Ali Abdur'Rahman, 49, making him second in line behind Philip Workman to be executed this year. Abdur'Rahman, formerly James Lee Jones Jr., was convicted in 1987 of killing a Melrose-area pot dealer and leaving the dealer's girlfriend for dead with a knife in her back. . . . **Just seven months** after accepting a $1-million signing bonus to be president of Gaylord Entertainment Co.'s creative content group, Tim DuBois abruptly resigns from the post. The departure of DuBois, the Music Row insider who founded Arista Records' Nashville office in 1989,

Frazier also rekindled interest and support among members of the business community. Project PENCIL, now called the PENCIL Foundation, was begun in 1982 to match businesses and civic institutions with Metro schools on a one-to-one basis. In 1987, former school board member Annette Eskind established another not-for-profit group, the Metropolitan Public Education Foundation, and funded its launch with a personal donation of $1 million. The foundation is attracting private-sector support for a wide range of initiatives in the Metro schools.

Even with what appeared to be renewed community interest, however, public education could not claim a high place in the priorities of our local civic culture. At the same time the schools seemed to be gaining strength under Frazier, the physical plant was in decline, and no major construction or renovation projects were in prospect. Lacking the civic and financial support to address both instructional and capital needs, school officials had focused their resources on the classroom and left maintenance issues unattended.

In 1989 and 1990, as the school system was reeling from back-to-back years of punishing, multimillion-dollar budget cuts, a grassroots organization called Parents for Public Education was energized to promote a restoration of confidence and funding to the school system. Some civic groups and a few high-profile individuals endorsed this campaign, but the Metro Council turned a deaf ear to their plea. Undeterred, the activist parents and others formed a coalition that persuaded a reluctant school board to call for a public referendum—in effect, a vote of confidence in the public schools—but that August 1990 vote failed by almost 2 to 1, a disaster for the schools and their supporters.

The effort was costly in more ways than one. Before-and-after polls of public opinion showed that the school system's high-approval rating (A or B) among Davidson County residents fell from an already-low 31 percent to just 17 percent. On both sides of the campaign, negative images of the schools took over, with supporters emphasizing all the unmet needs and opponents describing a system that was not deserving of new funds. The combination proved deadly, both in the voting booth and in the arena of

With their budgets for classroom supplies cut to the bone, Metro teachers like Kathy Johnson from Fall-Hamilton Elementary looked to the nonprofit Community Resource Center as a vital source for donated materials.

Suburban growth and the expansion of private schools through the 1970s and '80s were two forces that contributed to increased segregation by race and economic class. White flight was the defining cultural trend of that 20-year period.

public opinion. The school system's reputation recovered a bit in the years that followed, but negative opinions, well-informed or not, still outpoll positive ones.

Another prevalent attitude was also working against public education. I heard a private school parent tell a friend at the time of the referendum that she wouldn't support a tax levy for schools because she couldn't afford it, given the private-school tuitions she was paying for her children. This cuts to the very heart of the problem. Years ago, private schools were attended by children whose families could afford the tuition and still support public education through taxes. That dual obligation has been altered dramatically since 1970, when the proportion of children in private schools here was only about 6 percent (it's now more like 18 percent, which is roughly twice the national average). And just as important as the revenue loss has been the loss of interest, energy, and talent from people who could have helped build a strong urban school system dedicated to giving all children a fair chance to succeed.

The 1990s were years of renewed focus on education, both locally and nationally. Schools returned to the spotlight because of a changing economy that required an educated and literate workforce. The age-old pattern of school dropouts finding their way into the workforce no longer applied. Business and political leaders became alarmed at the number of youths who were entering adulthood unable to read, write, do math, and think at a level considered essential in a fast-paced technological society. And in the rapidly globalizing economy, students in other parts of the world were consistently outperforming Americans on international tests. A national alarm bell was sounding.

In 1992, Phil Bredesen became Nashville's mayor and announced in his first

does nothing to stem worries that Gaylord has lost its direction and focus. For one thing, Gaylord's corporate culture is getting increasingly conservative. The company drew snickers when it recently imposed a coat-and-tie dress code on habitually casual Music Row employees. . . . **Rocker Joan Jett,** looking bald, muscular and 10 kinds of fierce, puts on an incendiary display of unflagging punk energy in the odd environs of the Nashville Motor Speedway, where she and her band, the Blackhearts, play as part of the Tennessee State Fair. When she fires up her anthem "I Love Rock 'n' Roll," the pulsing stage lights illuminate a crowd of muscle-shirted mulletheads, pot-smoking truckers, dreadlocked

State of Metro address that education should be the community's top priority. Bredesen believed in the importance of high-quality public schools, and as a businessman, he recognized the important role a good school system plays in attracting and retaining new businesses. He also underscored the importance of maintaining racially integrated schools, noting that it would "kill our dreams as a city" if we didn't maintain a commitment to a "truly integrated, truly fair school system." Bredesen called for the creation of a citizens' committee to recommend changes that would bring quality and equality to the public schools. He and newly appointed Director of Schools Richard Benjamin, who replaced the retiring Charles Frazier in 1992, sought a plan that would attest to Nashville's commitment to equal educational opportunity for all children. With such a plan in place, the new leaders hoped, Metro might be able to bring its long-languishing school desegregation lawsuit to a satisfactory conclusion.

Development of that blueprint was a long and evolutionary process. It started with the creation of a 21-member group, the Advisory Committee on Excellence and Equity. The school board, the plaintiffs in the desegregation lawsuit, and the mayor's office each appointed seven of its members. They met for almost a year before submitting a report in December 1993 that laid out twelve specific goals for the school system. The board and staff, with various others assisting, worked for another two years to develop a comprehensive, long-range educational plan consistent with the advisory committee's recommendations. That plan, spelled out in a report called "Commitment to the Future," was a visionary attempt to revitalize public education in Nashville. It addressed a wide range of issues, from curriculum reforms and teacher accountability to school safety and targeted funding for at-risk students.

Seeming anything but impressed, Mayor Bredesen dismissed the document as cumbersome and overly complicated rendering. Out of its dense verbiage and his own instinctive notions of what was pragmatically possible, he molded a budget request and sent it to the council. The mayor boldly called for a large property tax increase, with more than half of the new funds devoted to the school priorities and a major expansion of the city library system. Bredesen's wish-list included reducing class sizes in the elementary grades (as mandated by state law); providing art and music teachers for all elementary schools; funding a new "core curriculum" (an idea he was pushing on his own), with planning time factored in to help teachers implement it; and eliminating most (but by no means all) of the hundreds of portable classrooms then in use around the city.

On the day before the Metro Council's crucial vote on the tax increase, Ronnie Steine, chairman of the budget and finance committee, a longtime

During Phil Bredesen's two terms as Metro's mayor in the 1990s, he gave public school advocates numerous reasons to praise him—and some to question his judgment. On balance, he spurred more improvements in the school system's physical plant than any mayor before him.

Rastas, purple-haired teens, civic leaders and music journalists rekindling their '80s youths. All shake their fists on the beat. . . . **Union workers** at Bridgestone/Firestone's La Vergne plant overwhelmingly ratify their new contract. . . . **Elvis Presley's** prescription-happy doctor, George Nichopoulos, is again denied reinstatement by the Tennessee State Board of Medical Examiners. The notorious "Dr. Nick" lost his license in 1995 for having overprescribed addictive drugs to more than a dozen patients, including Jerry Lee Lewis.

14—The baby's name is McKennah Keys. The infant girl abandoned yesterday in front of Trevecca Community Church today awaits her father and grandmother, who are fast on their way from Chicago to get her. The father was located through a Chicago church brochure left among the belongings accompanying the little girl. Police still seek the girl's mother, Allyssa Keys, last seen in a dark-blue 1992 Mazda with the license plate GOD IOU. . . . **Cinema North 6**, the Rivergate discount theater that offered 50-cent weekday admissions, becomes the last of more than 20 discount screens in the city to close its doors. Over the past three years, the rise of multiscreened megaplex theaters has forced more than a dozen smaller moviehouses to close and about 80 screens to fade to black. . . . The *Nashville Scene* runs a rare interview with singer Bobby Hebb, a native Nashvillian whose 1966 hit "Sunny" remains a staple of oldies stations the world over. On the occasion of a German label issuing a CD of 16 "Sunny" cover versions, performed by artists ranging from Cher and Dusty Springfield to actor Robert Mitchum, Hebb recalls his days at the Del Morocco club on Jefferson Street and his many encounters with jazz and R&B greats. Interviewer Jonathan Marx, a horn player for the local band Lambchop and a chronicler of Nashville's 1960s rock and R&B scene, catches up public school supporter, offered a smaller alternative budget, saying it was "the best we can do." The compromise took away fully one-third of the mayor's new funds for the school system. Though he had argued that the substitute package would cripple the system's budget and "send the wrong message as to what we care about in this community," Bredesen seemed resigned to defeat, and stood aside as a handful of council members fought in vain to restore the cuts. With almost 90 percent of his library expansion funds and two-thirds of his new school money assured, Bredesen was in no mood to fight. "All's well that ends well," he said.

But all had not ended well. It appeared that the council was six votes shy of an emphatic YES for schools that could have been read as a rough equivalent of the YES for sports that had built the city's new arena and stadium. By coincidence, six senior members of the council who had given Bredesen all he asked for in the campaigns that funded almost a half-billion dollars in sports facilities, now voted in favor of the compromise plan that slashed the mayor's request for schools. The school system was left without class-size reductions in grades four through six, and its capital improvement fund request was slashed from $213 million to $96 million.

Many citizens had complained loudly when efforts to bring professional sports to Nashville dominated Bredesen's first term as mayor. They argued that his priorities were wrong, that schools and libraries should be given their needed attention before a downtown arena and stadium were built. Bredesen had tried to calm the naysayers by asserting that Nashville could have both top-notch schools and professional sports.

The outcome in 1997 seemed to reinforce a familiar pattern in Nashville: "The best we can do" for public education was far short of what one of the local newspapers had called "the heroic efforts and dedication" of city leaders determined to boost Nashville into the big leagues of professional football. Or, to put it another way: Given a choice between doing the best thing for everyone and doing the best thing for those who needed it least, Nashville had chosen the latter option.

Meanwhile, the school board and plaintiffs' attorneys, using the "Commitment to the Future" document as their guide, continued to hammer out details of a plan that would satisfy the federal court's desegregation requirements and end the long-standing lawsuit. Their efforts led to adoption of the School Improvement Plan (SIP), a detailed blueprint for systemwide revitalization that is guiding major changes in the school system today.

Finally, Bredesen had what he was looking for. He embraced the recommendations and presented them to the council in 1998 as a package aimed at lifting the court order. The previous year, the council had lopped 10 cents, or one-third, off the mayor's tax increase proposal; this time around, he boldly asked for a 12-cent tax increase that would, among other things, restore most of the capital improvement funds that had been cut from the previous year's budget. This time around, a majority of the council voted for the tax measure with the hope and expectation that the new plan would finally bring an end to the desegregation orders that had hung over the schools for decades.

The SIP created a new student assignment pattern aimed at stabilizing desegregation while shortening bus rides. It set up a three-tiered system that, when fully implemented over the course of five years, would assure children who remain in the same residential area that they would

Metro Councilman Ronnie Steine (left) and Director of Schools Bill Wise worked together effectively through the ups and downs of the late 1990s, when issues involving budgets, curriculum, desegregation and council-school board relations tested the patience of all parties.

with Hebb at the annual Sevier Park reunion of people whose ties to the South Nashville neighborhood go back 50 years or more. Hebb grew up with seven siblings at 1708 12th Ave. S.

15—**Bradford Jason Lewis,** son of convicted gambler Jimmy Lewis, sues WTVF-Channel 5 for damaging his reputation in a series of reports on corruption in the Metro police department. Last month, the station reported that Lewis received special treatment from his former father-in-law, police Maj. Carl Dollarhide, when Lewis was detained in 1998 at a roadblock. Yes, he was carrying a sawed-off shotgun, paper receipts and lots of cash, Lewis says, but the station failed to report that the shotgun was legal, the slips of paper were credit-card receipts from his Madison bar, and the cash, also from the bar, was in a bank deposit bag. . . . **Citing doctrinal differences,** Nashville-based religious publisher Thomas Nelson pulls the plug on author Gwen Shamblin's third devotional weight-loss book. Shamblin, whose controversial religion-centered Weigh Down Diet has sold more than a million copies and whose weight-loss seminars meet regularly in more than 30,000 locations worldwide, recently stated her belief that the Christian Trinity of God, Jesus and the Holy Spirit expresses a hierarchical leadership with God at the top, rather than the generally accepted view that the Trinity represents the coexistence of three aspects of God. . . . **Allyssa Keys,** 24, expresses remorse to Metro police for abandoning her infant daughter, McKennah, on the steps of Trevecca Community Church two days ago. She reportedly wanted only to find a good home for the little girl, who is healthy and well-fed. Keys is arrested and charged with child neglect. . . . **The State Supreme Court** strikes down parts of Tennessee's abortion law as being too burdensome to women. Eliminated are the two-day waiting period, mandatory counseling and a requirement that second-trimester abortions take place in a hospital.

... **The air** in the Davidson County Courthouse is rated "poor" in a new environmental report, confirming the complaints of dozens of courthouse officials who cite increased allergies and asthma symptoms as a result of working in the building, whose air-handling system dates to 1963. ... **East Nashville residents** are saddened by the imminent closing of the Fatherland Street Market, the popular neighborhood grocery at 1401 Fatherland St., that offers gourmet foods, specialty items and a weekend organic farmers market to the area's mix of new, affluent young homeowners and longtime blue-collar residents. Owner Beverly Gamble says that high overhead has doomed the three-year-old store. "She probably has no idea how much she's loved by her neighborhood," says Rick Clark, president of the Lockeland Springs neighborhood association.

16—**More than 2,000** Middle Tennessee lesbians and gays celebrate their identity at Nashville Pride 2000, a daylong alternative-family festival at the Bicentennial Capitol Mall. Featured speakers include Pat and Wally Kutteles, mother and stepfather of Pfc. Barry Winchell, the Fort Campbell soldier murdered last year by fellow soldiers who discovered he was dating a female impersonator. ... **Mexican independence** is celebrated at an unlikely site: the Tennessee State Fair, where singer Jose Guadalupe Esparza is a headliner. The selection of Esparza, whose hits include "Corazon Ranchero (A Rancher's Heart)," is a sign that fair organizers recognize the spending power of the city's growing Hispanic community.

17—**The history of country music**, as seen by a time-traveling Irish lad, will form the basis for the first country-music film shot in the giant-screen IMAX format. The 45-minute film, produced in part by Gaylord Entertainment and directed by Nashville video filmmaker Steven Goldmann, features a huge cast of Nashville favorites, including Dolly Parton,

Mayor Bill Purcell encouraged parents to come to school with their children on the first day and to take part in a First-Day Festival at the Gaylord Entertainment Center, and some 10,000 people responded. On the walk from Hobson United Methodist Church to Cora Howe Elementary were numerous families, including Vesia and Linwood Hawkins with their son, Amiri, and daughter Imani.

change buildings only twice—to enter the fifth and ninth grades—during their thirteen years of schooling. In the past, children were moved three to five times during their public school careers.

Under the plan, many inner-city children would attend primary schools closer to home. Parental involvement and connection to the community had suffered during the years of busing, especially in black neighborhoods where families saw their youngest children sent off to schools far away. The new plan established additional magnet programs in the inner city, as well as several "enhanced-option" schools serving pre-kindergarten through fourth-grade students in their home neighborhoods. Enhanced-option schools offer extra programs and resources not available elsewhere, including smaller classes (maximum size: 15), an on-site teacher for gifted students who also provides academic enrichment for all children, and an added 35 days in the school year. By 2000, three had opened (Glenn, Napier, and Park Avenue), with three others to follow (Bordeaux, Fall-Hamilton, and Warner).

With the capital costs of the new plan finally funded, the plaintiffs in the Metro desegregation case agreed to go hand-in-hand with the school board to seek "unitary status" from the federal court—meaning that all parties in the litigation were finally agreed, after 43 years of dispute, that the last vestiges of forced segregation and discrimination had been removed. Judge Thomas Wiseman granted the request on September 28, 1998.

Phil Bredesen may be best remembered now for bringing professional football and hockey to Nashville, but he deserves more credit—and may be remembered longer—for building libraries, and for focusing the community's attention on the public schools and winning support for them in the Metro Council. The school system didn't gain full funding on his watch, but it made greater strides in the 1990s than ever before. Class sizes were reduced in the lower grades, and when the current five-year building plan is finished, the system will have completed 76 building projects in a decade—32 new schools, 30 additions to existing buildings, and fourteen modernizations—at a total cost of $383 million, all during Bredesen's administration. (Unfortunately, more than 425 portable classrooms still dot school grounds citywide.)

Bredesen's efforts went beyond buildings and class sizes. He pushed the school board to develop an "accountability framework" that sets specific, measurable goals and objectives for academic achievement—although the consequences for not meeting the goals have yet to be spelled out. In a quick strike reflecting his top-down management style, Bredesen more or less forced the school board and teachers to adopt the core curriculum that outlines in very specific and sequential detail the knowledge and skills to be mastered at every grade level and in every school.

At first, teachers were very divided about the core curriculum's value. Some complained that it took away their creativity, or didn't allow them to proceed at their own pace, or covered topics in such a shallow way that the information would not be remembered. But many teachers became strong supporters of it, and so did parents who appreciated the content added to what had been primarily a skills-based curriculum. Parents also have liked getting a summary of what is being covered each six weeks in their children's classrooms (a component of the new approach). Differences of opinion on the curriculum no doubt still exist among teachers, but complaints are seldom heard about it now. Test scores have risen in each subject area since the curriculum was adopted.

So as Nashville entered the 21st century, things were looking up for Metro schools in many ways. Political leadership in the city appeared committed to strengthening the schools. In the 1999 city elections, Bredesen bowed to the term-limits law, and former state legislator Bill Purcell won the mayor's job. There was a big turnover in the council, too. Just four years earlier, education issues were barely visible in the mayoral and councilmanic races, but this time, candidates tried to outdo one another in voicing their commitment to public education.

What Bredesen started, Purcell was expected to continue. His campaign focused on restoring stability to neighborhoods and public schools. During his first year of office, Purcell made it a point to visit each of the 127 Metro schools (one of which his daughter attends). He asked former state Board of Education Chairman Nelson Andrews to head up an education advisory committee. In the summer of 2000, the mayor announced that the school system would be the first of all the Metro departments to undergo a performance audit conducted by professional consultants who will be expected to show what works

When Purcell moved into the mayor's office after his election in 1999, he quickly staked out the school system as his first priority. Purcell visited every school in the system during his first year in office. Warner Elementary (above) in East Nashville was his 50th stop on the list of 127.

Loretta Lynn, Earl Scruggs, Alan Jackson, Vince Gill, the Dixie Chicks, Kathy Mattea, Guy Clark, Dwight Yoakam, LeAnn Rimes, Lyle Lovett and Alison Krauss. The film is scheduled to open at Opry Mills' IMAX theater, a seven-story-tall venue, in June 2001. . . .

Claiming that the state death penalty system is "flawed and unjust," some 60 demonstrators at War Memorial Plaza demand a moratorium on executions in Tennessee. "When you look at the death penalty as it is used right now," says former state legislator Tommy Burnett, "it is a bludgeon used upon poor people, minorities and those who are mentally ill and mentally retarded." The protesters, clad in T-shirts emblazoned with slogans such as "Don't kill for me," wave posters reading, "What would Jesus do?"

18—**Beloved neighborhood activist** Fannie Williams, 107, is in critical condition after a fire at her Woodbine home. Williams, the granddaughter of slaves, has lived in the neighborhood since before it was called Woodbine, when it was known as Flat Rock. She founded the Woodbine Community Organization, and for generations new residents who wanted to help the neighborhood have been told to "go ask Miss Fannie" what to do. She has lived in the little white house at 2703 Fannie Williams St., since 1922. . . .

Local entrepreneur Herb Fritch and Baptist Hospital officials confirm that Fritch will acquire a 50-percent stake in HealthNet Management. Baptist Hospital currently owns 80 percent of the struggling HMO. A board member for four years, Fritch was named interim CEO of HealthNet early this summer. Once the deal goes through, Baptist will retain 30 percent of the HMO and St. Thomas Hospital will keep its 20 percent. HealthNet lost $3.5 million in 1999 and $1.3 million in the first quarter of 2000. . . .

Some 30 protesters picket the offices of WKRN-Channel 2 on Murfreesboro Road, voicing their outrage over the new TV show starring talk-radio scold Dr. Laura Schlessinger. Gay and lesbian activists across the country are calling for a boycott of the show because of Schlessinger's well-documented slurs against homosexuals, whom the conservative gab sister terms "deviants."

19—Sumner County Judge Jane Wheatcraft orders the state to get input from the widow of drowned Mexican migrant worker Emiliano Almaraz Monjaraz before she sentences farmer Galen Dean Eidson, who has pleaded guilty to reckless homicide. The widow lives in a remote Mexican village and speaks only her native Indian dialect. The widow's attorney says Mrs. Monjaraz believes the plea agreement between the state and Eidson is inadequate. . . . **Plans are now circulating** for an upscale urban village in the Five Points area of East Nashville. The prospectus, a product of redevelopment goals formulated after the destructive 1998 tornado, is being passed among community groups, designers and the Metro Development and Housing Agency.

20—**Big news** for Little Miss Dynamite. Brenda Lee, the petite but powerful vocalist who has maintained a successful career for more than four decades, has been nominated to the Rock and Roll Hall of Fame. Lee was inducted into the Country Music Hall of Fame in 1997. . . . **In an attempt** to reduce costs at its Spring Hill plant, Saturn offers incentives to 400 workers to leave the company. The automaker is also encouraging remaining workers to take educational and other leaves. . . . **As testimony continues** over the proposed State Route 840 loop through Williamson County, the judge, jurors, attorneys and witnesses visit a natural spring near Leiper's Fork to see firsthand the need for greater environmental considerations in the pristine area the road is scheduled to cut through.

21—**In a tribute** to Nashville's beloved radio station WSM-AM, a crane lifts a 70-foot tower to the top of the new Country Music Hall of Fame and Museum

and doesn't work in the schools. And in the fall, Purcell committed $55 million to the school system for a list of capital improvements he first presented to the Metro Council. This was a nuts-and-bolts fund for roof replacements, air conditioning repairs, modernized restrooms, an upgrade of the management computer system, a bid for compliance with the Americans with Disabilities Act, and other such infrastructure changes. Using the opening day of school in August to focus the city's attention on its schools, he stressed the importance of parental involvement and community support. Through public service announcements and media coverage, Purcell encouraged parents to actually come to school with their children on the first day, and he hosted a citywide party called First Day Festival at the Gaylord Entertainment Center. About 10,000 people turned out.

Another noteworthy political change that fosters hope for the future of Metro schools is a new spirit of cooperation between the mayor, the Metro Council, and the school board. Historically, there has been a built-in tension because of a "structural disconnect" among the three entities. The mayor recommends a city budget that includes funding for the schools, and the council decides how much to approve, but they have no say-so over how the money is spent; that's the exclusive prerogative of the elected school board. This system makes it easy for resentments and distrust to develop. For years, school board and council members seldom talked except at budget time, and that leadership vacuum was harmful to both bodies. The ill will seems to have subsided since Purcell's election, with all parties uniting around the common goal of ensuring that the schools are working well for everyone.

Through the stressful decades of transition and change for the Metro school system, the nine-member board of education has carried a heavy burden. When desegregation began in earnest 30 years ago, board members were appointed by the mayor. As this process proceeded, they came increasingly under attack. In 1981, some Bellevue residents, angry over the closing of their high school, started a petition drive calling for a referendum that would create an elected school board. It passed. With relatively few exceptions over the years, both appointed and elected school board members have devoted countless hours to an essentially thankless civic task that carries with it no pay except the satisfaction of performing a valuable public service. The community owes them a debt of gratitude that is seldom expressed or even acknowledged. Other factors bode well for Metro schools today. Over the past decade, the business community has increasingly recognized that its own success is linked to that of the public schools. The Nashville Area Chamber of Commerce has pledged its long-term commitment to improve schools. It has set an ambitious goal of achieving 100 percent student success by the year 2010, meaning that every student would graduate from high school prepared for a successful transition to a career or to further study. To help reach that goal, the chamber sponsors a citizens' panel that has produced an annual "Report Card" on Metro schools since 1993. The data-driven report highlights in great detail the areas of encouragement and concern in the school system, and the school board and its staff have responded positively to the panel's recommendations. The chamber also established a committee in 1998 to identify and support highly qualified school board candidates, and is taking a significant interest in the selection process for a new director of schools.

A number of other community groups are working to help the school system do its job. Project STARFISH, for example, began as a privately funded summer program for academically at-risk children in grades K-3 that is producing significant academic gains among the children who participate. Tying Nashville Together, the interfaith social action organization, is monitoring the system's pledge to meet stated standards of excellence and equity in resources, facilities, and staff at every school. Project GRAD, a partnership between Metro schools and Vanderbilt University, uses a multipronged approach to encourage Nashville's inner-city children to graduate from high school and get a college education. Tennessee State University's Center for Basic Skills has partnered with the school system for the past five years, preparing elementary teachers to use hands-on science kits for their class experiments. And a new group called Friends of Public Schools was organized in 2000 with the aim of informing the community about the strengths and needs of the public school system.

One of the greatest of the school system's strengths often goes unnoticed and unappreciated by the general public. In a word, it is people—individuals by the hundreds who quietly and selflessly share their excellence with others. Any Metro parent,

Alexine Hamby started Project SEE in 1991 to help children like 6-year-old Diamond Crowell learn to succeed in school. The philosophy of compensatory help for children who face numerous obstacles outside the classroom has long since proved its worth, though it is not a guarantor of success.

graduate, or current student can cite inspiring examples of dedicated principals, classroom teachers, librarians, coaches, and others in instructional and supportive roles who fit this description.

Student achievement is far more noteworthy than might be generally assumed from public opinion about school quality. We hear plenty about those who fail—nonreaders, flunk-outs, dropouts—but not enough about those who score near the top on SAT or ACT examinations and other national achievement tests, the winners of national scholarships, the students who win honors in music and art and theater, in science and mathematics, in business and technology. Others are demonstrating their excellence in government and public service, in productive off-campus work-study experiences, and in student-led campaigns against school violence or for social responsibility. Outstanding athletes tend to get their due when it comes to recognition and rewards; it is past time for others to be recognized—or at least for poorly informed critics of the public schools to acknowledge and applaud exemplary performance by thousands of Metro students.

Those who have stayed with the Nashville public schools through thick and thin—parents and their children, teachers and administrators, board members, taxpayers, politicians—have tried to keep the long-term health of this community, their home city, foremost in their minds. Perhaps that is the ultimate explanation of why the Nashville school system is still viable and vital after so many years of distraction and conflict: The institution retains the loyalty of many people with deep faith in its potential to become a model urban school system, if and when the city summons the collective will to achieve it.

The operative word here is "potential." We are fortunate to have had so many committed individuals whose aggregated talents, energy, and vision have kept the Metro school system afloat through decades of uncertainty and discouragement. It would be comforting to find now that the worst is over, and Nashville is poised on the brink of a great breakthrough in public education. But plenty of weaknesses and problems remain to be addressed.

building at the corner of Demonbreun and Fourth Avenue downtown. The tower resembles the radio station's tower, now in Franklin, which was the tallest in the nation when it was built in 1932. That 878-foot metal structure helped to make the Grand Ole Opry famous across the nation. . . . **Texas Gov. George W. Bush** stumps for the presidency at Vandyland Restaurant on West End Avenue, greeting a cherry-picked assortment of senior citizens. From there, he makes a beeline for a Belle Meade residence for a $10,000-a-plate dinner and a $1,000-per-person reception. Bush next goes to Florida for a weeklong blitz. Vice president Al Gore has not appeared locally in six weeks. . . . **Metro Codes officials** have issued warrants to Opry Mills and LoJac Safety Company for installing illegal road signs for the mall over McGavock Pike at Music Valley Drive. Neither LoJac nor Opry Mills secured Metro Council approval for the signs before putting them up. . . . **Gwendolyn Anthony,** who will be La Vergne's first black alderman if she wins the Oct. 3 election, says she has been both surprised and terrified by acts of vandalism and anonymous death threats, but the 14-year resident of the town vows not to be deterred from campaigning for the office. . . . **In a mediation hearing** here, Albert E. Brumley & Sons wins its lawsuit against rapper Sean "Puffy" Combs for royalties over the use of eight words from the gospel favorite "I'll Fly Away" in his 1997 Grammy-winning record "I'll Be Missing You." The Combs single, a tribute to the slain rapper the Notorious B.I.G., sold 11 million copies. At the statutory rate of 7.5 cents per sale, Brumley's piece of the action would come to about $800,000. "I'll Fly Away" was written by Albert Brumley while he picked cotton in 1929. . . . **The Metro fire department** is called to Douglas Corner Café when more than 200 fans crowd the 130-seat club to see a reunion show for The Ranch, the band once led by current country sensation and former Australian Keith

22—**In his first public admission** of guilt, former Franklin financier John A. Hackney pleads guilty to receiving more than $7 million over the past nine years from indicted accomplice Martin Frankel. Hackney, who has long been a respected member of the Williamson County community, says he helped Frankel steal more than $200 million from insurance companies, and he was the front man for several of Frankel's other schemes. Hackney, who now faces 20 years in prison and $750,000 in fines, was released without posting bond. . . . **Fest de Ville,** a new arts festival, opens today at the Tennessee Performing Arts Center downtown. Early estimates say the three-day festival, which features music, theater, opera and ballet, could bring in as many as 60,000 visitors. . . . **The waters** of a Mill Creek tributary stream look like étouffée, thanks to a cable-drilling effort that kills large numbers of crayfish. Metro Public Works orders workers installing fiber-optic cable under the stream to stop drilling when large numbers of the pincered freshwater delicacies turn up dead. A quarter-mile of the stream has turned gray from mud drilling and is filled with crayfish casualties. As more and more counties across Tennessee install fiber-optic cable, which has vastly greater capacities for information transmission, environmentalists worry the state's water quality and wildlife will suffer. . . . **State Finance Commissioner** Warren Neel tells state legislators that tax collections are well below estimates, with August collections down by $29 million. Neel notes that the state faces a $115-million shortfall by year's end. . . . **Following a downgrade** of its credit rating earlier this month, Nashville-based Shop At Home Inc. announces it will sell one of its six television stations at a substantial profit for $37.5 million. . . . **Expect to feel** this winter's chill in your wallet, as natural gas dis-

Too often, the system has been reluctant to push forward with creative approaches to problem-solving, bowing instead to defensive resistance from within. For example, Metro has been hesitant to empower its local schools, as some innovative districts have done, by allowing principals to manage their own budgets, hire their own staffs, and plan their faculty's professional development based on the needs of that particular school—and then be held accountable for results. That's what the independent "charter school" movement is really about, and Metro has personnel who are up to that challenge—but it appears that many administrators and teachers are not eager to venture into this new territory.

The central administration has always been reluctant to confront the weaknesses of principals, no matter how apparent their poor performance becomes. Principals have pull in the system; it's practically part of the job description. Seniority also gives them some support and protection, and some remain in place simply because of bureaucratic inertia. Ineffective or actively obstructive principals who destroy teacher morale are too often left in place or simply shuffled to another school, rather than weeded out.

Schools Director Bill Wise, working with Annette Eskind's foundation and Vanderbilt University's Peabody College, is setting up a leadership academy aimed at raising the skills of prospective and current principals. That is a good thing, but not enough in itself. The school system needs better methods of holding people accountable, whether they are in the classroom or the front office.

The administration also has been too slow in becoming a data-driven operation, and too quick to blame a lack of resources or outmoded technology for tasks done poorly or not at all. For example, data has been available for years from annual state reports indicating which schools are making good academic gains and which are not, but little has been done to examine the reasons and share the strategies of success. Gross inequities in performance among schools with similar student populations have been accepted without enough critical analysis of the causes. And, given the scores of textbooks and teaching materials, school improvement programs, new curricula and the like that Metro has introduced over the years, surprisingly little has been done to determine which actually produce the best academic results.

Teachers often are frustrated by demands imposed from above or by bureaucratic busywork required by administrators who tend to forget that they should be serving the teachers, not making their jobs more difficult. At the same time, teachers have problems of their own that need correcting. One is the "tyranny of low expectations" syndrome, which is rooted in the assumption that poor or minority children will do less well than affluent whites. The prejudgment becomes a self-fulfilling prophecy: expect less, get less. Good teachers—the majority—set high standards and push all their students to achieve them, but some teachers are content to simply get by and let their students do the same. These tend to be the same teachers who resist accountability and avoid opportunities to improve their own skills by learning new approaches to teaching or becoming more technologically savvy.

Another problem within the professional ranks has its roots in the great divide. Teachers and administrators who feel a strong commitment to the success of Metro schools have often felt demoralized by the consequences of white flight: declining test scores, loss of public support, and other related problems. For those who have stayed the course, it is especially dispiriting to see some of their own colleagues, in their role as parents, contribute to the problem by taking their children out of Metro. This is not an infrequent occurrence, and it provides a certain vindication to others, such as the private school parent who remarked, "Why should I eat at a restaurant where the cook won't eat the food?"

The local teachers' union, MNEA (Metropolitan Nashville Educators Association), has its own challenges to overcome. The organization's leaders won no friends when they refused to endorse the 1998 tax increase for schools, presumably because there was no money in it for teacher salaries. (The average Metro teacher's salary that year was close to $40,000—about 13 percent above the average for the Southeastern states.) At a time when the national teachers' organizations are promoting progressive ideas such as peer review (which the local group has not embraced), some longtime observers see the MNEA as a stumbling block to progress in the system. Classroom

Contract negotiations between the local teachers union (MNEA) and the school board are always intense but seldom hostile. Strikes are rare, though the MNEA did vote in 1998 to "work to the rule" (limit members' extracurricular duties) as part of its campaign for a major salary boost.

teachers alone should not bear total responsibility for the success of those in their charge, but demonstrable ineffectiveness cannot be supported. The MNEA developed a PALS (Peer Assistance Leadership and Support) program, which provides paid mentors to new teachers or those having difficulty, but there will never be enough funding to hire the number of such reinforcements required in a system this large. Another approach is needed.

At the same time, the school system and its teachers are facing new challenges in a city and society caught up in rapid and constant change. Twenty years ago, classroom teachers didn't have special education students in their classes, or children who couldn't speak English. The mainstreaming of children with mental and physical handicaps and the growing influx of immigrants have placed unprecedented demands on our teachers. Nashville, like the rest of the nation, has too many broken families, too many parents working extra jobs to make ends meet, too many latchkey children left to fend for themselves, too many families in crisis because of drugs or violence (and not all, by any means, in the inner-city slums, as witness the rash of suburban school shootings elsewhere). Children from these environments bring their troubles to schools where too few counselors and support personnel are available to assist them, and too few parents are volunteering. It's an all-too-familiar picture for teachers and principals who must deal with social and behavioral problems on a daily basis before they even get to the task of teaching.

I once knew an education writer who spent an entire year disguised as a public high school student in order to write a series of stories based on the hard realities of life there. Afterward he urged the rest of us at a national conference to spend more time inside the schools. I still remember his sobering conclusion. "We are chronicling the decline of a nation," he said, "and nowhere is it more evident than in our schools."

Nashville, no less than other American cities, is trying to prepare its children to make their mark in a society that seems at times to be spinning out of control. The dominant culture is driven by instant gratification and constant entertainment; schools must compete with television, music videos, cell phones, computers, virtual reality, sex and violence, cars, guns, drugs. Athletic success is more highly valued (and rewarded)

tributors prepare to pass on higher costs to customers. A Nashville Gas spokesman tells the city to expect winter heating bills to be at least 30 percent higher this year.

23—**Carl Rowan**, 75, the nationally syndicated columnist and longtime advocate for press freedom and racial equality, dies early this morning. A nominee for the Pulitzer Prize in 1995 and the author of seven books, Rowan was born in Warren County and raised in extreme poverty in McMinnville. While mopping floors at a tuberculosis hospital to earn money to attend Tennessee State University, Rowan won a national competition that led to his becoming one of the first 15 African-American commissioned officers in the U.S. Navy during World War II. He served in two presidential administrations: as deputy secretary of state for John F. Kennedy, and as director of the U.S. Information Agency under Lyndon B. Johnson. A trustee of the Freedom Forum, Rowan raised more than $79 million to help African-American students attend college. . . . **Heather Henderson** and Chris Neighbours marry tonight—with the assistance of 18 graduates of Henderson's Goodpasture Christian School kindergarten class. Dressed in white-satin dresses and tiny tuxedos, the children, now first-graders, participated in the ceremony at Madison Church of Christ. . . . **About 60 volunteers** gather at St. Vincent De Paul Church and fan out across North Nashville, documenting the condition of area neighborhoods. Sponsored by Tying Nashville Together, the Neighborhood Resource Center and Nashville Neighborhood Alliance, the audit will be used to ensure that city leaders get solid documentation of the conditions of specific neighborhoods. The volunteers note abandoned vehicles, vacant buildings, overgrown lots and trash piles. Over the next three weekends, volunteers hope to document conditions in all Nashville neighborhoods.
. . . **Three high-school boys** are

charged in the beating death of a middle-aged man on an East Nashville street corner. The teenagers claim that 51-year-old Salvador Perez was chasing a 15-year-old girl and her friend down the street, asking for sex. The boys got into an altercation with Perez after he allegedly threatened them with a knife. One boy hit him with a four-by-four board; another threw bricks at him. Perez died of blunt-force injuries to the head.

24—This morning's *Tennessean* features retired teacher Alexine Hamby, founder of Project SEE (Support, Education, Empowerment). Hamby, 76, has spent the last nine years building the after-school project to help children in the Cumberland View public-housing project realize their potential. Between 60 and 80 children are provided with tutoring, personal encouragement and food each day. . . . **Fest de Ville** concludes its three-day celebration with a tribute to legendary musician and singer/songwriter John Hartford, 62. More than a dozen artists perform songs in Hartford's honor, celebrating his artistry as well as his survival of a 15-year battle with cancer. Hartford's "Gentle on My Mind" remains one of the most recorded country music songs in history.

25—A robber in a gorilla mask shoots Metro police officer Linda Massengale in the thigh during a robbery at a Walgreens drug store on Clarksville Pike. At about 4:15 a.m., two Halloween-masked robbers burst through the door while another two wait outside; the gorilla-masked robber shoots Massengale almost immediately. Massengale, a 20-year veteran whose response to the surprise attack and its aftermath is calm and controlled, is in stable condition. The four robbers remain at large. . . . **Mayor Bill Purcell** names Bill Phillips, his former chief of staff, to the newly created post of deputy mayor. In Purcell's attempt to create a more corporate structure for city goverment, Phillips is now Purcell's stand-in, speaking for him and handling

than academic achievement. In the absence of strong families and supportive communities, the influence of peers increases. And yet, few voices are heard asking what we as a city can do to help nurture an environment that will support the teachers on whose shoulders we are placing such heavy demands.

Unlike many large cities where public schools have essentially become agencies for the warehousing of poor children, Nashville has a school system that remains racially diverse and where many good things are happening. The movement back in the direction of neighborhood schools offers greater freedom but an even greater responsibility. Nashville should not accept a return to school segregation by race or economic class. At the very least, it should be vigilant to ensure that schools in poorer neighborhoods get the resources they need to provide high-quality education, especially when our long period of economic prosperity ends. As we enter the new century, Nashville public schools have good support from the mayor and council. The schools are in the hands of a school board that appears productively engaged in trying to make schools more effective. A new plan is in place that can hold teachers and principals accountable, and stiffer promotion and retention policies have been implemented. The School Improvement Plan provides opportunity for more parental involvement, particularly for parents in the inner city.

In addition, more public information than ever before is available to help parents and citizens identify what is working well and what is not—school by school, and in the system as a whole. The State of Tennessee's annual report on every school shows not only the students' actual levels of achievement compared to their peers nationwide, but also how much they have gained from one year to the next in comparison to the national average gain on standardized tests. The very detailed annual review conducted by a citizens panel of the Nashville Area Chamber of Commerce is also a valuable yardstick, and so is the performance audit of the school system ordered by Mayor Purcell. The 2001 audit report should provide a detailed road map for the city to follow in its quest for a model urban school system. What such a model would look like is not yet clear. There appears to be no strategic plan that identifies where the school system is going and how it is going to get there—another major wrinkle to be ironed out.

These reports for 2000 present a mixed picture of the performance of Metro schools, with some areas showing improvement and others not. This year's data, for example, shows the dropout rate continuing to decline—reaching an all-time low of 16 percent, down from 22 percent two years before. Average achievement scores for third-grade math rose from 49 for the past two years to 56, compared to a national average of 50. The percent of students scoring competent or better on the writing assessments also rose significantly at all three grade levels tested: 64 percent of fourth graders, for example, scored competent or better, compared to 42 percent three years ago. Metro students are making greater academic gains than most of their peers across the nation but still lag behind state and national achievement averages on most measures. The gaps between rich-poor and white-nonwhite continue unabated. The combination of lower achievement and higher gains suggests that the students, half of whom come from low-income families, are coming to school without a good preparation for learning, but teachers are doing a good job of bringing them up to par. Are the gains great enough to catch us up completely? That is the challenge that still must be met.

In October 2000, the Nashville Area Chamber of Commerce brought the superintendent of the Seattle public schools to Nashville to explain the changes taking place in his city. Nashville business and community leaders had visited Seattle in the spring and were impressed by the dynamic profile they found there. A primary feature in that city is a "choice" system that allows all parents to select the public school or schools their children will attend, with transportation provided (subject to certain restrictions). A varying amount of money, depending on the child's background and handicapping condition

Surrounded by about half of the 40,000 achievement-test score sheets generated by students in grades one through eight during 2000, Metro testing and evaluation specialists Paul Changas (left) and Jim Schwarz prepare to sort the piles and send the scores out to the schools for distribution to the children.

(if any), follows the child to his/her chosen school.

Nashville parents already have many more choices than ever before. There are now eleven magnet schools drawing some 5,000 students, with more options on the way, and some of the enhanced-option elementary schools also provide an element of choice. But as yet, an open-choice system such as Seattle's has not been seriously considered here.

Whether or not a choice plan or any other new option becomes a part of Nashville's educational landscape will likely depend on the leadership that emerges under the new director of schools, following the retirement of Bill Wise. Many interested parties will be watching the school board closely as it moves into this new era. Good leadership will be essential to the success of Nashville's public schools in the coming years. The school system and the city need a strong leader who can work with the mayor and council, build confidence in and commitment to the public schools, articulate a vision and bring it to fulfillment, and make tough but necessary personnel and programmatic decisions. That's a tall order—for the new leader, the school system, and the city.

daily interactions between the mayor's staff and city departments. Vice Mayor Ronnie Steine remains second in line and would take over the mayor's duties should anything happen to Purcell. . . . **At the Olympic games** in Australia, Team U.S.A. wins the gold medal in women's softball when Middle Tennessee girls' softball instructor Jennifer McFalls scores the winning run in the championship game.

26—**The Nashville Predators** play a free preseason game for kids only. Metro students in grades 5-8 were invited last month to the special game, but the 17,000-seat arena isn't large enough to hold the 22,000 students invited, so those schools who requested tickets late are instead getting vouchers to attend a regular-season game for free. The Predators made the mistake of assuming not everyone would want tickets to the free event—but it turned out everyone did. . . . **Metro School Board** members approve a final budget, tacking on $128,000 to a dry textbook fund to ensure that hundreds of Metro students who don't have textbooks get them. But the $407.6-million budget still doesn't cover the cost of new textbooks needed for thousands of students taking vocational business, art and music classes, who must contend with six-year-old books despite plans to replace them this year.

27—**Dell Computer Corp.** executives announce at a ribbon-cutting ceremony for the Nashville location that the company is well ahead of its projected output and employment for its new Nashville and Lebanon plants. The Nashville plant, with 1,800 employees, has been operating since June, while the Lebanon plant, with 1,000 employees, opened its doors in August 1999. . . . **East Nashville residents** are pleased when the Tennessee Health Facilities Commission rejects a bid to locate in their neighborhood a methadone clinic for recovering drug addicts. Instead of opening the Center for

Not long ago, I watched *Remember the Titans*, a currently popular film based on a true story that unfolded in 1971, as a high school football team in Virginia grappled with the tensions that accompanied the school's first year of busing and desegregation. Similar challenges faced the Nashville schools as they moved through that same difficult year. My children had not yet started school then, but they were enrolled before all the dust had settled. As I watched the movie, I felt thankful that my own family had participated in this powerful and historic process that has moved the nation forward in significant ways.

In the movie, the team and its coaches found a way to come together in spite of their differences, gradually learning to respect each other as they united in the common mission of achieving victory on the football field. And they did achieve, going all the way to the state championship in their division. It is easy to imagine—it is, in fact, implicit in the film—that the internal challenges they faced and overcame together actually made them stronger and gave them a competitive edge.

The heart of the story, captured in the title, is a message of inspiration for us all: Remember the Titans (practically everyone around Nashville could rally to that). Remember the benefits and virtues of overcoming adversity, finding strength in unity, discovering that the whole is greater than the sum of its parts. Remember the Titans expresses an age-old wisdom, a universal truth. We find it embodied in such all-American mottos as "United we stand, divided we fall" and *E pluribus unum*: Out of many, one.

In this city, we have been divided over public school issues for the past half-century. We haven't found an equitable way to unite under the common banner of

Behavioral Health, which would have been Nashville's second methadone clinic, commission members will move the city's existing clinic, the for-profit Middle Tennessee Treatment Center, to larger offices on Charlotte Pike, putting it closer to local hospitals and businesses. . . . **Former Franklin financier** John A. Hackney pleads guilty to more charges in relation to his decade-long ties to indicted financier Martin Frankel. According to state prosecutors, Hackney helped Frankel bilk Tennesseans out of more than $17 million.

28—**The director** of the Tennessee Human Rights Commission, Julius Sloss, is himself charged with discrimination by the federal Equal Employment Opportunity Commission, which says Sloss and the THRC have unfairly favored whites over African-American employees. An investigation began in early spring after one of Sloss' Memphis investigators, Patricia Batts, lodged a complaint with the EEOC. Sloss, an African-American, filed an appeal last week. The THRC investigates allegations of discrimination in employment and housing. . . . **The pregnancy rate** among state teens dropped 8.8 percent last year, according to figures announced by Gov. Don Sundquist. The significant decrease gives the state its lowest teen pregnancy rate since 1975, when the state Department of Health began keeping records. Even so, "one out of every 20 babies born in Tennessee is born to a mother who's not even qualified to register to vote," says Sundquist, which means "we still have a lot of work to do.". . . **Emergency workers** participate in a disaster drill at the Adelphia Coliseum to evaluate Nashville's readiness to respond to a terrorist attack by biological or chemical weapons. . . . **Plans to turn** the historic Shelby Avenue Bridge between downtown and East Nashville into a pedestrian thoroughfare are under way, thanks to a money swap. Gov. Don Sundquist and Nashville Mayor Bill Purcell jointly announce the

providing an excellent education for all our children. Instead, individualism (a hallmark of American culture for ages) prompted a mass exodus from the public schools and created in the process a two-tiered educational system—one a well-supported private network for the more advantaged families, the other an often-ignored public structure for the rest of the city's children.

In 1999, the chamber-sponsored citizen's panel that evaluates the Metro school system every year decided to give the community itself a grade on its support of the schools. The grade chosen was "Incomplete," with the following explanation: "The majority want Nashville to have world-class school buildings, comparable to our new sports facilities—but few have stepped forward to support additional funding for equipping and staffing our buildings to achieve better student results. . . . General public apathy and skepticism about public schools continue to create barriers to the kind of fully engaged and supportive community necessary to develop and sustain a truly world-class school system."

As we enter the new century, Nashville is at a turning point. Will we become engaged as a community in a united effort to ensure that all schools provide excellent opportunities for all children? Will our political and civic leaders accept this challenge as the community's highest priority and do whatever it takes to accomplish the goal? Will we, as a people, turn in that direction ourselves?

It won't necessarily be the easiest path to take. Inevitably, conflicts will arise as people with different views try to influence the many decisions that will have to be made. These are a few:

• Who should be in charge of educating our children? What powers should be given to the school board, the mayor, the parents? Should we establish independent charter schools, or create a system that brings competition and even free enterprise into the educational arena?

• How should education be funded? What can we do to ensure that every school has the resources it needs to provide the fullest and most complete education for its students?

• What should the school calendar look like? Should we extend the school year, or require more time in school for those students who need it? And what should be included in the curriculum? Should all teachers have to be certified? Again, who should make these decisions?

• What teaching strategies should be used? Should traditional approaches replace the more progressive methods that have dominated the classroom for decades? How can we harness the potential of technology to transform our schools? And how can we make sure our children's teachers are up to the task of doing what is needed?

• What accountability systems should be put into place? What standards must be met, and what should happen if schools or students do not meet those standards? Should they be held back or promoted? Should there be alternative schools for them?

Such questions should elicit thoughtful and provocative debate, not just among those seated at the school board table but throughout the community. Yes, there will be strong differences of opinion, but it is a healthy community that can acknowledge its differences and move beyond to find common ground.

A big part of me remains optimistic that I will see Nashville become the community I always hoped for—a city that is known for its excellent schools. This could well be a more favorable time than ever before for such advances to be made. From the local to the national level, improved public education is high on almost everyone's list of priorities. The Nashville school system has a good foundation upon which to build. What is needed now is an unequivocal public commitment to the task—a willingness

Alex Green Elementary third-grader Sharae Cockrill had a lot to smile about after she was chosen state handwriting champion and invited to participate in the 2000 National Handwriting Competition.

to embrace the Children's Defense Fund motto (recently adopted by President Bush): "leave no child behind."

Nothing could strengthen our sense of community more than a vital, stable public education system for Nashville. Idealistically, it's the right thing to do for the children of the next generation—but there are many other very pragmatic reasons as well. Effective and productive schools will sustain our economic strength by enabling us to attract new businesses that are drawn to cities with an educated workforce. Education also raises the level of culture in the community, making it a more interesting and stimulating place to live. And finally, well-educated children, who sense the love of their community, are more apt to become the kind of citizens, neighbors, and coworkers we can all proudly claim as fellow Nashvillians.

Perhaps former Director of Schools Charles Frazier said it best: "I used to think that the best thing I could do for my child was to provide him with the best education possible. I now think that the best thing I can do for my child is to provide my neighbor's child with the best education possible."

exchange of $6 million in federal highway funds, which can't be used for the bridge, for $6 million in state transportation money, which can. The more flexible state funds will move the bridge project toward its goal of opening as a walkway by 2002.

29—**Judge Jane Wheatcraft** sends Cottontown farmer Galen Dean Eidson to prison for reckless homicide in the drowning death of migrant worker Emiliano Almaraz Monjaraz. Citing Eidson's repeated lies and lack of remorse for the killing, and noting that Monjaraz leaves a widow and four fatherless children, Wheatcraft offers no leniency, giving Eidson four years, the maximum sentence under the charge. . . . **Nashville artist Michael Aurbach** will be the first local artist to open a solo show at the Frist Center for the Visual Arts. Aurbach's installation "The Administrator" will be part of the center's grand opening in April 2001 and will run through August. Aurbach, who teaches at Vanderbilt University, was chosen from among nearly 150 artists from across the nation who submitted proposals. . . . **Belmont University's** new president, Robert C. Fisher, announces during his inauguration today the establishment of a new affirmative-action hiring plan to bring greater diversity to the mostly white campus. Currently, just four of 200 professors are minorities. Fisher, who has actually been on the job for six months, notes that a similar hiring plan was beneficial at Arkansas State University, where he last worked.

30—**Rosh Hashanah begins.** The Temple celebrates its 150th anniversary beginning with tonight's Jewish New Year. With more than 900 families, The Temple, located on Harding Road, is Nashville's oldest and largest Jewish congregation. . . . **Meanwhile,** Nashville's pagan community celebrates the autumn harvest with a ritual thanksgiving as part of Pagan Awareness Day at Two Rivers Park.

If I Had a Magic Wand. . . .

by Lamar Alexander

Lamar Alexander was governor of Tennessee from 1979 to 1987. He subsequently served as president of the University of Tennessee and as the U.S. Secretary of Education. In 1996 and 2000, he sought the Republican nomination for President of the United States. These are some of his thoughts and ideas for improving the public schools in Nashville, where he now lives.

Let parents choose the best public schools for their children.

Each January, the Metro Board of Education should ask all parents to list their first three school choices for the next year, and then do its best to honor the parents' requests. Nashville's experience with magnet schools (which have waiting lists) and nonpublic schools shows that parents who choose a school are more apt to be involved in their child's education. Parental involvement is the single most important predictor of a child's academic success.

If such school choices were allowed, my guess is that most parents would choose the same school their child now attends. If not, my guess is that most parents' choices could be accommodated more easily than perpetuating the byzantine zoning system we now have. As for transportation, in the 1980s Memphis was able to introduce a broad public school choice program that offered every child a ride and saved $2 million annually, money that was shifted to the classroom. Of course, some schools will stick out as schools too few want to attend. If so, then why should my child or yours be made to go there? Fix it or close it. Nothing is more offensive than reading that some Metro parents have violated the law by trying to get their child into a better public school. Metro is already moving to reinstitute the neighborhood schools that busing destroyed. Explicitly offering every parent a choice of schools would speed that process and build new support for public schools.

Having the best schools is, in concept, very simple: A great school has high standards in an environment that values education, involves parents, and attracts the best teachers. It can happen anywhere—in an independent school in northwest Nashville, a 100-year-old downtown building, or a suburban public high school with children of 30 different nationalities.

Pay good teachers a lot more.

In 1984, Tennessee became the first state to pay good teachers more for teaching well. Almost every teacher received a 20 percent increase in the state share of their pay, and the best teachers were offered up to a 70 percent increase. Eventually, 10,000 Tennessee teachers (1,100 of them in Metro Nashville schools) earned the Master Teacher honor and with it extra pay and a more generous retirement plan. If the teachers union had spent as much time trying to improve this career ladder program as it did to kill it, Tennessee teachers would today be among the best and best-paid in the country. Tennessee should reinstate the career ladder. That would be much easier now because it could be based upon the National Board of Professional Teaching Certification process to which the unions have agreed. While twenty states are paying annual salary increases of up to $10,000 for teachers who become board certified, Tennessee is adding no new teachers to the career ladder. Reinstating the plan could also incorporate the state's new "value-added" testing, which measures how much children learn from year to year.

Get rid of most of the school overhead and paperwork.

The way to do this, over time, is to make every Metro school a charter school. Charter schools are public schools with fewer government rules and union regulations. They are based on the presumption that the faculty has enough good judgment to decide what helps children learn. The new annual school-by-school achievement report card will tell us if the faculty is succeeding. Almost every state except Tennessee now has charter schools. In the presidential race of 2000, Governor Bush and Vice President Gore competed to see who could be the strongest advocate of charter schools. Yet, ironically, again it is the teachers' union that is blocking legislative efforts to give its own members more freedom to use their good judgment about how to educate children in our state.

Why were there so many Cs, Ds, and Fs on Metro's school-by-school achievement report cards in 1999-2000? And why is it so hard to make the common-sense changes that would improve these marks? The blunt answers are that parents are too busy, teacher unions are unreasonable about keeping control, and administrators are reluctant to change.

Tennessee's academic standards are among the nation's best. Our summer schools for gifted students are nationally admired. We're among the nation's leaders in connecting students to the internet. Using that same network, we can lead the nation in helping busy parents become more involved in their children's education. We still pay more teachers more for teaching well than any other state (even though we are adding no new master teachers). What remains to be done is frustratingly simple: give parents a real choice of schools, pay the best teachers more, get rid of most of the overhead and paperwork, and let teachers and principals use their own professional judgment to help our children succeed. Nashville could do nothing more effective to make this a better place to live than taking these steps to create the best schools for our children.

Welcome to the Virtual Campus

by RICHARD G. RHODA

The traditional notion of a college experience presupposes a campus, a library, classrooms and lecture halls, athletic and cultural events, student social life. Most of us could not imagine earning a degree without spending some time in residence and forming lasting personal relationships with a variety of classmates and professors. Sone would even argue that the social and cultural experiences, more than the things we learn in classrooms and laboratories, come closest to capturing the essence of an undergraduate education.

If you are among the fortunate minority of Americans (about 1 in every 4) and Tennesseans (1 in 6) who have completed a bachelor's or higher degree, the odds are astronomical that your time as a college student included most or all of the experiences described above. In all probability, your choice of a college was based on a wide range of cultural characteristics that combined to give the institution its identity and made it attractive to you. Those would include academic standards, emphasis, style, and quality, but many other extracurricular aspects as well, such as location, facilities, housing, student profile, athletics, affiliation (public, private, religious), and special features (music, employment opportunities, advanced degree programs and the like).

Higher education in Nashville has provided an important dimension of community life since early in the city's history. There are about fifteen institutions of higher learning here now that have been serving students at least since the post-World War II period (a third of them since the post-Civil War era), and in the aggregate they enroll close to 30,000 students. These facts help to explain why Nashville's reputation is based in part on its academic image.

This picture is certain to change dramatically in the near future. As the technological revolution accelerates, the traditional definition of higher education is expanding to connect with a much more diverse and dispersed student population. People for whom the campus experience has been neither an option nor an interest are rapidly going via the internet to visit websites that in time will open the minds of scholars and the libraries and laboratories of the world to anyone with a literate and intuitive command of the keys to the information kingdom.

The current 21st-century buzz word in higher education is "distance learning." In essence, it's all about transmitting information through a variety of media to and from widely separated parties—a professor in a campus lecture hall, for example, and an infinite number of students at their computers anywhere in the world. Through these forms of visual and verbal communication, a "virtual" college emerges—not the same as the ones we attended in times past, but a new entity capable of providing much the same informational and intellectual content.

Much of the enabling technology for online distance-learning classes is already in use here in Nashville, across Tennessee, and throughout the country—even in some remote corners of the world. Students can register for courses by telephone or the internet. They can call up library materials, watch and listen to lectures, take tests via e-mail, engage in interactive communication with teachers, join in class discussions—and arrange all of these to suit a clock and calendar of convenience or necessity. The virtual college, like the modern drugstore or grocery, is open all the time.

So much about this brave new technological world is truly exciting and filled with promise. The ever-increasing flexibility, convenience, variety, and speed of the internet should make higher education accessible to a far greater segment of the population at a reduced cost—and both of these changes will surely benefit any democratic society striving to make equal opportunity a reality. Furthermore, for rising generations of young citizens growing up in an internet-connected world, the electronic media will seem like natural extensions of their hands and ears and eyes, just as television, radio, and the telephone did to us, their elders.

The excitement comes from thinking about what tremendous new opportunities there will be for earning a college education. The possibilities truly are boundless, as infinitely elastic as our imagination and our vision. But as with all revolutionary changes, from the discovery of fire to the invention of the combustion engine to the development of computers, there is always a tradeoff, another side to the newly minted coin. Several such possibilities suggest themselves now; they lie along the distant horizon like storm systems, blinking with little flashes of lightning and muffled thunder. These are a few that could someday rain on our parade:

• Distance learning may worsen the growing sense of isolation that so many people experience in modern society. This feeling is heightened at present by two forces pulling in opposite directions. One is the phenomenon of "electronic obsession" that keeps millions of people glued to their terminals. The other is "electronic avoidance," seen especially among older citizens who, for a variety of reasons, are unable to get aboard the electronic rocket. Isolation is a common symptom of both—the one set apart by too much exposure, the other by not enough.

• Although technology is making possible some economies of scale by constantly increasing the universe of users, there looms the possibility that those who control information systems will become gatekeepers regulating the tolls of users. Information is power—and absolute power, as history has taught us, is a force to be dreaded.

• Finally, there is still no substitute for human interaction—and perhaps no more productive place to nurture it than on a college campus. So many intellectual and social possibilities blossom in that environment, and most of them cannot be replicated on a computer screen. As long as life is sustainable on the planet, there will be a central place for colleges and universities such as we proudly claim as our own here in Nashville.

Rich Rhoda is executive director of the Tennessee Higher Education Commission.

Words and Music

by SUSAN FORD WILTSHIRE

As he works along on his creations, such as the monumental Athena in the Parthenon, sculptor Alan LeQuire feels a certain kinship with the songwriters of his native Nashville. "Songwriters tell stories," he explained. "So do I, in another medium. We both deal in narratives. Nashville hasn't always had a strong visual arts community, but it has long been full of poets and pickers and storytellers. You can't live here without feeling the influence of their art."

Indeed, you can't. Thousands of people in this city of words and music must fantasize about harnessing the power of words to do their will on the printed page or in the narrow confines of a haunting ballad. And hundreds of those creative dreamers succeed, at least to the extent that their words are published or recorded.

Stories are privileged conversation in Nashville, and words are the preferred currency. Lots of people around here love to write. Many more love to make music, both instrumentally and with words. And of course everyone loves to talk, and some—lawyers, teachers, actors, politicians, preachers, waitresses, auctioneers—are really good at it. A confluence of reasons helps to account for this unusual profile: history and geography; a large and varied establishment of religious and educational institutions; the music industry; and, not least, a vast economic infrastructure that has grown up to support them all—an integrated network for the creation, production, printing, recording, and distribution of words and music.

Nashville's first settlers were remarkably literate. Only one of the 256 signatories of the Cumberland Compact signed that founding document in 1780 with an "X" instead of his name. Mrs. Ann Johnston, sister of James Robertson, taught the children on the flatboats that brought the first settlers to Nashville. The civic narrative was enriched significantly by well-educated clergy who articulated the vision of a new Athens on the frontier. One of them, Philip Lindsley, turned down the presidency of Princeton University to come to Nashville in 1824 as president of the University of Nashville. Largely through his leadership, some twenty schools and colleges had been founded in Tennessee by midcentury.

Nashville has been a book town almost from the beginning. Twenty-two year-old John Buchanan produced Nashville's first book, a handmade arithmetic primer, in 1781, just two years after he arrived with the first party of settlers. John Inston opened the first bookshop here in 1811. Reuben Mills was just 18 years old when he opened his first store in 1892. For nearly a century, Mills Book Store was a beacon of enlightenment and a magnet for writers and book lovers, especially in the years after World War II, when it was run by Bernie Schweid and his wife, Adele, Reuben's daughter. The Zibart brothers, Carl and Alan, inherited the book business started by their father, Leon, and his brother, Sam, in a newsstand on Church Street in 1898. Until they sold the business in 1982, the Zibarts continually operated a string of shops that brought together devoted readers and dedicated writers. The Schweids and Zibarts loved and respected good books and the people who made them. It was in no small part due to them that Nashville gained a sterling reputation as a favorite port in the book trade. Ron Watson, a longtime associate of the Schweids and later owner of Mills Book Store, said many of the sales representatives who came calling from the publishing companies "told Mr. Schweid that Nashville was a better book town than Atlanta."

Libraries are another measure of a city's commitment to words in print, and here again, Nashville ranks high. The university libraries in the city are generally excellent. So, too, are the Tennessee State Library and Archives, the city's grand new downtown public library (plus its branches and the Metro Archives), and even the Country Music Foundation's new, state-of-the-art research library.

The founding of the Southern Festival of Books in Nashville illustrates the level of creative energy generated by collaborations of various book- and word-related individuals and groups. In 1986, Tennesseans celebrated a year-long homecoming that featured a literary conference of prominent writers with Tennessee roots. The event was so successful that a number of writers and book people came to believe that Nashville should establish an annual festival. The Tennessee Humanities Council joined this effort, and the first Southern Festival of Books was launched in 1989.

Ingram Book Company was vital to this initiative, and not only for its financial backing. From its modest origins as the Tennessee Book Company, founded in 1935, Ingram had grown into the largest book wholesaler in the country. Major publishers took a chance on sending representatives to a book festival in a town no larger than Nashville because they had reasons to please Ingram. Ingram had a complete working knowledge of the book chain; they understood that writers need publishers, publishers need distributors, distributors need bookstores, stores need avid readers. Without Ingram, the Southern Festival of Books would never have happened.

Books and words are never far out of reach in this city. The Nashville chapter of the Women's National Book Association is the largest and most active in the country. *BookPage*, a bimonthly tabloid review with a circulation of 500,000 to bookstores and libraries nationwide, was founded here in 1989 by Michael Zibart, son of the late Alan Zibart. Photographers, illustrators, designers, publishers, printers, binders, and others in more specialized subdivisions of the book industry are here in impressive numbers. Basic literacy programs for adults, children, immigrants, and others with special needs operate in schools, churches, libraries, and community centers all over the city. Here you will also find bookshops and booksellers specializing in new books, old books, religious books, children's books, and technical books. The city boasts professors who write and writers who teach; clergy who weekly put their faith into words; journalists who report and comment upon the words of the day; a multitude of librarians; and, of course, countless readers.

Informed reviewers help to develop and sustain the audience for books. John Seigenthaler hosts one of the longest-running book review/author interview television programs in the country, *A Word on Words*, produced locally by Nashville Public Television. Rebecca Bain's inspired interviews with authors on Nashville's public radio station WPLN attract a wide following.

Religious publishing has long been a major industry in Nashville. The United Methodist Publishing House, established here in 1854, operates the largest church-owned printing plant in the world. The Southern Baptists, National Baptists, and others are based in Nashville as well. Several men of my acquaintance worked their way through college selling Bibles door-to-door for the Southwestern Company. Warner Books opened a division here in July, 2000, choosing Nashville over Atlanta, Louisville, and other Southern cities because of the printers, publishers, and other agents here involved with the crossover between books and music.

Nashville's universities have contributed to the city's literary ferment, too. Author Arna Bontemps, one of the leading intellectuals of the Harlem Renaissance, was for many years a professor at Fisk University; James Weldon Johnson, famed for his contributions to both books and music, was another of Fisk's luminaries. The creative output of a handful of Vanderbilt University faculty and students who called themselves the Fugitives brought attention and some notoriety to the institution in the 1920s and '30s. In their circle was Robert Penn Warren, who was to become the first poet laureate of the United States and the only winner of Pulitzer Prizes in both fiction and poetry. Other celebrated Fugitive poets were Allen Tate, John Crowe Ransom, and Donald Davidson.

The music industry draws thousands of creative people to Nashville, and that fact alone explains why the largest and most successful colony of writers in Nashville is the community of songwriters. A well-known writer and performer lives a few doors up the street from me. My cobbler is a songwriter. So is the daughter of a woman I work with every day. A Vanderbilt Ph.D. who wrote his dissertation on Vergil's *Aeneid* makes a living writing songs on Music Row. Songwriter/storyteller Tom T. Hall writes novels and short stories as well as poems set to music. Poet/songwriter Tom House, newspaperman/musician Tommy Goldsmith, and singer/songwriter Dave Olney have collaborated in recent years on musical operas based closely on the works of William Faulkner, Lee Smith, and others. Another Nashville resident, former pro football player Mike Reid, has won favorable recognition in his post-athletic career as a composer. Songwriters Marty Stuart and Don Schlitz are writing scores for stage and screen, as the late Roger Miller did a generation ago.

The technology of capturing words in print is changing, and Nashville is a leader in fashioning that revolution. Lightning Source, an outgrowth of Ingram Book Company, is electronically reproducing single copies of books on demand, thus renewing the life of important volumes that have long since gone out of print. These so-called "e-books," or DRMs (digitally recorded materials) may be the wave of the future in book publishing.

The last of the big independent bookstores in Nashville was Davis-Kidd Booksellers, founded in 1980 by two local women, Karen Davis and Thelma Kidd. Their Green Hills-area stores became gathering places for readers and writers, in the tradition established by Mills and Zibart's years before. Now Davis-Kidd is also part of a chain (albeit a small one), in competition with the nationally prominent Barnes & Noble and Borders chains, both of which have built impressive outlets in greater Nashville.

The city's universities are becoming more fully integrated into the life of Nashville. A striking example is the 1995 agreement between Vanderbilt University Press and the Country Music Foundation to co-publish books about country music. It should come as no surprise that local colleges and universities have scholars who write books and graduates who later win recognition as writers—but probably few cities can claim as many doctors, lawyers, judges, and ministers who are published novelists, poets, and nonfiction writers.

The music of words rises far above a whisper in Nashville. It seems safe to predict that words will not only endure here; they will thrive and prosper, whether rendered on paper, in the electronic sphere, or on the wings of poetry put to music.

Susan Ford Wiltshire, professor of classics at Vanderbilt University, is the author of several works of scholarship, as well as fiction, poetry, and a family memoir, Seasons of Grief and Grace.

SING ME
BACK TO NASHVILLE

by BRUCE FEILER

O ctober is music month in Nashville—a time when Music Row bestows its annual songwriting laurels, the Country Music Association hosts its glittering prime-time gala, and the Grand Ole Opry celebrates its birthday. On October 14, 2000, both the country music industry and its hometown were aglow for a particularly nostalgic event: The Opry, Nashville's most beloved, most maligned, and, in many ways, most misunderstood institution, was stepping out in style on the 75th anniversary of its founding.

At just after six o'clock in the evening, dozens of music celebrities began making their way alongside the Opryland Hotel, up the avenue that once led to the Opryland theme park (now a sprawling shopping venue called Opry Mills), and into a side door of the newly refurbished Grand Ole Opry House. About 500 early-bird fans had gathered alongside the red-carpeted runway to greet their favorite artists— Dolly Parton, Reba McEntire, Travis Tritt, Trisha Yearwood, and others. Some of the superstars, including Garth Brooks, snuck around to the back entrance to avoid the fans, but most were accommodating, and a few of the older entertainers seemed surprised by all the attention. "I didn't know we were this hot," said Larry Gatlin with a smile.

Neither did anyone else. "I haven't seen these guys in 20 years," said announcer Keith Bilbrey of WSM radio, broadcasting live on the AM dial, and also on the internet. "It looks like the Oscars out here, with TV cameras, paparazzi, and press crews from around the world. Nashville is hot tonight!"

Backstage, the usual bustle of Opry nights was accentuated by scurrying camera-and-light crews from the CBS television network, which was taping the historic evening for broadcast as a two-hour special on Thanksgiving night. The white-tiled corridors were crowded with dignitaries, industry personnel, and hangers-on. Loretta Lynn breezed in wearing red jeans tucked into her red cowboy boots and a long, red-beaded coat that sported a "Bush-Cheney" button. She was followed by her twin daughters, Peggy and Patsy, the latter holding her 3-week-old baby—the coal miner's great-grandson. A pyramid of champagne bottles stood near the door, each bearing the label "Saluting Our Treasured Members During Our 75th Year" and the name of an Opry stalwart: Charley Pride . . . Skeeter Davis . . . Alan Jackson . . . Tom T. Hall . . . Ricky Skaggs . . . They all belonged to one of Nashville's most exclusive clubs: the official cast of the Grand Ole Opry, a total of 72 acts.

To the casual eye, the scene reflected a glitz, glamour, and international sex appeal that the founders of the Grand Ole Opry could not have dreamed would attend the genre called country music when they put it on a radio show in downtown Nashville in the autumn of 1925. Now, national magazine reporters were jostling with the camera crews, Hollywood makeup artists schmoozed with New York fashion designers, and performers who had sold 100 million records worked amiably alongside high-school tappers from the Melvin Sloan Dancers. The Opry was like a big family picnic with guests from all around the country—and from other countries, too.

Inside Dressing Room 5, Music Row's most visible honeymooners, Vince Gill and Amy Grant, were talking about Nashville's new international status. Recently married (after high-profile divorces), Vince

1—In ceremonies at the Vatican, the Pope canonizes Katherine Drexel, the Philadelphia heiress for whom Nashville's Drexel Street, between Seventh and Eighth avenues, is named. At the age of 30, Drexel took a vow of poverty using her $20-million inheritance to start an order of nuns, Sisters of the Blessed Sacrament. The order started schools for African Americans and Native Americans in several cities, including Nashville. Several Nashvillians, alumni of schools she founded here, attend the ceremonies.

and Amy had just announced they were having a baby. While Vince folded a crocheted baby blanket they had received as a gift, Amy told a reporter from *People* magazine that the two had been listening to the WSM broadcast on their way to the Opry House: "They were interviewing people about where they were from, and we heard everything from Pennsylvania to Montreal and Ireland. We both choked up. What a beautiful thing that people made a pilgrimage to this location on this night. It's really moving." Echoed Vince: "This place really symbolizes what country music is in its entirety—not just the flavor of the month and who's the most popular artist of today. You can see 60 years of country music history in one night. People that are still performing here have been here since the '40s, and it's just a magical place to be."

But for all the glorification of the Grand Ole Opry's remarkable status as the longest-running regular broadcast in the history of radio, and for all the heavy breathing about country music's supposed new globalism, the scene backstage at the Grand Ole Opry was also unsettling. It hinted at the deep fissures within the country music community, and at a crisis of cultural identity on its home turf, Nashville. The town's hottest new stars—Faith Hill, Shania Twain, the Dixie Chicks—had been shunned by the Opry because they were too sexy, too pop, too controversial, or all three. The breakout artists of the 1990s—the uninomynous Alan, Vince, Reba, and Garth—all seemed to be losing some of their clout. And the stars of the past—Little Jimmy Dickens, Porter Wagoner, Jean Shepard, Brenda Lee—were all but ignored by the "new country" generation. Nashville, too, was blasé. It had a practiced habit of not liking its new stars, not liking its old stars, not liking its wanna-be stars. After three-quarters of a century in the entertainment business, it seemed that Nashville didn't like stars at all.

Throughout its history, country music, like all forms of entertainment, has gone through periods of tension between its devotees of traditional styles (as presently personified by picker-singer Porter Wagoner, above) and its constantly evolving cast of experimentalists such as the Dixie Chicks, (facing page), winners of the Country Music Association's 2000 award for Album of the Year.

But, of course, it has always liked money, which is what brought the stars to Nashville in the first place, and what made the city fathers want them to stay. But this uneasy commercial alliance is one reason the two sides have never seemed to know quite what to do with each other. Country music, an entertainment form that has always had a keen sense of place, has always felt out of place in its own hometown.

And tonight was no exception. Just behind the Opry stage is a small waiting area where visitors can get a cup of pink lemonade from 82-year-old Rosa Mae Hodge, a 31-year veteran of the Opry, who sits in front of a plaque signed by President Richard Nixon on the night in 1973 when he opened the new facility and yo-yoed with Roy Acuff. Across from Rosa, a short, elderly woman was sitting by herself in a puffy, bright fuchsia dress with black polka dots. No camera crews tried to film her; no autograph-seekers asked for her signature. Wilma Lee Cooper is actually older than the Opry (she was born in 1921), and first performed on the show in January 1946, almost 30 years before it left the Ryman Auditorium downtown. "My knees were shaky, because I knew I was going on the stage where a lot of greats had been and a lot of greats still were," she recalled wistfully. She had worn a gingham stage dress that night. "Back then, you didn't have the kind you could wash and hang up to dry. You had to starch them all and iron them."

Like many, Wilma Lee was perplexed and concerned by all the recent changes in country music: "I don't like what I see. What I see is not real. The real country has last-ed 75 years. It won't go another 75 on this new music." And why not? "The new music is more like pop music. It's mechanical, not written from the heart. And anything that's mechanical like that fails in time. It's like a car: It can't keep going too long before it breaks down. I'd like to see them reject all this rock-and-roll stuff and go back to family

2—**The Tennessee Repertory Theatre** continues its superb production of *Wit*, Margaret Edson's Pulitzer Prize-winning play about a scholar facing the end of her terminal illness. The featured actor, Tandy Cronyn, is the daughter of Broadway legends Jessica Tandy and Hume Cronyn. Nashville is in the midst of its fall theater season: current offerings (with top ticket prices) include the Broadway touring company of *Les Miserables* ($57); *Smoke on the Mountain* ($30) at the Ryman Auditorium; Circle Players' production of *42nd Street* ($14) in TPAC's Johnson Theater; an adaptation of *The Hound of the Baskervilles* ($35) at Chaffin's Barn Dinner Theater; the Nashville Children's Theater production of *Trickster Tales* ($8.75); the Dark-horse Theater's presentation of

Pygmalion ($10); and *Backstage Pass* ($12), an evening of one-acts about stage life performed by the Razors Edge company, which occupies the small stage at the Nashville Music Institute on McMillan Street.

3—**Mayor Bill Purcell** shocks the Metro school board, but with good news. As part of the capital-improvement budget he will present tonight to the Metro Council, the mayor tells school board members he is recommending an unprecedented $55 million in school repairs, computer technology, new school buses and other improvements. The sum is part of a $170.8-million plan to shore up the city's infrastructure, including sidewalk repairs ($15 million), renovations to the Metro Court-house ($28.7 million) and reloca-tion of all General Sessions court-rooms to the nearby Ben West Building, which will be expanded to include a 100,000-square-foot addition on top of its parking garage ($14.9 million). "I've had to bite my tongue for a week," says Metro Schools Director Bill Wise. "I doubt there is a school system in America that can say it's about to fix all its roofs.". . . **As Israeli and Palestinian forces** clash in the Middle East, police arrest a woman who may be responsible for sending anti-Semitic, anti-Israeli notes to Nash-ville synagogues. Rebecca Hasan Obedala, 31, is arrested outside Sherith Israel Congregation on West End after she allegedly tells a woman picking up her child that she should die because she is a Jew. She is charged with assault by intimidation.

4—**A Lebanon resident** is at home watching television at about 10 p.m., when two men knock on his front door. After allegedly refusing to identify themselves, the armed men kick in the door. The resident goes for his shotgun, thinking his wife is being threatened and his home invaded. A minute later, John Adams, 64, lies mortally wounded on the floor—and Lebanon police officers discover that they have the wrong man. The man police

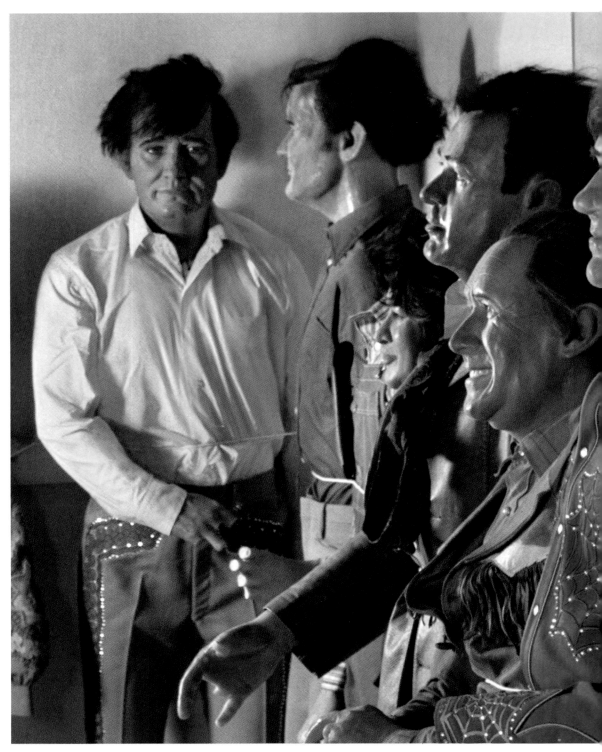

Eerily symbolic of the turn-of-the-century shelving of traditional country music by some media companies, dozens of wax images of country performers (including Bill Anderson, far end) fill a Music Row storeroom, waiting in suspended animation for a new home.

entertainment. If they do, they'll have people standing in line again." After a pause she added, "The Grand Ole Opry was a national treasure. Now it's a national disgrace."

After a few minutes, a stagehand came to summon her. She stood, straightened her dress, and prepared to take her turn in the lights. As she did, the stagehand re-marked that she was in the same half-hour segment as Garth Brooks. "Oops," she responded dryly, "I forgot to bring my rope swing." Then she put on her performer's smile and sashayed out onto the stage.

wanted, a suspected drug dealer, was at the house next door. Adams' friends and family are enraged. "They murdered my best friend," exclaims former Wilson County Commissioner Natchel Palmer. "It was a severe, costly mistake," says Lebanon Police Chief Billy Weeks, with considerable understatement. Officers Kyle Shedran and Greg Day are placed on paid administrative leave. . . . **Six-year-old Tzipora March's** fondest wish, expressed to Judge Aleta Trauger, is for her father, Perry, and his new wife, Carmen, to come to Nashville, so she can give them and her grandparents, Lawrence and Carolyn Levine, hugs at the same time. That will not be happening. Instead, in U.S. District Court, Judge Trauger orders the Levines to return March's two children to his home in Ajijic, Mexico. The children seem "relaxed" and "happy" after three months with the Levines, Judge Trauger writes in a 52-page opinion, but in the judge's chambers the children say they miss their father, stepmother and step-siblings. However, the Levines later obtain a ruling that they can keep the children while they appeal the decision. . . . **The Dixie Chicks** take the Country Music Association's top honor, Entertainer of the Year, at the CMA Awards ceremony at the Grand Ole Opry House. The Chicks also take home three other awards, including Album of the Year.

5—**The Tennessee Supreme Court** sets a new date, Jan. 31, 2001, for Death Row inmate Philip Workman's execution. . . . **In a deal that could boost** its revenue by more than $100 million a year, Ingram Entertainment Inc. becomes one of only three companies that will distribute videos for Universal Studios Home Video. La Vergne-based Ingram is already the world's largest distributor of home videos, with annual revenues of approximately $1.1 billion. Competitors worry that Ingram could wind up controlling 50 percent of the wholesale home-video market, and some of them are even dropping the

At the turn of the 21st century, country music was at its weakest point in more than a generation—its economic foundation cracking, its primary institutions wobbling, its basic purpose in question, its future direction unclear. Record sales, the industry's measuring stick, were down 20 percent from their peak in the mid-1990s. Radio listenership, the town's calling card, was down close to 40 percent. These two facts alone had deep repercussions in Nashville, and grave consequences for the entire industry. Because of declining record sales and corporate conglomeration, the number of record labels on Music Row, which had ballooned from single digits to over 30 in the boom

"A" word: antitrust. . . . **Dell Computer executives** forecast a rosy long-term outlook for the company, despite an anticipated drop in third-quarter earnings that has sent stock prices plunging. In five weeks, the computer company's stock has plummeted 42 percent, to a grim $25.19 a share. . . . **For lovers of traditional country music**, the week belongs not to the CMA but to WSM. The Air Castle of the South, WSM-AM, celebrates its 75th anniversary today with a marathon live broadcast from the Grand Ole Opry's sentimental homestead, the Ryman Auditorium. At 5 a.m., the broadcast kicks off with the very first artist and song WSM played in 1925: the Al Menah Shrine Brass Band performing the "Star-Spangled Banner." The day is devoted to on-air performances and reminiscences from Opry greats past and present, including Brenda Lee, Porter Wagoner, Charlie Louvin, Jack Greene, Earl Scruggs and Bill Carlisle. Also on hand are a gallery of personalities who gave the country station its warmth and homey rapport, including Ralph Emery, Tom Perryman, Teddy Bart and Jud Collins—who began his tenure with WSM in 1940. "WSM was important to everybody associated with it," says steel guitar great Don Helms, 73, who performed with Hank Williams on the Opry in August 1949. "It was the thing. Still is."

6—**On this day every year**, Fisk University pays tribute to the group that saved the school more than a century ago: the legendary Jubilee Singers, whose national tour in 1871 settled the school's debts, bought land for the campus, and built the university's Jubilee Hall. This Jubilee Day is doubly special, for it celebrates two of the university's most distinguished alumni: author W.E.B. Du Bois, and his Pulitzer Prize-winning biographer, David Levering Lewis. In his keynote address, Lewis, a 1956 Fisk graduate, reminds students of a speech Du Bois once made at Fisk in which he challenged school leaders' coziness with the white power

In the 1950s, two decades before leaving the Ryman Auditorium for the new Opry House, the Grand Ole Opry drew thousands of fans to its Fifth Avenue entrance every weekend.

years from 1989 through 1995, suddenly shrank to around eight again and appeared headed toward more consolidation. Sony Tree, one of the top songwriting factories in the industry, laid off half its staff.

The carnage didn't stop there. *New Country* magazine, *Music City News*, and *Country America* magazine all ceased publication within a couple of years of each other. Hundreds of country radio stations changed formats. Country television programs performed anemically. The 2000 Country Music Association Awards, broadcast in three-plus hours of prime time on CBS on October 4, drew a meager 17 million viewers, down a steep 25 percent from the year before—and the show's 1999 rating had set a new low. Perhaps even more frightening, cable television, which long had been Nashville's secret weapon, enabling the town to bypass hostile programmers in New York and Los Angeles, also seemed to be abandoning country music. In 1997, the Oklahoma-based Gaylord Entertainment Company (which had bought the Opry properties and WSM radio from the National Life and Accident Insurance Company fifteen years earlier), completely overturned its marketing strategy by closing the Opryland theme park in Nashville and selling its cable TV operations—The Nashville Network (TNN) and Country Music Television (CMT)—to CBS. Any hope that this deal would result in a bigger stage for country music on the nation's fiber-optic cables was quickly dashed. Once Gaylord sold its cable stations to CBS, the network promptly merged with Viacom, owners of MTV and VH-1. Music Row watched with horror as TNN, home of the weekly Opry broadcast, a nightly Nashville-themed talk show, and daily blocks of music videos, slowly whittled its country programming to almost nothing. In 2000, Viacom announced it was changing the name of the 17-year-old cable channel from The Nashville Network to The *National* Network—not quite what Music Row had in mind when it set out to become the home of "America's Music."

"It's bleak," said Luke Lewis, president of the Nashville division of Mercury Records, "and I don't see it getting any better. I've spent most of this year halfway out the window." The billion-dollar question on his mind, and on the minds of many people throughout the music industry, was simple and stark: Does country music have a future? Will it live for another 75 years?

Those lucky enough to get a seat inside delighted in performers such as comedienne Minnie Pearl and singer-guitar player Hank Snow.

These questions can best be answered by looking at the history of country music in Nashville. On the one hand, the industry's millennial downturn was different in degree but not in kind from the ebb and flow of country music over the past 75 years. Creative decisions (or, more accurately, *un*creative decisions) may have exaggerated the down periods, but the cyclical pattern is common in other styles of music, other parts of the entertainment business, and other areas of the general economy. Still, because country is the dominant form of music produced in Nashville, Music Row can't easily paper over its losses with profits from other genres that happen to be in vogue. As a result, the extremes of boom and bust appear to be more pronounced in Nashville—and have been for decades.

On the other hand, technological changes in American life, demographic changes in the population (as well as the performers), and changes in the nature of life in the South all suggest that Nashville may be in more than a cyclical downturn. Perhaps the nation has moved on and has less need for country music. In this scenario, Nashville and its music may be experiencing a more permanent ebbing of popularity.

The early history of country music can be told as a simple story—country comes to town. It's the story of rural Americans who left their agricultural roots for greater opportunities in the city, then used music as a way to preserve and reclaim what they'd left behind. The music that came to be called "country" was first assembled about a century ago from an eclectic array of sources, including Irish and Scottish string music, Mississippi blues, folk songs, Christian hymns (and, later, jazz and rock). At the time, few people considered any of this music more valuable than, say, nursery rhymes. By the 1920s, when the phonograph and the radio were being introduced into many homes, big-city businessmen gradually came to realize the financial potential for selling the music—and using the music to sell other products, such as mail-order goods and insurance.

The seminal moment in country music, known then as "old-time" or "hillbilly" music, occurred in August 1927 when Ralph Peer, an admittedly condescending carpetbagger from New York, recorded songs by the Carter Family and Mississippi crooner Jimmie Rodgers within days of each other in Bristol, Tennessee. Eventually this music found a home in the burgeoning new medium of commercial radio,

structure. The scholar and biographer also tells *The Tennessean* the school needs to shore up its endowment, possibly by selling some of the artwork in Fisk's famous collection. "It wouldn't be a felonious idea," Lewis says, "to sell one, two or three of those works of art in a seemly way to build up the resources of the institution.". . . ***Billboard*** **magazine's** internet site confirms one of Music Row's most persistent rumors: Garth Brooks and his wife, Sandy, are calling it quits after 14 years of marriage. "Right now, we're focusing on the impact it will have on our three children," Brooks tells reporter Melinda Newman, "and how to handle that best—to remain parents even if we don't remain husband and wife.". . . **Singer Michael English** gets three years' probation on 12 counts of fraudulently obtaining prescription painkillers for his own use. English, who rose to fame as a contemporary-Christian vocalist, became addicted after surgery in 1996. In a statement filed as part of his pre-sentence report, the singer says the drugs made him "more and more alone" and filled him with self-loathing. He adds that Philip Taylor, the Metro police investigator who charged him with prescription fraud last January, likely "saved my life."

7—The century-old stained-glass skylight in Nashville's Union Station is re-lighted tonight, as part of a weekend celebration of the historic train-station-turned-hotel's 100th anniversary. The news will not be as rosy for the station's adjacent train shed, now used as a parking facility.

8—The Tennessee Titans beat the Cincinnati Bengals 23-14, but at significant cost to Titans guard Bruce Matthews, who ends up with a sprained ligament in his right knee. "This is the most pain I've ever experienced on the field," says Matthews, 39, who has started in 202 consecutive games. Will Matthews play in the Titans' Oct. 16 game against the Jacksonville Jaguars, or will his streak come to an end?

especially after rural listeners flooded myopic big-city programmers with letters of heartfelt appreciation.

As contradictory as it seems, one principal reason for the success of country music at that time was that vast numbers of people were actually *leaving* the countryside. The first 40 years of the 20th century witnessed a mass exodus of rural Southerners in flight from bone-grinding poverty, discrimination, and lack of opportunity. Most, especially blacks, ended up in factory towns and cities in the North, but the cities of the South also grew rapidly. Nashville's population more than doubled, to 167,000, in the first four decades of the century, and rural in-migration accounted for most of that growth. Country music, with its themes of religion, family, and home, became a link to the places these people had left behind.

"It evokes a warm image of the culture of the common folk in the South, and a plea to preserve it against incursions of the modern world," wrote Andrew Lytle, one of the band of Vanderbilt Agrarians whose social criticism in the early 1930s was a collective lament for the feudal (and racist) society that was slowly crumbling. "Throw out the radio and take down the fiddle from the wall," Lytle wrote. "Forsake the movies for the play-parties and the square dance." But the radio, in fact, was the modern instrument that preserved and spread the music. The performers who joined the Opry in those early decades, such as the Delmore Brothers from northern Alabama, Roy Acuff from East Tennessee, Bill Monroe from western Kentucky, and Nashville-born harmonica wizard Deford Bailey, the only black star in the entire troupe, expertly captured this sense of loss and nostalgia.

World War II was a boon for country music, as it was for the entire South. First, it intensified the rural migration of previous decades. The war brought millions of Northerners to the South for military training and brought millions of Southerners into service with Northerners. Country music was uniquely suited to telling the stories of these soldiers. "I'll Be Back in a Year, Little Darlin' " became "Have I Stayed Away Too Long," giving way to "Stars and Stripes on Iwo Jima" and then "The Soldier's Last Letter." This exposure, coupled with huge population shifts, led to unprecedented growth after the war and to a golden era of traditional country music. In 1944, *Billboard* magazine estimated that there were 600 regular country radio shows in the United States and that they played to a combined audience of around 40 million people—one-third of the population at the time.

As would be the case throughout its history, country grew by adapting to the times. In the 1940s, it was popularly called "country and Western," reflecting the attempt to rope it together with the swing music of Texas and the Southwest. While early country music had been based around fiddles, harmonicas, and assorted backyard instruments, the new sound (called honky-tonk, after the spreading breed of beer joints located on the outskirts of Southern towns) included brasher instrumentation—string bass, more rhythmic guitar, even electric guitar—and edgier, more modern themes. There were fewer songs about rural dislocation and poor Grandma back on the farm, and more talk of drinking, sex, and families falling apart. With new stars—Hank Snow, Hank Thompson, and the prince of urban dislocation, Hank Williams—the Opry, in particular, reached more listeners than ever. Country was also popular in the Far West, with Okies who had gone to California from the Dust Bowl, and in the Northeast as well. A group of Opry stars played Carnegie Hall in October 1947 and sold the place out (this more than a half-century before the Nashville Symphony's Carnegie concert in September 2000). "The barriers were coming down," boasted Minnie Pearl, one of the performers on the 1947 show. "I think that was the first time I realized how far-flung country music had become."

Meanwhile, at exactly the same time country music was spreading across the nation, the industry was consolidating its base in a city that had shown more hostility than affection for it: Nashville. Country music set up shop here for three basic reasons, all of which came to a head in the 1940s. The first was money. Before the war, the performing rights organization ASCAP, which collects royalties for music publishers, more

9—**In the Middle East**, the Jewish holy day of Yom Kippur is marked by gunfire, gasoline bombs and fighting between Palestinians and Israelis in Israel's West Bank. In Nashville, a world apart, Jews and Muslims both pray for an end to the violence. As Metro police keep watch, following threats sent last week to area synagogues, thousands of Jewish residents attend services at local temples. "What we don't want—because it's bloodshed—is that Israel will be forced to defend itself," says Rabbi Zalman Posner of Sherith Israel Congregation. Meanwhile, Nashville's Muslim community plans a public prayer session for the coming weekend. "We want everyone to know we have human rights that have been violated," explains Salah Ayesh, a Palestinian and former Tennessee State University student who was born in the Gaza Strip. **. . . In what a Metro detective** describes as "a real whodunit," the body of Middle Tennessee psychiatric worker Charles W. Bender is discovered in his next-door neighbor's driveway on Whites Creek Pike. Bender, 49, has been shot to death, although police are withholding further details. They will say, however, that it appears Bender either chased someone or was chased through his neighbor's back yard. Bender, says Metro Murder Squad Detective Clinton Vogel, "was no bad dude. He had no history of drugs, no booze, no gambling—he was just a hardworking man that somebody killed.". . . **The Rev. Paul Durham**, pastor of Radnor Baptist Church and a political aspirant, is voted out of his longtime position as chairman of Metro's Traffic and Parking Commission. The ouster is believed to be the doing of Mayor Bill Purcell, who ensures that former Metro Planning Commission staffer Ed Owens gets the post. In the last mayoral election, Durham endorsed Purcell's opponent, former Mayor Richard Fulton.

10—**Two months after announcing** a recall of 6.5 million potentially defective tires, Bridgestone/Firestone Inc. has a new

Forty years after they founded one of the first and finest Nashville music publishing companies in 1942, Fred Rose (left) and Roy Acuff reveled in their role as elder statesmen of the country music industry. Acuff-Rose set the tone for what would later be known as Music City U.S.A.

chief. Executive Vice President John T. Lampe replaces Masatoshi Ono as chairman, CEO and president of the troubled tire manufacturer. The news comes as Bridgestone/Firestone continues rounds of depositions at the Loews Vanderbilt Plaza Hotel in conjunction with the tire recall. . . . **The tech wreck continues:** Gaylord Entertainment's expensive, much-ballyhooed internet venture called Gaylord Digital lays off 22 people, making it the latest in a string of Nashville "dot.coms" to hit hard times. . . . **After a decade** of some of the city's most memorable shows, concert promoter and club owner Steve West sells his no-frills Fourth Avenue venue, 328 Performance Hall, for an undisclosed sum. The buyer, Dave Wachtel III, son of Nashville restaurateur David Wachtel Jr., currently runs the Second Avenue club Jack Legs' Speakeasy with booker Jason Pitzer. Despite its concrete-bunker vibe, 328 brought a stunning variety of talent to Nashville: rap artists Public Enemy and Ice-T; rockers Beck, Alanis Morissette, the Smashing Pumpkins and Los Lobos; country stars Garth Brooks and Johnny Paycheck; and hometown heroes Jason & the Scorchers and BR5-49.

11—**After sustaining a week of criticisms** about his performance in the first presidential debate—his eye-rolling, his haughty sighs, his know-it-all demeanor—Vice President Al Gore seems almost chastened in tonight's rematch. At one point, he even apologizes to Texas Gov. George W. Bush for misstating some figures in the previous debate. Still, Bush manages once again to hold his own with his more experienced opponent. "I think he kicked [Gore's] rear end," says Gov. Don Sundquist, who has become well acquainted with the feel of boots on his own backside. . . . **Nashville loses a civic humanitarian** who gave decades of service to the community. Leah Rose Werthan, 92, the widow of the late Nashville businessman and philanthropist Bernard Werthan, was instrumental in the founding

or less ignored Nashville songwriters. When ASCAP raised its rates in 1941, though, a rival organization, BMI, arose to challenge it. BMI not only broke the monopoly, but also welcomed country writers into the fold—and, in the process, caused more music money to stay in Nashville.

The second reason was geography. By the mid-1940s, with growing numbers of musicians being drawn to Nashville by the Opry, producers found it convenient and economical to cut records here. Most of the musicians also preferred Nashville over, say, Atlanta or Dallas (which had Oprylike programs of their own), because of its central location. Thirty states are within 600 miles of Nashville—a distance that's significant because it's the range a tour bus can cover overnight. In the early 1950s, Owen Bradley, a former WSM engineer, set up a Quonset-hut studio in a run-down neighborhood not far from Vanderbilt. That temporary facility became the magnet for a ramshackle collection of recording studios, labels, and management offices that opened shop in old Victorian homes and nondescript low-rises through the 1950s and into the '60s. Like Tin Pan Alley in New York, Nashville's Music Row didn't develop—it simply happened.

The third reason the industry congregated in Nashville was music publishing. (The term carries over from the era when music was "published" in sheet form). As with other forms of music, publishing, as distinct from records, has always been the linchpin to country music because published songs have the capacity to keep on making money years after they are first recorded. They can be cut—or "covered," as the term of Nashville Memorial Hospital, the Nashville Family Shelter, the Green Hills Health Center and the Bill Wilkerson Speech and Hearing Center. Her last hours are spent at Memorial, the hospital she helped bring into being. . . . **A process called chelation** is the subject of a heated public meeting today before the Tennessee Board of Medical Examiners. Chelation, used to treat battery-factory workers for lead poisoning during the late 1940s, hinges upon a synthetic amino acid that "chelates," or binds, to heavy metals, allowing them to be passed from the body in urine. The blood-cleaning process is also reported to be successful in treating some symptoms of heart disease and even cataracts. The board, however, is considering a rule that would restrict its use to academic settings because its results are as yet unproven. Outraged patients want full access now. . . . **From 1995 to 1996,** a North Nashville branch of the

goes—by other artists, or they may be used in television shows, movies, or commercials. In 1942, Fred Rose, a songwriter with a Tin Pan Alley background, moved to Nashville from Los Angeles because his wife, a Nashville native, was homesick. With Roy Acuff, he founded a publishing company that coddled Nashville artists precisely because New York companies so cavalierly ignored them. One Acuff-Rose song in particular, "Tennessee Waltz," first recorded in 1948 and then recut by Patti Page in 1950, sold 4.8 million records in a single year, earning the publishers $330,000 and single-handedly paving the way for Nashville's "overnight" success in the musical mainstream. By 1960, *Broadcasting* magazine reported that half of all American recordings came from Nashville. The city that liked to portray itself as the "Athens of the South" had become home to 1,100 musicians, 350 songwriters, 110 publishing houses, and 35 recording studios—and the industry that liked to think of itself as a hillbilly family business was bringing in more than $40 million a year in record sales.

The presence of all that infrastructure dramatically transformed the music industry in Nashville. Suddenly, making money—feeding the beast, as it were—had become as important as making music. This was particularly noticeable during the first big challenge to the country gold rush. When Elvis Presley burst onto the music scene in the mid-1950s, he and the rock-and-roll revolution he ignited immediately sucked fans, particularly young people, out of country audiences. Radio dropped country like a hot rock—to pick up rock. Even the Grand Ole Opry lost half its audience. This left Nashville with a choice: adapt or shut down. The response was the Nashville Sound— Music Row's first significant attempt to tinker with country music and make it more appealing to mainstream American audiences.

Stretching into the 1970s, the era of the Nashville Sound (a sweeter, softer, smoother country, with more strings and less twang) was viewed in some quarters with deep ambivalence. Some saw it as a brilliant adjustment, or "Chet's Compromise," after Chet Atkins, the virtuoso guitarist-turned-RCA producer, who, with Billy Sherrill, Owen Bradley, and others, added strings, drums, and creamy background "ooohs" to the records of such artists as Jim Reeves and Bill Anderson. Others viewed it as "putting on

George Jones is to country music what Pavarotti is to opera: the master's voice. Fans and fellow performers alike have rated the Jones recording of "He Stopped Loving Her Today" at the top of the all-time hit list.

The early 1980s were years of great creative ferment for country music. Emmylou Harris attracted fans from across the spectrum of American music.

Johnny Cash and his wife, June Carter Cash, were among country music's elite. His superstardom dates from the 1950s. Her family's musical heritage predates the Grand Ole Opry.

The "outlaw" period of country was both a reference to long-haired Texans like Waylon Jennings (above) and Willie Nelson, and a spirit of rebellion against the more straitlaced image of the Grand Ole Opry.

airs"—a crass abandonment of tradition and authenticity. Both Reeves and Patsy Cline, for example, had begun as honky-tonk singers wearing Western clothes, but soon drifted into evening wear and cocktail-party stylings. What was clear was that country music had (at least temporarily) abandoned its dusty boots for a new uptown image. Commercially, it worked. During the 1960s, the number of radio stations playing the music increased more than seven times over. By 1970, country music was earning $200 million a year, five times the amount of a decade earlier. Even the stuffed shirts of Belle Meade could no longer ignore the reality of the new money machine on Music Row. Country had not only come to town, it was reshaping the place, year by year—one guitar-shaped swimming pool at a time.

Though many socialites still snubbed the music and resisted the intrusion of

notorious Gangster Disciples was responsible for a string of robberies and a half-dozen murders, including the fatal shooting of 12-year-old Adriane Dickerson in 1996 outside an Antioch supermarket. Today, former gang members Yakou Kenyatta Murphy, 25, and Dimitrice Martin, 23, receive reduced sentences for their testimony against other Disciples. Murphy gets 23 years, Martin gets 20. Prosecutors say the two did not kill anyone and helped convict others who did.

12—**For his role** in the botched Oct. 4 police raid that caused the shooting death of Lebanon resident John Adams, a 10-year veteran of the Lebanon police force is fired. Lt. Steven Nokes, supervisor of the Lebanon Police Department's narcotics unit, loses his job for what Police Chief Bill Weeks terms "serious policy and procedures violations." Another officer present at the raid, Tommy Maggart, is placed on unpaid leave. Both Nokes and Maggart were involved in the surveillance that resulted in the wrong house being described in the arrest warrant. . . . **Public transportation** is pitiful in Nashville, and native-born workers are treated better than immigrants, regardless of race, ethnicity or job experience. Even so, Middle Tennessee is a relatively friendly place to live, according to 156 Hispanic participants in a focus-group study sponsored by the Woodbine Community Organization, the United Way and several local groups. The participants say Nashville seems safer than hot spots in California and Texas, where school violence, street gangs and drug deals are an ever-present threat. . . . **Hal Holbrook**, now in his fourth decade of white mane, white suit, bushy mustache and prop cigar, performs his famous one-man show *Mark Twain Tonight!* at TPAC. *Tennessean* theater critic Kevin Nance calls it "a treasure of the American theater." . . . **There is no end** to worrisome news when the subject is the state's fiscal health. Lawmakers learn today that Tennessee could wind up $202 million short of its tax-collection estimates by the end of the fiscal year. For the first two months of the fiscal year, State Finance Commissioner Warren Neel tells legislators, sales-tax collections are down $48 million. Senate Speaker Pro Tem Bob Rochelle says lawmakers have had warnings of financial crisis for two years, and now the dire forecast threatens all the legislature's planned improvements. Thunders Rochelle, "That is before you consider we are just the absolute pits of the world in regard to services we provide to children, the services we provide to sick people and the services we provide to elderly people."

13—**Roger Sovine,** one of Music Row's best-known executives, announces he will leave his post as BMI's vice president of writer/publisher relations come January. The son of rock balladeer Red Sovine, he began his career at Nashville's Cedarwood Publishing Company in 1965. Except for a six-year hiatus in the 1980s, Sovine has been with BMI since 1972. . . . **Off the Row,** the music-industry trade journal *Gavin* announces that it is pulling the plug on its Americana chart, one of the only ways of tabulating the success of artists and albums in the nebulous "alternative country" and "roots music" genres. In its five-year life-span, the chart gave recognition to Nashville-based artists such as Steve Earle, Steve Forbert, Lucinda Williams, Gillian Welch & David Rawlings, BR5-49 and Tim O'Brien, along with many other singers, bands and musicians whose work incorporated elements of folk, rock, country and bluegrass. But there was little evidence the chart had any effect on sales. . . . **Matthew Drumright**, a Brentwood High School student, rides high today as the male homecoming attendant elected to represent his sophomore class. Drumright, 17, looks sharp in black tie and tails, seated next to sophomore female class attendant Kristin Barry, 16, in the Brentwood High homecoming parade. Drumright has a busy weekend in store. Tomorrow

this new money, town elders eventually came to realize that the phenomenon, including expanded tourism, meant more prosperity for everyone. In 1967, the city donated land on Music Row for a museum and hall of fame; in 1969, *The Tennessean* hired its first reporter to cover the music industry; and in 1972, National Life invested the first $60 million of what would eventually approach $1 billion to build the Opryland USA theme park, the new Grand Ole Opry House, and the Opryland Hotel in a bend of the Cumberland River northeast of the city. By mid-decade, 7 million people a year were visiting what filmmaker Robert Altman called America's "new Hollywood." Nashville, indeed, was increasingly given over to Hollywood theatrics—an impulse fed in part by Altman's big-screen use of the city as a metaphor for latter-day American decadence.

The rest of the nation finally discovered that country artists and their fans could no longer be dismissed as toothless, penniless hillbillies; cruel stereotypes of that sort reflected more on the ignorance of the perpetrators than on such gifted entertainers as Johnny Cash and George Jones. Country had succeeded in penetrating the leading edge of American pop culture—middle-class youth—and other segments of the market inevitably followed. They discovered that Johnny Cash was an established TV star, and both George Jones and Tammy Wynette kept on rising even after their D-I-V-O-R-C-E. Rock fans drawn in by the likes of Waylon Jennings and Willie Nelson, folkies attracted to Emmylou Harris and Anne Murray, pop lovers grooving on the country glamour of Dolly Parton and Kenny Rogers, revivalists discovering a genre genius like Bill Monroe—all these and many others were beginning to embrace this once déclassé form.

This national love affair with country music reached its peak in 1980 with the release of a spate of Hollywood films, including Willie Nelson's *Honeysuckle Rose*, Dolly Parton's *9 to 5*, and Loretta Lynn's *Coal Miner's Daughter*. The most important of all was *Urban Cowboy*, a brilliant honky-tonk travel poster starring Debra Winger and John Travolta, then the undisputed icon of American pop chic. The number of country radio stations doubled to 2,100 between 1978 and 1982. Record sales, which had hovered around 10 percent of the market, soared to 15 percent, or $400 million a year. The *New York Times*' Stephen Holden went so far as to claim that country had "supplanted rock for the time being as the dominant commercial mode of popular music."

And then came the mega-bust of the mid-1980s, ending more than two decades of mostly upward mobility and enrichment for the country music industry. When fickle listeners began searching for new sounds and found none, they quickly abandoned country. Audiences seemed to vanish overnight. In 1986, country album sales shrank to around 9 percent of the market, their lowest level in twenty years. A front-page story in the *New York Times,* this one by reporter/critic Robert Palmer, flatly declared that country music was dead.

Paradoxically, this happened just as Nashville and Music Row were at last reaching a tentative and delicate social truce, a mutual accommodation that they had been slowly moving toward for years. As country music's popularity and profitability expanded through the 1960s and '70s, Nashville had gradually surrendered its elitist pretensions and embraced the nickname that Music Row had been using for years: "Music City U.S.A." (The term, incidentally, didn't originate in the music industry but in the saga of Fisk University's Jubilee Singers, who were so successful touring Europe in the 1870s that Nashvillians who visited the continent afterward were asked, "Are you from the 'Music City?'") The Nashville Chamber of Commerce even replaced the Parthenon as its public symbol with a more fulsome image: Dolly Parton's profile.

But the city's timing was terrible; it stumbled onto the stage just as the national audience was tiring of Nashville's product. By the mid-1980s, not just Music Row but Nashville itself was entering an unsettling period of economic restructuring. One by one, the city's major financial institutions and some of its other prime properties were being snatched up by larger, out-of-town interests. The local elite was losing its power and control. Newcomers with money suddenly had an opening to power that would have been unthinkable a few years earlier. Social standing, once the defining distinction in Nashville, had been all but eliminated; in its place, *earned* money was the new calling

Giving tribute to the late Tammy Wynette in May 2000, five of country music's biggest female stars (from left: Martina McBride, Patty Loveless, Dolly Parton and Wynonna and Naomi Judd) sang one of Wynette's biggest hits, "Stand by Your Man."

card—and in the music industry, there was no other kind. No longer could Old Nashville look down its collective nose at the country performers. New money had leveled the playing field. A fresh wave of middle-class artists and musicians from across America was paving over country's rural roots. ("Vince Gill's different from Hank Williams," said a Belle Meade socialite, by way of explaining her newfound affection for country music. "He knows how to use a fork.") By the beginning of the '90s, both sides in the long and awkward arranged marriage between Nashville and country music were finally becoming resigned to the fact that neither of them could advance without the other. In the last decade of the century, Nashville became the embodiment of a new American reality, one in which roots were replaced by rootlessness, class background by social mobility, and being Southern by being American.

The country music boom of the 1990s was not media hype. It was real, and reflected real shifts in the country, and in the town. In a span of less than five years, what had been a quaint if listless corner of the entertainment industry exploded into *the* mainstream American music of the decade. At its peak around 1994, country music was the choice of 70 million Americans, a total of 42 percent of all radio listeners. It was the top-rated format in 55 of the nation's 100 largest cities, from Buffalo to San Diego. The largest country station in the world, New York's WYNY, had a million listeners.

This audience changed the complexion of the record business. Country album sales soared to a peak of $2 billion a year, five times what they were in 1980. In 1985, just before the last big bust, seventeen new country albums sold between 500,000 and

he tees up in the first Special Olympics Golf National Invitational Tournament in Murfreesboro and Smyrna. He will compete in the alternate shot format with the tournament's oldest contestant: Wayne Timby, 72, his grandfather. . . . **More than 1,100** pre-addressed newsletters are stolen from The Center, a Berry Hill center for gays and lesbians. More than likely, police say, the newsletters were taken by someone wanting an instant mailing list. But fears persist that the names and addresses will be sent to conservative employers or used for acts of vandalism. . . . **Clutching armloads of books,** a line of people winds around the atrium of the War Memorial Building. Novelist Bobbie Ann Mason is overheard shyly asking someone in the queue, "Are all these people here for me?" Indeed they are, as the 12th-annual Southern Festival of Books begins its three-day run at Legislative Plaza. Festival staffers Galyn Martin and Serenity Gerbman are seen wandering the plaza with cell phones, searching for wayward authors. They should search the Metro-Center quarters of public radio station WPLN-FM, where the congested hallways resemble an allergist's office in goldenrod season. Scribes mill around waiting to tape segments with popular on-air personality Rebecca Bain, whose Sunday-morning *The Fine Print* program can boost a book's local sales by hundreds of copies.

14—**Nicole Hastings**, a senior at Hunters Lane High School, works at her part-time job until midnight. She gets up at 6 a.m. just to work without pay until 2 p.m., and then she has to go to her regular job again. Hastings is one of an estimated 1,000 people who volunteer for Hands On Nashville Day, the city's annual day of community service. From Bordeaux Hospital to the Nashville Zoo at Grassmere, from Ross Elementary School to the Joe C. Davis YMCA Camp Widjiwagan, citizens spread out across the city, armed with mops and brooms and shovels. "I think it's worth it," Hastings says, "just to make a difference.". . . **Hundreds of book lovers** turn out to see novelist Tony Earley and country band-leader Paul Burch join forces at the Southern Festival of Books. Earley, one of the country's most acclaimed young authors and a Vanderbilt writer-in-residence, reads passages from his new book *Jim the Boy*, a lyrical novel written from the viewpoint of a fatherless 12-year-old boy. Meanwhile, Burch and his band, the WPA Ball-club, perform original string-band tunes suggested by the selections. Also enthusiastically received are novelists Ha Jin, Peter Matthiessen and Kent Haruf, as are local writers Bill Carey, Ken Beck and Jim Clark. . . . **As the book festival**

Garth Brooks took country music's national popularity to a new level in the early 1990s. One of his albums, *No Fences*, sold more than 10 million units—far and away the biggest commercial success of any Music Row product.

1 million units; eight years later, three times as many recordings posted such numbers, and ten of them sold 2 million or more. One of those, Garth Brooks' *No Fences*, broke all records with sales of more than 10 million units.

The conventional explanation for such phenomenal growth tended to focus on changes within the music industry itself. According to this theory, as contemporary music became more ethnic—with rap, salsa, and urban dance music suddenly dominating the airwaves—many listeners grew disenchanted and began searching the dial for new buttons to push. Another argument focuses on the change in the way album sales were recorded. In 1991, a new, computerized monitoring system was introduced in record stores, and for the first time it was possible to make actual calculations, rather than projections, of album sales. By coincidence (or fate, as Nashville would have it), the week the new system was put into place, Garth Brooks debuted at the top of both the country and pop charts with his third album, *Ropin' the Wind*—the first recording ever to achieve such a double.

The final and most frequently heard argument stressed changes within the music itself. According to this view, Ricky Skaggs, George Strait, and Randy Travis reacted to the post-*Urban Cowboy* bust by turning the music away from its crossover amalgam and back to its traditional roots. While there is some truth to this—Randy Travis did sell 3 million copies of *Storms of Life* without a crossover hit—the music of these artists, the so-called New Traditionalists, still had strikingly mainstream sensibilities. The fact remains that while these changes may have contributed to the renewed interest in country music, and certainly to its surge in media popularity, they ultimately did little to change the basic nature of the music itself. In the end, country music stayed where it was, while a larger audience moved to the music.

The leading edge of the baby-boomer generation was just turning 40 at the beginning of the 1990s, and it was these people who first reached out to Nashville music. "Country music is about lyric-oriented songs with adult themes," said Lon Helton, country editor of *Radio & Records*, the industry's leading trade publication. "You've probably got to be 24 or 25 to even understand a country song. Life has to slap you around a little bit, and then you go: 'Now I get what they're singing about.'" Two-thirds of country music listeners are between the ages of 25 and 54.

An even bigger demographic shift that fed country music was the movement of these baby boomers away from downtown. In the first half of the century, Americans moved in large numbers from the country to the city. Jazz, blues, even rock-and-roll reflected, in one way or another, this change, while country music remained predominantly a rural music. The second half of the century saw another shift as Americans moved from the cities to the suburbs—where more than 50 percent of the population lives today. Country music, more than any other format, was a direct beneficiary of this change. Middle-aged suburbanites were increasingly interested in issues that have long been the mainstay of Nashville songwriters. While popular music was still focused on sex, drugs, and other forms of license, country pounded out tales of love, heartache, and renewal.

More than any other singer, Garth Brooks showed his mastery of this kind of 40-somethings' ballad, a sort of fanfare for the reconciled. He mixed songs of middle-aged angst ("If Tomorrow Never Comes") with raucous, feel-good party anthems, like "Friends in Low Places." And he brewed these together into an upbeat pop sensibility that was perfectly pitched to his audience. When U2's Bono shocked the Grammy audience in 1993 by saying he intended to continue to "fuck the musical mainstream," Garth Brooks followed soon after with an acceptance speech taking offense at Bono's words. "The message I would send to the youth is not to screw up the mainstream," he said later, "but work with it to make it what you want."

What contributed to Brooks' connection to the mainstream audience is that he, like so many other country artists these days, was one of them—a native of Tulsa, said to be the nation's most demographically "typical" city. Brooks graduated from Oklahoma State University with a degree in advertising. Vince Gill, a former pop star with Pure Prairie League, grew up the son of a lawyer in an Oklahoma City suburb. Trisha Yearwood's father was the vice president of a bank. Typical, middle-class Americans—college-educated, worldly, as influenced by Dan Fogleberg as by Hank Williams.

That so many of them could find a place for themselves in the Nashville of the '90s also spoke to another fundamental change in American life: the revitalized American South. From pariah region—hot, isolated, racist, poverty-stricken—the South over the past 30 years had become the chief engine of growth and change in American life. A massive population shift (3 million people since 1975 alone) was reversing the trend of out-migration that had started a century earlier. The newcomers were drawn by service jobs and air-conditioned suburbs, by the weather and the slower pace, by old family ties and

continues with another huge crowd, the morning paper reports that Tennessee is alone among Southern states in not having a state-funded reading initiative to promote literacy. Amount of money spent by Mississippi on its reading initiative: $30 million. Amount spent by Tennessee: zero. . . . **Mabel Robinson Love**, who taught at Fisk University for 24 years and founded the school's Orchesis dance troupe almost 50 years ago, dies at age 95 in Los Angeles. Love is as well-remembered for Orchesis as for the ballet lessons she gave to generations of North Nashville girls, many of whom attended Fisk as a result of her influence. . . . . **Someone's eating brats** in Germantown! Bratwurst is just one of the delicacies on the menu at the 21st-annual Oktoberfest celebration, held today at the corner of Seventh Avenue North and Monroe Street in Nashville's historic Germantown district. More than a few brave souls also polka.

15—**Former Metropolitan Opera** soprano Regina Resnik headlines the "Kurt Weill Centenary Concert" at Belmont College in commemoration of the 100th birthday of the composer of *The Threepenny Opera* and *Street Scene*. . . . **The old Green Hills Branch Library** closes its doors for the last time today. The library is moving to a brand new facility at 3701 Benham Ave., where a public grand opening will take place Oct. 28. The Metro Archives, another division of the library, will move into the old Green Hills facility.

16—**Titans offensive lineman** Bruce Matthews, who sustained a knee injury eight days ago against the Cincinnati Bengals, shows up for work against the Jacksonville Jaguars and extends his streak to 203 consecutive starts, the longest in the NFL. Matthews has not missed a game since 1987. . . . **The Union Station train shed**, a magnificent rickety skeleton of a structure, may become Nashville's latest historic casualty. Developer Henry Sender wants to remove part of the shed that was damaged in a 1996 fire; he would replace it with a parking deck topped by either a hotel, office space or a marketplace. The shed is a national historic landmark, but because Sender's development company owns it, its fate is entirely in his hands. . . . **Gov. Don Sundquist** hails the state's new online driver's-license renewal as an advance that will "save a lot of frustration and a lot of time." That said, it takes the governor 20 frustrating minutes at a computer terminal in the Bordeaux Public Library to become the first driver renewed online. Eventually, the development will permit Tennesseans to renew their licenses 24 hours a day with no extra charge. . . . **A steady stream** of friends, admirers and relatives of Philip G. Davidson Jr. flows into Christ Church Cathedral this afternoon to honor the memory of the former Vanderbilt provost, University of Louisville president and lay leader of the Episcopal Diocese of Tennessee. The 98-year-old historian died three days ago, witty and uncomplaining to the end, after years of declining health.

17—Assistant Metro Police **Chief** Charles Smith makes his first arrest of the day—and the year—before he has even had breakfast. At 7:15 a.m., after his workout at the downtown YMCA, Smith is driving down Eighth Avenue North near Commerce Street when he spots a man chasing someone down the street. The two men scuffle, and by the time Smith pulls over, one has run off. The man left behind, David Grant, tells Smith he was chasing a purse snatcher who knocked down a co-worker at LifeWay Christian Resources on 9th Avenue North. In an odd twist of fate, Smith had just seen the victim, Kay Blackburn, at the Y. Smith gives chase down Commerce, catching up when the suspect stumbles. The thief puts up a fight, even biting Smith's hand, but after assistance from a pedestrian and a motorcycle officer, Smith cuffs Kevin Lenox, 27. He hasn't made an arrest in so long, Smith says, that he may need

In marriage and in music, Faith Hill and Tim McGraw were in the forefront of the country music parade as the industry entered the 21st century. Hill's songs—and her fan base—spilled over from country into pop.

easy-to-meet strangers, by politics—especially suburban Republican politics. As the cultural form most closely associated with the South, country music crept its way into the mainstream of American life that the gatekeepers on both coasts had so closely guarded.

Perhaps the biggest score of the country era was its penetration into the youth market. According to *Radio & Records*, teenage country music listeners tripled in number between 1988 and 1994, and in the next bracket, up to age 24, the number increased by half. Suddenly, 43 percent of Americans between 18 and 34 were listening to country music. "When I first started in country radio back in 1971," said *R&R*'s Helton, "you had to convince young people that country music didn't cause cancer. People in that age group always had a very negative connotation of country. It wasn't just neutral, it was negative. So for the first time ever, we went from having a whole generation of people with a negative view to having one with a positive view. We didn't even go through neutral; we went right to positive." What emerged in America was a new moral consensus, a coalescing around certain shared values: sincerity, earnestness, a longing for real emotion instead of constant ironic detachment. Boiled down to its core, the appeal of country music was in the lyrics, the content of its stories—simple, direct, not too heavy, and not too far in any direction from the centrist themes of the listening audience.

How could this demographic-cultural-corporate juggernaut derail so quickly, as it did near the end of the century? The most commonly heard explanation was also the oldest: that this was just another bust following another boom, the same old pattern repeating itself. Indeed, it would have been far more newsworthy had there *not* been a bust after the mega-boom of the early 1990s. Industry analysts, as they are wont to do, looked at the slippage almost entirely in terms of industry factors.

They noted first that radio station ownership had undergone dramatic changes near the end of the decade, when new telecommunications laws passed by Congress allowed one company to own upwards of four or five stations in each market. Suddenly, country radio programmers could narrow their playlists to appeal almost entirely to women in their 30s and 40s. Programmers concluded that they didn't need to worry about the male listeners such formatting decisions would affect; their classic-rock formula or bubblegum pop stations broadcasting out of the same building would pick

Brooks and Dunn, country's hottest duo, struck the right chords across the scale of old and new styles for millions of listeners at the turn of the century, giving Kix Brooks and Ronnie Dunn plenty to smile about.

Among the most popular "hat acts" of the 1990s were two country traditionalists, George Strait (left) and Alan Jackson, who performed their barbed and satirical "Murder on Music Row" song to wild applause at the 2000 Association of Country Music Awards ceremony.

help with the paperwork. . . . **Vice President Al Gore** makes his strongest showing yet in the third and final presidential debate, held tonight at Washington University in St. Louis. The "town hall" format proves Gore's grasp of issues and allows him to show backbone and appealing humility. Whether it will be enough to turn the tide of this hat-band tight election is another story. . . . **Jim Stackable**, a 55-year-old veteran awaiting a heart transplant at the Veterans Administration Hospital on 24th Avenue South, gets a cruel setback tonight: his parked van is stolen. Metro police later find the van wrecked, its windshield and steering column broken. Thieves have used the van in a robbery. The police decide to step in above and beyond the call of duty. . . . **Tonight at the Ryman Auditorium**: a benefit concert called "Shattering the Silence of Addiction," sponsored by Grace Ministries. The headliner is singer Michael English.

18—**For one hour today,** 50 Metro health and public-service workers are hounded by creditors, spurned by indifferent clerks, preyed upon by drug dealers and given food stamps and rubber checks to live on. The social workers are participating in the University of Tennessee's State of Poverty Welfare Simulation Program at Lentz Public Health Center, which is designed to make social agencies more sympathetic to the people they serve. Nutritionist Rosetta Bradford, for example, is given the role of a 36-year-old single mother with a part-time minimum-wage job, no benefits and three starving kids, including a learning-disabled 12-year-old daughter. She must provide for her family while contending with volunteers who portray debt collectors, landlords, bureaucrats, even pushers. After only 45 minutes, *The Tennessean*'s Monica Whitaker reports, Bradford is frazzled. . . . **Woodbine community activist** Fannie Williams, a slave's granddaughter who lived to see the entirety of the 20th century, succumbs today to injuries sustained a month ago to the day in a house fire. In the course of her 107 years, she fought to get food for those in need, faced down government officials no matter what their rank and steamrolled anything that stood in the path of making her neighborhood better. Her legacy is the Woodbine Community Center, which originated when "Miss Fannie" started a sewing circle in the 1930s. It's now one of the city's strongest multicultural community organizations. . . . **The bodies of four** young Guatemalan men, employees at a local chicken-processing plant, are found in a Monterey residence, murdered. The investigation proceeds slowly because of the language barrier and because some of the men used different names at work.

19—Willa Fitzgerald, a St. Bernard Academy fourth-grader, wins $1,000 and a set of 100 state quarters from *National Geographic World* magazine. Her essay on the topic "What makes your state great?" makes her one of 25 national winners in the magazine's 25th-birthday contest. She intends to use the money for her college education.

20—Due to years of legal wrangling, the 75-year-old Turner School on Nolensville Road has sat unused since 1989, during which time the school has become a safety hazard and a haven for street dwellers. In his State of Metro address earlier this year, Mayor Bill Purcell called the situation a "case study" that should not be allowed to happen again. Now, though, the property is reverting to the five heirs of Nashville developer R.W. Turner, who gave the city two acres for a school building in 1899, on the condition that it be maintained as a school. The building and property are on sale for $900,000. . . . **The four Guatemalan men** found murdered two days ago in a house in Monterey have finally been identified. They are Francisco Nicolas Francisco, 25; Diego Nicolas Francisco, 23; Julio Bartolome Nicolas,19; and Pascual

At dusk on the boulevard of broken dreams, a 10-second time exposure captured an itinerant country picker as he paused for traffic at Broadway and Fourth Avenue before moving on toward the riverfront.

them up. Narrow-casting had become even more narrow as consolidation of station ownership increased.

Second, pop music, which had withered in the 1990s, suddenly came soaring back to life, with bands such as the Backstreet Boys and N'Sync, teenage stars like Britney Spears and Christina Aguilera, and high-profile balladeers like Mariah Carey and Celine Dion. Even the greatest Vince Gill song of all time could not keep listeners from changing radio stations in 1998 to hear Celine Dion sing—and re-sing—"My Heart Will Go On," the theme song from *Titanic*. Once those listeners switched, they found no compelling reason to go back. So country songstresses went out after them: LeAnn Rimes, Shania Twain, and Faith Hill quickly overcame the long taboo against abandoning the country format for pop—and found fertile fields there for the taking. Only the hard-core country fan base remained.

A third industry factor, less clearly understood at the retail counters, was the rapid consolidation and globalization of control over the entertainment dollar. The old free-enterprise model that allowed coal miners' daughters and cotton-pickers' sons to become country music stars had vanished. Now it took a million dollars to "produce" a successful new act. In music, as in virtually every other industry, the talk was of competition amd free markets and cream rising to the top—but the action followed a gravitational pull toward monopoly, toward cornering markets, driving out competition, and controlling the pyramid from the top (up where the cream was). Seen from that

perspective, it was perhaps easier to interpret the phenomena of McGraw-Hill, the Dixie Chicks, George Strait, Alan Jackson, Brooks and Dunn, and the world according to Garth. Even the names sounded more like Madison Avenue or Sunset Boulevard than Music Row or Lower Broad. And the ownership—of radio stations and air time, recording and publishing, touring and cable TV and technological access—devolved to fewer and fewer bank vaults. Was it any wonder that Cash and Parton, Waylon and Willie, Jones and Loretta couldn't be heard on the contemporary airwaves?

All these factors may have played a part in country's latest downswing, but the more unsettling fact was that underlying changes in the social and cultural fabric of the nation were shaking up the market for country music in ways that seemed unthinkable even five years earlier. In oversimplified terms, these changes were an inevitable result of the electronic age: computers, the internet, cell phones—the blinding speed of life

Country music's entire reason for being was that it told the stories of people rooted in a certain place. But regionalism as an identity was always based primarily on economic limits; in other words, people were rooted to the places where they lived in large measure because they were tied financially to those places. Fifty years ago, when the Grand Ole Opry was at its peak, a majority of Americans lived in rural areas, and half of them didn't have electricity. As a result, they were less mobile, less wealthy, more isolated, and more inclined to define themselves by their communities. (Fewer than half of American homes had telephones in 1945, and in the South, the percentage was even lower.) By 1970, when the "outlaws" of country music were just beginning to shock Nashville out of its stodginess, the cumulative impact of rural electrification, jet airplanes, interstate highways, and network television was rapidly liberating Americans from their regional shackles. With greater mobility and prosperity, people began defining themselves less by their immediate surroundings and more by such broader social identifiers as race, gender, youth, and affluence. Regional identity was less important than ever. The foundations for a modern Pan-American culture were being laid.

In an era when computers, chain stores, and cable TV dominated American life, the sense of isolation and disenfranchisement that were once central to Southern identity had all but disappeared, to be replaced by a general sense of well-being and good fortune—so much so that outsiders starting flocking to the region. Once here, they generally were so enamored of their new digs that they began to identify with the region—something unthinkable two generations earlier, when the dominant images of the South were of racist white men, oppressed minorities, and suppressed women.

On top of all that, the internet rapidly etched its impact into the nation's cultural DNA. The buzzwords alone tell the story: America was "wireless," we were all part of "virtual communities," we were all caught up in a "world wide web." How could a musical form called country, with its tired images of cowboy hats, denim shirts, and pickup trucks, hope to appeal to young people on the move—to anyone who wanted to be current? Even more bluntly: What did Nashville have to say to the nation anymore that would warrant the kind of attention—and sales—that the industry demands?

The future of country music now rests in the answer to that question. There may, indeed, be an answer that the industry has yet to find. Certainly history would indicate that Music Row eventually will solve the riddle and return to the competition, stronger than ever. The difference is that the question now taps into an identity issue that the entire region is grappling with, namely: What is there about the South that's different from other parts of the country? In an age of instant communication, when physical place seems to be less important than cyberplace, do regional values still exist, and if so, what is their purpose?

Miguel Sebastian, 25. No suspect or motive has been found. . . . **Alarmed by the growing** conservatism of the Nashville-based Southern Baptist Convention, Texas Baptists say they will protest by withholding $1 million in support from two local SBC agencies. Says Ken Camp, a spokesman for the Baptist General Convention of Texas, "We won't just have Nashville calling the shots for us." The matter will be put to a vote Oct. 30. . . . **A motorized platform** carries R&B legend Tina Turner above the heads of the crowd at the climax of her sold-out show at the Gaylord Entertainment Center.

21—**Class action suits** brought by two Nashville women, Addie D. Coleman and Betty T. Cason, allege that Tennessee African Americans are charged higher finance rates on certain cars than whites, *The Tennessean*'s John Shiffman reports. Court documents unsealed at the request of the *New York Times* and ABC-TV offer evidence that many paid more than necessary if they financed through the defendants, General Motors Acceptance Corp. (GMAC) and Nissan Motor Acceptance Corp. (NMAC). . . . **Nashville Opera's** production of *Don Giovanni* opens tonight for two performances in TPAC's Jackson Hall.

22—**Brilliantly costumed dancers** and brassy salsa music are among the attractions at a daylong celebration of Latin cultures at Riverfront Park. Som Brasiliero, the nine-piece Brazilian jazz band led by Frank Marino, is among the featured acts at today's second-annual Latin American Festival, sponsored by the Nashville Area Hispanic Chamber of Commerce. According to chamber board member Steve Uria Jr., it's a chance not only to bring the city's many cultures together, but to "eliminate stereotypes that we're all laborers." Some 10,000 people attend, doubling last year's inaugural crowd at Greer Stadium.

23—Is Music Row going gaga for Gore or batty for Bush? The country music industry seems as divided as the nation. The Gore camp is said to include singers Mary Chapin Carpenter, Kim Richey, K.T. Oslin, Patty Loveless and Terri Clark, while Bush backers count Hank Williams Jr., Travis Tritt, Ricky Skaggs, Montgomery Gentry and Loretta Lynn among their supporters. Brooks and Dunn will be headlining the Republicans' election-night shindig at the Wildhorse Saloon, but their producer, Don Cook, is throwing a $250-a-head fundraiser for Gore at his home in two days. . . . **Seen in the parking lot** at the Green Hills Starbucks: a blue sedan with a metallic fish emblem that reads, GEFILTE.

24—**A presidential candidate's** home turf is rarely thought of as a battleground state, especially when that candidate is a sitting vice president. But the race is so close in Tennessee that Vice President Al Gore enlists Titans star Eddie George and singer Tony Bennett on his behalf for a star-studded rally at the Wildhorse Saloon. Expected emcee Rosie O'Donnell does not show, but Gore, his wife Tipper, his running mate Sen. Joseph Lieberman and Lieberman's wife, Hadassah, are all on hand. . . . **Condemned man Philip Workman** gets support from a startling source: former Memphis chief prosecutor John W. Pierotti, who signs on to head Workman's defense team. "It would have been a lot easier for me to say, 'I don't want to fool with this,'" Pierotti says, "but when I saw what had been developed, I became really interested in it and felt like I should get involved." Pierotti was an assistant D.A. in Memphis in the early 1980s, when Workman was convicted of killing a police officer, but he did not work on the case. . . . **Diners run screaming** into the back of a Shoney's restaurant on Harding Place when a gunman draws on a Metro police officer in the parking lot. The man had been drunk and disorderly inside the restaurant, an employee tells police. Officer J.R. Malone tries to

When the history of American culture is written in 2100, it seems possible—perhaps even likely—that country music will be looked upon as a 20th-century phenomenon that memorably and powerfully reflected the culture of its time and place. In its second century, by contrast, if Nashville is to continue in its role as a music powerhouse, it will likely have to move even further from its roots and towards a more Pan-American sound. This speculation applies primarily to Nashville as a commercial center of music. As long as songwriters and musicians continue to live and work here, Nashville will retain a role, if only as a sort of museum piece of living country music, much like New Orleans is for jazz or Memphis for the blues.

But Nashville's claim to be "Music City U.S.A." never rested on the music it played for itself; the claim applied to the music it exported to others. In this regard, the decline of traditional country may not be a bad thing after all. Music Row never had as its purpose the preservation of regional culture; its purpose has been to serve its audience, and thereby to serve itself. Doing that successfully in the future will mean creating a broader form of American popular music, with a set of values distinct from the coasts, and with echoes of Southern and mid-American regionalism. What will those echoes sound like? Will the music be vital? Will the quality remain high? Will anyone really care? The answers are not on the internet and not on Music Row. They're in the future of "place" itself. The answers are in the country.

Nothing captures the embracing spirit of country music more truly than the sight and sound of a couple of pickers (in this instance, bluegrass banjo legend Earl Scruggs and singer-songwriter-guitarist Marty Stuart) exploring familiar and unmapped melodies together.

Practice, Man, Practice

by E. Thomas Wood

As the last *Andante moderato* strains of Charles Ives' Second Symphony faded into the air, hundreds of Nashville's leading citizens burst into excited applause. Bounding to their feet from the best seats in Carnegie Hall, before the eyes of the city that never sleeps, the proud visitors hailed a moment of triumph for the maestro and orchestra.

With his back to the audience, conductor Kenneth Schermerhorn appeared, for the barest fraction of a second, to stiffen. Then he raised his baton to begin the second movement of the Ives piece. In her orchestra-level seat, Martha Ingram, the true orchestrator of this event, closed her eyes. *We still have miles to go*, she must have thought, *if the most privileged people in town don't know not to applaud between movements.*

The audience faux pas may or may not have registered negatively on the New Yorkers whom the Nashville Symphony—and, by strong implication, Nashville itself—was trying to impress in this self-financed appearance on a cold Monday night in Manhattan. But it wouldn't keep a music critic of the newspaper of record from showing an appreciation for the performance almost as deep as the Nashvillians'.

At intermission, the crowd was abuzz with the mere fact that the *New York Times*—that great validator—had seen fit to send a reviewer to the September 25 concert. Nashville Mayor Bill Purcell was one of the heralds of the scribe's presence among the milling throng. And then came the assessment, in black and white, a couple of days later: The show, wrote critic Allan Kozinn, was "mostly a knockout." A qualified rave, to be sure, but one couched in respectful language about musicians who "played with the energy of an ensemble that was out to impress."

All in all, the Carnegie foray was a grand success. The performance was nearly sold out, with a full complement of non-Nashville attendees as well as the 1,336 who purchased tickets in Nashville for the excursion north. Other national press attention brought on by the Carnegie initiative, including a glowing profile on the arts page of the *Wall Street Journal*, was encouraging, too. For the assembled boosters and backers, though, the paramount achievement was that they had made all these things happen by a well-planned and well-executed act of will.

Of all the upward trajectories that Nashville had launched since the 1980s—up from real estate recession, up from political dysfunction, up in population and affluence and good restaurants—the symphony's thirteen-year journey up from bankruptcy was one of the most dramatic. Without question, it was the most carefully scripted. The power elite in Nashville set out to do this, and they did it.

They re-established the symphony on a financially sound basis, applying Carnegie Fever as the touchstone for an endowment campaign that netted contributions of more than $1 million each from philanthropists Monroe Carell, Tommy Frist, and Ben Rechter, from the Bank of America, and, naturally, from the Ingram Charitable Fund—all leading patrons of the arts. They got religion about the need for cultural amenities in a city competing to attract major businesses. And they took a step toward broadening the definition of Nashville music.

The program of works performed at Carnegie Hall reflected a heartland vigor, but at the same time a careful distancing from the music played on Music Row. The Ives symphony, with its bars from "Camptown Races" and "Turkey in the Straw," was closer to "country" than the "Double Violin Concerto" of former Nashville session fiddler Mark O'Connor—which echoed Stephane Grappelli more than any country influence.

It was merely coincidental that the symphony made this musical statement just days after Viacom had erased the "Nashville" from The Nashville Network. Martha Ingram was not weeping over that development. "There are those who say it's better to be known for something rather than nothing," she said, crediting TNN for having boosted the city's visibility over the years. "But for a long time, I and some others have felt we just need to balance it out, and not have it so single file that Nashville's image is just country music, *Hee-Haw*, and the rest of it."

On the floor at Carnegie, an ebullient Purcell struck a similar tone: "I think, for a long time, we have been 'Music City.' We haven't been one kind of music or one kind of city. My sense is that people from New York and other places are just now learning that we have had all of these pieces as part of our mix. The rest of the world will come around to understanding that in the years ahead."

At the Redeye Grill, a ritzy raw bar across Seventh Avenue from the hall, the Nashville contingent threw a party after the show. The crowd, noshing on five varieties of smoked fish as cool jazz lent background, included a who's who of the New Nashville—Gordon Gee, just installed as Vanderbilt's chancellor; Chase Rynd, recruited from Tacoma to run the Frist Center for the Visual Arts; Rob McCabe, the former First American executive whose start-up Pinnacle Bank was about to go public.

Ingram and Schermerhorn ascended to a balcony over the restaurant with officials of the symphony, the Nashville Area Chamber of Commerce, and other involved organizations. They beamed as Marty Dickens, Tennessee president of BellSouth and chair of the Chamber's Partnership 2000 economic development program, declared, "Tonight, we experienced another Music City Miracle." The assembled city fathers and mothers cheered as though the Titans had just won the Super Bowl.

One of many Nashville-based bands with a trans-country flavor is the Gypsy Hombres, featuring percussionist Pino Squillace and violinist Peter Hynka.

REVISITING MUSIC CITY

by BILL FRISKICS-WARREN

So if you're living in some distant town
Brother, pack your bags and come on down
They used to call it Nashville but I'm here to say
That now they call it Music City U.S.A.

Today these lines read like a plug for Nashville's top tourist draw: country music. But back in 1950, the year Nashvillians first heard them on honky-tonker Dick Stratton's prophetically titled 78-rpm single, "Music City U.S.A.," the town didn't have much of a country music scene to shout about. Sure, the Grand Ole Opry was already the envy of the nation's radio barn dances, and the show was luring more "hillbilly" singers to Nashville all the time. A fair amount of recording was also going on, and had been, on an ad hoc basis, since the end of World War II, including sessions with the likes of Opry stars Ernest Tubb and Eddy Arnold. But at the midpoint of the 20th century, Nashville was still a good five to ten years away from becoming the "Country Music Capital of the World." It was a music city all right, but hardly the exclusive haven of honky-tonkers many historians make it out to be. The Nashville that Stratton was so dazzled by was home to a free-wheeling, kaleidoscopic music scene where everybody—blues, R&B, gospel, and pop singers—was "jumpin' to the solid beat of a guitar pickin' out an eight-to-the-bar."

That was no anomaly; to varying degrees—and this is Nashville's longstanding secret—the city's music scene has always been this diverse. Before the war, for example, the town could crow about a whole lot more than just the hoedown bands that anchored the Opry. All of the big downtown hotels had in-house dance orchestras, which is where pop stars like Dinah Shore and Snooky Lanson (who succeeded Frank Sinatra as the host of *Your Hit Parade* on nationwide radio) got their start. The city's two clear-channel radio stations, WSM and WLAC, beamed all manner of music, including live studio performances, out across most of the U.S. Jazz flourished as well; future giants like pianist Lil Hardin (soon to marry Louis Armstrong), bandleader Jimmie Lunceford, and trumpeter Doc Cheatham all gigged in Nashville's clubs before going on to greater fame elsewhere. And all this was more than half a century after the Fisk Jubilee Singers had first lifted their voices on stages from New York to London and Paris.

Nashville circa the year 2000 is little different. The big headline-grabbers, of course, are here: country sweethearts Faith Hill and Tim McGraw, the brand-new Country Music Hall of Fame and Museum, the country conglomerates that line Music Row. But, among many other things, the city also sustains first-rate symphony and chamber orchestras; the Blair School of Music; scores of professional-class church choirs and gospel quartets; an African-American Pentecostal denomination that is the sole repository of the 65-year-old art of sacred steel guitar; an expanding hip-hop scene; and a thriving pop and rock underground that has spawned bands ranging from Bare Jr., a hard-rock troupe fronted by the scion of country star Bobby Bare, to contemporary Christian rockers Sixpence None the Richer, whose single "Kiss Me" recently crossed over and topped the pop charts.

The career trajectories of many Nashville artists and ensembles exemplify this diversity as well. Reba McEntire, the show queen who has charted a busload of country hits, now draws rave reviews for her leading role in *Annie Get Your Gun* on Broadway. Mark O'Connor, the fiddle prodigy whose playing galvanized hundreds of country recording sessions during the '90s, composed the most frequently performed violin concerto since World War II. The hottest string trio in the world of classical music these days is a masterful union of O'Connor, virtuoso bassist Edgar Meyer of Nashville, and the renowned cellist Yo-Yo Ma. Working as studio musicians, the Nashville Symphony Orchestra's finest string players have added luster to such country classics as Patsy Cline's "Crazy," Ray Price's "For the Good Times," and Dolly Parton's "I Will Always Love You."

Too often, though, Nashville's variegated musical legacy is obscured by the vast shadow cast by the country music industry, or worse, defined over and against it. This isn't to deny that the city's musical identity—and its bread and butter as a tourist destination—is tied to country music; it's simply to recognize that, far from being a monochromatic music maker, Nashville is, and long has been, Music City U.S.A., not merely Country Music City U.S.A. This latter twang-centric sobriquet may suit the country wax museum that is Branson, Missouri, but it's not broad enough for Nashville, which continually nurtures music of virtually every imaginable tone and rhythm.

Piano prodigy Thomas Szczarkowski of Brentwood was 11 years old when he was awarded a scholarship to Vanderbilt's Blair School of Music.

stop the man from driving off, but instead the man walks up to Malone's patrol car and fires at the vehicle. Malone returns fire, killing the man, who is identified as Terry J. Trouten, 30. He had called police less than a month ago threatening to kill himself.

25—**Distrust of police** among Middle Tennessee's Hispanic community, which has been preyed upon by law-enforcement officers and security guards in well-publicized cases, leaves investigators no closer to solving the shooting deaths of four Guatemalan workers a week ago in Monterey. Meanwhile, in Guatemala, the families of the four men try to scrape together the funds to ship their bodies home for burial, using money the men had sent home for family support. The needed amount: $12,000. . . . **Anti-Gore sentiments** are surfacing in *The Tennessean* from an unexpected source: former Davidson County Sheriff Hank Hillin, who wrote not one but two glowing biographies of the Man from Carthage, one of which was called *Al Gore Jr.—Born to Lead.* Hillin has apparently changed his mind, judging from the classified ads he has placed in the morning daily. "I no longer admire the VP, no longer trust his character or integrity," writes Hillin. "Al, I mistook your ambition for leadership.". . . **Metro police officers** present Jim and Jeanne Stackable with a beautiful sight: their stolen van restored to tip-top condition. The van was taken by thieves Oct. 17 with a wheelchair inside belonging to Jim, a heart-transplant candidate. When the vehicle was found wrecked, Metro robbery, auto theft and burglary officers chipped in for a rental car and lined up companies to perform free repairs on the van. "They seem deserving," says Metro auto-theft officer Sgt. David Elmore. . . . **John Hiatt and Emmylou Harris**, two of Music City's most formidable talents, team up for a joint bill at the Ryman Auditorium. Hiatt performs songs from his new *Crossing Muddy Waters* album, while

Harris showcases her new collection of almost exclusively self-penned songs, *Red Dirt Girl*.

. . . To the titles of congressman, mayor, state representative, state senator, educator, coach, umpire, pallet manufacturer, talk-show host, talk-show guest and harmonica player, the unsinkable Bill Boner adds perhaps the last occupation left unclaimed on his resume: lobbyist. Most recently a teacher and administrator at the Tennessee Preparatory School for neglected and unruly youth, Boner will use his experience to lobby for the state Department of Children's Services. Legislators beware.

26—**"I'm here to announce** my retirement," Garth Brooks tells reporters at a morning press conference. Of course, "retirement" for the country superstar entails at least one new record in the coming year, the possibility of six or seven concerts to promote it and a slew of film and recording projects up in the air. Nine hours after dropping this bombshell, Brooks arrives at Gaylord Entertainment Center, where a crowd of 1,150 invitation-only black-tie bigwigs toasts his career-to-date sales of 100 million albums. . . . **As fast as it appears** in local toy stores, the PlayStation2 video-game system sells out its limited supplies in a matter of hours. Despite a hefty $300 price tag, the system's high-quality graphics—and scarcity—lead hundreds of clamoring videodrones to spend the night camped outside area retailers at Hickory Hollow and Rivergate.

27—**Goodbye Music City Mix Factory,** hello Trafalgar Square. The former Second Avenue dance club, infamous for its frequent fights, guns, drugs and underage drinking, reopens tonight as a British-themed multilevel nightspot. Hoping to attract an older, richer and more staid crowd, the club constitutes a virtual Norman conquest of Anglophilia, what with five floors of medieval feasts, Beatlemania, pub paintings, dance music, even jousting. The concept was created by Paul Eichel, the Mix Factory's

At a party to celebrate the release of a new album by Southern gospel diva Vestal Goodman, an all-star quintet joined pianist Andrae Crouch, another gospel star, in a stirring rendition of "Amazing Grace." Gathered round (from left): contemporary Christian entertainer Carman, lead tenor Jake Hess of the Statesman Quartet, Dolly Parton, George Jones and Goodman. The impromptu performance was typical of the musical convergences that come naturally in Nashville's music community.

It fosters cross-pollination, too, in countless combinations of sound. Any number of examples leap quickly to mind: legendary country session guitarist Hank Garland heading up after-hours jam sessions in Nashville's jazz clubs; the Oak Ridge Boys adopting the black gospel harmonies of the Fairfield Four; soulman Joe Tex making records with country producer Buddy Killen; songwriters Don Schlitz and Marty Stuart composing scores for movies and Broadway musicals; fiddler-songwriter John Hartford using the financial independence he got from a giant hit, "Gentle on My Mind," to

Proudly bearing a 130-year-old tradition, Fisk University student Ayesha Porter (front) and fellow members of the contemporary edition of the Fisk Jubilee Singers make practice an integral part of their weekly routine.

spend the rest of his career in a far-ranging exploration of folk and acoustic music; rockabilly band BR5-49 adding echoes of swing and punk to country standards; producer Don Was fusing signature styles and voices in a musical marriage of country with rhythm and blues; Jason and the Scorchers running the honky-tonk hits of Hank Williams and Faron Young through their punk-rock blender; space-walking banjoist Bela Fleck and mandolin master Sam Bush blazing new trails of instrumental discovery; Southern country rocker Marshall Chapman and others sticking to their individualistic performing styles yet thriving in Nashville's pluralistic musical milieu. Undergirding these genre-spanning creations—and, for that matter, much of the music that has been made in Nashville over the years—is an infrastructure, a circle of pickers, singers, songwriters, producers, and arrangers, committed not just to making music, but to coining new musical vocabularies.

This complementary framework has been evident at many points throughout the years, but never so much as in the 1950s creation of the Nashville Sound, the town's first intentionally rendered musical signature. The birth of this new musical identity, ironically, was a defensive reaction to the rockabilly phenomenon that was sweeping the nation's airwaves by 1956. The country music establishment, fearing that Elvis Presley, Carl Perkins, and other rockers would permanently supplant honky-tonk in the hearts of young record buyers, tried to recoup some of their losses by wooing adult pop audiences. Producers Chet Atkins, Owen Bradley, and Don Law started presiding over recording sessions that yielded country singles with a new uptown sheen. With these records came a loose, improvisational approach to playing, a less-is-more aesthetic as well as a communal, or team-oriented, ethic (the most frequently employed musicians were known collectively as the A-Team) that soon caught the attention of many who stood outside country's proverbial circle. Among the first to employ the sound were a few of the same rock-and-rollers who had so alarmed the Nashville brass to begin with—including "that Presley boy" himself. Before long, everyone from the Everly Brothers to Roy Orbison was cutting pop hits in Nashville, and using the very same pickers who played on the cocktail country chartbusters of Jim Reeves and Patsy Cline.

Much the same thing happened in the mid-1960s, when tambourine man Bob

controversial former partner, who is set for trial Dec. 5 on charges of money laundering related to drug trafficking. Eichel is limited to a consultant's role in the new club. Joe Savage, the bald-pated rocker whose snake-handling stage act once filled Nashville clubs, will put together the club's entertainment. . . . **The Monsters of Pop**, a three-day festival of local, regional and national pop music groups, is underway at the Exit/In and The End on Elliston Place. Among the Nashville artists performing are Bill Lloyd, Pat Buchanan, Lifeboy, The Shazam, SWAG, Jay Joyce, and Joe, Marc's Brother. . . . **Safety concerns** close the historic Union Station train shed to further parking, placing one of Nashville's architectural wonders a step closer to the wrecking ball. The century-old structure, noted for its single-span gabled roof, contains decaying wood and steel trusses up to 200 feet long.

28—**Abby Fuller,** 6, gets her first library card today. She is now able to check out books at the Green Hills Public Library, which opens today in its new facility at 3701 Benham Ave., near Hillsboro High School. The new 25,000-square-foot white-brick building is more than three times the size of the old Green Hills location a few blocks away, with the capacity for more than 110,000 volumes. . . . **Less than a mile** from the new library, another Nashville literary institution celebrates its 20th birthday. In 1980, long-time friends Karen Davis and Thelma Kidd acted on their dream of opening a bookstore, setting up shop on Hillsboro Pike. Today, the bookstore they founded, Davis-Kidd Booksellers, resides across the street in the center of Grace's Plaza, and it retains the name of its founders even though they sold it to the Cincinnati-based Joseph-Beth chain in 1997. The store's ambassador to book lovers everywhere, Roger Bishop, is still indefatigably serving customers. . . . **The city's art galleries** are mobbed tonight as the gala ARTrageous benefit for Nashville CARES, a support-advocacy organization for people with HIV/AIDS, celebrates its 13th year. Limousines filled with tipsy revelers rush from gallery to gallery, converging on the Gaylord Entertainment Center for a late-night silent auction and a concert by Mandy Barnett and dance diva Kristine W.

29—**More than 6,000 pedestrians** get their pulses racing at the seventh-annual American Heart Walk, the third-largest event of its kind in the country. Participants congregate at the corner of Natchez Trace and Jess Neely Drive on the Vanderbilt campus. The walk has been scheduled in the midst of one of the most colorful autumn seasons Nashville has seen in recent

Dylan led a parade of pop, rock, and folk singers to Music City. All were itching to record with the mythical Nashville cats to whom the Lovin' Spoonful paid tribute in their 1966 pop hit of the same name. Soon "hillbilly" pickers like harmonica whiz Charlie McCoy, piano man Hargus "Pig" Robbins, and steel guitarist Pete Drake found themselves with hip-status to burn; well into the '70s, their names appeared regularly in the credits of albums being released on both coasts.

Nashville continued to attract pop and rock stars during the '80s and '90s as well. Some, such as twang-leaning rocker Neil Young, just came to town to make records. Others, from arena-rock holdover Peter Frampton and blue-eyed soul singer Steve Winwood to former Greenwich Village folkie Janis Ian and disco chanteuse Donna Summer, pulled up stakes and moved to Music City. By no means were all of them, as neo-honky-tonker Alan Jackson put it, carpetbaggers "gone country." Many of them never even dabbled in what could pass for country music. To most, Nashville simply offered something they couldn't find anywhere else: a loose, relaxed approach to writing and playing, a singular focus on making music, a strong sense of community—in short, a richly diverse and vibrant colony of professional musicians of the highest caliber.

Lambchop, a post-punk collective made up of between ten and fourteen musicians—many of whom grew up in Nashville during the 1960s—embodies these virtues as well as anyone. Out to create a new Nashville Sound, the band specializes in a sweeping,

lyrical din that places much the same premium on beauty, nuance, and restraint as Bradley and Atkins did in their day. Increasingly, Lambchop has also drawn on the Southern R&B and soul music that the group's members heard on Nashville's WLAC during the '60s, just as producers Billy Sherrill and Jim Malloy did with the country-politan changes they wrought on the Nashville Sound in the late 1960s and early '70s. Due to the obsessive niche marketing of today's music industry, though, Lambchop is not under contract to a major label on Music Row, but to a North Carolina-based independent rock label called Merge Records. And despite being profiled twice on National Public Radio, the group remains something of an underground phenomenon at home. Not so overseas. Less category conscious than their stateside counterparts, Lambchop's European audiences, ardent fans who pack houses from Hamburg to Barcelona to see the band, hear their music as something that's not just uniquely American, but quintessentially Nashvillian as well.

It would be a shame if Nashvillians didn't follow suit and embrace Lambchop as their own, as proponents of a Nashville Sound for the 21st century. But with the corporatization of the entertainment industry contributing to the homogenization of so much music of late, the group's singular, at times quixotic, blend of tradition and innovation might not conform to what many today recognize as any sort of hometown sound. That's certainly the fate that has befallen so many others acts, both young and old, who've been squeezed off the increasingly narrow playlists of country and other radio formats, where programming tends more and more to reward only the most rootless, faceless performers.

Yet in Nashville, of all places, this need not be the case. Cities such as Memphis and New Orleans might concentrate most of their energies on preserving and promoting their musical heritage—that is, their musical past. Nashville, by contrast, continues to sustain a large and versatile infrastructure of creative artists (the Nashville Songwriters Association, for example, has 4,000 members, and the musicians' union local about 3,400) that gives it the capacity to produce music that grows and changes with the times, even as it nurtures its variegated roots.

It is by no means a stretch to argue that Nashville is more fittingly the capital of American music than any other city—even New York or Los Angeles, where music-making is a relatively small part of the total fabric of everyday life. Making music is Nashville's core identity, the one thing above all else that makes it uniquely itself. The city's heart beats to it, and its life has revolved around it since long before Dick Stratton first called it Music City U.S.A. 50 years ago.

Nashville-based music writer Bill Friskics-Warren's work has appeared in the New York Times, *the* Washington Post, *and the* Rolling Stone Encyclopedia of Rock & Roll.

Lambchop lead singer and songwriter Kurt Wagner likened the band's weekly practice sessions in his basement to their version of bowling night—a regular time when as many as possible of the dozen or so members come together to hone their skills and enjoy a diversion from their other responsibilities.

years. Proceeds go to the American Heart Association.

30—**In Corpus Christi, Texas,** 6,000 representatives of that state's 2.7 million Baptists vote to withhold $5 million in support funds from the Nashville-based Southern Baptist Convention. At issue is the growing conservatism of the convention, which caused an outrage earlier this year when it inveighed against women in the pulpit. Former President Jimmy Carter has also cut his ties to the convention over its "increasingly rigid" doctrines. **. . . Giving a whole new meaning** to "degrees of separation," the Tennessee Board of Regents announces that next fall, 17 Tennessee colleges will offer students a choice of five degrees via the internet. Some courses will require all students to be online at once; others will let students set their own hours. The degrees, which include four-year bachelor's degrees in general and professional studies, are intended to boost college enrollment across the state. Currently only 1 in 6 adult Tennesseans has a college degree.

31—**Midnight at the Waffle House,** Hermitage. Three men, fresh from watching the Titans game on the tube, are sitting at the counter when one turns to a diner in a nearby booth and asks, "Am I pretty?" Perhaps the guy doesn't hear so well, so the question is asked again. This happens, that happens, the booth guy winds up on the floor. He pulls a gun and starts shooting. No one is killed, but one man is shot in the skull (he's treated and released). The three who started the ruckus end up shot, hurt, pissed and unrepentant. The gunman—white male, late 30s, camouflage baseball cap—speeds off into the night in a GMC Sonoma pickup. It's Halloween in Nashville.

Portrait artist Ralph Earl's famous study of "General Andrew Jackson, President of the United States" (inset) was painted in 1833, at the start of the Nashville war hero's second term in the White House. When he first ran for the office in 1824, Jackson won the popular vote but was narrowly defeated in the electoral college. After a similar lightning bolt struck another Tennessean, Albert Gore Jr., in the 2000 presidential election, Nashville artist Nancy Blackwelder was inspired to link the two men in art as they are bound by historic coincidence.

FAVORITE SONS

by PHILIP ASHFORD

W hen it finally ended in the United States Supreme Court on the night of December 12, the historic presidential election of 2000 (which actually took place on November 7) had held a weary nation in suspense for five agonizing weeks. By a vote of five to four, the high court effectively put a stop to any further scrutiny of disputed ballots in Florida, and that, in turn, gave Governor George W. Bush of Texas the victory there. It also gave him a total of 271 electoral votes nationwide—just one more than he needed to defeat Tennessee's Democratic favorite son, Vice President Albert Gore Jr.

This improbable and surrealistic ending to one of the closest elections in American history turned on a mere handful of votes in Florida—a few hundred out of more than six million cast. It was a statistical dead heat, a photo finish, a razor-thin decision on a disputed call in sudden-death overtime. Bush did not win so much as he ran out the clock; Gore didn't lose so much as he ran out of time.

The national tally was almost as close as Florida's—so close that both candidates rolled up more than 50 million votes, or 48-and-a-fraction percent. Gore actually got 540,000 more popular votes than Bush, his lead gradually widening as the last tallies straggled in.

Only thrice before in U.S. history had a candidate won the popular vote but lost the election—most recently in 1889, when Republican Benjamin Harrison received a substantial majority in the electoral college even though Democrat Grover Cleveland had won at the polls; and most famously in 1825, when Andrew Jackson, another Tennessee favorite son, was the people's choice and even had a plurality in the electoral college, but lost the White House when partisans in the House of Representatives chose runner-up John Quincy Adams. Jackson came back four years later to oust Adams by a large margin, and four years after that he scored an easy re-election victory over another opponent.

As a lawyer, a general, and a politician, the fiery Jackson had soared to national prominence. Barely 20 when he rode into Nashville on horseback in 1788, he systematically acquired wealth, property, influence, and notoriety over the next two decades. As the tough and resilient hero of the Battle of New Orleans in 1815, when the last British invasion of this country was repulsed, Jackson earned the nickname "Old Hickory" from his admiring soldiers. A more populist spirit attended his eight-year tenure as president, causing historians to look upon him as the father of the modern Democratic Party. In his rise to power, Andrew Jackson gave Tennessee sustained visibility in national affairs for the first time, and Nashville, his hometown, basked in the same warm glow of recognition.

Twice more after Jackson, Tennessee sent men to the White House—first James K. Polk in 1844 (though he, like Gore, didn't carry his home state), and then Andrew Johnson in 1865, following the assassination of Abraham Lincoln. Now, after a hiatus of 135 years, another Tennessean was at the gate—and he would have gone all the way, if only his campaign staff had figured out how to carry Tennessee. Although it can be said that Al Gore lost the presidency because he lost Florida by less than one-tenth of 1 percent, it is also true that he was defeated because he lost his home state by more than 80,000 votes.

He carried his home county, Smith, and 34 other Tennessee counties; George W. Bush won the remaining 60, including Weakley County in West Tennessee, the home of popular former Governor Ned

1—"**Nashville's waited 93 years for this,**" blares the headline of the city's new daily newspaper. With an initial free circulation of 30,000, the *City Paper* arrives in driveways this morning, just in time for the presidential election—not that national matters will concern the paper much. The blue-and-white tabloid is positioning itself as a source for local news and nothing but. Reads the opening editorial, "We think you're hearing too much about East Timor and too little about East Nashville." . . . The *Nashville Scene's* notorious "City Crier" gossip column accuses Mayor Bill Purcell of badmouthing one of his loyal supporters, council member Chris Ferrell. Purcell is reportedly not pleased that Ferrell said the council might need time to study the mayor's recent bond package—a package Ferrell supported. . . . **Charlton Heston,** National Rifle Association president and erstwhile Moses, appears at the Opryland Hotel to rally support for Texas Gov. George W. Bush. . . . **Robert Timbs, 28,** is charged with indecent exposure after he rides through the community of Milton on horseback without a stitch of clothing. Timbs, dubbed "Mr. Godiva" by the wits on WSMV-Channel 4, says he made the bareback ride to settle a bet. The month is beginning on an appropriately weird note.

2—**Fisk University drama students** Charles Martin and Bennie Smith portray an HIV-positive musician and his male lover in the play *Before It Hits Home*, directed by Persephone Felder-Fentress. The production opens tonight for a four-night run in Fisk Memorial Chapel. Some students say acting in the play will make the audience think they are gay, especially on a campus as small as Fisk. But cast member Shonka White puts the matter in perspective. "If I played a lesbian," White says, "and the student body didn't look and say, 'I wonder,' I wouldn't have done

Gore's opponent, Texas Gov. George W. Bush, sensed early that Tennessee's neoconservative political tastes gave him a good chance to carry the state, and he came often to campaign, all the way up to the day before the election.

After 24 years of service in both houses of Congress and the vice presidency, Al Gore's string of political victories came to a shocking end when he lost his home state by 80,000 votes. Had he done as well in the rest of Tennessee as he did in Carthage and Smith County, his home base (above), he would have won the presidency and the debacle in Florida would be a footnote in history.

Ray McWherter and state Senator Roy Herron, two high-visibility Democratic first-stringers on the vice president's campaign team. Gore carried Nashville-Davidson County by 35,000-plus votes, and Memphis-Shelby County by 50,000; he lost the rest of the state by a landslide. The Tennessee Democratic Party, while still holding nominal majorities in both houses of the state legislature, was so inept that it could not muster enough votes to defeat a Republican state party consumed with bitterness over second-

Republican supporters of Gov. Bush, Sen. Bill Frist and other candidates of their party packed the Wildhorse Saloon on Second Avenue to follow the election returns and celebrate victory. Frist won easy re-election, but it was a roller-coaster night in the presidential race.

term Governor Don Sundquist's advocacy of tax reform against the objections of practically every GOP officeholder in the state.

While Republicans cheered Senators Bill Frist and Fred Thompson at their election-night victory party at the Wildhorse Saloon on Second Avenue, Sundquist was hissed and booed for having had the audacity to propose earlier that Tennessee might want to consider replacing parts of its anemic and inequitable sales tax with a general state income tax on its wealthiest citizens. In a time of great abundance, Tennessee was one of only ten states not enjoying a budget surplus.

Having won the national popular election and most of the biggest states (New York, California, Illinois, Michigan, Pennsylvania), Gore needed only Florida to lock up a majority of electoral votes. Many analysts concluded he would have eked out a win in the Sunshine State, had the hand count of disputed ballots been allowed to continue. (Over 185,000 Florida ballots had been thrown out because they didn't indicate a clear choice of candidates in the electronic tabulations; these "undervotes" and "overvotes" were concentrated in areas where Democrats appeared to have an edge.)

The ugly details of electile dysfunction, not just

Prominent Nashville heart surgeon Bill Frist handily defeated Congressman Jim Cooper in 1994 as the Republicans swept both of Tennessee's U.S. Senate seats. Six years later, Frist gave his Wildhorse Saloon supporters an early boost on election night when he was re-elected in a landslide over Democrat Jeff Clark.

a good job. To me, that would be a compliment.". . . **A related issue** affects a different campus, across town and a world apart. At Vanderbilt's Sarratt Cinema, an open forum addresses an incident Oct. 20 at a school parade, in which members of a campus fraternity allegedly yelled slurs and threw rocks, mud and candy at a float representing Vanderbilt's gay and lesbian Lambda Association. The fraternity, Sigma Chi, says a videotape of the parade exonerates them, but the accusation raises general issues about how the estimated 500 gay students on campus are treated. Only a fraction of them have come out. At the forum, gay students complain of steady harassment, name-calling, even vandalism. . . . **Members of Nashville Premieres**, a grassroots cinema club, were so determined to secure the city's first-ever screening of French director Robert Bresson's 1966 film *Au hasard, Balthazar* that they enlisted the help of the French consulate. Tonight at the Belcourt, Nashville Premieres founders Scott and Mimi Manzler and F. Clark Williams bite their nails, waiting to see if anyone will turn out for the admittedly difficult film. To their astonishment, the film—an account of a donkey's life told with non-professional actors—draws more than 140 viewers for its final evening.

3—**Fraud reports are up** 17 percent this year in Middle Tennessee, the Better Business Bureau announces. In the ruse of the moment, a letter writer pretends to be an International Red Cross worker with the inside track on a cache of diamonds and $20 million in cash in Sierra Leone; if you will give him your bank-account number to use for a transfer, he will graciously cut you in for 20 percent—while, in fact, he is cleaning out your account. Another popular scam involves trying to get cash advances for slavery reparations. . . . **The second issue** of Nashville's newest Spanish-language newspaper hits the streets. *La Campana del Sur* (The Southern Bell), founded and edited by Ramon Cisneros, aims its press run of up to 7,000 copies at the area's ever-expanding Spanish-speaking population. The paper is the fourth publication to start up in Nashville in recent months, joining the daily *City Paper*, Gannett's new pamphlet-sized entertainment weekly *The Rage* and the new tabloid *Urban Flavor*, founded by Morris Tipton and former WTVF-Channel 5 reporter Dwann Holmes-Olsen and targeted to an African-American readership. . . . **A Wilson County** grand jury indicts former Lebanon Police Lt. Steve Nokes on three felony counts, which stem from the bungled police raid Oct. 4 that led to the shooting of Lebanon resident John Adams.

4—**The current issue** of *Rolling Stone* magazine carries a photo of Vice President Al Gore. For the past week, the internet has buzzed that the photo had to be retouched because an unseemly bulge in the veep's khakis made him appear, as one wag puts it, "stiffer than usual." At this point, Gore needs anything that will arouse Tennessee voters: Polls show him trailing Texas Gov. George W. Bush by 4 percentage points in his own home state.

5—*The Tennessean* **profiles** Jackie Page, 68, a Metro program coordinator who has made it her mission to see that people with disabilities are neither pitied, patronized nor ignored. Born with a condition that left her paralyzed below the neck, except for limited use of one hand and arm, Page enrolled in Peabody College in 1959 at a time when people with disabilities were often either institutionalized or shut away. In 1981, she joined Metro's Disability Information Office, where she has made sure the city gives more than lip service to disability issues. Outside her office at Howard School, Page relies on a personal assistant, Gwendolyn Eddy, for help with daily routines and uses Metro's AccessRide van service for transportation. In her spare time, she attends Brookmeade Congregational Church, watches TV and videos, and reads, using her "third arm," a dessert fork taped

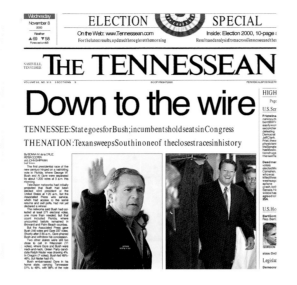

As election night dragged on into the morning after, *The Tennessean's* front-page makeup, like the election itself, remained unresolved. To be prepared for every possible outcome, the editors had four tentative layouts. Two of them (above) made it into print. The other two—BUSH WINS and GORE WINS—were tossed away. The first edition went "down to the wire." The final was "a heart-stopper" with no winner. The outcome was still five long weeks away.

Tension was etched on the faces of Gore supporters who waited in the rain at War Memorial Plaza for a winner to emerge. Close to 10,000 people were there in the early evening; less than one-fourth that many remained at three the next morning, when the partisans were told there would be a recount of ballots in Florida.

in Florida but all across the country, would emerge slowly, day by agonizing day, keeping partisans on both sides in a suspended state of anxiety and outrage. But one fact was absolutely clear to the Gore campaign on election night: Their man had come up short at home—and in Arkansas, President Bill Clinton's home state, and West Virginia, which never goes Republican, and indeed in every single Southern state, any one of which would have put the vice president above the requisite 270 electoral votes and made the outcome in Florida moot. Gore's margin of defeat in the eleven states of the Old Confederacy was an astonishing 3,267,000 votes. Third-party candidates Ralph Nader, Harry Browne (of Williamson County), and Patrick Buchanan, far from being spoilers, were practically no-shows; their combined vote total in the entire South didn't come close to a million, and even in Tennessee, they could have given all their paltry total of 28,000 votes to Gore and he still would have lost decisively.

It would take until long past election night, all the way to the end, for every astonishing twist and turn of this epic struggle to be played out, climaxing in the unprecedented intrusion of more lawyers and judges than might have been thought to inhabit the jurisdictions of Tallahassee and Washington. The entire drama will surely be debated—no doubt inconclusively—for many years to come.

Although Gore twice prevailed in the Florida Supreme Court in his attempts to get the disputed votes counted by hand, Republicans each time persuaded the U.S. Supreme Court to put aside its normally firm and consistent deference to state courts in interpreting state laws and block the Florida recount. The Supreme Court's decision to stop the count finally ended the battle, and Gore was forced to concede. The official certified result in Florida gave Bush a 537-vote margin, although that narrowed to about 100 votes with the inclusion of amended tallies approved by the Florida high court before the recounting was stopped.

Clearly, supporters of Gore came away feeling they had been robbed. Random error is inevitable in any counting process of such magnitude, but the problem in Florida went beyond that, they argued. The inequitable distribution of modern voting machines was such that Bush held a flimsy lead due to structural flaws that consistently short-changed Gore, they contended, and it seemed only fair to conduct a supervised hand count of the contested ballots. Florida Republicans, led by Governor Jeb Bush, the presidential candidate's brother, vigorously disagreed. Speculative analysis and post-election counting by various newspapers and watchdog organizations would keep alive into the distant future a deep conviction that Gore would have won the state if a higher standard of accuracy in counting had been achieved.

But life is not ruled by best-case scenarios and absolute truths, and so Gore's

After five weeks of high drama, the U.S. Supreme Court finally brought the presidential election of 2000 to an absolute conclusion with a late-evening, 5-to-4 ruling that put George W. Bush in the White House. Hundreds of reporters, as well as partisans from both sides, were kept back by court and congressional security officers while the court was deliberating.

to a metal rod, to turn pages. At all times, she deploys her skills in "people engineering" to defuse others' obvious discomfort, using her own example to make them consider people with disabilities as human beings, flaws and all.

6—**Singer David Allan Coe** will not be performing his benefit concert at the Ryman Auditorium, scheduled three days from now. New York attorney Robert Arleo, the promoter and opening act, says he is canceling the show on account of bad press. The controversy springs from some racist, sexually explicit underground recordings Coe made in the mid-1970s that resurfaced during his recent opening dates with white Detroit rapper Kid Rock. The intended beneficiary, the charity organization Make a Wish, had already pulled out before the story ran in Brad Schmitt's *Tennessean* gossip column. Nevertheless, Arleo tells Schmitt "the show can't go on because you screwed it up." . . . **Dickerson Road residents** and merchants get a boost today in their fight to clean up the crime-ridden avenue. Metro government files temporary restraining orders against three strip clubs that reportedly flout city laws and zoning ordinances. Charges range from nude dancing to offering sex acts for cash. Neighbors applaud the move, saying nightspots such as Charlie's Angels and Private Fantasy have given the area "a dirty name."

7—**At 6:30 a.m.**, 30 voters are already lined up at the Woodbine Presbyterian Church, site of the 16th District voting booths. By the time the polls open a half-hour later, the line has grown to 100 people. "Don't you feel like you're in one of those science-fiction movies where everybody lines up to get on the spaceship," one apprehensive woman asks the man behind her, "but the aliens are really going to eat them?" "Aw, I'm not sweatin' it," the man reassures her. "It'll all be over tonight anyway." Outside the voting area, Krispy Kreme conducts its own exit poll: boxes of doughnuts labeled with each candidate's name. The count, as of 7:15: four doughnuts taken for Gore, three for Bush, one for Nader and an untouched box for Buchanan. . . . **Endorsing the only brand** of pork-barrel politics it can stomach, the *Nashville Scene* greets the returns and visitors to its Eighth Avenue offices with tubs of barbecue. Fate Thomas Jr. and his restaurant, Fate's Pig & Pie, supply heaps of smoked pork, cooked according to the recipe his late father used to cap many a Nashville political function. Turnout of Gore supporters is heavy, Nashville Mayor Bill Purcell among them.

8—**A monthlong election-night hangover** is just beginning, starting with the news that the presidential race is far from over. "Don't get snippy about it," Al Gore tells his surly rival, George W. Bush, in the wee morning hours. It may be the first retraction of a concession call in the history of American politics. Come daybreak, the shock for many Tennesseans—among them Gore—is that this state went for Bush. Had Gore held the home ground, there'd be none of this electoral-college nonsense being bandied about by pundits still groggy from the night before. Instead, the eyes of the nation now turn to Florida, where the election may turn on a confusing "butterfly" ballot form and various snafus on Gov. Jeb Bush's watch. Here at home, to no one's surprise, Republican Sen. Bill Frist is re-elected by a more than 2-to-1 margin over his Democratic challenger Jeff Clark. . . . **Randall Gilmore** didn't like waiting for Nashville landscaper Stephen Taylor to pull his tractor off Tusculum Road last year. When Gilmore honked his horn, he liked even less the obscene gesture Taylor made in response. So he made a U-turn, came back, and ran down Taylor with his car. Taylor was not seriously injured. Gilmore, 19, is convicted today of assault.

9—**A cold rain** sends temperatures plunging into the mid-30s across Middle Tennessee, testing

chance of victory slipped away into the mists of ambiguity. In a December 13 concession speech to the nation that was widely praised for its graciousness, the vice president yielded to Governor Bush, saying that the Supreme Court had ruled, and he was "honor-bound to accept that." He offered his congratulations to Bush on "becoming" the next president, not on "winning" the presidency. Whether Gore would return in four years to challenge his incumbent rival—as Andrew Jackson had done in 1828—was beyond anyone's knowing as the year 2000 drew to a close.

Al Gore's defeat in the 2000 presidential election may have marked the end of a noteworthy twenty-year period in which Tennessee political leaders of both parties were positioned near center stage on many of the important issues of the day. During those years, former Senator Howard Baker was Senate majority leader, then chief of staff for President Ronald Reagan, and a Republican "wise elder" advising incumbents and candidates alike. (It was he who commented on television in the midst of the Gore-Bush donnybrook that "we're going to get a president and a hero out of this—not necessarily both in the same man.") Former Governor Lamar Alexander served as the elder George Bush's secretary of education, and thus joined the national debate over the ways and means of schooling just as the subject was becoming a major public and partisan issue. Gore served as both a congressman and senator in the 1980s, was elected vice president twice, and ran twice for the White House. Democrat James Sasser chaired the Senate Budget Committee and was considered a leading contender for the post of majority leader when the voters sent him home. More recently, Republicans Fred Thompson and Bill Frist have held the state's two Senate seats.

Those days in the spotlight were set up by the transformation that occurred throughout Southern politics in the quarter-century after World War II, as the region gradually moved from the era of Jim Crow to a more nuanced pattern of two-party politics. Tennessee had its battlegrounds in the civil rights wars, but it emerged from the

In the 1948 elections, Nashville and Middle Tennessee gave U.S. Senate candidate Estes Kefauver the backing he needed to dismantle the statewide Democratic Party machine built up over decades by Memphis Mayor E. H. (Boss) Crump. The balance of political power in the state thus shifted to the center, both philosophically and geographically.

period perhaps better adapted to the new realities of politics than some of its neighbors to the south—and thus the state's politicians may have moved a bit more easily onto the national stage.

Nashville's evolution as the fulcrum of Tennessee Democratic politics can be traced back to the election of 1948, when gubernatorial contender Gordon Browning and Estes Kefauver, who was running for the U.S. Senate, defeated Democratic primary candidates backed by the organization of E.H. "Boss" Crump of Memphis. Crump had been the dominant figure in Tennessee politics in the first half of the century by virtue of his iron grip on the votes of Memphis and West Tennessee. Moving eastward with the massive force of numbers, Crump skillfully bargained for alliances as he went, and confidently racked up victories at will in most statewide contests. But the defeats of 1948 signaled the beginning of the end for Boss Crump. He maintained his iron grip on Memphis politics, but his statewide power was substantially diminished. Crump died in 1954.

In the years that followed, Tennessee was noteworthy in Southern politics for two things: its moderation (compared to other Southern states) on the volatile issue of race and, paradoxically, its hospitable openness to conservative political philosophy. It was here that the Republicans established their first new bases inside the Democratic "Solid South."

The racial moderation was probably best underscored when the state's two senators, Kefauver and Albert Gore Sr., refused to sign the Southern Manifesto in 1956—an anti-integrationist broadside that defied the U.S. Supreme Court's *Brown* v. *Board of Education* decision outlawing school segregation. By refusing to affirm the notorious document, both men (along with Lyndon B. Johnson of Texas, the only other Southern senator to stand with them) distanced themselves from the diehards—and in the process, gained visibility and influence on the national political scene. Indeed, when Democratic nominee Adlai Stevenson threw open the vice presidential nomination to the will of the Democratic Convention in 1956, Kefauver won in a spirited fight with Senator John F. Kennedy of Massachusetts and Gore, who finished third. Later, Nashville Congressman Richard Fulton would gain a reputation for quiet courage as one of a handful of Southerners to support the 1964 Civil Rights Act and 1965 Voting Rights Act.

Middle Tennessee Congressman Albert Gore Sr. followed Kefauver to the Senate in 1952 by defeating the longtime incumbent and Crump dynasty factotum, Kenneth McKellar. In contrast to their predecessors, and to the rest of the South, the Kefauver-Gore wing of the Tennessee Democratic Party gave the state a more moderate image in national politics.

the readiness of local homeless shelters for the winter months. The Nashville Union Rescue Mission sends its "Cold Patrol" van to search for homeless people under the city's overpasses and bridge spans. By night's end, some 450 people have been given shelter and a hot breakfast. Other facilities are filled to capacity. The Room at the Inn program, which finds space for 185 homeless men, women and children at area churches, is forced to turn away 30 more. . . . **The ongoing electoral confusion** in Florida, with competing lawsuits, hand recounts and talk of misleading ballot forms, leaves Nashvillians as bewildered as everyone else. "Just from how the ballot has been described in the media, I understand it," says John Brown, 51, a 20-year Internal Revenue Service veteran, "and I'm as blind as a box of rocks." . . . **Hispanic residents** deluge the city's Spanish-language radio stations with requests for updates and explanations of the voting arcana. Jesus Ybanez, morning host at WHEW-AM, says callers are mystified that the election still hasn't been decided. "This usually happens in our own countries," says the Mexican-born Ybanez, "but not in the U.S."

10—**At present,** London-based EMI Group Inc. is the only major music company left that hasn't been swallowed by a larger conglomerate. That may change, though, as the German juggernaut Bertelsmann AG announces a possible merger of EMI with its BMG subsidiary. EMI owns Capitol Nashville, Garth Brooks' label, while BMG is the label home of Alan Jackson and Martina McBride. Bertelsmann also made an offer recently to infuse the controversial free-music website Napster with sufficient cash to make it a "legitimate" part of the music industry. . . . **The *Gavin Report'*s** Americana chart for alternative country music may be dead, but the music itself is very much alive. The first-annual Americana Music Association convention, held at the new

downtown Hilton and strategically situated across from the new
Country Music Hall of Fame,
draws more than twice the
expected number of people. Conventioneers hear artists ranging
from Rodney Crowell to rootsy
Nashville pop performer/producer
Bill Lloyd, and they leave more
convinced than ever that these
acts deserve the push they're not
getting from Music Row. . . .
**Based largely on citizen
support**, Nashville's library system
ranks among the 20 best in the
country, according to the *American Library Association* magazine.
But it's bad news for the state as a
whole: Tennessee ranks lower
than every other state except Mississippi. . . . **Charles O. Bissell**,
whose political cartoons and cari-
catures graced *The Tennessean* for
more than 50 years, dies today in
his sleep at age 92. A tall man
with a trim mustache, Bissell is
remembered as much for his
courtliness and impeccable bearing as for his artwork, which ran
in the daily paper from 1942
until 1996. . . . **"It's as if you
crammed** all 500 of Nashville's
liberals into a phone booth," says
one of them, gazing out over the
dinner crowd in the dining room
of the University Club on Vanderbilt's campus. The occasion: the
annual awards banquet of the
American Civil Liberties Union's
Tennessee chapter. Texas-based
political columnist Molly Ivins, the
featured speaker, is outrageously
funny some of the time, but not
electric enough to lift the spirits
of a crowd still in shock from
the Gore defeat in Tennessee—
and probably in Florida and
the nation.

11—Hundreds of Nashvillians
gather along Broadway for the
city's annual Veterans Day parade,
an assemblage of soldiers, Scout
troops, Shriners, clowns in funny
cars and marines in town for a
convention of Korean War vets.
Given the country's current political confusion, the many groups
marching underneath the American flag are a reassuring sign.
Says spectator Ruby Carmen,
"These young people don't know
how blessed they are to have a

Republicans scored unprecedented victories in the election cycles of 1966-70, with Howard Baker
winning one senate seat, Bill Brock defeating Albert Gore for the other and Winfield Dunn capturing
the governor's office. Then, in 1976, Democrat Jim Sasser (left) ousted Brock, and Bob Clement
(right), son of former Gov. Frank Clement, got in line for future opportunities.

Tennessee's status as a Republican breakthrough state in the South largely reflects
the fact that it started with a stronger Republican base than most states. East Tennessee,
where pro-Union sentiment prevailed during the Civil War, traces its GOP allegiance to
that period, and remains solidly Republican today. What's more, Republican majorities
carried the state for Dwight Eisenhower in 1952 and 1956, and for Richard Nixon in 1960.
But Republicans seldom won races for state office (except in occasional alliances with
Crump) until a new strain of Republicanism began to emerge in West Tennessee in the
early 1960s, largely in reaction against the civil rights movement. East Tennessee Republicanism was much more populist, not having been shaped in the crucible of racial politics. The Memphis-area GOP was a different story—built from the top of the economic
ladder downward, with an allegiance to traditional social values and laissez-faire economics in the wake of Barry Goldwater's 1964 presidential campaign.

The emergence of a second wing made it possible for Republicans to move
beyond their mountain strongholds and start contending in statewide contests. Howard
Baker scored the first victory when he was elected to the Senate in 1966. Victories in
1970 by Bill Brock for a senate seat over the elder Gore (in a campaign with ugly racial
overtones), and by Winfield Dunn over John Jay Hooker for governor, gave the party all
three of the state's top offices. Conservative Democrat Ray Blanton recaptured the governorship in 1974, only to see it fall back into the hands of the Republicans in 1978
after the Blanton administration collapsed in a heap of scandals and malfeasances.

The Democrats' long, grinding struggle to recapture their majority in Tennessee
can probably more accurately be dated from Sasser's victory over Brock in 1976, followed by the younger Gore's elevation to the Senate in his bid to succeed Baker in 1984,
and Ned McWherter's victory over Dunn in the 1986 gubernatorial race.

Throughout the early years of young Al Gore's political career, many Democrats
had him sized up as presidential timber. In his first term as a congressman from Middle
Tennessee in 1977, he earned high marks for his ardent advocacy of consumer interests.

Then he put together an impressive team for his first Senate campaign in 1984, and, once elected, positioned himself as a thoughtful moderate and gained considerable notice as a voice of change in the Democratic Party. His brief presidential campaign in 1988 did little to dim his luster in the Senate or back home—but his eight years as vice president were in some ways costly. They took him away from his state base, threw him in with the more liberal policies of the national Democratic Party, and linked him closely with Bill Clinton (whose popularity in his native South was not high to begin with and slid lower over the years).

Here in Tennessee, what had emerged in that period was a seesaw balance: a strongly Democratic Middle Tennessee, with its tradition of New Deal politics and racial moderation, contending against the atavistic Old Republicans of the east and the conservative New Republicans in the west. The relatively small black population in Tennessee—about 15 percent, compared to roughly twice that in the Deep South states—was overwhelmingly Democratic, offsetting the virtually all-white and all-Republican counties in the upper East Tennessee. Even so, a few rural and mostly white counties traditionally supported New Deal and Great Society Democrats and didn't get caught up in the virulent politics of race. This was especially true in the Upper Cumberland region, which has few minorities and is quite poor. In Jackson County, for example, the Democratic presidential nominee got 58 percent of the vote in 1984, even as Ronald Reagan was sweeping the state with 59 percent of the vote.

Ironically, Nashville was more important as a political center after Tennessee became a genuine two-party state than it had been in the heyday of Boss Crump. The increasing independence of the General Assembly, once a gubernatorial rubber stamp, meant that Nashville would be more of a center ring where the state's power blocs came to fight their legal, political, and economic battles. And, as state politics became more focused on money than on organization, the richest city was the right place for such fights—located as it was near the geographical and ideological center of the state.

free country." . . . **For 41 years,** James Edward Polly kept his Belmont Boulevard gas station, Jim Polly's Amoco, an oasis of full service in a self-service world. Polly's many loyal customers learn with regret today of his death at home, from cancer. He was 64. . . . **Corn cakes,** Cajun fried turkey and helpings from the "world's largest pot of turnip greens" are dished out in generous quantities at the annual Turnip Green Festival at the Farmers Market. . . . **Just three hours** after her husband, DeWitt Ezell Sr., dies of an aneurysm at Baptist Hospital, Angie Merritt Donelson Ezell succumbs to a stroke at her home, surrounded by family. The mother of federal Judge Gilbert Merritt, Ezell was known as "the first lady of Donelson-Hermitage" for her work on behalf of the Hermitage, President Andrew Jackson's home, and the Donelson community. She was 85; her husband was 88.

12—**With no sign** of resolving its long-term budget woes, the state must find ways to shave costs for the long haul. But no one likes the newest method on the table: giving up control of five state parks, including Middle Tennessee's Dunbar Cave and Bledsoe Falls. The state would cede jurisdiction—and funding—of these areas to local governments and outside agencies, at an annual savings of approximately $500,000. . . . **It's not Al Del Greco's day.** With 2:30 left against the Baltimore Ravens, after a touchdown by teammate Perry Phenix, the Tennessee Titans placekicker prepares to hammer home the extra point. Instead, Del Greco dings it off the left upright, leaving the Titans ahead 23-17—until the Ravens turn the tide 24-23. The doinked kick ends a consecutive string of 228 successful extra points by Del Greco, 38, who hadn't missed since Nov. 7, 1993. In the final moments he attempts a 43-yard field goal, but the ball veers wide right and the Titans tumble. On talk radio, fans show Al no love, even though his kicks last week against the Philadelphia Eagles won the game.

It was also in the 1976 election that Albert Gore Jr. first won election to his father's old congressional seat in Middle Tennessee and started along the road that eventually led him into the historic presidential contest of 2000.

The new face of the Republican Party in Tennessee in the 1980s closely reflected that of the GOP nationally. When President Ronald Reagan and his wife, Nancy, visited the state, they were warmly welcomed by the leadership of the party, including Senator-turned-White House Chief of Staff Howard Baker (between President and Mrs. Reagan) and Gov. Lamar Alexander (right).

13—It's another business day at Marivuana Hempalot, the East Nashville (h)emporium that carries clothes, salves and oils made from the hemp plant. The building also serves as the headquarters for Tennessee's Organization for the Reform of Marijuana Law (TORML), a coalition that seeks an end to the $27-billion drug war, starting with the legalization of cannabis. . . . **Some bumper stickers** seen in a random swing

These trends all culminated in the big switch of 1994, when the face of Tennessee politics changed overnight. Nationwide, the 1994 election was the revolutionary event in which Republicans rode general voter resentments about life, politics, and the excesses of protracted Democratic congressional rule to a sweeping cross-country victory. And if those old grievances weren't enough, there was plenty of voter backlash against heavy-handed political overreaching in the first two years of the Clinton presidency. Republicans captured control of both houses of Congress for the first time since 1954 and reduced Bill Clinton, at one point, to babbling about how he was not irrelevant.

In Tennessee, the Republican flood tide ran swift and deep, taking everything in its path—including the Democratic Party, whose peculiar misfortune it was to be contending for the three top statewide jobs (governor and both U.S. Senate seats) when the tidal wave struck. Before the vote, all three offices had been held by Democrats; afterward, all three belonged to the Republicans, who also gained two seats and a 5-to-4 edge in the state's delegation to the U.S. House of Representatives.

Part of the turnover was attributable to the national voter tantrum; part of it

In the first off-year elections after the Clinton-Gore Democratic triumph in 1992, a massive Republican reaction nationwide was particularly fruitful for the Tennessee GOP. In one day, they captured the governor's office and both U.S. Senate seats. One of the new senators, Fred Thompson (above), led the stampede across the state in a rented red pickup truck.

No statewide Democrat survived the Republican tidal wave of 1994. Sen. Jim Sasser (speaking, above) lost to Bill Frist; Gov. Ned Ray McWherter (left) retired and Nashville Mayor Phil Bredesen (center) failed in his attempt to replace him, losing to Don Sundquist; and Vice President Al Gore (right) saw his vacant senate seat go to Nashville lawyer Fred Thompson.

about town: TAKE CONGRESS OFF WELFARE. CAGE THE MONKEYS IN THE LEGISLATURE. FREE TIBET. 840 = NASHLANTA. DON'T BLAME ME: I THOUGHT I WAS VOTING FOR HIS FATHER.

14—**Cal Turner Sr.,** founder of the Goodlettsville-based Dollar General chain of stores, dies of pneumonia related to a bout with cancer. He was 85. Turner left college in 1934 to open his first store in Dupontonia, Tenn., now known as Lakewood. In the 1950s, he took note of the success large department stores in Nashville and Louisville were having with their monthly "dollar day" sales and devised a retail plan for selling low-cost items to low- and middle-income patrons. In 1955 he converted a store in Springfield, Ky., into the first Dollar General Store, where "every day is dollar day." The dollar-store concept survives to this day; Dollar General is now a multibillion-dollar corporation with 4,800 stores in 25 states. More merchant than moneyman, Turner is remembered for his combination of frugality and generosity: The same man who reused paper sacks to carry his lunch gave $1,000 to every church in Allen County, Ky. "Plow to the end of the row," he said, as advice for getting ahead. He did. . . . **At a meeting** of the city's board of education, Metro Schools Director Bill Wise announces his resignation. Wise, 65, says he wants to give the board enough time to select his replacement before his contract expires next June.

15—**After receiving more than 200 letters,** along with a petition signed by 6,500 supporters, the Tennessee Board of Medical Examiners decides not to restrict the use of chelation, a process that uses a synthetic amino acid to remove heavy metals from the blood. "That's the end of these rules," says Dr. David L. Starnes, president of the board, at today's hearing, as more than 80 chelation advocates cheer the decision. The therapy, created to treat lead poisoning in factory workers, has shown promise for relieving

symptoms of heart disease. . . .
Boxing trainer Ricky Brigman
pleads not guilty to molesting six
boys he met through the Police
Athletic League boxing program
over the past seven years. The
case is scheduled to go to trial
next January. . . . **An adult
nightspot** called the Boobie Bungalow is the center of an ongoing
dispute in the community of Elkton, Tenn. The strip bar, which
draws a steady tourist trade off
I-65, is a major tax generator for
Elkton, and the town wants to
regulate the club only to the
extent of levying a $1 tax per cus-
tomer. But residents who oppose
the club want Giles County to
have jurisdiction over adult entertainment in Elkton—an idea that
annoys many of the town's residents. "We have been running for
75 years, and we don't need their
help now," says Elkton Council
member Sam Turner. Nashville
newscasts fan the issue for days,
largely because newscasters are
visibly amused by the phrase
"Boobie Bungalow."

16—Nearly 112,000 parents
click onto a website today that
posts citywide report cards—but
the grades do not belong to their
children. The state Department of
Education issues "report cards" to
Tennessee's 1,611 public schools,
assigning grades of A, B, C, D or
F based on test scores, attendance, promotion to higher
grades and how much students
learned as compared to national
standards. In a ranking of Metro
schools according to the number
of A grades they received, the
best are Meigs Magnet School,
Harpeth Valley Elementary School,
Eakin Elementary School and M.L.
King Magnet School, with 12
each. The worst, based on the
number of F's, are Bass Middle
School, Isaac Litton Middle
School, Shwab Elementary
School, John Early Middle School,
Highland Heights Middle School,
Bellshire Elementary School, Johnson Middle School and Kirkpatrick
Elementary School, with six failing
grades each. On achievement test
scores, which compare to the
national average, Metro K-12 stu-
dents get D's overall in reading,

was a genuine change in the balance of political power. In the three election cycles prior to 1994, Democrats in Tennessee had received some 58 percent of the generic congres-sional vote, but in that flip-over year, their total dropped to 44 percent. (They rebound-ed to 49 percent two years later, but Republicans remained firmly in control.)

Another key element in the transformation of Tennessee politics has been the emergence of a third branch of the Republican Party in the Middle Tennessee suburbs clustered around Nashville. Voters in this group tend to be drawn to the Republican Party because of economic and social concerns rather than as a reaction to the racial struggles of either the 1860s or 1960s. The potency of this faction was forcefully illus-trated in the Senate Republican primary of 1994 between wealthy Chattanooga devel-oper Bob Corker and wealthy Nashville surgeon Bill Frist.

Corker, following conventional wisdom, devoted most of his resources to cam-paigning in East Tennessee, where the bulk of the Republican primary vote had tradi-tionally come from. Frist split his resources more evenly, spending more time and money in Middle Tennessee, and was rewarded with victory. It was the first major pri-mary election in state history to record a Republican turnout larger than that of the Democrats. In the years since 1994, the Democrats have been unable to regain their standing as a statewide force, offering only token opposition to the re-election of incumbents Frist and Sundquist, who rose to power in that turnover year.

And then along came Gore to run for president in 2000. Not since 1990 had he been on the ballot in his own right, rather than as the understudy of a controversial president. Back then, he was running for re-election to the Senate, and the Republicans virtually conceded him the victory; he carried all 95 counties. What a difference a decade would make in the relative fortunes of Tennessee's two major political parties.

If there's anyone in Tennessee who could truly know how Al Gore must have felt dur-ing the agonizing death throes of his presidential campaign, it would probably be Lamar Alexander. Starting in 1979, he had guided the fortunes of the state (as gover-nor), the University of Tennessee (as president), and the U.S. Department of Education (as secretary), and had made two bids of his own for the Republican presidential nomination.

On December 7, as Gore's options were narrowing, Alexander penned a witty little piece for the *Wall Street Journal* editorial page, trying to talk Gore down from the cliff of electoral disaster. "Come home to Tennessee," he cooed; life is sweeter after pol-itics (you get to watch ESPN instead of CNN)—and remember the immortal words of Davy Crockett, another Tennessee native son, after he had lost his seat in Congress ("I'm going to Texas, and you can all go to hell"). The headline over Alexander's clever missive said "Losing can be liberating, Al"—but the empathetic tone had a wistful, bit-tersweet tinge. No one who knows him truly believes the former governor feels more liberated outside of politics than he felt when he was in the hunt for the White House.

Alexander had taken his own good shot at the nomination in 1996, focusing tightly on the key initial states of Iowa and New Hampshire. He had built good organ-izations in both states and spent a lot of personal time there. Bob Dole, the Republican front-runner, was making his third bid for the presidency. Alexander figured that if he could establish himself as the moderate alternative to the aging party warhorse, the other candidates would begin to fade, and he would get the nomination. A respectable showing in the Iowa caucuses and a finish ahead of Dole in the New Hampshire pri-mary just might be enough for him to break out of the pack.

But two wild-card candidates spoiled his plan. The rich-man's-vanity campaign of billionaire eccentric Steve Forbes fogged the windows in Iowa, and the nativist can-didacy of ultra-right-winger Patrick Buchanan took the prize in New Hampshire. Alexander might have prevailed over their different brands of extremism further down the road, had he been able to prove himself more of a vote-getter than Dole. But after a credible top-three showing in Iowa, the Tennessean was blindsided in the closing days before the New Hampshire vote when Dole made a tactical move of his own.

In the final weekend, Dole pulled all of the conventional advertisements boosting

Former Gov. Lamar Alexander's bid for the GOP presidential nomination in 1996 might have succeeded, had not Sen. Bob Dole of Kansas undercut him in the New Hampshire primary. Later, when Dole came to Nashville, Tennessee Republican leaders (from left) Winfield Dunn, Alexander, Bill Frist and Howard Baker closed ranks behind the eventual nominee at a War Memorial Auditorium rally.

his candidacy and unleashed a barrage of TV attacks on Alexander, painting him as a closet liberal, too weak and indecisive to run the country. The offensive worked; Dole got just enough of a boost to edge out Alexander for second place behind Buchanan. Thinking he was tantalizingly close to capturing the lightning that would make him the Republican nominee, Alexander found to his shock and dismay that he had suffered a mortal blow. After that, his campaign limped on, but he had no other opportunities to knock Dole out of the race before they got to the primary in Tennessee. "I didn't respond effectively to [what happened in New Hampshire]," he recalled later. "They were able to label me as 'Liberal Lamar,' and I couldn't overcome that in time to climb back up."

Forbes and Buchanan had a few more minutes of fame, but Dole had calculated correctly that the nomination would be his if he could get the only conventional challenger out of the race. People might toy with the idea of casting protest votes for Forbes or Buchanan, but not if either of them appeared likely to win the whole thing.

Nothing galls Alexander more than the knowledge of how close he came to winning the nomination without anyone much realizing it. A couple-thousand more votes in New Hampshire would have pushed him past Dole—and probably forced the Kansan out of the race. Against Forbes and Buchanan, Alexander probably would have inherited most of Dole's support.

So in 2000, he tried again. "I thought all you had to do was work hard and run a second time," he said. But when he went back to Iowa, he faced a barrage of press questions about being a perennial candidate, in the mold of Minnesota's oft-defeated Harold Stassen years ago. The same doubting questions somehow weren't directed at

math, science and social studies. The city currently has 68,345 students enrolled at 128 public schools; its 4,528 teachers make an average salary of $41,072.
. . . **As a reward** for earning money to buy new school computers, students at Tusculum Elementary School get a big slice of a big pie. Caesar Randazzo, owner of Caesar's Ristorante Italiano, brings students a pizza 5 feet in diameter. . . . **A Thanksgiving meal** at Franklin's Moore Elementary School gives students and faculty nothing to be thankful for. At least 20 students and two staff members suffer vomiting and diarrhea after downing a meal of turkey, dressing, sweet potatoes and cranberry sauce.
. . . **A thorny issue** is settled

today in Davidson County Circuit Court: Should a Catholic priest who admitted molesting two boys be addressed in court as "Father"? Judge Walter Kurtz says no. Attorneys for former priest Edward J. McKeown argued that his victims' lawyers were referring to him as "Father" to sensationalize the case. McKeown's victims are suing him, the Catholic Diocese of Nashville, two physicians who treated him and the Metro government for $70 million.

17—The sounds of Music City's past are very much present this morning on "Nashville Jumps," a radio show on the Vanderbilt college station WRVU-FM. Host Pete Wilson and his guest, jazz critic Ron Wynn, play selections from a new eight-CD box set, also called *Nashville Jumps*, that documents Nashville's oft-unsung rhythm-and-blues history between the years 1945 and 1955. Car radios around the city crackle with long-forgotten cuts from locally based R&B labels such as Bullet, Tennessee and Excello, featuring Nashville artists Cecil Gant and Christine Kittrell.
    . . . **As its sales continue to crash**, embattled tire manufacturer Bridgestone/Firestone announces it will lay off 400 employees at its La Vergne plant at the first of the year. That is nearly a third of the plant's workers. . . . **Prepare for a soaking** at the pumps this coming Thanksgiving weekend. Gas prices are running just under $1.42 a gallon, approximately 20¢ higher than a year ago. But that apparently isn't deterring travelers. AAA estimates that a record 38.9 million motorists will be on the nation's roads this Thanksgiving, an increase of 4 percent over last year.

18—For more than 40 years of helping disadvantaged children learn to read, Georgeanne Chapman, 54, becomes the first recipient of the Tennessee Titans' Community Quarterback Award. With the honor comes a check for $11,000 to the Martha O'Bryan Center at the James A. Cayce Homes, where Chapman is a

Undaunted, Alexander tried again to become the Republican choice for the White House in 2000—which would have set up a rare clash between two nominees from the same state. But George W. Bush stopped him early, and there was no Alexander-Gore contest. The former Tennessee governor (above, with his wife, Honey) retired from active pursuit of political candidacy after the defeat.

chronic candidates Buchanan and Forbes. When pollsters started assessing the contenders for the Republican nomination, Texas Governor George W. Bush was surprisingly near the front of the pack, and the big-money backers quickly jumped on his bandwagon.

If ever there was proof of the randomness of political success in America, it comes from this development. Many respondents to the polls apparently thought they were selecting the former president, not his son—then just two years into his first term in public office. Yet on that shaky foundation, Bush built a financial juggernaut that carried him to the Republican nomination, and ultimately to the White House.

Looking back on it, Alexander could say, "I had a convergence of good luck in 1995 and 1996, and I could have provided a real alternative. But the second time, Governor Bush had it from the beginning, and I simply couldn't get very much attention." For the most part, Alexander's second campaign was feeble. He lost valuable time trying to do things that had worked for him before in politics—wearing his plaid shirts and walking across various parts of America. (His walk across Tennessee helped him win the governorship in 1978.) This time, though, he got mocked for resorting to gimmicks. He struggled to raise money, even in Tennessee, where many old supporters had grown weary of being pursued and dunned. Press coverage mainly focused on the haplessness of the campaign—comic relief beside the Bush machine. Alexander made his last stand in the Republican straw poll conducted at the Iowa State Fair. After trailing just about everyone, he finally heard the voice of the people. They said go home. And so he did.

"Maybe there was something else I could have done, but I wasn't smart enough to think of it," Alexander concluded. By the time he got around to writing his *Wall Street Journal* piece, he appeared to have come to terms with defeat, and his sense of humor was back in place. Like Gore, Alexander deserves his high rank among the truly intelligent politicians ever to come out of Tennessee. Like Gore, he lacked the common touch, but had applied his considerable intelligence and will to create that kind of appeal. And again like Gore, he suffered because his attempts at popular campaigning were inexpertly stitched together, and the seams were too visible.

Both as an attorney and as a character actor in Hollywood films, Fred Thompson gained valuable experience and name/face recognition for his 1994 smash debut as a real politician. His generally favorable marks as an incumbent senator have made him not only unbeatable in Tennessee but a person with genuine star quality in national politics.

There is one politician left in Tennessee who still gets to strut on the national stage. Republican Senator Fred Thompson has no trouble playing the part of a great man with the common touch. "A lot of politicians would kill to have Fred's personality," Alexander has observed.

Thompson, a Nashville lawyer, first gained notice as an investigative staff attorney during the Watergate scandal of the 1970s. He then parlayed the theatrical skills he had developed as a public advocate into a part-time acting career, playing big shots in the movies. From there, it was a short leap to becoming a big shot in politics. In the Republican sweep of 1994, Thompson crushed the Democratic candidate, Congressman Jim Cooper. His campaign performance was so impressive that Thompson immediately was touted as a future presidential contender. In Washington, his party rewarded him with a high-profile slot as chairman of a Senate committee investigating campaign finance irregularities, and he was often called upon to offer the Republican response to Democratic speeches.

But while Thompson may have the kind of touch that would make him a star in national politics, he may not have the ambition. He has tended to go his own way in Washington, breaking with party orthodoxy on issues such as those related to the trial lawyers' lobby and spending his free hours dating starlets and other entertainers (Thompson is divorced). During the contentious Republican presidential primaries of 2000, he backed Senate colleague John McCain against Governor Bush. So far, Thompson has not focused on building the kind of network within and beyond the Senate that would be necessary to take him higher, and he seems content with that. For people like Gore and Alexander—blessed with plenty of substance and personal ambition but not much public charm—such nonchalance must be absolutely maddening. Even when rumors circulated that Thompson was considering retiring from politics to renew his alliances in the film industry, he casually let the stories run their course.

volunteer. "I really think that if you put a book in the hands of children, they will read," Chapman says as she accepts her award. She and nine other finalists, including Myrna King from the Rape & Sexual Abuse Center and 17-year-old Stephanie Beatty from the Oasis Center, are treated to a luncheon and a tour of the Titans' training facility. Every team in the NFL selects its own candidate, and if Chapman is chosen above the 30 other recipients next month, the charity of her choice will receive $25,000. . . . **Former Washington, D.C.** Mayor Marion Barry, who attended Fisk University as a graduate student in 1960 and took part in Nashville's civil-rights struggle, says today that African Americans must seize the "mantle of leadership" to galvanize their communities. "We have had to fight for every gain we have made," says Barry, addressing the 26th-annual retreat and training conference of the Tennessee Legislative Black Caucus. Barry, who received a six-month sentence in 1990 for misdemeanor cocaine possession while in office, tells the mostly black crowd that mandatory minimum sentences account for the high number of black males in American prisons. More African-American men are in prison now, he observes, than in college.

19—Of the 1,273 adults in Nashville who were reported missing in 1999, two have not been found. A candlelight vigil is held for one, on the anniversary of her disappearance. On Nov. 19, 1999, Laresha Deana Walker, 23, dropped off her toddler son with relatives, planning to get her car appraised in Rutherford County the next day. She was never heard from again. Hers is one of 20 unsolved missing-persons cases dating back to 1980 that Metro police continue to work. A hundred people turn out tonight to share her family's hopes for closure. For the first 10 months of this year, 714 people have been reported missing. Only two have not been found: Delores Rogers, 46, and Mayme Hart Johnson, 85. . . . **By 2003,** if all goes as planned, pedestrians could be strolling the expanse of a stunning new Shelby Street Bridge—walking on broad 10-foot sidewalks, standing on specially built observation decks to gaze out at the city's downtown scene. The reopening to foot traffic only is two years behind the timetable announced when the bridge was closed to cars in Feb. 1998. The project stayed on hold until Mayor Bill Purcell and Gov. Don Sundquist agreed to trade funds—the mayor's stash of $6 million in federal dollars that couldn't be used on the bridge project for the governor's state matching funds that could. Work will begin next year on the final phase, which is expected to take 18 months.

20—**About 1,000 people** attend today's ninth-annual Family Re-Union Conference at Vanderbilt, a daylong seminar on issues affecting families and senior citizens. But the event receives more attention for someone who does not attend: Vice President Al Gore, who, after two weeks of recounts, court battles and national unease, is still no closer to resolving what is now generally known as "Indecision 2000." Gore, who has chaired every Family Re-Union Conference since 1992, appears by satellite only. . . . **Four decades** after his parents, Harry and Mary Zimmerman, founded the Nashville-based Service Merchandise retail chain, Raymond Zimmerman relinquishes his role as chairman. He passes the title to Sam Cusano, who succeeded Zimmerman as CEO in March 1999, at the time the chain filed for Chapter 11 bankruptcy reorganization. By that point, competition from larger retailers and electronics stores had weakened the company. Zimmerman, who now lives in Florida, will concentrate on his latest venture, a retail chain called 99 Cent Stuff. . . . **Little more than a month** after celebrating the Grand Ole Opry's 75th birthday, Gaylord Entertainment gives loyal Opry manager Jerry Strobel a token of its regard: a pink slip. The 30-year Opry veteran falls

When he finally accepted defeat in his brief and generous concession speech, Al Gore got the best reviews of his entire campaign. Some came from Republicans eager to hasten his journey off the national stage. Democrats also gave him fulsome praise, but their reasons were more complex. At one end were those who angrily or sorrowfully felt that the best man and the best party had suffered an unfair defeat; at the other were those who wished good riddance to a candidate who had lost a winnable election and henceforth would be a millstone around the party's neck. Scattered between these two were dozens of perspectives on Gore's inability to carry Tennessee—and, consequently, the nation.

The big national story has already been told at great length, and there is little more to add here. Gore's untelegenic personality, the drag of President Clinton's anchor, the diversion of former Senator Bill Bradley's challenge in the primaries, the disappointing outcome of the debates with Bush, the deep pockets of the Republicans, the third-party candidacy of Ralph Nader, the increasingly negative influences of the press, and the strategic decision to distance the campaign from the Clinton administration all contributed to the vice president's failure to hold the fort in an era of relative peace abroad and unprecedented prosperity at home.

Democrats staggered away from the debacle, finding consolation only in the thought that George W. Bush and the Republicans had captured a debased prize, and that control of Congress would be up for grabs again in just two years. But the historic presidential election had developed its own complex dynamic in Tennessee, and the outcome no doubt will have repercussions for the political process in Nashville and across the state for a long time to come.

In an election so close—and with the benefit of hindsight—it is easy to imagine innumerable ways that Gore could have found the last three electoral votes he needed. But his defeat in Tennessee was the one setback above all others that reasonably could have been foreseen and prevented. That is why the battle in Tennessee—and what it says about the changing face of politics in the South—is worth looking at again.

On a tactical level, the inside story of the Gore campaign in Tennessee reveals many of the flaws typically seen in most losing campaigns: erratic management, dysfunctional staffing, misplaced priorities. (Such failures can also be found in a lot of winning campaigns, but the things that look like fatal defects for a loser are mere foibles when the winner gets away with them.) Campaigns, after all, are ad hoc affairs that pull together lots of very different people with all sorts of personal agendas. It's probably too much to expect that these ragtag teams should be as efficient and well-managed as a neighborhood Wal-Mart.

But leaving aside the nuts and bolts of micromanagement and the painful recriminations, there remain three interconnected reasons—cultural, demographic, and operational—for Gore's failure at home, and there were limits to what he might have done to address them. Indeed, given the man that he had become by the beginning of the presidential race, nobody would have expected him to carry Tennessee if it hadn't been his home state.

The cultural factor had to do with a social cleavage lingering from the 1960s. Although the nation (including the South) had changed enormously since those tumultuous years, both the speed and direction of the changes varied greatly from one region to another. Much of the North and the West Coast have tended to be more permissive socially and more supportive of government action to ensure the general welfare, while the South, the Midwest, and the Mountain States have retained more of a commitment to conservative social values and a greater skepticism about the usefulness of government programs. Entangled in all this is a lingering reality concerning racial politics: The white South has changed, but it hasn't quite discarded its resentments about having to change.

Some of these philosophical differences carry a taint of hypocrisy in their real-world application, but there is some truth too—and it was enough to create a serious problem for Gore. As much as political scientists like to point to elections as exercises in self-interest, the fact remains that in this election, the states with the lowest median incomes gave the strongest support to Bush. This meant that working-class citizens with

Even though Tennessee Republicans were deeply split over tax issues, they showed their unity for George Bush at the party's national convention in Philadelphia. Cheers welled up from the Tennessee delegation when Gov. Don Sundquist announced that all their votes were for Bush.

victim to belt-tightening measures at Gaylord, which says Strobel's duties are already spread among several people. The news comes the same day Gaylord announces it is merging the staffs and rosters of its contemporary-Christian labels, Word Records and Myrrh Records, making several job cuts in the process. But to observers, the firing of Strobel is even more significant. "It's another indication of how the Nashville music industry is losing control of its own art form," says Opry chronicler and country music authority Charles Wolfe. "Now we're in a situation where decisions are made by people in corporate boardrooms in L.A. or New York or wherever."

21—**Downtown rush-hour traffic** is made even more congested by a broken water main, a cast-iron relic dating back at least to the 1920s, which sends streams gushing down 1st Avenue in the early-morning hours. Several businesses report water damage, including the Wildhorse Saloon, which closes until an employee area downstairs can be drained. The street is closed today and tomorrow from Church Street down to Demonbreun. . . . **Public support** may not be enough to avert the wrecking ball from the Union Station train shed, if a town meeting tonight is any sign. More than 125 citizens, including historic preservationists, beseech owner Henry Sender and the Metro Development and Housing Agency to shore up the frame's rotting trusses and rusted girders. But Sender does not want to spend the estimated $5.1 million and eight months necessary to restore the rickety, century-old historic structure. MDHA has until Dec. 6 to issue Sender a demolition permit. . . . **Porter Wagoner** flips a switch, and a glow suddenly appears on the horizon over Briley Parkway. The Christmas lights at the Opryland Hotel—all 2 million of them—blink on, turning every nearby tree and bush into a glistening ball of light. Visitors' pockets are also lighter, now that parking at the hotel has gone up to $10.

the least to gain from a Bush victory and passage of his tax plan were most likely to vote for him. Those with the most to gain from a Democratic victory—in the South and the Great Plains—also voted their philosophy not their wallets.

Tennessee is the only Southern state that Gore came close to carrying—if you ignore Florida, which left the cultural South long ago. The politics of race was a catalyst for the regional divergences, although it is now more context than active ingredient. Those Democrats who survived in the South did so by following regional gravity rather than the platform of their national party. Eight years as a national Democrat had stripped Gore of that luxury.

22—Reward checks totaling $73,000 go to six people who helped put convicted killer Paul Dennis Reid on Death Row. The largest amount, $28,400, goes to Juan Gonzalez, the 33-year-old man Reid stabbed and left for dead at a Hermitage McDonald's in 1997. Gonzalez's testimony helped convict Reid of the murders of three co-workers. Even with Reid behind bars, Gonzalez still doesn't sleep well at night.

23—**Thanksgiving.** The demand is especially great this season at local emergency food-distribution agencies such as Second Harvest Food Bank, which serves 7.4 million meals to 400,000 people in Middle Tennessee each year. The agency started canning its own food this year, using bulk quantities of donated foods to produce 600,000 cans of chili, stew and soups. As *The Tennessean*'s Jay Hamburg reports, Second Harvest's turkey-rice soup alone required a nationwide network of donors. Vice president of donor relations Larry Reynolds got Kroger trucks to give a free ride to 2,500 pounds of celery from a farming company in California, which joined two tons of carrots, 600 pounds of food starch, 625 pounds of vegetable oil and 2,500 pounds of turkey left over from a commissary company. The resulting dish filled 140,000 cans.
. . . **At the Catholic Church** of the Assumption in North Nashville's Germantown neighborhood, meanwhile, a throng of more than 1,400 of the grateful— a yeasty mix of poor people, social activists, politicians and church volunteers—turns out for neighborhood guardian angel Gerry Searcy's annual Thanksgiving dinner, whipped up by Searcy and a few dozen of her friends.
. . . **Tennessee's wild turkey** population, which fell to about 1,000 in the 1940s, now numbers more than 200,000. That includes the half-dozen gobblers that show up every morning at James and Katherine Brewer's home in Spring Hill, waiting for handouts of cracked corn. The Brewers

Al Gore's campaign for the presidency reached its apex in August with his widely applauded choice of Connecticut Sen. Joseph Lieberman as his running mate and their formal nomination at the Democratic Convention in Los Angeles. Their joint appearance on the plaza in front of the Tennessee Capitol following the selection of Lieberman drew a massive throng of supporters.

Responding to cheers of the Tennessee faithful, Gore and his wife, Tipper, joined by Lieberman and his wife, Hadassah, gave the state's Democrats hope of November victory that would not only keep the White House in the party's hands but also stall the Republicans' takeover of Tennessee. Those hopes would die when George Bush carried the state.

The demographic factor that played a big part in Gore's Tennessee loss was the rise of the suburbs—partly a result of regional in-migration and partly one of greater prosperity. Around the cities of the South, as in other regions, significant numbers of young families with high incomes have moved into handsome new homes in sprawling subdivisions that market themselves as destinations—exclusive, detached, self-contained. Here, upward mobility is the norm, and in such transient places, there is not much evidence of old political organizations or old loyalties. They tend to develop rather anemic patterns of political participation, until something big comes up, like an important local sewer bond issue, or a close and heated presidential election. The pocketbook perspectives are paramount—and here, the vote was all with Bush. Gore lost five of the six counties adjacent to Metro Nashville, carrying only Robertson, the most agricultural of the bunch.

The organizational factor in Gore's defeat was the poor execution of the campaign. This was the phase in which Gore was supposed to make up for the cultural and demographic indicators so unfavorable to him. If the Democrats had run a good campaign, they might have turned things around. They didn't.

In losing Tennessee, probably the most decisive fact was that Gore had not run a serious statewide campaign of his own since 1984, when he beat Victor Ashe of Knoxville to take over the Senate seat formerly held by Howard Baker, the Republican majority leader. In the intervening years, Gore had sought the Democratic nomination for president in 1988 and had won re-election to the Senate in a clean sweep of every Tennessee county in 1990. He had also endured two painful family losses, written a book, and won national election twice as the lesser half of the Clinton-Gore presidential team.

During his early Senate years, Gore had remained attentive to the state, keeping up the same kind of demanding, every-weekend-at-home schedule that had served him so well as an up-and-coming House member. The first presidential bid, and the near-tragedy that occurred when his only son was struck by a car as the two were leaving a

today are eating store-bought turkey. . . . **Jamie Taylor,** a Watertown 10th-grader and vegan, wins a vegetarian Thanksgiving dinner in an essay contest sponsored by People for the Ethical Treatment of Animals. For her essay, Taylor receives a "tofurky," a turkey substitute made of textured soy-based vegetable protein down to the drumsticks. . . . **Former Franklin High School** student Alan Parish does 5 miles in 25 minutes and 28 seconds, finishing first out of 5,500 entrants in the seventh-annual Boulevard Bolt on Belle Meade Boulevard. The race raises $55,000 for Nashville's homeless.

24—**Two unrelated bank robberies** in one afternoon have Metro police and FBI agents scrambling. A grandmotherly woman dubbed the "Granny Robber" tried to stick up SunTrust

Away from the rallies, the debates, and other public appearances, Gore worried that his deeply rooted base in Tennessee Democratic politics was eroding. But no one in the party or on his staff worried enough to head off an amBush out of Texas by an urban cowboy with an accent and a philosophy that appealed to conservative Tennesseans.

Bank branches on Nolensville Road and Hillsboro Pike before robbing the Regions Bank on Franklin Pike. Police are on the lookout for a 5-foot-tall redhead in a thick car coat and prescription glasses. In the other robbery, a man in his mid-20s asked the teller at the Bank of America branch on Gallatin Road if she had a nice Thanksgiving. He then told her he had a gun and demanded all her $100, $50 and $20 bills. He's wanted for six other Nashville bank robberies since July. The two stickups today bring the total of bank robberies this year in Nashville to 27, two less than all of last year.

25—The overconfident UT **Vols** come to Adelphia Coliseum for what should be their annual cakewalk against the hapless

At one airport rally after another, Bush kept dropping by to say howdy—in Memphis, Nashville, Chattanooga and the Tri-Cities. As early as May, six months before the election, he was openly predicting that Tennesseans would find his stand on guns, abortion, school prayer, privatization and other issues more palatable than Gore's.

The erosion of Democratic political power in Tennessee since the Republican sweep of 1994 was a factor in the 2000 election that few Democrats took seriously. But in fact, homegrown figures of any real stature in the party were down to a mere handful, perhaps the best-known being (from left) Congressman Bart Gordon (who holds the former Gore seat), Congressman Harold Ford of Memphis and retired former Gov. Ned McWherter.

baseball game in Baltimore, somewhat diminished his focus, but his reputation remained strongly positive, both in the Senate and in Tennessee.

The vice presidential nomination in 1992 came unexpectedly. Gore had not been on any of the speculative lists of vice presidential candidates, most observers having assumed that he was too much of an echo of Clinton (moderate-to-progressive white Southerner) to add anything to the ticket. But Clinton chose Gore precisely because their similarity underscored the point he had been trying to make about "a different kind of Democrat"—centrist, pragmatic, inclusive. This so-called "Double Bubba Ticket" was good news for the party in Tennessee, which had endured some fractious and unhappy months following Governor Ned McWherter's fitful and ultimately failed attempt to pass a state income tax and find ways to fund his package of education reforms. But none of that did much to hold together the county-by-county network Gore had pulled together previously. By the time he needed it in the presidential race, a lot of it was gone.

Gore had originally set up his campaign headquarters in Washington early in 1999, hoping to discourage the candidacy of any other prominent Democrats. While the strategy was largely successful until the late entry of the all-but-forgotten former Senator Bill Bradley, the sluggish, expensive start to Gore's campaign reflected the way he had sought to forestall opposition: by putting all the top Democratic operatives on his payroll. By fall, when the drive was stalled, Gore heeded the counsel of some of his closest advisers—including his wife Tipper—and relocated the campaign headquarters to Nashville, paring away some of the excess salaries in the process.

While the tactic was successful on many levels, the relocated campaign apparatus never really took root as an organic part of the city. The key people who headed the

Vanderbilt Commodores. Instead, UT fans are stunned to see Vandy QB Greg Zolman spark a scrappy offense that shoves touchdown after touchdown past the Vols' flummoxed defense. Vandy ultimately loses 28-26 in the game's final minutes—this is, after all, Vandy—but it's a better-than-average moral victory, and more tellingly, a moral defeat for the Vols, whose orange blood runs cold at the very thought of losing to the 'Dores.

26—It's hard to say which news some Tennesseans find more exasperating: that George W. Bush has been certified the winner today in Florida by the state's top election official, who also happens to be Bush's state campaign manager—or that Vice President Al Gore is prolonging the matter by contesting the results. "They're gonna call him 'Almost Al' when this is all over," says a woman in the checkout line at the Melrose Kroger. "Thank God For Chad," reads a cryptic message on a Nolensville Road Texaco sign. . . . **With a little more** than three minutes left against the hated Jacksonville Jaguars, the Titans once again go to their placekicker, Al Del Greco. In a replay of the Titans' loss two weeks ago to the Baltimore Ravens, Del Greco misses again— this time from a mere 28 yards— and the Jaguars claim the day, 16-13. On sports-talk radio, the topic of Del Greco rouses callers into a figurative mob bearing pitchforks.

27—Just after 1 a.m., Hohenwald police officer Alan Ragsdale responds to a burglar alarm at a local car dealership. As he approaches the building, an intruder inside fires three bullets through the plate-glass window. Ragsdale is wearing a bulletproof vest, but a slug strikes him under the arm where he is not protected. Alan Ragsdale, 32, described by friends, co-workers and townspeople as an all-around good guy, becomes the first Hohenwald officer ever to be killed in the line of duty. Ricky L. Grayson, 18, is charged with the crime.

campaign organization, chairman Bill Daley and campaign manager Donna Brazile, spent little of their time in Nashville, and even the resident leadership tended to be from out of town. Without homegrown leadership, it was inevitable that little attention would be paid to the pleas of the few who cautioned that Tennessee was not by any means in the bag. Veteran Tennessee activists complained of being dismissed as dumb hillbillies trying to enhance their stature by presenting their area of expertise—the Tennessee electorate—as a voter segment of outsized importance.

To be sure, the hard evidence didn't really start to show up in the polling data until September, but the threat should have been apparent much earlier. After all, Clinton and Gore had carried the state by less than 2 percent against Republican Bob Dole in 1996, and had gotten less than 48 percent of the vote in so doing. And, as early as May 2000, the Republicans were making well-publicized boasts about carrying the state. Most Democrats dismissed that as election-year posturing.

Gore was also undermined by his own earlier success. Many of the Democrats in the state from his own generation who would have hoped to ride a winning home-state presidential candidacy to an appointment in Washington had already done so during his vice-presidential tenure. Johnny Hayes, his longtime top money man, resigned his position as a director of the Tennessee Valley Authority to start shaking the money tree again, but others had already served their time, gotten their rewards, and retired from the hand-to-hand combat of politics. They were no longer out raising money or putting together plans to deliver counties.

The modern Democratic strategy for carrying Tennessee has three components: Roll up a big vote in Nashville and Memphis, hang on to the traditionally Democratic rural counties of Middle and West Tennessee, and force the Republicans to defend their traditional turf in East Tennessee and the new suburban counties.

On the first point, Gore succeeded admirably. He took an 85,000-vote edge out of those two big cities, although his success in Nashville didn't come easily. As late as September, much of the local campaign was in disarray as many of the top local power brokers stood on the sidelines, uncontacted by the young, out-of-state operatives put in charge of running the vital Davidson County operation. Only the timely intervention of some old Gore veterans pulled it together at the end. Nashville Mayor Bill Purcell, just elected in 1999, had been the state campaign chairman for the presidential ticket in 1996, but had come away from that experience estranged from Gore, who was said to harbor a feeling that Purcell had mainly used his position to advance his own gubernatorial ambitions. Purcell was largely inactive during the 2000 campaign. So too were Congressman Bob Clement of Nashville, former mayors Phil Bredesen and Richard Fulton, and even former Governor Ned McWherter. The nominal head of the Gore-Lieberman campaign in Tennessee, state Senator Roy Herron, appeared to be tagging along quietly throughout.

On the second strategic element—holding the traditionally Democratic counties—Gore had mixed results. He carried many of the counties in his old congressional district, although not the big suburban ones around Nashville. But in the farther reaches of Middle and West Tennessee, he did less well. Many of those counties have been slowly slipping out of the Democratic column, particularly in the west, where white have been more susceptible to racial backlash politics, presumably because blacks are numerous enough to have a political impact. In the largely white rural counties of the Upper Cumberland region, where voters mainly think of the Democratic Party in terms of TVA and the New Deal instead of civil rights, the Democrats remain strong. Gore was helped in that region by the organizational support of Congressman Bart Gordon, probably the state's best political technician, whose county-by-county operation has remained vital due to recurrent Republican challenges. Less useful was Congressman John Tanner in West Tennessee, whose hold on his district is more tenuous.

Probably the best-organized opposition to Gore in Middle Tennessee came from two powerful pressure groups, the National Rifle Association and the Christian Coalition. The NRA's relentless word-of-mouth campaign painted Gore as a government agent intent on taking away people's guns; the religious organization bound Gore and Clinton together as backsliding Southern Baptists who had stripped their high offices of decency and morality.

On the third element of a victory strategy—forcing the Republicans to defend the suburbs—the Gore campaign failed utterly. Assuming that local pride would carry Gore to victory, the campaign never put any resources into local advertising. Even bumper stickers and yard signs were hard to come by. It was a costly miscalculation. Bush visited these suburban areas around the state repeatedly, each time warning that he intended to whip Gore in his own back yard. He did exactly that, and decisively, winning roughly two of every three counties.

But the technical fine points of defeat are transitory; the larger consequences are much more enduring. By failing to run a well-planned and effective campaign, Gore just made it easier for the trends of electoral history to continue. In the end, he proved to be susceptible to those trends, which continue to shape the politics of Nashville and Tennessee.

For all the fury of the election and its aftermath, the consequences in Tennessee seemed remarkably small. The morning after Bush took the oath of office, the state's leading politicians were once again focusing on their usual daily crises and small ambitions. The General Assembly continued to wrestle haplessly with its tax woes and budget disputes; aspiring candidates great and small were plotting the paths still open to them; local governments went about patrolling the streets and collecting the garbage in the same old way. But the outcome was not meaningless, except in this sense: The irrelevance to everyday life of so much of the national political process was underscored once again.

The message of the election was a mixed one for the Republicans. At the top of the state ticket, the steady onslaught of Republican gains continued as the party re-elected another U.S. senator and put the state in the win column for the presidential

because it was, after all, the Waldorf. The Primms arrive tonight to find champagne and chocolate-dipped strawberries awaiting them on a silver tray. They spend their honeymoon anniversary taking in plays, the Christmas window displays and the show at Radio City Music Hall.

28—**The Rev. Morgan Babb** is on the air on WMDB-AM, the station affectionately known to listeners as "The Big Mouth." Babb, the first African American in Nashville to start his own radio station, has been broadcasting his "gumbo music in black" since 1983 over the 2,500-watt signal, along with listener greetings, comments about songs, even reminiscences about his many decades in the music industry as an artist, broadcaster and A&R man. During the daylight hours, the only time WMDB broadcasts, listeners might hear anything from Marvin Gaye to the Mighty Clouds of Joy; on Sundays, Babb preaches at the King Solomon Missionary Baptist Church on 10th Avenue North, which he founded in 1965. A *Nashville Scene* profile by Ron Wynn says Babb represents a bygone era when black radio stations reflected the tastes and personalities of individual DJs, offering community news and public events in place of the depersonalized "churban" (contemporary hits plus urban) format dictated today by programmers. . . . **Berry Hill, Woodbine,** Oak Hill and Tusculum residents have something back that they sorely missed: the neighborhood Krispy Kreme. The old building at 408 Thompson Ln., was razed in May to make room for a new, improved $1.5-million doughnut dispensary with extra seating and an expanded drive-through. The red light blinks on in the window at 5:30 this morning. From then on, 250 dozen doughnuts roll off the assembly line every hour. . . . **The Catholic Diocese** of Nashville wins a major victory today in court, as Judge Walter Kurtz dismisses much of the $35-million lawsuit filed by two boys who were molested by former priest

Gov. Don Sundquist (at microphone) was part of the big Republican sweep of 1994 that drove the Democrats from power, and Nashville Mayor Phil Bredesen (left) was the man he defeated. But less than two years later, they teamed up on a financial package to lure the Houston Oilers of the National Football League to a new stadium and home base in Nashville.

Edward McKeown. Kurtz rules that too much time had passed between the current abuse charges and the abuse of McKeown's earlier victims for the diocese to be held responsible.

29—**Metro is no closer today** to having a comprehensive solid waste plan than it was at the first of the month, when a report was due that was supposed to outline the costs of different options. Under consideration is the future of the controversial Nashville Thermal Transfer Plant, which burns garbage to heat and cool some 40 downtown buildings. Some community activists contend that burning is more costly, inefficient and environmentally harmful than recycling and composting, but there is not unanimity on these assertions. Metro officials say the report has been pushed back to the end of the year. When it came on line 25 years ago, Nashville Thermal was hailed as an economic and environmental stroke of genius that would conserve energy, get rid of trash, reduce pollution and save money all at once. The downtown land on which the plant sits is coveted for a more stylish use than garbage disposal, so its days appear to be numbered.

30—**Ricky Grayson,** the 18-year-old suspect who shot and killed Hohenwald police officer Alan Ragsdale, tells the Columbia *Daily Herald* that he wishes he had been shot instead of the fallen officer. Grayson says he didn't mean to shoot Ragsdale, just scare him away from the car dealership the suspect was burglarizing. "I am probably going to get the death penalty anyway, which is better than being in hell," Grayson says, "and this is hell."

. . . **Two weeks to the day** after Tennessee public schools received "report cards" grading their quality, the state's higher-learning institutions get their own marks. These grades would get most any student expelled. In an assessment of the 50 states released by the National Center for Public Policy and Higher Education, Tennessee public and private colleges

candidate. The Republicans also held their majority in the state delegation to the U.S. House—if only because the Democrats were too feeble to mount a serious challenge. But there were also setbacks for the Republicans, most notably the party's failure to capture the state Senate despite a determined effort to target key incumbent Democrats and open seats in the suburban and exurban areas around Nashville. Democrats also kept their huge advantage in the state House of Representatives. Among other things, those two successes meant that the Democrats would retain control of the redistricting process before the 2002 elections. Ten years earlier, House Democrats had artfully redrawn district lines to squeeze eight Republican legislators into the districts of eight other Republican incumbents. Party operatives say they aren't too worried about a repeat performance this time, because the Democrats so efficiently gerrymandered them in 1992 that there are no places left to hide any more Republicans.

And then there is the nagging question of the governorship. The job will be vacant in 2002 and offers the best chance for the Democrats to return to the political wars as a statewide force. Don Sundquist's effort to revamp the state tax structure has destroyed his personal popularity, but most of the Republicans kept their distance once he started talking up an income tax. There was no "pro-tax" faction in the party; there was only Sundquist. It seemed unlikely that his quixotic venture would put a drag on Republican efforts to keep the office in 2002. Senator Thompson was thought to be a shoo-in for the Republican nomination until he threw cold water on that idea.

The most significant impact of the 2000 election on Nashville and Tennessee may have been to prevent the city from becoming a key power base of the president (Gore), and to make it instead just another state that voted for the winner (Bush). Even Knoxville, whose mayor, Victor Ashe, was a Yale classmate of Bush's, may now have a better claim than anyone in Nashville to an inside position in the presidential orbit. Taking Tennessee away from Gore may have provided Bush with the margin of victory—but from his vantage point in Washington, Bush probably cares little about the poetry of that. A Gore victory would have created another long list of ambitious Tennesseans who wanted something for themselves—a judgeship, an ambassadorship, a federal appointment. That list is much shorter after a Bush victory; a seat on the Tennessee Valley Authority board of directors appears to be the most attractive plum.

The Democrats, meanwhile, are facing a vertical climb out of a deep hole. For starters, they have to find 80,000 more votes in the state just to return to par—and the trend has been running steadily in the other direction for almost a decade. It's not that the party is totally without resources—they still control four of the state's nine congressional seats and both houses of the legislature. The problem is that they have not been able to win elections across broad (rather than local) constituencies, or when the focus has been on national issues.

After the collapse of 1994, the Democrats could take comfort in Gore's status as vice president and Clinton's success in carrying the state in 1996. Party activists and aspirants could still look to the possibility of a federal appointment while waiting for their own election day to come. But with Bush's victory, the stakes for the 2002 governor's race went up. There would be no satisfactory explanations for another defeat. Knowing this, party leaders appeared to be working cooperatively (an uncommon style for them) to recruit strong candidates with a real chance to win, rather than leaving the field to freelance lightweights whose single-shot issues and overstimulated egos become a recipe for disaster. One person who figures prominently in such planning is Congressman John Tanner, a West Tennessee lawyer who projects the homespun qualities of a thinner, sleeker version of former Governor Ned Ray McWherter while still keeping healthy ties to the business community. Tanner has also positioned himself on the right-wing side of the cultural divide, once having voted to eliminate funding for the National Endowment for the Arts at a time when it was under conservative fire for failing to represent mainstream values.

Other candidates may emerge, but the serious ones will be those who try to create a special Tennessee brand of the Democratic Party, in the spirit of McWherter and the early Al Gore Jr.: concerned about those with less while not being antagonistic to those who have succeeded, tolerant on racial issues, carefully tuned to the dominant cultural values of the state, and silent on unpopular national Democratic issues when speaking out fails to improve the silence. Nashville will remain the hub of the party—

The Gore family has played a central role in Tennessee and national politics for more than 60 years, starting with the election of Albert Gore Sr. to Congress in 1938. Al Gore the younger won that same congressional seat in 1976, and went on to serve eight years each as representative, senator and vice president. The outcome of the 2000 presidential election closed a chapter in the family political saga for Al and Tipper Gore, son Albert III (not pictured), and (from left) Sarah, Karenna (holding son Wyatt), her husband, Drew Schiff, and Kristin. Whether it closed the book was less certain.

the best place to raise money and the surest place to gather votes. If the Democrats are to recover, they must find common ground among urban, suburban, and rural interests.

For Gore, another presidential run in 2004 is not out of the question, especially if the business cycle turns against Bush. Winning the popular vote to some degree absolves him of the ignominy of blowing a highly winnable election and turns his defeat into something more like electoral theft, especially given the way the systemic imperfections of the Florida vote count weighed against him. Realistically speaking, though, Gore may already have had his best shot. He may have a tough time persuading members of his own party that he is still their best candidate, especially when there are so many other ambitious Democrats panting in the wings.

If it is the end of his political career, he may do well to ponder the advice he gave his father after the 1970 election. In his autobiography, *Let the Glory Out*, the elder Gore wrote this in the wake of his loss to William Brock:

"I not only had wanted those next six years, but had felt that the country needed my Senate votes and accrued experience. But my son had the correct attitude about that situation. When I asked him how he would feel if after 32 years in Congress—good record, very clean nose, etc. . . . he lost to an opponent who had no accomplishments except to have been consistently wrong for eight years, his calm reply was, 'Dad, I would take the 32 years.'"

get C's or worse in affordability, the preparedness of students and how quickly students complete their degrees. The state scores a shocking D- in the number of students who actually pursue a college education. In the top five states, an average 42 percent of the 18-to-24-year-old population attends college; in Tennessee, as of 1998, that figure is 27 percent.

by Liz Murray Garrigan

With a confidence bordering on cockiness, George W. Bush stood before a cheering crowd of close to 10,000 supporters in the Memphis suburb of Bartlett and declared flat out that he would take the state of Tennessee from its favorite-son candidate, Al Gore, in the November presidential election.

The day was Friday, August 18, 2000, and it was already hot and muggy at 11 a.m., but Bush was as cool as an East Tennessee cucumber. By no coincidence, this was the morning after Gore's acceptance speech at the Democratic convention in Los Angeles. Before the celebrants were out of bed on the West Coast, Bush was delivering their wake-up call in person.

The Texas governor's handlers had been bringing their man to the Volunteer State at every opportunity. They smelled a delicious upset in the making. Steadily since the turbulent 1960s, affluent and conservative suburbanites around the state's major cities had given the Republican Party a new and powerful base. Bush's campaign strategists calculated that if they could score an early election-night victory in Tennessee, the outcome might have great impact in states farther west, where the polls would still be open. They could hardly have imagined just how big such a triumph would be.

Tuesday, November 7: It's election day, and Tennessee Republicans wake up feeling good—not gloating, not smirking, but hopeful, eager, positive. "We had people mad at us because we didn't have enough buttons and signs," says Governor Don Sundquist, chairman of the Bush campaign in the state. "We thought we had plenty, but the demand was overwhelming."

Still, Senator Fred Thompson cautiously notes, it would be a mistake to let overconfidence creep in. "Al Gore hasn't made it home as often as people expected," he says, "and the GOP hasn't quite known how to read that. It's as if they know something we don't." But by noon today, there are signs—quite literally—that people think the great struggle is about to end in Bush's favor. A giant Gore/Lieberman poster, too big to carry

except on a truck, is shoved in between two garbage dumpsters behind the Metro Courthouse. Talking-head prognosticators are saying the electorate will know sooner rather than later the conclusion to this political drama, at least in Tennessee.

On the streets of downtown Nashville, satellite trucks are moving into position, press stands are being erected, and wandering TV crewmen are roaming from building to building, scouting out the most promising free-food prospects. Numerous creative entrepreneurs—hucksters in campaign garb, donkey and elephant sales reps—peddle a highly perishable inventory of throwaway memorabilia, including Gore Beanie Baby rip-off dolls.

Former Nashville Mayor Phil Bredesen, walking through the downtown Arcade, stops to say hello to an ink-stained wretch, and the guessing game begins. "I think Bush will win the popular vote," he says, with only a faint ray of hope for his man Gore. "And I think Bush will win Tennessee." The only question in Bredesen's mind is whether Gore can somehow manage to squeeze out a bare majority of electoral votes nationwide.

By late afternoon, the loyalists are starting to swarm their nests for the evening. The GOP has commandeered the Wildhorse Saloon on Second Avenue for its election-night festivities, and the Democrats are in two locations—Gore and the bigwigs at the Loews Vanderbilt Plaza Hotel, and thousands of the rank and file on War Memorial Plaza. In addition to pulling the Bush bandwagon, the Wildhorse Republicans are poised to celebrate Senator Bill Frist's re-election. As Thompson and even most Democrats acknowledge, Frist's no-name challenger, Jeff Clark, offers little opposition. "I don't think it'll go down to the wire," Thompson says diplomatically—and indeed, just minutes after the local polls close at 7 p.m., Frist is tagged the apparent winner.

But this anticipated outcome brings only a ripple of applause from the assembled GOPs. They're in shock from a devastating blow delivered at about ten minutes before the hour by CBS's Dan Rather, who declared Gore the winner in Florida—considered a vital state by both sides. The other networks quickly followed suit. No one in the Wildhorse is willing to concede Florida yet, but the intended celebration of Frist's easy victory now feels more like a funeral home visitation.

The Dems are on their own emotional roller-coaster ride. Things start out well for them in the big Eastern states, and then comes the call for Gore in Florida, setting off raucous cheering and high-fiving. The underdog look has fled. A red-faced Chris Ferrell, an idealistic young Democrat doing time as an at-large Metro Council member until higher office calls, says with a gleeful gleam in his eyes, "Al Gore's going to be the next president." Frist's easy win doesn't hurt the Dems much—they didn't expect to beat him anyway—but worse news is lurking.

Still expectant, if no longer smugly confident, the ever-hopeful GOPs bounce back with a vengeance shortly after 8 o'clock when the networks and their local affiliates declare Bush the winner over Gore in Tennessee. The Wildhorses go wild. Uptown, of course, this news turns the other party's worst nightmare into stark reality. The favorite son of loyal Democrats—and the man most Tennessee Republicans love to hate—has been trounced on his home court.

It was one of those nights, one for the record books and the storybooks—close, tense, emotional. With everything on the line, the last two guys left standing were duking it out like there was no tomorrow, which there wasn't supposed to be (but in fact, there would be 36 more tomorrows for Bush and Gore to endure before it all got settled in a courtroom far from Nashville).

In all the excitement, a subplot in the ongoing political drama surfaced briefly, noted only by those who witnessed it. The party at the Wildhorse was just getting its legs when the networks gave Florida to Gore, and the news stung like a cold shower. Dejected Republicans stood motionless and silent, morose and surly. It was right after this catastrophe that Governor Sundquist came strolling into the saloon.

There were formalities to be endured—introductions, exhortations, pleas for all to stick together and keep the faith. Gamely, Senator Frist gathered the leaders—Sundquist and his wife, Martha, former Governor Lamar Alexander, state GOP chairman Chip Saltsman, and others. Both as governor and as chairman of the Bush campaign in Tennessee, Sundquist was the state's official Republican leader. But when he stepped forward to acknowledge his introduction, he was greeted with a lusty round of boos.

At that moment, Senator Thompson was on the floor of the hall, doing an interview with an NBC reporter. Hearing the commotion, he first thought that the unruly crowd was attacking Gore. Then he realized, to his chagrin, that some of the frustrated and enraged partisans were turning on their own kind. Sundquist was still bearing bruises from a verbal mugging he had endured at the hands of lawmakers and voters alike for his advocacy of an income tax. Jaw clenched, he took another hit.

The cohesion of the previous hour had evaporated. Some of the revelers, finding themselves at a wake, downed their drinks and headed for home, seeking consolation and shelter. Former GOP congressional candidate and talk-radio gab man Steve Gill was offering commentary for WKRN-Channel 2, trying to ignore "the sick feeling in the pit of my stomach." At one point, in a room backstage, Frist and Thompson got on the phone to Bush election headquarters in Austin, their faces grim, their voices low. Sundquist himself later admitted, "It was kind of a downer for me"—both the news from Florida and the bum's rush from his own troops. Perhaps by way of reassuring himself, he explained, "You know, in some cases it was the liquor talking. I don't think it was party regulars; I think it was just the antis."

On the way home, Sundquist learned via telephone that the networks were retracting their call on Florida. Back at the residence, he scribbled various state electoral vote combinations on a pad, trying to figure out how Bush could still win if Florida went to Gore. Much later—well past midnight—the usually reliable television networks again miscalculated the outcome in Florida, this time in Bush's favor. Neither party knew quite how to respond. Sundquist finally spoke to Bush himself on the phone. "He was very happy about winning Tennessee," the governor reported. "He was very calm."

By 2 a.m., Sundquist was all alone in front of the TV. Thompson was back home alone, too—because, he said, "In a national election as close as this, the best place you can be is by yourself with the clicker." And so they sat, the two most prominent Republicans in Tennessee, each in his own cozy Nashville bunker, watching the Democratic Party diehards as they waited in the rain at War Memorial Plaza, hoping for a miracle, then flipping channels to check on the Republican hard-cores in Austin, praying for their own version of divine intervention.

Nearly all the way to daylight, the governor and the senator stayed glued to the tube, the net, the cell—whatever electronic umbilical cord might best relieve their anxiety. They were watching at 2 a.m. when word came that Gore had phoned Bush to concede, and then they saw the vice president's motorcade crawling down Broadway in the rain. They waited for Gore to step out onto the plaza stage and surrender. Tension mounted as an hour dragged by. The networks, having nothing else to show, switched back and forth between two scenes: the cortege of limousines strung out behind the War Memorial Building, and the remaining 2,000 or so thoroughly soaked true believers on the plaza, waiting patiently in the drizzle for history to happen. Then came the shocking report that Gore had retracted his concession, that the two candidates had had another exchange, frosty and inconclusive at the end. And shortly after 3 a.m., the networks, on their third try, finally got Florida right: too close to call.

In the gray gloom of the morning after, Sundquist and Thompson were as uncertain of the outcome as the networks, the partisans, and the candidates themselves. Hours after the polls had closed, the monumentally historic presidential election of 2000 was still unsettled, still up in the air. And it would stay up there, swinging in the wind, for another five weeks.

Liz Murray Garrigan covers politics for the Nashville Scene.

November 7, 2000: A Democrat's Diary

by NATILEE DUNING

In the last hour before dawn on election day, Al Gore sprinted up onto a temporary stage in a Tampa parking lot. "It's almost 5:30, Texas time, and George W. Bush is still asleep, and I'm still speaking to the people of Florida!" the presidential candidate shouted, to the cheers of a sleepy-eyed assemblage. The vice president and his running mate, Senator Joe Lieberman, who was at his side, were nearing the end of a 30-hour "Sprint for Victory" that would finally end in Nashville and Carthage at mid-morning.

A short time later, as Air Force Two sped northward, I was slowly getting up to speed at my house in the hills south of Nashville, preparing for what was sure to be a hectic but exciting day. At the Williamson County elementary school down the hill from my house, poll workers were welcoming the day's first voters. It was drizzling rain, warmer than usual for early November.

I had already voted weeks before. For the second time in a presidential election, Tennesseans had the option of early voting, and we later learned that nearly one-fourth of the 3.1 million registered voters in the state had done so. Republicans had originally fought that provision in the legislature—but in the end, it would be the Republicans who profited most from it.

Shortly after 8, I'm out the door, going to a general-aviation terminal on the back side of the Nashville International Airport, where the Gores will land. Then they will go home to vote in Smith County, returning to Nashville later in the day to await the returns. As I merge into the morning traffic on Interstate 65, I'm reading the bumper stickers. There's a smattering of Gore-Liebermans, but many more Bush-Cheneys. Why has it been so hard to get Gore bumper stickers? I called headquarters several times and finally ordered them from a vendor on the campaign website. Even then, it took six weeks before they arrived.

Soon I'm parked and moving with a gathering crowd through security checkpoints and onto the tarmac. The clouds overhead are breaking up. It's great to see the sun, and to witness political history being made today by a son of Tennessee.

After what seems like a long wait, we finally see the sky-blue jet touching down. It taxis to a stop before what has grown into a cheering, waving, stomping, screaming throng of 300 or more. Out comes Tipper, looking great as always. She must be exhausted, but she's beaming, buoyed by the crowd.

"Al, Al, Al!" we're all chanting. He bounds down the stairs, big smile, punching the sky with a fist. "Get out the vote!" he yells. "Get out the vote!" He's working the rope line, high-fiving, hugging, posing for pictures. Then, swiftly, the welcome party is over, and two shiny helicopters whisk the Gore entourage away to Carthage, 50 miles east. Smart move—no roadblocks. This isn't a good day to tie up I-40 traffic.

Heading back into town, I loop around the business district and exit at MetroCenter Boulevard, bound for the national headquarters of Gore-Lieberman 2000. I need credentials for what will surely be a victory celebration tonight. The offices are in a low-slung brick building on Mainstream Drive (did they choose this location for its name?). It's the campaign's third headquarters, its second in Nashville.

There's not a billboard in sight on this reclaimed floodplain—the better to avoid embarrassments such as the opposition engineered at Gore 2000's first Nashville location. Shortly after the campaign moved from $60,000-a-month offices in downtown Washington to a $2,000-a-month building at Charlotte and 25th avenues (behind HCA, fount of Tennessee Republican Senator Bill Frist's considerable wealth), the Republican National Committee leased the oversized billboard commanding the airspace above the site. They slapped up a huge photo of Gore hugging Bill Clinton. The caption ("One of Our Greatest Presidents") was a Gore quote—words spoken just after Clinton was impeached by the House. The only way Gore 2000 could get away from that sign was to move. Getting away from Clinton has been much harder.

Inside the heavily secured office building, I see a steady influx of staffers and volunteers, including some just in from the airport. There's Donna Brazile, the national campaign manager, looking disheveled and sleep-deprived. Free at last from the punishing marathon just ended, she's carrying an armload of briefing books and dragging a wheeled suitcase through the front door.

It takes me several minutes to get my credentials for admission to the War Memorial Plaza victory celebration. Then I'm off to Franklin to do my volunteer bit for the beleaguered Democrats of Williamson County. In the party's cramped headquarters at the corner of South Margin and Columbia Avenue in Franklin (a space that, post-election, will house the Rebel's Rest Civil War Artifact Shop), I'm assigned to work the polls located at the police station.

In three hours on the line there, I encounter exactly two Democrats: a middle-aged couple. "How's it going?" they ask. I have to say the news for Williamson Countians of our persuasion isn't good—but then, who would expect otherwise in this Republican stronghold?

"Gore's got to win," says the man. "He's got to. It's too important for the nation and the world. I just spent two days flying back from Russia to vote." He's a businessman with extensive dealings in the former Soviet Union. He says his friends and associates there are "scared to death" that a Bush victory would bring back the Cold War. "All we can do is vote and hope," says his wife as they depart.

Back home at 4, I turn on CNN—loud, so I can listen as I get ready for the evening. At about 5:45 p.m. Central Time, I hear the first two states—Indiana and Kentucky—being called for George W. Bush before all the polls are even closed there. On my way out the door at 6:05, I catch a glimpse as Gore gets on the boards with a win in Vermont. By 6:45, when the networks assign Virginia and Georgia to Bush, I'm exiting the freeway in Nashville to pick up my daughter, Kate, in Sylvan Park. She and I will join other Gore friends and family at Loews Vanderbilt Plaza Hotel to watch the returns. I arrive at her place on Idaho Street at 6:52, just in time to celebrate breathtaking news: Based on Voter News Service exit polls, all the networks have called the crucial state of Florida for Gore.

When we enter the hotel lobby at a few minutes past 7, Tennessee's polls have officially closed. Even so, many people who showed up before 7 remain in line at Middle and West Tennessee polling places, delayed by glitches in the state's new "motor-voter" registration system. Meanwhile, results stream in from other states. The networks are calling Illinois and the District of Columbia for Gore; Kansas for Bush; Maryland, New Jersey, and Massachusetts for Gore; Oklahoma, Texas, Mississippi, and Alabama for Bush; New York and Michigan for Gore; North and South Carolina for Bush.

Kate and I are directed to a private dining room on the mezzanine, where Pauline Gore (Al's mother), the Liebermans, and numerous family members and friends are finishing dinner and following the news on television sets placed around the room. (Newspapers will later report that a somber George W. Bush and family are leaving an Austin restaurant at this moment, returning to the privacy of the governor's mansion rather than to the Four Seasons Hotel, where a victory celebration has been planned. The *New York Times* will carry a restaurant patron's account of the tearful, apologetic embrace given the Texas governor by his brother, Florida Governor Jeb Bush, after the Sunshine State is called for Gore.)

As the wait staff move in to clear away the dinner dishes, the 80 or so of us in the room disperse. The presidential candidate's mother and her closest friends and family members move to an upstairs suite, as do the Liebermans. Most of the rest of us head to a large room down the hall, walking in at about 7:40, just as Maine goes to Gore. Five minutes later, our guy takes Pennsylvania, and the room erupts in cheers and shouts. With Michigan and Florida already in Gore's column, the crowd relaxes into comfortable confidence: The Democrats will win. Al Gore will be our next president. The room hums with a giddy buzz, and cell phones beep and chortle in every corner. Someone is pouring wine, and there's a run on bottled water and cold drinks. Champagne is chilling in ice buckets, but no one dares to jinx the victory by prematurely uncorking it.

Shortly after 8, Tipper Gore enters the room. Moving slowly through the crowd, she embraces the guests, poses for pictures, speaks with each person in turn. She seems calm, but distracted—from exhaustion, no doubt. Ohio and Louisiana go to Bush at 8:15, but few of us are paying close attention. Then at 8:18, with 40 percent of the Tennessee vote counted, CBS calls the state for Bush—*Bush!*—and a stunned silence falls over us, followed by shouts of "No!," angry protests, soft moans. We're all staring at Tipper, trying to grasp what has happened, to understand what this means. Of course she knew, she must have known, before she came in. The Tennesseans in the room flush with embarrassment. We thought it would be close, yes—all those Bush-Cheney yard signs, even in Wilson County!—but how can Al Gore lose his own state? He has won handily in Davidson County, but that's small consolation. We still believe he'll win the election, but this loss, Gore's first ever in Tennessee, will tarnish the victory. Tipper leaves soon after. Only much later will we fully realize the fatal significance of the Tennessee vote, and fully grasp how devastating this loss has been.

Minnesota and New Mexico have just been called for Gore when Bush appears at 8:50 in a live feed from the Texas governor's mansion. He's "not conceding anything" in Florida and Pennsylvania he says. Then, at 8:54, CNN pulls Florida out of the Gore column—too close to call. This is shocking news, almost unbelievable. At 8:59, the Associated Press—more restrained in its calls all evening—follows suit with the networks. Immediately after, New Hampshire and Missouri go to Bush. In just one hour, the euphoria has vanished, swept away by the chill wind of doubt.

It's quiet in the room now. People wander in and out, mumbling into their phones. When the West Coast polls close at 10 p.m. Central, it's still a muggy 60 degrees in Nashville. Snow is falling on the huge crowds at the Texas Capitol in Austin at 10:05 when the networks call California for Gore. Though still shaken by the Florida recall, we take this as a positive sign. There's little comment when Colorado goes to Bush, as expected, at 10:10.

The hours are stretching out, and it's clear this contest will go on into the early morning. At 11 p.m. Alaska goes to Bush; at 11:08 Arkansas rebuffs Bill Clinton and does the same, completing a Republican run of the entire South (not yet counting Florida). Washington state's assignment to Gore at 11:10 puts the electoral vote dead even at 242 each. Soon, Nevada goes to Bush. Only Wisconsin, Iowa, Oregon, and Florida are still out. At midnight, they're still out. Still out at half past 12.

Gore picks up Iowa at 1:05 a.m., but it's clear now that neither man can win without Florida's 25 electoral votes. Florida will decide the election. The snow has changed to rain in Austin, and it's raining in Nashville, too, where some 5,000 people still hold vigil at War Memorial Plaza. In Florida, with 94 percent of the vote in, Bush is leading by 20,000 votes. Jittery, numbed by the flood of figures and television's flashing maps, we stand, stretch, wander into the hall. There, Ted Koppel (remarkably short of stature, considering his gravitas on TV) is asking insiders why Gore failed to take Tennessee. Down the way, Jesse Jackson stands in the glare of television lights, talking about America's growing conservatism and about "voting irregularities" in Florida's African-American precincts.

At 1:16 a.m., Fox News calls Florida for Bush, and the other networks follow suit almost immediately. Local affiliate stations show Tennessee Republicans at the Wildhorse Saloon erupting into cheers. In Austin, whooping, screaming Texans dance in the streets to "Signed, Sealed, Delivered I'm Yours." (Stevie Wonder, whose song it is, must find that ironic. He campaigned with Gore only 24 hours before in Miami.)

Here at the Vanderbilt Plaza, muffled sobs provide a background chorus for the droning voices of TV anchors. After endless hours of waiting and hoping, the race is suddenly over; Al Gore's White House hopes are dead. There remains just one more duty for the faithful. Slowly, one by one, we rise and ready for the bus trip downtown, where Al will concede before his soaked followers and a huge, sodden flag unfurled behind the War Memorial's massive pillars.

"Never surrender. It's not over yet." So says Donna Brazile in an e-mail message to Al Gore at 1:20 from campaign headquarters across town, we'll later learn. But by 1:30, campaign chairman Bill Daley is calling Don Evans of the Bush campaign to tell him Gore will concede, and Al's on the ninth floor with Tipper, waking the kids, breaking the news. In a few minutes, he phones Bush, then prepares to leave for the plaza.

At 1:37, the Associated Press moves an urgent update to newsrooms nationwide that the "race is still up for grabs." But Gore friends, family members, and campaign staffers are now filing slowly onto waiting buses, unaware that any hope remains. On our bus, the only sounds are of soft weeping as we roll through deserted streets, city lights blurred by rain and tears. It's 2 a.m. as we pass the parking lot jammed with satellite trucks and stop before barricades closing off Charlotte at 7th Avenue. Despite the steady rain, several thousand supporters still wait on the plaza to hear the final word from Gore himself. Few have raincoats or umbrellas; they huddle together under pieces of scavenged plastic sheeting. We file off the buses like mourners come late to the cemetery, splashing through puddles and overstepping TV cables as we move to a reserved spot up front near the stage.

"Down with the umbrellas!" comes a hiss from behind. Forewarned of the rain, many of the just-arrived are blocking the view of those who've been here all night. The umbrellas—most of them—disappear. Now the misery is shared equally. The Jumbotron screens set up on either side of the stage are dark; no one wants to watch the Austin celebration anyhow. Where are the Gores, we whisper. What will he say? What happens now?

Nothing for a soggy half-hour. Then, at 2:30, someone throws a switch. We flinch at the sudden sound of television voices, and the giant screens begin to glow, bathing

upturned faces in election-map reds and blues. Mesmerized, we watch as George Bush's victory disappears, his 50,000-vote lead in Florida dwindling to 6,000, then dropping down, down into the hundreds—only the tiniest fraction of a single percentage point now separating him from Gore. Network anchors and commentators grasp for words and gasp for breath as Election 2000 careens off the tracks.

We hear the words "automatic recount" spoken by a Florida election official whose telephone connection to CNN goes dead shortly after. And now this: *Al Gore has retracted his concession!* Exuberant screams of surprise and relief split the night. We are leaping, bouncing, dancing, crying, hugging, chanting. "Recount! Recount! Recount!" segues into "Stay and fight!" On the giant screens, we see Austin, where cold rain drenches dumbstruck and despondent Bush supporters, even as our rain is ending. Just before 3 a.m. the networks pull Florida back into the undecided column. All bets are off now.

We watch the podium that extends like a ship's prow from the high plaza stage, its rainproof tarp removed in preparation for a speaker. The TVs go dark, and campaign chairman Bill Daley strides out from behind the great pillars. We search the shadows behind him for some sign of Al Gore and Joe Lieberman.

"I've been in politics a very long time," Daley says, "and I don't think there's ever been a night like this one." The crowd reacts with an explosive roar. But then he goes on to say that Gore will not appear, and a deep sigh rises up, shot through with boos. "We want Al! We want Al!" The chant starts strong, then tails away in disappointment. "Our campaign continues," Daley declares. "When the votes are all in, I hope we will meet back here for a great celebration."

And that's the end. For now. Slowly we move toward the buses that will return us to the hotel. This time, the trip smells of wet wool, fatigue, and, faintly, of hope. It's much quicker than the trip down.

By the time I've dropped Kate off in Sylvan Park and turned for home, it's 4 a.m. Patches of early-morning fog are drifting across Hillsboro Road. Occasionally I see flickers of television light in the windows of darkened houses. At home, I sink into the couch, too tired to move and too obsessed to sleep without checking one last time for any news I may have missed. But there is no more news, only a weary retelling of all I've just witnessed. At 5 a.m. on November 8, I stumble up the stairs to bed, hoping against hope that Al Gore will be president when I awake.

It was past 2:30 on the morning after Election Night 2000 when Al Gore's inner circle crowded into a basement room of the War Memorial Auditorium to hear advisor Carter Eskew (back to camera), report that the race in Florida, the state on which the entire election would turn, had ended in a virtual tie. Early in the evening, the TV networks had projected a win for Al Gore and Joe Lieberman there; later, they reversed themselves and called the state for George W. Bush and Dick Cheney; now they were saying it was deadlocked. Also listening, besides the remarkably composed candidates Gore and Lieberman, were (from left) Gore's brother-in-law Frank Hunger, legal adviser and former Tennessee Attorney General Charles Burson, and Gore's daughter, Karenna Gore Schiff. Seated next to Eskew is campaign chairman Bill Daley.

*B*ut of course, he wasn't. And five weeks later, when the U.S. Supreme Court finally put an end to Election 2000, he still wasn't. George W. Bush was declared the winner and would become the 43rd president of the United States. During the 35 days between November 7 and December 12, all eyes were locked on Florida's recount efforts and courtroom battles. But the war itself had been lost on November 7, when Tennesseans handed the state's 11 electoral votes to Bush. True, Gore victories in other states could also have changed the equation, tipped the balance to him. But Tennessee was the one that should have been his. It had supported him in every election for 24 years, the state he called home. Had Al Gore taken Tennessee, the Florida mess would've been moot. When the dust finally settled, that was what we saw and what we had to accept. "I don't know what happened," Gore strategist Carter Eskew told The Tennessean *on election night. "I thought we were going to win the state."*

How did Gore lose Tennessee? The analysis and finger-pointing began in earnest after his second concession speech on December 13. Donna Brazile told a group of Maryland Democrats what she saw as the "greatest mistake." "We should have started the campaign off in Tennessee. By the time we got there, it was too late." Brazile blamed the Democrats' "pollsters and media consultants" who diverted money away from Tennessee to the battleground states. This complaint surfaced again in post-election anecdotes that floated through state Democratic circles. Some Tennesseans who had contributed money to get out the vote at home later learned their contributions had left the state for Florida.

Other analysts cited other factors. The state had grown increasingly Republican over the past few years. The National Rifle Association sent in Charlton Heston and financed its own anti-Gore media campaign, which resonated strongly with hunters in this still largely rural state. The Clinton White House scandal doomed Gore from the start. A whole generation of new voters—voters who had never known Al Gore as their congressman or senator—came of age. And the Christian Coalition, with 30 chapters statewide, sent out 1 million voter guides to conservative church congregations in Tennessee just before Election Day.

But Gore's longtime friend and close adviser, two-term Tennessee governor Ned Ray McWherter, put blame for the loss squarely on the candidate's shoulders. McWherter said Gore misjudged the support of Tennessee voters and failed to come home enough during his eight years as vice president. "They vote for the person, and you've got to reach out to them," McWherter told an Associated Press reporter. He said the national campaign failed to take Tennessee seriously until "about two weeks before the election." That complaint was echoed by Tennessee's Gore-Lieberman campaign chair, Roy Herron, a state senator from McWherter's own hometown of Dresden in Weakley County (which, embarrassingly enough, went for Bush). "We thought that more media (advertising) should have been bought sooner," Herron told the Memphis Commercial Appeal, "but the folks making those decisions in the national campaign came to a different conclusion."

Ten days after George Bush was inaugurated, Gore adviser Eskew wrote in the Washington Post: "We failed as a campaign because we didn't do enough to reassure voters about what is true: Al Gore is a man of strong values and bedrock integrity."

With the eyes of the world on Nashville that momentous November night, Al Gore had come close enough to victory to smell it, touch it, taste it. But for the second time in a historic year of endings and beginnings, the home team had been stopped a yard short of the big prize. The clock ran out, the dream expired, and—for the moment, at least—Music City had run out of miracles.

Former Tennessean *reporter Natilee Duning is senior editor of the First Amendment Center at Vanderbilt University.*

Whimsically rendered in caricature as a modern Athena, the formidable Dame Nashville, as sketched by local artist W.J. Cunningham, stands tall at the portal of the modern age, bringing with her the cumbersome baggage of the past, the expansive appetites of the present, and an adapt-or-die readiness for the future.

"WELCOME TO AMERICA, DARLIN'"

by JEAN BETHKE ELSHTAIN

For my sins, I am a social and political philosopher. Not content to live in the world of ancient texts, I rummage about in the cluttered rooms of the present, trying to figure out what gives us meaning, purpose, and hope as individuals and as participants in a shared way of life. Almost as an occupational necessity, you might say, I stay alert to the wide range of social and cultural perceptions people bring to new situations.

When my family made the decision in 1988 to leave western Massachusetts, where we had lived since 1973, and move to Nashville, where I was to take up a post at Vanderbilt University, many of our friends were horrified. To them, Nashville was surely a place where reason goes to die. We found it instead a place where civil society goes to live.

Of course, this incomprehension of regions runs in both directions. Shortly after we moved to Nashville, in the steamy trough of a mid-August heat wave, I collapsed into a chair in a Green Hills beauty salon for a long overdue haircut. The country was just then entering a presidential campaign, and the overly serious former Massachusetts governor, Michael S. Dukakis, was running against the man who would become President George Bush the First. The haircut man and I exchanged a few words about the presidential campaign. He noticed the absence of any discernible Southern accent as I spoke, and this exchange ensued:

"Not from around here, are you?"

"No, we just moved here from Massachusetts."

"Well, welcome to America, darlin'."

I love that story. The comment "welcome to America, darlin' " seems very Nashville to me, and not in the usual Rebel-versus-Yankee way, or at least not exclusively that. The haircut man spoke more truth than he realized. As much of the United States over the past two to three decades has witnessed a withering of what social and political analysts call "civil society," associational enthusiasm is alive and well in Nashville. That was one of the things that struck me most about this city, and it manifests itself in palpable, plural ways.

Over the past six or seven years, social scientists who make it their business to study so-called "trend data" have noticed a disquieting change in American society: Many of the informal, voluntary associations that for generations have made up so much of the warp and woof of American civic life appear to be dying on the vine. Many fewer people—measured in the millions—are doing the hard, hands-on work of community, ranging from involvement in parent-teacher associations and Rotary clubs to participation in the outreach social ministries of mainline Protestant churches. Time was, especially in the industrial Northeast and the so-called Rust Belt in the Upper Midwest and Ohio Valley, when labor unions provided a rich social context for millions of American lives, but that spirit of solidarity and mutual support has been fading away. The phenomenon of civic disengagement is also measured in a strikingly steep decline in the number of folks rolling up their sleeves and going to work in politics at the local, precinct

1—**It must be Christmastime:** The Trees of Christmas stand lighted and decorated at Cheekwood. A Nashville tradition for the past 35 years, the event this year is organized around the theme, "Come! Sing a Song of Christmas." Each of the 14 living trees is decorated to commemorate a different carol. . . . **After a year of steadily declining sales,** the Tower Books location across from Vanderbilt on West End Avenue announces it will close after the first of the year. The bookstore has been in business since the late 1980s, but competition from the recently opened Borders superstore down the street proves too fierce. Christmas shoppers pounce immediately upon the bookstore's discounted merchandise.

2—**The baby Jesus is born** a few weeks early on the grounds at St. Luke Christian Methodist Episcopal Church, 2008 28th Ave. N. Last year's live, outdoor nativity scene, held in celebration of Jesus' 2000th birthday, drew unexpectedly huge crowds to St. Luke. "People came by from all over the community, they drove through or just sat down on that cold ground and started crying," recalls church member Allie Cage. Police officers will direct traffic tonight and tomorrow, and two shifts of volunteers will pose in St. Luke's manger. . . . **For $3,** Nashville residents can enjoy the illusion of living in a much colder city. RiverSkate, the city's small, seasonal, outdoor ice-skating rink, opens for the holidays at Riverfront Park. It stands next to the Tennessee Fox Trot Carousel designed by former Nashville artist Red Grooms. Nashville's mild winters keep the life span of the rink short, since it's hard to skate in puddles of melting slush. Today, though, a whistling wind off the Cumberland provides a wind-chill factor of 25 degrees.

level. More and more, politics seems irrelevant to them, or worse, sullied and corrupt—so why contribute in any way to such an enterprise? On and on, the litany of estrangement is intoned. As a civil society, we are in trouble. Political theorist Michael Walzer described the current moment vividly when he wrote:

> We are perhaps the most individualist society that ever existed in human history. Compared certainly to earlier Old World societies, we are radically liberated, all of us. Free to plot our own course. To plan our own lives. To choose a career. To choose a partner or a succession of partners. To choose a religion or no religion. To choose a politics or an anti-politics. To choose a lifestyle—any style. Free to do our own thing. This freedom, energizing and exciting as it is, is also profoundly disintegrative, making it very difficult for individuals to find any stable communal support, very difficult for any community to count on the responsible participation of its individual members. It opens solitary men and women to the impact of a lowest-common-denominator commercial culture. It works against commitment to the larger democratic union and also against the solidarity of all cultural groups that constitute our multiculturalism.

Why is this a worry? It troubles observers of the American democratic scene in particular because civil society—the existence of strong, plural associations—has been the very hallmark of American civic life. Such associations help to shape persons as citizens; help to draw them into community life and sustain them in doing so. Without the flesh and sinew of civil society, a democracy is much more susceptible to personal lassitude and withdrawal. Even disorder and instability may follow as people are less likely to know or interact with their neighbors, and more likely to see themselves as isolated individuals. They become more fearful as a result, more convinced that others are out to get them. They view their fellow citizens as competitors at best, menaces at worst. The upshot is that more control from above, so to speak, is sought in order to mitigate, however slightly, the disintegrative effects of civil society's decline. The sense that, as a people, we are all in this together is disappearing, supplanted by the conviction that we are all out for ourselves.

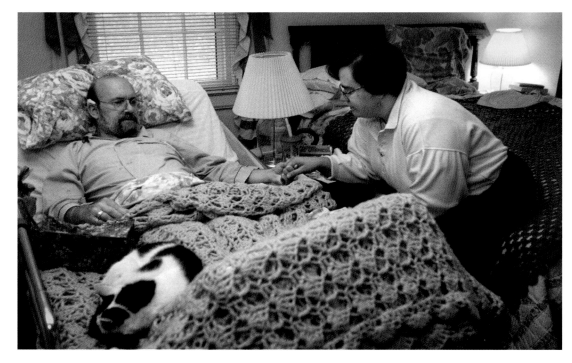

Cleburne Bender was terminally ill and reaching for a helping hand when volunteers from the Nashville support group Alive Hospice reached back. Chaplain Kathleen McGraw made frequent visits to Bender and his faithful cat, Freckles.

Almost like an abstract painting, the footprints of a lone pedestrian cut across the grain of tire tracks in the snow on Sixth Avenue, blending to create a winter cityscape of opposites: urban solitude, strength and vulnerability, the individual and the machine.

Life in such an atmosphere takes on a more temporary aspect. We see the place in which we just happen to live as a temporary resting point, one that is convenient, for now, until we pack up and move on to where the pastures are greener. Why bother with getting to know your neighbors, or making a contribution to your community, if it really isn't your community in any meaningful sense? Under such conditions, temporariness becomes a more constant feature of American life.

Not long ago I had a brief experience with the transient lifestyle, and I didn't like it much. I was conducting a three-week seminar for college teachers at the National Humanities Center in North Carolina. The center is a wonderful place to work but, of course, I also needed a place to sleep. The center staff found a place that was convenient and fully furnished. It was located in a vast complex that lacked any distinctive markers of any kind, whether to differentiate blocks and units or, indeed, to mark off one such residential complex from another. Being temporary, whether short- or long-term (and even the concept of long-term temporariness is weird), the dwellers had no particular incentive to add individual or idiosyncratic markers to their own upscale Brand X units. Research Triangle Park is loaded up with such complexes. They have names like "The Hamptons," conjuring up the exotic playgrounds of the rich and famous. I turned into one of these on my way home from work the first day and meandered for at least five minutes before I realized that I was not in the right one. There were three or four such places in a row. Mine was called "The Easthampton," I think. Even after I got to the right complex, though, it was almost impossible for me to locate my own unit. Once I did, I found the interior entirely faux, replete with a fake tree in a corner of the living room and fake French impressionist paintings on the walls. Driving in and out, I saw few children or elderly people. It was a place for yuppies, mostly single, a few paired. All the units were painted the same. This is but one example of what recent critics have called the destruction of place in America, and it is tied to the loss of community and the decline of civil society.

But Nashville is a different story. Oh, of course, it's the same story, too. It's not hard to find Nashville versions of The Easthampton, and areas of the city that are marked by temporariness. What stands out, however, is just how committed so many people are to this place—to their neighborhood, their circle, their city. A whole host of charitable service organizations here—Alive Hospice, Family & Children's Service,

3—**Cornerstone Church,** an Assemblies of God congregation in Madison, dedicates its new 3,500-seat, $15-million sanctuary, one of the largest in the state. Just nine years ago, the church was a declining congregation of about 200 people. But in 1991, it took a chance on an unconventional minister named Maury Davis, an ex-convict from Texas who served time for a murder he committed at age 18. Davis turned his life around with the help of a Texas minister, and he dedicated his life to the Lord, inspired by the apostle Paul's belief that the "low and despised" could spread the Gospel. Under Davis' guidance, the church's membership has risen to 2,000, and the pastor now envisions building a retirement home on its campus as well as a Western-themed Chuck E. Cheese family park. Davis' sermon today is titled "Where Dreams Come True." . . . **Few dreams come true** at the city's 24th-annual Christmas Parade, which creeps down Broadway before a disappointingly small turnout. Despite the presence of new Country Music Hall of Fame inductee Charley Pride as grand marshal, plus Mayor Bill Purcell and his 12-year-old daughter, Jesse, perched atop a Metro fire truck, the people in the parade almost outnumber the people watching it. The low turnout is blamed on a cold spell, as well as the Tennessee Titans' afternoon face-off against the Philadelphia Eagles. . . . **While the parade goes by** in Nashville, it's just beginning for the Titans in Philadelphia—especially for Al Del Greco, who of late has taken a hail of verbal abuse from fans. After blowing crucial kicks that cost the Titans two games in the past three weeks, the 38-year-old placekicker comes to the field with his career on the line. He responds by booting field goal after field goal through the Eagles' uprights, single-footedly scoring every Titans' point. To cap off a career-high day, Del Greco nails a 50-yarder as the clock runs out, plucking the Eagles 15-13. On talk radio, Al is forgiven—for now.

Second Harvest Food Bank, and Buddies of Nashville, to name only a few—have been giving continuous and dedicated assistance to people in need for more than 25 years. Even at the neighborhood level, there is much evidence of stability and dependability. On our block in Green Hills, we are surrounded by good neighbors who have been here since before we moved in. My husband estimates that 75 percent of the people on our street have not moved in the past twelve years—a rather remarkable figure for American cities, if we can trust the demographic data.

This is so important from a community point of view, because it is only through long-term relationships that we build the mutual trust, competence, and character that are the hallmarks of civil society. Trust is no easy thing to cultivate; it takes years, and the mulch of mutual experience. It is social trust that helps us to get out of the house, to go next door, to organize the block party, to volunteer. Stability in living patterns gives people a basis from which to work. Such stability is no guarantee that civil society will flourish. But without a measure of stability, we *know* that community is a much harder thing to come by and that even those whose stock in trade is building up the civic muscle of community—like professional community organizers—cannot do this unless the basic framework, the skeleton and some flesh on the bones, is in place. On the everyday level, community means that folks pause to pass the time of day; that the cash and credit card nexus doesn't dominate all exchanges; that the pace of life isn't quite so frantic. It means that a city is also a place of neighborhoods in which people help one another, keep watch mutually, find ways to get together, and get along.

There is another important piece to the civil society story told by the experts, and it is one that many of them at first resisted, even when their own data screamed out the truth of their findings: It is that the hard work of community-building is being done nowadays primarily by America's churches and synagogues and, increasingly, her mosques and temples. The social scientists resisted their own evidence because, like most academics, they had been trained in one variation or another of the famous (or infamous) "secularization hypothesis," the view that as societies "progressed" they would invariably, inevitably, and surely for the better, move from religion to secularism. This is what can best be called a failed hypothesis. That doesn't stop people believing in it, of course. But it does mean that honest researchers are compelled to rethink a fond truism when their own data tells a different story. And that story is this: If the work of civic stewardship is going to be done anywhere by anyone to any great extent, it is going to be done by religious groups. And why not? Virtually all the people who attend America's houses of worship subscribe to a faith that we are all children of a good God who also makes some pretty heavy demands on us (loving your neighbor as yourself is no easy thing). Of course, there is no guarantee that the behavior of worshipers will always rise above narrow self-interest—but it does mean that the so-called faith communities are more likely to look beyond themselves than are those who subscribe to no religion that makes demands on its followers.

Because Nashville is such an extraordinarily "churched" place (I drive past no fewer than five houses of worship to get to our house from the Hillsboro/21st Avenue exit off I-440, about a 2-mile jaunt), the strength and visibility of the social ministries of these institutions is extraordinary. There are about a thousand congregations in Metro Nashville-Davidson County. This feature of local life struck me when we first moved here, and it still impresses me. Just as a routine matter, churches involve large numbers of people conducting organized visits to the infirm, to shut-ins, to the elderly, creating soup kitchens and programs for children at many levels, sponsoring neighborhood cleanups, manning suicide hotlines, and so on. If a natural disaster strikes anywhere in the United States, particularly somewhere in the South, the response is simply amazing. Trailers to be hauled by semis bloom overnight in church parking lots, destined to be loaded with foodstuffs, clothing, household wares, cleanup equipment. People take unpaid leave from their jobs to go to South Carolina or Texas or some other spot in order to assist personally in the cleanup. And when tragedy strikes close to home—as in 1998, when a devastating tornado whipped through Nashville—it is as if every resident feels the impact and rushes to help. In East Nashville, the hardest-hit area, volunteers kept coming for weeks to lend assistance, and tree plantings to "re-leaf" the once shady streets are still taking place.

Mayor Bill Purcell, who lives in East Nashville, was seen frequently moving

In the days and weeks following the massively destructive Nashville tornado of 1998, hundreds of volunteers turned out regularly for assignment to repair teams (left) that went by bus to designated areas. In East Nashville on a rainy Saturday 10 days after the big blow, volunteers like Paula Barker and Brad Sapp (above) found plenty of work to do. The tornado damage in East Nashville alone exceeded $150 million, and the estimate citywide was close to a half-billion—but miraculously, there was only one fatality.

about the city in his work clothes, giving hands-on help wherever he saw a need. It may have been good public relations, good politics, but it was much more than that. Civil society has little or nothing to do with partisanship or explicitly political activity. Rather, it refers to everything that builds up and sustains communities as safe, strong, decent, pluralistic places where people can raise their children, live their lives, make their own contributions. It also refers to a determination to help other communities, whether near or far, do the same.

This is the world that astonished the great observer of American democracy, the famous Frenchman Alexis de Tocqueville, when he toured America in the Jacksonian era of the 1830s and turned his observations into a heralded masterwork, *Democracy in America*. He claimed that it was something entirely new under the civic sun: all that associational enthusiasm! But Tocqueville also issued a warning. He urged Americans to take to heart a possible corruption of their way of life. In his worst-case scenario, narrowly self-interested individualists, disengaged from the saving constraints and nurture of the overlapping associations of social life, would require more and more controls in order to mute, at least somewhat, the disintegrative effects of narrow individualism. Keep the peripheries alive! Political spaces other than or beneath those of the state need to be cherished and nourished. Only such small-scale civic spaces enable citizens to play an active role in the drama of democracy. Such participation depends on meaningful involvement in some form of community. Tocqueville distinguished the bad individualism he warned against—he called it "egoism"—from the notions of human dignity and self-responsibility central to a flourishing, democratic way of life. This is a fancy way of saying that we wouldn't even be ourselves without the presence of others.

There's a lot of talk in America today about difference. We need to celebrate difference, we are told. Too often, however, this difference-talk seems to assume that variety is just a fact of life, like so much dew on the morning grass. It isn't so. I can't be different all by myself. In a democracy, differences must be made visible publicly in such

literally leave people in the cold. Those residents who didn't request assistance have been either shifted elsewhere in Metro's 6,200-unit public-housing system or placed in subsidized private rentals. At the ceremony, William Jones, a 44-year-old Nashvillian who grew up at Preston Taylor, photographs the empty lot where his childhood home once stood.

5—**Two gunmen** and a red-haired woman with a spiderweb tattooed on one hand are sought in the robbery of more than a dozen Hispanic residents on Welworth Drive. Many of the victims, who work at Opryland, were ordered from the back of a van at gunpoint, and the three robbers attempted to stick up several more onlookers at the scene. . . . . **A "once-in-a-lifetime opportunity"** ends today, as an eBay auction for what is billed as Tennessee's electric chair closes several days ahead of schedule. The seller, who is revealed as Arthur Rosenblatt, a Florida-based dealer in "crime and punishment collectibles," tells *The Tennessean* that bids topped out at $25,000. The winner is the Ripley's Believe It or Not Museum in Gatlinburg, believe it or not. . . . **Still more bad news** from Gaylord Entertainment: The company is slashing 116 more jobs, including the 85 employees of its cash-bleeding albatross Gaylord Digital. Gaylord will unload or close its failed internet venture by the end of the year, taking a $35-million hit that swells its paper losses this year to $90 million. . . . **After almost half a century** on West End Avenue, Free Will Baptist College surveys the site of its new 123-acre, $18-million home in Joelton. Some 300 alumni, faculty, students and supporters are present for a ground-breaking ceremony at the new location on Highway 41A. The school, which has an enrollment of 318, hopes to get $14 million for the West End property it has occupied since 1942. . . . **A very pregnant** Amy Grant and her husband, Vince Gill, host the first of two sold-out nights of Grant's annual Tennessee's Christmas celebration at the Gaylord Entertainment Center.

6—**Henry Sender,** owner of the Union Station train shed, has a deal for Metro: He will dismantle the historic shed and let the city reconstruct it anywhere else it wants, as long as he can build his new parking deck and stop his monthly $48,000 loss on the facility. Deputy Mayor Bill Phillips is iffy about the idea: "What would you call it if it were at the Parthenon? The Grecian Shed?" . . . **Metro police** bust up a four-man ring responsible for 44 armed robberies in the Nashville area. After a month of surveillance by 30 detectives, police arrest ringleader Kevin DeWitt Ford, 29, and his 20-year-old cousin, Clifford Sylvester Wright, for robbing an auto-parts store on Clarksville Highway. They are believed to have been involved either together or separately in robbing more than three dozen

a way that they can be shared. Otherwise, difference turns into solipsism or destructive division. Positive differences are made visible when they take shape within living communities. America's religious groups, while they continue to reflect largely segregated social, economic, and cultural patterns that play out as racial and ethnic differences, are nevertheless committed to a principle of stewardship that calls them to move out of the pews and into the neighborhood, onto the streets and beyond. And wherever you find strong patterns of cross-racial and cross-ethnic association anywhere in the United States, it is likely that organizations made up of various religious groups are the basis and the bond.

This means that immediate needs are tended to—but larger problems also are tackled, such as long-term issues of housing, drug and alcohol addiction, teen pregnancy, the loneliness and lostness of too many of our elderly, violence and safety in the schools, and so on. This sort of commitment is visible all across Nashville. And, there are other, quieter ways of creating living communities committed to pluralism. For example, many churches in the city make their sanctuaries available to other faiths that are small, new to Nashville, and without a place of their own at present. This is not only ecumenism in practice, it is commitment to pluralistic community at its most generous.

In the film *The Apostle*, the protagonist (played by Robert Duvall in a transcendent performance) is a charismatic Pentecostal preacher who goes by the name of E.F. Witnessing a "Blessing of the Fleet" by the local Catholic priest, E.F. comments, "By God, you do it your way and I do it mine. But we sure do get it done." Whether a Pentecostalist in real life would be that open to Catholicism (or vice versa) is an open question, but the principle is well-taken: respect for just how we all get it done. This was also clearly the case during the 2000 presidential election when Senator Joseph Lieberman was chosen by Vice President Al Gore to be his running mate. Lieberman, an Orthodox Jew, openly expressed his religious faith and intoned the name of "our awesome God" throughout the campaign, nowhere more so than when he was introduced officially to the American electorate at a Nashville rally organized by Gore campaign officials. The Nashville news reports and the local commentary were overwhelmingly positive. Not only was there no overt anti-Semitism; Lieberman's religious faith was seen as a clear

Dorothy Beard's home near the Boston community in west Williamson County was slated for destruction to make way for State Road 840. As she waited and worried, Beard took comfort in the cheerfulness and support of her six grandchildren (clockwise from top left): Christina Beard, Rebecca Beard, Sara Edwards, Philip Holt, Courtney Beard and Stephanie Holt.

Stability, continuity and longevity rode along with Mary Pope Booker and Monroe J. Booker when the limousine reserved by their 12 children took them to their golden wedding anniversary dinner in Franklin. The strength of family ties such as the Bookers display is widely regarded as a central and paramount prerequisite to the restoration of neighborhoods and communities in urban centers such as Nashville.

additional sites, including cash-advance stores, markets and fast-food restaurants. To date this year, more than 2,000 robberies have been reported in Nashville.

7—The brilliant athletic career that John Henderson began as a Nashville grade-schooler reaches its peak to date tonight in Orlando, Fla. Henderson, a UT junior tackle, receives the coveted Outland Trophy for the nation's top interior offensive or defensive lineman. The award is significant because the past 10 recipients were drafted by the NFL—and six honorees went on to become Pro Football Hall of Famers. As a Nashville eighth-grader at St. Pius X, Henderson won the nickname "Baby Shaq" on the basketball court, and he was a high-school football star at Pearl-Cohn. . . . A **7-foot totem pole** planted on

positive. How things have changed since John F. Kennedy's Roman Catholicism was something he had to reassure people about by more or less insisting that his faith would never get in the way of his governing when, to a committed believer, it should surely be the other way around. In today's Nashville, and today's America, it wouldn't have been necessary for Kennedy to run so scared.

No place is perfect. But some ways of being in the world are better than others if you care anything about the quality of our lives together. At Grandparents Day at our granddaughter's school, it was standing room only. Some of those present had traveled across the United States to be there for their grandchildren. I had to turn my own schedule upside down in order to make it, but make it I did. Of course, I did it for my granddaughter. But I also did it because I was expected to. Communities help to keep us honest. There are all sorts of good things we do because we belong to a community that claims us. Absent that, it is far easier to offer excuses and fail to make the necessary effort.

Every election day in Nashville, we vote at the elementary at the end of our street. We try to arrive early. The line usually stretches for a half-block or so by opening time. People bring their kids and dogs, and chat amiably while they wait. It is a civic ritual that would be ruined if those who want computerized or mail ballots have their way. There are all sorts of bad ideas and that (save for citizens who really cannot make it out of the house because of infirmity) is one of them. Civic life calls us out. In Nashville, that call seems more compelling than it does in much of America. And, by the way, critical reason goes on here, too. It just isn't so full of itself as it is in many other parts of our driven, diverse, flourishing, and faltering society.

Welcome to America, darlin'.

In the same spring of 2000 when the Bookers celebrated 50 years together, Tom Yarbrough and his bride, Jennifer Liache, said their vows at Wightman Chapel on the campus of the Scarritt-Bennett Center. Explaining that the pre-wedding wait was making him "a little giddy," Yarbrough hunkered down on a stone wall to the amusement of Liache.

Strangers when they met for dinner (above) on a February evening in 2001, these nine young Nashvillians quickly found their comfort level—and plenty to talk about. From left: Chris Ferrell, Eleanor Fleming, Melissa Hogan, Cory Warfield, Katie Hill, Holly Shepherd, Scott Kozicki, Renata Soto and Alden Smith. (Personal notes on the nine are on page 356.)

Tomorrow's Nashville

At the end of this book on Nashville's journey into the 21st century, we wanted to listen to a select group of young people. So far, our collective self-profile has been composed by older writers who have tended to look at Nashville in the present tense, with an eye to the past. That makes sense when you think of the book as a sort of time capsule in which a wealth of information has been stored for the primary benefit of future generations. If this intentional artifact is to be useful in 50 or 100 years, it must provide an accurate and reasonably full account of life in the city now, informed by an understanding of what life was like here in the past, and further enhanced by some thoughtful inquiries and speculations about the future.

It seemed to us appropriate to ask people over 30 (most over 40, some well past 65) to look at Nashville now in the light of history; a certain amount of lived experience seemed appropriate, even necessary. But by 2025, most of the city's power and influence will be held by people who are now members of the under-30 generation. As this book clearly shows, our legacy to them is a mixture of triumphs and disasters, of great accomplishments and painful failures, all of which they must deal with as best they can. The future belongs to them. It seemed only fair that they should have the last words here—words of judgment on the city they are inheriting, and words of anticipation about tomorrow's Nashville in the state, the nation, and the world.

To get such fresh perspectives, we decided to make an unscientific selection of a few young Nashvillians and bring them together for a day or more of conversations about their city and its future, and then to draw out excerpts from those exchanges for the book's closing section. We sought help from a team of facilitators, Jenny Yancey and Dan Siegel, who had broad experience in conducting small-group discussions. In various places around the country and abroad, Yancey and Siegel had earned a solid reputation for their skill in drawing out participants in an exercise called "envisioning." The process was based on structured group conversations designed to encourage all participants, as individuals and as a group, to look beyond present trends to their possible and plausible consequences—in other words, to envision the future.

That doesn't mean we expected them to be visionaries whose conclusions would later prove to be prophetic; it might well be that their projections will land far off target. We were not looking for answers, but for strong, forceful, reasoned, passionate language that embraced hopes and fears as much as facts. We wanted good talkers, debaters, thinkers. We dreamed of getting spontaneous, unrehearsed eloquence.

Selection was the hardest part of this exercise, because an infinite number of combinations was possible, each yielding a different outcome. Getting the right chemistry was more a matter of luck than perception. We gambled that the combination of people we chose would click (or clash) in constructive ways, producing a rich and substantive conversation.

The "Nashville Nine," as we came to call them, met for the first time at an informal dinner hosted by Ellen and Townes Duncan on an evening in February 2001. The next morning, in a conference room of the First Amendment Center at Vanderbilt University, they came together for an all-day conversation guided by Yancey and Siegel, photographed by Dana Thomas, and recorded on audiotape by Jason Price. In the following pages, we offer a partial transcript.

The Editors

The way to the future is through the past. To begin thinking about Nashville's future, the nine participants were asked to recall some of their earliest encounters with the city, and to talk about coming to terms with the place in which they lived—their home and neighborhood, their city and state, their region and nation.

Centennial Park's First Amendment Hill is uprooted and placed in storage, against the wishes of the artist, an Alaska native who calls himself Blackfoot. "It was meant to stay there right where it was," says Blackfoot, who planted the pole a few weeks ago to protect the area and to honor the native drummers who play for peace there on weekends. Sadly, Metro Parks cannot accept a gift of art without a formal offer to the city and formal acceptance. The pole now sits in a nearby building, awaiting that sunny day. . . . **At 1:03 a.m.,** a policeman pulls over a 1987 Chevrolet Caprice on Ed Temple Boulevard for speeding and a broken taillight. During a weapons check, a passenger gets out and scuffles with the officer, then hits him on the side of the head with a gun and flees. As backup policemen give chase, the man runs onto Walter Davis Boulevard. Tracey Lamont Chadwick, 32, wanted on charges of aggravated robbery, rape and parole violation, decides he does not want to spend any more time in prison. At 1:22 a.m., he puts his gun to his head and pulls the trigger.

8—**Just when Vice President Al Gore's hopes** for the presidency seem dashed, the Florida Supreme Court orders a statewide hand recount of approximately 45,000 disputed ballots in 64 of Florida's 67 counties. Gore is suddenly a viable contender again, and Texas Gov. George W. Bush's lead is cut to a precarious 154-vote margin. The next day, the situation will reverse again when the U.S. Supreme Court calls a halt to the recount. Deanna McFarland, a Republican voter from Hendersonville, expresses the opinion of most Americans when she tells *The Tennessean* she's "tired of the whole thing."

9—**Every December** in Franklin's Rebel Meadows subdivision, lines of cars, limos, even tour buses parade past Chuck Smith's annual "Planet Christmas" extravaganza, a lighting display elaborate enough to have its own website

Holly Shepherd: Well, I grew up here, and I think the earliest memory I have is when they closed Harveys, a famous department store downtown. My mother grew

Holly Shepherd

up here, my grandmother grew up here, and they used to tell stories about how the only place to go shopping was downtown by bus. By the time I grew up, downtown was dirty and unattractive, and not many people went down there. We would go down once in a while and do Candyland—that was a restaurant—and we would go see the horses at Harveys. They had these big carousel horses. But the most vivid memory I have is when they closed it. In my mind, it seemed like the entire town was there the day they closed.

Scott Kozicki: The day after I moved down here, just to get away from my family—because I was pissed at them for making me come down here with them—I drove around and wandered into a Jim Dandy store just to buy some burritos and a Coke. The guy says, "Do you want a sack with that?" And I couldn't understand a word he was saying. "What?" "Do you want a sack with that?" "I don't know, whatever you're saying. Can I have a bag?" They guy looks at me and says "*Whuuut?*" We just completely did not understand each other. I think the conversation only lasted about 45 seconds, but it felt like it lasted an hour, and it was very frustrating, I'm sure, for both sides. So I grab my stuff, throw my money on the counter, and walk out— and I hear, "Y'all have a Jim Dandy day!" That was my first taste of moving here. I was out of sync with everything. It was like moving to another planet. I couldn't understand anybody, didn't understand the language, clothes, food. The sky is a different color blue here, no kidding. Then, just a couple of weeks ago, I had my first integrated-with-Nashville moment. I was at the Pie Wagon, and one of my co-workers was yapping about something. I tuned her out and was listening to all the other conversations around me. Suddenly I realized that I could understand the

Scott Kozicki

accents, for one thing, and that the topics they were talking about were things that resonated with me—the Titans, politics, the potholes in the road. That moment is when I realized: I'm a Nashvillian now. I've been here long enough, and I've integrated into the place. It took eleven years.

Renata Soto: That makes me feel better. I've been here only four years. We moved here because of my husband's job, and I got a job, too. And as I was getting to know people at work and meeting some colleagues of my husband, I soon realized that I was the first person they had ever met with a foreign accent, their first experience meeting somebody from another country. That was pretty amazing to me. We came here from Atlanta, where

Renata Soto

the Latino community is much larger. I just hadn't realized how small Nashville was—but also how great, maybe, the opportunities were. I can see now, four years after, how much that picture has changed for many people. Now I'm just one of many foreigners they encounter on Nolensville Road or at the Farmers Market, or in other areas of town.

I think one important experience that was shared by many, in terms of feeling something different about Nashville, was right after the tornado hit in 1998. It was amazing, in terms of the numbers, how many volunteers responded to the call for help, and also the intensity with which the people in East Nashville were working. Just the experience of being in East Nashville, cleaning up yards with people I didn't even know and would never have known otherwise—that was something special. This was not just people putting in a few hours of volunteer work. We were really *engaged* with the people we were trying to help. That was pretty amazing.

I call Nashville home now, but I don't think of it as my single home. There's something about when I go back to Costa Rica—the smell in the streets, the sounds and the noise—and I realize, "This is home." But I do see Nashville as my second home or parallel home. Sometimes the possibility of moving to another city is like a ghost in my house, and I'm uncomfortable with it. I like the connections and relationships I have made in this city, and I feel I would be giving up too much to leave it now. I wouldn't have dreamed four years ago that I would feel as rooted in Nashville as I do. And when my second child—a native Nashvillian—is born a few months from now, I'm sure I will feel even more rooted here.

Eleanor Fleming: I'm originally from Franklin, and so I always think of Franklin, and that white house with the black shutters where I grew up, as home. There's something about flying back from New York or Washington—when I see the airport I start to get excited. Then we're on the interstate, or we're on Hillsboro Road headed to Franklin, and it's like, "Oh yes, I'm home, this is it!" Those familiar sights, those people, connect everything together for me.

Chris Ferrell: This really has become my home in a few short years. The time I first realized it was once when I flew to Jacksonville, where I grew up. As I was walking through the Jacksonville airport, I heard a song playing, and it was a song a friend of mine here in Nashville had written. I just had this epiphany: "Wow! The sounds of home, the songs your friends write, being played all over the world." It made me realize that I had become a Nashvillian.

Melissa Hogan: I grew up in the newer suburbs of Cincinnati—one of those planned kind of communities, the houses neatly lining each street. In East Nashville, where we live now, there is a different feel. The first week we were there, a neighbor on one side of our house stopped me by the fence. She had her dog out, and I had my dog out, and we proceeded to talk through the fence. And then a couple of days later, a neighbor behind us brought us some brownies he had made. And then the neighbor on

and low-power FM radio station. After complaints from neighbors last year about traffic and sensory overload, former Franklin school board member Smith has scaled back his display. Visitors now have to settle for 10 motion-controlled light-up reindeer instead of 52; only a couple of "singing penguins"; and a mere 53,205 lights, as opposed to last year's 143,268. The helicopter still works, though.

10—**At the Jewish Community Center's** annual Hanukkah Festival, a large-screen TV has been set up to accommodate Titans fans, whose playoff hopes depend on the outcome of today's Titans-Cincinnati Bengals battle. The Flamin' Thumbtacks do not disappoint. The Titans trounce the Bengals 35-3, thus securing a berth in the upcoming NFL playoffs.

11—**A plan to use $8 million** in federal funds to save the historic Union Station train shed is dead. Since owner Henry Sender wants to build a for-profit enterprise on the shed site, federal tax funds cannot be used—and there is still the grim fact that the rickety shed has been condemned. Its fate is virtually sealed.

12—**Clean, green and lean.** Those three words are used to describe the city's long-awaited solid waste plan, to be presented tomorrow by Mayor Bill Purcell. Among the recommendations: converting or shutting down Nashville's 26-year-old Thermal Transfer Plant, and using natural gas instead of garbage as fuel to heat and cool downtown office buildings. The proposal is applauded by some environmentalists, even though the plant was hailed as a major advance by that group a quarter-century ago. Recycling advocates love the proposal to triple the city's recycling under the new plan. . . . **Last seen sticking up** a First Union Bank branch with tinfoil on his teeth, the robber who has hit eight area banks since July returns to the scene of an earlier crime—and robs it again. Clad in a dark trench coat and leather baseball cap, the robber enters the

SouthTrust Bank on West End Avenue, which he is suspected of holding up on Nov. 8, and claims to have a bomb. He asks for all the tellers' $100, $50 and $20 bills, same as before, and he gets them. Police are looking for a gold pickup truck used in the getaway.

13—**In Washington, D.C.,** Vice President Al Gore puts an end to the closest and most bitterly contested presidential election in American history. He sets the tone for his concession speech by announcing that he had just called President-elect George W. Bush to offer his congratulations, "and I promised him that I would not call him back this time." The veep is reportedly still devastated by losing his home state. His succinct, eloquent speech shows the humility and warmth his detractors claimed he lacked. Within weeks, this bumper sticker will be circulating: "Re-Elect Gore in 2004." . . . **Flames and black smoke** billow from the windows of a vacant building on Eighth Avenue South, which once housed the Nashville Union Rescue Mission and was built by a women's activist group, the Centennial Club, in 1914. The building was sold last year by the mission to First Baptist Church. At first firefighters think the mission itself is on fire, and more than 60 homeless men are evacuated from the building next door. The fire is contained, but the structure, which had been on Historic Nashville's endangered list, is gutted. Investigators suspect arson.

14—**For defrauding Medicare** and other federal health-care programs, Nashville-based HCA will cough up nearly a billion dollars. In a high-stakes pre-trial settlement, the corporation agrees to plead guilty to fraud charges that include allegations of false billing and overcharging the U.S. government. In response, the government slaps HCA with what Attorney General Janet Reno says is the largest fraud settlement in its history: $840 million, including $95.3 million for criminal conduct. . . . **One day after** Vice President Al Gore concedes the

the other side stopped me as I was coming in, and she had a picture of our house before it was renovated and wanted me to see: "Look at your house before they gutted it and made it look all nice." So that was really a sense of community. The neighbors all around us knew somebody new had moved in. And now there's an internet listserv specifically for East Nashville. People talk about how this crime happened here, or they found this dog and does anyone know whose it is. I must get three to five e-mails every day from these lists. It's technology combined with old-style community.

Cory Warfield: My first experience of realizing that Nashville was home had to be when I was very small, because I've always lived here. I was born here, raised here. My family is originally from southern Kentucky; they moved here in the '60s, and we've lived north of downtown ever since. I think I really didn't get a larger sense of Nashville until I went to my current school, MLK, which pulls people from around the county. I've met people from Bellevue and Hermitage and

Cory Warfield

Antioch, people I wouldn't normally meet. That made me open up about Nashville and see there are some differences as well as some common characteristics.

Ferrell: One of the things that struck me the first time I ran for office was when I went to parts of the city I had never been to before and discovered all of these little internal communities within the greater community of Nashville. Throughout the city, there are these little pockets of long-established communities that often do not interact with each other.

Katie Hill: My experience is kind of like Cory's. I grew up here, and I grew into it. I guess I went through a stage when I was 12 or 13 when I was not anti-Nashville, but, you know, "I want to get out of here, I can't wait 'til college, I want to get away, go up North or out West or wherever. And maybe I'll come back here and raise a family,

Katie Hill

but probably not." But then during my last years of high school I started thinking and talking more and more with my friends and my parents about what it means, good and bad, to be Southern and from Nashville. There is something unique about being Southern—even though there are a lot of things about the South, and Nashville, that aren't great. Now, especially since going off to college, I find that I have a bond with other people I know from Nashville. There really is something that binds us together.

What was it that you wanted to get away from?

Hill: I think it was this feeling I had that Nashville and the South were very backward. Part of it was just being naïve and young, wanting to go live in New York City and live it up. And I'm not saying I don't still want to do that.

Kozicki: I've always been fascinated with Southerners' self-esteem. Up North, we don't care. Southerners, you guys have something very precious, but it takes some kind of cathartic process for you to realize what that is. What Katie just said is exactly the statement I hear all the time: "I wanted to get out, because it's kind of backward and podunk." But then I've also heard "You don't understand what the South is until you leave it." I don't claim to understand what it is, but I can tell you that you guys don't understand what you have until you leave it. You walk through life wearing this "I'm proud to be a Southerner" attitude if you're in a conversation with somebody like me, but inside you're asking, "Where do I fit in? I live in a place that's not like the rest of the world, and I'm not sure I like it, and it's kind of bizarre." I've noticed that about many people born and raised in this area. They have that dichotomy.

Alden Smith: That's actually a nice cue for me, the word "dichotomy." As I have become more attached to New England, where I've been living for several years now, I have consciously kept one foot back in Tennessee, and specifically in Nashville. Part of that is the emotional resonance of childhood memories, of family still here, of friends still here. And as those years have moved along, it actually takes more energy to split my devotion between two places. I feel mysteriously called back to my roots, in a way, but I have to be honest and say I'm not feeling as certain about that these days, and I'm even experiencing some grief about how Nashville has changed. Returning here intermittently, season by season throughout the years, I've seen the place grow and develop, and change in the same way you might see a niece or nephew change when you only see them rarely. That's been difficult for me to come to terms with.

Alden Smith

I'm from Belle Meade; I had a very privileged upbringing. When I was a junior in high school, we did a service project for a group in North Nashville. It was just a clothes drive, really easy. All I had to do was take these clothes, drive them across town to North Nashville just off Jefferson Street, and give them to someone at St. Vincent De Paul. When I got there, I met a nun and talked to her for a pretty long time. I had not expected to. I had this very sudden but welcoming introduction into a different Nashville—and a sudden understanding that it was so close to where I came from, right down the road maybe 5 miles, and yet so far from where I came from. And then I spent the next few summers working there, trying to make sense of the drive from Belle Meade to North Nashville. Now I feel like, in some ways, I'm trying to negotiate that same conflict between Nashville and someplace else. I'm trying to put things together and make sense of what is home for me.

Did you think of Belle Meade as a community, a neighborhood, when you were growing up?

Smith: It was all I knew. It was a neighborhood for me. What I remember about it is the space. I remember the feeling of being able to ride my bike into the countryside. I don't know about the sense of community. I didn't know my neighbors very well.

Shepherd: I grew up in the 'burbs here, where there was no sense of community. Growing up, I didn't know my neighbors. As an adult, I choose now to live in an area where I do know all my neighbors and I can walk to the grocery store. That was the greatest thing about New York City for me, believe it or not. All my relatives said, "Oh my

presidency, his friend Craven Crowell, 57, a Nashvillian and Clinton appointee, announces he is stepping down as chairman of the Tennessee Valley Authority, the nation's largest public power provider. Crowell will retire in April, thus giving incoming President Bush time to appoint a replacement and handle the accompanying transition.

15—Drawling newshound **Larry Brinton**, 70, announces he will retire early next year from day-to-day activities at WTVF-Channel 5, after 45 years in local news. In the 1960s, former *Nashville Banner* reporter Brinton duked it out with *The Tennessean*'s Jerry Thompson for dominance of the city's colorful police beat, back when rivalry between the two dailies was ballistic. For the past 21 years, Brinton has been at News Channel 5. He'll keep doing his weekly "Street Talk" segment, a viewer favorite, but he is giving up his co-host's slot on the 7:30 a.m. *Morning Line* show. . . . **James Brooks**, an associate dean of liberal arts at Middle Tennessee State University, will replace the outgoing Brian McQuistion as president of the Watkins Institute College of Art & Design. For more than a century, Watkins was a part of downtown life on Church Street, but attendance had dipped precipitously by the early 1990s. During McQuistion's tenure, the school reversed its fortunes, shoring up attendance by adding a film school and winning accreditation. The school's longtime home was razed to make room for construction of the new downtown public library. In exchange Watkins plans to move into the old Ben West Library building. Until its new home is ready, the school is housed in a temporary location across from 100 Oaks Mall.

16—New country hitmaker Brad Paisley ("He Didn't Have to Be") gets an early Christmas present tonight onstage at the Grand Ole Opry. "You've been a good boy," says Opry stalwart Little Jimmy Dickens, dressed in an

God, you're going to die the second you step off the flight, you're gonna get killed"—
but there was a diner, a club across the street, an Irish pub, and a cleaners, and pretty
soon I knew all of those people by name, and their families. I didn't know anyone like
that growing up. I went to public schools when they were really doing some major busing, so I went to a middle school that was 80 percent African-American, where I was in
the minority. Cultural awareness was brought to us in the 'burbs [by busing]. Now I look
at it and say, "Wow. I was made to be culturally aware when I didn't even know I was
being made culturally aware."

Warfield: I don't consider Nashville a true city, in the sense that it mainly has
a suburban feel. But the community has always been brought to me. I have not had to
go and seek it, because of where I went to school, because of this citywide desegregation plan. I'm a product of busing across town. My schools have been predominantly
white. With my generation now, we're all just people. The past experience of those
things has taught me to get outside that neighborhood that otherwise you might feel
confined to. I really appreciate that the community was in some way brought to me.
Now I do feel I want to go out and seek it.

Of what benefit is Nashville's history to you? Do you think of the city as hav-ing a useable past?

Fleming: The notion of a useable past is a good one. It immediately reminds me
of a singular moment that, I think, made Nashville a community. In 1960, when the
sit-ins were going on downtown, Diane Nash, a student at Fisk, confronted Ben West,
the mayor of Nashville, on the steps of the courthouse. She challenged him with a question about the morality of segregation and got him to say that he thought it was wrong.
At that moment, different communities—worlds apart, whether in race or class or any
of the differences that we dwell on—were brought together. At that point, Nashville
became a community and a city. And that has been working and weaving its way into
our present.

Ferrell: I thought of that same moment, too.

Hogan: One of the things that I think is important about Nashville—and it has
come from the past, and I think it's one of the things that really drew me here—is the
civility, the courtesy, the gentlemanly nature of Southerners and of Nashvillians in particular. I think that's something from the past that people need to strive not to lose.
People who come into the city consider that very valuable—especially if you come from
the North. It's not something that's very common up there. I lived in Pittsburgh, and
then outside of Cleveland, before moving here. It's just so heartwarming for people to
say "hello" on the street, for men to hold the elevator for women and let you on and
off first. It's those tiny little things. I know they're not that important, but I think it's
that fabric that underlies a
lot of the bigger issues that
we face in this city.

Warfield: We should
not lose our charm, but as we
strive to become "major
league," we should remem-
ber who we are, and not try
to transform our city into
another New York or Atlanta.
It's O.K. to go slow and take
things at an easier pace.

Kozicki: I was born
and raised in Detroit. I lived
in a wealthy suburb and

Melissa Hogan

went to an urban high school. The first thing I noticed when I came down here was how segregated things were. Blacks acted different than what I was used to. When I first started meeting people in Franklin, peers my age, they were mostly white. Every once in a while the N-word would get thrown around. I couldn't believe how people were talking to me. I couldn't believe that in this day and age, people would still think like that. It was very sobering. There's a lot more needs to happen in this community in order to integrate it. Busing is just the tip of the iceberg.

Soto: Civil Rights is one useful tradition. We are already facing a growing number of residents whose native language is not English, and that is creating a lot of the same struggles that blacks have with whites. Social injustice and inequality are so much a part of our community. Even though there's a lot of work to do, there's something to build on as we think about relationships with other groups of people.

How aware do you think people are of that history?

Soto: People bring other struggles with them. Sometimes my fear is that there is more competition, that now African Americans have to compete with yet another group for some of those resources they have fought so hard to gain. I hope that's not what is emphasized, but it's an issue that affects us all.

Ferrell: There still is a lot of pain in certain communities about the closing of Bellevue, Dupont, Cameron, Litton, and other high schools.

Fleming: I think part of the concern comes from letting the past stay in the past. More specifically, we're not re-creating the memory of a time when everyone came together and we thought more progressively about issues of ethnicity and race and economic resources. There needs to be a time in our future when we return to sitting down at the table and talking about how we can come together to work for the good of us all—as opposed to "I want this, you want that, but I'm gonna get it because I've been here longer."

Eleanor Fleming

Was the cost of school desegregation worth it?

Smith: It's such a difficult question to answer. I believe in people coming together, and yet I believe in neighborhoods.

Hogan: Busing and the desegregation programs were totally worth it.

Smith: As a teacher, and also just as a native Nashvillian, I'm depressed by what I have seen described as "the inevitability of outward expansion." I worry that we surrender control of our future by buying into what feels like an inevitable prospect. The expansion of Nashville is part of a story that's been going on for a long time. I want to believe there's a useful connection between the depair that I feel over places and things that are lost and, at the same time, the hope that I feel about diversity.

How about religion? What role does it play in your view of the city?

Shepherd: The Southern Baptist Convention has had a huge negative impact on the arts community in Nashville, and throughout the Bible Belt.

Soto: Four years ago when we moved here, we learned that asking "What

over 100 people in Nashville will die by gunshot in 2000. . . . **Urban planning** in Nashville gets a major boost with today's announcement of a new Nashville Civic Design Center, to be housed temporarily in the old Neuhoff meat-packing facility on Monroe Street in Germantown. Addressing department heads, architects, planners and community advocates at the Vanderbilt Institute for Public Policy Studies, Mayor Bill Purcell says the new center will be a combination think tank and bully pulpit, for matters as large as building heights and as small as sidewalks. . . . **Commuters who take I-65 North** to work each morning can expect to encounter some roadwork problems for a while—say, until 2004. The state approves a $47.3-million project to improve the interchange at Briley Parkway and expand I-65 North from six to 10 lanes all the way to the Old Hickory exit. It's not too soon to move.

19—A housewarming party is thrown today for Mercreshia Greer in the downtown Hope Gardens neighborhood. The party celebrates two months of home ownership for Greer, a 22-year-old single mother with two children, custody of two young siblings and a mother who lives with her. To get this far, she had to finish school at Stratford High, get off federal and local assistance and take the extra computer courses she needed for a job at Dell. Through the efforts of the Woodbine Community Organization, which built the house, and the Bank of America's Community Development Group, which offers discounted mortgages to working families making less than 80 percent of the local median income of $58,800, Greer was able to buy her three-bedroom home for $87,000. . . . **The issue of paying reparations** to African Americans because of slavery tonight comes before the Metro Council, which debates a nonbinding resolution urging a federal commission to study the matter. Despite misgivings by some members, who question the $8-million cost of church do you go to?" is still part of the fabric of the community, just like asking "What's your name?" I realized that not being a churchgoer and not having any religious identification was an uncomfortable response to make. I had to develop my own little speech so I wouldn't offend anybody.

Ferrell: I can think of at least six church-related colleges in Nashville that shape the character of the community and the type of people we attract.

Soto: Religion's economic power here is pretty amazing. There is such a disconnect for me between the economic resources that churches manage in Nashville and how much of that we see at work in the community. I really can't see a relationship between the presence of so many churches and the quality of social justice here.

Kozicki: I think the influence of religion in Nashville has waned tremendously over the past ten years. It doesn't seem to exert nearly as much power as it once did.

Chris Ferrell

Ferrell: The large denominations that are here are historically very evangelical. The focus is put on saving souls and not on transforming society. But there are some things that have happened within the past decade, the most important of which was the founding of Tying Nashville Together. TNT and some other groups are beginning to work across denominational lines and racial lines, and now there are some congregations that are actually trying to transform their communities in these ways.

Fleming: The black church, regardless of the denomination, is still a force.

How does Nashville compare to other Southern models in having a useable past?

Ferrell: I think we in Nashville still have a sense of frontier spirit. This is a city that has a sense it can accomplish things. We want to try new things. We're willing to take risks. I think you can trace a lot of it back to our frontier past.

Smith: I'm not comfortable with that. When we look back to a frontier destiny, we suffer the illusion that we're not *choosing* this way of life. We start assuming that expansion is a given and inevitable. There is another perspective, though. It's not as organized. It doesn't have nearly as much money. But there are lots of individuals who believe in a different way of living. A way that feels like it retains some of the character and soul of the place.

Our focus is shifting to the present. What is it like to live in Nashville today? What does it feel like as a city?

Ferrell: I feel like Nashville right now is a city of incredible opportunity. Part of that is the times we've been through, and I'm not sure we'll continue to feel that way over the next year or two. But, for the last decade, Nashville has been a place where, if you wanted a job, you could find one. If you wanted to change careers, you could do that. As a city, we had a sense that if we wanted to make something happen, we could. A lot of that is attributable to Mayor Bredesen. A lot of it is just attributable to the community as a whole. That's not to say that there aren't problems, and that there aren't some real concerns about growth and people who are being left behind, and things that remain to be done to make this the kind of city we really want to live in. But I feel like there's a sense in this city that we can actually do the things that are important to us, and that if we are able to agree on what those things are, then we can make them happen.

Hogan: I tell people that this is a city on the verge, and not necessarily in the sense that it's sprawling and things are being torn down, although that's happening. I think the positive things that are happening and the intentions of the people that live here speak with one voice—that people are essentially trying to go to the same place. We just need to decide how to get there.

Hill: I agree. When people ask what Nashville is like, I say that it's a city in transition. I just think it doesn't know quite what it wants to be yet.

Soto: Today, Nashvillians are awakening to a kind of otherness in the city, these other new people that we have never had before. I see it through very concrete examples. I get many phone calls from nonprofit providers, banks, and just companies interested in the Latino market. They want to know who can sit on their boards and where to distribute information in Spanish, and so on. There's a lot of movement toward trying to learn about this new population.

We moved here because of a job, but I want to stay: I have found that Nashville is closer to the setting that I would have in Costa Rica in terms of the relationships among people. Social networks are much tighter here than they were in Atlanta, where I was for two years. People here tend to invite you to their homes for dinner as opposed to just gathering in a restaurant. That completely changes the tone of a meeting or an encounter. There's more reciprocity in relationships among people. Friends that I've found here are just more accessible. I see them more.

Renata Soto

Warfield: I view Nashville today as very similar to myself. It's like a teenager, which is parallel to my life. I'm at a crossroads, and the city is, too. We're trying to move beyond our past. We're trying to grow into something new—something we're not quite meant to be. Nashville doesn't have the luxury to reflect and look at its past and avoid what Atlanta has done wrong. The question is: Are we going to step up to the plate and become this major-league city, or are we going to really embrace who we are and not deny our heritage and the essence of what has made us? What works for Atlanta, New York, or Chicago may not work here. As a teenager, you want to be part of the group, but by the end of the teens, you want to be an individual. I think Nashville is at a point where we have to decide if we're going to be like everyone else, or if we're going to contribute something greater to the whole society. That takes a lot of guts and boldness, and I think we have to look within ourselves and be who we truly are.

Kozicki: Nashville has, almost by accident, found itself with an opportunity to be a great place, a great city, a great community. And now everyone is worried that we'll blow it. We're spending all this time comparing ourselves and not being the best we can be. You don't want analysis paralysis, and that's where I think the city is right now.

Smith: When I describe Nashville, I use some of the same words I've already heard here—verge, crossroads, trend. It strikes me that Nashville is a friendly place to

construction of a planned University of Tennessee campus in Nashville, which Geier believed would lead to further separation of black and white students. . . . **At 8:30 a.m.,** a wall heater bursts into flames in the Second Street basement apartment of Mary and Edward Lee Batey Jr. The family's belongings are destroyed, along with their Christmas tree and the presents for their two children. It is only five days before Christmas.

21—**The Rev. Becca Stevens, 37,** is named Nashvillian of the Year by the *Nashville Scene*. An Episcopal minister, mother of three and wife of songwriter Marcus Hummon, Stevens is executive director of the Magdalene Project, an organization that helps prostitutes escape the hazards of life on the streets and the grim cycles of abuse, degradation and addiction. According to Metro police, an estimated 300 prostitutes work Nashville's streets, performing an average of seven sexual acts a day. The typical prostitute serves an average of three months in jail and is arrested seven times a year. . . . **A lone trumpet** plays "Taps" at Riverfront Park, as a few dozen gatherers stand in honor of the 25 homeless people who died on Nashville's streets this year. Two street people, Betty Rippy and Cedric Moon, just died in the past few days. The group sings "Amazing Grace" near the so-called "hot rock," an outdoor heating vent warmed by the nearby Thermal Tranfer Plant, where homeless people frequently sleep. Of the 25 people remembered today, the names of six are still not known. . . . **Calls pour in** from people offering help to the Batey family, whose apartment home of six years was destroyed in a fire yesterday. Callers offer everything from money and dog food to clothes and a full living-room suite. "I just want to thank everybody," Mary Batey says.

22—**Autumn Millar, 9,** is getting the Christmas gift she told Santa she wanted this year. Earlier this week, Betty Eddington, a Nashville postal worker who helps answer the many letters mailed by children to the North Pole, opens an envelope addressed to "Santa Clause." Inside she finds a letter written in Autumn's slanted cursive handwriting. "What I want for Christmas," the letter begins, "is a new wheelchair and walker for Nicky." Nicky Millar, 8, was born with developmental disabilities; according to *Tennessean* writer Sylvia Slaughter, his family just moved to Hendersonville from California six months ago. Eddington puts in a call to Ty Johnson, one of a network of Middle Tennesseans who help Santa deliver his gifts. In less than 24 hours, calling on customers, vendors and other dealers, Johnson and his co-workers at the Hendersonville CarSmart manage to put together $2,400. Today, Nicky Millar is measured for his new wheelchair.

23—**A deer hunter** who ventured onto a Sumner County man's property lies dead tonight. Shortly after 4 p.m., Tim Butler, 23, and a 16-year-old companion shoot a deer on property north of Gallatin belonging to Joel Summerlin. They return with a vehicle to haul their kill when Summerlin spots them. Summerlin fires on them with a high-powered rifle, striking and mortally wounding Butler. His companion is unhurt. Authorities are now searching for Summerlin, 39.

24—**Two years after a tornado** demolished its century-old sanctuary, the congregation of St. Ann's Episcopal Church in East Nashville comes home, starting with this evening's emotional Christmas Eve services. Led by construction committee member Mark Brown, who bears a vessel of burning incense, church members march in procession from Holy Name Catholic Church, their temporary home of the past two years, down Woodland Street to their refurbished parish hall. Built in 1882, the church's Victorian Gothic sanctuary was left in rubble by the tornado that ravaged East Nashville in April 1998. The sanctuary will not be rebuilt for another few years, but the Southern Baptist Executive Committee

live. It's a place that still has trees. It's a place that has a Farmers Market, a Bicentennial Mall, and some commitment to restoring an urban core. At the same time, it's a place with a lot of tension between an obsession with economic development and the desire to retain local character, a healthy landscape, and communities. I live somewhere else, so I feel like I'm playing with a different model, experiencing it, and learning about it. My hope is to bring that experience back here and be a part of the community and be committed to the health of children through good, supportive schools.

Fleming: In making a decision about where to go to graduate school, I was actually torn between staying here and going off to Columbia. I decided to stay here because, essentially, this is my home. But the more I think about my future, the more I think that at some point I'll have to leave. What I'm looking for, Nashville doesn't have. I want a cultural center, an intellectual center, a center where you know all of these different people, and you don't have to drive 5 miles to see them. I think that Nashville as it stands now has a ways to go. I mean, this is still a place where the traffic lights go into flashing mode at midnight.

Shepherd: I struggle with these questions. I'm an actress and singer. So, what is it like for me to live in Nashville today? Well, I can be the lead in a play, but I have to have two other jobs to supplement that in Nashville. Unless you're in the country music business, this is really a starving-artist town. No theaters here do many musical productions. By the same token, I can go into a theater where I work often, and I don't

Holly Shepherd

have to audition much for parts anymore. They'll call me and say, "Do you want to do this?" And that's nice, because that was not happening in New York City. I've been trying since I was 17 years old to get out of this city. I have done it, yet I continue to come back. My family is here, and my theater world is a family here, too. I can own my own home here. Still, I think Nashville has a long way to go when it comes to the arts.

Hill: Yes, it's pretty amazing that we're just now getting a real art museum.

Fleming: I find the city really stifling. You rarely find anyone who's thinking about big-picture questions.

Ferrell: I would challenge that. I think there are an extraordinary number of people here thinking seriously about what cities look like as they grow up. I think Bredesen was the right man to be mayor at the time. In the late '80s, this was a city that was embarrassed, that had lost its belief in itself, and that needed a different kind of person to look to as mayor. Bredesen was an entrepreneur first and foremost. He liked the deal, and as mayor, he made a lot of them. I didn't always agree with Bredesen, but I think he was the right man for the time. And Purcell is the right man for this time. We've moved the city forward a notch. Now the question is: How do we move the sense of community and neighborhood forward?

Fleming: You can say that but it still seems to me that the city's focus is more on business, as opposed to political or social ideas. Just look at the fact that there's only one major newspaper here.

Kozicki: But you have to realize that business is really the driver for all those other things. Nashville is certainly moving forward, but it's not Chicago, it's not New York, and it's not San Francisco. That's what makes it beautiful in a lot of ways. Yeah, we don't have a thriving, mature artistic community. It's more grassroots. But when you push the scale all the way to the red line, you have to deal with all kinds of other problems that aren't fun.

Scott Kozicki

Soto: You could argue and say there's benefits to these investments and new businesses coming to Nashville, I hope we remember that there are many, many people in Nashville who have not seen any improvements in the quality of their lives as a product of a new stadium or Dell coming. In terms of some quality-of-life indicators, we rank pretty poorly. Those of us here in this room belong to a group that might benefit from enjoying the Frist Center for the Visual Arts, but many people still are trying to think about very basic needs like how to feed their kids. We still have many neglected communities and neighborhoods. They are struggling with the same issues they faced ten or fifteen years ago.

What are Nashville's weaknesses? What holds us back from being a great city?

Kozicki: I believe the media is extremely weak.

Hogan: The media just doesn't look professional. Our daily newspaper doesn't feel like the authoritative voice where people go for hard-core news.

Kozicki: All of the things we've discussed as opportunities and challenges are going to be harder to accomplish if we can't communicate past our differences. The media is our primary vehicle for doing that. If it continues to disintegrate, everything will be much harder.

Ferrell: Another problem is that there's not a lot of confidence in the public school system.

Hill: Nashvillians tend to ignore what goes on in surrounding counties. I think it's really dangerous to ignore what's going on in Williamson County. Just look at State Road 840. There are citizens groups opposing it for environmental reasons, but it also has the potential to create horrible sprawl like the I-285 Loop did in Atlanta.

Melissa Hogan

continues to store St. Ann's treasured stained-glass windows, which date back to 1859. . . . **On the eve of** the Tennessee Titans' game against the Dallas Cowboys, Coach Jeff Fisher is selected as the Tennessean of the Year by *The Tennessean*. Under Fisher's leadership, the paper explains, the Titans have put an end to the acrimony and regional resentments fueled by their arrival, chiefly the rivalry between sister cities Nashville and Memphis.

25—At 9:47 a.m., a thumbnail of shadow edges onto the sun. Christmas Day begins in Nashville with a partial eclipse, as the passing moon obscures 35 percent of the solar disk visible to Middle Tennesseans. Enjoy it while it lasts, for there will not be another solar eclipse on Christmas Day for 307 more years. . . . **Nashville residents** get another unexpected gift today: mail. Twenty-five postal workers deliver cards, letters and parcels on Christmas Day, which falls this year on Monday. The post office even handed out mail yesterday on Christmas Eve, a Sunday! This holiday season, Nashville postal workers have been handling some 7 million pieces of mail each day, a 3 percent volume increase over last year. . . . **Who needs Christmas Day** with the family when the Titans are in town? Any worries that Adelphia Stadium would be left empty on Jesus' birthday in the buckle of the Bible Belt are groundless, as hard-core fans turn out en masse to watch the Titans trample the Dallas Cowboys in a 31-0 shutout. It is only the third Monday-night game played on Christmas Day in NFL history, and the temperature inside the stadium is a wind-whipped 29 degrees.

26—While watching the Titans-Cowboys game the previous night with old friends, NFL great Joe Gilliam Jr. reportedly nods off on the couch. When friends fail to rouse him, an ambulance is called, but it is too late. Gilliam is pronounced dead on arrival at Baptist Hospital, just four days shy of his 50th birthday.

His heart attack ends what has been a long, sad and intermittently hopeful cycle of relapse and recovery. The man known as "Jefferson Street Joe" was named an All-American at Tennessee State in 1970 and '71 before being signed by the Pittsburgh Steelers. During the Steelers' 1974 season, he became the first black starting quarterback in the NFL, and he seemed destined for a brilliant career. But Gilliam began having trouble with drugs, and the QB slot went instead to Terry Bradshaw. Bradshaw went on to NFL glory; Gilliam was waived by the Steelers and spiraled downward into addiction. At one point, he was reduced to a street-dwelling junkie who pawned his two Super Bowl rings for dope. Today, though, he is remembered as Jefferson Street Joe everlasting, the man with the golden hands.

27—Five thousand Middle Tennessee Muslims gather at TSU's Gentry Center to celebrate *Eid al-Fitr*, the holiday that ends the sacred month of Ramadan. The Muslim community in Middle Tennessee was small enough in the 1970s that the Ramadan celebration was held in a private home. A Muslim leader estimates the local population at 15,000, and he foresees the day when the celebration grows large enough to warrant a football stadium.

28—Shooting suspect Joel Summerlin, wanted in the Dec. 23 killing of a hunter who trespassed on his property, surrenders to Sumner County police. He is accused of shooting Tim Butler of Gallatin, who felled a deer on Summerlin's property without permission. . . . **Waylon Jennings fans** with leftover Christmas cash are in for a bargain. Jennings and his wife, Jessi Colter, are moving to a new home in Arizona that is much smaller than their Brentwood mansion. The country singers throw a three-day estate sale that lets fans troop through their Old Hickory Boulevard residence. Items for sale include posters, guns, one of the 1969 "General Lee" Dodge Chargers used in *The Dukes of Hazzard* TV

Warfield: I see a lost generation of African-American males as a problem here. A high number of us go into jails. We die at a younger age than other segments of the population. There's not much of a positive image in the media of the African-American male. My friends and I are very conscious, particularly at school, that we have to break these stereotypes, but it's hard to do.

Katie Hill

Kozicki: I think most of what's wrong with Nashville can be fixed. But the question is how we're going to pay for it. Until we get a fair tax system figured out, we're not going to go as far as we would like. Also, we have to to rethink our education system completely. It's based on the needs of an industrialized society. We are training our kids to go to classes when the bell rings, just like they do in a factory, and drill and repeat their exercises just like they do on an assembly line. That's not the kind of work force that they are expected to go into. Those systems were built in the '30s and '40s to educate for an industrialized country, not what we have today, which is an information economy. It's going to take a couple of generations to make that adjustment.

Soto: One of the things that amazes me about our public educational system in this country is that even though we talk about a global economy, learning a second language is not a priority. I think that's a weakness here in Nashville. You hear a lot about newcomers learning English, but nobody says much about the value of being bilingual. Those whose native tongue is English obviously aren't all that eager to learn Spanish or any other language.

At this point, the Nashville Nine broke up into smaller groups and spent time imagining a future as it might evolve for them personally and for the larger community—the Greater Nashville that they would like to see emerge in another 25 years.

Hogan: In our fantasy future, I am 51 years old. Chris, Cory, and I are the advisors to a group called the Nashville Vision Council, which was started in 2001 as an outgrowth of the writing of a book. We are now the advisors because we're too old to be on the Nashville Vision Council. The age limit is 32. Chris is the Speaker of the U.S. House, I am a judge on the Sixth Circuit U.S. Court of Appeals, and Cory is the junior senator from the state of Tennessee.

Ferrell: O.K. It's 2025, and Nashville has slowed its growth and has close to 2 million people in its metropolitan statistical area, and we've managed to reverse the effects of sprawl. We've modified our metropolitan government to expand to a regional metropolitan government, with a mayor and council that govern the entire MSA. We now have commuter rail running along five corridors to bring people from outlying areas into the city and

Chris Ferrell

vice versa. Every Nashvillian has the opportunity to live in safe, affordable housing. We have it in mixed income communities, and we have also managed to increase density close to downtown and around the rail stops. We have created opportunities for people to live, work, play, and go to school within their communities.

We have an excellent public school system that features a high degree of choice. In the business community, we have managed to maintain and foster an entrepreneurial environment, where people are founding companies in the city with a diversified economy. We have been able to attract more publicly held company headquarters here, but mostly we've managed to grow our own here. Our biotech sector has emerged as a national leader in that field, growing out of relationships at Vanderbilt and in our cooperative public-private health-care sector. We just celebrated the best Olympics of all time right here in Nashville in 2024. We continue to have a very vibrant entertainment district downtown. Replacing the Thermal Transfer Plant with an entertainment district on the river was a phenomenal idea.

Kozicki: In our parallel Nashville, Renata is 52 years old and is the CEO of the largest and most important regional foundation of the Southeast, which is based in Nashville. Katie is 43 and the first woman governor of Tennessee. I'm 52, and I live on an island after starting a couple of businesses here that have done well. I fly in on weekends in my private plane.

Years ago, the city went to a localized, neighborhood political zone concept. Each area or political zone is focused around an institutional focal point like a church, a school, or some other civic or social institution. Each political zone is relatively self-sufficient. It includes retail, commercial, and residential areas that are established with a neighborhood flavor. Gradually, this zone concept broke down the infrastructure problems we had and the political and socioeconomic barriers we had to break through. Meanwhile, telecommuting and technology drastically reduced the need to drive.

Fleming: I'm now 46. In listening to the conversation we're having so far, it seems to me that if everyone has decided that education and quality of life are what's most important, then there needs to be some kind of change in our community values. Until we reassess and change our emphasis, not just as a government but as citizens in the voting booths, we'll just be talking around in circles—and in 2025, this same conversation will still be going on. We need to draw on all our community resources to make our public schools our first priority. That means using professional people like lawyers and doctors and engineers. And I don't understand why we're not using retired teachers, who have boundless knowledge but whose gifts we ignore.

Smith: I'm 53. I don't live in Nashville currently. I live up on the Cumberland Plateau, where I help run a small school. I occasionally get into my very small, fuel-cell car and come into

Eleanor Fleming

Nashville to consult with the public schools about how to build place-based, interdisciplinary initiatives into their programs. In the past 25 years, there has been a groundswell in Nashville to build a culture of creativity. We have a vibrant arts community now. We have found creative ways to celebrate the traditions of Middle Tennessee. The core of the city is now a pedestrian center with local gardens, lots of arts, and places where people walk, meet, and greet. Where people live.

show and Jennings' old mascot, a wooden Indian named Leon.

29—A hearse carries Joe Gilliam Jr. down the street that gave him his nickname, as more than 1,000 people turn out to bid Jefferson Street Joe farewell. Today would have been his 50th birthday. At TSU's Kean Hall, where the young Gilliam once played pickup basketball games, he is honored by a crowd that includes NFL Hall of Famer Franco Harris, his former teammate, and Doug Williams, the first black quarterback to start a Super Bowl.

30—The Christmas holidays are over, but the celebration of Kwanza is just beginning tonight at the Martha O'Bryan Center off Shelby Street. The Village Cultural Arts Center, the multipurpose Charlotte Pike teaching facility, presents its annual Kwanza Celebration for a crowd of approving families and neighborhood residents. When it opened in 1995, The Village offered mainly music and drumming lessons; under the guidance of director Kysa Novichi Estes, its mission has expanded to include computer labs, tae kwon do classes, tutoring, community guidance and studies in African history and culture.

31—It is a calmer city that greets what is actually the first day of the next century and the new millennium. In the early morning hours, a fine snow of glittering crystal flakes sifts through the beams of the Union Station train shed. Two months hence, the historic shed will be gone. A year passes, a year begins; the snow drifts down on us all. Whether asleep or awake in these last hours before dawn, we the living hang by a slender thread between our history and the unknowable future. Somewhere in the city is a child whose date of birth is 01-01-00 and who bears the name of the Christian savior. His first birthday is greeted by a flashing sign atop the Eighth Avenue Carpet Barn. Silently, it blinks its lonely question into the star-spangled night: What would Jesus do?

Chris Ferrell, 31, grew up in a Jacksonville, Florida, suburb, graduated from Furman University in South Carolina, and moved to Nashville in 1991 to enter Vanderbilt Divinity School. In 1995, he became the youngest person ever to be elected to the Metro Council, and four years later he was re-elected to that at-large seat. Ferrell is president of MarketingOps.com., an internet marketing company. Previously, he was a vice president of Telalink, a Nashville-based internet service provider. He is married and the father of three children.

Eleanor Fleming, 22, has lived all her life in Williamson County, where her family has deep roots. She was salutatorian of her graduating class at Battle Ground Academy in 1996, and four years later graduated summa cum laude from Vanderbilt University, where she is now pursuing a Ph.D. in political science. She has been working since she was 15, primarily at the Boys & Girls Club of Franklin, which she describes as "my internship for a career in teaching, politics, and other ways of helping people, especially children."

Katie Hill, 19, a freshman in the honors program at the University of Virginia, spent all her years prior to college in Davidson and Williamson counties. She attended public schools through eighth grade and finished at Harpeth Hall, where she was president of the Honor Council and editor of the student newspaper. In her spare time, she has worked as a sales clerk, a tutor in English as a second language, and an intern in the district attorney's office. Her career interests include politics and classical archaeology.

Melissa Hogan, 27, grew up in Cincinnati, attended public schools, and graduated from Georgetown College in Kentucky in 1994. She worked for a year before going on to earn a degree at the University of Pittsburgh Law School. During college, she often came to Nashville with a classmate whose home was here. Hogan clerked for a federal judge on the Sixth Circuit Court of Appeals and also for the Nashville law firm of Bass, Berry & Sims. She joined the BB&S firm in 1998. She and her husband live in East Nashville.

Scott Kozicki, 29, has lived in the Nashville area since 1989, moving here with his parents from Detroit when his father was hired to help build the first Saturn automobiles in Spring Hill. A self-described "drummer, piano player, and nonconformist," Kozicki tried college but dropped out in his second year at Middle Tennessee State University. In the mid-1990s he made a niche for himself in technology, founding BlueStar Communications and then launching Factory 23, an internet firm providing specialized services to small and mid-sized tech companies.

Holly Shepherd, 30, was born in Nashville and graduated from Overton High School in 1987 with a burning ambition to be an actress. She went to Florida State University for a year and then finished at the University of Tennessee in 1992. Shepherd lived and worked in New York and elsewhere as a band singer, dancer, actress, and entertainer until 1995, when she returned to Nashville "to be a full-time artist, rather than a really good waitress who also works onstage." Today she teaches theater arts, performs and directs with the Tennessee Repertory Theater and other theater companies, and sings with a band.

Alden Smith, 29, grew up in Belle Meade, sailed through Ensworth and Montgomery Bell Academy, and graduated from Davidson College with high honors as president of the student body, captain of the football team, and an English major with a 3.8 GPA. Over the next five years, Smith studied part-time at Middlebury College's Breadloaf School of English, earning a master's degree in 2000. He has worked at an outreach center in North Nashville, an inner-city school in Charlotte, and a boarding school in Connecticut. Since 1999 he has served as assistant director of the Mountain School in rural Vermont.

Renata Soto, 28, grew up in a middle-class family in Costa Rica, attended Kenyon College in Ohio and Georgia State University, and graduated from the Universidad de Costa Rica in 1995. She lived in Atlanta for two years, working as a language teacher and social service program director for Latino immigrants, before moving to Nashville. Here she works for United Way of Metropolitan Nashville as director of a task force to extend the Davidson County Family Resource Center network into underserved parts of the city. Soto and her husband, a Floridian, and their two children live in South Nashville.

Cory Warfield, 17, is president of the junior class at Martin Luther King High School, an academic magnet in the Metro public school system. Born and raised in Nashville, he lives now in the Madison area, north of the city. His mother works the night shift at Aladdin Industries; his father passed away last year. Fleming has acted in videos and had other part-time jobs, but in the main he has been able to concentrate on his studies. He is keenly interested in politics, is looking at Georgetown University in Washington for college, and thinks, at this point, that he will eventually study law.

At the end of their daylong conversations, the young Nashvillians gathered for a farewell portrait. From left, sitting: Holly Shepherd, Alden Smith, Renata Soto, Cory Warfield, Melissa Hogan and Scott Kozicki. From left, standing: Katie Hill, Eleanor Fleming and Chris Ferrell.

In a period of just under fourteen months, beginning on July 4, 2000, and ending on August 24, 2001, the editorial side of *Nashville: An American Self-Portrait* was completed. On the latter date, as the final details were being added to the front and back—table of contents, credits, index—about 90 percent of the book had already been printed on flat sheets 40 inches long by 25.5 inches wide. Front and back, these sheets held sixteen-page impressions (called a signature in the trade); when folded and trimmed, the total of 24 signatures would be gathered and bound to make, in the initial printing, 12,500 copies of the 384-page volume.

The paper had been selected through a local supplier, Athens Paper Company, an old and respected name in the Nashville printing industry. The chosen paper was an 80-pound LOE (for Lustro Offset Enamel) acid-free coated stock produced from Northern hardwoods and manufactured in a Michigan mill by an international company based in South Africa. On the advice of a Nashville bookbinder with a half-century of experience, a "short grain" stock was specified to assure that the direction of the paper's grain would be parallel to the spine of the book, rather than perpendicular to it, thus producing a stronger, smoother, longer-lasting sewn spine. BINDTECH, Inc. of Nashville would be responsible for the binding process.

The first two signatures had been delivered to the printer on July 19, four days ahead of the target date; the last two signatures were handed over on August 24, a month late. We were just four weeks away from our first scheduled presentation of the book itself when the last words were finally written and given on computer disk to the prepress team at Lithographics, Inc., our Nashville-based printing company. The most advanced high-tech application of Johann Gutenberg's invention of the "modern" printing press five and a half centuries ago was now turning blank sheets of paper into printed signatures for us at speeds of up to 7,500 sheets per hour.

Speed and quality beyond Gutenberg's wildest imagining have become the norm in today's best printing operations. At Lithographics, two Heidelberg Speedmaster five-color presses, guided by direct computer-to-plate electronic digital prepress technology, printed 665,000 sheets of paper on both sides in less than 175 total hours of running time. On August 7, in the middle of this process, a dozen or so of the approximately 200 people who played some part in the bookmaking venture paused in the pressroom at Lithographics for a photographer's "working portrait" documenting the phenomenon of simultaneous editorial and production work on a book in the making. With one of the Heidelberg presses humming contently in the background, the individuals present proudly represented most of the specialties having a part to play in the process—writing, editing, photography, design, paper supply, prepress, printing, and binding. They held printed flat sheets of the book, a blank dummy of the finished work, and even an uncorrected proof of the cover. They also wore the pleased expressions of experienced professionals far enough along in a complex undertaking to look toward its completion with great expectation and confidence.

Less than a mile from the Lithographics plant, a historical marker notes the placement, in 1780, of Buchanan's Station, one of a half-dozen or so forts erected in a 5-mile radius of Fort Nashborough by the parties of settlers led into the area by John Donelson and James Robertson a few months prior to that. Twenty-year-old John Buchanan, with his parents and two brothers, had joined the Robertson group on its way through Kentucky in the fall of 1779; they crossed the frozen Cumberland with him on Christmas Day. A year or so later, while he was living at the outpost near the present intersection of Elm Hill Pike and Massman Drive, young Buchanan did something that ties him in spirit to the printers and binders and other principals in this city's publishing community: He produced, entirely by hand, Nashville's first printed and bound volume, called *John Buchanan's Book of Arithmetic*. The Tennessee State Library and Archives holds the only known copy. That leather-bound text is symbolic of a book-publishing heritage as old as the city itself. In *Nashville: An American Self-Portrait*, the legacy continues.

The editors are grateful for the confidence and encouragement extended by the following people, businesses, and institutions in whose names early and significant support was generously provided for the creation and development of this book.

Lucy and Stanford Adams

David and Lissa Allen

Thomas E. Allen

AmSouth Bank

Bill Armistead, III

Mr. and Mrs. Robert H.F. Armistead

Walt Baker

Bank of America

The Bank of Nashville

Barrett, Johnston & Parsley

Barry and Jean Ann Banker

Bass, Berry & Sims, PLC

Belmont University

Don and Joyce Beisswenger

Bob Bogen

Boult, Cummings, Conners & Berry, PLC

Dr. and Mrs. T.B. Boyd, III & Family

Branstetter, Kilgore, Stranch & Jennings

Katherine Brick

Anne Brown

Betty and Martin Brown

Margaret W. Brown

Richard L. Burtner

Eliza Brown and Hal Candee

Dr. and Mrs. George K. Carpenter, III

Neal Clayton

Mr. and Mrs. William H. Van Cleave

John Lawrence Connelly

John and Diane Cooke

Ron Watson and Jeffrey Corvin

N.A. Crippens

Jack and Jennifer Cunningham

Mr. and Mrs. Robert V. Dale

David Dingess

Ellen and Townes Duncan

Ruth Duncan

Walker Duncan

Mr. and Mrs. William H. Eberle

Ensworth School

Alice Randall and David Ewing

Chloe Fort

Madge Franklin

Mr. and Mrs. K. Martin Grafton-Grattan

B. Dallas Hagewood

Ed and Linda Hamlett

Sharon Hels and Brad Reed

Hoyt and Martha Hickman

Barnie Allen Higgs and Mary Egerton Higgs

Betty G. Hobbs and Doug Wonder

Michael Hodges

Eli Horton

Pete and Bette Horton

M.S. Joyce

S.A. Joyce

Donna Paz Kaufman and Mark Kaufman
Leigh Walton and Cliff Knowles
Jay Langford
Lattimore, Black, Morgan & Cain
Loews Vanderbilt Plaza Hotel
Lovell Communications, Inc.
Judith Lovin
Mrs. Jack C. Massey
Dr. and Mrs. Frank Mastrapasqua
Robert C.H. Mathews
Jack and Lynn May
Mr. and Mrs. Joseph P. McAllister
Jessie Morris
Julia and John Morris
Miller Morris
Sara Morris
Bruce and Dorothy Mosher
Jack Murrah
Mr. and Mrs. Edward G. Nelson
Sandra Davis Owen
Frank and Micki Pendleton
The Family of William H. Polk, M.D.
Mr. and Mrs. Kirk A. Porter
Friends of Bill Purcell
Ms. Elizabeth M. Queener
Sandra Roberts
Mike Rollins

Anne and Charles E. Roos
Anne and Joe Russell
Sherry Shaw
Joan and Herbert Shayne
Jo Silveman
Mr. and Mrs. David F. Smith
Mr. and Mrs. Sam B. Smith
Solidus Company
Christopher "Butch" Spyridon
St. Thomas Hospital
Michael, Kim and Matthew Stagg
Elizabeth May Stern
Willy Stern
Zachariah L. Stern
Howard G., Thomas G. and Jeffrey G. Stovall
Vanderbilt University
John and Debbie Van Mol
Vietti Chili
Waller Lansden Dortch & Davis, PLLC
A.J. Walton
Simon and Jane Waterlow
Ann and Charles Wells
Jamye and McDonald Williams
Richard and Sally Williams
Susan and Ashley Wiltshire
Stephen F. and Nancy B. Wood
Victor and Denise Zirilli

APPRECIATION

In large ways and small, the people named below have cheerfully aided and encouraged this venture as it evolved from abstraction to reality. At the risk of slighting a few who may have been overlooked in the rush to finish the book on schedule, we take this final opportunity to express our sincere thanks to all those listed alphabetically below; to the electronic prepress, pressroom, and bindery employees of Lithographics, Inc. and BINDTECH, Inc.; and to the people of Nashville, who always provide such rich subject matter for writers, photographers, and other students of the human condition.

Charlie Allen
Joan Anderson
Peter Applebome
The Arts Company staff
Lynne Bachleda
David Bailey Sr.
Boyer Barner
George Barrett
Kay Beasley
Don and Joyce Beisswenger
Roger Bishop
Anne Blake
Diann Blakely
Bob Bogen
Tom Bond
Daniel Boone
Ellen Bradbury
Bobby Braddock
Cecil and Charlotte Branstetter
Anne Brown
Bonnie Buckner
Carol Bucy
Dan and Pat Burton
Benjamin H. Caldwell
Linda Center
Lindsay Chappell
Mary Ann Clayton
Brenda Colladay
Jeff Colvin
Toby Compton
Kathy Conkwright
Jack Corn
Debbie Cox
Tamara Crabtree
Nathaniel A. Crippens
J. T. Culbertson
Roy Cunningham
Ruth Cunningham
Clarice DeQuasie
Dean Dixon
Bruce Dobie
Ellen Duncan
Ruth Duncan
Natilee Duning

Kay Durham
Walter Durham
Susan Dyer
John T. Edge
Ann B. Egerton
David Ewing
Ken Fieth
Jamie Fisher
Chloe Fort
Nancy Blackwelder Fort
David A. Fox
Madge Franklin
Frye Gaillard
Tony Garr
Susan Gordon
Fred Graham
Hugh Davis Graham
Wes Green
Frank Grisham
Red Grooms
Phila Hach
Cherie Hamilton
Ed and Linda Hamlett
Kay Hammock
Bill Hance
Erwin Hargrove
Diane Hayes
Alexander Heard
Mary Glenn Hearne
Eddie Henderson
Martha Whitmore Hickman
Skip Higgs
Laura Hill
Michael Hodges
James A. Hoobler
Robin Hood
Angie Howard
Judi Hudgins
Marylin Hughes
Keel Hunt
Jackie Jones
Carol Kaplan
Dolly Kelly
John Kincer

Edd Keefe
Bert Knight
Phil Krakouriak
Bill LaFevor
John Lancaster
Adrienne Latham
Jim Leeson
Ellen Lehman
Andree LeQuire
Janet Lethgo
Dwight Lewis
Jim Lockhart
Candy Markman
Gloria and Henry Martin
Joe Maxwell
Debbie May
Sue McClure
Karinna McDaniel
Robert A. McGaw
Kenny McLemore
Tony Mize
Annette Morrison
Bruce and Dorothy Mosher
John Netherton
Donna Nicely
Charles S. Nichols
Maria-Elena Orbea
Libby Page
Wesley Paine
Laurie Parker
Jessica Pasley
Bev Peery
Vickie Phelps
Mike Piggott
Julia B. Polk
Craig Pollock
Jason Price
Ellen and Bill Pryor
Don Radcliffe
Alice Randall
Sallie Ray
Brad Reed
Pam Reese
Margaret Renkl

Jim Riddle
Gregory Ridley
Sandra Roberts
Carolyn Russell
David C. Rutherford
Barbara Sammons
David Sanders
John S. Sanders
James M. Sandlin
Lindy B. Sayers
Jessie Schmidt
Adele Mills Schweid
John Seigenthaler
Audrey Seitz
Michael Sims
Anne Meador Shayne
Jon Shayne
Dan Siegel
Kathy Smith
Sam and Sue Smith
Chantay Steptoe
Nancy Stewart
Tom and Virginia Stovall
Thomas G. Stovall
Barbara Stovall
Marty Stuart
Bob Summer
Jim Summerville
Frank Sutherland
Joseph Sweat
Phil Thomason
Brandy Vickers
Evelyn Wakefield
Sam E. Wallace Sr.
Jane Waterlow
Ron Watson
Dick and Sally Williams
Patsy Williams
Carolyn Wilson
Nicki Pendleton Wood
Larry and Saralee Woods
Steve Womack
Jenny Yancey
Michael Zibart

STAFF FOR THE BOOK

Nashville has long taken pride in the high level of professional skill it can bring to bear on the multi-task process of creating books. From the germ of an idea to the successful completion of a marketing campaign, all of the necessary talents are at hand here, in corporations and cottage industries alike, to make words and pictures assume a permanent place on the printed page. At one point or another, the approximately 150 people named below made a direct contribution to the creation of this book; so did another 50 or more in the printing and binding process. The end result of this collaboration is living proof that Nashville remains "a great book town" in the fullest meaning of that phrase.

Senior Editor: John Egerton
Editor: E. Thomas Wood
Writers: D. Michelle Adkerson, Lamar Alexander, Leon Alligood, Phil Ashford, Gloria Ballard, Roy Blount Jr., Gordon Bonnyman, Will D. Campbell, Bill Carey, jeff obafemi carr, Paul Clements, Hal Crowther, Larry Daughtrey, Natilee Duning, Jean Bethke Elshtain, Bruce Feiler, Carrie Ferguson, Bill Friskics-Warren, Liz Murray Garrigan, Steve Gill, David Halberstam, Beverly Keel, Christine Kreyling, Amy Lynch, Jim Molpus, Madeena Spray Nolan, Anne Paine, Dana Pride, Rich Rhoda, Jim Ridley, Fred Russell, Richard Schweid, John Sergent, Sandra Smithson, Willy Stern, Reginald Stuart, Ray Waddle, Jeff Wilkinson, Susan Ford Wiltshire, and the "Nashville Nine"—Chris Ferrell, Eleanor Fleming, Katie Hill, Melissa Hogan, Scott Kozicki, Holly Shepherd, Alden Smith, Renata Soto, and Cory Warfield
Illustrations Editor: Nancy Rhoda
Photographers: Jackie Bell, Michael Clancy, Al Clayton, Vic Cooley, Howard Cooper, Hal Crowther, P. Casey Daley, Delores Delvin, Billy Easley, Jimmy Ellis, Frank Empson, Jen Fairall, Don Foster, Ed Fulcher, D. Patrick Harding, Aubrey Haynes, Elmer Hinton, Peyton Hoge, Gerald Holly, Robert C. Holt Jr., Mark Humphrey, Robert Johnson, Delores Johnson, Billy Kingsley, Gary Layda, Jared Lazarus, Nina Long, Michelle Lord, Harold Lowe Jr., Larry McCormack, Dawn Majors, Shelley Mays, Rick Musacchio, Vince Musi, J. William Myers, Lisa Nipp, Sam Parrish, Eric Parsons, John Partipilo, Rex Perry, J.T. Phillips, Randy Piland, Bill Preston, Freeman Ramsey, Jeanne Reisel, Ricky Rogers, Joe Rudis, Amanda Saslow, Callie Shell, Bill Steber, Dana Thomas, George Walker
Artists: Nancy Blackwelder, W.J. Cunningham, Newton Holiday
Chief Copy Editor: Susan Chappell
Copy Editors: Beth Monin Harrington, Lynne Bachleda, Roy Cunningham, Ruth Cunningham, Dana Kopp Franklin, Cherie Hamilton, Diane Hayes, Mary E. Higgs, Jackie Jones, Michael Sims, Barbara Swift
Graphic Design: James A. Bateman and Harriette H. Bateman
Research: Tammy Binford and Chantay Steptoe
Indexing: Carolyn James
Technical Support: Jason Price, Mary McClean
Printing Coordinator: Ellen Bradbury
Binding Coordinator: Tom Bond
Distribution: Ron Watson and Chris Anderson
Marketing: Ned Horton and Audrey Seitz;
Roger Bishop, Angie Howard, Dolly Kelly, Tony Mize, Laurie Parker, Bev Peery, David Sanders
Finance & Administration: Townes Duncan, Kay Hammock, Edd Keefe, Julia Polk, Patsy Williams;
Martin S. Brown Jr., Whit Forehand, Larry D. Woods

PHOTOGRAPHIC CREDITS